ROMANS

Also by James Montgomery Boice

Witness and Revelation in the Gospel of John
Philippians: An Expositional Commentary
The Sermon on the Mount
How to Live the Christian Life (originally, *How to Live It Up*)
Ordinary Men Called by God (originally, *How God Can Use Nobodies*)
The Last and Future World
The Gospel of John: An Expositional Commentary (5 volumes in one)
"Galatians" in the *Expositor's Bible Commentary*
Can You Run Away from God?
Does Inerrancy Matter?
The Foundation of Biblical Authority, editor
The Epistles of John
Genesis: An Expositional Commentary (3 volumes)
The Parables of Jesus
The Christ of Christmas
The Minor Prophets: An Expositional Commentary (2 volumes)
Standing on the Rock
The Christ of the Open Tomb
Foundations of the Christian Faith (4 volumes in one)
Christ's Call to Discipleship
Transforming Our World: A Call to Action, editor
Ephesians: An Expositional Commentary
Daniel: An Expositional Commentary
Joshua: We Will Serve the Lord
Nehemiah: Learning to Lead

Volume 2
The Reign of Grace
Romans 5:1–8:39

JAMES
MONTGOMERY
BOICE

BAKER BOOK HOUSE
Grand Rapids, Michigan 49516

Copyright 1992 by
Baker Book House Company

Printed in the United States of America

Library of Congress Cataloging-in-Publication Data

Boice, James Montgomery, 1938-
    Romans / James Montgomery Boice.
       p.   cm.
    Includes bibliographical references and indexes.
    Contents: v. 2. The reign of grace, Romans 5:1–8:39.
    ISBN 0–8010–1003–9 (v. 2)
    1. Bible. N.T. Romans—Commentaries. I. Title.
BS2665.3.B58 1991
227'.1077—dc20   91-7204
                                          CIP

To **HIM**
who caused grace to reign
through righteousness
to bring us eternal life
through Jesus Christ our Lord

Contents

Preface

More than a year and a half has gone by since I wrote the preface to volume one of these expository studies of Paul's great letter to the Romans. Yet I did not expect to be writing the preface to volume two so soon. The reason for my change of plans is the very welcome decision by Baker Book House to publish simultaneously the first two volumes of what I project to be a four-volume set on the Book of Romans. By this means those who are interested in my attempts to sound the depths of Paul's teaching will be able to use both volumes to work through at least the first important half of Romans without undue delay.

The remaining two volumes, on chapters 9 through 11 and chapters 12 through 16, will follow as quickly as I am able to preach through them in the course of my regular ministry at Tenth Presbyterian Church in Philadelphia, which I have served now for nearly a quarter of a century.

In my introduction to volume one I mention how little I feel American evangelicals understand this great letter, the greatest of all biblical books, in the opinion of many. I say that very few understand chapters 1 through 4 deeply, though many suppose they do. But if that is the case with those earlier, easier, and fairly familiar chapters, how much more must it be true of chapters 5 through 8! Let me tell you what I think many evangelicals do. I think they read Romans 5:1–11, which they construe as listing only the fruit or benefits of the believer's justification through Jesus Christ, and then skip on to chapter 8 to assure themselves and others that, having been justified by God, they are now eternally secure in Christ and that nothing will ever separate them from the love of God in him.

That is correct, of course—if one is truly justified or genuinely born again. But the conviction that a person is secure in Christ—"once saved, always saved"—is mere presumption if there is not an inevitable, corresponding, and necessary growth in righteousness and victory over sin following conversion.

That is what these chapters show so convincingly. Their theme is the reign of grace, understood not (as some understand it) as God's being gracious to us regardless of what we may do, even if we continue in a very disobedient and dishonorable walk, but understood rather as grace triumphing in those who are Christ's in order to create a genuinely godly walk and righteousness. Even Romans 8 says this, for it states early on that God "condemned sin in sinful man, *in order that the righteous requirements of the law might be fully met in us,* who do not live according to the sinful nature but according to the Spirit" (vv. 3–4, emphasis added). Those who live according to the sinful nature are not Christians, Paul says in verses 5–8. Rather, Christians are those who are "controlled" by the Spirit (v. 9). Therefore, Christians are those who are having the righteous requirements of the law fulfilled in them.

I believe this is a message that American evangelicals desperately need to hear. For too long we have been subjected to a feeble proclamation of the gospel, which amounts in the end to a denial of it, since it says that it is possible to be regenerate without being sanctified, to be eternally secure in Christ and yet not show any evidence of having the life of Christ within.

No wonder so many so-called evangelicals are indistinguishable from the ungodly, unregenerate people surrounding them, and why the self-proclaimed evangelical churches have been failing to make any appreciable impact on the surrounding culture. We are ineffective because many who consider themselves to be Christians are not saved.

I invite you to walk through these great chapters with me, as my own congregation did from July 1988 through July 1990. (The same studies were also aired over the internationally heard "Bible Study Hour" broadcast after about a six-month delay.)

In these studies of Romans, I have been strengthened in my own awareness of the sovereignty, grace, and holiness of God and of the need for holiness in his people, that is, for holiness in those who profess to be Christians. We are not a holy people, not very. But we can become increasingly holy as we draw near to God and live in the mental universe of these great Bible teachings. Indeed, we must!

As usual, I want to thank the congregation of Tenth Presbyterian Church for allowing me to spend so much time in serious Bible study and in the preparation of these sermons, in particular. I trust the congregation has benefited from them.

May God bless us in these sad days of declining evangelicalism, and may we have a recovery of the whole counsel of God. I know no better way to move in that direction than by studying, meditating on, and once again preaching from the Book of Romans.

Philadelphia, Pennsylvania

PART SIX

Security in Christ

60

Peace with God

Romans 5:1

Therefore, since we have been justified through faith, we have peace with God through our Lord Jesus Christ.

A number of years ago, *Look* magazine ran a personality feature entitled "Peace of Mind." Sixteen prominent Americans had been asked how they were able to find peace in our stressful world, and the article consisted of their answers.

James Michener, the author of many best-selling books, said that he finds peace by taking his two dogs for a walk "along old streams and into fields that have not been plowed for half a century." Barry Goldwater, the former Senator from Arizona and Republican presidential candidate, said that he finds peace in his hobbies—photography, boating, flying, and camping— but above all by "walking in the Grand Canyon." (It was obvious that Goldwater had been elected to the Senate from "the Grand Canyon state.") Former CBS news anchorman Walter Cronkite finds peace in solitude, usually by "going to the sea by small boat." Margaret Mead, the well-known anthropologist and author of *Coming of Age in Samoa*, sought "a change of pace and scene." Sammy Davis, Jr., said he found peace by looking for "good in people." Bill Moyers, television personality and former press secretary to Lyndon Johnson, tried to find peace in a family "reunion, usually in some remote and quiet retreat."[1]

As I read these answers I was impressed with how subjective and dependent upon favorable circumstances most of the approaches were. But I noted something else, too. Although each of these prominent Americans differed in his or her methods, all were nevertheless seeking peace of mind and recognized that pursuing it was important. No one considered a search for peace to be irrelevant.

What is it that people are most seeking in life, once their basic physical needs are satisfied? Some say they are seeking "freedom." Movements for national liberation are usually based on this intense human desire. But Americans are free. We have been free of foreign domination for over two hundred years, and our constitution and legal system affirm our individual liberties. Yet most of us are as restless and discontented (perhaps even more so) as those living under strongly oppressive regimes. Is it wealth we are seeking? One of the richest men in the world once said, "I thought money could buy happiness. I have been miserably disillusioned." Others seek fulfillment through education, fame, sex, or power, but most are discontented even when they attain such goals. What is the reason? The explanation is that what people are really seeking is peace, and the ultimate and only genuine peace is found in a right relationship with God.

The great North African Christian, Saint Augustine, expressed it best more than a millennium and a half ago, when he wrote in his *Confessions,* "You made us for yourself, and our hearts find no peace until they rest in you."[2]

Peace Through Jesus Christ

If you are restless and seeking peace, the verse that begins the fifth chapter of Paul's magnificent letter to the Romans is addressed to you. For here Paul speaks of peace and tells how it may be found: "Therefore, since we have been justified through faith, we have peace with God through our Lord Jesus Christ."

I want to put this verse in its context, however. And to do that I need to have you think ahead to what we are going to find in this next major section of Paul's letter (chs. 5–8).

It is traditional among commentators to suggest that at this point in his letter, having explained the doctrine of justification by grace through faith, Paul lists what most writers call "the fruits of justification" and then moves on to discuss sanctification. Peace is one such "fruit," but there are others:

1. *Look* magazine, July 27, 1971, pp. 21–30.

2. Saint Augustine, *Confessions,* trans. R. S. Piné-Coffin (Baltimore: Penguin Books, 1961), p. 21.

access to God through prayer, hope, joy, perseverance, and a sense of being loved by God. According to this view, Paul interrupts his listing of these fruits of justification at verse 11 to deal with the parallel between Adam and Christ (Rom. 5:12–21) and sanctification (Rom. 6:1—8:17), before returning to the assurance that nothing can separate the believer from God's love, which is another fruit of justification (Rom. 8:18–39). Commentators taking this approach conclude that the chief concern of the apostle in this section of Romans is sanctification.

If the traditional approach is correct, Romans falls into four major sections: (1) a portion dealing with justification (chs. 1–4); (2) a discussion of sanctification (chs. 5–8); (3) the problem of God's dealing with the Jews (chs. 9–11); and (4) practical matters (chs. 12–16).

However, at this point I think that F. Godet and D. Martyn Lloyd-Jones (who follows him) are right when they suggest that what Paul is actually presenting in Romans 5:1–11 is not "the fruits of justification," though he mentions some of them, but the beginning of a well-developed statement of the security in Christ that comes to a believer as a result of his or her justification.[3]

There are a number of reasons for this interpretation, and there are reasons why it is important, which I will explain later.

I suggested one reason for approaching verses 1–11 in this way when I said that according to the traditional view, Paul *interrupts* his treatment of the "fruits" of justification to deal with the parallel between Adam and Christ and sanctification. Yet interruptions are not what we have been led to expect in this letter. One German commentator sees this to be a real problem, and he does not hesitate to say that at this point "the systematic order of our epistle leaves something to be desired."[4] But is that really so? Any suggestion that Paul is not being systematic should make us pause in our interpretation of his teaching, at least in this letter, which up to now has been a model of consistent and systematic argumentation.

The best arguments against the traditional view are from verses 1–11 themselves. Look at the first sentence. In the New International Version there is a period in the middle of verse 2, separating the sentence "And we rejoice in the hope of the glory of God" from the previous one. But in the Greek text this is actually a continuation and climax. In Greek the passage says what the King James Version allows it to say, namely: "Therefore being justified by faith, we have peace with God through our Lord Jesus Christ: By whom also we have access by faith into this grace in which we stand, and rejoice in hope of the glory of God." Since "hope of the glory of God" refers to what theologians call glorification, the opening sentence of

---

3. See F. Godet, *Commentary on St. Paul's Epistle to the Romans,* trans. A. Cusin (Edinburgh: T. & T. Clark, n.d.), vol. 1, pp. 313–315; and D. M. Lloyd-Jones, *Romans: An Exposition of Chapter 5, Assurance* (Grand Rapids: Zondervan, 1972), pp. 2–7.

4. Reuss. See Godet, *Commentary on St. Paul's Epistle to the Romans,* p. 314.

Romans 5 actually directs our minds to the final glorified state of those who have been justified. And that is exactly where we come out at the end of Romans 8, where Paul argues that nothing is "able to separate us from the love of God that is in Christ Jesus our Lord" (v. 39). This suggests that Paul has chapter 8 in mind as he begins chapter 5 and that he moves consistently toward his conclusion in the intervening material.

There is another argument as well. In Romans 5:1–2, Paul moves from justification to glorification without mentioning sanctification, the matter that traditionalists suppose to be his main concern. In Romans 8:30, he does the same thing, writing: "And those he predestined, he also called; those he called, he also justified; those he justified, he also glorified." Justification, then glorification! In both of these texts, one at the beginning of Romans 5–8 and one at the end, the one idea (justification) leads directly to the other (glorification).

It is true that a great deal of sanctification takes place between justification and glorification and that much of what is found in Romans 5–8 bears upon it. But we could well ask why Paul does not mention sanctification either at the start of this section (Rom. 5:1–11) or at the end of it (Rom. 8:18–39), if this is the primary subject he is writing about. Is it not the case that the reason he does not mention sanctification is that he is not *chiefly* concerned about it and that these chapters are actually focused on another matter entirely?

What is that matter? It is the believer's security in Christ or, as we also often say, the "assurance of salvation."

D. Martyn-Lloyd Jones, who sees Romans 5–8 in this light, says that "the apostle is concerned primarily, from this point onwards, to show us the absolute character, the fullness and the finality of the salvation which comes to us in the way he has already described, namely, as the result of justification by faith."[5]

In my opinion, this is the proper and most profitable approach to Romans 5–8.

"Peace with God" and "Peace of God"

When I began my analysis of Romans 5–8, I said that it was *important* to have this approach to these chapters and that I would come back to its importance later. I want to do that now. But to do so I want to make another distinction. It is the distinction between having "peace with God," which is what this section treats, and having the "peace of God," which is another matter.

Most Christians are acquainted with Philippians 4:6–7, which tells us about the peace *of* God: "Do not be anxious about anything, but in everything, by prayer and petition, with thanksgiving, present your requests to

---

5. Lloyd-Jones, *Romans: An Exposition of Chapter 5, Assurance,* p. 3.

God. And the peace of God, which transcends all understanding, will guard your hearts and your minds in Christ Jesus." Those two verses envision upsetting situations that come into our lives. Perhaps we have lost a job and are worried about earning enough money to provide for our families. Perhaps we are sick, or a friend is sick. Perhaps a person who has been very close to us has died, and suddenly everything seems in turmoil. One writer argues that the death of a close family member or friend is like having an eggbeater thrust into the mixing bowl of our emotional lives. Elisabeth Elliot, who had one husband murdered by Auca Indians in Ecuador and another slowly consumed by cancer, said that this is a time when the earth seems to be giving way, the waters are roaring, and the mountains are being cast into the sea (cf. Ps. 46:2–3).[6] In such times of stress we need personal peace in our lives, and it is this about which Philippians 4:6–7 is speaking: We can have personal peace by asking God for it.

And it works! I regularly cite these verses when I am writing to people who have lost a close family member, encouraging them to believe that God, who loves them and cares for them, will give them a peace that "transcends all human understanding." Many tell me that this is exactly what God has done for them. He has given them peace in the midst of their emotional turmoil.

But this is not the peace that Romans 5:1 is talking about. Romans 5 is not referring to the "peace *of* God," but to "peace *with* God." The idea here is not that we are upset and therefore need to become trusting and more tranquil, but rather that we have been at war with God and he with us, because of our sin, and that peace has nevertheless been provided for us by God—if we have been justified through faith in Jesus Christ.

When we see this, we realize that nothing is more appropriate and logical at this point in Romans than such a reference. For what Paul has been saying in the previous section is that God is not at peace with us but is at war with us because of our ungodly and wicked behavior. The word he has been using is "wrath." "The wrath of God is being revealed from heaven against all the godlessness and wickedness of men who suppress the truth by their wickedness" (Rom. 1:18). Having shown what this means and having answered the objections of those who feel that it is an appropriate description of the condition of *other* people, but not of themselves, Paul then reveals what God has done to satisfy his wrath against men in Jesus Christ. The Son bore the Father's wrath in our place. He died for us, and we receive the benefits of his atonement by believing on him and in what he has done. This is the point at which the fourth chapter of Romans ended.

But where does this lead? Obviously to peace *with* God! Since we have been justified by faith, the cause of the warfare between ourselves and God

---

6. Elisabeth Elliot, *Facing the Death of Someone You Love* (Westchester, Ill.: Good News Publishers, 1980), p. 8. First published as an article in *Christianity Today*, 1973.

has been removed, and peace is the result. We therefore *have* peace with God through the Lord Jesus Christ.

Peace has been provided from God's side, for he has removed the cause of the enmity through Jesus' death.

Peace has been received on our side, for we have "believed God" and have found the righteousness of the Lord Jesus Christ to be credited to us by God as our righteousness.

One commentator summarizes the point of Romans 5:1 by saying: "Every soul has been at war with God, and therefore every soul must have peace with God through cessation of the hostilities which exist between the individual and the Creator. How is the warfare to be brought to an end? . . . God has made peace, and no other peace can be made except that which he has already made. . . . If you come in unconditional surrender, you will find him all peace toward you."[7]

First Peace, Then Blessing

There are some practical applications that we need to make at this point, and they are important enough to be remembered as we make our way through these chapters.

1. *The starting point for all spiritual blessings, in this life and in the life to come, is the peace that God has made with us through the death of Jesus Christ.*

It is no accident that Paul begins Romans 5 with this theme. Many people would like the peace *of* God (or some other kind of peace) in difficult circumstances. They would like to be calm under fire, self-assured in highly pressured situations—to be always under control. Many more would like other blessings. But if God is the ultimate source of all good things, as he clearly is, we can only have them when we have first entered into a right and proper relationship with him. How is that done? The only way is by faith in Christ, as Paul has been arguing. But suppose you will not come that way. In that case, what can you possibly expect but a continuation of the wrath of God—a wrath greatly intensified, in your case, by your rejection of Jesus?

2. *Having been justified by God through faith in Jesus Christ, believers can know that their salvation is secured forever and that now nothing can separate them from God's love.*

This is the point I have been making in this study, and the reason is that it is the chief point of the passage. We have already seen how the first two verses of Romans 5 pass directly from justification to glorification, just as Romans 8:30 also does. These chapters also move inexorably to the great

7. Donald Grey Barnhouse, *God's River: Exposition of Bible Doctrines, Taking the Epistle to the Romans as a Point of Departure*, vol. 4, Romans 5:1–11 (Grand Rapids: Wm. B. Eerdmans, 1959), pp. 20, 22.

conclusion: "For I am convinced that neither death nor life, neither angels nor demons, neither the present nor the future, nor any powers, neither height nor depth, nor anything else in all creation, will be able to separate us from the love of God that is in Christ Jesus our Lord" (Rom. 8:38–39).

If this were not enough, we should be led to the same conclusion by the fact that the text itself speaks, not of *seeking* peace with God, but of *having* peace. "*Having* been justified, we *have* peace with God" is what it says.

It is hard to emphasize this too much, since all Christians need to be sure of their salvation. True, there is a false security about which we need to be warned. Mere intellectual assent to doctrine is not saving faith, and boasting of one's security while continuing to sin is presumption. But such qualifications aside, it is important to know that we have been saved by God, that peace has been made between God and ourselves, and that the peace made by God will last forever. Only those who are sure of this salvation can be a help to others.

3. It is possible to be at peace with God and know that we are at peace with God while, at the same time, fail to experience peace in a given situation.

It is important to point this out because, if we do not know this in advance and cling to it, we can be thrown into paralyzing doubt whenever tragic circumstances or upsetting situations arise. Death will come into our experience, and we will be agitated. "Bad breaks" will come, and we will be confused by them. Disappointments will shake us. In such situations we will need to come to God for the help we desperately need. That is why Paul tells the Philippians not to be anxious, "but in everything, by prayer and petition, with thanksgiving, present your requests to God" and, as a result, "the peace of God, which transcends all understanding, will guard your hearts and your minds in Christ Jesus" (Phil. 4:6–7). One great secret of the Christian life is to bring all troubling matters to God in prayer so as to find peace even in the midst of them. But the fact that these situations sometimes cause us to lose our sense of the peace *of* God does not mean that peace *with* God has been destroyed. In fact, knowing that God has made peace with us and that nothing will destroy the peace he has made will enable us to come to him quickly and boldly when we need help.

It will be an evidence of the fact that we have peace with God that we do so. D. Martyn Lloyd-Jones says that faith in this matter is like the needle of a compass that always points to the magnetic north. It is possible to deflect it—by a hard blow, for example, or by bringing another magnet close alongside. But these deflections are temporary, and the needle will always return to the proper position. That is what faith is like. It can be jarred or deflected, but it will always return to God—because God has made peace with us. Faith knows this, and God is faith's true home.

4. *These blessings are nevertheless only through the Lord Jesus Christ, as Paul says.*

Paul has been writing about Jesus at the end of Romans 4; he has spoken of his death and resurrection. In this chapter we might have expected him merely to assume the earlier references as a given and say simply, "Therefore, since we have been justified through faith, we have peace with God," stopping there. But Paul does not do that. Although he has already mentioned Jesus Christ, he now mentions him again, because he does not want us to imagine that we can get anywhere without him. He understands that any feeling of acceptance by God that is not based upon the work of Jesus Christ is an illusion!

At the start of this study I mentioned the feature in *Look* magazine in which sixteen prominent Americans told of the techniques they had developed for finding "peace of mind." There was one person I omitted, and that was Norman Vincent Peale. I did not mention him then because I was holding his reply until now. Peale is known for his philosophy of "positive thinking," which, in the judgment of many people, is not strongly Christian. But Peale nevertheless is a Christian, and in this feature he responded in a truly Christian way. Peale said, "I find peace of mind through a committed relationship with Jesus Christ and through faith in God. . . . Jesus alone can give you peace. That I've found to be a fact."[8]

So have countless others, and the reason is clear. Jesus gives us peace of mind because he has first made peace between our rebellious souls and God. I commend that peace to you and urge you to put your faith in him.

8. *Look* magazine, July 27, 1971.

61

Standing in Grace

Romans 5:1–2

Therefore, since we have been justified through faith, we have peace with God through our Lord Jesus Christ, through whom we have gained access by faith into this grace in which we now stand. . . .

One of the most important principles of sound Bible interpretation is that not everything written in the Bible is for everybody. This seems strange and wrong to some people. But it should not be, because we acknowledge this principle widely in everyday life.

What would you think of a postman who mixed up the addresses on the mail he was entrusted with delivering? Suppose he gave a letter containing a birth announcement to a person who didn't even know the child's parents. Or a bank statement showing an overdrawn account to someone who actually had a large balance. What about death notices? Or invitations to a party? Or bills? It is obvious that unless a letter is delivered to the right person, the postman is not doing his duty. A preacher is something like a postal worker. The Bible is his bag of messages, and his duty is to see that the right message gets to the right individual.

I emphasize this because we have passed from a section of Romans in which Paul has been explaining the gospel for the benefit of those who have not yet believed it and moved to a section of Romans in which he presents the benefits that belong to those who *have* believed. This means that while the first four chapters have, in a sense, been for everybody—an offer of salvation for the lost and an explanation of the nature of salvation for those who have received it—this present section (chs. 5–8) is only for those who have believed in Jesus Christ.

This is clear from the opening words of Romans 5: "Therefore, since we have been justified through faith. . . ." *If* you have been justified through faith in Jesus Christ, the benefits now to be listed are for you, says Paul. If you have not been justified, they are not for you. You must begin by believing in Jesus.

Peace: The Foundation

We have already seen one of these benefits in our study of the very first verse. It is "peace with God." This is a military metaphor, of course, and we have seen that it points to the fact that before our justification by God on the basis of Christ's work, we were not at peace with God. We might be inclined to say, as Henry David Thoreau is quoted as having said, "I am not at war with God." But we are lying if we say that. The Lord Jesus Christ said that man's chief responsibility is to "love the Lord your God with all your heart and with all your soul and with all your mind," and that the second is to "love your neighbor as yourself" (Matt. 22:37, 39; cf. Deut. 6:5; Lev. 19:18). But we do not do that. We actually hate God, hate others, and hate ourselves. We would do away with God if we could. We murder others when we can. And we commit spiritual suicide every day of our lives.

But, having been justified by grace through faith in Jesus Christ, this state of spiritual warfare has been changed to one of peace. We have peace with God, make peace with others, and experience a new measure of personal peace ourselves. This is the first great benefit of our justification.

A Few Important Definitions

In Romans 5:2, we come to a second benefit. But unlike verse 1, which speaks clearly of having peace with God, this verse is a bit hard to understand. There is a textual variation, for one thing, though it is not of great importance. Some Bible versions—the New International Version is among them—have the words "by faith" in verse 2, so the text reads: "we have gained access *by faith* into this grace in which we now stand" (emphasis added). Other versions—the Revised Standard Version is an example—omit "by faith." This is not an example of any supposed tendency of the RSV editors to eliminate faith from the Bible, but only a reflection of the fact that the words *tē pistei* are omitted in some of the earliest Greek texts.

The words should probably be retained, as the New International Version does. But this does not really matter. Since "access" is a benefit of justification and since justification has already been explained as coming to us through faith, faith is implied here, even if it is not stated. Or, to look at it in another way, the sentence begins "through whom"—that is, "through Christ." But we have Christ only through faith, and therefore faith is demanded by this expression also.

No, the really difficult thing is not the textual variation, though it has given us different translations of the verse, but the meaning of the words themselves. There are a number of very important words in this verse: *access, faith, grace,* and *stand.* But these can be used in different ways, and it is not easy to see how they all go together in this sentence.

Let me make an attempt to define each one, taking them in the order I think will get us to the meaning of this verse most quickly.

1. *Grace.* Grace is usually defined as "God's unmerited favor," and that is sometimes rightly strengthened to read "God's favor to those who actually deserve the opposite." In this sense, grace is what lies behind God's entire plan of redemption. That is why Paul can use it in writing to the Ephesians, saying, "For it is by grace you have been saved, through faith—and this not from yourselves, it is the gift of God—not by works, so that no one can boast" (Eph. 2:8–9).

But this is not the meaning of the word here. One clue to the fact that Paul is giving "grace" another meaning in Romans 5:2 is that he prefaces it with "this." "*This* grace!" "This" indicates that he has a specific grace in mind. Another clue is that Paul speaks of it as a grace "in which we now stand." What grace is that? In the context of Romans 5, it is clear that the grace in which we now stand is our state of justification.[1] It still means grace. But it specifically means that, while we were previously "under law and wrath," we are now "under grace" because we stand before God as justified men and women—if we have been justified through faith in Jesus Christ.

2. *Faith.* Faith also has a variety of meanings. It always means "believing God and acting upon that belief." But the emphasis can be either upon the acting (being faithful) or upon the believing (taking God at his word), or it can relate to a variety of things we are called upon to believe. Since the word is linked to "grace" in this sentence and since this grace is the grace of justification, the faith referred to here is the faith in Jesus Christ by which we are justified.

In other words, "faith" in this verse has the same meaning as "faith" in verse 1, which is why I said earlier that it does not matter much whether the words "by faith" are omitted in line with the textual variants. The faith by which we are justified is implied throughout.

1. See Charles Hodge, who writes, "The grace to which we have access, or into which we have been introduced, is the state of justification" (*A Commentary on Romans* [Edinburgh and Carlisle, Pa.: The Banner of Truth Trust, 1972], p. 133).

3. *Access.* The Greek term lying behind this word is *prosagōgē,* which can mean "access" or "right to enter" or "freedom to enter" or even "introduction." Since it is used of the work of the Holy Spirit in prayer in Ephesians 2:18, it has sometimes been said that the Holy Spirit "introduces" us to God.

What does the word mean here? The important thing to see about its use in Romans 5:2 is that it is preceded by the verb "have gained" and that this verb is in the past perfect tense. The New International Version says "have gained" in order to make the point I am making. But the word is actually "have," and in the past perfect tense the proper translation is "have had." What Paul is therefore saying is that we "*have had* our access into the grace of justification." Paul uses this special past tense to show that the justification in which we stand is something that has been accomplished for us and into which we have already entered. It has a present significance, too, of course. But the reason it has a present significance is that it is something that has already happened to us. We have been justified; therefore we remain justified. We have had our access, and it is because of this that we still have it.

4. *Stand.* The final key word in Romans 5:2 is the verb "stand." By now we can see how it should be taken. By the mercy of God we have been brought into the grace of justification, and that is the grace in which we now have the privilege to stand. Before, we were standing without, as children of wrath. Now we are standing within, not as enemies or even as pardoned criminals, but as sons and daughters of Almighty God.

Can I sum this up? You will remember that in the last study, when we were attempting to get a handle on the central purpose of Paul in Romans 5–8, I pointed out that the overriding theme of these chapters is assurance. So, although there is a progression in these first benefits of being justified—from having peace with God, to access, to rejoicing in hope of the coming glory—all nevertheless are also evidence that we have been made secure in Christ, and that forever. As Martyn Lloyd-Jones has written, "We have entered . . . into a position of grace, we have had our introduction to God and we [now] stand before him in an entirely new manner."[2]

Access to the King

In his short but valuable commentary on Romans, Ray C. Stedman illustrates the nature of our standing in grace by the Old Testament story of Queen Esther.[3]

Esther was a young Jewish woman living in the days following the fall of Jerusalem, as a result of which the majority of the Jewish people had been car-

2. D. M. Lloyd-Jones, *Romans: An Exposition of Chapter 5, Assurance* (Grand Rapids: Zondervan, 1972), p. 33.

3. Ray C. Stedman, *From Guilt to Glory,* vol. 1, *Hope for the Helpless* (Portland: Multnomah Press, 1978), pp. 134–136.

ried off to Babylon. At the time of her story, the king was Xerxes and he was ruling at Susa. Xerxes sought a bride to replace the deposed Queen Vashti and found one in Esther. She became his queen after being taken from the home of her cousin and guardian, Mordecai, to live in Xerxes' palace. A great enemy of the Jews named Haman was also living in the palace. Haman hatched a plot against the Jews in which Xerxes unwittingly signed a decree that would result in death for all the Jews in Persia. Mordecai got a message to Esther, telling her about the plot and saying that she must go to the king and tell him what was about to happen and prevent it.

Alas, explained Esther, there was a problem. It was a law of the Persians that no one could approach the king unbidden. If a person approached the king in the inner court without being summoned, there was only one result: death—unless the king held out his golden scepter to that person and thus spared his or her life. Although Queen Esther had not been summoned to the king for thirty days, even she could not approach him without danger of being put to death.

Mordecai explained to Esther that she had undoubtedly been brought to her royal position "for such a time as this" and that there was no one else who could intervene to save her people.

Esther agreed to go to the king. She spent three days in prayer and fasting, asking the Jews through Mordecai also to fast and pray with her. Then, at the end of her period of preparation, she put on her most royal robes and stepped into the king's inner hall. The king was sitting on his throne, facing the entrance. When he saw Esther he was so pleased with her beauty that he stretched out the scepter that was in his hand and thus accepted her. So Esther had access to the king, and through her the Jews were eventually spared.

This is what Paul says has happened to us through the work of Jesus Christ and the application of that work to us in our justification.

But the parallel is not exact, and for us the result is even more wonderful. Esther was beautiful, and the king was pleased with her. But, in our case, sin has made us highly offensive to God and we have not even tried to approach him. Still God has loved us. He sought us when we were far from him. He sent his Son to die for us, taking the punishment of our sin upon himself. Now, because of Christ's work, we have been brought into the palace where we enjoy God's favor and have continuing access to him.

The author of Hebrews puts it this way: "Therefore, brothers, since we have confidence to enter the Most Holy Place by the blood of Jesus . . . let us draw near to God with a sincere heart in full assurance of faith, having our hearts sprinkled to cleanse us from a guilty conscience . . ." (Heb. 10:19, 22).

Freedom and Confidence

That aforementioned verse from Hebrews obviously deals with prayer. This suggests that, although Romans 5:2 is not speaking explicitly about prayer (its concern is chiefly with assurance), all this obviously has bearing on our right to approach God in prayer and receive things from him.

Besides, we are encouraged in this thinking by the fact that one of the key words of Romans 5:2, "access" (*prosagōgē*), occurs in two other passages in the New Testament and that each of these has to do with prayer. Both are in Ephesians. The first is Ephesians 2:18—"For through him we both have access to the Father by one Spirit." The second is Ephesians 3:12—"In him and through faith in him we may approach God with freedom and confidence." These passages teach two things about prayer, which are based on the fact that we have been given access to God through his work of justification.

1. *Our access to God is direct.* I mean by this that we do not have to use mediators to get us to God, since the one true Mediator, the Lord Jesus Christ, has opened the door to heaven and given us access to the Father once and forever.

This truth is taught in the first of the two passages from Ephesians, for it comes at the end of a paragraph in which Paul has been referring to the barriers that once divided men and women from God and from each other. In the Jewish temple, to which he refers, there were walls designed to protect the approach to God. If you were to have approached the Temple Mount in Jerusalem at the time of Jesus Christ, you would have been confronted with a wall that divided the Courtyard of the Gentiles from what lay beyond. That wall meant what it said. No Gentile could go beyond it, and the penalty for thus violating the sanctity of the inner courtyard was death. Even the Romans upheld this penalty, and there were signs placed in warning, two of which have since been discovered and are in museums.

Jews could go forward, of course. But even Jewish worshipers would soon come to a second wall. This wall divided the Courtyard of the Women from the Courtyard of the Men. Here all Jewish women had to stop.

Beyond that was still another wall, and past it only Jewish priests could go. They could perform the sacrifices and enter the Holy Place of the temple. But here there was a final barrier, the great curtain that separated the Holy Place from the Most Holy Place. Beyond that barrier only one person could ever go, and that was the High Priest, who could enter only on the Day of Atonement to present the blood of the sacrifice that had been offered for the sins of the people moments before in the outer courtyard.

That elaborate system taught that the way to God was barred even for the elect people of Israel. God could be approached, but only through the mediation of the priests. Gentiles were without access at all, unless they first became Jews and approached by the Jewish route of priestly mediation.

But now, says Paul, those dividing walls of partition have been broken down, and the reason is that when Jesus died, God removed the ultimate barrier, the curtain that divided the Holy Place from the Most Holy Place. Do you remember how the great curtain was torn in two from top to bottom when Jesus died on the cross (Matt. 27:51)? This signified that atonement for sin had been made and accepted. The barriers of sin were now gone for all who would approach God on the basis of the death of Christ. For these—everyone who has been justified by the grace of God in Christ—access to God is now direct. There are no mediators needed, none save Jesus! Hence, we can come to God directly at any time of day or in any place and know that he hears us and will answer our prayers.

2. *Our access to God is effective.* This truth is taught by the second of the texts from Ephesians, for it emphasizes that through faith in Christ "we may approach God with freedom and confidence." Confidence in what? Obviously that he will hear us and answer our prayers according to his wise and perfect will.

We can pray wrongly, of course, and we often do. But when we pray according to the wise will of God, we can be confident that he will both hear us and answer our prayers.

My favorite story in this respect is about Martin Luther and his good friend and assistant Frederick Myconius. One day Myconius became sick and was expected to die within a short time. On his bed he wrote a loving farewell note to Luther, but when Luther received it he sat down instantly and wrote this reply: "I command thee in the name of God to live, because I still have need of thee in the work of reforming the church. . . . The Lord will never let me hear that thou art dead, but will permit thee to survive me. For this I am praying. This is my will, and may my will be done, because I seek only to glorify the name of God."

The words seem shocking to us, because we live in less fervent times. But Luther's prayer was clearly of God and therefore effective. For, although Myconius had already lost the ability to speak when Luther's letter came, in a short time he revived, and he lived six more years, surviving Luther by two months.

Can we be bold in prayer, as Luther was? There is a hymn by John Newton, the former slavetrader and preacher, that puts it quite well:

> Come, my soul, thy suit prepare:
> Jesus loves to answer prayer.
> He himself has bid thee pray,
> Therefore will not say thee nay.
>
> Thou art coming to a King,
> Large petitions with thee bring.
> For his grace and power are such,
> None can ever ask too much.

Abba, **Father**

My final point does not come specifically from either Romans 5:2 or the texts in Ephesians, though it occurs later in Romans (8:15) and in Galatians 4:6. But it is important to remember it whenever we speak about praying. It is that our approach to God may be intimate. We know this because Jesus taught us to use the intimate term *abba,* meaning "daddy," when we pray. It is the term Jesus used when praying, and it is the term he passed on to us: "Our *Abba,* who art in heaven."

God may be our King—the greatest king of all—which is why we can be bold in bringing large requests to him. But he is also our dear heavenly Father, and the access that we have as a result of our justification through the work of Christ has brought us into his home as beloved sons and daughters.

62

Hope of Glory

Romans 5:1–2

Therefore, since we have been justified through faith, we have peace with God through our Lord Jesus Christ, through whom we have gained access by faith into this grace in which we now stand. And we rejoice in the hope of the glory of God.

P aul wrote the fifth chapter of Romans to teach those who have been justified by God through faith in Jesus Christ that they are secure in their salvation. We have already seen two initial ways he has done this. He has spoken of the "peace" that has been made between God and ourselves by the work of Christ, and he has spoken of the "access" to God that we have been given as a result of that peace. In the final sentence of verse 2 we come to a third evidence of our security, namely that "we rejoice in the hope of the glory of God."

What does that mean?

In an earlier study I pointed out that "hope of the glory of God" concerns our final destiny as believers, in a manner parallel to the great statement in Romans 8:30: "And those he predestined, he also called; those he called, he also justified; those he justified, he also glorified." I pointed out that justification inevitably leads to glorification; that is, since God has justified us, he will also glorify us. Therefore, not only our present status, including both peace and access, but our final end, the hope of the glory of God, assure us that God's purposes for us will never be frustrated.

But this third benefit of justification is richer than anything I have expressed thus far, and for that reason, I want to take time to look at it carefully.

The Glory of Jesus Christ

I begin with the high priestly prayer of Jesus uttered just before his crucifixion:

> Father, the time has come. Glorify your Son, that your Son may glorify you.
> . . . I have brought you glory on earth by completing the work you gave me
> to do. And now, Father, glorify me in your presence with the glory I had with
> you before the world began. . . . Father, I want those you have given me to be
> with me where I am, and to see my glory, the glory you have given me
> because you loved me before the creation of the world.
>
> John 17:1, 4–5, 24

These verses teach that Jesus possessed a certain glory before his incarnation and laid this glory aside when he became man, but that now, having finished the earthly work God had given him to do, he was to take up that glory again. What was that glory? We have a few good intimations of it in Scripture, and there are a number of references to it beyond that.

First, when Peter, James, and John were with Jesus on the Mount of Transfiguration, we read that Jesus "was transfigured before them. His face shone like the sun, and his clothes became as white as the light" (Matt. 17:2). This was not a full manifestation of his heavenly glory, but it was enough to dazzle and even frighten the disciples. Peter, especially, was amazed at what he saw. At the time he had only a foolish suggestion: "Lord, it is good for us to be here. If you wish, I will put up three shelters—one for you, one for Moses and one for Elijah" (v. 4). But Peter always remembered this experience and later wrote, "We did not follow cleverly invented stories when we told you about the power and coming of our Lord Jesus Christ, but we were eyewitnesses of his majesty. For he received honor and glory from God the Father when the voice came to him from the Majestic Glory, saying, 'This is my Son, whom I love; with him I am well pleased.' We ourselves heard this voice that came from heaven when we were with him on the sacred mountain" (2 Peter 1:16–18).

The second intimation of Jesus' heavenly glory was Paul's vision of Jesus on the road to Damascus. That vision blinded Paul, and he was without sight for three days until God sent Ananias to heal him.

The glory of Jesus is a wonderful thing. So it is significant that in the Lord's great priestly prayer he asks not only that it might be restored to him following his crucifixion, resurrection, and ascension into heaven, which it clearly was, but also that those who belong to him might have the privilege of beholding him thus glorified. In light of this, when Paul speaks of "the hope of the glory of God" in Romans, at the very least he is looking forward to the time when we will see Jesus in the full manifestation of his glory. He had seen this glory on the way to Damascus and perhaps on one other occasion (2 Cor. 12:1–6), and he longed to see it again.

"Changed from Glory into Glory"

But we have to go further in understanding this idea, for it also has to do with the fact that we shall be glorified, as I suggested at the beginning. This is necessary, of course, because without our own glorification we would never be able to see the glory of the Lord (Heb. 12:14).

The best New Testament expression of this theme is 2 Corinthians 3:12–18, but to understand it we need to remember something that happened to Moses as a result of his having spent time with God on Mount Sinai (Exod. 34:29–35). When Moses came down from the mountain his face glowed with a transferred brilliance, and this was so bright that the people were unable to look directly at him. To converse with them Moses had to cover his face with a veil until the heavenly glory faded.

In 2 Corinthians 3, Paul picks up on this story, suggesting that today the veil is actually over the hearts of unbelievers and that believers, by contrast, are themselves unveiled and are becoming increasingly glorious, rather than having the glory fade from them, which is what happened to Moses. He says, "And we, who with unveiled faces all reflect the Lord's glory, are being transformed into his likeness with ever-increasing glory, which comes from the Lord, who is the Spirit" (v. 18). This means that the experience of Christians is to become increasingly glorified even now. We are to become like the Lord Jesus Christ in his perfections.

D. Martyn Lloyd-Jones has an excellent discussion of this progressive transformation, and one of its valuable features is his citing of hymns that use the idea of glory to express being transformed into Christ's likeness.[1]

One of the best known of Charles Wesley's hymns is "Love Divine, All Loves Excelling." The theme of this hymn is sanctification, and in it the sanctifying roles of the Son, Holy Spirit, and Father are reviewed successively while the corresponding progress of the believer is unfolded. The last verse says:

> Finish, then, thy new creation;
> Pure and spotless let us be:

---

1. D. M. Lloyd-Jones, *Romans: An Exposition of Chapter 5, Assurance* (Grand Rapids: Zondervan, 1972), pp. 53, 54.

> Let us see thy great salvation
> Perfectly restored in thee!
> *Changed from glory into glory,*
> Till in heaven we take our place,
> Till we cast our crowns before thee,
> Lost in wonder, love, and praise.

The central line, "changed from glory into glory," refers to the growth in holiness that is being achieved in believers now.

Here is another hymn, one by Isaac Watts: "Come, We That Love the Lord." One verse especially captures our idea, saying:

> The men of grace have found
> *Glory begun below;*
> Celestial fruits on earthly ground
> From faith and hope may grow.

The fact that we are going to be like Jesus one day is a marvelous expectation. But it is encouraging to know that this transformation has already begun for those who have been justified. In fact, sanctification proves to us that we are on the path to that glory.

The Glory of God

Yet I have still not reached the greatest part of the Christian's blessed hope, which I am expounding in this study.

Going back to Romans 5:2, we notice that, although Romans 5:2 is parallel to Romans 8:30 (as I have already indicated several times), the words Paul uses are not "glorification" or even "the glory of Jesus Christ," but "the glory of God." What is this "glory"? We have already touched on aspects of this word in treating the glory of Jesus. But glory is one of the richest concepts in the Bible, and for that reason it is worth backing up just a bit to define it more fully.

1. *The meaning of "glory" in Greek.* In the early days of the Greek language, when many Greek words were still developing freely, there was a verb (*dokeō*) that meant "to believe," "to think," or (in an intransitive form) "to seem," "to appear," or "to have the appearance of." Thus, the sentence *dokei moi* means "it seems good to me." From this verb came the noun (*doxa*), which is the word we translate as "glory" but which in those early stages naturally referred to how a thing seems or appears to someone. In other words, it meant "an opinion." This early meaning of *doxa* has been preserved in such theological terms as orthodox, paradox, and heterodox. An orthodox statement is one in which a person holds a "right" opinion. A

paradox is a "contrary" or inherently "contradictory" opinion. A heterodox opinion is one "other than" the right one.

In those early days the opinion one held could be either a good opinion or a bad one. But, as time went on, the word came to be used almost exclusively of a good opinion—it meant "renown," "reputation," or "honor"—and finally meant only the very best opinion of only the very best individuals. This is why the ancients came in time to speak of the "glory" of kings and eventually of God as "the King of glory" (Ps. 24:7–10). God is the King of glory because he is the most glorious of all beings. He is the one of whom only the highest opinions should be held.

When we express these high opinions of God what do we do? We "glorify" him, don't we? So, in this sense, to "glorify" God, "worship" God, and "praise" God are the same thing. To worship God means to assign him his true worth.

2. *The meaning of "glory" in Hebrew.* In the Hebrew language the words translated "glory" are a bit different, and to complicate matters a bit more, there are also two very distinct ideas. Nevertheless, it is important to have this background as well.

The common Hebrew word for "glory" is *kabod.* It is closest to the Greek word and is therefore (in the Septuagint) usually so translated. *Kabod* can mean "reputation" or "renown." But the root meaning actually refers to something that is "weighty" as opposed to something that is "weightless." We can define the glory of God in one sense by saying that God alone has real gravity or that he is the only really weighty being in the universe. To expand the idea a bit further, we can say that when the created order moves closer to God it takes on weight—like matter rushing toward a black hole—and that when created things move away from him they become lighter. Thus, the idols are accounted as being mere "nothings" (they have no weight), and God's judgment upon godless rulers is expressed by God's saying, as in the case of King Belshazzar, "*Mene, mene, tekel, parsin*" (Dan. 5:25). *Tekel* meant "You have been weighed on the scales and found wanting" (v. 27).

The other distinctly Hebrew idea is the *shekinah.* This was a visible manifestation of God's glory, generally understood as light so brilliant as to be unapproachable. This was the glory transferred to the face of Moses as a result of his having spent time with God on Mount Sinai (Exod. 34:29–35; cf. 2 Cor. 3:12–18), which I have previously noted. It was also the glory, veiled in a cloud, that descended to fill the Most Holy Place of the Israelites' wilderness tabernacle and later of the temple in Jerusalem (Exod. 40:34–38; 1 Kings 8:10–11).[2]

2. The linguistic history of "glory" is covered comprehensively in the long article on *dokeō, doxa* in Gerhard Kittel, ed., *Theological Dictionary of the New Testament,* vol. 2 (Grand Rapids: Wm. B. Eerdmans, 1964), pp. 232–255.

With this important background in place, let me refer now to one of the most interesting stories in the Old Testament. Moses had led the people of Israel to Mount Sinai and there had received the law of God. But the time to move on was coming, and Moses was not at all sure of his ability to lead the people forward. He shared his anxiety with God, and God replied, "My Presence will go with you, and I will give you rest" (Exod. 33:14).

Moses was still not satisfied. "If your Presence does not go with us, do not send us up from here. How will anyone know that you are pleased with me and with your people unless you go with us? What else will distinguish me and your people from all the other people on the face of the earth?" (vv. 15–16).

God said he would do what Moses asked. He would go with them.

Then Moses asked the most daring thing of all. "Show me your glory," he said.

To this God replied, "I will cause all my goodness to pass in front of you, and I will proclaim my name, the LORD, in your presence. I will have mercy on whom I will have mercy, and I will have compassion on whom I will have compassion. But . . . you cannot see my face, for no one may see me and live. . . . There is a place near me where you may stand on a rock. When my glory passes by, I will put you in a cleft in the rock and cover you with my hand until I have passed by. Then I will remove my hand and you will see my back; but my face must not be seen" (vv. 19–23).

In these verses, seeing the glory of God and seeing the face of God are treated as identical. This means, in the final analysis, that "hope of the glory of God," the phrase Paul uses in Romans 5:2, is nothing less than what theologians have called the Beatific Vision. It is the vision of God—the goal of our faith, the climax.

So what Paul is telling us is that the boon for which Moses prayed, and for which the saints of the ages have longed for fervently, is to be ours, and it is to be ours because of our gracious justification by the Father. Those who have been justified will see God. Therefore, as Paul wrote elsewhere, "Now we see but a poor reflection as in a mirror; then we shall see face to face. Now I know in part; then I shall know fully, even as I am fully known" (1 Cor. 13:12).

A Sure and Certain Hope

I need to make two more points to unfold fully what Paul is getting at in this section of Romans. The first is that this glorious culmination of our salvation by God is certain.

I have been saying this in different ways ever since we began these studies of Romans 5, but it is especially necessary to emphasize this now because of Paul's use of the noun *hope* in our text: "*hope* of the glory of God." In our day "hope" is a rather weak word. One dictionary defines it pretty well when it says: "desire with expectation of obtaining what is desired," listing "trust" and "reliance" as synonyms. But in common speech we usually mean much less than this. We speak of "hoping against hope" or "hoping for the best," which implies that we are not very hopeful. Or we even say, like John Milton, "Our final hope is flat despair" (*Paradise Lost,* book 2, line 139).

But this is not what hope means in the Bible, and even the dictionary definition (which I said was not bad) falls short of it. In the Bible, "hope" means certainty, and the only reason it is called hope rather than certainty is that we do not possess what is hoped for *yet,* although we will. Here are some examples of how "hope" is used in the New Testament:

Acts 2:26–27—"'. . . my body also will live in hope, because you will not abandon me to the grave . . .'" (cf. Ps. 16:8–11).

1 Corinthians 13:13a—"And now these three remain: faith, hope and love."

2 Corinthians 1:7—"And our hope for you is firm. . . ."

Colossians 1:5—"The faith and love that spring from the hope that is stored up for you in heaven. . . ."

Colossians 1:27—". . . Christ in you, the hope of glory."

Titus 1:2—". . . hope of eternal life, which God, who does not lie, promised before the beginning of time."

Titus 2:13—"While we wait for the blessed hope—the glorious appearing of our great God and Savior, Jesus Christ."

Hebrews 6:19–20—"We have this hope as an anchor for the soul, firm and secure. It enters the inner sanctuary behind the curtain, where Jesus, who went before us, has entered on our behalf. . . ."

1 Peter 1:3—". . . [God] has given us new birth into a living hope through the resurrection of Jesus Christ from the dead."

In each of those passages, hope refers to certainty. For even though we are not yet in full possession of what is hoped for, we are nevertheless certain of it, since it has been won for us by Christ and has been promised to us by God "who does not lie." This is how Paul is speaking in Romans 5:2 when he says, "And we rejoice in the hope of the glory of God."

And there is something else. The Greek word for "rejoice" is a common one in the New Testament, being used seventy-two times in Paul's writings alone.[3] But this is not the word used here, though it is not incorrectly translated "rejoice." The word Paul used is *kauchōmetha,* which actually means "boast" or "glory in." So the meaning is even stronger than rejoicing. How

3. The verb *charein* is used seventy-two times, the noun *chara* sixty times more.

could it be possible to boast, glory, or exult in our "hope of glory" if that end result were not absolutely certain?

Clearly, those who have been justified are to look forward to their final and full glorification with great confidence.

Purified by This Hope

There is one last point. In 1 John 3:1–3, the apostle is speaking of the return of Jesus Christ and of the fact that when he appears we shall be like him. He calls this our "hope," which is an appropriate use of the word, as we have already seen. But this is not only something having to do with the future, says John. Hope has a present significance, too. Here is how he puts it: "Dear friends, now we are children of God, and what we will be has not yet been made known. But we know that when he appears, we shall be like him, for we shall see him as he is. *Everyone who has this hope in him purifies himself, just as he is pure*" (vv. 2–3, emphasis added). It is our hope, or confidence, that we will be like Jesus one day that motivates us to be like him now. It leads us to live as morally pure a life as possible.

I have already said that Romans 5–8 is not chiefly about sanctification. But it does not exclude it, and in fact the opposite is the case. These chapters are about assurance, about our certain hope. But for that very reason they also embrace our growth in holiness. It is because we know that we will be like the Lord one day that we must purify ourselves and strive to live for him now.

63

God's Purpose in Human Suffering

Romans 5:3–5

Not only so, but we also rejoice in our sufferings, because we know that suffering produces perseverance; perseverance, character; and character, hope. And hope does not disappoint us, because God has poured out his love into our hearts by the Holy Spirit, whom he has given us.

The fifth chapter of Romans lists the grounds on which a person who has been justified by God through faith in Jesus Christ can know that he is saved from sin and can be steadfast in that knowledge. Verses 1 and 2 have listed several ways a Christian can be sure of this. Verses 3–5 give one more reason. It is the way believers in Christ respond to the troubles, trials, and tribulations of this life.

Christians do have tribulations, just like anybody else.

How should they respond to these trials?

How does their response strengthen their confidence that they are truly converted persons?

Paul says that Christians respond to their trials by rejoicing in them, however strange, abnormal, or even irrational this may seem to unbelievers, and that this is itself another evidence of their salvation. His exact words are:

"Not only so, but we also rejoice in our sufferings, because we know that suffering produces perseverance; perseverance, character; and character, hope. And hope does not disappoint us, because God has poured out his love into our hearts by the Holy Spirit, whom he has given us."

A Matter of Knowledge

Each of the words in these verses is of great importance, and we are going to look at some of them in detail. But if someone should ask me, "What is the most important word?" I would say that it is the word *know* in verse 3. The phrase reads, "because we know. . . . " "Know" is important because knowledge is the secret to everything else in the sentence. Christians rejoice in suffering because of what they know about it.

You have all heard the tired atheistic rebuttal to Christian doctrine based upon the presence of suffering in the world. It has been expressed in different forms, depending on which unbeliever has uttered it. But one common form goes like this: "If God were good, he would wish to make his creatures happy, and if God were almighty he would be able to do what he wished. But his creatures are not happy. Therefore God lacks either goodness or power or both."[1] That objection is insulting in its simplicity, for it assumes that our lack of suffering is an ultimate good and that the only possible factors involved in our quandary are the alleged benevolence and alleged omniscience of God. The Christian *knows* that there is more to the problem than this.

Still, the problem of suffering is a big one, and it is not easy to answer it in a single essay or even in a single book.

A Number of Negatives

The place to begin is with some negatives, and the negatives we need to begin with are two non-Christian approaches to this problem.

1. *Epicureanism.* The first non-Christian approach to suffering goes by the name Epicureanism, from the name of the Greek philosopher Epicurus (342–270 B.C.). Epicurus taught that life is an inevitable mixture of good and bad experiences, and since there are always some bad experiences, which cannot be avoided, the way to handle them is by loading life with more pleasure than pain so that the bottom line is positive. This outlook is called "qualified hedonism." It is popular today. I suppose it is the basic

1. This is the way the great Christian apologist C. S. Lewis states it at the beginning of his study of human suffering, *The Problem of Pain* (New York: Macmillan, 1962), p. 26. It is also the way the problem is viewed by the Boston rabbi Harold S. Kushner in *When Bad Things Happen to Good People* (New York: Avon Publishers, 1981), though he solves the problem merely by abandoning the divine attribute of omnipotence. He advises us to love God and "forgive him despite his limitations" (p. 148).

"Yuppie" outlook or mentality. But, of course, this is not the Christian answer to unavoidable bad things.

2. *Stoicism.* The second inadequate answer also has a Greek name since it was developed by a body of Greek philosophers called Stoics. Their answer was what our English friends call "the stiff upper lip" or, as we say: trying to "grin and bear it."

Some years ago there was a war movie starring the quintessential Stoic actor, Jimmy Cagney. I forget the exact title of this film, but it involved a crew of air-force bomber pilots who were flying raids over Europe in support of the Allied invasion. Cagney was returning from one of these raids, but his plane had been fired upon and was damaged and it looked as if it would not be able to clear the cliffs of Dover and so be able to return to its base. The crew dropped everything they could to lighten the plane and give it height, but it was still too low. Finally the crew itself bailed out, leaving Cagney alone at the controls. The plane was close to the cliffs now, and they were looming larger and larger through the cockpit window. It was clear the plane was not going to make it. Finally, just as the plane got to the cliffs, Cagney leaned out the window and spit at the cliff—and a moment later the plane exploded in flame.

That is the Stoic temperament. It is the attitude of the man who takes whatever life brings to him and spits at fate. But, of course, this is not the approach of Christians any more than that of the Epicureans.

God's Many Purposes

I have called this chapter "God's Purpose in Human Suffering" because of the single purpose that Paul spells out in our text. But if the entire Word of God is to be taken into account, as I intend to do, it would be better to speak of "God's *purposes* in human suffering," since there are a number of them. Let me suggest a few as part of our general approach to this large topic.

1. *Corrective suffering.* The most obvious category of suffering for a Christian is what we can call corrective suffering, that is, suffering that is meant to get us back onto the path of righteousness when we have strayed from it. We have an example from family life in the spankings given to young children when they disobey and do wrong. If a child needs a spanking, he should receive one, and if he has the right kind of father or mother, he does. Why? Is it because the parent likes to inflict pain? Are good parents all naturally sadists? Not at all! Rather, they understand that a child has to learn that he or she is not free to do whatever seems desirable irrespective of the needs or feelings of others, and that there are painful consequences whenever anyone persists in wrongdoing.

It is the same in the case of the divine Father and those who are his spiritual children. The author of Hebrews quotes Proverbs 3:11–12—"'My son, do not make light of the Lord's discipline, and do not lose heart when he rebukes you, because the Lord disciplines those he loves, and he punishes everyone he accepts as a son'"—concluding that we should: "Endure hardship as discipline. . . . For what son is not disciplined by his father?" (Heb. 12:5–7).

I mention this form of suffering first, for the first thing we should do when suffering comes into our lives is ask God whether or not it is intended by him for our correction. If it is, we need to confess our wrongdoing and return to the path of righteousness.

2. *Suffering for the glory of God.* A second important reason for suffering in the lives of some Christians is God's glory. Therefore, although when *we* suffer we should always ask God whether or not the suffering is for our correction, we should never blithely assume that this is necessarily what God is doing in the life of someone else. On the contrary, another person's suffering may be an evidence only of God's special favor to him or her.

How can that be?

Well, in John 9 we are told of the healing of a man who had been blind from birth. The blind man was apparently sitting at one of the gates of the temple when Jesus and his disciples passed by. The disciples made the mistake I just referred to, supposing that the man's sufferings were the result of a one-to-one relationship to some sin. They asked Jesus, "Rabbi, who sinned, this man or his parents, that he was born blind?" (John 9:2).

Jesus answered, "Neither this man nor his parents sinned, but this happened so that the work of God might be displayed in his life" (v. 3). Clearly, Jesus was teaching that the sole cause of this man's having spent the many long years of his life in blindness was so that, at this moment, Jesus might heal him and thus bring glory to God.

That idea is hard for many people to accept, particularly non-Christians. But it is not so difficult when we remember that life is short when measured by the scope of eternity and that our chief end is to glorify God—by whatever means he may choose to have us do it.

It was this knowledge that enabled Hugh Latimer to cry out to Nicolas Ridley as they were being led to the stake in Oxford, England, in 1555, "Be of good comfort, Master Ridley, and play the man; we shall this day light such a candle, by God's grace, in England as (I trust) shall never be put out."

Only those who have their eyes on eternity can assume this perspective.

3. *Suffering as a part of cosmic warfare.* A third kind of suffering is illustrated by the story of Job from the Old Testament. The story begins with Job as a happy and favored man, with a fine family and many possessions. But suddenly he suffered the loss of his many herds and the death of his ten children, and he did not know why. His friends came to try to help him sort it through. In fact, the Book of Job is a record of the limitations of human

reasoning in wrestling through these tough problems. But *we* know why Job suffered, because the book tells us why at the very beginning. It was because of a conflict between Satan and God. Satan had made the accusation that Job loved and served God only because God had blessed Job physically. "But stretch out your hand and strike everything he has, and he will surely curse you to your face," said Satan (Job 1:11).

God knew that this was not so. But he allowed Satan to have his way to show that Job loved God for himself and not for what he could get out of him. Job lost everything, but in a posture of abject mourning he neverthe-less worshiped God, saying: "Naked I came from my mother's womb, and naked I will depart. The LORD gave and the LORD has taken away; may the name of the LORD be praised" (v. 21). Then we are told: "In all this, Job did not sin by charging God with wrongdoing" (v. 22).

This story explains a great deal (perhaps most) of the suffering some Christians endure. I imagine that for every believer who is suffering with a particular form of cancer there is also a nonbeliever in exactly the same condition and that the Christian praises and worships God in spite of his afflictions while the unbeliever curses God and bitterly resents his fate. God is showing that the purpose of life lies in a right relationship to him and not in pleasant circumstances. For every Christian who loses a son or daughter there is a non-Christian who experiences the same thing. For every Christian who loses a job there is a non-Christian in like circumstances. This is the explanation of life's struggles, in my opinion. It is the ultimate reason for the drama of history.

4. *Constructive suffering.* The fourth purpose of God in suffering is what Paul presents in Romans 5, namely, that God uses our troubles, trials, and tribulations to form Christian character.

Evangelist Billy Graham illustrated this by a story from the Great Depression. A friend of his had lost a job, a fortune, a wife, and a home. But he was a believer in Jesus Christ, and he hung to his faith tenaciously even though he could see no purpose in what was happening and was naturally oppressed by his circumstances. One day in the midst of his depression he was wandering through the city and stopped to watch masons doing stonework on a huge church. One was chiseling a triangular piece of stone. "What are you doing with that?" he asked.

The workman stopped and pointed to a tiny opening near the top of a nearly completed spire. "See that little opening up there near the top of the spire?" he said. "Well, I'm shaping this down here so that it will fit in up there." Graham's friend said that tears filled his eyes as he walked away, for it seemed to him that God had spoken to say that he was shaping him for heaven through his earthly ordeal.

The Benefits of Suffering

Having approached our subject from the perspective of God's purposes, we are now ready to see what Paul says suffering will do in the lives of Christians, and why this is reassuring. What benefits does suffering bring?

First, it produces *perseverance*. You may notice another word used to translate this idea in your Bible—if you are using other than the New International Version—because the word seems to most translators to call for a richness of expression. Some versions say "patience," others "endurance," still others "patient endurance."

The full meaning of this word emerges when we consider it together with the word for "suffering," which occurs just before it in the Greek text and which is what Paul says produces "patience" (KJV). There are a number of words for suffering in the Greek language, but this one is *thlipsis,* which has the idea of pressing something down. It was used for the effect of a sledge as it threshed grain, for instance. The sledge pressed down the stalks and thus broke apart the heads to separate the chaff from the grain. *Thlipsis* was also used of crushing olives to extract their oil or of grapes to press out wine.

With that in mind, think now of "perseverance." The word translated "perseverance" is *hypomonē*. The first part of this word is a prefix meaning "under" or "below." The second part is a word meaning an "abode" or "living place." So the word as a whole means to "live under something." If we take this word together with the word for tribulation, we get the full idea, which is to live under difficult circumstances without trying, as we would say, to wriggle out from under them. We express the idea positively when we say, "Hang in there, brother." It is hanging in when the going gets tough, as it always does sooner or later.

So here is one thing that separates the immature person from the mature one, the new Christian from one who has been in the Lord's school longer. The new believer tries to avoid the difficulties and get out from under them. The experienced Christian is steady under fire and does not quit his post.

Second, just as suffering produces steady perseverance, so (according to Paul) does perseverance produce *character.* Other versions translate this word as "experience." But again, it is richer even than these two very useful renderings.

The Greek word is *dokimē,* but *dokimē* is based on the similar word *dokimos,* which means something "tested" or "approved." There is an illustration that Paul himself provides. In 1 Corinthians 9:27 Paul is speaking of self-discipline and says, ". . . I beat my body and make it my slave so that after I have preached to others, I myself will not be disqualified for the prize." The word *disqualified* is our word, but with a negative particle in front of it. This suggests an image from the ancient world. Silver and gold coins were made quite roughly in those days, not milled to exact sizes as our coins are, and people would often cheat with them by carefully trimming off some of the excess metal. We know they did this because hundreds of laws were passed against the practice. After people had trimmed away enough metal, they would sell it for new coins.

When coins had been trimmed for a long time, they eventually got so light that the merchants would not take them anymore; then a coin was said to be *adokimos*, "disqualified." This is what Paul is referring to. He is saying that he does not want to be disqualified, but rather to be judged "fit" as a result of his sufferings and self-discipline.

It is the same in our Romans text, where Paul says that the sufferings of life or the pressures of merely trying to live for Christ in our godless environment produce endurance, which in turn proves that we are fit.

I think of it another way, too. A disapproved coin is a light coin, and I remember (from the previous study) that this is what happens to us when we draw away from God. We become increasingly weightless. But when we draw closer to God and he to us, working in us what is well pleasing to himself, we become "weighty," as he is. We become approved persons of great value.

Ray Stedman, who discusses these benefits well in his Romans commentary, tells at this point of a time he once asked a nine-year-old-boy, "What do you want to be when you grow up?"

The boy said, "A returned missionary."

He did not want to be just a missionary, but a returned one—one who had been through the fires, had them behind him, and was shown to have been of real value in God's work.[2]

Finally, Paul indicates that the steadfast, approved character created by perseverance in its turn produces *hope*. Here we have come full circle. We started with hope. We saw it as an assurance of what will one day be ours, though we do not possess it yet. Then we looked at our sufferings. We saw why we can rejoice in them. It is because they lead to endurance, endurance to an approved character, and character to an even more steadfast hope. And all this is further evidence of our security in Christ—when we share in Christ's sufferings and embrace them in like fashion.

The Church in China

Some years ago I had an opportunity to publish an article on suffering by one of the missionaries of Tenth Presbyterian Church, Dr. Jonathan Chao, an acknowledged expert on the state of the church in China. It made a comparison between the growth of the Chinese church during the relatively peaceful years of the nineteenth and early-twentieth centuries, and the years since 1950, when the Communists took over. By the end of the "mis-

2. Ray C. Stedman, *From Guilt to Glory*, vol. 1. *Hope for the Helpless* (Portland: Multnomah Press, 1978), p. 148.

sionary period," there were approximately 840,000 Christians in China. Today, however, after forty years of the most intense persecutions and suffering, the Chinese church, according to Chao's calculations, numbers fifty million. In Chao's opinion, it was the suffering of the church that produced character, the ability not only to survive the persecutions, but also to win many others even in hard times.

I mention this background for the sake of the following story. In this same article Chao told of an American student who came to Hong Kong to study the Chinese church. Before he had left the States a friend had asked him, "If God loves the Chinese church so much, why did he allow so much suffering to come upon it?"

The student confessed that he had no answer at the time. But after he had traveled to China and had made extensive and meaningful contacts with a number of Chinese Christians, he discovered an answer that he put like this: "Mr. Chao, I am going back to America and ask my friend this question: If God loves the American church so much, why hasn't he allowed us to suffer like the church in China?"[3]

It is a good question, because, according to the Bible, suffering is not harmful; on the contrary, it is a beneficial experience. It is beneficial because it accomplishes the beneficent purposes of Almighty God. It is part of all those circumstances that work "for the good of those who love him . . ." (Rom. 8:28).

3. Jonathan Chao, "The Place of Suffering in the Christian Life," in *Tenth: An Evangelical Quarterly*, vol. 14, no. 2 (April 1984), pp. 10–19.

64

God's Love Commended

Romans 5:6–8

You see, at just the right time, when we were still powerless, Christ died for the ungodly. Very rarely will anyone die for a righteous man, though for a good man someone might possibly dare to die. But God demonstrates his own love for us in this: While we were still sinners, Christ died for us.

There are a number of preachers today, some of them quite famous, who do not want to say anything unpleasant about sinful human nature. They describe their approach to Christianity as "possibility thinking" and argue that people are already so discouraged about themselves that they do not need to be told that they are wicked. I do not know how such preachers could possibly preach on our text.

They should want to, I think,

Romans 5:6–8 (and verse 5, which precedes this paragraph) speak about the love that God has for us. The greatness of this love, which is mentioned here in Romans for the very first time, is an uplifting and positive theme. Besides, it is brought into the argument at this point to assure us that all who have been justified by faith in Christ have been saved because of God's love for them and that nothing will ever be able to separate them from it. This is the climax to which we will also come at the end

535

of Romans 8. Nothing could be more positive or more edifying than this theme. Yet Paul's statement of the nature, scope, and permanence of God's love is placed against the black backdrop of human sin, and rightly so. For, as Paul tells us: "God demonstrates his own love for us in this: While we were still sinners, Christ died for us" (v. 8).

How can we appreciate or even understand that statement without speaking about the evil natures of those whom God has thus loved?

This is a very practical matter for two reasons. First, since Paul is describing the love of God against the dark background of human sin, he is saying that it is only against this background that we are able to form a true picture of how great the love of God is. In other words, if we think (as many do) that God loves us because we are somehow quite lovely or desirable, our appreciation of the love of God will be reduced by just that amount—just as a beautiful but very vain woman might have trouble appreciating the love of her husband, or of anyone else. If we think we deserve the best of everything, we will not appreciate the love we receive irrespective of our beauty, talent, or other supposedly admirable qualities.

The second point is this: If we think we deserve God's love, we cannot ever really be secure in it, because we will always be afraid that we may do something to lessen or destroy the depth of God's love for us. It is only those who know that God has loved them *in spite of* their sin who can trust him to continue to show them favor.

God's Love for Sinners

I begin with Paul's description of the people God loves and has saved, and I ask you to notice the four powerful words used to portray them, three in the passage we are studying and one additional word in verse 10. They are "powerless," "ungodly," "sinners," and "enemies." It is important to know that we are all rightly described by each of these words.

1. *Powerless.* This word is translated in a variety of ways in our Bible versions: "weak," "helpless," "without strength," "feeble," "sluggish in doing right," and so on. Only the strongest terms will do in this context, since the idea is that, left to ourselves, none of us is able to do even one small thing to please God or achieve salvation.

One commentator distinguishes between "conditional impossibilities" and "unconditional impossibilities" in order to show that this kind of inability is truly unconditional.[1] A conditional impossibility is one in which we are unable to do something *unless* something else happens. For example, I might find it impossible to repay a loan *unless* I should suddenly earn a large sum of money. Or I might be unable to accept an invitation to some

---

1. Donald Grey Barnhouse, *God's River: Exposition of Bible Doctrines, Taking the Epistle to the Romans as a Point of Departure,* vol. 4, Romans 5:1–11 (Grand Rapids: Wm. B. Eerdmans, 1959), pp. 161, 162.

social event *unless* a prior commitment is canceled. An unconditional impossibility is one which no possible change in circumstances can alter, and it is this that describes us in our pre-converted state.

What specifically were we unable to do? We were unable to understand spiritual things (1 Cor. 2:14). We were unable to see the kingdom of God or enter it (John 3:3, 5). We were unable to seek God (Rom. 3:11). Paul elsewhere describes this inability vividly when he says that before God saved us we were "dead in [our] transgressions and sins" (Eph. 2:1). That is, we were no more able to respond to or seek God than a corpse is able to respond to stimuli of any kind.

2. *Ungodly.* This word conveys the same idea Paul expressed at the beginning of his description of the race in its rebellion against God: "The wrath of God is being revealed from heaven against all the godlessness and wickedness of men who suppress the truth by their wickedness" (Rom. 1:18).

In these verses, "ungodly" and "godlessness" mean not so much that human beings are unlike God (though that is also true), but that in addition they are in a state of fierce opposition to him. God is sovereign, but they oppose him in his sovereignty. They do not want him to rule over them; they want to be free to do as they please. God is holy, and they oppose him in his holiness. This means that they do not accept his righteous and proper moral standards; they do not want their sinful acts and desires to be called into question. God is omniscient, and they oppose him for his omniscience. They are angry that he knows them perfectly, that nothing they think or do is hidden from his sight. They also oppose him for his immutability, since immutability means that God does not change in these or any of his other attributes.

3. *Sinners.* "Sinners" describes those who have fallen short of God's standards, as Romans 3:23 says: "For all have sinned and fall short of the glory of God." It means that we have broken God's law and in this sense is probably parallel to the word *wickedness* in Romans 1:18, which was cited above. "Godlessness" is being opposed to God; that is, to have broken the first table of the law, which tells us that we are to worship and serve God only (cf. Matt. 22:37–38). "Wickedness" means to have broken the second table of the law; we have failed to treat others properly, to have respected them, and to have loved them as we love ourselves (cf. Matt. 22:39).

4. *Enemies.* The final word Paul uses to describe human beings apart from the supernatural work of God in their lives is "enemies," though the word does not appear until verse 10. This summarizes what has been said by the first three terms, but it also goes beyond that. It affirms that not only are we unable to save ourselves, are unlike and opposed to God, and are violators of his law, but we are also opposed to God in the sense that we would attack him and destroy him if we could. Being like Satan in his desires, we would drag God from his throne, cast him to hell and crush

him into nothingness—if that were possible—which is what many people actually tried to do when God came among them in the person of Jesus Christ.

What a terrible picture of humanity! No wonder the possibility thinkers choose other, more uplifting themes to speak about!

Yet it is only against this background that we see the brightness of God's love. "You see," writes Paul, "at just the right time, when we were still powerless, Christ died for the ungodly. Very rarely will anyone die for a righteous man, though for a good man someone might possibly dare to die. But God demonstrates his own love for us in this: While we were still sinners, Christ died for us" (vv. 6–8).

Love at the Cross

Any contrast has two sides, of course, and thus far we have looked only at one side. We have looked at the dark side: ourselves. We have seen that God loved us, not when we were lovely people who were seeking him out and trying to obey him, but when we were actually fighting him and were willing to destroy him if we could. That alone makes the measure of God's love very great. However, we may also see the greatness of the love of God by looking at the bright side: God's side. And here we note that God did not merely reach out to give us a helping hand, bestowing what theologians call common grace—sending rain on the just and unjust alike (cf. Matt. 5:45), for instance—but that he actually sent his beloved Son, the Lord Jesus Christ, to die for us.

There is a further contrast, too, as Paul brings these great ideas together and compares what God has done in dying for sinners with what human beings might themselves do in certain circumstances. Paul points out that, while a human being might be willing to give his life for a righteous or, better yet, a morally superior woman or man under certain circumstances, Jesus died for us while we were still sinners, which is the precise opposite of being good, or righteous.

In his excellent study of this text Donald Grey Barnhouse gives two illustrations of exceptionally great human love.

In one story two men were trapped in a mine cave-in, and poisonous gas was escaping. One man had a wife and three children. He also had a gas mask, but his mask had been torn in the underground explosion and he would have perished apart from the act of the man who was trapped with him. This second man took off his own mask and forced it on the man who survived, saying, "You have Mary and the children; they need you. I am alone and can go." When we hear of an act like this, we sense we are on hallowed ground.

The other story concerns a tough youngster from the streets of one of our large cities. His sister had been crippled and needed an operation. The operation was provided for her. But after the operation the girl needed a blood transfusion, and the boy, her brother, was asked to volunteer. He was taken to her bedside and watched tight-lipped as a needle was inserted into his vein and blood was fed into his sister's body. When the transfusion was over, the doctor put his arm on the boy's shoulder and told him that he had been very brave. The youngster knew nothing about the nature of a blood transfusion. But the doctor knew even less about the actual bravery of the boy—until the boy looked up at him and asked steadily, "Doc, how long before I croak?"[2] He had gotten the idea that he would have to die to save his sister, and he had thought that he was dying drop by drop as his blood flowed into her veins. But he did it anyway!

These stories sober us, because in them we recognize something of the highest human love. Yet, when we read of the love of God in Romans 5, we learn that it was not for those who were close to him or who loved him that Jesus died—but for those who were opposed to God and were his enemies. It is on this basis that God commends his love to us.

An Argument for Hard Hearts

Isn't it astounding that God should need to commend his love to us? We are told in the Bible, though we should know it even without being told, that all good gifts come from God's hands (James 1:17). It is from God that we receive life and health, food and clothing, love from and fellowship with other people, and meaningful work. These blessings should prove the love of God beyond any possibility of our doubting it. Yet we do doubt it. We are insensitive to God's love, and God finds it necessary to commend his love by reminding us of the death of his Son.

So it is at the cross that we see the love of God in its fullness. What a great, great love this is!

You may recall that when the Swiss theologian Karl Barth was in this country some years before his death, someone asked a question at one of his question-and-answer sessions that went like this: "Dr. Barth, what is the greatest thought that has ever gone through your mind?"

The questioner probably expected some complicated and incomprehensible answer, as if Einstein were being asked to explain the theory of relativity. But after he had thought a long while, Barth replied by saying: "Jesus loves me, this I know. For the Bible tells me so."

This was a profound answer and a correct one. For there is nothing greater that any of us could think about or know than that Jesus loves us and has shown his love by dying in our place.

The Greatness of God's Love

I would like to close this study by reflecting on the greatness of God's love for us, but I wonder how anyone can do that adequately. How can any merely human words sufficiently express this wonder?

2. Barnhouse, *God's River*, p. 177.

Some years ago I was preaching through the Gospel of John and had come to that greatest of all verses about the love of God: John 3:16. "For God so loved the world that he gave his one and only Son, that whoever believes in him shall not perish but have eternal life." I wanted to say that the love of God is great, remembering that Ephesians 2:4 uses that very word: "But because of his *great* love for us. . . ." But the English word *great* is not great enough for this subject. The week before, I had been at Houghton College in New York, and I remembered having said that I thought the work of the college was *great*, that some of the points the other speakers had made were *great*, and that I had had a *great* time. I was sincere in my use of the word *great*. But what were such uses of the word compared to the use of the word to describe God's love?

Someone once tried to express the greatness of God's love by printing on a little card a special arrangement of John 3:16, with certain descriptive phrases added. The twelve parts of the verse were arranged down one side of the card, and the added phrases were printed across from them. It went like this:

God	the greatest Lover
so loved	the greatest degree
the world	the greatest company
that he gave	the greatest act
his only begotten Son	the greatest gift
that whosoever	the greatest opportunity
believeth	the greatest simplicity
in him	the greatest attraction
should not perish	the greatest promise
but	the greatest difference
have	the greatest certainty
everlasting life	the greatest possession

The title placed over the whole was: "Christ—the Greatest Gift."

Let me try to express the greatness of the love of God by the words of a hymn by F. M. Lehman. Lehman wrote most of this hymn, but the final stanza (the best, in my opinion) was added to it later, after it had been found scratched on the wall of a room in an asylum by a man said to have been insane. The first and last verses of the hymn and the chorus, go as follows:

> The love of God is greater far
> Than tongue or pen can ever tell;
> It goes beyond the highest star,
> And reaches to the lowest hell.
> The guilty pair, bowed down with care,

> God gave his Son to win:
> His erring child he reconciled
> And rescued from his sin.
>
> Could we with ink the ocean fill,
> And were the skies of parchment made;
> Were every stalk on earth a quill,
> And every man a scribe by trade;
> To write the love of God above
> Would drain the ocean dry;
> Nor could the scroll contain the whole,
> Tho stretched from sky to sky.
>
> Oh, love of God, how rich and pure!
> How measureless and strong!
> It shall forevermore endure—
> The saints' and angels' song.

Did you know that the love of God seemed so great to the biblical writers that they invented, or at least raised to an entirely new level of meaning, a brand-new word for love?

The Greek language was rich in words for love. There was the word *storgē,* which referred to affection, particularly within the family. There was *philia,* from which we get "philharmonic" and "philanthropy" and the place name "Philadelphia." It refers to a love between friends. A third word was *erōs,* which has given us "erotic," and which referred to sexual love. This was a rich linguistic heritage. Yet, when the Old Testament was translated into Greek and when the New Testament writers later wrote in Greek, they found that none of these common Greek words was able to express what they wanted. They therefore took another word without strong associations and poured their own, biblical meaning into it. The new word was *agapē,* which thereby came to mean the holy, gracious, sovereign, everlasting, and giving love of God that we are studying here.

Alas, I feel that even yet I have not begun to explain how great the love of God is. There is nothing to be done but to go back to our text and read again: "You see, at just the right time, when we were still powerless, Christ died for the ungodly. Very rarely will anyone die for a righteous man, though for a good man someone might possibly dare to die. But God demonstrates his own love for us in this: While we were still sinners, Christ died for us."

Perhaps I should say one more thing on this subject: If you do not yet fully appreciate (or perhaps have not even begun to appreciate) the greatness of the love God has for you, the explanation is probably that you have never really thought of yourself as God saw you in your fallen state.

Perhaps you have never thought of yourself as someone who was utterly without strength or powerless before God saved you.

Perhaps you have never considered yourself to have been ungodly.

Nor a sinner.

Nor God's enemy.

But that is what you were—and still are if you have never come to Christ in order to be justified. It is only if you can recognize the truth of these descriptions that you can begin to appreciate the love that God holds out to you through the death of his Son.

If you have never responded to this great overture of the divine love, let me encourage you to do that, assuring you that there is no greater truth in all the universe. Can you think of anything greater? Of course, you can't. How could anybody? God loves you. Jesus died for you. Let those truly great thoughts move you to abandon your sin, love God in return, and live for Jesus.

65

Full Salvation

Romans 5:9-11

Since we have now been justified by his blood, how much more shall we be saved from God's wrath through him! For if, when we were God's enemies, we were reconciled to him through the death of his Son, how much more, having been reconciled, shall we be saved by his life! Not only is this so, but we also rejoice in God through our Lord Jesus Christ, through whom we have now received reconciliation.

I have been expounding Romans 5:1–11 for five studies now—this is the sixth—and in every one of these studies I have said that the point of these verses is to assure Christians of their salvation. They are to know that they are eternally secure in Christ so that they might be able to rejoice in God fully. In this study we find the same idea. I might be inclined to apologize for this repetition were it not for the fact that this is clearly the emphasis of the chapter—and that it is going to continue in one form or another until the end of chapter 8.

This has not been mere repetition, however, since the thesis (which *is* repeated) has been supported by a variety of arguments:

1. We can be assured of salvation because God has made peace with us through the atoning work of Jesus Christ.

543

2. We can be assured of salvation because, through that same work of Christ, we have been brought into a new relationship with God in which we continue to stand.

3. We can be assured of salvation because of the sure and certain hope that we shall see God.

4. We can be assured of salvation because of the way we are able to react to sufferings in this life. We see God's purposes in them and therefore rejoice in them, which unbelievers cannot do.

5. We can be assured of salvation because God sent Jesus Christ to die for us, not when we were saved people, as we are now, but when we were God's sworn enemies.

In this last section, Paul provides yet another argument or, what is probably more accurate to say, draws his previous arguments together: "Since we have now been justified by his blood, how much more shall we be saved from God's wrath through him! For if, when we were God's enemies, we were reconciled to him through the death of his Son, how much more, having been reconciled, shall we be saved by his life! Not only is this so, but we also rejoice in God through our Lord Jesus Christ, through whom we have now received reconciliation."

Sound Logic

In the sayings that have come down to us from the great Rabbi Hillel there are some principles for Bible interpretation that Paul, as a Jewish thinker, frequently used in his writings. One is called *qal w'chomer*, from the Hebrew words for "light" and "heavy." It refers to a form of arguing in which, if a lesser thing is true, a greater thing must clearly be true also. Here is an example from the teaching of Jesus: "If you, then, though you are evil, know how to give good gifts to your children, how much more will your Father in heaven give good gifts to those who ask him!" (Matt. 7:11). Obviously, if we who are evil know how to do good to those who are close to us (this is the "light" part of the comparison), God, who is utterly good (this is the "heavy" part), will do good to his children.

A second principle related to the light/heavy argument is the opposite, an argument from the "heavy" to the "light." It argues that if something great is true, then something lesser in the same category will obviously be true also. Paul uses this principle twice in these verses:

1. "Since we have now been justified by his blood, how much more shall we be saved from God's wrath through him!" (v. 9), and

2. "For if, when we were God's enemies, we were reconciled to him through the death of his Son, how much more, having been reconciled, shall we be saved by his life!" (v. 10).

Each of these arguments is based upon things God has already done for us through the death of Christ. They are great works: justification on the one hand, and reconciliation on the other. They are so great that they are used by God to commend his love to us, as Paul stated earlier. But if God has already done such great works on our behalf, justifying us in Christ when we were ungodly and reconciling us to himself when we were his enemies, God will obviously continue his work in the lesser task of seeing us through life and through the final judgment.

Saved from God's Wrath

When we look at verse 9, we have a tendency to think that we have already heard everything this verse has to teach. After all, "wrath" is the term we began with back in Romans 1:18, and the doctrine of "justification" was developed fully and compellingly in Romans 3. Besides, Romans 5:9 seems to be almost an identical repeat of verse 1 of this chapter. It is true, of course, that this is the first time we have encountered the word *saved* in the letter. But what have we been talking about all this time if it has not been salvation?

To understand what is happening we have to realize that "saved" is used in at least three different ways in the Bible, in three different tenses. Sometimes it refers to something past, at other times to something present, sometimes to things yet to come.

Let me illustrate. Suppose you are a Christian and that someone asks you, "Are you saved?"

How do you respond? I suppose you would most likely just say, "Yes, I am." But it would be possible for you to answer in three different ways, the answer you gave ("Yes, I am") being only one of them. If you are thinking of what Jesus accomplished on your behalf by dying for you on the cross, it would be correct to have answered as you did, for Jesus did save you by his substitutionary death.

But if you are thinking of the present and of what God is accomplishing in you day by day, it would also be correct to say, "I am being saved." Paul himself uses the word this second way in 1 Corinthians 1:18: "For the message of the cross is foolishness to those who are perishing, but to us who are being saved it is the power of God." This verse means that God works through the power of the cross to save us from sin now.

Third, you could think in future terms and answer the question by saying, "No, I am not saved yet, but I will be when Jesus returns." In this case you would be looking forward to your future glorification when the work begun in the past by Jesus and continued into the present by the power of the Holy Spirit, who works in us, will be perfected. In that day we will be delivered even from the presence of sin and made like Jesus forever.

I mention these three tenses of the word, because it is important to see that it is in the third sense, the future sense of salvation, that Paul speaks here. He is not denying the other tenses, particularly not the first. But he is thinking of the judgment to come and is saying that because we have already been justified by God on the basis of the death of Christ, we can be certain of being saved from the outpouring of God's wrath in the final day. D. Martyn Lloyd-Jones says, "The apostle's argument is that this method, this way of salvation that God has planned, is a complete whole, and therefore, if we have been justified by Christ's blood we are joined to Christ, we are in Christ, and we shall therefore be saved by him completely and perfectly."[1]

Or we could put it like this: If God has already justified us on the basis of Jesus' atoning death, if he has already pronounced his verdict, any verdict rendered at the final judgment will be only a confirming formality.

Reconciled

Arguing from the "heavy" to the "light" is, if anything, even more apparent in verse 10, where Paul speaks of reconciliation. I begin with the "heavy" part. What is this "heavy" thing God has done for us?

It is the very work we were looking at in detail in the last study. There we were dealing with the love of God, and we saw that the basis upon which God commends his love to us is that it caused him to send his Son, the Lord Jesus Christ, to die for us while we were yet sinners. Our sinfulness was spelled out in three powerful terms, and these (as we saw) are followed by a fourth term in verse 10. Paul describes us as powerless, ungodly, sinners, and enemies. Let us review those terms:

1. "*Powerless*" means that we are unable to help ourselves. It is what theologians mean by total depravity, not that we are all as bad as we could possibly be, but that we are all equally and totally incapable of doing anything to save ourselves. We are not able to seek out and eventually come even to understand the way of salvation.

2. "*Ungodly*" means that we are opposed to God in his godly nature. We do not like him for being who he is.

3. "*Sinners*" means that we are violators of God's moral law, particularly that second table of the law meant to govern our conduct toward other persons.

4. "*Enemies*," the word used in the verses we are studying now, is the worst term of all. It means not only that we dislike God in his godly nature, but that we are so opposed to God in that nature that we would destroy him if we could. Like a soldier approaching his counterpart in an enemy army in wartime, we consider it a matter of "kill or be killed." We think of God's law as suffocatingly oppressive and destructive of who we want to be. So we are

1. D. M. Lloyd-Jones, *Romans: An Exposition of Chapter 5, Assurance* (Grand Rapids: Zondervan, 1972), p. 135.

set on destroying God or at least destroying his influence so far as the living of our lives is concerned.

But, says Paul, it is while we were like this that God reconciled us to himself through Jesus' death. "Reconcile" means to remove the grounds of hostility and transform the relationship, changing it from one of enmity to one of friendship. In our case, as Paul has shown earlier, it meant taking us out of the category of enemies and bringing us into God's family as privileged sons and daughters. If God did that for us while we were enemies, Paul reasons, he is certainly going to save us from the final outpouring of his wrath on the day of judgment, now that we are family members.

If God has done the greater thing, he will do the lesser. If he has saved us while we were enemies, he will certainly save us as friends.

Rejoice in God

The last verse of our text, which also marks the end of the first half of Romans 5, says that now, having been reconciled to God, "we also rejoice in God through our Lord Jesus Christ. . . ."

There is a sense in which this idea returns us to where we started out, since the first sentence of Romans 5 speaks of just such a rejoicing: "we rejoice in the hope of the glory of God."[2] But careful reading will show that the object of our rejoicing is not the same in both cases. In verse 2, our rejoicing is in "hope of the glory of God." That is, it is in our glorification. Knowing that we are going to be glorified is a cause of great joy for us. However, in verse 11, the object of our rejoicing is not our glorification, important as that is, but God himself who will accomplish it. And, of course, of the two ideas the second is obviously the greater. To rejoice in God is the greatest of all human activities.

We affirm this in the response to the first question of the Westminster Shorter Catechism.

Question: "What is the chief end of man?"

Answer: "Man's chief end is to glorify God and to enjoy him forever."

Up to this point I have not marked the number of ways and times Paul has referred to God in the first half of Romans 5, but this is the place to do it. In the first paragraph, he has referred to each person of the Trinity: ". . . we have peace with *God* through our *Lord Jesus Christ.* . . . And we rejoice in the hope of the glory of God. . . . And hope does not disappoint us, because God has poured out his love into our hearts by *the Holy Spirit*. . ." (vv. 1–2, 5, emphasis added). In the passage as a whole, the Holy Spirit is referred to once, God the Father seven times, and the Lord Jesus Christ five times, plus four more times in which Jesus is referred to by a personal pronoun.

2. In the Greek text there is no break in verse 2, as the NIV has it. Rather, the one sentence runs directly on from justification to glorification.

What exactly shall we rejoice in, if we are to "rejoice in God"? We can rejoice in any one or all of his attributes. Our passage suggests these:

1. *God's wisdom.* Several chapters further on in Romans, after Paul has traced the marvels of God's great and gradually unfolding salvation work in history, he will cry out: "Oh, the depth of the riches of the wisdom and knowledge of God! How unsearchable his judgments, and his paths beyond tracing out!" (Rom. 11:33). But even at this point in our study we can marvel at a wisdom so great as to be able to save powerless, ungodly, sinful enemies.

The question is: How can God save sinners without ignoring or otherwise condoning their sin? How can he save those who are filthy without dirtying himself? How can he be both just and the justifier of the ungodly? The answer is: through Christ, through his death for us. But we would not have known this or even have been able to suggest it by ourselves. It took the wisdom of the all-wise God to devise such a plan of salvation.

There is also a special display of God's wisdom in the way suffering works for our good, as Paul has shown in verses 3 and 4.

2. *God's grace.* Grace is usually defined as God's favor to the undeserving. But we rejoice in God's grace because, in our case, grace is favor not merely to the undeserving but to those who actually deserve the opposite. What do "enemies" deserve, after all? They deserve defeat and destruction. God did not treat us that way, however. Rather, he saved us through the work of Christ.

3. *God's power.* We often forget God's power when we think about salvation, reserving this theme for when we contemplate creation. But the Scripture speaks of God's power being displayed preeminently at the cross. In fact, the earliest reference to the cross in the Bible does this: Genesis 3:15. In this verse God is speaking to Satan, describing what will happen when the Mediator comes: "And I will put enmity between you and the woman, and between your offspring and hers; he will crush your head, and you will strike his heel." In this verse the cross is portrayed as a battlefield on which Satan and his hosts will be defeated. And so it was! The power of God was revealed at the cross when Satan's power over us was broken. We rejoice in God's power when we think of the cross, as well as in his other attributes.[3]

4. *God's love.* There are a number of attributes of God that may be learned from nature, chiefly his power and wisdom, and perhaps his grace.

---

3. The Swedish theologian Gustaf Aulen, more than anyone else, has reminded contemporary Bible students of this theme through his popular study of the three main ways of looking at the atonement: *Christus Victor,* trans. A. G. Hebert (London: S.P.C.K., 1961). J. R. W. Stott gives a chapter to this theme in *The Cross of Christ* (Downers Grove, Ill.: InterVarsity Press, 1986).

But the only place we can learn of God's love is at the cross. Perhaps that is why this attribute is the only one explicitly developed in our passage: "But God demonstrates his own love for us in this: While we were still sinners, Christ died for us" (v. 8). It is when we look to the cross that we begin to understand what love is and how much God has loved us.

5. *God's immutability.* Several times in these studies I have referred to immutability as something for which unregenerate men and women hate God, because he does not change in any of his other attributes. But it is important to say that, although in our unregenerate state we may hate God for his unchanging nature, in our regenerate state we find this something to rejoice in, since it means that God will not waver in his love and favor toward us. Having loved us and having sent the Lord Jesus Christ to save us from our sin, God will not now somehow suddenly change his mind and cast us off. His love, grace, wisdom, and other attributes will always remain as they have been, because he is immutable.

Arthur W. Pink wrote of God's immutability: "Herein is solid comfort. Human nature cannot be relied upon; but God can! However unstable I may be, however fickle my friends may prove, God changes not. If he varied as we do, if he willed one thing today and another tomorrow, if he were controlled by caprice, who could confide in him? But, all praise to his glorious name, he is ever the same."[4]

Do We Rejoice?

The last verse of this section says, "Not only is this so, but we also rejoice in God through our Lord Jesus Christ. . . ." This is a positive statement: "We rejoice!" It has led one commentator to say, "The one clear mark of a true Christian is that he always rejoices."[5] But do we rejoice? Have we actually come as far as Paul assumes we have in verse 11?

Honesty compels us to admit that often we do not rejoice in God.

Why is that? D. Martyn Lloyd-Jones gives a number of reasons, which I list for the sake of our self-examination:

1. A failure to grasp the truth of justification by faith only.

2. A failure to meditate as we ought, that is, a failure to think about what we do know.

3. A failure to draw the necessary conclusions from the Scriptures.[6]

I do not know if these are your failures (if you have failed to rejoice in God) or whether there is some other hindrance in your case, as there may be. But whatever the cause, anything that keeps us from rejoicing in God is

4. Arthur W. Pink, *The Attributes of God* (Grand Rapids: Baker Book House, n.d.), p. 41.
5. Ray C. Stedman, *From Guilt to Glory*, vol. 1, *Hope for the Hopeless* (Portland: Multnomah Press, 1978), p. 155.
6. Lloyd-Jones, *Romans: An Exposition of Chapter 5, Assurance*, pp. 158–162.

inappropriate and should be overcome by us. I challenge you to overcome it. I challenge you to think about these great truths, meditate upon them, learn how great the love, power, wisdom, and grace of God toward you are. Then glory in God, as those who have known God throughout the long ages of human history have done before you. It will make a profound difference in your life, and you will be a blessing to others.

PART SEVEN

Union with Christ

66

Union with Jesus Christ

Romans 5:12

Therefore, just as sin entered the world through one man, and death through sin, and in this way death came to all men, because all sinned—

The last ten verses of Romans 5 are a new section of the letter. They deal with mankind's union with Adam on the one hand, a union which has led to death and condemnation, and with the believer's union with the Lord Jesus Christ on the other. This latter union leads to life and righteousness. This is a difficult section of the letter, possibly the most difficult in all the Bible. But it is also very important.

Union with Christ! The Scottish pastor and theologian James S. Stewart called union with Christ "the heart of Paul's religion," adding that "this, more than any other conception—more than justification, more than sanctification, more even than reconciliation—is the key which unlocks the secrets of his soul."[1] John Murray went even further, saying, "Union with Christ is the central truth of the whole doctrine of salvation."[2] Yet, strangely,

1. James S. Stewart, *A Man in Christ: The Vital Elements of St. Paul's Religion* (New York: Harper and Brothers, n.d.), p. 147.
2. John Murray, *Redemption Accomplished and Applied* (Grand Rapids: Wm. B. Eerdmans, 1955), p. 170.

this is a widely neglected theme even in many otherwise helpful expositions of theology. Arthur W. Pink states the situation fairly:

> The subject of spiritual union is the most important, the most profound, and yet the most blessed of any that is set forth in the sacred Scriptures; and yet, sad to say, there is hardly any which is now more generally neglected. The very expression "spiritual union" is unknown in most professing Christian circles, and even where it is employed it is given such a protracted meaning as to take in only a fragment of this precious truth. Probably its very profundity is the reason why it is so largely ignored. . . .[3]

Many preachers avoid such subjects, thinking it better to avoid matters that most of their hearers may be unable or unwilling to understand. But it is not wise to neglect anything God has seen fit to reveal to us, particularly something as important as this. And, in any case, union with Christ cannot be neglected in any faithful exposition of Romans.

The Theme in Context

Where are we in our exposition of this letter? How does Romans 5:12–21 fit into its context?

At this point it may be worth thinking back to what I said at the beginning of this volume when I introduced the very first words of chapter 5. I rejected the view that Romans 5 introduces an entirely new section of the letter in the sense that in chapters 1–4 Paul has been speaking about justification and that now, in chapters 5–8, he speaks about sanctification. He does speak about sanctification, of course, but not as a radically new theme. On the contrary, as I pointed out (the word *therefore* in Rom. 5:1 is a clue to this), Paul is carrying forward the argument begun earlier, showing that the work of justification, about which he has been speaking, is a sure thing and will inevitably carry through to the believer's full glorification in heaven at the end of life.

Thus far, Paul's arguments have had to do with the nature of our justification:

1. We can be assured of salvation because God has made peace with us through the atoning work of Jesus Christ.

2. We can be assured of salvation because, through that same work of Christ, we have been brought into a new relationship with God in which we continue to stand.

3. We can be assured of salvation because of the sure and certain hope that we shall see God.

3. Arthur W. Pink, *Spiritual Union and Communion* (Grand Rapids: Baker Book House, 1971), p. 7.

4. We can be assured of salvation because of the way we are able to endure sufferings in this life.

5. We can be assured of salvation because God sent Jesus Christ to die for us, not when we were saved people but when we were enemies.

6. We can be assured of our salvation because, if God has justified us, which is a greater thing and demands more of God than glorification, he will surely do the lesser.

But now we have something new, as I said at the beginning of this study—and yet not new, because the apostle's objective remains the same: to enhance our assurance. We have seen that Romans 5:1–11 argues the certainty and finality of salvation from the nature of justification by faith. Now Paul also argues that when God saved us through the work of Christ, justifying us by faith, justification was not the only thing involved. Justification is immensely important, of course. But in addition to justification, and in conjunction with it, we were also united to Christ in what theologians have come to call "the mystical union." This union with Christ has been revealed to us, although we do not fully understand it.

In my opinion, Paul has anticipated this theme in the verses we have already studied, although I did not point it out at the time and the point is hidden in most of our translations. I am referring to verse 10, which says, "For if, when we were God's enemies, we were reconciled to him through the death of his Son, how much more, being reconciled, shall we be saved through his life!"

In the Greek text the last three words are not "through his life," as we have them in the New International Version (or "by his life," as in most others), but literally "*in* his life." Is this important? Yes, in my opinion. For, when we say "through" or "by" his life, the words seem to mean either or both of two things to us: (1) that we are saved through Christ, that is, by his work on the cross, and/or (2) that we are saved through faith in that atonement. But this is not the idea here. The first part of verse 10 does say this, but the second part goes beyond it, making a contrast. The argument is: If God has saved us through the death of Christ (through faith in his atonement), he will certainly save us by our being "in his life." At this point of the letter we may not fully understand what that means. That is why verses 12–21 explain it. But I am making the point that union with Christ, which Paul develops in verses 12–21, is suggested earlier.

D. Martyn Lloyd-Jones says, "The word 'in' means 'in the sphere of,' or 'in the realm of,' or 'in connection with' his life."[4]

---

4. D. M. Lloyd-Jones, *Romans: An Exposition of Chapter 5, Assurance* (Grand Rapids: Zondervan, 1972), p. 175.

This union with Jesus makes possible the sequence of deliverances from sin, death, and the law, and the resulting spiritual victories that Paul will unfold in the next three chapters of Romans.

Probing the Mystery

Union with Christ is difficult to understand, however, and the treatment of it in Romans 5:12–21 is particularly mind-stretching. So I want to probe this doctrine a bit before we actually get into the verses. There are two important points to keep in mind.

First, the union of the believer with Christ is one of three great unions in Scripture. The first is the union of the persons of the Godhead in the Trinity. Christians, as well as Jews, speak of one God. Yet, on the basis of the revelation of God in Scripture, we who are Christians say we also believe that this one God exists in three persons as the Father, the Son, and the Holy Spirit. We cannot explain how these three persons of the Godhead are at the same time only one God, but the Bible teaches this and we believe it.

The second mystical union is that of the two natures of Christ in one person. The Lord Jesus Christ is one person. He is not a "multiple personality." Nevertheless, he is also both God and man, possessing two natures. The theological formulation of this truth at the Council of Chalcedon (A.D. 451) said that Jesus is "to be acknowledged in two natures, inconfusedly, unchangeably, indivisibly, inseparably; the distinction of natures being by no means taken away by the union, but rather the property of each nature being preserved, and concurring in one Person and one Subsistence, not parted or divided into persons, but one and the same Son."[5] If you understand that completely, you are a better theologian than I am. But though I do not fully understand it, I believe it since it seems to be what the Bible teaches.

We have a similar situation in the case of the union of believers with Christ. Probably we are never going to be able to understand this union fully either. But it is important. Therefore we should hold to it and try to gain understanding.

The second important point to keep in mind as we study this doctrine is that the union of the believer with Christ is not a concept that was invented by Paul; rather, it was first taught by Jesus and then built upon by the apostle. True, Jesus did not use the term "mystical union." But he taught it in other words and through analogies, which are frequent in Scripture, particularly in the later portions of the New Testament. Let me list a few examples.

1. *The vine and the branches.* The most important passage on this theme is the teaching in John 15. It occurs in one of Jesus' final discourses prior to

5. Philip Schaff, *The Creeds of Christendom with a History and Critical Notes*, vol. 2, *The Greek and Latin Creeds, with Translations* (New York: Harper & Brothers, 1877), p. 62.

his arrest and crucifixion. Jesus said, "I am the true vine. . . . Remain in me, and I will remain in you. No branch can bear fruit by itself; it must remain in the vine. Neither can you bear fruit unless you remain in me. I am the vine; you are the branches. If a man remains in me and I in him, he will bear much fruit; apart from me you can do nothing" (John 15:1, 4–5).

The emphasis in this passage is upon the power of Christ nourishing and working itself out through his disciples. Paul touches on this image in Romans 11:17–21, where he speaks of Jewish "branches" being broken off an olive tree so that Gentile "branches" might for a time be grafted in. He is thinking along similar lines in Galatians when he speaks of the "fruit of the Spirit" (Gal. 5:22–23).

2. *The Lord's Supper.* On the same evening that Jesus spoke about himself as the vine and his disciples as the branches, he gave instructions for observing the Lord's Supper in which he said, "This is my body" and "This is my blood of the covenant, which is poured out for many for the forgiveness of sins" (Matt. 26:26, 28). The sacrament clearly symbolizes our participation in the life of Christ. In the same way, Jesus discoursed on the bread of life ("I am the bread of life. He who comes to me will never go hungry, and he who believes in me will never be thirsty" [John 6:35]) and challenged the woman of Samaria ("Everyone who drinks this water will be thirsty again, but whoever drinks the water I give him will never thirst. Indeed, the water I give him will become in him a spring of water welling up to everlasting life" [John 4:13–14]).

The emphasis in this image is on empowering (as in the analogy of the vine) and permanence. By faith, Jesus becomes a permanent part of us, just as surely as what we eat.

3. *A foundation and the structure built upon it.* Jesus initiated this image when he spoke of himself as a solid foundation for building a successful life: "Therefore everyone who hears these words of mine and puts them into practice is like a wise man who built his house on the rock. The rain came down, the streams rose, and the winds blew and beat against that house; yet it did not fall, because it had its foundation on the rock" (Matt. 7:24–25).

Paul made ample use of this image. He told the Corinthians, "You are . . . God's building. . . . For no one can lay any foundation other than the one already laid, which is Jesus Christ" (1 Cor. 3:9b, 11). He told the Ephesians, ". . . you are no longer foreigners and aliens, but fellow citizens with God's people and members of God's household, built on the foundation of the apostles and prophets, with Christ Jesus himself as the chief cornerstone" (Eph. 2:19–20). In the next verse the building becomes a temple: "In him the whole building is joined together and rises to become a holy temple in the Lord" (v. 21). Notice the words "in him." It is only because we are "in Christ" that this is possible.

This image also shows that being joined to Christ means that we are at the same time joined to one another. We are part of the church.

4. *The head and members of the body.* This was one of Paul's favorite ways of speaking. "And God placed all things under [Christ's] feet and appointed him to be head over everything for the church, which is his body, the fullness of him who fills everything in every way" (Eph. 1:22–23). "It was he who gave some to be apostles, some to be prophets, some to be evangelists, and some to be pastors and teachers, to prepare God's people for works of service, so that the body of Christ may be built up. . . . Then we will no longer be infants, tossed back and forth by the waves, and blown here and there by every wind of teaching and by the cunning and craftiness of men in their deceitful scheming. Instead, speaking the truth in love, we will in all things grow up into him who is the Head, that is, Christ. From him the whole body, joined and held together by every supporting ligament, grows and builds itself up in love, as each part does its work" (Eph. 4:11–12, 14–16).

In these verses (and others like them) the emphasis is upon two things: (1) growth and (2) the proper functioning of the church under Christ's sure direction. In 1 Corinthians Paul uses this image to show that each Christian is needed if the church is to function properly (cf. 1 Cor. 12:12–27).

5. *Marriage.* By far the greatest of all illustrations of the union of the believer with Christ and of Christ with the believer is marriage, in which a man and a woman are joined to form one flesh and one family. This image is in the Old Testament—Hosea, for example. There God compares himself to the faithful husband who is deserted by Israel, the unfaithful wife (Hosea 1–3). Jesus picked up on this theme when speaking of a marriage supper to which all who have faith are invited (Matt. 22:1–14). However, it is chiefly Paul who develops the theme in what is probably the best-known passage from Ephesians, mixing it with the image of the church as Christ's body.

> Wives, submit to your husbands as to the Lord. For the husband is the head of the wife as Christ is the head of the church, his body, of which he is the Savior. Now as the church submits to Christ, so also wives should submit to their husbands in everything.
> Husbands, love your wives, just as Christ loved the church and gave himself up for her to make her holy, cleansing her by the washing with water through the word, and to present her to himself as a radiant church, without stain or wrinkle or any other blemish, but holy and blameless. In this same way, husbands ought to love their wives as their own bodies. . . . This is a profound mystery—but I am talking about Christ and the church.
>
> Ephesians 5:22–28, 32

The emphasis in this image is upon a love-bonding. This is indeed the one true "marriage made in heaven." It is a marriage not only for this life but for eternity.

Looking Back and Looking Forward

In the studies that follow we are going to be looking at the doctrine of our union with Christ in detail, comparing it initially with our corresponding but contrasting union with Adam. But I close here by trying to put our union with Christ in its widest possible setting, remembering that it is included at this point of the letter to assure us of our security. This is what we find as we look both backward and forward at this union.

Here I quote from the best statement of these themes I know: a chapter on "Union with Christ" in *Redemption Accomplished and Applied* by John Murray:

1. *Election.* "The fountain of salvation itself in the eternal election of the Father is 'in Christ.' Paul says: 'Blessed be the God and Father of our Lord Jesus Christ, who hath blessed us with all spiritual blessings in the heavenlies in Christ, even as he chose us in him before the foundation of the world' (Eph. 1:3, 4). The father elected from all eternity, but he elected in Christ. We are not able to understand all that is involved, but the fact is plain enough that there was no election of the Father in eternity apart from Christ. And that means that those who will be saved were not even contemplated by the Father in the ultimate counsel of his predestinating love apart from union with Christ—they were *chosen* in Christ. As far back as we can go in tracing salvation to its fountain we find 'union with Christ'; it is not something tacked on; it is there from the outset."

2. *Redemption.* "It is also because the people of God were in Christ when he gave his life a ransom and redeemed them by his blood that salvation has been secured for them; they are represented as united to Christ in his death, resurrection, and exaltation to heaven (Rom. 6:2–11; Eph. 2:4–6; Col. 3:3, 4). . . . Hence we may never think of the work of redemption wrought once for all by Christ apart from the union with his people which was effected in the election of the Father before the foundation of the world. . . . This is but another way of saying that the church is the body of Christ and 'Christ loved the church and gave himself for it' (Eph. 5:25)."

3. *Regeneration.* "It is in Christ that the people of God are created anew. 'We are his workmanship, created in Christ Jesus unto good works' (Eph. 2:10). . . . It should not surprise us that the beginning of salvation in actual possession should be in union with Christ because we have found already that it is in Christ that salvation had its origin in the eternal election of the Father and that it is in Christ salvation was once for all secured by Jesus' ransom blood. We could not think of such union with Christ as suspended

when the people of God become the actual partakers of redemption—they are created anew in Christ."

4. *Glorification.* "Finally, it is in Christ that the people of God will be resurrected and glorified. It is in Christ that they will be made alive when the last trumpet will sound and the dead will be raised incorruptible (1 Cor. 15:22)."[6]

This great scope of salvation from the electing counsels of God in eternity past to the glorification of the sons of God in eternity future is based on the union of the believer with Christ, and it is for this that the doctrine is so important for us. Assurance of salvation! Security in Christ! This is what we are dealing with in this doctrine, as also in the great middle chapters of Romans. While there are many things meant to encourage us in that security, the greatest of all is that we are "in Christ."

The question you must ask yourself is: "Am I really in him? Am I a Christian?"

How can you know? You cannot look into eternity past to pry into God's hidden counsels. You cannot look into eternity future to see yourself as one who has been glorified. All you have is the present. But if you probe the present, you can know. Do you remember the marriage illustration? Ask yourself: "Am I married to Jesus?" You are—if you have taken the vow, promising to "take Jesus to be your loving and faithful Savior, in plenty and in want, in joy and in sorrow, in sickness and in health, for this life and for eternity," and if you are living for him. God has pronounced the marriage. And what God has joined together no one will ever put asunder.

6. Murray, *Redemption Accomplished and Applied,* pp. 162–164.

67

Christ and Adam

Romans 5:12–14

Therefore, just as sin entered the world through one man, and death through sin, and in this way death came to all men, because all sinned—for before the law was given, sin was in the world. But sin is not taken into account when there is no law. Nevertheless, death reigned from the time of Adam to the time of Moses, even over those who did not sin by breaking a command, as did Adam, who was a pattern of the one to come.

We are studying a difficult, yet extremely important section of Romans, and we have begun by an overview of the doctrine of the mystical union of the Christian with Jesus Christ. This important New Testament theme is widely neglected, no doubt because it is so difficult. But without this doctrine we cannot understand Romans 5:12–21, and without understanding those verses the truths of this second major section of the letter (chs. 4–8) will be beyond us.

It works the other way, too. We must understand the believer's union with Christ to understand verses 12–21. But, in a parallel way, in order to understand how we are "in Christ" and what that means, we need to see how we were "in Adam," which is where the passage starts. Adam is the

561

"man" mentioned in verse 12: "Therefore, just as sin entered the world through one man, and death through sin, and in this way death came to all men, because all sinned. . . ." The passage starts with Adam and builds from him, showing, on the one hand, how the union of the race in Adam and the union of believers in Christ are similar and how, on the other hand, they are also quite different, the results of the first being evil and the results of the second being good.

Since the verses also deal with justification, to understand them is to move further in our understanding of this theme. Paul has been teaching that in the work of justification, righteousness has been imputed to us. But people are reluctant to accept that truth. Therefore, to help them understand and believe in the principle of imputed righteousness, Paul shows that we have already been treated on the basis of this same principle "in Adam."

The Flow of the Passage

We start with verse 12. It teaches that sin, followed by death, came into the world by Adam. But you will notice that at the end of verse 12 there is a dash, indicating that the thought breaks off at this point and that Paul inserts what we would call a parenthesis. It is even a bit more complicated than that, however. Verses 13 and 14 are a parenthesis. They explain what Paul meant when he said, at the end of verse 12, "because all sinned." But at the end of verse 14, the apostle throws in another parenthesis to elaborate the parallel between Adam and Christ, which he suggested in verse 14. This parenthesis, which is actually a parenthesis within a parenthesis, fills out verses 15–17. So it is not until verse 18 that we get the continuation of the thought begun in verse 12.

I point this out to show what is coming and to note the full parallelism between Christ and Adam. According to these verses, believers are now "in Christ," just as they once were "in Adam." That is the similarity. But there is also a contrast, since in Adam the race has experienced sin, leading to condemnation and death, while in Christ believers have experienced righteousness, leading to justification and eternal life. The two sequences are exactly parallel. Putting verses 12 and 18 together, we get something like this:

> On the one hand, just as sin entered the world through one man, and death through sin, and in this way death came to all men, because all sinned—that is, just as the result of one trespass was condemnation for all men. . . .
>
> So also, on the other hand, the result of one act of righteousness was justification that brings life for all men.

This teaches that there were two great acts in history: the act of Adam, which brought condemnation and death, and the act of Jesus, which brought justification and life. The results are "brought" to us by virtue of our union with Adam, on the one hand, and with Jesus Christ, on the other.

Sin and Death Through Adam

Verse 12 assumes two great truths: (1) the universality of sin, and (2) the universality of death. Paul can do so, because there is hardly anybody who would be foolish enough to challenge them. The most thoroughly secular person will not claim to be perfect. "After all, I am no saint," he might say, thus acknowledging Paul's claim that "all have sinned" (Rom. 3:23). Again, the universality of death is a given. "There is nothing certain in life but death and taxes," we say, using an absolute certainty to illustrate the nature of a lesser one.

But that raises some very big questions: How can we explain this situation? Why is sin universal? And why is death the universal experience of all? Just on the basis of the law of averages, shouldn't we expect that somewhere at some time there would or will have been a sinless person? And shouldn't we find that somewhere at some time there is a person who will not die?

In answering these questions we come to a parting of the ways between secular and Christian thought. The secular mind says two things: (1) there is no connection between sin and death at all, they are two utterly unrelated issues; and (2) each may be explained naturally.

As far as sin is concerned, the secular view assumes that sin is only an imperfection, soon to be overcome. This view of sin fits the prevailing evolutionary framework of our time, according to which all things are gradually evolving from less complex and less perfect forms to forms that are more complex and more perfect. The secular-minded person argues that sin means only that we are not yet where we hope to be and eventually will be.

There are two things wrong with this.

First, if sin is only an imperfection, then it is not really correct to call it sin, or even to look down on it as something less desirable than the next inevitable stage of the evolutionary process. "Sin" is not bad at all, which eliminates the possibility of any meaningful talk about virtue. Nobody can be said to be better or worse than someone else. No action can ever really be inherently wrong.

The second problem is this: If sin is only an imperfection to be eliminated in time as a result of the inevitable upward movement of the race, why has so much evil been around for so long? If sin is only a minor imperfection, why hasn't that imperfection been eliminated long before this? I can go further with such questions. Looking at the historical record left by human beings honestly, is it even possible to say that there has been such a thing as progress? Are we really better than our predecessors? Are we more virtuous than the Greeks? Are we more noble even than the barbarians? It is hard to say so. But if this is the case, doesn't this fact alone suggest that sin is a much greater problem than the secularist's framework allows?

The other inescapable reality is death. The secularist explains this as something inherent in nature itself. That is, it does not have anything to do with evolution—like sin, which *will* be overcome. It is just natural and inescapable for living things. All living things die. This point is better for the secular argument than the earlier one, since observation confirms that living things do indeed die. We can speak of a process in which organisms are born, grow, decline, and perish. The problem is that none of us really believes that this is right. We sense that we were meant to be immortal. We should not die. Hence arise those images of life beyond death—Mount Olympus, Valhalla, Hades, Sheol, the Underworld, Nirvana, Paradise, Heaven—found in all the world's civilizations and religions.

The Christian answer to the problem of the universality of sin and death is that death is not natural but that it is the punishment of God for sin. It says, moreover, that sin entered the world through the one act of Adam, who was the first man, and that—from Adam—sin and its consequence, death, passed to his descendants.

Four Views within Christianity

The Christian view is far more comprehensive than that brief statement, however. But, in order to develop it fully, I need to acknowledge that there are different views of Romans 5:12 in Christian thought. They arise out of an important question: Assuming that sin and death passed to the race from Adam, how exactly did that happen? And why should it have happened? Why should something that Adam did affect anyone?

1. *Pelagianism.* The first view is called by the name of Pelagius, the opponent of Saint Augustine, but it is not limited to him. Many contemporary liberal commentators on Romans also hold to it.[1] This view teaches that each human being sins in his or her own person, entirely apart from any relationship to Adam, and that the person's death, which follows, is a consequence of that sin only. There are several reasons why this view must be rejected, even apart from the fact that Pelagianism is wrong generally.

First, it is not observably true. Not all who die, die for their own sin. For example, babies die though they have not sinned themselves.

Second, it contradicts the explanation of the phrase "because all sinned," which Paul himself gives in verses 13 and 14. Those verses, as I have already indicated, are a parenthesis in which Paul breaks off his opening statement in order to explain what he is saying. He says that death reigned "even over those who did not sin by breaking a command, as did Adam. . . ." That is, they did not sin as Adam did. But this would be untrue if, as Pelagianism

1. See John Murray, *The Epistle to the Romans: The English Text with Introduction, Exposition and Notes* (Grand Rapids: Wm. B. Eerdmans, 1968), p. 183, footnote 20.

holds, every individual dies because of his or her own actual transgression, since that is exactly how Adam himself sinned and was judged.

Third, this interpretation of the universality of sin is inconsistent with the overall flow of the passage. The point of the argument is that we are declared righteous in Christ just as we have been declared sinful in Adam. But we are not declared righteous in Christ because of any righteousness of our own. Rather, it is on the basis of the righteousness of Christ imputed to us. If the parallel is to hold, we must also be declared sinful on the basis of Adam's sin and not merely on the fact that we sin personally.

Fourth, the Pelagian view is inconsistent with the tense of the verb *sinned*. It is an aorist. So it cannot mean that all people *do* sin or are *accustomed to sin* (that is, are sinners), but rather that they *have sinned* at a particular past moment. In the context of the passage this can only mean that they have sinned "in Adam."

2. *The view of John Calvin.* The second interpretation of the phrase "because all sinned" is attached to the name of John Calvin, though it seems to be inconsistent with what Calvin himself taught elsewhere. It seems to have been an uncharacteristic slip of interpretation on his part. Calvin took "sin" in Romans 5:12 to mean "corruption" and the verse to teach that sin passed upon all because all are corrupted. All *are* corrupted by sin, of course. Each would also be condemned for his or her own sin apart from Adam, were not the passage we are studying also true. But true as those points may be in themselves, Paul is nevertheless just not teaching this in Romans.

As in the case of the Pelagian interpretation, the "corruption" view is inconsistent with verses 13 and 14, and with the passage as a whole.

3. *Augustinianism.* The third view was proposed by the great Saint Augustine, but it has been held by many theologians in the Middle Ages and even into modern times. This view is also called the realistic or "seminal" view. It holds that the human race sinned in Adam because in a literal physical sense all future generations were in Adam at the time. So, when he acted the whole race acted, and when he was judged the whole race was judged literally in him.

Most people today would be inclined to discount this as a strange though uniquely medieval idea since, as we see things, the fact that we were in Adam "in embryo," as it were, cannot mean that we all actually sinned in him since we were not conscious entities capable of sinning at the time. But we should probably not dismiss this so quickly. This is because, as D. Martyn Lloyd-Jones points out, that very point is made in Hebrews 7:9–10, in the case of Levi, Melchizedek, and Abraham: "One might even say that Levi, who collects the tenth, paid the tenth through Abraham, because when Melchizedek met Abraham, Levi was still in the body of his ancestor." The point of the author is that the descendants of Levi paid tithes to

Melchizedek because they were in the loins of Abraham, their forefather, when he paid tithes. But, if that is so, then it must also be true to say that the entire human race was in Adam and therefore sinned when he did. Because of Hebrews 7, the Augustinian or realistic view can never be dismissed too lightly, though, in my opinion, it still does not capture the full meaning of the passage.[2]

4. *Federalism.* The fourth view, which is that of the best interpreters of virtually all Christian traditions—Calvinists, Arminians, Lutherans, even Rationalists—is that God appointed Adam the head or representative of the race, so that he would stand for them and they would be accounted either just or sinful on the basis of his obedience to or disobedience of God's command. This view is called federalism because of the analogy to the way an ambassador might act on behalf of his country. When he signs a document or takes an action, he does so for each of the country's citizens, and they are therefore bound by what he does.

In this view, the point is not that all people sin, though they do, but rather that Adam stood for them so that, when he sinned, not only was Adam judged but they were judged, too. It is because Adam sinned that death passed upon all. Here is how Lloyd-Jones puts it: "Adam's sin is imputed to us in exactly the same way that Christ's righteousness is imputed to us. We inherit, of course, a sinful nature from Adam. . . . But that is not what condemns us. What condemns us, and makes us subject to death, is the fact that we have all sinned in Adam, and that we are all held guilty of sin. . . . It is our union with Adam that accounts for all our trouble. It is our corresponding union with Christ that accounts for our salvation."[3]

Proof of the Christian View

There are many reasons why federalism is the right interpretation of this passage. Charles Hodge gives nine reasons.[4] But we do not need these or any other additional reasons. We need only the two that Paul himself gives in these verses: (1) the fact that death was in the world before the giving of the law of Moses, and (2) the fact that all die, including innocents. If sin is the transgression of law and people who did not have the law were punished, what other explanation of the universality of death can there be, except that we were all judged in Adam?

2. See D. M. Lloyd-Jones, *Romans: An Exposition of Chapter 5, Assurance* (Grand Rapids: Zondervan, 1972), pp. 214–216.

3. Lloyd-Jones, *Romans: An Exposition of Chapter 5, Assurance*, p. 210. For helpful discussions of these four views see Charles Hodge, *A Commentary on Romans* (Edinburgh and Carlisle, Pa.: The Banner of Truth Trust, 1972; first edition 1835), pp. 148–155; Murray, *The Epistle to the Romans*, pp. 182–187; and Lloyd-Jones, pp. 204–206, 213–218.

4. Hodge, *A Commentary on Romans*, pp. 151–154.

Or, to make it even more pointed, why do infants die unless they, along with the rest of the race, have been judged for Adam's sin? Or for that matter, why do they even suffer? Why do newborns get cancer or have colic?

As far as I can see, there are only two possible answers other than the Christian one, and each is clearly inadequate. The first is the doctrine of an eternity of evil: that sin, death, and evil have simply always existed. The problem with this, as I pointed out in discussing the view of sin as mere imperfection, is that the moral dimensions then vanish and there is no reason why sin should be called sin at all or why evil should be called evil. Besides, although it is possible to understand sin as a corruption of the good—that is, as something that came along to defile God's originally good creation—it is hardly possible to see good as a development out of something that is evil. Satan can be a fallen angel. But no fallen angel can become God.

The other explanation of the universality of suffering and death is reincarnation, the argument being that infants (the most striking example) suffer for the sins done in a previous life. This explains the problem for this life, of course. But it does not solve the real problem, since it only pushes it into a future life and into a life beyond that and so on. At some point the big questions inevitably reemerge.

The only really valid explanation is the one Paul gives, namely, that Adam had been appointed by God to be the representative of the race so that if *he* stood, we too would stand, and if *he* fell, we would fall with him. Adam did fall, as we know. So death passed upon everyone.

"But isn't that terribly unfair?" someone protests. "Isn't it cruel for God to act in this fashion?"

We are going to be studying this at greater length as we go on, but let me state here that far from being unfair or cruel, the federal way of dealing with us was actually the fairest and kindest of all the ways God could have operated. Besides, it was the only way it would later be possible for God to save us once we had sinned. In other words, federalism is actually a proof of God's grace, which is the point the passage comes to (vv. 15 ff.).

It was gracious to Adam first of all. Why? Because it was a deterrent to his sin. God must have explained to Adam that he was to represent his posterity. That might have restrained him from sinning. A father who might be tempted to steal his employer's funds (and would if only he himself were involved), might well decide not to do it if he knew that his crime would hurt his children if he should get caught. If something as limited as that can be a restraining influence, how much more would Adam's knowledge that what he would do would affect untold billions of his descendants?

This way of operating is also an example of God's grace to us, because to be tried in Adam was the best of all ways to stand trial. The great Charles Simeon of Cambridge wrote more than a century ago that if each human being were asked whether he would prefer to be judged in Adam or in himself, every thinking person would answer "in Adam." After all, Adam faced only one temptation and that a mere trifle. He was not to eat of one tree. Besides, he was as yet unfallen. He did not have a sinful nature. He was possessed of his full faculties (which were undoubtedly superior to our own). He lived in a perfect environment and had a perfect companion. For our part, we are sinful, weak, and ignorant, and we live in a world filled with all kinds of temptations. Was it not merciful of God to judge us in Adam? Was God not gracious in that choice?[5]

And there is this great fact as well: If God had chosen to judge us as each of us think we would like to be judged, that is, in and for ourselves with no relationship to any other person, then we would all inevitably perish. For our only hope of salvation is that we may also be judged in Christ, he being our representative, just as we have been judged in Adam. If we were like the angels who are entities in themselves, who do not exist in families and who have no relationship to one another, then there would be no hope for us, just as there is no hope for them. But because we have been judged in Adam, we may also be judged in Christ and be acquitted.

That is what happens for those who are called by God and joined to Jesus Christ through the channel of saving faith. We do not deserve it, but this is the way grace acts. It is grace from the beginning to the end.

5. Simeon's point is paraphrased by Donald Grey Barnhouse, *God's Grace: Exposition of Bible Doctrines, Taking the Epistle to the Romans as a Point of Departure*, vol. 5, Romans 5:12–21 (Grand Rapids: Wm. B. Eerdmans, 1959), p. 55.

68

The Reign of Death

Romans 5:14

Nevertheless, death reigned from the time of Adam to the time of Moses, even over those who did not sin by breaking a command, as did Adam, who was a pattern of the one to come.

In Romans 5:14 there is a phrase that we have not yet adequately studied but to which we return now: "death reigned from the time of Adam to the time of Moses." It is important to do so for several reasons. First, it is repeated more than once. We find it in verse 14, which we are studying here, but it also appears in verse 17 ("death reigned through that one man"), and a variation of the thought appears in verse 21 ("sin reigned in death"). An idea stated (or implied) three times in just ten verses must obviously be important for our understanding of the passage.

Again, as we have seen in our study of the parallel between our natural, physical union with Adam and our supernatural, spiritual union with Jesus Christ, the fact that death reigns over all persons proves that God has judged everyone in Adam. In other words, the reign of death proves the principles of representation and imputation, both of which are indispensable to Paul's argument. And these principles are indispensable for salvation, since it is only because God determined to treat the entire race representationally—either in Adam or in Christ—that Jesus could die in our place and be our Savior.

Finally, the phrase "death [or sin] reigned" has its counterpart in the words "so also grace might reign through righteousness" in verse 21. Since we want to understand the latter, we must first understand the former.

From Adam to Moses

The first thing to notice about the reign of death is that for the sake of Paul's argument it is linked to a specific time period: "from the time of Adam to the time of Moses." It is a fact (which we are going to treat explicitly later) that death also reigns in our own day and will continue to reign to the end of human history. But Paul specifies the time period from Adam to Moses because he means something different merely than that all persons die.

Why does Paul cite this specific time period? The answer has to do with what we were exploring in the last study, namely, that death passed upon the race as a result of God's judgment upon all for the sin of Adam.

When we were looking at this point earlier, I focused on the death of infants, who have not committed any conscious sin, because the point is easier to grasp in that fashion. The only adequate explanation for the death of infants is that they, along with the rest of us, have been judged guilty for what Adam did. Paul's argument does not particularly specify infants, however, though they are included in what he says.[1] Rather, he is focusing on all persons, and his argument is that in the time between Adam and Moses all persons died, even though there was no specific law for them to have broken. They were sinners, of course. The judgments of the great flood of Noah's time and the destruction of Sodom and Gomorrah in Abraham's day prove it. But the race as a whole was judged by universal death, not for the specific sins of the individuals involved, but for Adam's transgression.

The critical idea here is "imputation" or, as Paul expresses it in verse 13, the fact that sin was "not taken into account." He means that, although all were sinners, God did not take their own personal sin into account when he punished them. But since they all nevertheless died, their death must have been for Adam's disobedience and not for their own sinfulness.

---

1. Some have taken the words "even over those who did not sin by breaking a command, as did Adam" in this way, however. They would see the first phrase ("death reigned from the time of Adam to the time of Moses") as referring to all persons, young and old alike, and the second phrase ("even over those who did not sin by breaking a command, as did Adam") as referring to a second category included within the first, that is, to infants particularly. For a helpful discussion of this possibility see John Murray, *The Epistle to the Romans* (Grand Rapids: Wm. B. Eerdmans, 1968), pp. 190, 191.

This is the meaning of the phrase "those who did not sin by breaking a command, *as did Adam.*" People sinned during this period, but it was not by breaking a specific command of God, as Adam did, since there was no specific command for them to break. Adam sinned by breaking a command: he disobeyed God's explicit warning not to eat of the tree of the knowledge of good and evil (Gen. 2:16–17; 3:6).

This is so important that I want to make the point once more, this time by quoting William Barclay. The sad thing is that Barclay does not believe this teaching himself. He understands it, but he thinks that it is only a Jewish argument, which he is free to reject. Nevertheless, Barclay's is the most succinct statement of the argument I have found anywhere:

1. Adam sinned because he broke a direct commandment of God—the commandment not to eat of the fruit of the forbidden tree—and because Adam sinned, Adam, who was meant to be immortal, died.

2. The law did not come until the time of Moses; now, if there is no law, there can be no breach of the law; that is to say, if there is no law and no commandment, there can be no sin. Therefore, the men who lived between Adam and Moses did in fact sin, but it was not reckoned against them because there was as yet no law, and they could not be condemned for breaking a law which did not exist.

3. But, in spite of the fact that sin could not be reckoned to them, they still died. Death reigned over them although they could not be accused of breaking a non-existent law.

4. Why, then, did they die? They died because they had sinned in Adam. It was their involvement in the sin of Adam that caused their deaths, although there was no law for them to break. That, in fact, is Paul's proof that all men did sin in Adam.[2]

In my judgment, the strongest passage in the entire Bible for teaching this is Genesis 5, a chapter that contains the genealogy, not of the ungodly descendants of Adam, who were filling the earth at this time (their genealogy is in chapter 4), but of the godly line of Adam, containing the names of people like Enoch, Methuselah, and Noah. What is powerful about it is the repeated refrain: "and then he died."

The sentences need to be read together for their intended effect: "Altogether, Adam lived 930 years, *and then he died.* . . . Altogether, Seth lived 921 years, *and then he died.* . . . Altogether, Enosh lived 905 years, *and then he died.* . . . Altogether, Kenan lived 910 years, *and then he died.* . . . Altogether, Mahalalel lived 895 years, *and then he died.* . . . Altogether, Jared lived 962 years, *and then he died.* . . . Altogether, Methuselah lived 969 years, *and then he died.* . . . Altogether, Lamech lived 777 years, *and then he died*" (vv. 4, 7, 11, 14, 17, 20, 27, 31, emphasis added). These were long life spans, from 365

---

2. William Barclay, *The Letter to the Romans,* in "The Daily Study Bible" series (Edinburgh: The Saint Andrew Press, 1969), p. 80.

(in the case of Enoch, who did not die but was translated) to 969 years (in the case of Methuselah, who lived longer than any other man), but each was cut off by death. Death reigned during this period, just as it has reigned over every other period of human history.

All Must Die

We must apply this now in a way that will enable us to benefit from it. This is because, even though Paul is developing an argument for the imputation both of sin and righteousness, he is not concerned merely with his argument but also with our current great dilemma—all have sinned and must die—and with the solution for it.

Do you know that you must die?

Years ago, when young girls used to learn to read and write by making samplers, the rhymes they would work out in needlepoint often came from the *New England Primer*, which taught Bible truths through couplets based on the English alphabet. Under "A" the child would write:

> In Adam's fall we sinned all.

Under "X," toward the end of the exercise, she would write:

> Xerxes the Great did die,
> And so must you and I.

That is exactly what Romans 5 is all about: (1) "A" is for Adam ("sin entered the world through one man"); (2) "X" is for Xerxes ("death came to all men").

Nothing is as certain as death and taxes, we say. Yet we go to great lengths to avoid this inescapable reality.

Franz Borkenau is an historian who believes that cultures can be analyzed in terms of their attitudes toward death. He says that there are three basic attitudes. In ancient Greece he finds a *death-accepting* attitude. In our modern, post-Christian era he finds a *death-denying* attitude. In the Judeo-Christian system he finds a *death-defying* attitude.[3]

1. *A death-accepting culture.* The chief example of the death-accepting attitude of ancient Greek culture is the death of Socrates, one of the best-known deaths of all time. Socrates had been sentenced to death by the rulers of Athens for corrupting the city's youth by his "atheism," which meant that he did not accept the literal existence of the Greek gods. He was to die by drinking hemlock. The moment came. His students were

3. Cited by Richard W. Doss, *The Last Enemy: A Christian Understanding of Death* (New York: Harper & Row, 1974), p. 4.

gathered around him. They were weeping. But Socrates did not weep. Instead of bemoaning his fate or shrinking from death, Socrates used the occasion to reason with his sorrowing students about immortality, a discourse that Plato recorded in the "Phaedo." Socrates argued that the soul is immortal and that death is the only way the individual can escape the curse of bodily existence.

The problem, of course, is that it is difficult to die serenely with just a philosophic hope. Socrates may have done it, though we do not know for sure what he was actually experiencing. But few others have. Even Plato confessed that when his mentor drank the poison he, along with the others, burst into tears at losing such a just and wise companion.[4]

2. *A death-denying culture.* The second classification of cultures includes our own. Its attitude is death-denying, which Borkenau finds the most inadequate of all. Why does our culture deny death's inescapable reality? It is all about us, confronting us constantly. Why do we go to such lengths to avoid even speaking about death?

Some years ago the Forest Lawn Foundation, a large West Coast funeral institution, commissioned an American Baptist seminary professor by the name of Richard W. Doss to investigate this question and write a book on a proper understanding of death. Doss suggested several reasons why our society is death-denying. The first is *psychological.* Sigmund Freud, the father of modern psychology, spoke of death as an unconscious fear of man. Therefore, the more one is faced with death, as we are through the newspapers and television, the more one denies it personally. We see reminders of death every day. So we deny death vigorously.

The second reason for our denial of death is *cultural.* American society emphasizes youthfulness, vitality, and productivity. The worth of individuals is measured by what they contribute. Wholeness is measured by one's ability to think and act young. In America death is not the last enemy to be defeated at the last trump, as the Bible describes it, but an enemy to be defeated now—through gyms, health spas, facelifts, diets, health foods, and a variety of other body-enhancing pastimes and procedures.

This cultural attitude is best expressed by one modern advertising slogan for face cream: "I don't intend to grow old gracefully. I intend to fight it every step of the way."

However, in Doss's judgment the chief reason for America's having become a death-denying culture is *religious.* The nation has lost its religious consciousness:

Religion has been a major force in shaping the ideas and life-style of the American people. Our forefathers came to this country with a clearly

---

4. Plato, "Phaedo" in *The Works of Plato*, trans. B. Jowett (New York: Tudor Publishing Company, n.d.), vol. 3, pp. 185–271.

defined view of man and the world. From the Puritan settlement of New England to nineteenth-century life on the western frontier, a theological framework supported and interpreted man's place in society and his relationship with nature and God. Man believed and felt that God had a purpose for life, and more, that every man could know and understand God's plan. Death was one element within this religious framework and thus could be dealt with openly and treated as a natural part of life. Burial of the dead was carried out with religious rites which gave expression to this view of God's purposes for man.

[But] the twentieth century has seen a virtual abolition of the traditional Christian framework with no new proposal to take its place. Secularization has separated modern man from older understandings of man and society, and in so doing has separated death from the means by which it has been isolated and denuded. With no meaningful framework for understanding death, our culture has adopted a style of denial and avoidance.[5]

But death cannot be avoided. That is the reality. Death reigns, the very point Paul is making. We may treat death as a fiction. But suddenly death turns our corner, walks down our street, and forces its form across our threshold or enters the home of our neighbor—and we tremble before it.

Death Defeated

3. *A death-defying culture.* The third class of culture that Franz Borkenau lists is death-defying, which he discovers in Judaism and Christianity.[6] The Old Testament Jew looked forward to an afterlife, like Job, who declared:

> I know that my Redeemer lives,
>   and that in the end he will stand upon the earth.
> And after my skin has been destroyed,
>   yet in my flesh I will see God;
> I myself will see him
>   with my own eyes—I and not another. . . .
>
>   Job 19:25–27

Paul also looked forward. In fact, Paul is the chief example of a death-defying attitude. He wrote in 1 Corinthians 15:54–55: "'Death has been swallowed up in victory.' [cf. Isa. 25:8]

> 'Where, O death, is your victory?
>   Where, O death, is your sting? [cf. Hos. 13:14]'"

5. Doss, *The Last Enemy*, pp. 7, 8.
6. I have borrowed a portion of the discussion of death-accepting, death-denying, and death-defying cultures, based on Borkenau, from James Montgomery Boice, *Genesis: An Expositional Commentary*, vol. 3 (Grand Rapids: Zondervan, 1987), pp. 319–321.

The sting of death is sin, and the power of sin is the law. But thanks be to God! He gives us the victory through our Lord Jesus Christ."

How did the apostle arrive at this answer? How did he and Job sustain their defiance of death? The answer is: through Jesus Christ! It is the solution Job anticipated ("I know that my Redeemer lives"), and Paul, with his later and greater understanding, proclaimed it boldly.

Here is the bottom line:

1. *Christianity has the only explanation for the universal reign of death, and*

2. *Christianity has the only solution for it.*

Let me share some words written by Horatius Bonar, one of the great Scottish divines of about a century ago and a father of the Scottish Free Church. They are from his volume on Genesis, where he is writing about Adam but thinking also of our text from Romans:

> The first Adam dies, and we die in him; but the second Adam dies, and we live in him! The first Adam's grave proclaims only death; the second Adam's grave announces life—"I am the resurrection and the life." We look into the grave of the one, and we see only darkness, corruption and death; we look into the grave of the other, and we find there only light, incorruption and life. We look into the grave of the one and find that he is still there, his dust still mingling with its fellow dust about it; we look into the grave of the other and find that he is not there. He is risen—risen as our forerunner into the heavenly paradise, the home of the risen and redeemed. We look into the grave of the first Adam and see in him the first-fruits of them that have died, the millions that have gone down to that prisonhouse whose gates he opened; we look into the tomb of the second Adam, and we see in him the first-fruits of that bright multitude, that glorified band, who are to come forth from that cell, triumphing over death and rising to the immortal life; not through the tree which grew in the earthly paradise, but through him whom that tree prefigured—through him who was dead and is alive, and who liveth for evermore, and who has the keys of hell and death.[7]

How did Jesus accomplish this great transformation? He did it by dying in our place, by taking the punishment for our sins upon himself. He became our representative, just as Adam had been our representative before him. He endured the punishment of our death, and then he rose again so that we might enjoy the reality of eternal life.

In his small volume on Romans, the great Bible teacher Harry Ironside included an epitaph that is inscribed on the tombstone of four children in a graveyard in St. Andrews, Scotland. It presupposes that children who die in infancy are saved by God's grace in Jesus Christ. It reads like this:

7. Horatius Bonar, *Thoughts on Genesis* (Grand Rapids: Kregel, n.d.), pp. 274, 275. (Original edition 1875.)

> Bold infidelity, turn pale and die.
> Beneath this stone four sleeping infants lie:
> Say, are they lost or saved?
> If death's by sin, they sinned, for they are here.
> If heaven's by works, in heaven they can't appear.
> Reason, ah, how depraved!
> Turn to the Bible's sacred page, the knot's untied:
> They died, for Adam sinned;
> They live, for Jesus died.[8]

Do you follow that argument? We know the infants sinned because they died. Question: How is that possible? Answer: They sinned in Adam. Second question: Can they have been saved, then? Answer: Not by works certainly, because they had not performed any. Third question: Then, they must have been lost? The epitaph answers: No, they were saved—but it was by the death of Jesus Christ.

Union with Christ is the only way of salvation for anyone.

---

8. H. A. Ironside, *Lectures on the Epistle to the Romans* (Neptune, N.J.: Loizeaux Brothers, 1928), p. 71.

69

Adam: A Pattern of the One to Come

Romans 5:14

Nevertheless, death reigned from the time of Adam to the time of Moses, even over those who did not sin by breaking a command, as did Adam, who was a pattern of the one to come.

W hat would you say are the most important events of human history? Would you cite the discovery of fire? The invention of the wheel, whenever that may have been? The introduction of printing? How about Caesar's crossing of the Rubicon? Or the invasion of England by the Normans in the fall of 1066? Or the invention of the atomic bomb?

Listing the great moments of history can go on almost indefinitely, and the items listed can all be quite interesting—at least to specific individuals or races. But important as these events may have been, they pale before the two stupendous events that the apostle Paul cites in Romans 5: the fall of the race in Adam, and the redemption of the race by the Lord Jesus Christ. These are the pivotal points of history, and they overwhelm all other events because of two things: (1) the significance of what Adam and Jesus did, though what they did and the results of what they did were quite different;

577

and (2) the people affected. Paul summarizes the importance of these events in Romans 5:18, saying, ". . . just as the result of one trespass was condemnation for all men, so also the result of one act of righteousness was justification that brings life for all men."

The New International Version captures the force of these actions by the subtitle given to verses 12–21: "Death Through Adam, Life Through Christ."

A "Type" of Jesus

Whenever we link these two events, as I have just done (following Paul's example), we stress the contrast: Adam brought death, Jesus brought life. But we need to see that although the contrast is important—verses 15–17 will develop this at some length—the ways in which Adam and Christ are *similar* are also important, perhaps even more so. This is because our understanding of salvation depends upon this similarity, which Paul points to by the phrase: "Adam, who was a pattern of the one to come" (v. 14).

What does this mean? We can understand how Adam might be a pattern of other human beings in his choice to sin against God. We sin, too, of course. But how can he be a pattern of Jesus Christ? How can sinful Adam, a mere man, represent the sinless Son of God?

We begin with the critical term in this passage: "pattern." It is translated "figure" in the King James Version and "type" in the Revised Standard Version. The New English Bible resorts to a verbal paraphrase, saying, "Adam foreshadows the Man who was to come." J. B. Phillips says, "Adam, the first man, corresponds in some degree to the man who was to come."

The Greek word is *typos*. It comes from the verb *typtō*, meaning "strike," which is why we have derived the words *type* and *typing* from it. A piece of type is a steel character made to fit into a printing press and strike a piece of paper, leaving an impression of the letter of the alphabet or the symbol it has been made to represent. Typing is a process by which several characters strike a piece of paper in succession. In the Greek world, *typos* referred to the mark left by an object that for some reason or another hit something else, a wound, for example. When Thomas told the other disciples, "Unless I see the nail marks in his hands and put my finger where the nails were, and put my hand into his side, I will not believe it" (John 20:25), the word translated "marks" is *typos*. It refers to the wounds left by the nails of Jesus' crucifixion.

Along the way, *typos* took on a wider set of meanings. It came to mean a "figure" or "form" of something, a figure of a god, for instance. It appears that way in Acts 7:43, where it is translated (in a plural form) as "idols."

More commonly, *typos* is translated "example." Thus, in 1 Corinthians 10:6 and 11 we read, "Now these things occurred as examples, to keep us from setting our hearts on evil things as they did" and "These things happened to them as examples and were written down as warnings for us. . . ." Similarly,

Philippians 3:17 declares, "Join with others in following my example, brothers, and take note of those who live according to the pattern we gave you."

Eventually *typos* came also to mean a person, object, or event that typified or prefigured something greater than itself. This is the way it is used in our text, where we are taught that Adam was "a pattern of," or "prefigured," Jesus Christ.[1]

Adam is not the only "type" of the Lord Jesus Christ in the Bible, of course. Much (if not all) of the Old Testament prefigures Christ. I think here of that wonderful scene in which Jesus appeared to the Emmaus disciples following his resurrection and "opened the Scriptures" to them (Luke 24:32). He began with "Moses and all the Prophets" and "explained to them what was said in all the Scriptures concerning himself" (v. 27). That is, he taught them from the whole Bible. I am sure that after this great opening of the Scriptures, neither of these disciples ever looked at the Bible as they had before. From this point on, everything in the Old Testament would in one way or another have been a "type" of Christ.

They would have turned to Genesis, and it would have been an entirely new book for them. They would have read of the "seed of the woman" and known that this was Christ. They would have seen him in the promises to Abraham and recognized him, too, in the moving story of Joseph. As they turned to Exodus, they would have seen Christ in the Passover Lamb.

In Numbers he would be the rock in the wilderness from which the people received the water of life freely (Num. 20:2–11; cf. 1 Cor. 10:4). Manna would have further typified Jesus (cf. John 6:32–33), and he would also have been seen in the cloud that led the Israelites during their desert pilgrimage and overshadowed them for their protection.

Deuteronomy pictures Christ as "the righteous one" and defines that righteousness.

In Joshua he is "the commander of the army of the Lord."

So on throughout the Bible. In Malachi, the last book of the Old Testament, he is the "sun of righteousness" risen with healing in his wings.

Four Similarities

What about Adam? Our study of "types" has not yet answered the question of how Adam can be said to represent Jesus Christ. But it has put us on the right track in the sense that we have seen that "types" represent their fulfillments in certain great particulars, though not in all respects. This means, then, that we are not looking for a perfect correspondence between

1. For the best study of *typos* and *typtō*, see the articles by Leonhard Goppelt and Gustav Staehlin in Gerhard Friedrick, *Theological Dictionary of the New Testament*, trans. Geoffrey W. Bromiley, vol. 8 (Grand Rapids: Wm. B. Eerdmans, 1972), pp. 246–269. There is a good though much shorter study in Charles Hodge, *A Commentary on Romans* (Edinburgh and Carlisle, Pa.: The Banner of Truth Trust, 1972), p. 162. (Original edition 1935.)

Adam and Jesus Christ. As a matter of fact, in the next study we are going to see some important differences. What we are looking for here are the important similarities.

So we ask again: "How can Adam be said rightly to represent Jesus Christ? How can sinful Adam typify the sinless Son of God?" There are four important parallels.

1. *Both Adam and Jesus Christ were appointed by God to be representatives for other men.* We have already seen how God appointed Adam to stand for humanity as our federal head or representative, so that if he stood firm in righteousness, we would stand with him, and if he fell, we too would fall. Jesus was also appointed to be a representative. We find this, for example, in Hebrews 10:5–7:

> Therefore, when Christ came into the world, he said:
>
> > "Sacrifice and offering you did not desire,
> >   but a body you prepared for me;
> > with burnt offerings and sin offerings
> >   you were not pleased.
> > Then I said, 'Here I am—it is written about me in the scroll—
> >   I have come to do your will, O God.'"

According to this and other texts, Jesus was appointed to be a federal head of the race to accomplish our salvation.

2. *Both Adam and Jesus Christ became heads of particular bodies of people, a race or descendants.* Thus, each is the source of what can be called either the old or the new humanity.

The old humanity is the race as it stands apart from Jesus Christ, lost in its sin and headed for destruction. It is what we see about us in the world. The new humanity is that redeemed people who have been saved by Jesus. In Romans 5, Paul speaks of this as "the many [who] were made sinners" in contrast to "the many [who] will be made righteous" (v. 19). In 1 Corinthians 15 he speaks of it again, saying that "in Adam all die" and "in Christ all will be made alive" (v. 22). And again: "'The first Adam became a living being'; the last Adam, a life-giving spirit" (v. 45).

Notice the words "first Adam" and "last Adam." Paul did not say, "first" and "second," but rather "first" and "last," because he was thinking of Adam and Christ, not as mere men, but in this representative capacity. It is a way of saying that there are only two humanities (not three or four or more), only two representative heads of these humanities—there will never be a third—and that the entire race is divided into these two humanities by virtue of people's relationships to these representatives.

3. *Both Adam and Jesus Christ had covenants made with them by God.* A covenant is an agreement between two parties, usually confirmed by a sym-

bolic act or oath. We have many examples, particularly in the Old Testament: the covenant with Noah; the covenant with Abraham, Isaac, and Jacob; the Deuteronomic covenant; the covenant with David; and so on.

The word *covenant* is not used in the Bible specifically of Adam, but there can be little doubt that God established a covenant with him. The pertinent words are in Genesis 2, where God says, "You are free to eat from any tree in the garden; but you must not eat from the tree of the knowledge of good and evil, for when you eat of it you will surely die" (vv. 16–17). That is a short statement. But in light of Romans 5 and similar teaching elsewhere, it can surely be expanded to mean: "If you obey me by refusing to eat of the tree of the knowledge of good and evil, which I have placed in the garden, then you will be established in righteousness and live forever. Moreover, all who descend from you will also be established in righteousness and enjoy the fruit of righteousness, which is eternal life. But if you disobey me and eat of the tree of the knowledge of good and evil, you will die. And not only will you die; death will also come to your descendants. You will be their ruin, and they will be condemned for your act." (We explored that idea in a previous study.)

In the same way, a covenant was made by God with Jesus Christ. It would have gone as follows: "If you will become the federal head or representative of a new humanity, taking upon yourself the task of fulfilling my divine law and then dying to make satisfaction for the sins of a people I will give to you, then that people shall be freed from sin's bondage, be given eternal life, and be raised to life to reign with you in heaven throughout eternity."

This is a great covenant, which is why the author of Hebrews contrasts it with the covenant made with Israel (which was similar to the covenant made with Adam), saying, ". . . the covenant of which he [Jesus] is mediator is superior to the old one, and it is founded on better promises" (Heb. 8:6).

4. *Both Adam and Jesus Christ passed on to others the effects of their disobedience or obedience.* The effect of Adam's disobedience was sin, condemnation, and death. The effect of Jesus' obedience was righteousness, justification, and eternal life.

D. Martyn Lloyd-Jones, who has an excellent summary of these important similarities, says, "Adam's sin and its consequences was passed on to us all without exception: Christ's obedience and righteousness is passed on to all who believe in him."[2]

Robert Haldane also makes the point nicely: "The two Adams are the heads of the two covenants. The one the representative of all who are under the covenant of works, communicating his image unto them; the other the representative of all who are under the covenant of grace, and communicat-

---

2. D. M. Lloyd-Jones, *Romans: An Exposition of Chapter 5, Assurance* (Grand Rapids: Zondervan, 1972), p. 224. For Lloyd-Jones's *five* similarities see pp. 223–225.

ing his image to them. By the one man's disobedience many were made sinners, and by the obedience of the other many shall be made righteous."[3]

A Historical Adam

In the next study we will explore the other side of the comparison between Adam and Christ, namely, the differences between them. But before we do, we need to remind ourselves of what the comparison itself, including both the similarities and the differences, teaches about Adam and the events that surround him in Genesis.

The first point is that Adam was an actual historical character, every bit as real as ourselves.

There has been a tendency in recent times, perhaps since the middle of the last century, to dismiss Adam (as well as many other parts of the Book of Genesis) as mythology. A myth is a story meant to tell a religious truth. It differs from a fable, which is an imaginary story with a moral, like Aesop's fables, in which animals speak. It also differs from a legend, which is an heroic saga involving larger-than-life characters. The tales of King Arthur fit the legend category. On the other hand, a myth is a *religious* story. It does not necessarily have to do with gods and goddesses or heroes or heroines, though it often does. But a myth deals with timeless or religious truths and—this is the important point—it is not meant to be taken literally. This is why so many liberal scholars in particular have viewed the story of Adam as mythology.

Whenever I hear that judgment, I think of a contrasting judgment by the great English literary scholar and Christian apologist, C. S. Lewis, who made his reputation writing about mythology. Lewis was dealing with claims that the New Testament is mythology, but his points apply to the Genesis accounts equally well. He wrote:

> A man who has spent his youth and manhood in the minute study of New Testament texts and of other people's studies of them, whose literary experiences of those texts lacks any standard of comparison such as can only grow from a wide and deep and genial experience of literature in general, is, I should think, very likely to miss the obvious things about them. If he tells me that something in a gospel is legend or romance, I want to know how many legends or romances he has read, how well his palate is trained in detecting them by the flavor; not how many years he has spent on that gospel.[4]

3. Robert Haldane, *An Exposition of the Epistle to the Romans* (MacDill AFB: MacDonald Publishing, 1958), p. 213.
4. C. S. Lewis, "Faulting the Bible Critics," *Christianity Today*, June 9, 1967, p. 895. The article later appeared in *Christian Reflections* (Grand Rapids: Wm. B. Eerdmans, 1967).

Lewis then introduced the Gospel of John as an example of biblical material considered to be mythology, concluding, "I have been reading poems, romances, vision-literature, legends, myths all my life. I know what they are like. I know that not one of them is like this."[5]

Nor are they like Genesis. If the story of Adam is a myth, then we are going to have to find a new definition for the word! For there *was* an historical Adam; his story *is* to be taken literally.

The real proof of the historicity of Adam is the parallel the apostle Paul draws between the person of Adam and the person of Christ, which we have been studying. Jesus was a specific historical character. He came to earth at a specific past time—in the days of Herod the king, when Caesar Augustus was the ruler of the Roman Empire and Quirinius was governor of Syria (Luke 1:5; 2:1–2)—and he accomplished a literal redemption for us by his death at the hands of Pontius Pilate. Jesus came into our history to undo the effects of Adam's literal transgression. Therefore, Adam himself (and his deeds) must have been historical.

You do not need an historical atonement to undo a mythological fall or a mythological transgression. All you need is another myth. But if Christ needed to be real to save us, then Adam was real, too. It is because Adam was real that Christ also had to be real to make atonement.

That brings us to the second thing the comparison between Adam and Jesus Christ teaches: that the fall of the human race was also historical. It was a real event. That is important because it involves guilt before God—true guilt, not merely imagined guilt or a feeling of guilt.

I am convinced that the major reason why the liberal scholars want to regard the opening chapters of Genesis as mythology is that they do not want to face the reality of the fall of the race in Adam or the guilt that flows from it. If there was no fall, then all this business about Adam and Eve and the serpent and the Garden of Eden is meant only to describe our unfortunate but inevitable human condition. It is meant only to say that we live in an imperfect world and must therefore continually struggle against imperfection. Rather than involving guilt, a framework like that actually gives us cause for pride and an imagined heroic stature. We are not to be blamed for anything. We have simply inherited imperfection and are, if anything, to be praised for how well we are struggling against it. In fact, we can be said to be doing better and better all the time.

But it is not that way. We are not doing better and better, nor are we merely struggling against imperfections. We were once right with God in Adam. But we rebelled. Now we are actually falling away from God as rapidly as our depraved powers and the downward-spiraling flow of our culture will take us. Romans 1 describes this decline. If we are to be saved, it

5. Ibid.

must be by another historical act. The Lord Jesus Christ, who entered history precisely for that reason, must perform it.

In Adam or in Christ?

I close with these paragraphs from Donald Grey Barnhouse:

Apart from the story of his fall, it is remarkable how little is written in the Bible concerning Adam. He was created by God; he was commanded to take dominion over creation; he fell; for him the first blood sacrifice was made. He had several children, the first of whom was a murderer; the second, a type of those who believe and follow Christ; and the third, the progenitor of the race and fulfillment of the promises of God. There is also recorded Adam's age at death—an extremely meager biography. But two stupendous facts make Adam one of the most famous names in history. He was the first man, and he was the first sinner. He dissipated his children's heritage, and we have all been in spiritual poverty ever since. But as we peer at him through the shadows of time we do not judge him too harshly, for we know that he did exactly what we would have done in his place.

And, indeed, we can look rather kindly upon Adam, because through him we learn the principle of the one standing for the many. At the cross of Jesus Christ we see that other one also standing for the many. As Adam stood for many and brought death upon all, so our Lord Jesus stood for many and brings life to all who believe.

Without question everyone of us is in Adam.

Can you look away to Calvary and know that you are in Christ? Having been defiled by the stream that flows from Adam, you can find cleansing only by plunging into the stream that flows from the Lord Jesus Christ dying for us, as head of the new race.[6]

6. Donald Grey Barnhouse, *God's River: Exposition of Bible Doctrines, Taking the Epistle to the Romans as a Point of Departure*, vol. 4, Romans 5:1–11 (Grand Rapids: Wm. B. Eerdmans, 1959), pp. 55, 56.

70

Three Great Contrasts

Romans 5:15–17

But the gift is not like the trespass. For if the many died by the trespass of the one man, how much more did God's grace and the gift that came by the grace of the one man, Jesus Christ, overflow to the many! Again, the gift of God is not like the result of the one man's sin: The judgment followed one sin and brought condemnation, but the gift followed many trespasses and brought justification. For if, by the trespass of the one man, death reigned through that one man, how much more will those who receive God's abundant provision of grace and of the gift of righteousness reign in life through the one man, Jesus Christ.

The paragraph to which we come now, Romans 5:15–17, is one in which Paul develops the differences between our being in Adam and our being in Christ. But in order to understand it we have to go back to the overall analysis of Romans 5:12–21, which I did earlier. If you remember that analysis, you will recall that in those verses Paul is writing about Christ and Adam and that, at the beginning of the section, he started to develop an important comparison: "Therefore, just as sin entered the world through one man [he means Adam], and death through sin, and in this way death came to all men, because all sinned. . . ."

At this point Paul obviously intended to go on with something like what we find in verse 18: ". . . so also the result of one act of righteousness was justification that brings life to all men." But when he got to the point of saying, "and in this way death came to all men, *because all sinned,*" he interrupted his thought, as we have already seen. Apparently he sensed that the majority of his readers (if not all) would be confused by the words "because all sinned." They would not have even the faintest idea what he was really talking about. They would think he meant only that all people sin, when actually he meant that all have been accounted sinners because of Adam's first transgression. So Paul did the only sensible thing. He broke off what he was saying to explain himself.

Verses 13 and 14 are that explanation. In them he shows that the punishment for sin, which is death, was in the world even before the law was given through Moses. Therefore, since people everywhere died during this period, though they were not technically transgressors of the law, which was not yet given, they must have been condemned, not for their own transgressions (though they were guilty of them), but for the sin of Adam. Paul's point is that we were condemned by reason of our union with Adam, just as we have now been saved by virtue of our union with Jesus Christ. It is an important and great similarity.

Parenthesis within a Parenthesis

Here we might have expected Paul to have resumed the contrast with which he began the section, as I indicated he does do when he gets to verse 18. But he does not do this immediately, and the reason must be that when he got to the end of verse 14 he began to think that a further clarification was needed. He had shown that we are united to Christ, just as we were united to Adam. But he must have said to himself, "I cannot give the impression that the parallel holds true on every level. Although it is true that we are justified in Christ, just as we have been condemned in Adam, that is only part of the story. Actually, the differences are as great as the similarities. We are condemned in Adam, true. But the salvation that we have because of our union with Christ is far greater and more glorious."

For this reason, Paul interjects here what I have called a parenthesis within a parenthesis or, as you might prefer to say, a further digression. In verses 13 and 14 he has explained how we have "sinned in Adam." In verses 15–17 he digresses further to explain how union with Christ is greater in its nature and effects than our original union with Adam.

I have called this study "Three Great Contrasts," because of the way Paul sets out his contrasts in the three verses we are studying here, verses 15, 16, and 17. But actually the paragraph is filled with contrasts:

trespass *versus* gift
death *versus* eternal life

condemnation *versus* justification
one *versus* many
sin *versus* righteousness
Adam *versus* Christ

The comparisons continue in verses 18–21:

disobedience *versus* obedience
sinners *versus* those who have been made righteous
law *versus* grace.

The final idea, the triumph of grace over law and the "reign" of grace, is a climax to which the entire chapter moves. It supports the position with which Romans 5 began: that the one who has been joined to Christ by faith is secure in that relationship.

Natural *Versus* Supernatural

Of these three verses (vv. 15–17), the hardest to understand is the first, because it is least explicit. It says: "But the gift is not like the trespass. For if the many died by the trespass of the one man, how much more did God's grace and the gift that came by the grace of the one man, Jesus Christ, over-flow to the many!" In what way is the gift of salvation in Christ *not* like the trespass? In what sense is the gift *much more?*

Let me begin by saying that there is a sense in which this verse is a generic or inclusive statement of the contrasts that follow, so that the remainder of the chapter might be considered exposition. But that aside, it is still right to ask: What is the particular contrast, the unique idea, that verse 15 introduces?

I suggest that the contrast is found in the first key word Paul uses, after having said that "the gift is not like the trespass." It is the word *died.* The sin of Adam brought death. It brought death to all. By contrast, the gift of God brought life to many.

We must not be misled by Paul's use of the word *many.* To most people today "many" suggests "number." So we immediately begin to weigh the "many" who sinned and therefore fell in Adam with the "many" who are being saved in Christ and ask which is greater. Does this verse teach that the saved will outnumber the lost eventually? (There are expositors who say this.) Does it perhaps teach that eventually all will be saved, that is, universalism? I maintain that it is not teaching either one of these things. Paul has been thinking of the union of the race with Adam and the union of the saved with Christ. He is not thinking quantitatively at all. So when he writes of "the many" who died because of Adam's transgression, he means just that: the many who died in Adam, that is, all persons. And when he writes of "the many" to whom the gift of life overflows, he also means many, for surely "many" are being saved.

But what is the contrast, if it is not between a smaller number and a greater number, or between numbers at all? It is, as I suggested, between *death,* which has come upon all because of Adam, and *life,* which has been given to every believer in Christ.

Death is a natural thing, "natural" in the sense that if we are left to ourselves without any supernatural intervention, death simply comes. God told Adam and Eve that if they ate of the fruit of the forbidden tree, they would die. They ate of it, and they did die. It did not require any special intervention of God to produce the effect. Sin always produces death. Moreover, it produces death equally for all. Because Adam sinned, death passed in a natural and inevitable way upon the human race. To that extent, the secularists are right when they speak of a normal biological sequence in which organisms are born, mature, grow old, and eventually die. This is so natural and so understandable that Oswald Spengler used it to explain the equally natural and equally understandable rise and decline of nations. He even used it to prophesy the decline of the western nations in the title of his monumental history, *The Decline of the West.*[1]

Is death natural? Of course.

Even taxes are not as inescapable as mortality.

"But the gift is not like the trespass." Over against the natural outworking of the sin of our first parent, resulting in the death of all, stands the supernatural working of the gracious God. Left to ourselves, the cause is hopeless. Nothing is more characteristic of the presence of man upon earth than graveyards. But God has not left us to ourselves. He has intervened to save us, apart from anything we can do or could ever have done. It is what Paul says in Ephesians 2:1–7:

> As for you, you were dead in your transgressions and sins, in which you used to live when you followed the ways of this world and of the ruler of the kingdom of the air, the spirit who is now at work in those who are disobedient. All of us also lived among them at one time, gratifying the cravings of our sinful nature and following its desires and thoughts. Like the rest, we were by nature objects of wrath. But because of his great love for us, God, who is rich in mercy, made us alive with Christ even when we were dead in transgressions—it is by grace you have been saved. And God raised us up with Christ and seated us with him in the heavenly realms in Christ Jesus, in order that in the coming ages he might show the incomparable riches of his grace, expressed in his kindness to us in Christ Jesus.

1. Oswald Spengler, *The Decline of the West,* 2 vols., trans. Charles Francis Atkinson (New York: Alfred A. Knopf, 1926, 1928).

This is what Paul will write about later on in Romans, though more briefly: "For the wages of sin is death [that is natural part], but the gift of God is eternal life in Christ Jesus our Lord [this part is supernatural]" (Rom. 6:23). Think of what follows from this:

1. Glory goes to God and not man, and

2. Salvation is certain, because the work of God is a lasting thing, unlike our own weak achievements. It is because the work is of God and not man that nothing in creation "will be able to separate us from the love of God that is in Christ Jesus our Lord" (Rom. 8:39).

One Sin *Versus* Many Sins

Verse 16 carries the contrast between the effects of Adam's sin and the effects of God's work in Christ further, pointing out that "the gift of God is not like the result of the one man's sin: The judgment followed one sin and brought condemnation, but the gift followed many trespasses and brought justification."

As I suggested earlier, this verse is easier to understand than the previous one, which is generic and somewhat understated. It is hard to see the precise contrast in verse 15, but this is not true of verse 16. Here a clear contrast is found between the "one sin" that brought condemnation, that is, the sin of Adam in eating from the forbidden tree, and the "many trespasses," which Adam and all who followed him have committed but which are atoned for by the blood of Christ.

Let me elaborate: If in some way—which we know is impossible, but I put it like this only for the sake of argument—the one sin of Adam in eating of the forbidden tree turned out to be the only sin Adam ever committed, and if no one who came after him in all the long ages of human history (including Eve and Cain and Abel and all the rest of mankind down to and including ourselves and our contemporaries) ever committed another sin in thought, word, or deed, it would still have been necessary for Jesus to die to save us. Since we are condemned for Adam's sin, he having been our federal representative, we would still need a Savior to rescue us from that original sin and God's consequent condemnation. And even if that had been the situation and Jesus had come to save us from the effects of only that one sin, salvation would still have been glorious, and the angels would still rightly have used their time singing: "You are worthy to take the scroll and to open its seals, because you were slain, and with your blood you purchased men for God from every tribe and language and people and nation" (Rev. 5:9).

But that is *not* the situation! Adam's one sin did bring condemnation to all, from which Christ alone has redeemed us. But Adam's one sin was not the only sin Christ died for. Adam, having become a sinner, sinned many more times before he died. In fact, it would have been as true of him as Scripture later says it is of the entire race that "every inclination of the thoughts of [man's] heart was only evil all the time" (Gen. 6:5). And Adam's many sins were followed by countless billions of sins by countless billions of sinners, all of whom added their own evils, arrogance, brutality, malice, and other vices to the grim moral history of mankind.

What is the essence of human history? From God's point of view, is it not what Paul has already summarized in Romans 1:29–32?

> They have become filled with every kind of wickedness, evil, greed and depravity. They are full of envy, murder, strife, deceit and malice. They are gossips, slanderers, God-haters, insolent, arrogant and boastful; they invent ways of doing evil; they disobey their parents; they are senseless, faithless, heartless, ruthless. Although they know God's righteous decree that those who do such things deserve death, they not only continue to do these very things but also approve those who practice them.

Since Christ died for such a vast accumulation of sins, is it any wonder that Paul marvels in Romans 5 how "judgment followed one sin and brought condemnation, but the gift followed *many trespasses* and brought justification" (v. 16, emphasis added).

Death *Versus* the Reign of Life

The third and final great contrast is in verse 17: "For if, by the trespass of the one man, death reigned through that one man, how much more will those who receive God's abundant provision of grace and of the gift of righteousness reign in life through the one man, Jesus Christ."

What does that mean?

The key to understanding this verse is to emphasize the word *abundant* in the phrase "God's abundant provision of grace and of the gift of righteousness," and the thought that those who have been thus abundantly blessed are enabled to *reign in life* now through Jesus. To put it simply, the work of Christ in dying for us did not merely restore us to the position in which Adam stood before the fall, but rather carries us beyond that. One commentator says, "Those redeemed by the death of Christ are not merely recovered from the fall, but made to reign through Jesus Christ, to which they had no title in Adam's communion."[2]

D. Martyn Lloyd-Jones, rightly noting the reappearance of the word *justification* in this section, says,

> It is not only that we are forgiven, but over and above being forgiven, the righteousness of Jesus Christ is put to our account, is put upon us. . . . Unfallen Adam was righteous, but it was his own righteousness as a created being, it was the righteousness of a man. Adam never had the righteousness

2. Robert Haldane, *An Exposition of the Epistle to the Romans* (MacDill AFB: MacDonald Publishing, 1958), p. 214.

of Jesus Christ upon him. What he lost was his own righteousness. But you and I are not merely given back a human righteousness, the righteousness that Adam had before he fell—we are given the righteousness of Jesus Christ. "Much more"—abundance, superabundance—give full weight to it! We receive this abundance of grace and the gift of righteousness.[3]

If Adam had remained in a state of righteousness, he could have sung: "In my own righteousness I stand,/Soon to join God's glorious band." But Adam did not stand. He fell, because he was not able by his own strength to confirm himself in righteousness. Similarly, were we to attempt to stand in our own righteousness, assuming that we could attain to it in the first place, we would fall also. But we do not fall. We stand instead, and the reason we stand is that we do not stand in our own righteousness. So we sing:

> Jesus *thy* Blood and righteousness
> My beauty are, my glorious dress;
> 'Midst flaming worlds in these arrayed,
> With joy shall I lift up my head.

Moreover, it is not only that we will stand in that final day of divine judgment. We stand now, which is what the phrase "reigning in life" refers to. It means that by the grace of the Lord Jesus Christ, the love of God, and the communion and empowering of the Holy Spirit, we are victorious *now*. In this way, the gift of God in Christ far surpasses the effects of Adam's and all other transgressions.

Through Jesus Christ

I close by noting some words that Paul has kept repeating in these verses and that also occur later. They are "through the one man," that is, "through Jesus Christ." They occur in verse 17, but we have already encountered a similar phrase in verse 15: "by the grace of the one man, Jesus Christ." And the same idea is found later, in verses 19 and 21: "through the obedience of the one man" and "through Jesus Christ our Lord."

The apostle never leaves this idea out because, as we have been seeing, it is the one glorious and absolutely essential truth in this passage. We were in Adam once, and we fell in him. His sin brought death on the human race. What then? Good news! We can escape the effects of Adam's fall, Paul tells us. More than that, we can rise above the position in which Adam first stood. We can stand in a divine righteousness, which is perfect and which can never be taken away from us. It enables us to reign in life, triumphing over sin, as Adam, in his own human (though once perfect) righteousness, could not. Therefore we can sing:

3. D. M. Lloyd-Jones, *Romans: An Exposition of Chapter 5, Assurance* (Grand Rapids: Zondervan, 1972), p. 262.

On Christ the solid rock I stand;
All other ground is sinking sand.

Are you "in Jesus"? Adam was not "in Jesus," and he fell, even from his high pinnacle of human perfection. If he who was once humanly perfect fell, what chance do *you* have to stand, you who are corrupted by many sins and wholly disposed to unrighteousness?

Your only hope is to believe on Jesus and be joined to him. It is to stand in him, as you originally stood (but also fell) in Adam.

71

Grace

Romans 5:15–17

But the gift is not like the trespass. For if the many died by the trespass of the one man, how much more did God's grace and the gift that came by the grace of the one man, Jesus Christ, overflow to the many! Again, the gift of God is not like the result of the one man's sin: The judgment followed one sin and brought condemnation, but the gift followed many trespasses and brought justification. For if, by the trespass of the one man, death reigned through that one man, how much more will those who receive God's abundant provision of grace and of the gift of righteousness reign in life through the one man, Jesus Christ.

I n the preceding five studies, we have been looking at Romans 5:12–21 with attention to its outline and great themes, trying to follow Paul's thought as he compares our natural union with Adam, on the one hand, with our spiritual union with Christ, on the other. It is a comparison that has involved both similarities and differences. Now we must look at just one word: *grace*. It is a wonderful, magnificent word. "Grace" occurs five times in this passage, three times in verses 15–17, which we are particularly studying here, and twice more in verses 20 and 21. In these verses Paul says that grace is of God and that it comes to us through the Lord Jesus Christ. It is free, triumphant, and overflowing.

593

What is grace? It is God's favor toward the undeserving. Grace lies behind the plan of salvation, but it is also what brings that salvation to us individually and effectively, which is why the great Baptist preacher of the last century, Charles Haddon Spurgeon, called it both the "fountain" and "stream" of salvation.[1] Someone has made grace into an acrostic, calling it: "God's Riches At Christ's Expense." Another has said, "Grace is favor shown to people who do not deserve any favor at all, who, indeed, deserve the exact opposite."[2]

Amazing Grace!

Whenever I come to a word like "grace" and want to capture something of its special meaning for a sermon, I frequently turn to a hymnbook to see how it has been described in poetry by earlier Christians. When I do this for grace, I find that I am almost overpowered by the words and hymns available. In the hymnbook I commonly use there is a table of contents that is organized theologically, and when I turn to it I find that "grace" appears not only in one section or category but in many. It appears under the doctrine of God in two listings: "His [that is, God's] Love and Grace" and "The Covenant of Grace." Under "Jesus" I find "His Love and Grace." Later on there are listings for "Salvation and Grace" and "God's Refreshing Grace."

In the back of this hymnbook there are listings for "converting grace," "efficacious grace," "magnified grace," "refreshing grace," "regenerating grace," "sanctifying grace," "saving grace," and "sovereign grace."

The hymns themselves swell this powerful verbal litany, using phrases like "amazing grace," "abounding grace," "matchless grace," "marvelous grace," and "pardoning grace." A number of these are among the great literary treasures of the English language.

There are the classic lines of John Newton:

> Amazing grace—how sweet the sound—
> That saved a wretch like me!
> I once was lost, but now am found,
> Was blind, but now I see.

Or these by Philip Doddridge:

> Grace! 'Tis a charming sound,
> Harmonious to the ear;
> Heaven with the echo shall resound,
> And all the earth shall hear.

1. C. H. Spurgeon, *All of Grace* (Chicago: Moody Press, n.d.), p. 42.
2. D. M. Lloyd-Jones, *Romans: An Exposition of Chapter 5, Assurance* (Grand Rapids: Zondervan, 1972), p. 232.

My favorite hymn about grace was written by Samuel Davies, a former president of Princeton University:

> Great God of wonders! All thy ways
> Are worthy of thyself—divine;
> And the bright glories of thy grace
> Among thine other wonders shine;
> Who is a pardoning God like thee?
> Or who has grace so rich and free?
>
> Pardon from an offended God!
> Pardon for sins of deepest dye!
> Pardon bestowed through Jesus' blood!
> Pardon that brings the rebel nigh!
> Who is a pardoning God like thee?
> Or who has grace so rich and free?
>
> O may this glorious, matchless love,
> This God-like miracle of grace,
> Teach mortal tongues, like those above,
> To raise this song of lofty praise:
> Who is a pardoning God like thee?
> Or who has grace so rich and free?

Theologians speak of "common grace," "saving grace," "irresistible grace," and "persevering grace." "Sovereign grace" is among the most powerful of all theological expressions.

No wonder Spurgeon said of grace: "What an abyss is the grace of God! Who can measure its breadth? Who can fathom its depth? Like all the rest of the divine attributes, it is infinite. God is full of love, for 'God is love.' God is full of goodness; the very name 'God' is short for 'good.' Unbounded goodness and love enter into the very essence of the Godhead. It is because 'his mercy endureth for ever' that men are not destroyed; because 'his compassions fail not' that sinners are brought to him and forgiven."[3]

Boring Grace?

Despite all this, there are today in most of our churches probably only a small percentage of people who really believe in grace, much less appreciate it. They pay lip service to grace; they know we are "saved by grace" apart from our own good works. But there they stop. If they were to tell the truth, most would probably say that they find the topic of "grace" boring.

3. Spurgeon, *All of Grace*, p. 41.

The great English theologian J. I. Packer has noted this, observing of such people,

> Their conception of grace is not so much debased as non-existent. The thought means nothing to them; it does not touch their experience at all. Talk to them about the church's heating, or last year's accounts, and they are with you at once; but speak to them about the realities to which the word "grace" points, and their attitude is one of deferential blankness. They do not accuse you of talking nonsense; they do not doubt that your words have meaning; but they feel that, whatever it is you are talking about, it is beyond them, and the longer they have lived without it the surer they are that at their stage of life they do not really need it.[4]

What could possibly have caused such indifference, particularly to such a sublime concept? Packer believes that it reflects a failure to understand, acknowledge, and "feel in one's heart" the four great truths that the biblical doctrine of grace presupposes:

1. *The moral ill-desert of man.* Modern man is complacent about his grim spiritual condition, and he assumes that God is also. "The thought of himself as a creature fallen from God's image, a rebel against God's rule, guilty and unclean in God's sight, fit only for God's condemnation, never enters his head."

2. *The retributive justice of God.* "The idea that retribution might be the moral law of God's world, and an expression of his holy character, seems to modern man quite fantastic."

3. *The spiritual impotence of man.* "To mend our own relationship with God, regaining God's favor after having once lost it, is beyond the power of any of us." Yet few think this in our century.

4. *The sovereign freedom of God.* Most people think God owes them something. But, says Packer rightly, "The God of the Bible does not depend on his human creatures for his well-being . . . nor, now that we have sinned, is he bound to show us favor. . . . God does not owe it to anyone to stop justice taking its course. . . . Only when it is seen that what decides each man's destiny is whether or not God resolves to save him from his sins, and that this is a decision which God need not make in any single case, can one begin to grasp the biblical view of grace."[5]

Grace upon Grace

Each of these missed points, so well defined by Packer, has already been spelled out in Romans. Therefore, if we have come to this point having understood what has been taught earlier, we know what grace is and are prepared to marvel at it, as Paul himself does in this section. In fact, this is what we are going to do in the studies that close out our treatment of

---

4. J. I. Packer, *Knowing God* (Downers Grove, Ill.: InterVarsity Press, 1973), p. 117.
5. These four truths are described by Packer in *Knowing God*, pp. 117–120.

Romans 5. They are entitled: "Justification by Grace," "Law and Grace," "Abounding Grace," "God's Motives for Grace," and "The Reign of Grace." Each will help us to explore this marvelous concept further.

But what should we do here? In this first study of grace, I want to set the subject in its broadest context, showing how the grace of God operates. There are five main categories.

1. *Electing grace.* As soon as we see that grace really is apart from any possible merit in its object, we understand that God is utterly sovereign in his choices. Most people probably think of God's saving men and women (if they think of this at all) on the basis of some good in them, either seen or foreseen. That is, most people think that God waits to see the good we are capable of performing and then saves us, if the good is good enough. Or, if we insist with such people, as the Bible teaches, that God has made a decision to save whom he will save in eternity past—before we were created and thus had any opportunity of doing anything—they answer that the decision must have been made on the basis of the good God foresees. Even those who think they believe in grace will sometimes argue this way, supposing that what God foresees is the "faith" that enables him to save us.

But answer this: If men and women really are as corrupt as the Bible describes us as being, what possible "good" in us could God foresee, unless he himself should first decide to put it there? If, as Genesis 6:5 maintains, "every inclination of the thoughts of [our hearts is] only evil all the time," even faith must be created in us sovereignly as an expression of God's grace.

Another way of saying this is to say that grace is eternal; it is before all things.

Still another way is to say that grace is the source or fountainhead of salvation; it is not dependent on anything.

Some years ago, Dr. John H. Gerstner, a former Professor of Church History at Pittsburgh Theological Seminary, was preaching a series of sermons on Romans and had just gotten around to teaching about election in what had turned out to be the eighth sermon in the series. There was a question period afterward, and one man asked, "Why are you Presbyterians always talking about predestination? Why don't you focus on the atonement?" This was the eighth sermon in the series, remember. Gerstner had actually been talking about the atonement for the previous seven messages. But he overlooked that matter and instead pointed out to the man who had asked the question that there would have been no atonement at all if there were no predestination. "If God had not unconditionally elected you to salvation, can you suppose for one moment that he would have sent his precious Son into the world to redeem you?" Gerstner asked.[6]

6. John H. Gerstner, "The Atonement and the Purpose of God" in James M. Boice, ed., *Our Savior God: Man, Christ, and the Atonement, Addresses Presented to the Philadelphia Conference on Reformed Theology 1977–1979* (Grand Rapids: Baker Book House, 1980), p. 110.

We can never pre-distance grace. The grace of God, like God himself, is before all other things. It is from grace that all good comes.

2. *Pursuing grace.* Do you remember what happened to Adam and Eve when they sinned by eating of the forbidden tree? We might have expected that God would have cast them off, abandoning them to hell, since that is what they deserved. But, instead of this, Adam had not moved far from the place of his rebellion when God came to him, calling him by name, and eventually pursuing him into the grove of trees where he and Eve were hiding. There he made great promises of grace, announcing that the Messiah would one day be sent to destroy Satan and restore the guilty pair to Paradise.

It has always been like this. Saul, the self-righteous Pharisee fled God, kicking even against the "goads" of conscience. He fled God by religious activity and zeal, even to the point of hunting out, arresting, and killing Christians. But God pursued Paul. He pursued him to Damascus, stopping him in his furious outward flight. He called to him: "Saul, Saul, why do you persecute me?" (Acts 9:4). Grace did that, and Paul never forgot the fact.

The God of grace has been called "The Hound of Heaven," who pursues rebellious man down the long corridors of time and circumstance.

We may think at times that we have sought God. But as we grow in grace and increasingly learn the nature of our own sinful hearts, we discover that we have sought him only because he first sought us.

> I sought the Lord, and afterward I knew
> He moved my soul to seek him, seeking me;
> It was not I that found, O Savior true.
>   No, I was found of thee.

3. *Pardoning grace.* Samuel Davies marveled at this when he wrote: "Who is a pardoning God like thee? Or who has grace so rich and free?" And no wonder! What he was marveling at was no less than the very core of salvation. We are more accustomed to speak of this core as justification by faith, but that is only a convenient theological shorthand. What we mean when we speak of justification by faith is justification by the grace of God through faith, according to which we are moved from "the status of a condemned criminal awaiting a terrible sentence to that of an heir awaiting a fabulous inheritance."[7] And that is grace! Why was it that God "spared not his own Son, but delivered him up for us all"? (Rom. 8:32), asks J. I. Packer. It is grace alone!

We did not deserve it. We could never deserve it. "But because of his great love for us, God, who is rich in mercy, made us alive with Christ even

---

7. Packer, *Knowing God*, p. 121.

when we were dead in transgressions—it is by grace you have been saved"
(Eph. 2:4–5).

4. *Persevering grace.* Reformed Christians refer to the last of the well-
known points of Calvinism as "the perseverance of the saints" and explain
rightly that those who have been saved by grace persevere. They note Jesus'
saying that "he who stands firm to the end will be saved" (Matt. 10:22). This
is a sound emphasis. The Christian life is not passive on our part. We are
active in it. When Christ calls us we come running, and we keep on running. But notice: We persevere because he perseveres. We endure to the
end because the grace of God preserves us. Indeed, it is absurd to suppose
that we are able to keep ourselves in grace even for a single moment. If it
were up to us, in the final analysis all would be lost.

Do you remember the third verse of John Newton's hymn?

> Through many dangers, toils, and snares,
> I have already come;
> 'Tis grace has brought me safe thus far,
> And grace will lead me home.

That is it exactly. Grace has brought us to where we are now, and that same
grace, persevering grace, will lead us to glory.

5. *Saving grace.* I have left the category of "saving grace" until now
because, although salvation is usually thought of in reference to our being
justified or pardoned only, salvation is actually a more embracing concept.
It refers to the past: God saved us from sin's penalty in Christ. It concerns
the present: God is saving us from sin's power now. It looks to the future:
God will save us from sin's very presence when we are given our resurrection bodies and are taken into his holy presence forever.

How? It is by grace, grace only.

Grace in God's People

I have two main conclusions in this study. First, if we have been saved
entirely by grace, as we see we have, this very fact should draw us closer to
God. Why? Because without him we are lost. We must never trust ourselves.

> Oh, to grace how great a debtor
> Daily I'm constrained to be;
> Let that grace now, like a fetter,
> Bind my wandering heart to thee.
> Prone to wander, Lord, I feel it,
> Prone to leave the God I love;

> Here's my heart, Oh, take and seal it,
> Seal it for thy courts above.
>
> Robert Robinson, 1758

Second, let us revel in grace, abounding in it even as it is abounding. Why? Because, as D. Martyn Lloyd-Jones says, "It is only when you and I, and others who are members of the Christian Church, are rejoicing in this abounding grace as we ought to be, that we shall begin to attract the people who are outside the church."[8] There are lots of things about Christianity that will always be unattractive to the world: holiness, discipleship, self-sacrifice, and more. There are scores of them. But grace is not one. Grace is attractive, and those who have received grace should be attractive, too.

Later on, Paul is going to speak of grace "abounding." Let it abound! He is going to speak of grace "reigning." Let it reign! Let it reign until all about turn to you and say, "If that is Christianity, then that is what I want." Do not live like a pauper when God has made you a king.

---

8. Lloyd-Jones, *Romans: An Exposition of Chapter 5, Assurance,* pp. 238, 239.

72

Justification by Grace

Romans 5:18–19

Consequently, just as the result of one trespass was condemnation for all men, so also the result of one act of righteousness was justification that brings life for all men. For just as through the disobedience of the one man the many were made sinners, so also through the obedience of the one man the many will be made righteous.

I do not know when or where it happened, but somebody was sitting in his apartment, getting ready to go to bed, when he heard his neighbor drop a shoe on the floor above him. The upstairs neighbor was obviously getting ready for bed, too, and the man below him waited for the thud of the other shoe. Afterward he must have talked about it, and the expression "waiting for the other shoe to drop" became an expressive figure of speech in our language.

Now we come to what we have been waiting for ever since we started to study Romans 5:12–21. Our expectation arose because Paul began this great passage with a contrast: "Therefore, just as sin entered the world through one man, and death through sin, and in this way death came to all men, because all sinned. . . ." But just when we were expecting the second half of that thought, he broke it off, and everything we have been studying since has in a sense been a digression, or parenthesis.

In fact, there have been two major digressions, which it might be helpful to review before proceeding.

First, Paul explained the sense in which "all sinned." He did not mean that all have become sinners and have therefore sinned, though we would naturally think this, but rather that each of us was declared a sinner because of Adam's original sin or transgression. It is true that we also sin and should be condemned for that, if there were nothing more to be said. But that is not Paul's meaning. He meant that all have been accounted sinners in Adam, so that those who were going to be saved could be accounted righteous in the Lord Jesus Christ.

Since this digression finished at the end of verse 14, we again expected the other shoe to drop. But instead of completing the contrast introduced by verse 12, Paul worked in another long parenthesis to show the differences between our union with Adam, on the one hand, and our union with Jesus Christ, on the other. This second digression started at verse 15 and occupied the next three verses.

It is only when we get to verse 18 that the second shoe finally falls and we get the full impact of the contrast. Paul backs up to give it, restating the first part again, although in slightly different words: "[1] Consequently, just as the result of one trespass was condemnation for all men, [2] so also the result of one act of righteousness was justification that brings life for all men."

There we have it!

But then, lest we have fallen asleep in the meantime and have somehow missed the point after this long wait, Paul makes it again in verse 19, adding: "[1] For just as through the disobedience of the one man the many were made sinners, [2] so also through the obedience of the one man the many will be made righteous."

What a great list of contrasts is implied here! In a previous study we have already seen "Three Great Contrasts" in verses 15–17. They were intended to show the ways in which the work of Adam and the work of Christ were dissimilar. The new list of contrasts in verses 18 and 19 shows the fullness of what Paul is teaching and serves as a summary. Those contrasts are:

Adam *versus* Christ
The one trespass of Adam *versus* the one act of righteousness of Christ
The disobedience of Adam *versus* the obedience of Christ
Death *versus* life
Condemnation *versus* justification.

Of these five contrasts, the greatest is the one between condemnation and justification, since this is what the chapter has been dealing with in one way or another all along.

By Faith or By Grace?

In the previous study, I said that we would be dealing with the subject of God's grace through the end of Romans 5, and for that reason I have called this study "Justification by Grace." But I wonder if that sounds right to you. We already know about "justification by faith." It was the rallying cry of the Protestant Reformation, Martin Luther having said that it is the doctrine by which the church stands or falls.[1] But if that is so, why should we speak of justification by *grace*? The answer, of course, is that both statements are parts of the same truth, since the justification that is received by faith alone (*sola fide*) is also by grace alone (*sola gratia*).

A full statement of the doctrine would be: "Justification by the grace of God alone, received through faith alone."

Justification is an act of God as judge by which he declares us to be in a right standing before him so far as his justice is concerned. We are not just in ourselves, of course. So the only way by which we can be declared to be in a right standing before God is on the basis of the death of Jesus Christ for our sins, he bearing our punishment, and by the application of Christ's righteousness to us by God's grace. This grace is received through the channel of human faith, but it is nevertheless utterly of grace. It is apart from all deserving.

Is Etymology Helpful Here?

"Justification" is what this great section of Romans is all about, and we need to see the passage's force. But before getting into the text, let me mention another reason why some people might be confused about justification and thus misunderstand it—the problem lies with the word's etymology, its linguistic history.

Anyone who knows Latin can tell at a glance that "justification" is constructed out of two Latin words: *iustus* and *facio, facere*. The first word is an adjective meaning "just," "equitable," "fair," or "proper." In legal terminology it means "having a right status in reference to a law." We have preserved the Latin term in English words like "just," "justice," and "justify." The second word is a verb; it means "to make" or "to do." We have it in such words as "factory," which is a place where things are made, or "manufacture," which literally means "to make a thing by hand." Putting these two Latin words together, we have a meaning for "justification" that would go some-

---

1. "When the article of justification has fallen, everything has fallen. . . . This is the chief article from which all other doctrines have flowed" (in *What Luther Says: An Anthology*, compiled by Ewald M. Plass, vol. 2 [Saint Louis: Concordia, 1959], pp. 715, 702).

thing like this: "to make just, right, or equitable." Used of people, this would suggest that they are literally to be made righteous.

But here the etymology of the word *justification* is misleading to most English speakers.[2] The reason is that "justification" actually refers *not* to a righteousness attained by or produced in an individual, but to the act of God by which the righteousness of Christ is credited to that person.

The context of Romans 5 is of great help in coming to understand and appreciate this term. You will remember from the list of contrasts I presented earlier that justification is contrasted with condemnation in verse 18: "Consequently, just as the result of one trespass was *condemnation* for all men, so also the result of one act of righteousness was *justification* that brings life for all men." If this is the contrast, we need to ask what happens when people are "condemned." Does the act of condemnation make them lawbreakers? To use biblical terminology: Does it make them sinners? Or does it merely mean that they are declared to be such? The answer is: It means that they are *declared* to be sinners. They are lawbreakers already. The act of condemnation merely declares this to be so and subjects them to whatever penalty the law in the case prescribes.

The same idea applies to justification. Even though the etymology would suggest that justification means "to make just or righteous," the term actually means "to declare one to be in a right standing before God's law." In human courts, this might be on the basis of the individual's own personal righteousness. But this can never be the basis in God's court, since no one is truly righteous, as Paul has shown in the preceding chapters.

How can God declare us to be righteous, then? Only on the grounds of Jesus' own perfect righteousness imputed to us. That is, we are justified by God by grace alone.

There is another explanation derived from the wording of verse 19. Paul says that on the basis of Adam's one act of disobedience many "were made sinners." We have already seen how that is to be taken. It does not mean that all were affected by sin and thus became sinning individuals, though that did happen and is true. Rather, here it means that the entire race was declared to be sinful because of Adam's sin. That is why death passed upon all, even upon those (like infants) who died before they had any opportunity to sin. If "the many were made sinners" in that sense, it must be in a corresponding sense that "the many will be made righteous," namely, through the one act of obedience by Jesus Christ.

2. I say "most," because an accurate understanding of *iustus* would keep a good Latin student from the error I am discussing. He would know that the term chiefly refers to one's status before the law and only secondarily to whether such a person is indeed a just or upright individual.

The Obedience of Christ

This brings us to another important idea: the obedience of Jesus. Paul mentions this in verse 19, and it is the first time he has used the word. He has really been speaking of the difference between Adam's disobedience and Christ's obedience all along, but up to this point he has used different terminology. What is the significance of his use of the phrase "through the *obedience* of the one man" here?

In discussing the obedience of Christ, theologians usually distinguish between what is called the active obedience of Jesus and the passive obedience of Jesus.

The *active* obedience of Jesus refers to his submission to and active conformity to the law of Moses. Do you remember how in Galatians Jesus is described as having been "born under law, to redeem those under law" (Gal. 4:4–5)? This means that when Jesus became man he deliberately subjected himself to the law of Moses, so that when he went to the cross to die for our sin, it might be known that he did so as a perfect sin-bearer, "a lamb without blemish or defect" (1 Peter 1:19).

Jesus' baptism signified the same thing. When Jesus came to John to be baptized, John protested at first, saying, "I need to be baptized by you, and do you come to me?" (Matt. 3:14). He meant that Jesus was perfect, that he needed no baptism of repentance from his sins. But Jesus replied, "Let it be so now; it is proper for us to do this to fulfill all righteousness" (v. 15). In other words, Jesus did not come to John for a baptism of repentance, as the others were doing, for he had no sin for which to repent. By his baptism he identified with us, putting himself under law as our federal head or representative. The law was there to be kept, and Jesus kept it. Throughout his life he exercised a full and active obedience to God's standards and thus showed himself to be the only acceptable sacrifice for sin.

The *passive* obedience of Jesus Christ is something else. It refers to his submission to the cross. Do you recall how Jesus wrestled with this in Gethsemane? He prayed, "My Father, if it is possible, may this cup be taken from me . . ." (Matt. 26:39). Jesus was not asking if he could somehow escape the cruel death of crucifixion. It was his being made sin for us that troubled him. He was to be placed on the cross, and the full weight of the sin of men and women was to be placed on him and punished there. The Father was even going to turn his back upon him. That is what Jesus dreaded and what he referred to when he asked if there were not some other way open.

This was Jesus' passive obedience, and it is what Paul is referring to when he speaks of "the obedience of the one man" through which "the many will be made righteous." Christ's active obedience qualified him for this role. But it was his one act of passive obedience, corresponding to Adam's one act of disobedience, that atoned for our sin and made it possible for the Father to credit Jesus' righteousness to our account.

Where Are Your Sins?

But enough explanation. Here is an illustration from the life of Donald Grey Barnhouse, one of my predecessors as pastor of the Tenth Presbyterian Church of Philadelphia. It is the story of his conversion.[3]

When Barnhouse was about fifteen years old he heard the testimony of a man who had been a narcotics addict but had been delivered from that life and become a minister of the gospel. Barnhouse approached the man and asked about his experience of Christ, because he believed that the preacher had something he himself lacked. The preacher gave him an object lesson. He took Barnhouse's left hand, turned it palm upward and then said intently, "This hand represents you." On it he placed a hymnbook, saying, "This book represents your sin. The weight of it is on you. God hates sin, and his wrath must bear down against sin. Therefore, his wrath is bearing down on you, and you have no peace in your heart or life." It was a good statement of the truths in Romans 1, and Barnhouse knew it was true.

Then the preacher took the young man's other hand and said, "This hand represents the Lord Jesus Christ, the Savior. There is no sin upon him, and the Father must love him, because he is without spot or blemish. He is the beloved Son in whom the Father is well pleased." There were Donald's two hands, the one weighted down by the heavy book, the other empty. Again he knew it was true. He had the sin. Jesus had none.

Then the older man put his hand under Barnhouse's left hand and turned it over so that the book now came down on the hand that previously had been empty. He released the left hand, its burden now transferred to the hand that stood for Jesus. Then he said, "This is what happened when the Lord Jesus Christ took your place on the cross. He was the Lamb of God, bearing away the sin of the world."

While the hymnbook representing Barnhouse's sin still rested on the hand representing Jesus Christ, the preacher turned to his Bible and began to read verses that taught what he had just illustrated.

First Peter 2:23–24: "When they hurled their insults at him, he did not retaliate; when he suffered, he made no threats. Instead, he entrusted himself to him who judges justly. He himself bore our sin in his own body on the tree, so that we might die to sins and live for righteousness. . . ."

Isaiah 53:4–6 (the verses to which Peter was referring):

> Surely he took up our infirmities
>   and carried our sorrows,
> yet we considered him stricken by God,
>   smitten by him, and afflicted.

3. Barnhouse tells this conversion story in Donald Grey Barnhouse, *God's Grace: Exposition of Bible Doctrines, Taking the Epistle to the Romans as a Point of Departure*, vol. 5, Romans 5:12–21 (Grand Rapids: Wm. B. Eerdmans, 1959), pp. 86–88.

> But he was pierced for our transgressions,
>> he was crushed for our iniquities;
> the punishment that brought us peace was upon him,
>> and by his wounds we are healed.
> We all, like sheep, have gone astray,
>> each of us has turned to his own way;
> and the LORD has laid on him
>> the iniquity of us all.

The preacher stopped reading and addressed the young man directly. "Whose sins were laid on Jesus?" he asked.

"Our sins," Barnhouse replied.

"Whose sins does that mean?" the preacher probed.

"Our sins," came the same answer.

"Yes, but whose sins are those?"

"Well, everybody's sins—your sins, my sins . . ."

The older man interrupted and caught the words almost before they were out of Barnhouse's mouth. "*My* sins; yes, that's it," he said. "That's what I want. Say it again."

Young Barnhouse obeyed. "My sins," he repeated.

The preacher then went back to Isaiah 53:6. He put the hymnbook back on Barnhouse's left hand and pressed down upon it as he read, "We all, like sheep, have gone astray, each of us has turned to his own way." The pressure was strong. But then he turned the book and hand over once again, so that the burden was transferred to the hand that represented Jesus Christ, and he continued his reading: "and the LORD has laid on him the iniquity of us all."

Barnhouse understood it then, and he never forgot it. In fact, he used that very illustration to teach many others about justification and lead them to the Savior. He also expanded it. For just as the transfer of the hymnbook showed the transfer of our sin to Jesus, where it has been punished, so also is it possible to show the transfer of the righteousness of Christ to us by movement in the opposite direction. As I showed when we were studying Romans 4, a double transfer is involved.[4] Barnhouse used a Bible to show this corresponding reality.

Horatio G. Spafford knew these truths. He wrote:

> My sin—O the bliss of this glorious thought!—
>> My sin, not in part, but the whole,
> Is nailed to the cross, and I bear it no more:
>> Praise the Lord!
>> Praise the Lord! O my soul.

---

4. "David's Testimony" (Romans 4:6–8) in James Montgomery Boice, *Romans*, vol. 1, *Justification by Faith* (Grand Rapids: Baker Book House, 1991).

All of Grace

But this double transfer is all of grace! Nothing compelled God to act this way toward us. Nothing made Christ die for your sin or made God credit the righteousness of his Son to you. There was nothing in you, under that great blanketing weight of sin, that drew his love downward. God did it because it pleased him to do it, and because it is his nature to be gracious.

At the end of his very excellent treatment of these verses, D. Martyn Lloyd-Jones asks whether we have understood the doctrine of justification by grace, and suggests (rightly I think) that there is a connection between understanding this and being truly saved. He does not mean that everyone who is saved understands everything about justification, of course. None of us does. He means that if these truths seem impossible or even crazy to you—if you are objecting, "But how could God possibly treat us as if we were in Adam and as if we are in Christ? How can he save us because of something someone else has done?"—it is probably because you are not saved.[5]

For those who are not saved, these doctrines will always sound foolish. They may even sound like an invitation to sin, which is the objection Paul deals with in the very next chapter of Romans. It will always be thus, for how can those who do not possess the Spirit of God understand spiritual matters? Ah, but to those who are saved, these truths are wonderful. They are the very essence of life—which is, of course, what Paul speaks about here: "Justification that brings life for all men."

If you understand this and it seems right to you—not pointless, incorrect, or irrational—and if you believe it, you are one of those saved persons.

5. D. M. Lloyd-Jones, *Romans: An Exposition of Chapter 5, Assurance* (Grand Rapids: Zondervan, 1972), pp. 279, 280.

73

Law and Grace

Romans 5:20

The law was added so that the trespass might increase. But where sin increased, grace increased all the more.

At the end of Romans 5 is a short paragraph of two verses that a careless reader might be inclined to overlook, because at first glance the verses seem merely to be tacked on as an afterthought. We have followed Paul's argument in the previous nineteen verses of this chapter in detail, particularly from verse 12 on, and we have seen that the contrast between the sin of Adam and its consequences, on the one hand, and the obedience of Christ and its consequences, on the other, has at last been wrapped up. The sin of Adam led to condemnation and death. The righteousness of Christ led to justification and eternal life. This was so important to state that Paul has actually done so twice, once in verse 18 and a second time in verse 19.

Why, then, do we have a reintroduction of the "law," "trespass," "sin," "grace," "death," "righteousness" and "eternal life" in this short paragraph? Isn't it redundant? Wouldn't we be better served by moving on directly to chapters 6 and 7?

Well, the words are not redundant, and they are not unimportant. They are important for three reasons. First, they are a summary of what Paul has already been saying. That is why so many of the key terms of verses 12–19 are repeated. Second, they are a capsule treatment of the themes that chapters 6 and 7 will develop in detail. One commentator says that the following chapters are "virtually nothing but an extended commentary" on these verses.[1] Third, verses 20 and 21 answer a question that has not been answered but has been suggested by something Paul wrote earlier. It is this question (and the answer) that concern us now.

Why Was the Law Given?

Verse 20 begins by mentioning the law. So let's back up a moment to what Paul has already said in Romans about the law of God. He has said two important things.

First, he has pointed out that the law was not given as a way by which we can be justified. The Jewish people thought differently. They believed that one could be justified by observing the law, which was Judaism's greatest treasure. But Paul has been at pains to disabuse the Jew of this opinion. "The law tells you what you should do," he says, "but it does not enable you to do it. All it does is reveal that you are a sinner." Paul made this clear in Romans 3, where he said: "Now we know that whatever the law says, it says to those who are under the law, so that every mouth may be silenced and the whole world held accountable to God. Therefore no one will be declared righteous in his sight by observing the law; rather, through the law we become conscious of sin" (vv. 19–20).

Second, in Romans 5:12–19 Paul has gone further, showing that the law was not even necessary to condemn us, since we have all already been condemned for the sin of our first parent, Adam. It is because of his trespass, not our own, that "the many were made sinners" (v. 19).

Can you see how someone might be confused at this point? A person might say, "Paul, you have shown us that the law was not given as a means of justification, and we accept that. You have also shown that the law was not even necessary to condemn us, since we have all already been condemned for the sin of Adam. That is harder for us to understand, but we are willing to accept that, too. But look: If these two things are so, then please tell us, what was the purpose of the law? If we cannot be saved by the law and if the law is not even necessary for our condemnation, why was it given? What does it do? Does it, in fact, do anything? As we look at it now, the law of God seems to be without a real purpose."

This is the question that has not been answered but was suggested by Paul's mention of the law earlier in Romans 5, particularly in verses 13 and

1. D. M. Lloyd-Jones, *Romans: An Exposition of Chapter 5, Assurance* (Grand Rapids: Zondervan, 1972), p. 298.

14. His answer is in verse 20, our text: "The law was given so that the trespass might increase. . . ."

But that creates an entirely new set of problems, doesn't it? It seems to say that God wanted more sin and that he decided to create sin by giving the law. That can't be true. That is an obvious error. God is not the author of sin, nor does he encourage it. James says that he does not even tempt us: ". . . God cannot be tempted by evil, nor does he tempt anyone; but each one is tempted when, by his own evil desire, he is dragged away and enticed" (James 1:13–14). If Romans 5:20 does not mean what on the surface it seems to mean, what does it mean? Why was the law "added"?

A proper approach to this verse is suggested by the word *added*. The Greek word is translated in various ways in the versions: "came in" (RSV and NASB), "keeps slipping into the picture" (Phillips), "intruded" (NEB), "was introduced" (TEV). But this is the same word that was used for the entrance of sin into the world in verse 12 ("therefore, just as sin *entered* the world through one man"), but with the prefix *para* (meaning "alongside of") joined to it. The literal meaning is: "the law entered alongside of."

Alongside of what? Obviously, alongside of the sin that had already entered into the world. I point this out because, as soon as we see that God sent the law to be *alongside of sin*, we understand that the law was meant to exist in relationship to the sin that was already there. In other words, it does not cause sin, but rather does something to it. Since the sentence goes on to say that this was done "so that the trespass might increase," it must mean that the law somehow brought out the true nature and magnitude of sin so that it could be seen for what it truly is.

Moreover, as we are going to see, it was because of grace and in order that the grace of God might abound that God did this.

But we need to spell this out carefully. I have been greatly assisted at this point by D. Martyn Lloyd-Jones's careful treatment of this subject, and I want to follow his outline as I explore the ways in which the law increased (and was meant to increase) sin. There are three of them.

"I Would Not Have Known Sin, Except . . ."

The first way in which the law increased sin was by increasing our knowledge of it. This is what Paul is going to explain more fully in Romans 7, where he says, ". . . . I would not have known what sin was except through the law. For I would not have known what coveting really was if the law had not said, 'Do not covet'" (v. 7). Obviously, the law did not make Paul covetous. He was that already. It merely showed him that he was.

Lloyd-Jones breaks this down into four parts, asking: How does the law increase our knowledge of sin specifically? Then he answers:

1. *The law defines sin for us.* Before the giving of the law we were in a sense like children. You know how it is with children. They have the seeds of sin in them and also behave sinfully. But there is a sense in which they often do

not know that what they are doing or are inclined to do is sinful. They are selfish, for example. But they only begin to learn what selfishness is, and that it is wrong, when a teacher or parent explains that it is important to share the toys in nursery school. No one is allowed to hog them all. Or they are willful. But they discover what this is only when their wills are opposed by the wiser and steadier wills of their parents, expressed in a list of things they can and cannot do. In the same way, sin is defined for us by the written law of God.

Another way of saying this is that law turns sin into transgression. All wrong acts are sinful, even without the law. But they are only seen to be sin when they are exposed as transgressions of the law of God. Paul said this earlier in this letter: "For before the law was given, sin was in the world. But sin is not taken into account when there is no law" (5:13) and ". . . where there is no law there is no transgression" (4:15).

2. *The law reveals sin's nature.* The true essence of sin is that it is rebellion against God. But there is a sense in which we do not fully know that or understand it until we are confronted with the law pertaining to the case. I mean by this that most people have a God-given sense of right and wrong. Even the native in the jungle, without any knowledge of the Bible, has a certain moral code. But he does not know God, and as a result he does not know that violations of his code, which he knows he violates, are actually directed against the God who has given him his moral sensibilities.

To give an example: When David committed adultery with Bathsheba and then conspired to have her husband killed, he would have known, even if he were an unenlightened heathen, that he had done wrong. Adultery and murder are not condoned anywhere. But because he was also an instructed member of God's chosen race, David saw his sin on a deeper level and therefore confessed it to be against God, saying: "Against you, you only, have I sinned and done what is evil in your sight . . ." (Ps. 51:4). David had sinned against (as well as with) Bathsheba, Uriah, and the nation of Israel. But it was only when he saw his sin as being against God that its true horror gripped him and he was led to confess it openly.

3. *The law exposes sin's power.* Let me give an example here, too. There is a man who is a heavy smoker. A number of people suggest he should stop, and his reply is that he can stop smoking anytime he wants to. After all, he has proved it by stopping dozens of times. He really does not know (or will not admit) that he has a nicotine addiction. Then he visits his doctor, who examines him, tells him that his smoking is killing him, and orders him to stop. Now he has a law to deal with, the law of his doctor. "All right, doctor," he says. "I'll stop smoking." But when he tries to stop he finds that he really cannot do it. Before, he thought he could. Now, when the doctor's "law" commands him to stop, he discovers that he cannot. He needs help.

This is the way with us. And it is this sense of helplessness that has actually been a step in many persons' conversions. They supposed that the cure for sin was within their own power—until they were convicted by the law of God and actually attempted reformation. It was then they discovered their own spiritual inability and turned to Christ.

4. *The law unveils sin's deceit.* Until we are directly exposed to the law of God we excuse our conduct, calling sin by some lesser name or denying it. The written law shows us that sin is sin and that it has fooled us into taking it lightly. Only the law exposes the pitfalls on sin's primrose path.

Martyn Lloyd-Jones applies this first way in which the giving of the law increased sin by saying:

> One of the greatest troubles in the church today, as well as in the world, is that men do not have a knowledge of sin as they should have. Sin is regarded very lightly and loosely. . . . Men are prepared to admit that they need a little help, and that they are weak in this or that respect; but the Scripture teaches the depth and the foulness, and the exceeding sinfulness of sin. Our fathers, our grandfathers, and especially those who preceded them, knew all about this, and it was in such times that great spiritual revivals occurred. It is when men and women realize the depth of iniquity and sin that is in them that they begin to cry out to God. But if men have no real knowledge of sin, if they are lacking in the knowledge of sin which is given only by the law, then they will be content with a superficial evangelism. This is surely one of our main troubles today.[2]

Those words state the case exactly.

Conviction of Sin

But the law does not only bring a knowledge of sin by defining it and exposing its power and its true and deceitful nature. It convicts us of sin, which is where the points in the previous section have been leading. Does the law also do the opposite? Yes, it sometimes does that: It can harden the heart. But when the Spirit of God is moving, the preaching of the law brings conviction and teaches those who have been convicted of sin to recoil from it.

Why does that happen? It is because the law reveals sin to be an offense against God, as I said earlier. As long as we think of sin only as a violation of some abstract moral code, it will not trouble us very much. We will just try to get away with the sin if we can. Sin will not even trouble us if we think of it as violation of a law made by other human beings. Why should their will restrict us? However, when we discover sin to be against the God who has made us and who has provided us with all good things, when we see that it

2. Ibid., p. 289.

is a rebellion against our Creator—an offense and an insult to him—we then experience real conviction.

In Romans 7, where Paul is discussing the role of the law at length, he not only says that the entrance of the law gave knowledge of sin. He adds that it awoke sin and allowed sin to produce even more sinful desires: "But sin, seizing the opportunity afforded by the commandment, produced in me every kind of covetous desire . . ." (v. 8).

This idea is not hard to understand. Everyone knows how the knowledge of a law somehow produces the desire in us to break it. If we are going down the highway at what we regard as a reasonable speed and see a sign restricting us to a speed we judge to be unreasonable, often we do not slow down. We hold our speed constant, and at times we even increase it. Do you remember Prohibition? I am told that during those days people who did not drink before became drinkers, and the sale of alcoholic beverages went up. A related story is told about John Nance Garner (who later became vice-president of the United States under Franklin Delano Roosevelt). Supposedly, after the law prohibiting the sale of alcoholic beverages was passed, Garner would greet every visitor to his home by opening a cupboard, taking out a decanter and two glasses, pouring two drinks, and then saying solemnly, "Let us strike a blow for liberty."

This truly is the very nature of sin, and it is the coming of the law of God that reveals its stiff-necked nature within us.

Where Does Grace Come In?

Because we are studying grace in these concluding messages of Romans 5, at this point a person might well be asking, "Where, in the midst of all this definition and exposure of sin, can grace come in?" Or, to put it differently, "Why is this chapter entitled 'Law and Grace,' when thus far all we have talked about is law?"

There are several answers to those questions. Let me give two of them.

First, the very exposure of sin is an act of grace by God. He did not need to give the law. He could have left us in ignorance, allowing us to suppose in our blind sinfulness that all was well with us, when actually we were under his wrath and were perishing. He could have left us to compare ourselves with other persons, as a result of which we all inevitably suppose that we are fairly good. But, by giving us the law, God has disabused us of those fantasies and allowed us to see our condition as it truly is. The first step in seeking a doctor is to know that you are sick. In order to seek salvation you must know you need it.

Second, the law contained an anticipation of the gospel. The law was given at Mount Sinai amidst many visible demonstrations of God's presence. God declared what the people of Israel were and were not to do:

"I am the LORD your God, who brought you out of Egypt, out of the land of slavery.

"You shall have no other gods before me.

"You shall not make for yourself an idol in the form of anything in heaven above or on the earth beneath or in the waters below. You shall not bow down to them or worship them; for I, the LORD your God, am a jealous God, punishing the children for the sin of the fathers to the third and fourth generation of those who hate me, but showing love to thousands who love me and keep my commandments.

"You shall not misuse the name of the LORD your God, for the LORD will not hold anyone guiltless who misuses his name.

"Remember the Sabbath day by keeping it holy. Six days you shall labor and do all your work, but the seventh day is a Sabbath to the LORD your God. On it you shall not do any work, neither you, nor your son or daughter, nor your manservant or maidservant, nor your animals, nor the alien within your gates. . . .

"Honor your father and your mother, so that you may live long in the land the LORD your God is giving you.

"You shall not murder.

"You shall not commit adultery.

"You shall not steal.

"You shall not give false testimony against your neighbor.

"You shall not covet your neighbor's house. You shall not covet your neighbor's wife, or his manservant or maidservant, his ox or donkey, or anything that belongs to your neighbor."

Exodus 20:2–10, 12–17

But that is precisely the code of law we have broken! What can we do?

Here is where the grace of God comes in. For in addition to giving us the law, which exposes our sin and shows us our deep need, God at the same time also pointed to the sacrifices by which sin might be punished and the guilt of sin be removed. At the very time God gave Moses to the people, God also gave them Aaron and the priests.

God showed how, when the people sinned, they were to take an animal and present it to the priest, who would then kill it and offer it up on the altar. It was a way of acknowledging the grim nature and dread consequences of sin—"The soul who sins . . . will die" (Ezek. 18:4b)—while, at the same time, it was also a way of portraying the grace of God, who was thereby shown willing to accept the death of an innocent substitute rather than requiring the sinner's own death and condemnation.

All this pointed forward to the atonement provided by Jesus Christ.

And remember that *he* did not take the law lightly! Philip E. Hughes writes:

> Jesus when he came to save the world did not set aside the law: he fulfilled
> it—that is to say, he kept the law fully, without fault or lapse. In contrast to

all other men, who are law-breakers, he is the sole law-keeper. He alone is without sin (Heb. 4:15; 7:26; 1 Pet. 2:22). He alone is full of grace and truth (John 1:14; 14:6). He is Jesus Christ the righteous (1 John 2:1). This perfect obedience of Christ to the law is an essential element in the salvation which he came to procure for us. . . . The first stage of his work of salvation required that, *as man,* he should keep fully the law of God which mankind had broken. Only thus would he be qualified to offer himself, as the spotless Lamb of God (1 Peter 1:18–19), in sacrifice for man.[3]

Which is precisely what he did! For, as Paul writes in Galatians, "But when the time had fully come, God sent his Son, born of a woman, born under law, to redeem those under law, that we might receive the full rights of sons" (Gal. 4:4–5). At the cross of Christ the law of God and the grace of God met, and each was fully satisfied.

God's grace saves us from the law's condemnation. And what is more, as we will see in our study of Romans 6 and 7, that same grace of God enables those who were once law-breakers to become law-keepers. Both the law of God and the grace of God are magnified.

---

3. Philip Edgcumbe Hughes, *But for the Grace of God: Divine Initiative and Human Need* (Philadelphia: The Westminster Press, 1964), p. 36.

74

Abounding Grace

Romans 5:20

. . . But where sin increased, grace increased all the more.

The second half of Romans 5:20 is one of the truly great verses of the Bible. Even in the midst of a book in which every sentence is splendid, Romans 5:20 stands out like a brilliant beacon on a dark and dangerous night. The dark background is sin and its horrible proliferation in the world. But the beacon flashes, "Where sin increased, grace increased all the more."

This sentence is so wonderful that it is difficult to do justice to it, especially in translation. In the New International Version the word *increase* is used twice: once of sin, which is said to have "increased," and once of grace, which is said to have "increased all the more." This is a reasonably accurate translation. But it is weak, because Paul used two different Greek words for the two kinds of increase, and the strength of the verse is enhanced by the resulting contrast.

The Greek word that refers to the increase of sin is based on a term (*polys*) meaning "much" or "many." So the verb (*pleonazō*) has the idea of a numerical increase. The NIV translation of this first verb is not bad, since it

617

means "to increase in number," "grow," or "multiply." The second word is different, however. It is the verb *perisseuō*, which means "to abound," "overflow," or "have more than enough." This verb does not have to do with numbers so much as with "excess." However, lest we miss the point, Paul adds the prefix *hyper* (we would say "super"), which gives the word the sense of "superabundance" or "abundant excess."

Most people probably know this verse best in the Kings James translation, which uses the idea of "abundance" for both parts of the comparison: "But where sin abounded, grace did much more abound." The New American Standard and the Revised Standard Bibles do better by using "increase" for the first part and "abound" for the second: "Where sin increased, grace abounded all the more."

But how about this? The New English Bible says, "Where sin was thus multiplied, grace immeasurably exceeded it."

Or this? J. B. Phillips paraphrases the verse, saying, "Though sin is shown to be wide and deep, thank God his grace is wider and deeper still."

Even this does not seem to satisfy the commentators, however. One of them suggests, "Where sin reached a high-water mark, grace completely flooded the world."[1] Another says, "The idea is that of an overflowing, as if a mighty flood were let loose, sweeping everything before it. Indeed, we might well use the term 'engulfed'; such an abundance, such a superabundance that it drowns and engulfs everything."[2]

What Paul says of grace in this verse prepares us for what he is going to say in the continuation of the sentence. In verse 21 he is going to show that although sin has triumphed over us, grace has now triumphed over sin and reigns victoriously.

John Bunyan's Text

Romans 5:20 is the text of John Bunyan, the English Puritan preacher who is best known as the author of *The Pilgrim's Progress*. But although that book reflects his spiritual experience, Bunyan's life and religious progress is spelled out best in his classic devotional autobiography, *Grace Abounding to the Chief of Sinners*. The title is taken from our verse and 1 Timothy 1:13–16.

Bunyan was born in 1628. His parents were poor. His father was a traveling tinker, that is, a mender of pots and pans, and Bunyan practiced this trade for a time, as a result of which he was known as "the tinker of Bedford." He had little formal education, though he was an avid reader. In his youth he was quite profligate and in time became greatly troubled by an acute sense of personal sin. He wrote of himself in those days that it seemed

1. Donald Grey Barnhouse, *God's Grace: Exposition of Bible Doctrines, Taking the Epistle to the Romans as a Point of Departure*, vol. 5, Romans 5:12–21 (Grand Rapids: Wm. B. Eerdmans, 1959), p. 122.

2. D. M. Lloyd-Jones, *Romans: An Exposition of Chapter 5, Assurance* (Grand Rapids: Zondervan, 1972), p. 299.

"as if the sun that shineth in the heavens did grudge to give light, and as if the very stones in the street, and tiles upon the houses, did bend themselves against me; methought that they all combined together to banish me out of the world; I was abhorred of them, and unfit to dwell among them, or be partaker of their benefits, because I had sinned against the Savior."[3]

God saved Bunyan and gave him great peace, and the title of his autobiography is testimony to what he discovered. He had learned that, no matter how great his sin was, the grace of God proved itself to be greater.

No Withholding of Grace

I want to make two points about this superabounding grace of God, and the first is this: *Grace is not withheld because of sin.* We need to understand this clearly, because in normal life you and I do not operate this way. If we are offended by someone, we tend to withdraw from that person and restrain any natural favor we might otherwise show. If someone offends us greatly, we find it hard even to be civil. God is not like this. On the contrary, where sin increases, grace superabounds.

What happened when Adam and Eve sinned? They feared that God would withdraw his grace, as he had every right to do. Although God had been good to them, they rebelled against his command concerning the forbidden tree, and God had said, "You must not eat from the tree of the knowledge of good and evil, for when you eat of it you will surely die" (Gen. 2:17). When God came to them, calling in the garden, they hid in terror, thinking that the threatened judgment would now be fully executed. Instead, they found grace abundant.

Donald Grey Barnhouse has written:

> Adam had not gone very far from the scene of his rebellion before the grace of God sought him, called him by name, pursued him in the obscurity of the grove where he was hiding. . . . God did not withhold his grace because of Adam's sin. Instead, he made great promises of grace, announcing that the Messiah would come, the Deliverer, the Seed of the woman, the Lord Jesus Christ, who would destroy the destroyer and bring man back into fellowship with himself. Although man . . . sought to cover his shame with fig leaves, God intervened in grace and clothed the guilty pair with coats of skins, in the very garden where they had rebelled. The first blood ever shed upon this planet was shed by God Almighty to provide covering for the man and woman who believed his word about the redemption that would be provided. Grace was not withheld because of sin; grace was given in spite of sin.[4]

3. John Bunyan, *Grace Abounding to the Chief of Sinners* (Grand Rapids: Baker Book House, 1986), p. 87. (Written in 1666.)

4. Barnhouse, *God's Grace*, p. 123.

It was the same in the days of Moses, when the people had come to Mount Sinai and the law was being given. On the mountain God told Moses, "I am the LORD your God, who brought you out of Egypt, out of the land of slavery. You shall have no other gods before me" (Exod. 20:2–3). But, while God was saying that, the people he had brought out of Egypt were breaking not only this command, but also all the other commands he was giving. They were taking his name in vain, dishonoring their fathers and mothers, committing adultery, stealing, bearing false witness, coveting, and other things besides.

Was this a barrier to God's grace? Barnhouse, from whom I am quoting freely, replies, "Not at all. On the very mount whence God looked down on the awful sin of this people, he gave the specifications for the tabernacle, altar, priesthood, and the method of approach that honored his holiness and was consistent with his justice. 'Where sin abounded, grace did much more abound.' Sin rolled as high as Mount Sinai; the grace of God rolled as high as heaven."[5]

When we come to the New Testament, the same principle unfolds with ever-increasing splendor. Peter denied his Lord, even with oaths and cursings. But Jesus did not condemn Peter. Instead, Jesus appeared to him personally following the resurrection (1 Cor. 15:5) and recommissioned Peter to service (John 21:15–19):

"Simon son of John, do you truly love me more than these?" asked Jesus.

"Yes, Lord, you know that I love you," Peter answered.

"Then you must feed my lambs and take care of my sheep," Jesus countered.

The same thing was true of Paul, the apostle used by God to give us the text we are studying here. Paul's testimony is nearly identical to Bunyan's, which is why Bunyan paraphrased Paul's words to describe his own experience. Paul told the Corinthians, "For I am the least of the apostles and do not even deserve to be called an apostle, because I persecuted the church of God. But by the grace of God I am what I am, and his grace to me was not without effect. No, I worked harder than all of them—yet not I, but the grace of God that was with me" (1 Cor. 15:8–10).

Near the end of his life Paul wrote to his young co-worker Timothy:

Even though I was once a blasphemer and a persecutor and a violent man, I was shown mercy because I acted in ignorance and unbelief. The grace of our Lord was poured out on me abundantly [here he uses a combination of the two words found in Romans 5:20, the first of the two verbs plus the emphasizing prefix *hyper,* which is part of the second], along with the faith and love that are in Christ Jesus. Here is a trustworthy saying that deserves full acceptance: Christ Jesus came into the world to save sinners—of whom I am the worst. But for that very reason I was shown mercy so that in me, the

5. Ibid., p. 125.

worst of sinners, Christ Jesus might display his unlimited patience as an example for those who would believe on him and receive eternal life.

1 Timothy 1:13–16

Now we come to you. Today most people have very little awareness of their sin, which shows how desperate their condition has become. But perhaps you are one who, like John Bunyan, is very conscious of your sinfulness. You may consider yourself to have forfeited all hope of salvation by some sinful action that rises up before you like a great concrete dam against grace. I do not know what that transgression is. It may be some gross sexual sin or adultery. Or it may be a perversion.

Perhaps you have stolen from your employer or your parents or someone else who is close to you.

Have you destroyed somebody's life work or reputation?

Committed murder?

Perhaps you remember a time in your life when you were so tyrannized by sin that you lashed out against God with blasphemies. Perhaps you cursed God. Perhaps you called down damnation on yourself. When you think back on those days—and they may not be long in the past—you shudder and tremble. You are sure you have passed beyond all bounds of hope, that you are destined to be lost eternally.

If you are such a person—fortunate at least in your knowledge of your sinfulness—then this text is a great cry of hope for you: "Where sin increased, grace increased all the more." Where sin multiplied, grace overflowed! No dam erected by sin can hold back the abundant flow of God's grace. Grace is never withheld because of sin—not Adam's sin, not the sin of the people at Sinai, not Peter's sin, not Paul's sin, not John Bunyan's sin—not *your* sin. Therefore, you may come to God through Jesus Christ. Right now. Regardless of what you have done, you can repent and find full forgiveness in Jesus.

Have you done that? If not, will you do it now? Paul said that even "God's kindness leads you toward repentance" (Rom. 2:4).

No Depletion of Grace

The second point I want to make about the superabounding grace of God is that *God's grace is never reduced because of sin.* There is an unlimited supply of grace available.

Some people mistakenly suppose that there is only so much grace to go around. They envision God as looking down on mankind and seeing a great variety of sinners in need of salvation. One man is fairly good, but he is not perfect. He can only be saved by grace, of course, so God dips into his bucket of grace and splashes out just enough for this man to find Christ and salvation. Here is another person, a woman. She is not as "good" as the man. She needs more grace. Finally, here is a very terrible person. He has committed every sin in the book and is not the least bit inclined toward God or godliness. This man is also saved by grace, but it takes a lot of grace to save him. God has to scrape the very bottom of the bucket to get this vile profligate in.

All this is a gross misunderstanding. Grace is not something that is depleted as it covers our deficiencies. Furthermore, by grace God provides one hundred percent of what is necessary for the salvation of one hundred percent of the people he is saving. Grace is not doled out in proportion to our misdeeds. And God's superabundant supply never runs dry!

There is another error related to the first. Imagine a man who was once walking close to God but who fell into some great sin. I do not care what sin it was. It may have been Moses' sin, David's sin, your sin. Having fallen into sin, this man now thinks that he has forfeited something of God's grace. It is as if he had originally been given one hundred percent of God's grace but now supposes that he is slowly wasting away this treasury of grace by his major transgressions.

Do you ever find yourself thinking that? Are you thinking that now? That you were saved in the past and you were once a first-class Christian; but now, having sinned, you are condemned to be only a second-class or third-class Christian forever? Forget that idea. Your sin did not keep God's grace from flowing to you in full measure when you came to Christ. It will not keep grace from you now.

I do not mean to suggest even for a moment that God condones sin. God hates sin so much that he sent Jesus Christ to die to rescue men and women from its destructive rule and tyranny. He hates sin in you. He will continually work to remove it and give you victory over it. But the point I am making here is that God will never diminish his grace toward you because of your sin. In fact (Can I say it this way and not be misunderstood?), it is in your sin that you will most find grace to be abundant. The reason Paul was such a champion of grace was that he had been forgiven a great deal.

And do not think that you can fall from grace! I know that phrase is in the Bible. It is in Galatians 5:4, which in the New International Version is translated, "You have fallen away from grace." But let me tell you what that means. It does not mean, "You have lost your salvation." It means, "You have fallen into law as a way of living."

The Galatians had been taught the true gospel of salvation through faith in Jesus Christ, but they had been confused by Jewish legalists, who had been teaching that it was necessary for them to keep the law of Moses to be saved. Particularly, they had been insisting that Gentile believers must be circumcised. Paul's letter to the Galatian church was written to refute that heresy and encourage the Galatians to stand firm in the freedom Christ had purchased for them and not be entangled again in legal bondage. The related text says, "Mark my words! I, Paul, tell you that if you let yourselves be circumcised, Christ will be of no value to you at all. Again, I declare to every man who lets himself be circumcised that he is obligated to obey the whole law. You who are trying to be justified by law have been alienated from Christ; you have fallen away from grace" (Gal. 5:2–4).

What happens when you fall away from grace?

You do not lose your salvation. If you could, that sin of yours in falling from grace would diminish grace, and we have already seen that grace is neither withheld nor reduced because of sin. What happens is that you fall *into* law! You become a miserable legalist instead of a joyous thriving Christian.

But, even then, grace will still be working to deliver you from your bondage.

Grace to a Slave of Slaves

In the first volume of these studies, in a commentary on Romans 3:22–24, I told the story of John Newton, the "slave of slaves" who was miraculously delivered by God. I want to tell it again here, since we are dealing with the text that, of all texts in Scripture, most aptly describes Newton's experience.

Newton lived from 1725 to 1807. He was raised in a Christian home in which he was taught verses of the Bible. But his mother died when he was only six years old, and he was sent to live with a relative who hated the Bible and mocked Christianity. One day, at an early age, Newton went to sea as an apprenticed seaman. He was wild and dissolute in those years, as John Bunyan had been. He had the dubious reputation of being able to swear for two hours without repeating himself. At one point Newton was conscripted into the British Navy, but he deserted, was captured, and then beaten publicly as a punishment. Eventually he was released into the merchant marine and went to Africa. Why Africa? In his memoirs he wrote that he went there for one reason only: "that I might sin my fill."

In Africa Newton fell in with a Portuguese slavetrader in whose home he was cruelly treated. This man often went away on slaving expeditions, and when he was gone the power in the home passed to the trader's African wife, the chief woman of his harem. This woman hated all white men, and she took out her hatred on Newton. For months he was forced to grovel in the dirt, eating his food from the ground like a dog and beaten unmercifully if he touched it with his hands. In time, thin and emaciated, Newton made his way to the sea, where he was picked up by a British ship on its way up the African coast to England.

When the captain of the ship learned that the young man knew something about navigation as a result of his time in the British Navy, he made him a ship's mate. Even then Newton fell into trouble. One day, when the captain was ashore, Newton broke out the ship's supply of rum and got the crew drunk. He was so drunk himself that when the captain returned and struck him on the head, Newton fell overboard and would have drowned if one of the sailors had not hauled him back on deck just in the nick of time.

Near the end of the voyage, as they were approaching Scotland, the ship ran into bad weather and was blown off course. Water poured in, and she began to sink. The young profligate was sent down into the hold to pump water. The storm lasted for days. Newton was terrified, sure that the ship would sink and he would drown. But, there in the hold of the ship, as he pumped water desperately for life, the God of grace—whom he had tried to forget but who had never forgotten him—brought to his mind Bible verses he had learned in his home as a child. The way of salvation opened up to him. He was born again and transformed. Later, when the storm had passed and he was again in England, Newton began to study theology and eventually became a distinguished preacher, first in a little town called Olney and later in London.

Of this storm, William Cowper, the British poet who became a personal friend of Newton and lived with him for many years, wrote:

> God moves in a mysterious way,
> His wonders to perform;
> He plants his footsteps in the sea
> And rides upon the storm.

And Newton, who became a poet as well as a preacher, declared:

> Amazing grace—how sweet the sound—
> That saved a wretch like me!
> I once was lost, but now am found,
> Was blind, but now I see.

Newton was a great preacher of grace, for he had learned on a very personal level that where sin increased, grace abounded all the more. He is an outstanding example of the truth that grace is neither withheld nor reduced because of sin. He is proof of the fact that God can save anybody.

75

God's Motives for Grace

Romans 5:20-21

The law was added so that the trespass might increase. But where sin increased, grace increased all the more, so that, just as sin reigned in death, so also grace might reign through righteousness to bring eternal life through Jesus Christ our Lord.

There are many times in life when we examine another person's motives. And it is right that we should be acutely aware of them. A person can do something that turns out badly, but we may excuse the failure if his or her motivations were commendable. Or, by contrast, a person may do something good, but we will discount the apparently worthy act if, for example, it was done only to enhance the person's reputation or outdo someone else.

We have been talking about the grace of God for the past few studies, and probably at this point someone is beginning to ask about God's motives. We have seen that God operates by grace in saving men and women. If he did not, no one could be saved. But you may now want to ask whether the Bible reveals a reason for God's grace. Are there motives behind it? Why has God functioned in this manner?

Since these are valid questions, they might have occurred to anyone entirely "out of the blue," as we say. But even if they did not, they would certainly have been suggested by our text—for two reasons.

First, we have explored the contrast in verses 20 and 21 between the law of God and the grace of God. The first verse gives a motive for the entry of God's law, saying: "The law was added *so that* the trespass might increase. . . ." When we studied that verse we saw what "increasing" the trespass meant: (1) the law increased sin by increasing our knowledge of it, that is, defining it for us, which is good; (2) the law increased sin by convicting us of sin, thus showing it to be an offense against God, which is also good for us to know; and (3) the law provoked even more sin in us, thereby uncovering sin's true nature. All this opened us up to grace. But if God's motives for giving the law are suggested and if the verse contains a contrast between the law and grace (as we have seen), what about the motivation underlying grace? The very fact that the first half of the contrast involves God's motives for the giving of the law causes us to look for his motives for the operation of grace also.

Then, too, the text itself encourages us to search for God's motives. The key word here is "so" or "so that," which occurs three times in verses 20 and 21. The first time is in reference to the law: "The law was added *so that* the trespass might increase." The second and third times are in reference to grace, in the first case comparing grace to sin (or law), and in the second case linking grace to its accomplishments. The sentence says: "Grace increased all the more, *so that*, just as sin reigned in death, *so also* grace might reign through righteousness to bring eternal life through Jesus Christ our Lord."

The point is even clearer in the Greek text. For, after having stated in verse 20 that "grace superabounded," Paul writes the word *hina*, which means "in order that," thereby marking off what follows as an explanation of why God has been gracious.

In exploring this subject I have been helped by an excellent treatment of "God's Motives for Grace" by Donald Grey Barnhouse. It is a chapter in his multi-volume study of the Book of Romans. Barnhouse lists five motives for grace, and I want to follow his outline in this study.[1]

To Do Us Good

The first motive for the superabounding grace of God is stated in our text, which says that God acted in grace in order "to bring eternal life through Jesus Christ our Lord." This refers to all redeemed men and

1. Donald Grey Barnhouse, *God's Grace: Exposition of Bible Doctrines, Taking the Epistle to the Romans as a Point of Departure*, vol. 5, Romans 5:12–21 (Grand Rapids: Wm. B. Eerdmans, 1959), pp. 142–148.

women, and it is a statement that one reason why God acts in grace, an initial reason, is that he might do us good.

Here is another verse that says exactly the same thing in Jesus' own words. You know it well: John 3:16—"For God so loved the world that he gave his one and only Son, that whoever believes in him shall not perish but have eternal life." Like Romans 5:21, John 3:16 also has a purpose clause introduced by the important Greek word *hina*. But in John 3:16 the purpose for grace is expressed both negatively and positively. The negative statement is that we "shall not perish." The positive statement is that we "have eternal life." Some people have considered a motivation like this to be unworthy of God, as if the only reason for grace is that Christians might escape hell's fires. If that were *all* there were to grace, there might be some point to the objection. Nevertheless, the desire of God to do us good is not unworthy of being mentioned, even by itself. For it means that *God* is good. Remember that: *God is good!* That is wonderful, is it not? It is something we should converse about and even shout about, because if God were not good, there would be no hope for any of us.

Barnhouse comments rightly: "The sinner who comes to Christ discovers this motive for grace. He can say: God does not want me to perish; God wants me to have everlasting life. God has done something about it. . . . How wonderful to me that God did not want me to perish! For I deserve to perish. How wonderful that God wanted me to have eternal life, for I deserve death."[2]

To Enable Us to Do Good

The second motive for grace flows from the first, for if God is gracious to us because he is good, it is natural that he acts also in grace so that we, in our turn, might do good. The key text is Ephesians 2:8–10: "For it is by grace you have been saved, through faith—and this not from yourselves, it is the gift of God—not by works, so that no one can boast. For we are God's workmanship, created in Christ Jesus to do good works, which God prepared in advance for us to do."

It has been pointed out by more than one commentator that there is a striking repetition of the word *works* in verses 9 and 10. The first mention of works is negative. It tells us that because we have been saved by grace through faith, we are not saved "by works." Otherwise, it would be possible for a person who was saved "by works" to boast over another person who did not do these works and therefore was not saved. There would be boasting on earth and in heaven. But verse 9 utterly repudiates works as contributing to justification in any way. If we imagine that our good works have anything to do with our justification, we are not justified. We are still in our sins and therefore not saved.

2. Ibid., p. 143.

On the other hand, no sooner has Paul emphatically repudiated works as having anything to do with the Christian's justification than he brings works in again, saying that God has created us precisely "to do good works." This is said in such strong language—"good works, which God prepared in advance for us to do"—that we are correct in saying that if there are no good works, the person involved is not justified.

This may sound confusing to some. But the problem vanishes as soon as we realize that the "good works" Christians are called upon to do are the *result* of God's prior working in them. It is why, in verse 10, Paul prefaces his demand for good works by the statement "we are God's workmanship" and why, in his letter to the Philippians, he says in a similar vein, "Therefore, my dear friends . . . continue to work out your salvation with fear and trembling, for it is God who works in you to will and to act according to his good pleasure" (Phil. 2:12–13).

Let me say this another way. One reason why God has saved us by grace regardless of any merit on our part is that we might be enabled to be gracious to others regardless of any merit on *their* part. In other words, we are to do good to others as God has done good to us.

This is important, because it is only through such an altruistic and unselfish approach to benevolence that any uniquely original and compelling good works are done. What is wrong with so much of the "good works" of this world is that they are done for selfish reasons, for what the "do-gooders" can get out of it themselves. For example, a man will be helpful to those who can advance him up the career ladder or improve his social status, or a woman will be charitable because this will enhance her reputation. It is obvious that such "good works" do nothing to advance true goodness. What really advances goodness is when someone does good simply to do it—out of love for others—with no hidden, self-serving motive, such as getting something for oneself.

That is what God does in salvation, of course. And that is why those who have learned from God can actually be agents for good in this world.

To Make God's Wisdom Known

A third motive for God's grace is stated in another important verse in Ephesians. Paul has been speaking in Ephesians 3 of the way in which God has saved men and women from all walks of life and ethnic backgrounds and has brought them together into one new body, which is the church, thereby overcoming the formidable natural barriers that formerly existed. He then says of God, "His intent was that now, through the church, the manifold wisdom of God should be made known to the rulers and authorities in the heavenly realms" (v. 10). The "rulers and authorities in the heavenly realms" are the fallen angels. So the text means that one of the motives for grace was to reveal the wisdom of God to these beings. This raises the subject of God's motivation to the cosmic level, beyond the merely human level.

How does this principle operate?

Barnhouse writes:

> When Lucifer and the angels were created, power was given to them on various levels. Lucifer became Satan, and many of the angelic beings—the principalities and powers—followed him in his rebellion. They thought they had sufficient wisdom to govern, and to carry on the administration of creation without recourse to the authority and wisdom of God. The universe was engulfed, chaos came into the world, and sin's erosion became manifest to the uttermost part of creation. In the fullness of time, God revealed his plan of salvation. Christ would go down, down to the cross. Because of his death a great number of sinners would be called out of the world and form the true Church—the organism, not the organization. God would then exhibit these believers before the hosts of Satan as a demonstration of the true method of government and administration. Instead of seeking exaltation within themselves, all who have been redeemed recognize that there is no power within themselves. All that they accomplish is through total reliance upon the wisdom and power of God. Thus, in the very place where powerful and wise beings rebelled in their imagined self-sufficiency, God took from men, greatly inferior to angels, a company which accomplishes what the latter could never accomplish.
>
> The fallen angels sought to accomplish all by independence; we accomplish by total dependence. They followed Lucifer who said, "I will ascend . . . I will exalt my throne . . . I will be like the most High" (Isa. 14:14). We follow the Lord Jesus Christ, "who, though he was in the form of God did not count equality with God a thing to be grasped, but emptied himself, taking the form of a servant, being born in the likeness of men. And being found in human form he humbled himself and became obedient unto death, even the death on a cross" (Phil. 2:6–8).[3]

There is a wisdom here that the world will never understand. For the world says, "You've got to look out for number one" and "The devil take the hindmost." Yet, the way of the cross, not the way of self-seeking or self-advancement, is what overcomes evil and leads to true happiness.

His Body: The Fullness of Christ

The fourth motive for the superabounding grace of God in salvation is found in Ephesians 1:23, with its startling revelation of the church as "the fullness of him who fills everything in every way."

This is a difficult phrase to interpret, because it can be taken in three ways. First, it can be taken, not as a description of the church, but as a description of Christ, so that it would read: "[the church] which is the body

3. Ibid., pp. 145, 146.

of him [that is, Christ] who is the fullness of him [that is, God]] who fills all in all." This is appealing to many interpreters since the Bible elsewhere speaks of God as filling all things (Jer. 23:24) and asserts that the fullness of the Godhead does indeed dwell in Christ (Col. 1:19). On the other hand, this strength is also a weakness, since the Bible does not say anywhere that Christ is God's fullness. Besides, this interpretation just does not seem to be what the verse is talking about.

Second, it can be taken as referring to the church as that which somehow fills or completes Christ. Barnhouse holds to this view, illustrating it by the way a princess of relatively humble origins might be said to complete the glory of a great king, should he choose to marry her.[4] John Calvin held to this interpretation, too, writing that "our Lord Jesus Christ, and even God his Father, account themselves imperfect unless we are joined to him."[5] D. Martyn Lloyd-Jones holds it in a guarded fashion.[6]

Third, the phrase can be taken in a passive sense, that is, of the church as that which Christ fills. This is the view of John Stott, who considers it far more natural to say that Christ fills the church, just as he also fills the entire universe, than to say (unnaturally, Stott thinks) that the church somehow fills or completes Jesus.

I think Stott is right in holding to the third of these positions.[7] But I also realize that the difference between the third and the second is quite slight. Moreover, it is true beyond doubt that something of the splendors of Christ are to be seen only in his people, as they live for him and serve him—something of Christ that in any given historical situation would be seen in no other way. Just before his crucifixion Jesus prayed to the Father for those he was leaving behind, saying, "Glory has come to me through them" and "I have given them the glory that you gave me, that they may be one as we are one. I in them and you in me. May they be brought to complete unity to let the world know that you sent me and have loved them even as you have loved me" (John 17:10b, 22–23).

The point is that God has saved us by grace so that something of the nature of Christ, and even of the Godhead, might be seen in believers by the world outside. We might say that the chief place where the super-abounding grace of God is to be manifested is in the saints.

4. The illustration Barnhouse uses is of the late King George V and Queen Mary. Mary was only Princess Mary of Teck until she married the crown prince and thus came in time both to bask in his glory and reflect it.

5. John Calvin, *Sermons on the Epistle to the Ephesians* (Edinburgh and Carlisle, Pa.: Banner of Truth Trust, 1975), p. 122.

6. D. M. Lloyd-Jones, *God's Ultimate Purpose: An Exposition of Ephesians 1:1 to 2:23* (Grand Rapids: Baker Book House, 1979), pp. 430, 431.

7. See my own study in James Montgomery Boice, *Ephesians: An Expositional Commentary* (Grand Rapids: Zondervan, 1989), pp. 44–46.

To Exhibit God's Grace Eternally

The fifth motive for the salvational grace of God is "in order that in the coming ages he [that is, God] might show the incomparable riches of his grace, expressed in his kindness to us in Christ Jesus" (Eph. 2:7). This text brings us back to Romans, for the exhibit of grace in believers is one of the elements involved in the "reign" of grace, which Romans 5:21 speaks of. We will be looking at this more closely in the next study.

Lewis Sperry Chafer has some thoughts on this motive in his book *Grace*, where he calls it the "greatest" of God's motives. He writes:

> God's supreme motive is nothing less than his purpose to demonstrate before all intelligences—principalities and powers, celestial beings and ter-restrial beings—the exceeding riches of his grace. This God will do by means of that gracious thing which he does through Christ Jesus. All intelli-gences will know the depth of sin and the hopeless estate of the lost. They will, in turn, behold men redeemed and saved from that estate appearing in the highest glory—like Christ. This transformation will measure and dem-onstrate the "exceeding riches of his grace."
>
> The supreme purpose of God is to be realized through the salvation of men by grace alone. So fully does that supreme purpose now dominate the divine undertakings in the universe that everything in heaven and in the earth is contributing solely to the one end. To gain the realization of this supreme purpose, this age, which continues from the death of Christ to his coming again, was ushered in. These long centuries of human struggle were decreed for this one purpose. No vision which is less than this will prove suf-ficient. Men with blinded eyes do not see afar off. To such the world is mov-ing on by mere chance, or to the supposed consummation of some human glory on earth. Eyes thus blinded see naught of the glory of heaven; minds thus darkened understand nothing of the supreme purpose of God in the demonstration of the exceeding riches of his grace. But when this age is con-summated, it will be clearly seen by all beings in heaven and in the earth that these centuries of the on-moving universe have been designed for no other reason than the realization of the supreme purpose of God in the sal-vation of men by grace alone.[8]

We speak often of a Christian world-view, but nearly as often we also fail to define it. Well, here is a Christian world-view that is very well defined: namely, that history is the field upon which the manifold grace of God in the salvation of sinners is displayed.

I have sometimes compared history to a play, the title of which is "God's Grace." The angels are the audience. We are the actors. Satan is there to do everything he can think of to resist God's purposes and discredit his grace. This drama has unfolded across the centuries, and in its early acts has

8. Lewis Sperry Chafer, *Grace* (Chicago: The Bible Institute Colportage Association, 1939), pp. 29, 30.

starred such leading characters as Adam and Eve, Noah, Abraham, Moses, David, Isaiah, John the Baptist, Peter, Paul, and the other *dramatis personae* of the Old and New Testaments and church history. There have been dominant players and minor walk-ons, strong persons and weaklings, but each has been brought onto the stage to speak the words God has written and all have contributed to the movement of the drama.

You and I are now the actors in this long-running play. Satan is attacking, and the angels are all straining forward to look on. Are they seeing the "manifold wisdom" of God in you as you go through your part and speak your lines? What kind of contribution does your life make to the drama known as "God's Grace"?

At the end of Barnhouse's study, to which I have referred several times, this great champion of grace wrote:

> I have no doubt that in the ages to come—what we might call billions of years from now—there will be angels who will look at you and me with awe and wonder, and say to each other, "There are two of the saints! They were on earth in the times of the rebellion. They were dead in trespasses and sin. They were ungodly sinners, the enemies of God. But he loved them when they were like that. Think of that! How marvelous is his love! How great his condescension! How free his grace! He did all that for them!"
>
> And we will say to those angels: "You were right in giving all glory to him. He is the wonderful one. He is the gracious one. There is none like unto him." And amid all the ceaseless activities of heaven, while we are associated with him as the queen is with the king, we shall ever point to him as the source of all grace, and be, in ourselves, the exhibit of the exceeding riches of his grace.[9]

---

9. Barnhouse, *God's Grace*, p. 148.

76

The Reign of Grace

Romans 5:20–21

. . . But where sin increased, grace increased all the more, so that, just as sin reigned in death, so also grace might reign through righteousness to bring eternal life through Jesus Christ our Lord.

At the end of the last study I used the illustration of a play to show how God is exhibiting his grace in history and how you and I have been given important acting roles in that drama. I called the play "God's Grace."

The drama analogy is a good one, of course (or I would not have used it). But all such illustrations have a downhill side, and the downside of this one is that someone may think the theme is not a serious matter—just because I have called this a play. "After all," such a person might argue, "a play is just make-believe. It might be interesting, informative, even entertaining for a while. But nobody takes a play too seriously; after it is over, we all have to get back into the real world." If you found yourself thinking that way as a result of the last study, I want you to pay particular attention to this one. Because here I want to explore Paul's own illustration of what grace is about and show that the drama of "God's Grace"—Paul would call it "The Reign of Grace"—is as serious as it is real.

Rival Kingdoms

The illustration Paul uses is of two rival kingdoms, and the way he gets into his illustration is by personifying the power of sin, on the one hand, and the power of grace, on the other. He compares these powers to two monarchs, two kings, if you will. The one king is a despot. He has invaded our world and has established ruthless control over all men and women. The end of this king's rule is death, for all persons. This king's name is Sin. The other king is a gracious ruler. He has come to save us from sin and bring us into a realm of eternal happiness. The end of this king's rule is eternal life. His name is Grace.

This illustration tells us something about grace that we have not yet adequately considered. It tells us that grace is a power. We tend to think of grace as an attitude; and, of course, it is that. We even define it that way. We call grace "God's unmerited favor toward the undeserving," in fact, toward those who deserve the precise opposite. But grace is more than an attitude. It is also a power that reaches out to save those who, apart from the power of grace, would perish.

This means that grace is more than an offer of help. It is even more than help itself. To use the illustration of the two rival kingdoms, it would be possible to say that grace is an invasion by a good and legitimate king of territory that has been usurped by another. The battle is not always visible, because this is a matter of spiritual and not physical warfare. But the attack is every bit as massive and decisive as the invasion of the beaches of Normandy by the Allied Forces at the turning point of the Second World War. The Allies threw their maximum combined weight into that encounter and won the day. In a similar way, God has thrown his weight behind grace, and grace will triumph.

The Kingdom of Grace

All earthly kingdoms have a beginning, perhaps a military victory that brings a new monarch to the throne, perhaps a peaceful succession in which a new and particularly able ruler takes over a government and begins a new era of influence and prosperity, perhaps an election of an outstanding ruler in a democratic land.

What was the origin of the kingdom of grace about which Paul is writing? When was it inaugurated?

The answer, to use the classic phrase of the apostle Peter, is "before the creation of the world" (1 Peter 1:20). In that verse Peter is referring to the decision made in the eternal counsels of the Godhead in eternity past to send God's Son, the Lord Jesus Christ, to be our Redeemer. Theologians call this the Covenant of Redemption, and it took place before sin entered the world. In fact, it took place even before the world was created.

In that eternal covenant between the persons of the Godhead, God the Father said, "I want to demonstrate the nature and power of my grace before the hosts of heaven. To do that I am going to create a world of creatures to be known as men and women. I am going to allow them to fall into sin. I am going to allow sin to reign over them, enslaving them by its power and leading them at last to physical and spiritual death. But when sin has done its worst and the condition of the race seems most hopeless, I will send a heavenly being of infinite grace and power to rescue them and effect a new kingdom of love. Who will go for us? Who will accomplish the salvation of this yet-to-be-created race?"

The Lord Jesus Christ responded, "Here am I; send me. I will do what needs to be done. I will take the form of one of these creatures, thereby becoming man as well as God. I will die for them. I will die in their place, the innocent for the guilty, God for man. I will bear the punishment of their transgressions. Then, when I have paid the penalty for their sin so that they will never have to suffer for it, I will rise from the dead and be for them an ever-reigning and ever-gracious Lord."

So a covenant was enacted to establish a kingdom of grace, in which Jesus would die for a people whom God would give to him.

The Holy Spirit, who was also present at the inauguration of this kingdom, covenanted to lead those whom God had first chosen for this kingdom to faith in the crucified and risen Lord, by which alone they could enter it.

The Growth of God's Kingdom

Every earthly kingdom has a period of growth in which, the reign of the new monarch having been declared, territory is conquered and those who are to be part of the kingdom are drawn into it. There is also a parallel here to God's kingdom.

1. *The announcement of the kingdom.* God wasted no time in announcing the kingdom of grace. On the same day that Adam and Eve sinned, thus welcoming the contrary reign of sin and death into the world, God appeared in the Garden of Eden to foretell the coming of his Son. The words were spoken to Satan, who had been instrumental in our first parents' fall: "And I will put enmity between you and the woman, and between your offspring and hers; he will crush your head, and you will strike his heel" (Gen. 3:15). This was a prophecy of the incarnation of Jesus Christ and the atonement, and although Adam and Eve did not understand it fully, they understood enough of it to believe God and look for the coming of the Redeemer. As a result, they became the first citizens of the kingdom. They were saved by God's grace.

2. *The preparation for the kingdom.* The Old Testament records a long period of preparation for the new king's coming, and again the God of all

grace was doing it. God established a godly line in the midst of the world's ungodliness, a line in which his name was remembered and faith in the coming Redeemer was kept alive. Seth, the third son of Adam and Eve who replaced godly Abel after Cain had killed him, was the first of this new line. From Seth came the line of the godly antediluvians, including such persons as Enoch, who "walked with God," and Noah, who received grace at the time of the great flood. Later Abraham was chosen, and from Abraham came Isaac, Jacob, and Jacob's sons, the twelve patriarchs of Israel. There were priests like Aaron, prophets like Isaiah and Jeremiah, and godly kings like David. On the eve of the birth of Jesus, there were people like Zechariah and Elizabeth, Joseph and Mary, Simeon and Anna, and others, all of whom looked forward to Christ's coming.

"These were all commended for their faith, yet none of them received what had been promised" (Heb. 11:39). They were saved by grace. They were part of the preparation for God's kingdom. But "The true light that gives light to every man was [only then] coming into the world" (John 1:9).

3. *The atonement.* The death of the Lord Jesus Christ for sin is the very basis and center of God's kingdom. So we are not surprised to find Paul thinking of this specifically as he unfolds his illustration, saying that grace reigns "through righteousness to bring eternal life through Jesus Christ our Lord" (Rom. 5:21).

His words remind us that grace does not mean the setting aside of God's law or the waiving of justice, as if God were saying, "Well, you have been bad, but it does not matter; I forgive you." Sin does matter. Sin is a terrible thing. It leads to death, death in this life (life without righteousness is "a living hell," as we say) and death in the age to come. God does not overlook sin. He deals with sin. Christ dies for it, and God counts Christ's divine and utterly perfect righteousness as ours. This is what Paul has been writing the entire Book of Romans to explain. It is what chapter 3 is particularly about. It is the doctrine with which he now ends chapter 5.

Do you want to see the nature of the kingdom of grace? There is no place you will see it better than at Christ's cross. There, grace and righteousness come together. Each is satisfied. It is by the death of Jesus that eternal life is "poured out for many" (cf. Matt. 26:28).

4. *The citizens of the kingdom.* It takes more than territory to make a kingdom. No one has ever gotten very excited over a king who ruled nothing but a desert. A kingdom requires subjects. Therefore, God is in the business of providing subjects for this kingdom. How? Theologians speak of the *ordo salutis* or the "order of salvation." It refers to the steps God takes to bring individuals into the kingdom of his Son.

First, there is *foreknowledge.* It means that God takes saving notice of them and sets his favor on them.

Second, there is *predestination* or *election*. This means that, in the eternal counsels of his will, God has determined to save them by bringing them to Christ.

Third, there is *effectual calling*. This is the call of the gospel, which is not merely general but which actually produces a proper, believing response in those who hear it. It is like the calling of Lazarus, which brought him from death back into life.

The fourth step is *regeneration*. This is a spiritual quickening or making alive. Everything that becomes good in us, including each of the next two items, flows from it.

The fifth step is *repentance and faith*. We turn from sin and believe on Jesus because we have been made alive.

Sixth, *justification*. This is the act by which God reckons our sin to be punished in Christ and Christ's righteousness to be ours.

Seventh, *sanctification*. The new life of Christ within the believer works itself out in an increasing growth of holiness and good works.

The final step is our *glorification*, in which we are made into the image of Jesus Christ, without sin, forever.

No more glorious unfolding of the kingdom of grace toward individuals can be imagined. For it is the power of God, providing for and then actually saving those who apart from it would certainly be lost. If grace were only a handout or an offer to help, we would perish. The only reason any of us are saved is that grace first provides the way of salvation and then actually reaches out to turn us from sin, quicken us, and draw us to salvation.

A Bountiful Kingdom

Much of what I have written already speaks to the nature of the reign of grace. But it is worth looking at this in detail, since we know that some of this world's kingdoms, though beneficial, are nevertheless hard to live with. We have looked at the inauguration of God's kingdom and the unfolding of it in history. What can we say about the nature of the reign of God's grace?

1. *Grace is bountiful.* The first thing we can say is that the reign of grace is bountiful. I mean by this that it is overflowing with benefits. We can think of a kingdom as "good" though it is nevertheless a very stringent one. For example, following a war, a good kingdom might make hard demands on its people and even require them to live without what we would think of as necessities. Of course, God does demand obedience, and in the Christian life sacrifice is required. But when we think of the reign of grace, we usually do not consider it in terms of sacrifice and denial so much as fullness of life and provision. The reign of grace is not something that any of the children of grace find odious.

In preparing for this sermon I read through dozens of studies of this text (there are many such studies, since commentators seem naturally to have been attracted to it), and I found many memorable statements. But among them is one from D. Martyn Lloyd-Jones that I think is so on-target that I want to repeat it more than once. I even suggest you memorize it. It is this: *"Grace always gives, whereas sin always takes away."*[1] Let me say that again: *"Grace always gives, whereas sin always takes away."*

Sin—the despotic king—says the opposite. He tells us that he will give us all we have ever wanted, and that grace is the way of deprivation. Sin says, "Look at those Christians; they never have any fun!" Or, "Look at all the things they can't do." So, like the Prodigal, we listen to the bad king, take our inheritance and journey into a far country where we do not have to listen to the good king's voice or respond to the Father's wise will. What do we do there? You know the answer. We spend our assets on wild living. Because we waste our inheritance, when we come to the end of our days it is all gone. Sin has taken it all, and we find, as the Prodigal did, that no one will give us anything. In the end, when we look to the tyrant named Sin, whom we have followed, and ask for his help, Sin laughs at us as he reaches out to snatch away even life itself.

Follow sin, and sin will rob you of your innocence and character.

Follow sin, and sin will wither away your health.

Follow sin, and sin will turn to ashes even the common, precious things of life—things like friendship, love, laughter, the innocence of children, hope, and contentment.

Follow sin, and sin will usher you to damnation and smirk as you stagger through the door.

How different is the king whose name is Grace! Grace sees us staggering and comes alongside to help us and bear us up. Grace sees us destitute and pours the inexhaustible riches of Christ and the Father into our laps. Grace sees us dying and imparts eternal life. The Bible says through Paul that "the wages of sin is death, but the gift of God is eternal life in Christ Jesus our Lord" (Rom. 6:23).

Grace says, "What do you need? Tell me. Tell me anything at all." And then grace provides that need in accord with God's perfect wisdom, invincible power, and unlimited supply. It is because of grace that the author of Hebrews urges: "Let us then approach the throne of grace with confidence, so that we may receive mercy and find grace to help us in our time of need" (Heb. 4:16).

2. *Grace is invincible.* In this life it is not always true that the good triumph and the evil are defeated. Looking at this life, we might ask, "Can anything as good as grace really triumph in the end? To be sure, grace offers everything. But how can we know that in the end sin will not somehow still be there to assert its rule and snatch God's bountiful gifts from our hands?"

---

1. D. M. Lloyd-Jones, *Romans: An Exposition of Chapter 5, Assurance* (Grand Rapids: Zondervan, 1972), p. 356.

Ah, but that would be possible only if we were speaking of grace in human terms. If it were only my grace or your grace that we are talking about, sin would snatch our good gifts away. We could not stand against this powerful adversary. But it is not my grace or your grace that is reigning. It is the grace of God, and God is the Almighty One. Who or what can stand against God or his purposes? Paul writes in Romans 8:31–39:

> . . . If God is for us, who can be against us? He who did not spare his own Son, but gave him up for us all—how will he not also, along with him, graciously give us all things? Who will bring any charge against those whom God has chosen? It is God who justifies. Who is he that condemns? Christ Jesus, who died—more than that, who was raised to life—is at the right hand of God and is also interceding for us. Who shall separate us from the love of Christ? Shall trouble or hardship or persecution or famine or nakedness or danger or sword? As it is written:
>
> > "For your sake we face death all day long;
> > we are considered as sheep to be slaughtered."
>
> No, in all these things we are more than conquerors through him who loves us. For I am convinced that neither death nor life, neither angels nor demons, neither the present nor the future, nor any powers, neither height nor depth, nor anything else in all creation, will be able to separate us from the love of God that is in Christ Jesus our Lord.

This brings us back to the first study in this volume, where I pointed out that all of Romans 5 (indeed, all of chapters 5–8) is designed to assure us of salvation. We can be assured of salvation because, through Christ, we have gained permanent access by faith "into this grace in which we now stand" (Rom. 5:2).

Here are two hymns for us to think of as we end these six studies of God's grace. The first is by Augustus M. Toplady, who is also the author of the well-known hymn "Rock of Ages." The hymn I cite here is "A Debtor to Mercy Alone," and I refer to it because of the word *indelible*, which occurs in the third and final verse. It goes:

> My name from the palms of his hands
> Eternity will not erase;
> Impressed on his heart it remains,
> In marks of indelible grace.
> Yes, I to the end shall endure,
> As sure as the earnest is given;
> More happy, but not more secure,
> The glorified spirits in heaven.

Nothing can erase that which is indelible. So, if grace is written out in indelible characters, it is forever and ever. For the reign of grace there is no defeat, and there can be no end.

The other hymn is by Charles Wesley, and I would imagine every English-speaking Christian in the world has heard and probably also sung it:

> O for a thousand tongues to sing
> My great Redeemer's praise,
> The glories of my God and King,
> The triumphs of his grace!

There are no triumphs anywhere like those triumphs. There are none so happy or so certain. Let grace triumph in you. Yield to it. Yield to the grace of God in Christ. Open your arms to grace, and let grace draw you to the winning side.

77

Where Do We Go from Here?

Romans 6:1–2

What shall we say, then? Shall we go on sinning so that grace may increase? By no means! We died to sin; how can we live in it any longer?

The week before I was to start preaching in Philadelphia on Romans 6, I was at a Bible college for some meetings and mentioned my upcoming series to one of the school's professors. His reply was instantaneous: "Ah, that is a good Baptist chapter for a Presbyterian." The comment took me entirely off guard, because the chapter has nothing whatever to do with baptism, as I understand it. In fact, the only reason I can think of that this professor might have said what he did is that Paul uses the illustration of baptism in verses 3 and 4 to reinforce his earlier point about our being united to Jesus Christ by God's grace.

Actually, the sixth chapter of Romans is a parenthesis dealing with the first and most logical objection that anyone might bring against the gospel, namely, that it leads to Antinomianism or sinful conduct.

Two Parentheses

But let me back up a moment. I have called Romans 6 a parenthesis, following the approach to Romans 5–8 by the English preacher D. Martyn

Lloyd-Jones. But that arrangement is not universally accepted,[1] and I need to explain this position.

You will recall that when we began chapter 5, I pointed out that I was departing from the most common outline of Romans, according to which these chapters (and especially chapter 6) deal with sanctification. In the traditional division of Romans, chapters 1–4 deal with justification, chapters 5–8 with sanctification, chapters 9–11 with the problem of Israel, and chapters 12–16 with practical matters. There is some truth to this arrangement, of course. The first chapters obviously do present the great doctrine of justification. The next section does touch on sanctification, the next mentions the Jews, and so on. But, as I pointed out in the first study in this volume, to approach Romans as if it were arranged in four segregated compartments is to misunderstand it completely. And, of course, an error in the overall analysis will lead to errors in handling the parts, which is particularly the case here.

What did we see when we began Romans 5? Some people have approached the chapter as if it is listing the *results* of justification, a sort of wrap-up of the previous chapters, after which the author supposedly launches into his second important theme, which is sanctification. But we saw that this is not the case at all.

What Paul is concerned to show in chapter 5 is that our justification is permanent. In other words, his concern is not with the results of justification, though some of these results are mentioned, but with the *assurance* of it. That is why he writes at the start of the chapter that "we rejoice in the hope of the glory of God" (v. 2). Those words are a reference to the Christian's glorification, the ultimate and inevitable outcome of God's work in him or her. It is also why, a few verses further on, we find Paul saying, "Since we have now been justified by his blood, how much more shall we be saved from God's wrath through him!" (v. 9). These words anticipate the triumphant note on which the eighth chapter ends: ". . . If God is for us, who can be against us? He who did not spare his own Son, but gave him up for us all—how will he not also, along with him, graciously give us all things?" (Rom. 8:31–32).

In Romans 5, as well as in Romans 8, the apostle passes directly from justification to glorification, not because he is unaware that sanctification fits into the middle of that sequence, but because he wants to stress the permanent nature of our justification: "And those he predestined, he also called; those he called, he also justified; those he justified, he also glorified" (Rom. 8:30).

Since I have not explicitly made this point before, let me also point out that this is the direction the second half of Romans 5 has been heading. Verses 12–21 deal with the Christian's union with Jesus Christ, showing that

1. See footnote 1 in Leon Morris, *The Epistle to the Romans* (Grand Rapids: Wm. B. Eerdmans, and Leicester, England: Inter-Varsity Press, 1988), p. 243.

just as we were united to Adam, so that his fall became our fall and we were condemned in him, so also have Christians now become united to Jesus Christ, so that his death for sin became our death to it and his triumph ours. This, too, is permanent. So when Paul gets to the end of the chapter and speaks of the "reign" of grace "through righteousness to bring eternal life through Jesus Christ our Lord," his point is that nothing is going to defeat God's great plan for us. In terms of the overflow of thought, what follows immediately after chapter 5 is chapter 8.

But if that is so, if these middle chapters of Romans are dealing chiefly with assurance, why are chapters 6 and 7 here at all? Or to put it another way, since I have called chapter 6 a parenthesis, why does Paul interrupt the flow of the letter at this point?

The answer lies in what he said in chapter 5. In verse 20 he said that the law of God was given "so that the trespass might increase." Then, in verse 21, he spoke of the triumph of God's grace in us. Anyone who has been thinking carefully about these things will see immediately that this introduces two problems. First, if grace is destined to triumph in us, as Paul says it is, doesn't this inevitably lead to loose living? In fact, doesn't this even suggest that we should sin more so that grace might have even more space in which to be triumphant? That can't be right. But since it seems to follow from Paul's teaching, doesn't it discredit Paul's doctrine? The second problem concerns the law. In verses 12–21 Paul passed quickly from Adam to Jesus Christ. But everyone knows that between those two great historical events the law was given to Israel. The law must have had a purpose, or God would not have given it. But how can that be fit into Paul's teaching? If you retain the law, you destroy the gospel of salvation by the grace of God through Jesus Christ. But if, on the other hand, you retain the gospel, the law is superfluous.

These are valid questions. Rather than ignore them and pass on directly to what he says in chapter 8, the apostle stops at this point and answers them. He deals with the problem of Antinomianism in chapter 6 and with the problem of the law in chapter 7.

A Rational Objection

As we begin Romans 6, we see at once that we are not entering upon a radically new section, as if here for the first time Paul begins to address the problem of the Christian's sanctification. This is because the chapter begins with a question that immediately turns us back to chapter 5. "What shall we say, then?" Paul asks.

"Say about what?" we reply.

Obviously, about what he has just said in Romans 5: ". . . where sin increased, grace increased all the more, so that, just as sin reigned in death, so also grace might reign through righteousness to bring eternal life through Jesus Christ our Lord" (vv. 20–21). In other words, where does the doctrine of the triumph of God's grace lead us? There are two possibilities. On the one hand, it could lead to sinful conduct, the antinomian objection. If sin is going to be conquered by grace, let us keep sinning. Sin doesn't matter. On the other hand, the triumph of grace could lead to righteousness, the position that Paul will actually uphold.

In one way or another, the entire sixth chapter is going to be an answer to this question. But before we launch into it, we need to take time to feel the full force of the objector's argument. I want you to see three things about it.

1. *It is logical.* I mean by this that it is a reasonable question to ask after one has understood the true gospel. The gospel is one of salvation by grace apart from human works. If that is so, if works are not the basis of our salvation, why do we have to worry about works at all? Shouldn't we just go on sinning?

The presence of this question is in one sense a test of whether or not one's gospel really is Pauline. Most religious teaching is not. Most religions tell you that in order to get to heaven what you must do is stop sinning and do good works, that you will be saved if you do this well enough and long enough. If a person is preaching along those lines, it is inconceivable that anyone would ever ask him, "Shall we go on sinning so that grace may increase?" Such a teacher is not talking about grace but about works, and his whole point is that salvation comes by doing lots of them. To "go on sinning" is the exact opposite of his doctrine. Nobody ever raises that question to one who is teaching works-righteousness.

But if one teaches, as Paul did, that a person is saved by grace apart from works, the objection we are looking at is the first thing that comes to mind. It is the argument religious people raised with Martin Luther. It was the question repeatedly thrown up to George Whitefield. Ray Stedman suggests, "There is something about the grace of God and the glory of the good news that immediately raises this issue."[2]

2. *It is natural.* Stedman also talks about this point, saying that "sin is fun" and that "we like to do it."[3] That may be too strong when we are talking about Christians, since a reaction against sin as well as an attraction to it will be present. But the point is well taken, at least in the sense that our "flesh"—or "sinful nature," to use Paul's own term (cf. Rom. 7:5, 18, 25)—inclines to sin naturally. To put this another way: As far as our old nature is concerned, righteousness calls us to an unnatural path, the path of self-denial and cross bearing (cf. Luke 9:23).

2. Ray C. Stedman, *From Guilt to Glory*, vol. 1, *Hope for the Helpless* (Portland: The Multnomah Press, 1978), p. 171.
   3. Ibid.

3. *It is pious.* When I say that the objection that Paul's gospel leads to sin is "pious," I mean that it only occurs within a religious setting and among those who are at least somewhat concerned with being righteous. That is why it was it was such a major problem among the Jews.

In 1 Corinthians 1:23, Paul wrote of the gospel being "a stumbling block to Jews and foolishness to Gentiles." It was foolish to Gentiles, because it ran counter to their philosophy. They could not see how God could become man, since in their mind "spirit" was good while "flesh" was evil and, for God to become man, the "good" (God) would have to take on "sin" or in some way become "evil." Again, the Gentiles could not see how Jesus could be a Savior of others when, on the cross, he could not even save himself. These were their problems with the gospel. With the Jews it was different. The Jews had the law, and their religion was chiefly concerned with right conduct. Therefore, when Paul came along teaching that salvation could not be achieved by moral living but had to be a gift of God apart from good works, the Jews naturally saw this as an attack on practical righteousness and objected to it. It was their very religiosity that acted as a "stumbling block."

If you do not see or care about the problem Paul raises at the start of Romans 6, you are obviously missing something. Either: (1) you have not yet understood the gospel; (2) you are blind to your own sinful inclinations; or (3) you are not really concerned about religion. On the other hand, if any of these things are true of you, you will not only see the problem but will be troubled by it.

An Unthinkable Position

And yet, you should not be troubled long. This is because, as soon as we begin to explore this problem, as Paul does in Romans 6, we see that the inference that Christians should "go on sinning" is unthinkable.

Paul's response, after he has asked the question, "Shall we go on sinning so that grace may increase?" is, "By no means!" (v. 2). This expression has already occurred in a similar exchange in chapter 3, and it is a powerful one. The Greek words (*mē genoito*) literally mean "let it not be," and they have the force of a powerful negation. They actually mean, "It is inconceivable for it to be thus" or "It is unthinkable,"—"It should not even be considered." Some translators render the expression, "God forbid!"

Why is it unthinkable? "In fact," someone might ask, "isn't it even contradictory to suggest this? You have just said that the question posed in verse 1 is logical. You have admitted that it is both natural and pious. How then can you say that it should not even be considered?"

The answer, of course, is that although the objection is logical, natural, and pious on the superficial level to one who is newly hearing the gospel of salvation through faith by the grace of God, it is seen to be completely untenable as soon as one probes further. In fact, one does not even have to probe deeply. The answer, given quite simply, as Paul does in the assertion that immediately follows his vehement repudiation, is "We died to sin; how can we live in it any longer?" There have been so many misunderstandings of what Paul meant by the statement "we died to sin" that I want to devote our entire next study to explaining it. But even without a full investigation of this phrase we can already see the folly of the "let us go on sinning" position.

Why is this objection absurd? There are several reasons.

First, it overlooks God's *purpose* in the plan of salvation, which Paul has been unfolding. What is this purpose? Clearly, it is to save us from sin. What does that mean? Does it mean to save us only from the punishment due us because of our sin? It does mean that, but not only that. Yes, we are justified by God in order that we might be saved from wrath at the final judgment, but that is only one part of God's plan. Well, then, does salvation mean that God is saving us from sin's guilt? Yes, that too. But again, not only that. Sin brings guilt, so one of the blessings of salvation is to be delivered from guilt, knowing that sin has not merely been overlooked or forgiven but has also been punished in Jesus Christ. Still, deliverance from the guilt of sin is also only a part of what is involved. How about deliverance from sin's presence? Of course! But again, that only happens at the end, when we are glorified.

Each of these matters is important. But the one thing that has not been mentioned thus far is salvation from the practice of sin *now,* and that is clearly also part of God's purpose. No one part of our deliverance from sin can rightly be separated from any other. So, if we go on practicing sin now, we are contradicting the very purpose of God in our salvation.

Second, the antinomian objection is absurd because it overlooks God's *means* of saving sinners. Our discussion of the early chapters of Romans was concerned with justification, the act by which God declares a person to be in a right standing before his justice due to the death of Jesus Christ. This is basically a declaration. But at the same time we saw that this is not all that is involved. God justifies, but Christ also redeems. God forgives, but the Holy Spirit also makes us spiritually alive so that we can perceive and by faith embrace that forgiveness.

Indeed, what has Paul been talking about in Romans 5? He has been talking about the believer's union with Jesus Christ, hasn't he? And what is that union like? It is not a mechanical bonding, or legal only. It is as vital as the union between a vine and its branches or between a head and the other parts of a person's body. Therefore, if we are saved, we are "in Christ." And if we are "in Christ," he is in us and his life within us will inevitably turn us from sin to righteousness.

One commentator says, "Union with Christ, being the only source of holiness, cannot be the source of sin."[4] Therefore, if we find it possible to "go on sinning so that grace may increase," we only prove by our actions

4. Charles Hodge, *A Commentary on Romans* (Edinburgh and Carlisle, Pa.: The Banner of Truth Trust, 1972), p. 191. (Original edition 1935.)

that we are not really saved. It is as simple and as strong as that! "We died to sin," Paul says—"How can we live in it any longer?"

Third, it is absurd to think that we can "go on sinning so that grace may increase," because, if we think that way, we have never understood God's *grace*. In the previous six studies, I said that grace is neither diminished nor withdrawn because of sin. That is, God does not cease to be gracious to us because we fall into sin. But just because grace is not diminished by sin does not mean that it is ever defeated by it. In fact, the contrary is true. As Paul said, ". . . grace increased all the more, so that . . . grace might reign through righteousness to bring eternal life through Jesus Christ our Lord" (Rom. 5:20–21).

"What is the business of grace?" asks D. Martyn Lloyd-Jones. "Is it to allow us to continue in sin? No! It is to deliver us from the bondage and the reign of sin, and to put us under the reign of grace."[5] A reigning monarch is a triumphant monarch. If grace is reigning in us, grace is advancing its conquest over sin. Christians sin. But they are not defeated by sin, and they do not continue in it.

Do you understand the absurdity of the objector's question now?

"Shall we go on sinning so that grace may increase?" If you understand the nature of grace, you will understand that for grace to increase, sin must decrease, not increase. The goal of grace is to destroy and vanquish sin. Therefore, if a person goes on sinning, as the objection suggests, it shows that he or she actually has no part in grace and is not saved.

Two Warnings

I close with two warnings, the first being obvious from what I have said, and the second being a deduction from it.

The first is directed particularly to the many people in religious circles who have much head knowledge about doctrine and who suppose, just because they know such things and give mental assent to them, that all is therefore well with their souls, that they are saved. That is not necessarily the case. If you are such a person, I need to warn you that it is not enough for you only to believe these things. Salvation is not mere knowledge. It is a new life. It is union with Christ. Therefore, unless you are turning from sin and going on in righteousness, as you follow after Jesus Christ, you are not saved. It is presumptuous to believe you are. So examine your life. Make sure you are saved. The Bible warns you to "make your calling and election sure" (2 Peter 1:10). The very doctrines of justification, grace, and sanctification urge this upon you.

The other warning is to all Christians, and it is in the words of an old Puritan preacher who asked in relation to our passage from Romans: "Is

5. D. M. Lloyd-Jones, *Romans: An Exposition of Chapter 6, The New Man* (Grand Rapids: Zondervan, 1973), pp. 10, 11.

there anyone here who, by his conduct, gives occasion for this objection?" You may not believe—I hope you do not believe—that you can be saved and go on sinning. But is your life so careless that a unsaved person looking on might reasonably conclude that this is precisely where the doctrine of justification by grace leads Christians?

If that is the case, correct that impression at once. Remember our Lord's words: "Things that cause people to sin are bound to come, but woe to that person through whom they come. It would be better for him to be thrown into the sea with a millstone tied around his neck . . ." (Luke 17:1).

The writer to whom I was referring says, "It is a lamentable fact that one man who dishonors the gospel by an unholy walk does more injury to the souls of men than ten holy ones can do them good."[6] I urge you to be part of the solution, part of the ten, rather than part of the problem. Let your life be marked by righteousness, not marred by sin—for your own soul's good as well as for the good of other people.

6. Quoted without giving the name of the writer by Donald Grey Barnhouse, *God's Freedom: Exposition of Bible Doctrines, Taking the Epistle to the Romans as a Point of Departure*, vol. 6, Romans 6:1—7:25 (Grand Rapids: Wm. B. Eerdmans, 1961), p. 13.

78

Death to Sin

Romans 6:2

We died to sin; how can we live in it any longer?

From time to time in our Bible study we come across a verse that we immediately perceive to be of fundamental importance. Sometimes this is a personal matter; the verse speaks to us in a way we know it would not equally speak to others. If you have been a Christian for any length of time and have been faithful in Bible study, you probably have many verses like that and can even tie them to specific times of trial, growth, or blessing in your life. There are other verses that are important in a broader sense. They stand out as classic statements of basic Bible doctrines. The verse we come to now is in this second category.

John Murray calls Romans 6:2 the "fundamental premise" of the apostle's thought in this chapter.[1] That is quite literally true. In verse 1 Paul has raised an objection to his doctrine, asking the question that must have been asked him many times in the course of his ministry: "Shall we go on sinning so that grace may increase?" His answer is emphatic: "By no means!" His

1. John Murray, *The Epistle to the Romans* (Grand Rapids: Wm. B. Eerdmans, 1968), p. 213.

explanation is straightforward: "We died to sin; how can we live in it any longer?" (v. 2). That is the whole of his position. So there is a sense in which everything that follows in Romans 6 is an elaboration of that point. For one thing, he repeats the idea of our having died to sin in every verse up to and including verse 8. Verse 3—"All of us who were baptized into Christ Jesus were baptized into his death." Verse 4—"We were therefore buried with him through baptism into death." Verse 5—"We have been united with him like this in his death." Verse 6—"Our old self was crucified with him." Verse 7—"Anyone who has died has been freed from sin." Verse 8—"We died with Christ."

By the end of verse 10 Paul has explained his doctrine. Next he applies it, urging his readers: "In the same way, count yourselves dead to sin but alive to God in Christ Jesus" (v. 11). The application continues through verse 14. Then, in verse 15, Paul begins to do the same thing all over again but by using a different image, the image of slavery.

An analysis of the chapter shows that the idea of our death to sin is fundamental throughout. So our understanding of the statement "we died to sin" in verse 2 is critical to our understanding of the whole.

But the statement is even more important than that. For this is the first section of Romans in which Paul begins to talk about the Christian life specifically, that is, about living a life of holiness that is pleasing to God. If Romans 6:2 is the key to understanding this section, it is therefore also obviously the key to understanding the doctrine of sanctification. To understand this statement is to understand how to live a holy life. And *because* it is the key to sanctification, I would go so far as to say that Romans 6:2 is the most important verse in the Bible for believers in evangelical churches to understand today.

"We Died to Sin"

Yet this is not an easy verse to understand. I want to handle it by first analyzing a number of wrong or inadequate explanations of what the key words, "we died to sin," mean and then giving what I believe is the proper understanding. Before doing that, it will be helpful to note exactly what the verse says.

There are two things to keep in mind. First, there is an emphatic use of the word *we*. As you may know, in the Greek language the pronoun subjects of verbs are included in the verbal endings. So it is not necessary to have a separate pronoun. However, when an author wants to emphasize the subject the pronoun can be explicitly added to the sentence, which is the case here. The thrust of the statement is to contrast the "we" who are now in Christ with (1) others who are not in Christ but who are still in Adam, and (2) even ourselves as we were before God saved us. This is an important key to the right interpretation. As D. Martyn Lloyd-Jones says, "The whole emphasis is on our uniqueness, our special position, we 'being what we are.' That is what makes the question of verse 1 unthinkable."[2]

The second thing we need to keep in mind as we think through the various interpretations of this verse is the tense of the verb *died*. It is an aorist tense, which means that it refers to a single action that has taken place in and been completed in the past. We are going to see how important this is as we go along, since a number of people read the verse as if "died" were in a different tense entirely. Some treat it as if it were a present tense: "we are dying to sin." Some as a past imperfect tense: "we have died and are continuing to die to sin." Some as a future tense: "we shall die to sin." But "died" is none of these things in this verse. It is an aorist and refers to a finished past action.

Five Misinterpretations

Since this verse is so critical to our understanding of why and how we are to live a holy life, we must proceed very deliberately. To do that we must begin by eliminating some of the misinterpretations. I want to discuss five of them.

1. *The Christian is no longer responsive to sin.* This is a very popular view, though a harmful one. It is an argument from analogy, and it usually goes like this: What is it that most characterizes a dead body? It is that its senses cease to operate. It can no longer respond to stimuli. If you are walking along the street and see a dog lying by the curb and you are uncertain whether or not it is alive, all you have to do to find out is nudge it with your foot. If it immediately jumps up and runs away, it is alive. If it only lies there, it is dead. In the same way (so this argument goes), the one who has died to sin is unresponsive to it. Sin does not touch such a person. When temptation comes, the true believer neither feels nor responds to the temptation.

J. B. Phillips, the translator of one of the most popular New Testament paraphrases, seems to have held this view. I say this because his rendering of verse 7 reads, "a dead man can safely be said to be immune to the power of sin" and of verse 11, that we are to look upon ourselves as "dead to the appeal and power of sin."[3]

What should we say about this? The one thing in its favor is that it takes the tense of the Greek verb translated "died" at face value. It says that Christians have literally died to sin's appeal. But the problem with this inter-

2. D. M. Lloyd-Jones, *Romans: An Exposition of Chapter 6, The New Man* (Grand Rapids: Zondervan, 1973), p. 14.

3. John R. W. Stott cites two other contemporary expressions of it. C. J. Vaughan wrote, "A dead man cannot sin. And you are dead. . . . Be in relation to all sin as impassive, as insensible, as immoveable as is He who has already died." Similarly, H. P. Liddon comments, "This [death] has presumably made the Christian as insensible to sin as a dead man is to the objects of the world of sense." See *Men Made New: An Exposition of Romans 5–8* (Grand Rapids: Baker Book House, 1984), pp. 38, 39.

pretation is that it is patently untrue. There is no one like this, and anyone who is persuaded by this interpretation to think he or she is like this is due to be severely disillusioned. Moreover, it makes nonsense of Paul's appeal to Christians in verses 11–13, where he says to "count yourselves dead to sin but alive to God in Christ Jesus. Therefore, do not let sin reign in your mortal body. . . . Do not offer the parts of your body to sin, as instruments of wickedness. . . ." You do not urge one who is as unresponsive to sin as a corpse is to physical stimuli not to be responsive to it.

We can dismiss this interpretation, even though (unfortunately) it is held by many people.

2. *The Christian should die to sin.* This view has been common in a certain type of holiness meeting, where Christians are urged to die to sin. They are to "crucify the old man," which, they are told, is the secret to a "victorious" Christian life. The best thing that can be said for this view is that it is obviously correct to urge Christians not to sin. Indeed, that is what Paul himself will do later: "Do not let sin reign in your mortal body" (v. 12) and "Do not offer the parts of your body to sin" (v. 13). But aside from that, everything else about this view is in error. The starting point is wrong; it begins with man rather than with God. The image is wrong: one thing nobody can do is crucify himself. Above all, the tense of the verb is wrong; for Paul is not saying that we ought to crucify ourselves (or die) but rather that we *have* died. He is telling us something that is already true of us if we are Christians.

3. *The Christian is dying to sin day by day.* All this view means to say is that the one who is united to Christ will grow in holiness, and this is true. But it is not by increasingly dying to sin. It would be true to say that we will have to be as much on guard against sin's temptations at the very end of our lives as we need to be now, though we will do so more consistently and effectively then. To look at the verse that way, though it touches on something true, nevertheless gets us away from the proper and only effective way of dealing with sin. And what is equally important, the tense of the Greek verb for "died" is again wrong. This interpretation takes "died" as if it is an imperfect tense ("are dying"), rather than as an aorist ("have died"), which is what Paul actually says.

This is an important point, one that we are going to see again as we move through the chapter. I put it in this way: The secret of sanctification is not our present experience or emotions, however meaningful or intense they may be, but rather something that has already happened to us.

4. *The Christian cannot continue in sin, because he has renounced it.* This view carries no less weighty a name in its favor than that of Charles Hodge, and it is to be respected for that reason, if for no other. To begin with, the great former professor at Princeton Theological Seminary notes the full aorist tense of the verb *died,* saying rightly that "it refers to a specific act in our past history."

But what was that act? Hodge answers that it was "our accepting of Christ as our Savior." That act involved our firm renunciation of sin, since "no man can apply to Christ to be delivered from sin, in order that he may live in it." It is "a contradiction . . . to say that gratuitous justification is a license to sin, as much as to say that death is life, or that dying to a thing is living in it."[4] This is a good interpretation for two reasons: (1) it recognizes the full force of the aorist verb *died,* and (2) what it argues is true. Coming to Christ as Savior really does include a renunciation of sin, and to renounce sin and at the same time continue in it is a real contradiction. If we had no other possible interpretations to go on, this would be an attractive explanation.

But I cannot help but feel that D. Martyn Lloyd-Jones is correct when he rejects this as being other than Paul's meaning. Why? Because in Hodge's interpretation "dying to sin" is something we do. It is our act, the act of accepting Christ. However, in Paul's development of the idea, "dying to sin" is not something we do or have done but is something that has been done to us. It is the same as our being joined to Jesus Christ, which Paul is going to talk about in a moment under the figure of baptism. We did not join ourselves to Christ. Rather, we were in Adam, and then God by his grace took us from that position and transferred us into the kingdom of his Son.

It is because of what has happened to us that we are now no longer to continue in sin. It is because of God's work that our continuing in sin is unthinkable.

5. *The Christian has died to sin's guilt.* This last and, in my view, inadequate understanding of the phrase "we died to sin" is by Robert Haldane. He sees it as having nothing whatever to do with sanctification but rather as another way of talking about justification or one result of it. Haldane says, "It exclusively indicates the justification of believers and their freedom from the *guilt* of sin."[5] The problem with that statement is the word *exclusively.* I put it that way because what Haldane says is undoubtedly true as far as it goes. The justification of the believer has certainly freed him or her from the guilt of sin, and it is true that in this sense the person has indeed died to it. As far as the guilt of sin and its resulting condemnation are concerned, sin no longer touches the Christian. He has nothing to do with it.

But that does not go far enough. True, we have died to sin's guilt. But what Paul is dealing with in this chapter is why we can no longer live in sin. If all he is saying is that we are free from sin's condemnation, the question of verse 1 is unanswered: "Shall we go on sinning so that grace may increase?" At the end of chapter 5 the apostle spoke of the inevitable reign of grace; now (in chapter 6) we must be told why this is so.

4. Charles Hodge, *A Commentary on Romans* (Edinburgh and Carlisle, Pa.: The Banner of Truth Trust, 1972), p. 192. (Original edition 1935.)

5. Robert Haldane, *An Exposition of the Epistle to the Romans* (MacDill AFB: MacDonald Publishing, 1958), p. 239.

Our Old Life and Our New Life

It is obvious, having rejected five important interpretations of the phrase "we died to sin," including no less weighty interpretations than those of Charles Hodge and Robert Haldane, that I must have a better view in mind—presumptuous as that may seem. But I think that is exactly what I do have, though I have certainly not invented this new view. It is expressed in various forms by such scholars as F. Godet, John Murray, and D. Martyn Lloyd-Jones.[6] I have found the most helpful expression of it John R. W. Stott's *Men Made New: An Exposition of Romans 5–8*.

Stott begins by noting that there are three verses in Romans 6 in which Paul uses the phrase "died [or dead] to sin." It appears in verse 2, which we are studying, and it occurs again in verses 10 and 11. In two of those instances, the first and the last, the reference is to ourselves as Christian men and women. In the second of those verses the reference is to Christ. It is a sound principle of interpretation that whenever the same phrase occurs more than once in one context it should be taken in the same way unless there are powerful reasons to the contrary. If that is so, the first question we have to ask in order to understand how we have died to sin is how Christ died to it. How did Jesus Christ die to sin?

The first answer we are inclined to give is that he died to sin by suffering its penalty. He was punished for our sin in our place. If we carry that analogy through, we will come out near the position of Robert Haldane. We will be thinking of justification only and of our death to sin's guilt.

But I want you to notice two things. First, the reference to Jesus's death in verse 10 does not say that he died *for* sin, though he did, but that he died *to* sin—the exact thing that is said of us. That is a different idea, or at least it seems to be.

Second, Paul's statement does not say only that Christ "died to sin" but adds the very important words "once for all." The full verse reads, "The death he died, he died to sin once for all; but the life he lives, he lives to God." This means that as far as sin is concerned, Jesus' relationship to it is finished forever. While he lived upon earth he had a relationship to it. He had come to die for sin, to put an end to its claims upon us. But now, having died, that phase of his life is past and will never be repeated. Moreover, verse 9, which leads into verse 10, says exactly that: "For we know that since

6. Godet speaks of it as "an absolute breaking" with the past. He calls it "gradual in its realization, but absolute and conclusive in its principle" (F. Godet, *Commentary on St. Paul's Epistle to the Romans*, trans. A. Cusin [Edinburgh: T. & T. Clark, n.d.], vol. 1, p. 404). John Murray says, "What the apostle has in view is the once-for-all definitive breach with sin which constitutes the identity of the believer. A believer cannot therefore live in sin; if a man lives in sin he is not a believer" (Murray, *The Epistle to the Romans*, p. 213). D. Martyn Lloyd-Jones focuses on the reigns of sin and grace, arguing that "our Lord's death and resurrection have brought the reign of sin to an end in the case of all believers" (Lloyd-Jones, *Romans: An Exposition of Chapter 6, The New Man*, p. 20).

Christ was raised from the dead, he cannot die again; death no longer has mastery over him."

We must now apply that understanding of "death to sin" to the other two instances, which refer to us. How? By realizing that, as a result of our union with Christ in his death and resurrection, that old life of sin in Adam is past for us also. We can never go back to it. We have been brought from that old life, the end of which was death, into a new life, the end of which is righteousness. Therefore, since this is true of us, we must embrace the fact that it is true and live for righteousness.

But perhaps even this is not clear. Let me share an illustration that Stott uses:

> Suppose there is a man called John Jones, an elderly Christian believer, who is looking back upon his long life. His career is divided by his conversion into two parts, the old self—John Jones before his conversion—and the new self—John Jones after his conversion. The old self and the new self (or the "old man" and the "new man") are not John Jones' two natures; they are the two halves of his life, separated by the new birth. At conversion, signified in baptism, John Jones, the old self, died through union with Christ, the penalty of his sin borne. At the same time John Jones rose again from death, a new man, to live a new life to God.
>
> Now John Jones is every believer. We are John Jones, if we are in Christ. The way in which our old self died is that we were crucified with Christ.
>
> [*A little further on, Stott amplifies his illustration in this way:*] Our biography is written in two volumes. Volume one is the story of the old man, the old self, of me before my conversion. Volume two is the story of the new man, the new self, of me after I was made a new creation in Christ. Volume one of my biography ended with the judicial death of the old self. I was a sinner. I deserved to die. I did die. I received my deserts in my Substitute with whom I have become one. Volume two of my biography opened with my resurrection. My old life having finished, a new life to God has begun.[7]

Nowhere to Go but Forward

In the last study I asked the question: Where do we go from here? And I posed what seemed like two alternatives: Do we continue in a life of sin so that, as some might piously choose to put it, grace may increase? Or do we choose the other path, the path of God-like conduct? By now you should be able to see that there is no possible alternative to God's path, for those who are truly saved. The life of sin is what we have died to. There is no going back for us, any more than there could be a going back to suffer and die for sin again by our Lord. If there is no going back—if that possibility has been eliminated—there is no direction for us to go but forward!

This is why I say that a right understanding of Romans 6:2 is the key to sanctification.

7. Stott, *Men Made New: An Exposition of Romans 6–8*, pp. 48, 49.

Some people try to find the key in an intense emotional experience, thinking that if only they can make themselves feel close to God they will become holy. Others try to find sanctification through a special methodology. They think that if they do certain things or follow a prescribed ritual they will be sanctified. Godliness does not come in that fashion; in fact, approaches like these are deceiving. A holy life comes from *knowing*—I stress that word—*knowing* that you can't go back, that you have died to sin and been made alive to God. Stott says, "A born-again Christian should no more think of going back to the old life than an adult to his childhood, a married man to his bachelorhood, or a discharged prisoner to his prison cell."[8]

Can an adult still want to be a child or an infant? A happily married man a bachelor? A freed man a prisoner again? Well, I suppose some could. But no right-minded woman or man would want to.

8. Ibid., p. 51.

79

Baptized into Jesus Christ

Romans 6:3–4

Or don't you know that all of us who were baptized into Christ Jesus were baptized into his death? We were therefore buried with him through baptism into death in order that, just as Christ was raised from the dead through the glory of the Father, we too may live a new life.

After I had first preached the sermon that constitutes the previous study, a member of the congregation at Tenth Presbyterian Church said, "That message was so important and yet so hard to understand that you ought to preach it all over again next week." I felt that way myself, and that is what I did. However, I did it as Paul himself did it: by going on to Romans 6:3–4, which is what this study is. These two verses are a restatement of the principle for living a godly life laid down in verse 2.

I remind you of where we are. Paul has asked a question that must have been asked of him a thousand times in the course of his ministry: "Shall we go on sinning so that grace may increase?" He answered by saying: "By no means! We died to sin; how can we live in it any longer?"

The key words in this answer are "we died to sin." We saw in the last study that there have been many ways of interpreting those words: that the

657

Christian is no longer responsive to sin; that Christians should die to sin; that the Christian is dying to sin day by day; that Christians cannot continue in sin, because they have renounced it; that the Christian has died to sin's guilt. But we saw, too, that the real meaning of the phrase is that we died to our old life when God saved us. I used John Stott's illustrations of John Jones before his conversion and John Jones after his conversion, and of volumes one and two of "our biography."

The bottom line of this discussion has been that the key to a holy life is not our experiences or emotions, however meaningful or intense these may be, but rather our *knowledge* of what has happened to us. I stressed the word *knowledge* because the most important and basic reason for going forward in the Christian life is that we cannot go back.

Knowing and Growing

When you hear this for the first time, you may think that it is just too simple or even that it is a novel (and therefore questionable) interpretation of Romans 6:2. But I would argue that it is neither novel nor questionable, and in proof of this I refer to the very next words Paul writes: "Don't you know . . . ?" These words are the start of the question by which Paul reminds us of our identity with Jesus Christ.

Do not pass over those words lightly. Remember that Paul had never been to Rome, though he was planning to visit Rome on a proposed trip to Spain (Rom. 15:24). He had not taught the Christians in Rome personally. Moreover, so far as we know, the church had never had the benefit of any apostolic teaching. Yet, although the Christians in Rome had never had such teaching, Paul assumes their knowledge of this doctrine by these words. In other words, what he is referring to here was common Christian knowledge. Christians have died to sin! Or, to put it in the words he is going to use next, they have been "baptized into Christ Jesus . . . into his death." The apostle assumes that this was known to believers everywhere, and he appeals to our knowledge of it as the key to our growth in holiness.

So I say it again: The secret of sanctification is not some neat set of experiences or emotions, however meaningful or intense they may be. It is *knowing* what has happened to you.

The Meaning of "Baptism"

What Paul says we are to know in verses 3 and 4 also supports my interpretation of verse 2. But before we plunge into that we need to think about the meaning of the word *baptism,* since it is the key term he uses.

The reason we need to do this is that for the vast majority of today's people, the mere mention of baptism immediately sets them thinking about the sacrament of water baptism and blinds them to what any text that mentions baptism may actually be saying. It has blinded commentators, too, of course. They also think of the sacrament, and because they do they have produced many wrong interpretations of these verses based on their assumption. Some have taught that the sacrament joins us to Christ and is therefore necessary for salvation. This view is called "baptismal regeneration." Some assume that Paul is thinking of our baptismal vows, others that it is a matter of coming under Christ's influence, still others that what is important is our public testimony to our faith in Christ.[1] The last three of these actually do have something to do with water baptism. But Paul is not thinking along these lines at all in these verses, and therefore any approach to them with the idea of the sacrament of water baptism uppermost in our minds will be misleading.

What is "baptism"? A good answer starts by recognizing that there are two closely related words for baptism in the Greek language and that they do not necessarily have the same meaning. One word is *baptō*, which means "dip" or "immerse." The other word is *baptizō*, which may mean "immerse" but may have other meanings as well. This is a normal situation with Greek words. The simpler word usually conveys the most straightforward meaning. The longer word adds specialized and sometimes metaphorical meanings.

It is the longer word that is used for "baptism" in the New Testament. So we need to ask next what the precise meaning of the longer word is.

We gain help from classical literature. The Greeks used the word *baptizō* from about 400 B.C. to about the second century after Christ, and in their literature *baptizō* always pointed to a change having taken place by some means. Josephus used it of the crowds that flooded into Jerusalem and "wrecked the city."[2] Other examples are the dyeing of cloth and the drinking of too much wine. In each of these cases there is a liquid or something like it—the crowds were like a human "wave," a dye and wine are liquids—but the essential idea is actually that of a change. Jerusalem was wrecked. The dyed cloth changes color. The drinker becomes different; he misbehaves.

The clearest example I know that shows this meaning of *baptizō* is a text from the Greek poet and physician Nicander, who lived about 200 B.C. It is a recipe for making pickles, and it is helpful because it uses both words. Nicander says that to make a pickle, the vegetable should first be "dipped" (*baptō*) into boiling water and then "baptized" (*baptizō*) in the vinegar solution. Both verbs concern immersing the vegetable in a solution, but the first is temporary. The second, the act of "baptizing" the vegetable, produces a permanent change.

To get this distinction in mind is of enormous help in understanding the New Testament verses that refer to baptism, including our text in Romans, for which thoughts of a literal immersion in water would be nonsense.

1. See D. M. Lloyd-Jones, *Romans: An Exposition of Chapter 6, The New Man* (Grand Rapids: Zondervan, 1973), pp. 30–33, for a discussion of these wrong notions.
2. *Josephus in Nine Volumes*, trans. H. St. J. Thackeray, vol. 3, *The Jewish War*, books IV-VII (London: William Heinemann, and Cambridge, Mass.: Harvard University Press, 1961), pp. 40, 41.

Take 1 Corinthians 10:1–2, as an example. "For I do not want you to be
ignorant of the fact, brothers, that our forefathers were all under the cloud
and that they all passed through the sea. They were all baptized into Moses
in the cloud and in the sea." That cannot be referring to a water baptism,
because the only people who were immersed in water were the Egyptian soldiers, and they were drowned in it. The Israelites did not even get their feet
wet. What do the verses mean? Obviously, they refer to a permanent identification of the people with Moses as a result of the Red Sea crossing. Before
this they were still in Egypt and could have renounced Moses' leadership,
retaining their allegiance to Pharaoh. But once they crossed the Red Sea
they were joined to Moses for the duration of their desert wandering. They
were not able to go back.

By now you are probably beginning to see why this discussion of baptism
is important and why Paul used the words *baptized* and *baptism* in verses 3
and 4. But let me offer a few more texts that are clarified by understanding
baptism as change rather than mere immersion in water.

Galatians 3:27. "For all of you who were baptized into Christ have
clothed yourselves with Christ." This is not referring to water baptism,
because if it were, the illustration of being clothed with Christ would be
inappropriate. Rather, it refers to our being identified with Christ, like a
child identifies with her mother when she dresses in her mother's clothes
or a soldier identifies with the armed forces of his country when he dons a
uniform.

Mark 16:16 is well known. Jesus says here: "Whoever believes and is baptized will be saved. . . ." Scores of people have wrongly concluded from that
verse that unless a person first believes in Christ and then is also immersed
in water, he or she cannot be saved. But even the poorest Bible student
knows that this is not true. A person is saved by grace through faith in Jesus
Christ alone. If baptism in water is necessary for salvation, then the believing thief who was crucified with Christ is lost.

Once we get away from the mistaken idea that baptism always refers to
water baptism, the verse becomes clear. For what Jesus is saying in Mark
16:16 is that a person needs to be identified with him to be saved. He was
saying that mere intellectual assent to the doctrines of Christianity is not
enough. It is necessary, to use another of his teachings, that "If anyone
would come after me, he must deny himself and take up his cross daily and
follow me" (Luke 9:23). This last verse is an exact parallel to what the apostle is teaching in Romans 6:3–4, for it means that a true follower of Christ
has died to his past life—like a man on his way to execution. Only, in
Romans 6, the man has already died and been buried.[3]

3. I discuss the meaning of being baptized into Christ more extensively in James
Montgomery Boice, *Foundations of the Christian Faith: A Comprehensive and Readable Theology*

Buried Through Baptism

With this lengthy excursion into the meaning of the word *baptism* in mind, I return to our text to show how these ideas come together. What was the chief idea in Romans 5:12–31? It was the idea of our union with Christ, wasn't it? Before, we were in Adam; now, we are in Christ. And what is Paul's answer to "Shall we go on sinning so that grace may increase?" (Rom. 6:1). It is that we have died to sin: "We died to sin; how can we live in it any longer?" Union with Christ! And death to sin!

But notice: That is exactly what baptism signifies, and in that order. The most important idea is that we have been taken out of one state and put into another. We have had an experience similar to that of the Jews after they had been brought through the Red Sea. They were joined to Moses; we are joined to Christ. Or, to put it in the words of Galatians 3:27, we have been clothed with Christ. We are in Christ's uniform. And what that means, if we look backward, is that we have died to whatever has gone before. We died to the old life when Christ transferred us to the new one.

As soon as we see how these ideas go together, we see why Paul's thoughts turned to the word *baptism* as a way of unfolding what he had in mind when he said: "How can we live in [sin] any longer?"

I want you to notice something else, too. When theologians write about our being "baptized into Christ" and how this is the equivalent of our being united to him by the Holy Spirit, they stress that we are identified with Christ in all respects. That is, we are identified with him in (or baptized into) his death, burial, and resurrection.[4] One commentator got into this theme so deeply that he worked out parallels to our identification with Christ in his election, virgin birth, circumcision, physical growth, baptism by John the Baptist, suffering, crucifixion, burial, resurrection, and ascension into heaven.[5] Much of this is very true, of course. If we have been identified with Christ, as we have been, we are identified with him in many respects, particularly in his death and resurrection.

But what I want to point out is that Paul does not say here that we have been identified with Christ by baptism in these other respects. He does not, for example, even say that we have been baptized into Christ's resurrection,

(Downers Grove, Ill., and Leicester, England: InterVarsity Press, 1986), pp. 597–601. A study of the early history of these words may be found in Gerhard Kittel, ed., *Theological Dictionary of the New Testament*, trans. Geoffrey W. Bromiley (Grand Rapids: Wm. B. Eerdmans, 1964), vol. 1, p. 529 ff.

4. See Lloyd-Jones, *Romans: An Exposition of Chapter 6, The New Man*, pp. 42-54; John Murray, *The Epistle to the Romans* (Grand Rapids: Wm. B. Eerdmans, 1968), pp. 214–217; Leon Morris, *The Epistle to the Romans* (Grand Rapids: Wm. B. Eerdmans, and Leicester, England: InterVarsity Press, 1988), pp. 247, 248; and others.

5. Donald Grey Barnhouse, *God's Freedom: Exposition of Bible Doctrines, Taking the Epistle to the Romans as a Point of Departure*, vol. 6, Romans 6:1—7:25 (Grand Rapids: Wm. B. Eerdmans, 1961), pp. 32-84.

though he goes on to say that "just as Christ was raised from the dead through the glory of the Father, we too may live a new life" (v. 4) and later that we have been "united with him like this in his resurrection" (v. 5). In verse 3 he speaks of our baptism into Christ in one respect only: "into his death." And in the next phrase he shows that what he has particularly in mind is Christ's burial: "We were therefore buried with him through baptism into death."

This flow of thought is so strong that F. Godet rightly says, "According to these words, it is not to death, it is to the *internment of the dead,* that Paul compares baptism."[6]

This is striking, and quite puzzling, too. I notice, for example, that when theologians work out the parallels of our identification with Christ, they have little trouble showing how we have been crucified with him, raised with him or even made to ascend into heaven with him. But they have trouble with the burial. "How can we be said to be buried with Christ?" they ask. "And what does this add that is not already covered by our death to sin?"

Yet burial is the thing Paul emphasizes.

How do we account for this? And how do we account for the difficult way Paul puts it: "buried with him through baptism into death." More than one commentator has struggled with the awkwardness of that phrase, suggesting in some cases that it is even backward, since no one is buried into death (that is, buried to die) but rather is buried because he died.

I suggest that if this is approached as I have been suggesting, the problem is not difficult at all. The reason burial is an important step even beyond death is that burial puts the deceased person out of this world permanently. A corpse is dead to life. But there is a sense in which it can still be said to be in life, as long as it is around. When it is buried, when it is placed in the ground and covered with earth, it is removed from the sphere of this life permanently. It is gone. That is why Paul, who wanted to emphasize the finality of our being removed from the rule of sin and death to the rule of Christ, emphasizes it. He is repeating but also intensifying what he has already said about our death to sin. "You have not only died to it," he says. "You have been buried to it." To go back to sin once you have been joined to Christ is like digging up a dead body.

The Public Profession

I have been saying throughout this study that when Paul refers to our being baptized into Christ, he is not thinking chiefly of the sacrament of baptism but rather of our having been joined to Christ by the Holy Spirit. I do not want to go back on that. The very next verses prove this view, for in

---

6. F. Godet, *Commentary on St. Paul's Epistle to the Romans,* trans. A. Cusin (Edinburgh: T. & T. Clark, n.d.), vol. 1, p. 405.

them Paul speaks explicitly of our being "united with him in his death [and] resurrection." This is something the Holy Spirit does.

But, while emphasizing this, I do not want to miss the significance of the sacrament of baptism as a Christian's public renunciation of his past life and a profession of his new identification with Christ.

This is not so obvious to us today perhaps, since baptism is something that generally takes place in an exclusively Christian environment and for many people means very little. But it was not so in Paul's day. And it is not so in many places in the world even today. In the ancient world, to be identified with Christ in baptism was a bold and risky declaration. It often put the believer's life in jeopardy. There was nothing wrong with listening to Christian preaching or propaganda. But when a Christian was baptized, he was saying to the state as well as to his fellow believers that he was now a follower of Jesus Christ and that he was going to be loyal to him regardless of the outcome. It meant "Christ before Caesar."

Baptism was as nearly an irreversible step as a believer in Jesus Christ could take. Therefore, even though Paul is not thinking primarily about water baptism in Romans 6—water baptism is something we do; the baptism Paul is talking about is something that has been done to us—the sacrament of baptism is nevertheless a fit public testimony to what baptism into Christ by the Holy Spirit means: that we have been united to Christ and that the old life is done for us forever. That is what you have professed if you have been baptized, particularly if you have been baptized as an adult. You have told the world that you are not going back, that you are going forward with Jesus.

But I come to the questions that I know are in many people's minds, the same questions I touched on at the end of the last study: "But what if I do go back? What if I do sin?"

Here are three points to remember:

1. *It won't work.* Do you remember my illustration of an adult trying to return to childhood. Can he do it? Well, he can act childlike, though it would be a dishonor to him and an embarrassment to everyone else. But to become a child again? It can't be done. An adult can behave in an infantile manner. But an adult cannot *be* a child. In the same way, if you are a true Christian, you cannot return to sin in the same way you were in it previously. You can sin. We do sin. But it is not the same. If nothing else, you cannot enjoy sin as you did before. And you will not even be able to do it convincingly. You will be like Peter trying to swear that he did not know Jesus, after having spent three years in Jesus' school. People will look at you and say, "But surely you are one of his disciples."

2. *God will stop you.* God will not stop you from sinning, but he will stop you from continuing in it. And he will do it in one of two ways. Either he will make your life so miserable that you will curse the day you got into sin

and beg God to get you out of it, or God will put an end to your life. Paul told the Corinthians that because they had dishonored the Lord's Supper, God had actually taken some of them home to heaven (1 Cor. 11:30). If God did it to them for that offense, he will do it to you for persistence in more sinful things.

3. *If you do return to the life you lived before coming to Christ and if you are able to continue in it, you are not saved.* In fact, it is even worse than that. If you are able to go back once you have come to Christ, it means, not only that you are not saved, but that you even have been inoculated against Christianity.

I am sure that is why the author of Hebrews wrote, "It is impossible for those who have once been enlightened, who have tasted the heavenly gift, who have shared in the Holy Spirit, who have tasted the goodness of the word of God and the powers of the coming age, if they fall away, to be brought back to repentance . . ." (Heb. 6:4–6). Those verses are not referring to a true believer in Christ being lost—How could they in view of Paul's teaching in Romans 5 and 8?—but rather of one who was close enough to have tasted the reality of Christ and who nevertheless turned back. It teaches that the closer you are to Christ, if you do go back, the harder it will be to come to Christ again. In some cases, as in the case described here, it will be impossible.

So don't go back!

I say it again: *Don't go back!*

If you have been saved by Jesus, you have been saved forever. There is nothing before you but to go on growing in righteousness!

80

Living with Jesus Now

Romans 6:5-10

If we have been united with him like this in his death, we will certainly also be united with him in his resurrection. For we know that our old self was crucified with him so that the body of sin might be rendered powerless [done away with], that we should no longer be slaves to sin—because anyone who has died has been freed from sin.

Now if we died with Christ, we believe that we will also live with him. For we know that since Christ was raised from the dead, he cannot die again; death no longer has mastery over him. The death he died, he died to sin once for all; but the life he lives, he lives to God.

I t is a sad fact that many people perceive Christianity as being negative. It is viewed as a series of don'ts: "Don't drink; don't play cards; don't fool around; don't laugh too loud." In fact, "Don't have fun at all," because, if you do, God will be looking down from heaven to see it and say, "Now you cut that out!"

It is possible that some reader has taken our first studies of Romans 6 negatively, because the emphasis has been on the fact that once a person has been joined to Jesus Christ he or she can no longer go on sinning. "Shall we go on sinning so that grace may increase?" Paul asked. "By no

665

means!" he has answered. "We died to sin; how can we live in it any longer?" (vv. 1–2). That does indeed sound negative, particularly to the non-Christian. Death! And dying! If you do not know Christianity better than that, it sounds almost like "no more anything."

But that is not what real Christianity is, of course. In fact, it is just the opposite. It is sin that is negative. So to be freed from sin is to be freed to a brand new life, which is positive. Leon Morris, one of the newer and best commentators on Romans, says, "The Christian way is not negative. There is a death to an old way, it is true, but as the believer identifies with Christ in his death he enters into newness of life."[1] The Christian way of speaking about this is to say that, for the Christian, death is followed by a resurrection.

And not just at the end of time! True Christianity is living out a new, joyful, abundant, resurrected life with Jesus Christ *now*.

A New, Rich Section

We have already had more than one hint that this has been coming. Paul ended the fifth chapter of Romans by saying that the reign of grace has replaced the reign of sin and death, and in chapter 6 he has concluded that we were "buried with him [Christ] through baptism into death in order that, just as Christ was raised from the dead through the glory of the Father, we too may live a new life" (v. 4). Nevertheless, it is in the section to which we turn now (verses 5–10) that this new and abundant life is unfolded fully for the first time.

This is a long section compared to the several smaller units we have been studying in the previous chapters. In fact, it would be too long for one study if it were not that we have already dealt with most of the key terms. Most important, we have studied how we can be said to have died to sin. Jesus died to sin (not "for sin," though that is also true) by ending the phase of his life in which he was in sin's realm, and by returning to heaven. In the same way, our old relationships to sin have also ended. God fixed our future when we were taken out of Adam and joined to Christ. We cannot go back to the old life. As I have said several times, there is no place for us to go but forward.

The outline of these verses is a simple one. In verse 5, Paul states a thesis, which verses 6–10 develop. It has two parts: "If we have been united with him like this in his death . . ." (that is the first part; it is what he has already been talking about extensively) and ". . . we will certainly also be united with him in his resurrection" (that is the second part; it is the new idea to be developed). Paul unfolds the meaning of the first part in verses 6 and 7; he explains the second part in verses 8–10.

1. Leon Morris, *The Epistle to the Romans* (Grand Rapids: Wm. B. Eerdmans, and Leicester, England: Inter-Varsity Press, 1988), p. 254.

The Body of Sin

A few lines back I wrote that the first part of verse 5 (We have been united with Christ in his death) has already been dealt with extensively, and that is true. But when Paul unfolds the meaning of this sentence in verses 6 and 7, he is not just repeating himself. This is the point at which he is starting to talk about the Christian life, particularly the Christian's sure victory over sin. Now when he mentions our union with Christ in his death, it is to show how this frees us from sin's tyranny.

The best way to show what Paul is doing in these verses is by focusing on the two key phrases.

1. *Our old self.* The first phrase is "our old self" which, he says, "was crucified with" Christ. Our earlier studies have already indicated how this should be taken. "Old self" refers to our old life, that is, to what we were in Adam before God saved us. That old life is done for. We have died to it. That is why Paul says it "was (or 'has been') crucified."

Many commentators go astray at this point, because they confuse the "old self" with the Christian's "old (or 'sinful') nature," a phrase Paul uses later. Because the old nature remains with us, these teachers are always urging believers to crucify or kill the old self. They explain the persistence of sin in the believer by observing that crucifixion is a "long drawn out" process.[2] Now it *is* true that the Christian life is a long-drawn-out battle with sin. That is what Romans 7 is about, as I will show when we get to it. But the secret to victory over sin is not the crucifixion or killing of the old self, for the simple reason that the old self has already died. That is why the Bible never tells us to crucify the old man. How can we if he has already been put to death?

I make this point strongly because, although the Christian life is indeed a struggle, to equate killing our old self with that struggle (when the old self has already been crucified with Christ) is to miss the truth that has been given to us by God for our victory.

2. *The body of sin.* The second key phrase is "the body of sin." It occurs in the clause "so that the body of sin might be rendered powerless [done away with]." This is the first time we have seen this phrase, though it or some variation will occur a number of times more as we proceed. What does it refer to?

Our first inclination is to think of the body of sin as being the same thing as our old self, which has just been mentioned. This is probably because the old self is said to have been crucified; a body is crucified and, if the body of sin is crucified, it is therefore obviously rendered powerless, which is what

2. Donald Grey Barnhouse, *God's Freedom: Exposition of Bible Doctrines, Taking the Epistle to the Romans as a Point of Departure*, vol. 6, Romans 6:1—7:25 (Grand Rapids: Wm. B. Eerdmans, 1961), p. 100.

the text states. But that is not the idea. I think D. Martyn Lloyd-Jones is exactly right at this point when he says that by the term "body of sin" Paul *is* talking about the old nature,[3] and that to some extent he means the word *body* (that is, our physical body) literally.[4] Paul was not talking about this earlier. The old self (or old man) is not the old nature. The old self is the "old me," who has died. But here, in talking about "the body of sin," Paul *is* talking about the old nature, mentioning—for the first time in Romans—the Christian's actual inclination to sin, which must be dealt with.

That makes sense of verse 6, of course. For what Paul says in verse 6 is that God has taken us out of Adam and placed us in Christ, thereby causing us to die to the old life, in order that (1) our present inclinations to sin might be robbed of their power, and (2) we should be delivered from sin's slavery.

I want to give a personal reaction to the phrase "body of sin" at this point. If Paul were with us today and I had an opportunity to speak to him, I think I might say that I wished he had spoken of our sinful nature in some other fashion. This is because to locate the Christian's continuing inclination to sin in the "body," as this phrase does, seems to suggest two admittedly wrong ideas. First, it suggests: "I am not a sinner; it is only my body." We do not want to say that. John tells us that "if we claim to be without sin, we deceive ourselves" (1 John 1:8). And second, it suggests that the body is somehow intrinsically evil, and we know that this is a Greek or Hindu idea, rather than a Judeo-Christian one. "Couldn't you have thought of another phrase?" I would have asked the apostle.

Yet I confess that I cannot think of a better one. And the phrase is helpful as long as I realize that, although I am not ultimately my body, I am nevertheless so much formed by it that I cannot escape its influences. The wording teaches us that in our present physical state, prior to glorification, sin is in possession of our bodies and must be dealt with at that level.

Sin in the Body

Here are some examples of how sin operates in our bodies.

We sit down to eat, and our hostess sets a beautiful spread before us. There is nothing intrinsically wrong (sinful) in either her preparations or our eating. The body is from God; it needs to eat because God made it that way. But we become so enthralled by the food's appearance and taste that we take this natural bodily function and push it beyond where it was intended to go. We overeat. We indulge, we stuff ourselves. The overindulgence is sin, and it leads to even greater sin if it becomes a pattern. This

3. D. M. Lloyd-Jones, *Romans: An Exposition of Chapter 6, The New Man* (Grand Rapids: Zondervan, 1973), p. 69. Lloyd-Jones has an extensive discussion of this phrase, including many references to the word *body* elsewhere in the New Testament, on pages 70–80.
    4. Ibid., p. 72.

pattern of eating harms the body and in time makes us insensitive to the needs of others—others who are hungry, for example—and to God, who has given us the food. We become ungrateful, fail to thank him, and even complain if for some reason we are unable at some future point to indulge ourselves as freely.

Take sleeping as another example. The body needs rest. We cannot do without it. Sleep or relaxation refreshes us so that we feel good. But the body can draw us into the sins of sloth and apathy and then lead us to the even more sinful conviction that others should work for us so we can be at ease. We may even think ourselves superior to these other persons since they, in our view, exist chiefly to see that we are made comfortable.

Our glands and the hormones they produce are also parts of the body. They, too, are good, since they have been given to us by God. They feed our emotions. Danger causes our adrenaline to flow so that we can react quickly to escape a life-threatening situation. Sexual hormones awaken us to the qualities of the opposite sex and lead to love, marriage, and procreation. But these same glands also react wrongly and more strongly than they should. Adrenaline will flow just because someone has offended us, and we will fight back when we should show a spirit of meekness. Our sexual glands, particularly when they are stimulated by the world's culture, lead to lust, infidelity, promiscuity, and other vices. Indeed, they turn us against God when we are told that his law forbids such inclinations.

A person may say, with reason, that it is not the body that is at fault but our minds. Sin begins in the mind or spirit. But although I realize that the source of sin is in the mind or spirit and that the spirit is not the body, it is nevertheless impossible to separate the *mind* from the body. We are as we think, and the thinking process (so far as anyone can determine) is physiological. So even at this level it is clearly "the body of sin" from which we need to be delivered.

Posse Non Peccare

This is what our having died to sin by our union to Christ in his death is intended to accomplish. Paul says that our union with Christ in his death has been to render the body of sin powerless, so that we might "no longer be slaves to sin."

"Rendered powerless" (or "done away with"), as in the New International Version, is a better translation than the older word "destroyed" (KJV, RSV). But even this can mislead some people. The Greek word is *katargeō*, and it occurs twenty-seven times in the New Testament, including three prior instances in Romans. It occurs in Romans 3:3 and 31, where it is rendered "nullify" ("Will their lack of faith nullify God's faithfulness?" and "Do we, then, nullify the law by this faith?"). It also occurs in Romans 4:14, where it is rendered "has no value" ("For if those who live by law are heirs, faith has no value"). Two more instances in Romans are in chapter 7, where it is translated "released" ("If her husband dies, she is released from the law of marriage" [v. 2] and "We have been released from the law so that we serve in the new way of the Spirit" [v. 6]).

None of these instances mean "destroyed," and they do not mean "rendered powerless" in the sense that the thing involved can be said no longer to exert an influence. They mean rather: "no longer to exert a controlling force or power" or "to be made ineffective."

In other words, the reason God has removed us from our union with Adam and has joined us to Christ (so that we have died to our past) is so the inclinations to sin that operate so strongly in our bodies might no longer exercise effective power or control us. They are still there, but from this point on they will not dominate us. Before this, we were "slaves to sin" (v. 6), but having died to sin, we are now "freed" from it (v. 7).

Will we sin? Yes! But we do not need to, and we will do so less and less as we go on in the Christian life. You may remember how Saint Augustine put it when he was comparing Adam's state before the fall, Adam's state after the fall, the state of those who have been saved by God through the work of Christ, and our final state in glory as Christians.

Augustine said that before he fell Adam was *posse peccare* ("able to sin"). He had not sinned yet, but he was able to.

After his fall, according to Augustine, Adam became *non posse non peccare* ("not able not to sin"). By himself he was unable to break free from it.

The state of believers, those who have been saved by Christ, is now one of *posse non peccare* ("able not to sin"). That is the state Paul is writing about in Romans 6. For them, the tyranny of sin has been broken.

The glorified state, for which we yearn, is *non posse peccare* ("not able to sin"). In our glorified state we will not be tempted by sin or be able to fall into it again.

A Present Resurrection

The second half of Paul's topical sentence in verse 5 ("we will certainly also be united with him in his resurrection") is explained in verses 8–10, where Paul speaks of a present resurrection: "Now if we died with Christ, we believe that we will also live with him. For we know that since Christ was raised from the dead, he cannot die again; death no longer has mastery over him. The death he died, he died to sin once for all; but the life he lives, he lives to God."

I have quoted those verses in full, because unless we take them together we will perceive the words "we will also live with him" as referring to our future resurrection, when actually they refer to an experience of resurrection life here and now.

Don't misunderstand. There is a future resurrection, and the same union of the believer with Christ that we have been talking about is a guarantee of it. But that is not what these verses are about. We have already seen what they mean in the case of Christ.[5] They refer to his passage from the sphere where death reigned to the sphere of the resurrection, from where he was to where he is now. In the same way, they refer to *our* passage—from the reign of death to the reign of grace, to a present resurrection. This is what Paul says of himself in Philippians when he writes: "I want to know Christ and the power of his resurrection . . ." (Phil. 3:10). He means that he wants to be victorious over sin.

I have been reading Stephen W. Hawking's stimulating book on modern physics, entitled *A Brief History of Time.*[6] Hawking is the distinguished English physicist who has Lou Gehrig's disease and is confined to a wheelchair, but has done pioneer work in the analysis of what are commonly called "black holes" or "singularities." A black hole is a collapsed star of such density and gravity that nothing can escape from it, not even light, which is why it appears as a dark spot in the panorama of the heavens. Objects rushing toward it approach the speed of light as well as approach infinite mass; as a result, the normal laws of physics tend to lose meaning at the center. No one knows what happens when an object reaches the center, but some have speculated that for reasons beyond most people's ability to grasp, an object might shoot through the "hole" and pass into another time period or existence.

I understand a great deal less about black holes than scientists do, so I have no idea whether such speculations are true. But it occurs to me that passing through a black hole is an apt illustration of a Christian's having died to sin and having been raised to new life in Christ—if for no other reason than that he or she cannot come back. Anything that has gone through a black hole has passed through it forever. Similarly, anyone who has been united to Christ has died to sin, is on the way to God, and can never return to his or her former sphere of existence.

And there is this, too: For most of us, to pass through a black hole in space would be, in physical terms, the most important, monumental, irreversible, and life-changing experience we can imagine. But great as that might be, it would not be so great as the change that has already taken place in those who have been lifted out of the realm of sin and joined to Jesus Christ.

When all is said and done, passing through a black hole would still mean being limited to some kind of physical universe. But being joined to Christ means being joined to the One who made the universe itself and who will still be there when heaven and earth—including black holes, quasars, neutron stars, and all the rest—have passed away.

But I do not want to leave you there. This last point is a flight of fancy, so far as I know. But what I started to talk about is the positive Christian experi-

5. In the chapter "Death to Sin" (Romans 6:2).

6. Stephen W. Hawking, *A Brief History of Time from the Big Bang to Black Holes* (New York, etc.: Bantam Books, 1988).

ence of being delivered from the power of sin by the realities of Christ's life. I return to the key questions.

First: "Shall we go on sinning so that grace may increase?"

The answer: "By no means! We died to sin; how can we live in it any longer?"

Second, the question of this study: "How can we triumph over sin?"

The answer: "By knowing what God has done for us when he joined us to Christ." We are going to look at the meaning of that even more in the next study, when we consider verse 11. But I hope you have noticed, as we studied verses 5–10, that the important word *know*, which I have called the key to this entire matter of sanctification, is here again and not only once but twice. We saw it first in verse 2: "Or don't you *know* that all of us who were baptized into Christ Jesus were baptized into his death?" Here it appears in verse 6: "For we *know* that our old self was crucified with him," and in verse 9: "For we *know* that since Christ was raised from the dead, he cannot die again; death no longer has mastery over him."

What is true of Jesus is true of us. His relationship to sin, while he was in this life, has passed forever. It is true of us as well, since we are joined to him. The key to holiness is to know this and to press on.

81

You Can Count On It

Romans 6:11

In the same way, count yourselves dead to sin but alive to God in Christ Jesus.

I want to start this study with a brief quiz on the early chapters of Romans, and the question I want to ask is this: How many times in the letter up to this point has the apostle Paul urged his readers to do something? That is, how many exhortations have there been?

More than ten? Thirty? Less than five?

How many imperative statements occurred in chapter 1? Were there more exhortations in chapter 5 than in chapter 4?

What do you think? How many exhortations has Paul made so far?

The answer to this question is that there have been none at all! And the reason I emphasize this is to call attention to the most significant thing to be noted about Romans 6:11. This verse *is* an exhortation, and it is the *first* in the epistle. This is the first time in five and a half chapters that the apostle has urged his readers to do anything.

What are they to do? The text says: "In the same way, count yourselves dead to sin but alive to God in Christ Jesus."

This is an important enough statement in itself, but it becomes even more so when we realize that Romans 6:11 is also a turning point in the letter. I mean by this that, having gotten the first olive out of the bottle, so to speak, the other exhortative olives now tumble out naturally. The next verses are full of them: *"Do not let sin reign in your mortal body. . . . Do not offer* the parts of your body to sin . . . but rather *offer yourselves* to God . . . and *offer* the parts of your body to him . . ."* (vv. 12–14, emphasis added).

What God Has Done

Most modern Americans are activists. So we are inclined to think, as we come to this verse, that we are at last getting to what matters. But, at the risk of prolonging our discussion of the earlier chapters beyond the limits of most people's tolerance, I need to say that the point I am making—that this is the *first exhortation* in the letter—is of great practical importance.

Let me approach it this way. We live in an age of self-help books and seminars, in Christian circles as well as in the world at large, and these small books (they are usually small) and short (perhaps weekend-length) courses promise the consumer great things. The Christian versions offer formulas by which we are supposed to be able to move ahead quickly in our Christian lives. They teach us how to become great prayer warriors, perhaps even "change the world" through prayer. They show us how to relate to others successfully. They promise quick and effective methods of Bible study.

I do not want to suggest that these "quick fix" offerings are useless, of course. They are not useless. They are helpful to many, and I am sure they have their place, particularly in our fast-paced, solution-oriented culture. Still, if you have read any of these books or attended these seminars, isn't it the case that you have generally been disappointed at some level, perhaps even deeply frustrated? Perhaps you have even been frustrated enough to write off completely these methods for growing strong in the Christian faith. You have said, "I am sure they must work for other people, but not for me. They help, but not enough. Probably nothing will help me. I am probably called to be just a normal [read 'second-class'] Christian."

What is wrong here? I suggest that because of our characteristic North American impatience with matters of basic substance or with anything requiring hard and prolonged work, we have jumped ahead too quickly to the "exhortation" parts of Christianity and have not taken sufficient time to understand and appropriate the fundamental teachings. If this is so, then Paul's procedure in Romans should be of great help to us. Was Paul not interested in the spiritual growth of the Roman Christians? Of course, he was. But he knew that there was no use rushing ahead to tell them how to live the Christian life until he had first fully instructed them on what God had done for them in Jesus Christ. This is because the work of God in Christ is foundational to everything else about Christianity.

What Paul principally wanted his readers to understand here is what theologians call the mystical union of believers with Jesus Christ. Paul's way of talking about this is to say that Christians are "in Christ," "in Jesus Christ" or "in him." Those who count such things tell us that those phrases occur 164 times in Paul's writings. One of them is in our text, and it is the first time this exact phrase has occurred in Romans. Yet it is what Paul has really been talking about for several chapters. Romans 5 dealt with it directly, contrasting our former state of being in Adam with our present state of being in Christ. In Romans 6 this has already been presented indirectly in terms of our having died to sin and having been united to Jesus in his resurrection.

This has been done for us by God. It has been his work, not ours. We have no more joined ourselves to Jesus in his resurrection than we have died for our own sins. If we are Christians, everything that is necessary has been done for us by God.

A Bookkeeping Term

What we learn in a general way, by reflecting on the amount of teaching Paul has given in chapters 1–5 of Romans, is reinforced by the verb he uses in Romans 6:11. It is the word *count* (or "reckon," as some of the other versions have it). The Greek word is *logizomai*, and it is related to the more common term *logos*, meaning "word," "deed," or "fact."

In classical Greek, *logizomai* had two main uses:

1. It was used in commercial dealings in the sense of evaluating an object's worth or reckoning up a project's gain or losses. In other words, it was a bookkeeping term. We have preserved a bit of this in our English words *log, logistics,* and *logarithm*. A log refers to the numerical record of a ship's or airplane's progress. Logistics is a military term dealing with the numbers and movement of troops or supplies. A logarithm is the exponent to which a base number is raised to produce a given number.

2. *Logizomai* was also used in philosophy in the sense of objective or nonemotional reasoning. We have preserved this meaning in our English words "logic" and "logical."[1]

The common ground in these two uses of the word is that *logizomai* has to do with reality, with things as they truly are. In other words, it has nothing to do with wishful thinking. Nor is it an activity that makes something come to pass or happen. It is an acknowledgment of or an acting upon something that is already true or has already happened. In bookkeeping,

---

1. For a detailed study of the classical and biblical uses of *logizomai* and the related word *logismos* see the article by H. W. Heidland in *Theological Dictionary of the New Testament*, vol. 4, ed. Gerhard Kittel, trans. Geoffrey W. Bromiley (Grand Rapids: Wm. B. Eerdmans, 1967), pp. 284–292.

for example, it means posting in a ledger an amount corresponding to what actually exists. If I "reckon" in my passbook that I have $100, I must really have $100. If not, "reckoning" is the wrong word for me to be using. "Deceiving myself" (or others) would be more like it.

It will also help us in our understanding of Romans 6:11 to recognize that *logizomai* has already been used several times in Romans and that in every case it has referred to recognizing something that is factual. In fact, *logizomai* has appeared fourteen times before now, and it will occur again (in Romans 8 and 9).[2] The chief use has been in chapter 4 (eleven occurrences), where Paul employed it to show how our sins have been reckoned to Christ and punished there, and how his righteousness has been reckoned ("credited") to us. These two "reckonings" are the two parallel sides of justification, and when we studied them (in volume 1) we saw that their strength comes from knowing that they concern realities. They are not just imaginary transactions. Jesus really did die for our sin; he suffered for our transgressions. Similarly, his righteousness really has been transferred to our account, so that God accounts us righteous in him.

This has bearing on Paul's exhortation to us in Romans 6:11. For although he is proceeding in this chapter to the area of what we are to do and actions we are to take, his starting point is nevertheless our counting as true what God has himself already done for us.

This is so critical that I want to ask pointedly: Do you and I really understand this? We cannot go on until we do.

Can I possibly say it more clearly?

Try this: The first step in our growth in holiness is counting as true what is, in fact, true.

And this: The key to living the Christian life lies in first knowing that God has taken us out of Adam and has joined us to Jesus Christ, that we are no longer subject to the reign of sin and death but have been transferred to the kingdom of God's abounding grace.

And this: The secret to a holy life is believing God.

The First Reality: Dead to Sin

In our text Paul says there are two things God has done that we are to count on. First, that we are *dead to sin* if we are Christians. We have already seen how this is to be taken. It does not mean that we are immune to sin or temptation. It does not mean that we will not sin. It means that we are dead to the old life and cannot go back to it.

That is the reality Paul first stated explicitly at the beginning of Romans 6, in verse 2. "We died to sin," he said. In verses 3 and 4, he restated it: We were "baptized into his death" and "buried with him through baptism into death." It was also said in verse 5: "We have been united with him in his

2. Romans 2:15, 26; 4:3–6, 8–11, 22–24; 5:13; 6:11; 8:18; 9:8.

death." Verse 6 said it, too: "Our old self was crucified with him." Verse 7 again made the point that we "died" with Christ. All those statements have been factual. They describe something that has happened.

On the basis of this truth, Paul now tells us to "count" ourselves as having died to sin in Christ Jesus. D. Martyn Lloyd-Jones renders it: "Consider, and keep constantly before you, this truth about yourself."[3] In other words, learn to think of yourself as one who has been delivered from sin's realm.

This is such a pivotal text that it is worth adding a number of things that this statement does *not* mean. Lloyd-Jones lists six of them:

1. It does not mean that it is my duty as a Christian to die to sin. The text has nothing to do with duty. It is concerned with fact.

2. It is not a command for me to die to sin. How can I be told to do what has already been done to me?

3. It does not mean that I am to reckon that sin as a force in me is dead. That would not be true. Sin *is* a force in me, though it is a force whose effective power over me has been broken (v. 6).

4. It does not mean that sin in me has been eradicated.

5. It does not mean that I am dead to sin as long as I am in the process of gaining mastery over it. That would make the statement refer to something experimental, and it does not do that. It refers to a past event.

6. It does not mean that reckoning myself dead to sin makes me dead to sin. That is backwards. What Paul is saying is that, because we *have* died to sin, we are to count on it.[4]

The Second Reality: Alive to God

The second reality Paul says we are to count on is that we are now "alive to God in Christ Jesus." This statement completes the parallel to verse 5, in which Paul said, "If we have been united with him like this in his death, we will certainly also be united with him in his resurrection." It explains how the earlier verse is to be taken. You may remember that when we were discussing verse 5 in the previous study, I stressed that the resurrection referred to there is not the future resurrection of believers at the end of time but rather a present experience of Christ's resurrection life now. That is exactly where verse 11 has brought us. It tells us that just as we have died to sin (and must count on it), so also have we been made alive to God in Jesus Christ (and must count on that also).

This is the positive side of the matter, the side we were beginning to open up in the earlier study. But we only touched on it there. Here we can ask: "Just what does being made alive to God in Jesus Christ mean? What changes have taken place?" Let me suggest a few of them.

3. D. M. Lloyd-Jones, *Romans: An Exposition of Chapter 6, The New Man* (Grand Rapids: Zondervan, 1973), p. 113.
4. Ibid., pp. 116–118.

1. *We have been reconciled to God.* In the earlier chapters of Romans there has been a grim sequence of terms: sin, wrath, judgment, death. But God has lifted us out of that downward-spiraling sequence by a set of opposing realities: grace, obedience, righteousness, eternal life. This means that we were subject to the wrath of God but that now, being in Christ, we are in a favorable position before him. Before, we were God's enemies. Now, we are his friends and, what is more important, he is a friend to us. There is a new relationship.

2. *We have become new creatures in Christ.* Not only is there a new relationship between ourselves and God, which is wonderful in itself, but we have also become something we were not before. In 2 Corinthians, Paul puts it like this: "Therefore, if anyone is in Christ, he is a new creation; the old has gone, the new has come! All this is from God, who reconciled us to himself through Christ . . ." (2 Cor. 5:17–18).

Another way of putting this is to speak of regeneration, or of being born again, which was Jesus' term for it. He told Nicodemus, "You must be born again" (John 3:7). This was a deliberate backward reference to the way in which God breathed life into our first parent Adam, so that he became "a living being" (Gen. 2:7). Before that, Adam was utterly inert, a lifeless form. But when God breathed some of his breath into him Adam became alive to God and all things. Likewise, this is what happens when God breathes new spiritual life into us in the work known as regeneration. We become something we were not before. We have a new life. That life is responsive to the one who gave it.

Before this, the Bible meant nothing to us when we read it or it was read in our hearing. Now the Bible is intensely alive and interesting. We hear the voice of God in it.

Before this, we had no interest in God's people. Christians acted in ways that were foreign to us. Their priorities were different from our own. Now they are our very best friends and co-workers. We love their company and cannot seem to get enough of it.

Before this, coming to church was boring. Now we are alive to God's presence in the service. Our worship times are the very best times of our week.

Before this, service to others and witnessing to the lost seemed strange and senseless, even repulsive. Now they are our chief delight.

What has made the difference? The difference is ourselves. God has changed us. We have become alive to him. We are new creatures.

3. *We are freed from sin's bondage.* Before we died to sin and were made alive to God, we were slaves of our sinful natures. Sin was ruining us. But even when we could see that clearly and acknowledge it, which was not very often, we were still unable to do anything about it. We said, "I've got to stop drinking; it's killing me." Or, "I am going to ruin my reputation if I don't

stop these sexual indulgences." Or, "I've got to get control of my temper, or curb my spending [or whatever]." But we were unable to do it. And even if we did get some control of one important area of our lives, perhaps with the help of a good therapist or friends or a supportive family, the general downward and destructive drift was unchanged. We really were *non posse non peccare* ("not able not to sin"), as Saint Augustine described it.

But, being made alive to God, we discover that we are now freed from that destructive bondage. We still sin, but not always and not as often. And we know that we do not have to. We are now *posse non peccare* ("able not to sin"). We can achieve a real victory.

4. *We are pressing forward to a sure destiny and new goals.* Before, we were not. We were trapped by the world and by its time-bound, evil horizons. Being saved, we know that we are now destined for an eternity of fellowship and bliss with God. We have not reached it yet. We are not perfect. But we echo within what Paul said in describing his new life in Christ to the Philippians: "Not that I have already obtained all this, or have already been made perfect, but I press on to take hold of that for which Christ Jesus took hold of me. Brothers, I do not consider myself yet to have taken hold of it. But one thing I do: Forgetting what is behind and straining toward what is ahead, I press on toward the goal to win the prize for which God has called me heavenward in Christ Jesus" (Phil. 3:12–14).

5. *We can no longer be satisfied with this world and its offerings.* To be sure, the world never did really satisfy us. The world, which is finite, can never adequately fill beings who are made with an infinite capacity for fellowship with and enjoyment of God. But we *thought* the world and its values were satisfying. We expected to be filled.

Now we know that it will never work and that all we see about us, though it sometimes has value in a limited, earthly sense, is nevertheless passing away and will one day be completely forgotten. Our houses will be gone; our televisions will be gone; our beautiful furniture and cars and bank accounts (even our IRAs and Keoghs) will have passed away. So these tangible things no longer have any real hold on us. We have died to them, and in their place we have been made alive to God, who is intangible, invisible, and eternal, and of greater reality and substance than anything else we can imagine.

Therefore, we know ourselves to be only pilgrims here. We are passing through. Like Abraham, we are "looking forward to the city with foundations, whose architect and builder is God" (Heb. 11:10).

"A Man Like Me"

Count yourselves dead to sin but alive to God in Christ Jesus.

I think of Nehemiah as an illustration of what this means and of what our attitude should be. Nehemiah had determined to rebuild the wall of the ruined and abandoned city of Jerusalem, and he was being opposed by the rulers of the rival city-states around him. Two of his opponents were Sanballat of Samaria and Geshem the Arab. They invited him to a conference to be held about a day's journey from Jerusalem on the plain of Ono. This was a ploy to slow down Nehemiah's project and perhaps even to kidnap or murder him. Nehemiah refused to stop the work and go to the meeting. His words were classic: "I am carrying on a great project and cannot go down. Why should the work stop while I leave it and go down to you?" (Neh. 6:3).

Later when the same people tried to frighten him with rumors of a plot on his life, Nehemiah replied, "Should a man like me run away? Or should one like me go into the temple to save his life? I will not go!" (v. 11).

It is that courageous, self-aware attitude to life that I commend to you. "Shall I go on sinning so that grace may increase?" You should be able to answer, "How can such a one as I do it—I who have died to sin and been made alive to God in Christ Jesus?" For that is what has happened to you, if you are a Christian. You have been removed from your former state to another. Your job is to reckon it so, to count on it. You must say, "A person like me has better things to do than to keep sinning."

82

God's Instruments

Romans 6:12–14

Therefore do not let sin reign in your mortal body so that you obey its evil desires. Do not offer the parts of your body to sin, as instruments of wickedness, but rather offer yourselves to God, as those who have been brought from death to life; and offer the parts of your body to him as instruments of righteousness. For sin shall not be your master, because you are not under law, but under grace.

During my college years I majored in English literature, concentrating on the period from Edmund Spencer to William Wordsworth, and the instruction was so good that even now, in strange moments, parts of what I learned then come back to me. This happened as I began my study of Romans 6:12–14. The words that came to mind were from *The Prelude*. In the sixth book of that fourteen-book poem, William Wordsworth is telling of a walking tour he and a friend took from Switzerland up over the Simplon Pass into Italy. They did not know the route, got lost, descended into a ravine, and there inquired of a peasant where they could find the road to Italy. Wordsworth then wrote:

Every word that from the peasant's lips
Came in reply, translated by our feelings,
Ended in this—*that we had crossed the Alps.*

Those words came to mind as I began this study because, in a sense, that is what has happened to us. For more than five and a half chapters we have been laboring up the majestic mountain of doctrine concerning what God has done for us in salvation. Now, for the very first time, we have passed over the highest ridge to verses that tell what we are to do in response to God's action.

To put it in other words, after many detailed studies, our tour has at last enabled us to cross from the high doctrine of justification-by-grace-through-faith to the doctrine of sanctification.

We were already easing into it in our last study, for in Romans 6:11 we encountered Paul's first exhortation to his readers in this epistle. He told them to "count" upon everything he had previously told them, to "reckon" those things so. Now he comes to four specific exhortations, prefaced by the important connecting word *therefore.* Because of what he has said, believers are to do the following: "Therefore *do not let sin reign* in your mortal body so that you obey its evil desires. *Do not offer* the parts of your body to sin, as instruments of wickedness, but rather *offer yourselves* to God, as those who have been brought from death to life; and *offer* the parts of your body to him as instruments of righteousness. For sin shall not be your master, because you are not under law, but under grace" (emphases added).

Principles of Sanctification

Since this is the first direct teaching about sanctification in Romans, it is important that we understand what is being said. To do that, we need to look at this passage as a whole to see what principles about sanctification are taught here. Then we need to apply those teachings in the most practical terms possible.

We start with the principles. What are they?

1. *Sin is not dead in Christians, even in the most mature and pious Christians, but rather is something always to be struggled against.* I have already said this in a variety of ways in our previous studies, but it needs to be repeated here for two reasons. First, this principle is clear from the passage. There is no point in telling us not to offer the parts of our bodies to sin, as "instruments of wickedness," but rather to offer them to God, "as instruments of righteousness," unless we have a tendency to do the former. The reason we have to fight against sin is that we are sinners.

Second, there are some people who tend toward a kind of perfectionism in which they can claim either that sin is not in them or that the sin that *is* in them can in time somehow be eradicated. This doctrine is not only wrong (the whole of Scripture stands against it), but it is also a source of frustration for those who have come to believe in their own perfection but who nevertheless constantly find themselves fighting against sin.

2. *Sin's hold on us is in or through our bodies.* This is something we have not explored earlier (except in reference to Rom. 6:6). But it is very important, and we need to examine it carefully. When I say that sin's hold on us is in or through our bodies, I do not mean that sin is in our bodies as opposed to being in us, as if by saying that it is in our bodies we are claiming that we are not sinners or that sin is only external to us. Of course, we are sinners, and sin is not merely external to us but rather is within. But here is the point: So far as that new man about whom Paul has been writing is concerned—that new creature I have become by being taken out of Adam by God and by being joined to Christ—that new man is dead to sin, so that sin's hold is no longer actually on me but on my body.

Certainly we cannot miss noticing how directly, literally, and strongly Paul emphasizes our actual physical bodies in these verses. In verse 12 he refers to our "mortal body," that is, the body of our flesh that is dying. In verse 13 he twice refers to "the parts of" our bodies, that is, to our hands, feet, eyes, tongues and so forth. It is through these physical parts of our bodies that sin operates and through which it maintains its strong hold on us.

3. *Sin can reign in or dominate our bodies.* It cannot dominate or destroy that new person that I have become in Christ. That new "me" will always abhor sin and yearn for righteousness—and it will have it, because God is determined to produce the holy character of Christ in his people. But sin can certainly dominate my body. I can become a slave to its cravings. If this were not so, it would be pointless for Paul to say "Do not let sin reign in your mortal body so that you obey its evil desires," as he does.

4. *Although sin can reign in or dominate our bodies, it does not need to.* In other words, although it is possible for us to "offer the parts of [our] body to sin, as instruments of wickedness," we do not need to do this. On the contrary, being now joined to Jesus Christ, we have his new life within and his power available to us. Having been *non posse non peccare* ("not able not to sin"), to use Saint Augustine's phrase, we have now become *posse non peccare* ("able not to sin"). We often do sin; that is why Paul is urging us not to yield our bodies to it. But we no longer need to. We have an alternative.

5. This leads to the last and positive truth: *As Christians, we can now offer the parts of our bodies to God as instruments of righteousness.* This is the thrust of the passage. It is what Paul is urging on us.

The Parts of Our Bodies

There are many ways one can approach the subject of sanctification. Paul himself does it in several ways. But I do not know a more practical, balanced, or down-to-earth way of speaking about how to live a holy life or grow in righteousness than the way in which Paul does it here. He has given us one easy-to-grasp principle in verse 11: "Count yourselves dead to sin but alive to God in Christ Jesus." Now he tells us how to give practical expression to that great principle. It is by what we do with our bodies. What does that mean? The answers come by considering the body's parts and their potential for doing both good and evil.

The Mind

We begin with the mind because, although we like to think that who we are is largely defined by our minds, and thus separate our minds from our bodies, our minds are actually parts of our bodies, so the victory we need to achieve must begin here. I take you to Romans 12:1–2, where Paul is writing much as he does in Romans 6. "Therefore, I urge you, brothers, in view of God's mercy, to offer your bodies as living sacrifices, holy and pleasing to God—this is your spiritual act of worship. Do not conform any longer to the pattern of this world, but be transformed by *the renewing of your mind.* Then you will be able to test and approve what God's will is—his good, pleasing and perfect will" (emphasis added).

That text begins in nearly the same way as Romans 6:12–14 ("Therefore . . . offer the parts of your body to him . . ."). But when Paul begins to spell this out, strikingly the very first body part he mentions is the mind.

Have you ever carefully thought through that what you do with your mind will determine a great deal of what you will become as a Christian? If you fill your mind with the products of our secular culture, you will remain secular and sinful. If you fill your head with trashy "pop" novels, you will begin to live like the trashy heroes and heroines whose illicit romances you read about. If you do nothing but watch television, you will begin to think like the scoundrels on "Dallas" or "Falcon Crest" or the weekday soap operas. And you will act like them, too. On the other hand, if you feed your mind on the Bible and Christian publications, train it by godly conversation, and discipline it to critique what you see and hear elsewhere by applying biblical truths to those ideas, you will grow in godliness and become increasingly useful to God. Your mind will become an instrument for righteousness.

Some years ago, John R. W. Stott wrote a book entitled *Your Mind Matters* in which he bemoaned the growth of "mindless Christianity" and showed how a proper use of our minds is necessary for growth in all areas of our Christian experience. He related it to worship, faith, the quest for holiness, guidance, presenting the gospel to others, and exercising spiritual gifts.

He asks at one point, "Has God spoken to us, and shall we not listen to his words? Has God renewed our mind through Christ, and shall we not think with it? Is God going to judge us by his Word, and shall we not be wise and build our house upon this rock?"[1]

And there is something else: If Christians would offer their minds to God to be renewed by him, they would begin to think and express themselves as Christians and would begin to recover something of what Harry Blamires calls "a Christian mind."

Blamires writes:

There is no longer a Christian mind. There is still, of course, a Christian ethic, a Christian practice, and a Christian spirituality. As a moral being, the modern Christian subscribes to a code other than that of the non-Christian. As a member of the Church, he undertakes obligations and observances ignored by the non-Christian. As a spiritual being, in prayer and meditation, he strives to cultivate a dimension of life unexplored by the non-Christian. But as a *thinking* being, the modern Christian has succumbed to secularization. . . . Except over a very narrow field of thinking, chiefly touching questions of strictly personal conduct, we Christians in the modern world accept, for the purpose of mental activity, a frame of reference constructed by the secular mind and a set of criteria reflecting secular evaluations.[2]

If the use of the mind is important in sanctification, as I maintain it is, and if we lack "a Christian mind" in our day, as Blamires claims, is it any wonder that so many Christians today are for the most part indistinguishable from the non-Christians around them? Obviously, if we are going to grow in holiness, either as individuals or as a church, we must start here.

Here is a simple goal for you in this area. For every secular book you read, make it your goal also to read one good Christian book, a book that can stretch your mind spiritually.

Our Eyes and Ears

The mind is not the only part of our bodies through which we receive ideas and impressions and which must therefore be offered to God as an instrument of righteousness. We also receive impressions through our eyes and ears. These, too, must be surrendered to God.

Do you remember Achan? He was the Israelite soldier who participated in the battle of Jericho under Joshua but who disobeyed God's command not to take any of the spoils but rather to dedicate them to God. As Achan afterward confessed, "When I saw in the plunder a beautiful robe from Babylonia, two hundred shekels of silver and a wedge of gold weighing fifty

1. John R. W. Stott, *Your Mind Matters: The Place of the Mind in the Christian Life* (Downers Grove, Ill.: InterVarsity Press, 1972), p. 26.
2. Harry Blamires, *The Christian Mind: How Should a Christian Think?* (Ann Arbor, Mich.: Servant Books, 1963), pp. 3, 4.

shekels, I coveted them and took them. They are hidden in the ground inside my tent with the silver underneath" (Josh. 7:21). Achan was stoned for his sin. But what caused it? The "lust of his eyes" (1 John 2:16). Achan's eyes became instruments of wickedness instead of instruments for his growth in holiness.

It is no different today. Sociologists tell us that by the age of twenty-one the average young person has been bombarded by 300,000 commercial messages, all arguing from the identical basic assumption: *personal gratification is the dominant goal in life.*[3] Television and other modern means of communication put the acquisition of material things before godliness; in fact, they never mention godliness at all. How, then, are you going to grow in godliness if you are constantly watching television or reading printed ads or listening to secular radio?

Do not get me wrong. I am not advocating an evangelical monasticism in which we retreat from the culture, though it is far better to retreat from it than perish in it. But somehow the secular input must be overbalanced by the spiritual.

One simple goal might be for you to spend as many hours studying your Bible, praying, and going to church as watching television.

Our Tongues

The tongue is also part of the body, and what we do with it is important. James, the Lord's brother, must have thought about this a great deal, because he says more about the tongue and its power for either good or evil than any other writer of Scripture. He wrote, ". . . the tongue is a small part of the body, but it makes great boasts. Consider what a great forest is set on fire by a small spark. The tongue also is a fire, a world of evil among the parts of the body. It corrupts the whole person, sets the whole course of his life on fire, and is itself set on fire by hell" (James 3:5–6).

If your tongue is not given to God as an instrument of righteousness in his hands, what James writes will be true of you. You do not need to be a Hitler and plunge the world into armed conflict to do evil with your tongue. A little bit of gossip will do. A casual lie or slander will suffice.

What you need to do is use your tongue to praise and serve God. For one thing, you should learn how to recite Scripture with it. You probably can repeat many popular song lyrics. Can you not also use your tongue to speak God's words? How about worship? You should use your tongue to praise God by means of hymns and other Christian songs. Above all, you should use your tongue to witness to others about the person and work of Christ. That is the task Jesus gave you when he said, "You will be my witnesses" (Acts 1:8).

3. Mike Bellah, *Baby Boom Believers: Why We Think We Need It All and How to Survive When We Don't Get It* (Wheaton, Ill.: Tyndale House, 1988), p. 27.

Here is another goal for you if you want to grow in godliness: Use your tongue as much to tell others about Jesus as for idle conversation.

Our Hands and Feet

Our hands and feet determine what we do and where we go. So when we are considering how we might offer the parts of our body to God as instruments of righteousness, let us not forget them.

I think of several important passages in this regard. In 1 Thessalonians 4:11–12, Paul writes of using our hands profitably so we might be self-supporting and not dependent on anybody: "Make it your ambition to lead a quiet life, to mind your own business and to work with your hands, just as we told you, so that your daily life may win the respect of outsiders and so that you will not be dependent on anybody." Similarly, in Ephesians 4:28, Paul writes of working so that we will have something to give to others who are needy: "He who has been stealing must steal no longer, but must work, doing something useful with his own hands, that he may have something to share with those in need."

And what of our feet? A few chapters further on in Romans, Paul writes of the need that others have for the gospel: "How, then, can they call on the one they have not believed in? And how can they believe in the one of whom they have not heard? And how can they hear without someone preaching to them? And how can they preach unless they are sent? As it is written, 'How beautiful are the feet of those who bring good news!'" (Rom. 10:14–15).

Where do *your* feet take you?

Do you allow them to take you to where Christ is denied or blasphemed? Do they take you to places where sin is openly practiced? Are you spending most of your time soaking up the world's entertainment or loitering in bars or the "hot" singles clubs? You will not grow in godliness there. On the contrary, you will fall from righteous conduct. Instead, let your feet carry you into the company of those who love and serve the Lord. Or, when you go into the world, let it be for the purpose of serving the world and witnessing to its people in Christ's name.

Here is another goal: For every special secular function you attend, determine to attend a Christian function also. And when you go to a secular function, do so as a witness by word and action for the Lord Jesus Christ.

A Warfare and a Race

What we are actually engaged in is spiritual warfare, an ongoing battle against sin, for our own growth in grace and for the good of others. And, like all soldiers who are facing some great conflict, we are to train ourselves physically and steel our wills for the enterprise.

Paul thought in these terms, sometimes speaking of a warfare in which the followers of Christ are to clothe themselves with God's armor (cf. Eph.

6:10–18), sometimes speaking of a race. "Fight the good fight of the faith . . ." he says in 1 Timothy 6:12. "I have fought the good fight, I have finished the race, I have kept the faith," he says in 2 Timothy 4:7.

I like the way Paul puts it in 1 Corinthians: "Do you not know that in a race all the runners run, but only one gets the prize? Run in such a way as to get the prize. Everyone who competes in the games goes into strict training. They do it to get a crown that will not last; but we do it to get a crown that will last forever. Therefore I do not run like a man running aimlessly; I do not fight like a man beating the air. No, I beat my body and make it my slave so that after I have preached to others, I myself will not be disqualified for the prize" (1 Cor. 9:24–27).

Perhaps you have seen the recent television advertisement for a certain brand of athletic shoe in which six or seven very energetic young people are going through their workouts. The scenes shift quickly and the tempo increases rapidly throughout the commercial until it all suddenly comes to an abrupt halt and three words appear on the screen in bold black letters: "Just do it."

That is what I recommend to you. You have been waiting through five and a half chapters of Romans for something to do. Now you have that something. You know what it is. So do it. Just do it. "Do not offer the parts of your body to sin, as instruments of righteousness, but rather offer yourselves to God, as those who have been brought from death to life; and offer the parts of your body to him as instruments of righteousness."

Why should you do this? Why should you submit to such rigorous training? It is not because you are driven to do it. It is because you have been liberated from sin by the grace of the Lord Jesus Christ and want to do it. You want to live for him. This is why Paul ends by saying, "For sin shall not be your master, because you are not under law, but under grace" (v. 14).

83

Whose Slave Are You?

Romans 6:15–18

What then? Shall we sin because we are not under law but under grace? By no means! Don't you know that when you offer yourselves to someone to obey him as slaves, you are slaves to the one whom you obey—whether you are slaves to sin, which leads to death, or to obedience, which leads to righteousness? But thanks be to God that, though you used to be slaves to sin, you wholeheartedly obeyed the form of teaching to which you were entrusted. You have been set free from sin and have become slaves to righteousness.

The point of this next study is difficult for most people to accept, so I want to state it simply at the beginning and allow the rest of the chapter to expound and defend it. The point is this: *There is no such thing as absolute freedom for anyone.* No human is free to do everything he or she may want to do. There is one being in the universe who *is totally* free, of course. That is God. But all others are limited by or enslaved by someone or something. As a result, the only meaningful question in this area is: Who or what are you serving?

Ray C. Stedman, pastor of the Peninsula Bible Church in Palo Alto, California, tells of walking down the street in Los Angeles one day and seeing a man coming toward him with a sign hung over his shoulders. The sign read: "I am a slave for Christ." After the man had passed him, Stedman turned around to look after this rather eccentric individual and saw that on his back there was another sign that said: "Whose slave are you?"

That is exactly the point of this passage. Since you and I are human beings and not God, we can never be autonomous. We must either be slaves to sin or slaves of Jesus Christ.

But here is the wonderful and very striking thing: *To be a slave of Jesus Christ is true freedom.*

The Chapter's Second Half

All this flows from our study of Romans 6, but we need to back up a bit to find our place in Paul's argument.

The verses we are considering here are verses 15–18, the start of a longer section that extends to the end of the chapter. A glance at this section shows that it is parallel to the first half of the chapter, that is, to verses 1–14. Each section deals with a nearly identical question. The first verse of section one asks, "What shall we say, then? Shall we go on sinning so that grace may increase?" The first verse of section two raises the same issue: "What then? Shall we sin because we are not under law but under grace?" (v. 15).

These questions are followed by identical responses: "By no means!" (vv. 2, 15). From this point on, the two sections follow parallel tracks as Paul explains why it is impossible for the believer in Christ to continue in sin and why, by contrast, Christians must yield the parts of their bodies to God as instruments of righteousness. These arguments are so close to one another that it is possible to lift terms from one section and transfer them to the other without any real change in meaning.

Yet the two halves of Romans 6 are not identical. They have the same objective—to show that the believer in Christ cannot go on sinning. But they make this important point in different, though complementary, ways.

The first section comes out of the discussion in chapter 5, in which Paul argued that the Christian is not under law but is under grace and that grace will triumph. He shows that grace does not lead to sin, the reason being that we have been joined to Christ. If we have been joined to Christ, the past is behind and there is no place for us to go in life but forward in righteous conduct. The second section comes out of the discussion in Romans 6:1–14, particularly verse 14, in which Paul rejects law as a vehicle of righteousness. He argues that freedom from law does not lead to sin either. The reason he gives is that we have been freed from law, not to become autonomous creatures (which we cannot be on any account), but to be slaves of God. We must be slaves to righteousness.

Two Errors

Paul was answering objections to the doctrine of salvation by grace that were coming from two sides, just as they come to us today.

On one side were Jewish traditionalists with a commitment to the law of Moses. They argued that if law is rejected as a way of salvation, which Paul obviously was doing, immorality and all other vices inevitably follow. Paul shows that it does not work that way. In fact, he shows the opposite. He shows:

1. The law does not lead to righteousness, for the simple reason that it is unable to produce righteousness in anyone. The law can only condemn.

2. Paradoxically, it is only by being delivered from the law and its condemnation, through union with Jesus Christ, that we are empowered to do what the law requires.

The other objection came not from Jewish legalists, but from people we call Antinomians, those who reject the law not only as a way of salvation but even as an expression of proper conduct. Antinomianism says, "Since we are free from law, we can do anything we please. We are free to go on sinning. In fact, we can wallow in it."

Paul answers both of these errors in this chapter of Romans.

Five Sound Reasons

"Shall we sin because we are not under law but under grace?" The answer, as we already know by now, is: "By no means!"

"Why not?" we ask.

In this section Paul gives five sound reasons.

1. *Sin is slavery.* The first reason Christians must not sin, even though they are not under law but under grace, is that sin is actually slavery, and it would be folly to be delivered from slavery only to return to it again. The difficulty here is that sin is rarely seen by us in this way, that is, in its true colors. Instead of being presented as slavery, it is usually described as the very essence of freedom. This was what the devil told Eve in the Garden of Eden when he argued, "Don't be bound by God's word. Be free. Eat of the tree and become as God, knowing good and evil."

Years ago, before the current thaw in Sino-American relations, some Christians in Hong Kong had an interview with an eighty-two-year-old woman who had come out of China just a short while before. She was a believer in Christ, but her vocabulary was filled with the terminology of communism, which was all she had been hearing for decades. One of her favorite expressions was "the liberation."

The interviewers asked her, "When you were back in China, were you free to gather together with other Christians to worship?"

"Oh, no," she answered. "Since the liberation, no one is permitted to gather together for Christian services."

"But surely you were able to get together in small groups to discuss the Christian faith," they continued.

"No," she said. "We were not. Since the liberation, all such meetings are forbidden."

"Were you free to read your Bible?"

"Since the liberation, no one is free to read the Bible."

The conversation shows that "freedom" is not in the word but in the reality. Remember that, the next time someone suggests that you have to sin to be free. Merely attaching the word *freedom* to sin does not make sin a way of liberation. The truth is that sin is bondage. It enslaves us so that we are unable to escape its grasp later, even if we want to. If you give way to sensual passions, you will become a slave to those passions. If you give way to greed, you will become a slave to greed. So also for every other vice and wrongdoing.

2. *Sin leads to death.* The second reason we must not sin, even though we are not under law but under grace, is that sin leads to death. Paul says this several times in these verses: "sin, which leads to death" (v. 16), "Those things result in death!" (v. 21), and "For the wages of sin is death" (v. 23).

Again, this is not what we are usually told. It is not what the devil told Eve either. God had said, "You must not eat from the tree of the knowledge of good and evil, for when you eat of it you will surely die" (Gen. 2:17). The devil countered, "You will not surely die. . . . For God knows that when you eat of it your eyes will be opened, and you will be like God, knowing good and evil" (Gen. 3:4–5).

Here was a true crisis for the woman. God said, "You will die." The devil said, "You will not surely die." Who was right? Who was she to believe?

The woman decided to resolve the dilemma for herself. She examined the tree and saw that it was "good for food and pleasing to the eye, and also desirable for gaining wisdom" (Gen. 3:6). She concluded, "How can it be wrong when it feels so right?" So she took some of the fruit, ate it, and then gave some to Adam, who also ate of it.

What happened? They died! They died in their spirits instantly, for the fellowship they had enjoyed with God up to this point was broken, which they showed by hiding from God when he came to them later in the garden. Their personalities began to decay, for they started to lie and shift the blame to one another. At last their bodies also died, as God said: ". . . dust you are and to dust you will return" (Gen. 3:19).

The only bright spot was that God also graciously promised a Redeemer who would save them from their sin.

Do not listen to those who tell you that sin is harmless. Above all, do not trust your own judgment in these matters. You are not able to judge in such situations. You must trust God, who tells you that to sin is to die. In fact, being a sinner, you are already dying. Your moral life is decaying. Your body is inclining to the grave. One day you will experience the second death, which is to be separated from God in hell forever—unless God saves you first. The only sensible reaction to sin is to turn from it and seek salvation in the Lord Jesus Christ.

3. *Christians have been delivered from sin's slavery.* The third reason Christians are not to continue in sin, even though they are not under law but under grace, is that they have been delivered by Jesus from sin's tyranny if they truly are Christians. This is so wonderful that Paul actually breaks into a doxology or "praise to God" at this point, saying, "But thanks be to God that, though you used to be slaves to sin . . . you have been set free from sin and have become slaves to righteousness" (vv. 17–18).

This is the meaning of what former Princeton Seminary professor B. B. Warfield called the most "precious" terms in the Christian's vocabulary: "Redeemer" and "redemption."[1] Redemption means to buy out of slavery to sin. This was accomplished for us by Jesus, who is our Redeemer. We were slaves to sin, that cruel taskmaster. But Jesus paid the price of our redemption by his death. He purchased us with his blood: "For you know that it was not with perishable things such as silver or gold that you were redeemed from the empty way of life handed down to you from your forefathers, but with the precious blood of Christ, a lamb without blemish or defect" (1 Peter 1:18–19).

This is the very purpose of the atonement. How, then, can those who have been redeemed return to sinful living? To do so would be to repudiate Christ, to turn from everything he stands for. It would be apostasy. No true Christian can do it.

4. *The same work that has delivered Christians from sin's slavery has also made them slaves of God, which is true freedom.* The fourth of Paul's arguments for why Christians cannot continue in sin, even though they are not under law but under grace, is that the same act of Christ that has delivered us from sin has also made us "slaves of God" (v. 22). By his act of redemption, Jesus has purchased men and women for himself, that is, to serve him.

"Ah," says someone. "What gain is that? What advantage is it to be freed from one master if all it means is that we become slaves of another?"

Well, it would be a significant gain even if we were slaves in a physical sense and were set free from a cruel master to become a slave to one who was kind and had our best interests at heart. That would be a welcome change, and it is part of the picture, for God is as good, kind, and loving a

---

1. Benjamin Breckinridge Warfield, "'Redeemer' and 'Redemption,'" in *The Person and Work of Christ*, ed. Samuel G. Craig (Philadelphia: The Presbyterian and Reformed Publishing Company, 1970), pp. 325–348. The address first appeared in *The Princeton Theological Review*, vol. xiv, 1916, pp. 177–201.

master as sin is cruel and harmful. But there is more to it than that. The Bible teaches that this "slavery" actually brings freedom.

What is this freedom? It is not autonomy, a license to do absolutely anything at all. True freedom is "the ability to fulfill one's destiny, to function in terms of one's ultimate goal."[2]

Real freedom means doing what is right.

Do you remember the conversation the Lord Jesus Christ had with the Jewish religious leaders of his day, as recorded in John's Gospel? Jesus had been speaking about the source of his teachings, and some of the Jews had believed on him in a rudimentary way. So he encouraged them to remain with him and continue to learn from him, saying, "If you hold to my teaching [that is, continue in it], you are really my disciples. Then you will know the truth, and the truth will set you free" (John 8:31–32).

This infuriated some of his listeners, presumably those who were not true believers, because they did not like the suggestion that they were not free—just as many resent any similar suggestion today. They replied, "We are Abraham's descendants and have never been slaves of anyone. How can you say that we shall be set free?" (v. 33). This was a ridiculous answer, of course. The Jews had been slaves to the Egyptians for many years prior to the exodus. During the period of the judges there were at least seven occasions when the nation came under the rule of foreigners. There was also the seventy-year-long Babylonian captivity. In fact, even while they were talking to Jesus they were being watched over by occupying Roman soldiers, and they were carrying coins in their pockets that testified to Rome's domination of their economy. It was this latter fact that probably made them so sensitive to the suggestion that they were not truly free.

But instead of reminding them of these obvious facts, Jesus answered on a spiritual level, saying, "I tell you the truth, everyone who sins is a slave to sin. . . . So if the Son sets you free, you will be free indeed" (vv. 34, 36).

What kind of freedom was Jesus talking about? True freedom, of course, the only real freedom there is. It is not liberty to do just anything at all. If we choose sin, the result is bondage. True freedom comes through knowing the gospel and being committed to the Lord Jesus Christ in his service.

Can I put this sharply? The only real freedom you are ever going to know, either in this life or in the live to come, is the freedom of serving Jesus Christ. And this means a life of righteousness. Anything else is really slavery, regardless of what the world may promise you through its lies and false teaching.

5. *The end of this second, desirable slavery is righteousness.* This leads to Paul's last point, the fifth reason why Christians must not continue in sin, even though they have been freed from law and are under grace. It is that the end of this second, desirable slavery to God and Jesus Christ is righteous-

---

2. Roger R. Nicole, "Freedom and Law," *Tenth: An Evangelical Quarterly,* July 1976, p. 23.

ness. True Christianity can never lead to license, the accusation refuted by Paul in this passage. Since it is liberation from sin in order to become a servant of God and of Jesus Christ, Christianity must inevitably lead to what God desires, which is righteousness.

The Obedience of Faith

I close this study by asking you to look at one more word: *obedience*. It occurs in verse 16 in the phrase "slaves . . . to obedience," and it is amplified by the verb *obey*, which occurs three times more in these verses (once in verse 16, and twice in verse 17). This is an important idea.

It is puzzling, too, at least at first glance.

Why? Because in verse 16 it occurs as the opposite of sin ("slaves to *sin* . . . or to *obedience*"), which does not seem exactly right to us. Instead of "obedience" we would expect the word *righteousness*. Then, in verse 17, it occurs where we would normally expect the idea of "faith" ("you wholeheartedly *obeyed* the form of teaching to which you were entrusted"). We would more naturally say, "You wholeheartedly *believed* the gospel."

One reason why Paul uses the word *obedience* is that it carries through the image he has been developing, namely that of being a slave either to sin or of Jesus Christ. It is the function of a slave to obey his or her master. But the use of the term goes beyond this, since obedience is an essential requirement of all who would follow Christ. And not just afterward, as if we are called first to believe and then to obey. Obedience is the very essence of believing. It is what belief is all about.

When I am teaching about faith I usually say that faith has three elements: (1) an intellectual element (we must believe in something; this is the gospel); (2) an emotional element (the content of that gospel must touch us personally); and (3) commitment (we must give ourselves to Jesus in personal and often costly discipleship). It is in this last area that obedience is so critical. For, if obedience is not present, we have not committed ourselves to Christ, even though we may believe in him in some sense. And without that commitment we are not saved; we are not true Christians.

Have you ever considered how important obedience is in the Bible's treatment of its chief characters? I will cite two examples.

The first is Joshua. Obedience was the chief characteristic of this very great man's life, for at the beginning of his story he was challenged to obey God in all things—"Be careful to obey all the law my servant Moses gave you; do not turn from it to the right or to the left, that you may be successful wherever you go" (Josh. 1:7b)—and this is precisely what he did, to the very end. His whole life was marked by obedience.

The other example is Abraham, who was such a giant of faith that he is praised for his faith four times in Hebrews 11. His faith was so great that when God promised him a son in his old age, though he was past the age of engendering a child and his wife Sarah was past the age of conceiving one,

Abraham "did not waver through unbelief regarding the promise of God, but was strengthened in his faith and gave glory to God, being fully persuaded that God had power to do what he had promised" (Rom. 4:20–21).

But even this was not the highest achievement of Abraham's faith. It is not the act for which he is chiefly praised in Hebrews.

The high point of Abraham's long life of faith was reached when God told him to sacrifice his son Isaac on Mount Moriah. Abraham showed an incredible faith here, believing that if God told him to sacrifice his son and if his son had not yet had the children God had promised he would have, then God would have to raise Isaac from the dead in order to fulfill his promise (cf. Heb. 11:19). But, in Genesis, where the story is told, the quality for which Abraham is praised by God is not faith but obedience: "Because you have done this and have not withheld your son, your only son, I will surely bless you and make your descendants as numerous as the stars in the sky and as the sand on the seashore. Your descendants will take possession of the cities of their enemies, and through your offspring all nations on earth will be blessed, *because you have obeyed me*" (Gen. 22:15–18, emphasis added).

There is no escaping it! Either we obey sin, which leads to death, and are enslaved by it, or we have been freed from sin to serve God. If we have been freed from sin, we will serve God. There is just no other option.

84

The Bottom Line

Romans 6:19–22

I put this in human terms because you are weak in your natural selves. Just as you used to offer the parts of your body in slavery to impurity and to ever-increasing wickedness, so now offer them in slavery to righteousness leading to holiness. When you were slaves to sin, you were free from the control of righteousness. What benefit did you reap at that time from the things you are now ashamed of? Those things result in death! But now that you have been set free from sin and have become slaves to God, the benefit you reap leads to holiness, and the result is eternal life.

We are coming to the end of Romans 6 and therefore to the end of a very important Bible chapter dealing with the Christian life. Strangely, the chapter is something of a parenthesis, as I pointed out when we began to study it—just as the following chapter, Romans 7, is also a parenthesis.

Paul had been talking about the permanent nature of salvation. This was his theme in chapter 5, and it is the dominant note of the magnificent eighth chapter that is still to come. Between these two chapters he has been exploring the errors of people who would say, on the one hand, "If salvation by the grace of God in Jesus Christ is a sure thing—if it cannot be lost—why should we not go on living a life of sin? We will be saved anyway" and, on the other hand, "If we are saved by the grace of God apart from the Old Testament law, why shouldn't we be lawless?" In the verses immediately preceding the ones we will study here, the apostle has answered the first question by showing that being a Christian means being delivered from a slavery to sin so that we might become willing slaves of God, which is true freedom. We cannot go on serving the old master.

This means that "being a Christian" and "not being a Christian" are two mutually exclusive categories. Therefore, once we have passed from our former unbelieving state and become a Christian, we have no choice but to go forward in the Christian life, which means serving God in holiness.

John R. W. Stott puts it like this:

> Here then are two completely different lives, lives totally opposed to one another—the life of the old self, and the life of the new. They are what Jesus termed the broad road that leads to destruction, and the narrow road that leads to life. Paul calls them two slaveries. By birth we are slaves of sin; by grace and faith we have become slaves of God. The slavery of sin yields no return, except a steady, moral deterioration and finally death. The slavery of God yields the precious return of sanctification and finally eternal life. The argument of this section, then, is that our conversion—this act of yielding or surrender to God—leads to a status of slavery, and slavery involves obedience.[1]

Whom Will You Serve?

Paul has been using the analogy of slavery to make his point, a fact he alludes to in verse 19, saying, "I put this in human terms because you are weak in your natural selves."[2] And the point has been that in life we must serve either of two masters. Either we must serve sin, or we must serve God. There is no neutral ground.

This is Paul's main point. But do we really believe this? If we understood it and really believed it, would we sin as frequently or as easily as we sometimes do? Would we take sin lightly and be as casual in the pursuit of righteousness as we often are?

1. John R. W. Stott, *Men Made New: An Exposition of Romans 5–8* (Grand Rapids: Baker Book House, 1984), p. 55.
2. Paul's words do not mean that he is speaking as a mere man, rather than as an apostle, that is, giving an uninspired analogy. He means that he is borrowing an analogy from common life to assist those who might have trouble understanding spiritual things. And, like all analogies, it is not perfect. "After all, the new life in Christ is not 'slavery' as it exists among men; it is the highest and only freedom. But the institution of slavery does service to set forth the totality of our commitment to God in that emancipation from the bondage of sin which union with Christ involves" (John Murray, *The Epistle to the Romans* [Grand Rapids: Wm. B. Eerdmans, 1968], p. 233).

The Doctrine of the Two Ways

What Paul has been describing in these verses is the doctrine of the two ways, which is found throughout the Bible.

The best-known statement of it is in the words of Jesus recorded in the Sermon on the Mount. The last section of that sermon lists a series of contrasts among which choices must be made: two gates and two roads, two trees and their two types of fruit, two houses and two foundations. The part regarding the two ways says, "Enter through the narrow gate. For wide is the gate and broad is the road that leads to destruction, and many enter through it. But small is the gate and narrow the road that leads to life, and only a few find it" (Matt. 7:13–14). The point is that a person can be on only one of these two roads, because the roads are entirely different and lead in opposite directions.

The classic statement of the doctrine is in Psalm 1, which contains the very points Paul makes in Romans 6. It describes two different categories of people: "the wicked" and "the righteous."

The psalm shows the progression within each of these two categories. On the one hand, there is progression in wickedness. Those in the first category begin by "walk[ing] in the counsel of the wicked," then "stand in the way of sinners" and finally "sit in the seat of mockers" (v. 1). In other words, they become increasingly settled in ungodliness by their practice of it. Moreover, their lives bear no fruit. They are barren plants, "like chaff that the wind blows away" (v. 4). On the other hand, there is progression in godliness. The righteous man's "delight is in the law of the LORD," and he produces lasting fruit; he is like a "tree planted by streams of water, which yields its fruit in season and whose leaf does not wither. Whatever he does prospers" (vv. 2–3).

Finally, the psalm gives the ends of the two types of people: "Therefore the wicked will not stand in the judgment, nor sinners in the assembly of the righteous" (v. 5), that is, the company of the righteous in heaven. "For the LORD watches over the way of the righteous, but the way of the wicked will perish" (v. 6). The end of the righteous is eternal life. The end of the wicked is judgment.

It should be evident that this is exactly what Paul is saying in these verses, though his slavery analogy does not speak of scoundrels collecting by the gates of the city or the scattering of useless chaff at harvest time. Nor does he refer to the "slaves to God" as fruitful trees. But he does describe two different pathways.

The first path starts with slavery to sin. It is the condition into which each of us is born, for none of us is born righteous. Sin is our cruel master; it drives us along. By ourselves we are unable to escape this harsh tyranny.

This leads to "impurity and to ever-increasing wickedness" (v. 19). Impurity refers to sin as it affects the individual. It means personal defilement, particularly by sins that are opposed to chastity. Wickedness refers to violation of the divine or human laws. Robert Haldane says that the former "refers principally to the pollution, the other to the guilt of sin."[3] Moreover, this wickedness is progressive! The Greek text is particularly suggestive at this point, for it literally reads "you have yielded your members slaves . . . *to wickedness unto wickedness.*" In other words, sin is a downhill path, as Paul has already shown in Romans 1. Those who begin by walking in the counsel of the wicked soon find themselves standing in the way of sinners and eventually sitting in the seat of mockers.

The end of this destructive path is death, which Paul mentions three times in this section (vv. 16, 21, 23). This does not mean physical death, since the righteous as well as the wicked experience physical death. It means the full penalty of sin, which is eternal punishment.

The second path starts with slavery to God, which God accomplishes in us and which is actually freedom. This path leads to "righteousness," and righteousness leads to "holiness" (v. 19). These words parallel the principle that "impurity" leads to "ever-increasing wickedness" and describe the contrary experience of one who has been claimed by God. "Righteousness" in this context means primarily righteous acts. "Holiness" is an inner state characterized by conformity to the will and character of God. The phrase "righteousness leading to holiness" teaches that the practice of outward godliness leads to inward godliness; that is, doing right things actually brings a person along the pathway of spiritual growth.

The end of this healthy, developing path is eternal life (v. 22). In this context "eternal life" refers to the fruit, or end result, of a godly life, not the life itself or its reward. It refers to eternal fellowship with God, who is its source.

Just Do It!

The point of Paul's analysis is to exhort Christians to live holy lives, though the application is made at the beginning of the paragraph rather than at the end: "Just as you used to offer the parts of your body in slavery to impurity and to ever-increasing wickedness, so now offer the parts of your body in slavery to righteousness leading to holiness" (v. 19b).

What more can be said about this application?

The first thing we notice is that it is an almost identical exhortation to the one found in verse 13 in the first half of the chapter. At that point Paul had already shown that the one who has become a Christian has died to sin and been made alive to God in Christ. His argument was that, because this is so, it is for us to recognize this change and act on it: "Count yourselves dead to sin but alive to God in Christ." How are we to do that? What does it

3. Robert Haldane, *An Exposition of the Epistle to the Romans* (MacDill AFB: MacDonald Publishing, 1958), p. 263.

mean to count ourselves dead to sin but alive in Christ? The answer was: "Do not offer the parts of your body to sin, as instruments of wickedness, but rather offer yourselves to God, as those who have been brought from death to life; and offer the parts of your body to him as instruments of righteousness" (v. 13).

Notice that this is precisely what Paul says all over again in verse 19. He refers to the parts of our bodies and contrasts our former offering of them to sin with our present offering of them to righteousness. The only noticeable difference is that in verse 19 he speaks about *slavery* to sin versus *slavery* to righteousness, which fits in with the new analogy he is unfolding.

Why does Paul repeat himself like this? Obviously to make the point that there is just no other way for us to grow in righteousness. There is no secret formula for holiness, no magic recipe. The only means is to realize what God has done for us and then discipline the parts of our bodies—our minds, eyes, ears, tongues, hands, and feet—to act accordingly.

I cannot emphasize this point enough, because we live in a day in which Christian people are shirking hard work and are searching (if they even bother to search) for some easy solution or quick fix. We look for quick solutions in our physical and emotional lives on a regular basis. If we are depressed, we take in a movie, go shopping, or pop a pill. If we are having trouble with a personal relationship, we go to a weekend seminar to pick up pointers—or to a singles bar to pick up some new person.

We Christians find it easy to carry this outlook into our spiritual lives. Some who do this look for a special "victory" formula ("let go and let God," "take it by faith," or some other handy slogan). Some search for a powerful emotional experience. Still others pray for miracles.

But these are not God's answers. God is not withholding something from us, some secret we need to seek or for which we should pray. God has already done everything necessary for our salvation and given us everything we need to live a consistent Christian life. So, if we fail to do it, it is either because we have not been taught what God has done and therefore do not know how to conduct ourselves as Christians, or we are just too sinful or lazy.

D. Martyn Lloyd-Jones wrote, "You have already received 'all things that pertain unto a life of godliness.' You do not need another experience. You do not need some new gift. You have been given everything in Christ; you are 'in him' from the beginning of your Christian life. You are just a slacker and a cad, just lazy and indolent, indeed 'a liar,' if you are not living this life."[4] He says that this is the New Testament way of preaching holiness and sanctification, and he is right.

4. D. M. Lloyd-Jones, *Romans: An Exposition of Chapter 6, The New Man* (Grand Rapids: Zondervan, 1973), p. 269.

Our Reasonable Service

What is the bottom line? Lloyd-Jones spells it out in the six propositions.[5]

1. *The teaching about sanctification in verse 19, like the teaching in verses 11–13, is an exhortation.* In fact, it is a command. Before our conversion we were under the control of sin, and sin commanded us to give the parts of our body to it for wicked acts. We obeyed sin in those days; we had to. Now we have passed under the command of God, and God commands us to offer our bodies to him for acts of righteousness.

2. *Being an exhortation, the command to offer our bodies to God for his purposes is something we must do.* Indeed, it is something we can do. If this command had been laid upon us prior to our conversion, we would not have been able to do it. We would have been *non posse non peccare* ("not able not to sin"), as Augustine said. But being freed from bondage to sin and having been made willing slaves of God by the new birth, we are now *posse non peccare* ("able not to sin"). To put it in positive terms, we are now able to obey God, do good works, and live righteous lives.

3. *The command to yield the parts of our bodies as instruments of righteousness is based on something that has already happened to us.* That is, something that has *already* happened, not something that may happen or will yet happen to us.

Here is an exercise for you. Go through Romans 6 and underline the verbs that tell, in a past tense, what has happened to those of us who are Christians. You will find that you are underlining nearly every significant verb: "we *died* to sin" (v. 2); "all of us . . . *were baptized* into Christ Jesus . . . into his death" (v. 3); "we *were therefore buried* with him" (v. 4); "we *have been united* with him like this in his death" (v. 5); "our old self *was crucified* with him" (v. 6); "we *died* with Christ" (v. 8); "you wholeheartedly *obeyed* the form of teaching to which you were entrusted" (v. 17); "you *have been set free* from sin and *have become* slaves to righteousness" (v. 18); "you *have been set free* from sin and *have become* slaves to God" (v. 22). These verbs describe the experience of all who are truly Christians. It is because their experience can be described in these terms, because of what has *already* happened, that a life of holiness through the power of God is possible for them.

4. *The New Testament approach to sanctification is therefore to get us to realize our position and act accordingly.* The New Testament does not tell us to be what we will become. Rather, it tells us to be what we are. Lloyd-Jones says, "I cannot find anywhere in the New Testament, teaching which says, 'Christ has been crucified for you; what remains now is that you should be crucified with Christ.' That has been popular teaching; but it is not in the New Testament. Every man who is a Christian has already been crucified with

5. Ibid., pp. 258–265.

Christ. . . . It is because that has already happened, it is because that is true of us, that this command . . . is addressed to us."[6]

5. *This demand is utterly reasonable.* In fact, anything contrary to it is unreasonable. Before we were saved, we served sin; that was consistent and reasonable. But now that we are converted, it is equally reasonable that we should serve God.

Do you understand that Paul is reasoning with us here? A moment ago I said to look at Romans 6 for verbs that tell what has happened to us in our salvation. Now go back and look at it again, noting the deductions Paul draws from those actions: "We died to sin, *how can we* live in it any longer?" (v. 2); "If we have been united with him like this in his death, *we will certainly also* be united with him in his resurrection" (v. 5); "*Therefore* do not let sin reign in your mortal body so that you obey its evil desires" (v. 12); "For sin shall not be your master, *because you are not under law,* but under grace" (v. 14); "*What then? Shall we sin* because we are not under law but under grace? *By no means!*" (v. 15); "*Just as* you used to offer the parts of your body in slavery to impurity and to ever-increasing wickedness, *so now* offer them in slavery to righteousness . . ." (v. 19b).

The Bible says that if you are living a sinful life, your conduct is inconsistent with any Christian profession you might have made. If you claim to be a Christian, you must therefore straighten your life out, or you dare not long assume you are a true believer. That would be presumptuous! God forbid that any of us should continue sinning, thinking that grace will abound.

6. *The failures we have in trying to live a holy life are due almost entirely to our failure to realize these truths or to our laziness or sin in failing to apply them to our conduct.* Do you remember Jesus' words about sanctification? He said in his prayer for his disciples: "Sanctify them by the truth; your word is truth" (John 17:17). This is identical doctrine to what we have in Paul's writings. It is truth for today.

Not long ago I was rereading an essay by C. S. Lewis called "The Weight of Glory." As he ends this essay, Lewis urges us to think of people as eternal creatures who are daily becoming either more and more like God or more and more like the devil. He writes:

> It is a serious thing to live in a society of possible gods and goddesses, to remember that the dullest and most uninteresting person you can talk to may one day be a creature which, if you saw it now, you would be strongly tempted to worship, or else a horror and a corruption such as you now meet, if at all, only in a nightmare. . . . There are no *ordinary* people. You have never talked to a mere mortal. Nations, cultures, arts, civilizations—these are mortal, and their life is to ours as the life of a gnat. But it is immortals whom

6. Ibid., p. 262.

we joke with, work with, marry, snub, and exploit—immortal horrors or everlasting splendors.[7]

Lewis says that we would treat others better if we would learn to think of them in those terms. But if that is true of others, it is also obviously true of ourselves. What we do now has bearing on what we will one day be. And it works the other way, too. What we will be must determine what we do now. If we have been saved by Jesus and are going to be like Jesus, we must start living like him and for him, day by day.

7. C. S. Lewis, *The Weight of Glory and Other Addresses*, ed. Walter Hooper (New York: Collier Books, Macmillan, 1980), pp. 18, 19.

85

Sin's Wages and God's Gift

Romans 6:23

For the wages of sin is death, but the gift of God is eternal life in Christ Jesus our Lord.

Scattered throughout the Bible are verses that even the most casual reader at once perceives to be extraordinarily important. It is not that the other verses are unimportant, for "All Scripture is God-breathed and is useful . . ." (2 Tim. 3:16). But certain texts stand out above others as striking summaries of very important doctrines, particularly those that lie at the very heart of the gospel.

Romans 6:23 is one such verse. It says, "For the wages of sin is death, but the gift of God is eternal life in Christ Jesus our Lord."

This is one of the most familiar verses in the Bible. For one thing, it appears in Romans, a particularly well-known book. But it is also short and easy to memorize. There are only twenty words here (nineteen in Greek); only three of these have more than one syllable, and they are certainly not difficult: "wages," "eternal," and "Jesus." Romans 6:23 has been taught to millions of Sunday school children and has been incorporated into gospel presentations in scores of tracts, booklets, and studies. In many of these presentations the text comes immediately after Romans 3:23 ("for all have sinned and fall short of the glory of God") and before the best-known verse of all: John 3:16 ("For God so loved the world that he gave his one and only Son, that whoever believes in him shall not perish but have eternal life").

Charles Haddon Spurgeon called Romans 6:23 "a Christian proverb, a golden sentence, a divine statement of truth worthy to be written across the sky." He wrote, "As Jesus said of the woman who anointed him for his burial, 'Wherever this gospel shall be preached in the whole world, there shall also this, that this woman hath done, be told for a memorial of her'; so I may say, 'Wherever the gospel is preached, there shall this golden sentence, which the apostle has let fall, be repeated as proof of his clearness in the faith.' Here you have both the essence of the gospel and a statement of that misery from which the gospel delivers all who believe."[1]

Paul seems to have loved using short, expressive statements, no doubt because they were so useful in his front-line missionary teaching.

The Two Ways

The appeal of this verse is in its summary of the doctrine of the two ways, which we were officially introduced to in the last study but have been studying in one way or another throughout this entire chapter and even in Romans 5. This doctrine has been presented repeatedly, though in different formats.

In Romans 5 it was expressed as the distinction between being in Adam and being in Christ. The two ways were traced from the contrary actions of the two federal heads of mankind. Adam, we were told, disobeyed God; his disobedience brought condemnation and death to his posterity. Jesus obeyed God; his obedience resulted in justification and life for those who are joined to him. Toward the end of the chapter the contrast was described as being between the law and grace. Law worked sin, and the result of sin was death. Grace results in righteousness and eternal life.

In Romans 6 the case is similar, only here the two ways have been described as outworkings of two slaveries. On the one hand, there is a slavery to sin. Each of us is born into this slavery, which leads to "impurity and to ever-increasing wickedness" (v. 19). The end is death (v. 21). On the other hand, there is a slavery to God, which leads to "righteousness leading to holiness" (v. 19) and ends in life (v. 22).

This is what is summarized in our text. It is what Paul means when he says that "the wages of sin is death, but the gift of God is eternal life in Christ Jesus our Lord."

1. Charles Haddon Spurgeon, "Death and Life: The Wage and the Gift" in *Metropolitan Tabernacle Pulpit*, vol. 31 (London: The Banner of Truth Trust, 1971), p. 601.

The Way of Death

When the apostle contrasts "death" with "eternal life," as he does in this text, we immediately think of the state of souls beyond the grave. That is, we think of eternal life as the life of God's children in heaven and of eternal death (in Revelation it is called a "second death") as the death, accompanied by punishment, of those who die apart from Jesus Christ. That is part of the picture, of course, an important part. But we need to remember that, in Romans 6, Paul is writing about the *present* life of the believer and stressing that, having been freed from slavery to sin, a Christian must thereafter *live* to serve God.

Although these are eternal ends—death and life—we must not overlook that there is also a present death and a present life to be considered.

I would go even further than this to say that in this verse Paul is particularly concerned with the effects of sin and righteousness in *this* life and not with the life to come. My reason for thinking this is that he uses the word *opsōnia* ("wages") to describe sin's effects. This word was used of the daily food ration (literally, "fish ration") given to a Roman soldier for his service. In other words, it does not refer to a large payment dispensed at the end of the soldier's period of service but rather to something that was measured out to him day by day. It is the individual's present state, then, not his future state, that is in view.

In other words, we have a parallel in this verse to what we have already seen in Romans 1 regarding the "wrath" of God. To our minds, "wrath" also suggests something occurring at the end of time: God's final judgment on sin to be meted out at the last day. That is certainly one aspect of it. But what Paul is actually talking about in Romans 1 is the *present* outworking of God's wrath against men and women, as seen in the downward life-path of those who have rejected him.

This is extremely relevant.

Not long ago I was reading the classic study of sin, originally published in 1973 by Karl Menninger of the famous Menninger Clinic of Topeka, Kansas. It is called *Whatever Became of Sin?* Menninger is a psychiatrist, and what had disturbed him and caused him to write this book was an awareness, based on his careful observation and counseling, that as a concept "sin" has all but disappeared from our national consciousness—with disastrous results.

What is sin? Menninger defines it in classical language: "Sin is transgression of the law of God; disobedience of the divine will; moral failure. Sin is failure to realize in conduct and character the moral ideal, at least as fully as possible under existing circumstances; failure to do as one ought towards one's fellow man."[2]

2. Karl Menninger, *Whatever Became of Sin?* (New York: Bantam Books, 1978), p. 22. (The definition is from Webster's dictionary.)

What became of sin? Briefly put, "sin" first became "crime" (transgression of the law of man rather than transgression of the law of God), and then "crime" became "symptoms." Symptoms were caused by factors thought to be external to the offender and therefore things for which he or she was clearly not responsible.

Menninger refers to what happened by a satire about psychiatry written and sung by Anna Russell.

> At three I had a feeling of
> Ambivalence toward my brothers.
> And so it follows naturally
> I poisoned all my lovers.
> But now I'm happy; I have learned
> The lesson this has taught:
> *That everything I do that's wrong*
> *Is someone else's fault.*[3]

"Can we have moral health without responsibility?" asks Menninger. "Or mental health without moral health?" He suggests that psychiatrists may actually have compounded the problem by "neglecting the availability of help for some individuals whose sins are greater than their symptoms and whose burdens are greater than they can bear."[4]

But that is not the reason I refer to Menninger, though this background is necessary for understanding why I quote him. The reason I refer to him is that he is convinced from his own experience of dealing with many thousands of patients that sin is a reality, regardless of what we may have done with the idea of it—"There are no substitutes for words like 'sin' and 'grace,'" he argues[5]—and that sin is destructive. In one of the later sections of the book he analyzes what he calls "The Old Seven Deadly Sins (and Some New Ones)" and concludes wisely, "The long-term consequences of hate [the word that best summarizes the many types of sin, in his opinion] are self-destruction. Thus *the wages of sin really are death* (my emphasis)."[6]

How does this operate? Menninger suggests that self-destruction is observable in each of the old "deadly sins."

Pride (of power, knowledge, or virtue) destroys relationships. It turns us into people who look on others as possessions to be amassed, exploited, or controlled.

Lust (which embraces all sexual sins) destroys one's personality. It weakens loyalty, undercuts trust, and destroys integrity.

3. Anna Russell, "Psychiatric Folksong," in Menninger, *Whatever Became of Sin?*, pp. 210, 211.
4. Menninger, *Whatever Became of Sin?*, flyleaf.
5. Ibid., p. 54.
6. Ibid., p. 200.

Gluttony destroys the body—in whatever form it appears, whether as overindulgence in food, drink, or drugs. "Gluttony . . . is sinful [because] it represents a . . . love which is self-destructive."[7]

Anger destroys others, whether by violence or by words only. To wound another's pride or status by words is "to kill him" slowly.

Sloth destroys opportunities and ambitions.

Envy, greed, avarice, and affluence destroy contentment, even a proper sense of freedom and nobility. Menninger tells of a very rich man who had been brought to him by his relatives because he had tried to commit suicide. Life no longer held anything of interest for him. "I haven't the slightest idea what to do with all my money," he said. "I don't need it, but I can't bear to give it away."

"So you decide to kill yourself in order to get away from it," Menninger replied.

"What else can I do?"

"Could you establish a' memorial to your beloved father, endowing certain art forms in the smaller cities over the country, all named for him?" the doctor suggested.

The rich man brightened up. "That would be wonderful," he said. "My father would have loved that. Sure, I could do it easily. I would enjoy it. It would honor him, well, both of us, forever. Let me think about it. I might just do that."

But he didn't. He existed for a few more years, then died, prematurely, "to the satisfaction of his heirs and business associates who were not yet in his predicament, although they suffered from the same 'disease,'" says Menninger.[8]

Waste, cheating, stealing, lying, cruelty, and other vices—all are sins, and they are all destructive.

The wages of sin really is death, as the Bible states and Menninger confirms. And if it is death in this life, as it obviously is, it is surely death in the life to come.

The Way of Life

But enough about the first half of our text. It is time to look at the second half, with its great contrasts. The second half says, "but the gift of God is eternal life in Christ Jesus our Lord."

What marvelous contrasts these are:

death *versus* life

sin *versus* God

wages *versus* God's free gift

7. Ibid., p. 166.
8. Ibid., p. 178.

We have already looked at the first side of these great contrasts. Let us look at side two.

1. *Eternal life.* This means far more than mere physical life, of course, since the wicked also possess physical life for a time. It also means more than mere existence, for the wicked, too, will exist for eternity. "Eternal life" has to do with knowing God, as Jesus said: "Now this is eternal life: that they may know you, the only true God, and Jesus Christ, whom you have sent" (John 17:3). It is to know him in an ever-increasing measure. It means holiness coupled to all joy and blessedness. It means realization of that chief end for which we were created, namely, "to glorify God and to enjoy him forever" (*The Westminster Shorter Catechism*, Answer 1).

Moreover, eternal life is something that begins now. We have eternal life from the very beginning of our new relationships to Christ, from the moment we believe on him.

2. *God.* The first of these contrasts, the one between death and life, is what we naturally expect. Say one, and we think naturally of the other: life and death, death and life. This is not so with the second contrast. Sin does not suggest God as its opposite; it suggests the word *righteousness*. What we would expect the sentence to say is that "the wages of sin is death" and that "the wages of righteousness is eternal life."

There is a sense in which Paul could have said this, of course. The chain of terms he has been developing since chapter five leads to that idea: on the one hand, disobedience, wickedness, condemnation, death; and on the other hand, obedience, justification, righteousness, life. But if Paul had said "the wages of righteousness is life," we would immediately have assumed that we can earn salvation by our good works, and Paul is too wise a teacher to let that happen. Therefore, at the very point at which we might expect him to say "righteousness," he puts "God," to teach, as the Bible does throughout, that "salvation comes from the Lord" (Jon. 2:9).

In other words, no one but God can get us out of the predicament Karl Menninger describes in *Whatever Became of Sin?*

Do you know the Latin phrase *deus ex machina*? It is from classical drama, and it refers to the introduction of God into the action to resolve a problem. Aristotle had a rule for using God in the drama. He said that God must never be introduced as a *deus ex machina* unless the characters have gotten themselves into such a dilemma that only a god can get them out of it. This is the case here. That is exactly the kind of problem we have gotten ourselves into by our practice of sin. We are trapped in it, like elephants in quicksand or houses in a sinkhole. It takes God to get us out.

3. *The gift.* The Bible teaches that salvation is the gift of God. The Greek word is *charisma*, which actually means "a free gift." It means "grace." Wages are something we earn. They are the result of our working or doing. A gift is something that is unearned. It is free. That was the point to which we

came at the end of Romans 5, and it is a theme we will uncover again and again throughout this letter. In fact, we discover it in all our dealings with God in this life. We could translate Romans 6:23 to read: "The wages of sin is death, but the *grace* of God is eternal life in Christ Jesus our Lord."

Are You in Jesus?

I want you to notice one final thing about this verse. We have treated the contrasts, which are a sermon in themselves. But I am sure you have noticed that we still have one important phrase left over. It is the phrase "in Christ Jesus our Lord." It is not part of the contrast. "God" is set against "sin," "gift" against "wages," "eternal life" against "death." Why, then, does Paul include it?

Obviously, because it brings out what was all-important to him, indeed the great truth for which the entire Book of Romans has been written. We are now at the end of Romans 6. Paul has summarized the gospel as the free gift of God to his people, something they could never have earned. He is going to talk next about the use and limits of the law. But it is as if Paul stopped here and reflected: "I have said that salvation is the free gift of God. But surely I can't let it go at that. Salvation is the gift of God, yes! But how is it possible for God to be thus gracious to us? How can he have given us the gift of eternal life, we being the sinners that we are?" The answer, of course, is that it is *by*, *in* or *through* Jesus Christ, which is why he adds the phrase "in Christ Jesus our Lord." Paul never forgot that we are saved from sin only because of Jesus' work.

And that raises a final question—a personal one, because religion always is personal; it must be. *Are you in Jesus?* Is Jesus your Savior, your Lord? There are only two ways you can answer that question, either "Yes" or "No." He either is your Savior or he is not.

If he is, let me ask these follow-up questions: Are you living for Jesus? If you are not, why not? He gave himself for you. He died for you. He even lives for you. Paul's purpose in Romans 6 is to show that if you have been delivered from your bondage to sin by Jesus, it is so that you might thereafter be his, starting in this life. As Paul wrote to the Corinthians, ". . . You are not your own; you were bought at a price. Therefore honor God with your body" (1 Cor. 6:19b–20). In the midst of a world that is being swept along by the flood torrent of sin, you are to stand out as Jesus' servant. You are to live for and witness to him.

The other way you can answer my question is "No." And if that is the case, I ask why you would willingly keep going on such a self-destructive path, particularly when the way of salvation is known to you. Haven't you been trapped by sin long enough? Don't you long for deliverance?

I like the way Charles Haddon Spurgeon ended his sermon on this text. He referred to the question God asked the prophet Ezekiel when he stood in the Valley of Dry Bones. "Son of man, can these bones live?" (Ezek. 37:3).

Ezekiel was too wise to say what we probably would have answered in those circumstances. He said, "O Sovereign Lord, you alone know." (We would have said, "Not likely!") But when he was told to preach to them he did, and those dry bones came together, took on flesh, rose up, and became a great army.

That is what is necessary if you are to be delivered from sin, says Spurgeon. The wages of sin is death, and spiritually speaking you are as dead as those dry bones in the valley. No one but God can bring life out of death. No one but Jesus can make your dead bones live. God can do it. And he will as you come to him.[9] You need to come. You need to come now.

9. Spurgeon, "Death and Life: The Wage and the Gift," p. 612.

PART EIGHT

Freedom from Law

86

Freedom from the Law

Romans 7:1-4

Do you not know, brothers—for I am speaking to men who know the law—that the law has authority over a man only as long as he lives? For example, by law a married woman is bound to her husband as long as he is alive, but if her husband dies, she is released from the law of marriage. So then, if she marries another man while her husband is still alive, she is called an adulteress. But if her husband dies, she is released from that law and is not an adulteress, even though she marries another man.

So, my brothers, you also died to the law through the body of Christ, that you might belong to another, to him who was raised from the dead, in order that we might bear fruit to God.

The seventh chapter of Romans is one of the best-known chapters in the Word of God. It is an important chapter. But for anyone who sets out to explain and teach it, as I am doing, it is both formidable and frightening. Why? For several reasons.

First, it has been a focal point for much heated controversy. In this chapter, from verse 14 to the end, Paul writes of his own intense struggle against sin. But of what period of his life is he writing? Is Paul writing of himself as he was before his conversion? Or is he describing himself as he was at the time of writing, that is, after his conversion? Is he writing theoretically only? Or is he describing a real struggle? These verses continue to be a focal point of debate, since they bear upon current teaching concerning "the carnal Christian," if there is such a thing, and with what some call "lordship salvation."

The first section of the chapter (vv. 1–6) presents a problem, too. This is the section in which Paul introduces the illustration of marriage law to show how Christians have been freed from law in order to be married to Jesus Christ.

The illustration seems simple on the surface, but it has proven baffling to many. The main difficulty is that the illustration refers to a wife who is bound to her husband as long as he lives but is freed to marry another if he dies. It illustrates how the believer has died to the law in order that he or she might be married to Christ. But in the illustration it is the husband and not the wife who dies, and it is the wife who remarries. Besides, what does the husband represent? Is he the law? If so, what law? Law in general or the Old Testament law in particular? If not the law, what does he represent? Ray Stedman thinks the husband represents Adam.[1] Saint Augustine and some of the Reformers thought he represents our old, or corrupt, nature.[2]

There are even more problems in these verses, as an examination of nearly any commentary will show.

William Barclay said of Romans 7, "Seldom did Paul write so difficult and so complicated a passage."[3] C. H. Dodd is intemperate in his remarks, objecting that "the illustration . . . is confused from the outset." He advises us "to ignore the illustration, as far as may be, and ask what it is that Paul is really talking about in the realm of fact and experience."[4] That is hardly advice for the serious commentator to dispense.

The Most Difficult Problem: Application

I write as a preacher, however, and from my perspective the greatest problem with Romans 7 is not the interpretation of the chapter (which, in the final analysis, I do not believe is all that difficult) but rather the task of applying it to our own lawless age. Let me explain.

You will remember from our earlier studies that I have described Romans 6 and 7 as a parenthesis in a larger section embracing chapters 5–8. The larger section concerns the assurance and finality of salvation, beginning with the truth that, having been justified by the work of God in

1. Ray C. Stedman, *From Guilt to Glory,* vol. 1, *Hope for the Helpless* (Portland: Multnomah Press, 1978), p. 218.

2. Cf. Charles Hodge, *A Commentary on Romans* (Edinburgh and Carlisle, Pa.: The Banner of Truth Trust, 1972), p. 216. (Original edition 1935.)

3. William Barclay, *The Letter to the Romans* in "The Daily Study Bible" series (Edinburgh: Saint Andrews Press, 1969), p. 94.

4. C. H. Dodd, *The Epistle of Paul to the Romans* (London: Hodder and Stoughton, 1960), pp. 100, 101.

Christ, we now have "peace with God," and ending with the triumphal cry (in chapter 8) that nothing will be able to separate us from that relationship. In the course of this section the apostle deals with two questions that arise naturally from his thesis: (1) Doesn't a doctrine like this lead to immoral behavior, since it seems to be saying that we will be saved eventually regardless of what we do? and (2) Doesn't it make the law of no account, or useless? This second problem would be particularly acute for the Jew who had always rightly regarded the law as God's good gift.

Paul answers the first of these questions in chapter 6, showing that the gospel does not lead to immorality but rather to the reverse. This is because, in saving us from sin, God has joined us to Jesus Christ, as a result of which those who have been saved must and will live for him. Paul answers the second question—"But what about the law?"—in chapter 7.

But here is the problem. We live in a day when people have little concern for law, in fact, when most people try as hard as they can or dare to be lawless. So how do you say to people who do not care about law that the law is important? Or, harder yet, how do you tell them that they must be freed from law in order to live for righteousness (which is what Romans 7:1–6 says), when they are already acting as if they are freed from it—but in the wrong way? How do you make what you have to say about the law of God relevant?

A Universal Problem

Most commentators are agreed that "the law" referred to in Romans 7 is law in general and not the Old Testament law specifically, and that the word *brothers* in verse 1 refers to all Christians and not to believing Jews only. But the "all" includes the parts, and for that reason I begin with the problem that Paul's teaching must have presented to believing Jews. I also begin here because this part is the easiest to understand.

The problem was twofold. First, there was the problem I have already spoken about, namely that Paul's teaching about being justified by God apart from law seemed to make the law worthless or, worse yet, harmful. How could any true Jew accept that? The Jew knew that the law had been given through Moses from Mount Sinai, accompanied by frightening manifestations of God's presence. Nothing could have been more weighty or solemn than God's giving of the law on Sinai. The Jew rightly regarded the law as God's great, good, and beneficial gift to man. How could such an important gift be set aside?

The other problem was this: In a paradoxical manner, although the law was good, it was also an overwhelming burden. It imposed a strict code of legalistic behavior that was back-breaking for those who took it seriously. The Jews had a word for it. They called it a yoke, like those put upon animals to harness them for hard labor. That is what it was like to be a godly Jew. The Jew was proud of his yoke. It was from God; it set him apart from the godless peoples around him. Nevertheless it was still a yoke, and it was a great and overwhelming burden.

Do you remember how Peter spoke of this, in a moment of unusual clarity at the great Council of Jerusalem described in Acts 15? There were people at the council who wanted to impose the Old Testament law on Gentile believers, and Paul, followed by Peter, argued that this was a wrong thing to do. Peter's argument was telling: "Now then, why do you try to test God by putting on the necks of the disciples a yoke that neither we nor our fathers have been able to bear?" he asked (v. 10). His words were a candid admission that trying to live by the law of God had been onerous and impossible.

But is this only a Jewish problem? I said a moment ago that the whole includes the parts; therefore, the Jewish problem is included. But how is it that more than Jews are involved? How does the problem affect the Gentile?

In the following way. You remember perhaps that in the opening section of *Mere Christianity* the great Cambridge professor and Christian apologist C. S. Lewis argued that all persons recognize and feel bound to live by a certain moral standard. Lewis called it "the law of human nature," and he illustrated it from the way people argue. They say things like, "How'd you like it if anyone did the same to you?" "That's my seat, I was there first," "Leave him alone; he isn't doing you any harm," "Why should you shove in first?", "Give me a bit of your orange; I gave you a bit of mine," or "Come on, you promised."[5] Lewis believed—I am sure he is right—that statements like this show that all people everywhere recognize a standard of behavior to which they and others are supposed to measure up.

They may disagree about certain details of that standard, of course, and they may apply it wrongly. But all nevertheless believe in what used to be called Right and Wrong. And not only do they believe in it, they expect others to believe in it and live by the "right" standard, too. Thus the appeals for right conduct I have quoted.

Lewis also had another main point in his argument, and it is that we have all broken this law of nature. What is more, we feel guilty for breaking it, which is why we usually try to cover up for our bad behavior or make excuses for it.

These facts of human behavior show that in a certain sense the Gentile as well as the Jew is "under law" and knows himself to be condemned by it. Therefore the problem that Paul is dealing with in Romans 7 is a universal human problem.

In his study of Romans, Ray C. Stedman suggests four proofs that all persons are naturally "under law," even without possessing or being subjected to the specific law of the Old Testament. They are worth listing.

5. C. S. Lewis, *Mere Christianity* (New York: MacMillan, 1958), p. 3.

1. *We are proud of our achievements.* At first glance, this seems to prove recognition of a standard to which we have been able to measure up and to which others have perhaps not been able to measure up (at least not so well), not how we feel condemned by those standards. But it actually does show how we feel condemned, because our pointing to some area of moral achievement in our own lives is usually a diversion to keep people from looking at our failures in other areas. For example, the philanthropist may boast of the $100,000 he has given to some charity primarily because he is feeling guilty about how he or she acquired the money in the first place. Perhaps he neglected his family in order "to make his mark" or even cheated someone out of it. "The law reveals failure. Therefore, one of the first marks of a person who is living under the law is that he is always pointing out how well he is doing," says Stedman.[6]

2. *We are critical of others.* This is another diversionary tactic. It is the "scapegoat" ploy. Get people thinking about how others have failed, and perhaps they will overlook us. And there is this, too: In a strange way, we are usually most critical of others precisely in those areas where we are ourselves most at fault. It is the proud who most hate pride in others. It is cheaters who are most sensitive to being cheated by their associates.

3. *We are reluctant to admit our own failures.* This is the reverse side of boasting. It is because we instinctively feel the weight of the law over us that we attempt to cover up our failures. If we did not sense ourselves to be "under law" and rightly "under law," would we bother? We would not deny breaking a standard the validity of which we do not recognize.

4. *We suffer from depression, discouragement, and defeat.* This gets to the real heart of the problem, for it shows how futile it is for people to try to raise moral standards merely by enacting or proclaiming new laws. Social reformers generally think that all that is necessary to raise the moral standard of a community is to inform people of what is right and provide a few incentives for them to choose it. But it does not work that way. All of us are already "under law," and we are already breaking the law we have. What good does it do to have more laws? Or better laws? Or higher laws? All the so-called better laws do is increase our sense of failure and heighten our anxiety. We are defeated enough already.

"What a wretched man I am!" we might cry. "Who will rescue me from this body of death?" The answer, which Paul gives at the very end of Romans 7, where he asks those very questions, is not a new law but "God—though Jesus Christ our Lord!" (v. 25). The rescuer is a person!

6. Stedman, *From Guilt to Glory,* vol. 1, *Hope for the Helpless,* p. 216.

From Death to a New Life

Nevertheless, we are "under law." The Jew was (and is) under the law of the Old Testament. The Gentile is under the law of nature. And that is just the problem. The law cannot save us, as Paul proved early on in Romans. The law cannot sanctify us either, as he is showing now. Still we are under it. It is all very good to say that the answer to a holy life is not the law but a person, but that does little good if we are still under bondage to the former.

This is where Romans 7:1–4 comes in, of course. For what Paul tells us in these verses is that the solution is death. We must die to one (law) in order to be free for another (Jesus Christ). The law has an important role to play. Paul will explain that carefully in the next section (vv. 7–13). But his first teaching in reference to law is that we must be freed from it and that the only way we can be freed from it is by death.

This is where the argument gets difficult. But let's try to follow it carefully.

First, Paul states a fact upon which all can agree, namely, "that the law has authority over a man only as long as he lives" (v. 1). That should be self-evident. As long as we are alive we are bound by the laws of the country in which we live. But if we die, we are freed from those laws. Obviously you cannot require a dead person to do anything, nor punish him or her for failing to do it. Everyone can agree on this point.

Second, Paul gives an illustration from common experience, citing the case of a woman who is married to a certain man. His argument goes: "For example, by law a married woman is bound to her husband as long as he is alive, but if her husband dies, she is released from the law of marriage. So then, if she marries another man while her husband is still alive, she is called an adulteress. But if her husband dies, she is released from that law and is not an adulteress, even though she marries another man" (vv. 2–3). The point of the illustration is simplicity itself: The death of the husband releases the wife from the law that bound her to the marriage.

I am convinced that most errors in interpreting this passage come from trying to get it to teach more than that, more than Paul intended. We should remember that this is not a proof of Paul's point; it is only an illustration. More importantly, it is not an allegory. That is, it is not necessary to assign meanings to each of the illustration's parts. In fact, if we try to do that, we are at once led into difficulty, as I tried to indicate at the beginning when I mentioned the diverse meanings that have been assigned to the husband in the supposed illustration.

But why didn't Paul carry the illustration through in a way that would have avoided these problems? One reason is that it does not work out properly, no matter how you try it. If the husband represents the law, then the law dies in order that we might marry another, who is Christ. But the law does not die. It lives and has value. In verse 12, Paul is going to argue that "the law is holy, and the commandment is holy, righteous and good."

Actually, *we* are the ones who have died—in Christ, as Paul says in Galatians 2:20 ("I have been crucified with Christ and I no longer live . . .").

Try it that way, then. Make the husband who has died represent us. If we do that, the illustration falls apart because, being dead, we cannot marry another person, which is what Paul wants to suggest.

Why use an illustration at all, then? I think there are several good reasons. In his commentary, D. Martyn Lloyd-Jones gives four of them:[7]

1. *A woman who is married to a man is under the authority of that man.* This is not so true today, in our feminist age, but it was true of the age in which Paul wrote, just as it has been in most ages of human history and in virtually all places. Husbands had authority over wives, rather than each being equal in authority or wives having authority over husbands. This is what Paul wants to show. The human race is under obligation to the laws of nature and of God, and is bound by them. No one is free to write his or her own moral code or to abandon law entirely. We are responsible.

2. *The subjection of a wife to a husband in marriage is a life-long subjection.* Today we think of marriage as being easily broken by divorce, and by "no fault" divorce at that. But this was far from Paul's mind. He was thinking scripturally, as Christians still try to do today in marriage services. We have the parties repeat: "I, Mary, take thee, John [or I, John, take thee, Mary], to be my wedded husband [or wife]; and I do promise and covenant, before God and these witnesses, to be thy loving and faithful wife [or husband], in plenty and in want, in joy and in sorrow, in sickness and in health, as long as we both shall live." The illustration of marriage shows that we are under the authority of God's law for this life.

3. *In spite of the permanent nature of this relationship and the resulting authority, there is nevertheless the possibility of entering into another relationship.* How? It becomes possible if one of the parties dies.

This is the point Paul is particularly concerned to make, which we can see by the fact that, having made it one way in verse 2, he immediately states it all over again in verse 3, saying, "But if her husband dies, she is released from the law and is not an adulteress. . . ." What is Paul showing in this verse? Let me repeat that he is not working out an allegory in which the husband stands for something and the wife stands for something else. What he is stressing is that the law of marriage is not violated by the new relationship—if the husband has died. Rather, the law is upheld. The woman is freed from the law binding her to the first husband so that she might marry another *in a legal manner.*

Do you see how this is working out? Paul's opponents were saying, "But what about the law? Doesn't the gospel you have been preaching annul the

7. See D. M. Lloyd-Jones, *Romans: An Exposition of Chapters 7:1—8:4, The Law: Its Functions and Limits* (Grand Rapids: Zondervan, 1973), pp. 18–24.

law or set the law aside?" Paul's answer is that this is far from the case. In the gospel of God's free justification of the sinner, the law is fully honored, satisfied, and upheld. Salvation is a "fulfilling of the law." But at the same time it is liberation from it, which is necessary if you and I are to be able to step forward in Christ to live a morally fruitful life.

This leads to the fourth and most important point.

4. *The object of the new relationship is "that we might bear fruit to God"* (v. 4). Commentators seem afraid of this last point, no doubt feeling that the thought of bearing offspring to Christ is somehow indelicate. I do not feel this to be the case at all. Paul is concerned for righteousness, which is the fruit of God, and the idea is: How are we to attain this righteousness so long as we are married to law (or, if you prefer, to Adam or to our old sinful nature)? The old husband is impotent. The law never engendered righteousness in anybody. So how can we be fruitful? The answer is: Death must terminate the old relationship in order that we might enter into a new, fruitful relationship to Jesus Christ.

How does this happen? It happens by our dying to the law in Christ. That is, his death becomes our death. Therefore, when we die in him we die to the law, and when we rise in him we rise to the new relationship. Now God says to us, as he said to our first parents in the Garden of Eden, "Be fruitful and increase in number; fill the earth and subdue it" (Gen. 1:28a). Not with physical offspring, of course, but with righteousness produced by the Holy Spirit.

87

Our Second, Fruitful Union

Romans 7:4

So, my brothers, you also died to the law through the body of Christ, that you might belong to another, to him who was raised from the dead, in order that we might bear fruit to God.

Of all the scriptural illustrations of what it means to belong to the Lord Jesus Christ in salvation, none is more pleasing than the illustration of marriage. It is because love, courtship, and marriage are themselves pleasing and because our relationship to Jesus is a love relationship.

Many times, when I am asked to perform a wedding, either the man or the woman will mention that some of those coming to the service will not be Christians and inquire whether it might be possible for me to make the way of salvation clear as part of my marriage meditation. I always reply that I am glad to speak about the gospel and that it is easy in this context, for nothing so clearly illustrates what it means to be a Christian than the marriage service. In a service like this I will say that the Bible portrays Jesus as the passionate lover, devoted bridegroom, and faithful husband of his bride, the church, and that we are portrayed as that bride. Moreover, I will say that the marriage vows particularly illustrate the relationship.

Jesus took the vows first of all, for he sought us long before we knew him or had responded to him. He said:

> I, Jesus, take thee, Sinner [for that is what we are], to be my wedded wife; and I do promise and covenant, before God the heavenly Father, to be thy loving and faithful Savior, in plenty and in want, in joy and in sorrow, in sickness and in health, for this life and for all eternity.

After he had said that, the time came when we looked up into his loving face and repeated with corresponding ardor:

> I, Sinner, take thee, Jesus, to be my loving Bridegroom and Savior; and I do promise and covenant, before God the heavenly Father, to be thy loving and faithful wife, in plenty and in want, in joy and in sorrow, in sickness and in health, for this life and for all eternity.

I point out that it is the exchange of vows formally witnessed that makes the marriage, just as it is the fullness of saving faith that binds us to Jesus in salvation. For faith is not mere knowledge about Jesus any more than merely knowing about a man joins a woman to him or a man to a woman. Nor is faith even loving Jesus, important as that is. It is a promise to be his forever.

Joined to Jesus

This is the illustration Paul has been unfolding in the first verses of Romans 7, as we began to see in the previous chapter. He showed that the law is not abrogated by the manner in which God has saved us in Christ, but rather that the law has been both honored and satisfied. He did this by showing that law has a claim on people only as long as they live. Once they die, their relationship to the law is ended.

When we first began to look at this illustration—showing that "a married woman is bound to her husband as long as he is alive, but if her husband dies, she is released from the law of marriage"—I pointed out that confusion follows if we take the illustration as allegory. That is, as soon as we attempt to establish the identity of the husband who has died, we have trouble. He cannot be the law; the law is not dead. Nor can he be ourselves; for Paul's point is that those who are Christians have died to the one in order to be married to the other. (If we are to be identified with any one of the parties, it must be the woman.) When we studied the illustration in the last chapter, I argued that the comparison is not to be taken allegorically but only as an illustration to show that death releases any person from the law.

Yet, in verse 4, the last verse in which Paul uses the illustration, the apostle actually does work this out in terms of our relationship to Christ, showing how death to the law operates and how the result is a new and fruitful relationship. His teaching in verse 4 does not perfectly fit his illustration—no illustration is perfect—but it *is* the gospel.

What is Paul's point? Simply that the object of God's having freed us from the law, to which we were bound, was that we might be joined to Christ and be fruitful. In fact, it is even stronger than that. In Greek the sentence ends with the words "in order that we might bear fruit to God," which means that in this case it is the fruitfulness of the Christian, rather even than his union with Christ, that is emphasized.

And why not? Paul has been teaching that, having been saved by God, we must live a holy life. Now, by the image of a fruitful marriage, he teaches that this has been God's object in saving us all along.

Why has God saved us? In the context of today's self-centered culture, even as Christians we tend to answer this question in exclusively personal terms by talking about God's love for us. It is not wrong to do this, for Jesus told us that "God so loved the world that he gave his one and only Son, that whoever believes in him shall not perish but have eternal life" (John 3:16). But we might do far better to answer that God loved us and Jesus died for us *so that we might be holy.*

What was God's object in saving us? Let us state it clearly. According to these first few verses in Romans 7, *God saved us so that we, who beforehand were lost in sin and wickedness, might live a holy life.*

What I want to pursue in this study is how the union of the believer with Christ, illustrated by the marriage relationship, actually leads to this end. That is, I want to show how this new relationship produces holiness. It does so in several important ways.

Miss Sinner, Mrs. Christian

First, holiness is produced because when we become Christians we take the name of the Lord Jesus Christ as ours, just as a woman traditionally takes a man's name for hers when she marries him. She may have come into the church as Miss Jones, for example. But if the man she is marrying is named Smith, she goes out of the church as Mrs. Smith. This exchange takes place in most Christian marriage ceremonies. In fact, the part in which it does is my favorite part of the service. After the bride and groom have exchanged vows and rings and I have spoken about Christian marriage and prayed for the couple's marital union, I say: "Now, by the authority committed unto me as a minister of the church of Jesus Christ, I declare that John Smith and Mary Jones *Smith* are now husband and wife, according to the ordinance of God and the law of the state of Pennsylvania."

At that point both the new husband and the new wife generally relax a bit and smile, the bride with a sweet and contented joy that she at last belongs to her new husband and he with an equally wonderful joy that she is his.

That is what happens when you are joined to Jesus in fruitful Christian union. Before this, you were Miss Sinner, for you were under the law of God and rightly condemned by it. You were a sinner by choice and by divine decree. But when you have been set free from that old union by dying to it in Christ and are raised to another union "in him," God gives you Christ's name. So you who before were Miss Sinner are now Mrs. Christian—"Christian" means "Christ one"—and whatever you do from this point on will reflect either favorably or disfavorably upon him.

Does this have bearing on how we Christians now live our lives? It had better. If it does not, it is questionable whether we have actually been joined to him.

Have you noticed how people are often very proud of their names? Some belong to families with ancestors who came to this country on the Mayflower at the very beginning of our country's history. They are proud of that. Some have descended from patriots who fought in the American Revolution—the DAR (Daughters of the American Revolution) is a celebrated organization. Others point to soldiers of the Civil War in their family tree. Some have ancestors who made great fortunes or were known for their important contributions to politics, art, literature, or science. This, too, is a justifiable source of pride in many instances. But it cannot compare with the pride that should be ours as the bride of Jesus Christ. Paul's letter to the Philippians tells us that God has given Jesus "the name that is above every name" (Phil. 2:9b). There is no higher privilege than to bear the name of Jesus Christ, to be known as a Christian. How, then, can we dishonor it? How can we do anything other than strive constantly to live a holy life as Christians?

Daughters of the King

The second way this marriage to Christ leads to holiness is through the new status it gives us.

This is also true in an earthly marriage. A woman may have come from a distinguished family, but if she marries a man who is an alcoholic, thereafter she will be known as the wife of a ne'er-do-well. She is known by *his* status rather than the exalted qualities of her ancestors. On the other hand, she may have come from a very humble background, but if she marries the heir-apparent to a throne, she will be known thereafter as a princess and perhaps eventually as a queen. It is the same with us as Christians. Before we were saved we had the low status described by Paul in his letter to the Ephesians (most of whom were Gentiles). We were "separate from Christ, excluded from citizenship in Israel and foreigners to the covenants of promise, without hope and without God in the world" (Eph. 2:12). Now we are "no longer foreigners and aliens, but fellow citizens with God's people and members of God's household, built on the foundation of the apostles and prophets, with Christ Jesus himself as the chief cornerstone" (vv. 19–20).

By our union with Jesus Christ we have become sons and daughters of the great King of the universe, God the Father. There is no status anywhere that tops that! We should live accordingly. How can the children of God act like the devil's offspring?

"The Rights and Privileges Thereunto"

This leads to the privileges conveyed by our new, enhanced status. Not long ago I took part in a college graduation ceremony and heard again those words that are often pronounced to new graduates in such a setting. The president of the college welcomed the hundred or so graduates into "the society of learned men and women" and conveyed upon them "all the rights, privileges, and responsibilities pertaining thereunto." Similarly, because of the new status it imparts, marriage brings corresponding rights, privileges, and responsibilities. This is especially true of our marriage to Jesus Christ. As his bride—as Christians—we have many special privileges, all of which produce holiness in us.

1. *Access to God in prayer.* Earlier, when we were studying the phrase "we have gained access by faith into this grace in which we now stand" (Rom. 5:2), I pointed out that this is not referring to prayer so much as to our having gained the status before God of justified men and women. Now I must add that, although Romans 5:2 is not talking about prayer specifically, the status to which it refers nevertheless guarantees our access to God in prayer. It is because we are God's children that we may come to him.

"Do not be anxious about anything, but in everything, by prayer and petition, with thanksgiving, present your requests to God. And the peace of God, which transcends all understanding, will guard your hearts and minds in Christ Jesus," said Paul (Phil. 4:6–7).

We need no better proof of this than what Jesus told us: "I will do whatever you ask in my name, so that the Son may bring glory to the Father. You may ask me for anything in my name, and I will do it" (John 14:13–14).

2. *Provision for all our needs.* We live in a need-centered age, which means that most people are constantly thinking about what they want or think they want, and how to get it. It is a negative feature of contemporary life; it is frustrating. As Christians, instead of always thinking about our own needs, we need to be concentrating on the needs of others. However, it is certainly true that we do have needs, and one of the privileges of our new relationship to God the Father through Jesus Christ is that God promises to supply them. He is willing because it is his nature to do good to his creatures. He is able because, being omnipotent, he has an unlimited supply of riches at his disposal. Paul also wrote of this to the Philippians, saying, "And my God will

meet all your needs according to his glorious riches in Christ Jesus" (Phil. 4:19).

3. *Jesus' personal care and protection.* What would you think of a wife who was in serious trouble and whose husband refused to help her? You would say, "Well, he's not a very good husband. How could he be so indifferent, so callous toward his own wife?" No one will ever be able to make that complaint against Jesus. He is our faithful helper and constant protector.

Jesus, our Bridegroom, is with us each step of our journey through life. He said, "And surely I am with you always, to the very end of the age" (Matt. 28:20b). As he accompanies us, he also works with us to make us all that he would have us be. In Ephesians, where Paul also speaks of marriage, the apostle writes: "Husbands, love your wives, just as Christ loved the church and gave himself up for her to make her holy, cleansing her by the washing with water through the word, and to present her to himself as a radiant church, without stain or wrinkle or any other blemish, but holy and blameless" (Eph. 5:25–27). Jesus does this for us in full measure.

Again, Jesus is present to deliver us from temptation. Paul assures us that "No temptation has seized you except what is common to man. And God is faithful; he will not let you be tempted beyond what you can bear. But when you are tempted, he will also provide a way out so that you can stand up under it" (1 Cor. 10:13).

4. *The Bible.* There is a sense in which all the world has the Bible; it is available to be read by anyone. But having the Bible is much more than that if we are Christians. Together with the sacred text, we also have the ministry of the Holy Spirit so that, when we read its pages, the Holy Spirit interprets the Bible to us and we hear the voice of the Lord.

> Beyond the sacred page I see thee, Lord;
> My spirit pants for thee, O living Word.

It was of such moments of personal Bible study that another hymnwriter wrote so eloquently:

> I come to the garden alone
> While the dew is still on the roses,
> And the voice I hear, falling on my ear,
> The Son of God discloses.
> And he walks with me, and he talks with me,
> And tells me I am his own;
> And the joy we share as we tarry there
> None other has ever known.

D. Martyn Lloyd-Jones, who lists many of these privileges in his study of Romans 7:4, says,

> If you would know the love of Jesus "what it is," give him opportunities of telling you. He will meet you in the Scriptures, and he will tell you. Give time, give place, give opportunity. Set other things aside, and say to other people, "I cannot do what you ask me to do; I have another appointment, I know he is coming and I am waiting for him." Do you look for him, are you expecting him, do you allow him, do you give him opportunities to speak to you, and to let you know his love for you?[1]

It is through such quiet meetings more than in any other way that we will grow in holiness.

For This Life and for Eternity

The fourth way our new marriage to Jesus Christ produces holiness is by bringing us into a love that will never fade and a relationship that will never end. We died to our unfruitful first marriage to the law when we died in Christ. That marriage ended. But now, having been raised in Christ, who will never die, and having been joined to him, we are assured of a love that will last forever. As I say in my reworking of the marriage vows, it is "in plenty and in want, in joy and in sorrow, in sickness and in health, *for this life and for all eternity.*"

"But suppose my love is weak?" you ask.

Don't say "suppose." As a new bride of Christ, your love for him *is* weak, but it will grow. It will grow here on earth, and it will go on growing throughout eternity.

"Suppose my love should grow cold?" you wonder.

That is a sad thing to imagine since there is no excuse for it, but it is true that this sometimes happens. We get involved in the affairs of this world and forget the Lord for a time. We neglect prayer and Bible study. We do not pause to hear his voice. Like the beloved of Solomon's Song of Songs, we do not come to Jesus when he calls. We say, "I have taken off my robe—must I put it on again?/I have washed my feet—must I soil them again?" (Song of Songs 5:3). Then, when we turn to the Lord at last, he is not there. Ah, but he is still seeking us. He has only used our neglect of him to show us how much his love means and how empty our lives are without it.

"But suppose I betray his love, as Gomer betrayed the love of Hosea?" God forbid that you should ever do that! But even if that should happen, Jesus' love is greater even than your betrayal. He died to deliver you from the condemnation of the law and purchase you for himself. Do you think

---

1. D. M. Lloyd-Jones, *Romans: An Exposition of Chapters 7:1—8:4, The Law: Its Functions and Limits* (Grand Rapids: Zondervan, 1973), p. 62.

he will abandon you now? The Bible tells us, "If we are faithless, he will remain faithful, for he cannot disown himself" (2 Tim. 2:13).

One day the great God of the universe is going to throw a party. It will be the most magnificent party that has ever been held. The banquet will be spread in heaven. The guests will be numbered in the billions. The angelic legions will be there to serve these honored guests. Jesus, the Bridegroom, will be seated at his Father's right hand. And you will be there, too, for this is the great marriage supper of the Lamb. You will be there. Do you understand that? *You will be there.* Nothing is going to keep you from that great celebration—if you are really joined to Jesus Christ.

So what are you doing? Are you living a halfhearted life for Jesus Christ now? If you know where you are headed, you will be preparing for that day with every spiritual thought you have and with every deed you do. You will be bearing fruit for God, because on that day of celebration you will be able to lift it up and offer it to him with pure hands and with joy unspeakable.

88

Then and Now

Romans 7:5-6

For when we were controlled by the sinful nature, the sinful passions aroused by the law were at work in our bodies, so that we bore fruit for death. But now, by dying to what once bound us, we have been released from the law so that we serve in the new way of the Spirit, and not in the old way of the written code.

Our text here is the fifth and sixth verses of Romans 7, and in the very middle of these verses, linking them, as it were, are the marvelous words "But now." They have already occurred once in the previous chapter (v. 22). They point to the tremendous change that has taken place in the life of the one who has come to Christ as Savior, and they are so important that D. Martyn Lloyd-Jones was no doubt right in saying, "If the expression 'But now' does not move you, I take leave to query whether you are a Christian."[1]

This is a change Paul has been talking about all along, of course. He has been pointing to the difference in a person's life when one who formerly was apart from Christ becomes a believer.

1. D. M. Lloyd-Jones, *Romans: An Exposition of Chapters 7:1—8:4, The Law: Its Functions and Limits* (Grand Rapids: Zondervan, 1973), p. 83.

As far back as Romans 5, Paul contrasted our being in Adam with our being in Christ. The former is what we were before our conversion. The latter is what we have become after it—what we are now. In chapter 6 he contrasted our original slavery to sin with our new and happy slavery to God. In the first verses of chapter 7 he spoke of two marriages and explained how we have died to the former in order to have the latter. Paul is developing the same idea here. It is obvious that he is, because he begins with the word *for*, thus linking this section with what has gone before.

Paul wants us to know—Can we possibly doubt this after what he has said earlier?—that to be a Christian is to be "a new creation" in Christ (2 Cor. 5:17). To be saved means that we are no longer what we were and that we must live differently.

In the Flesh or in the Spirit

Since the strength of these verses is in the powerful terms Paul uses, we need to spend some time in understanding them. The first important term is "sinful nature" or, more literally, "flesh." "Flesh" (*sarx*) is the word the Greek text uses.

This term has already occurred several times in Romans.[2] But this is the first time it has occurred with the special theological meaning Paul so often gives it in his writings. In this fuller, theological sense it will appear many times more in the remainder of this chapter and through verse 13 of chapter 8.[3] It is so important and is used so often in these chapters that we must take special pains to understand it. If we fail to understand it, we will err not only in interpreting these two verses but also in interpreting the rest of Romans 7 and Romans 8. Some have made this error, of course, and the result has been at least one (and probably more than one) wrong doctrine.

The problem is that the word *flesh* is used in different senses, as many English words are. What does the word *mind* mean in English? It usually means "brain." But it can also mean "determination," as in "having a mind to do something." As a verb it can mean "be careful," as in "mind what you do." In philosophy "mind" can mean the controlling spirit of the universe. It is the same with *sarx* in the Greek language.

Basically *sarx* means the soft or fleshly parts of the body, which is how the resurrected Jesus used the word when he told the disciples that "a ghost does not have flesh and bones, as you see I have" (Luke 24:39). Sometimes "flesh" means the whole body, as in Galatians 2:20: ". . . the life which I now live in the flesh I live by the faith of the Son of God, who loved me and gave himself for me" (KJV). (The New International Version of that verse translates "in the flesh" as "in the body.") Sometimes *sarx* refers to the sensual part of our nature. That is why Paul can say in Galatians 5:17a, "For the sin-

2. In Romans 1:3; 2:28; 3:20; 4:1; 6:19.
3. In Romans 7:18, 25; 8:1, 3 (twice), 4, 5, 8, 9, 12, 13.

ful nature ['flesh'] desires what is contrary to the Spirit, and the Spirit what is contrary to the sinful nature." At still other times "flesh" can refer to the whole of mankind, as in the translation "all flesh" (KJV) in Isaiah 40:6; 1 Peter 1:24; and other passages.

What does "flesh" (*sarx*) mean in Romans 7:5? In this case it obviously does not mean the whole of mankind, because it is being used as a contrast to those who are "in the Spirit." And it is not referring to the body or even to any parts of the body. In Romans it is a term for the unregenerate, for unbelievers. It is what we were before God saved us.

We see this clearly in Romans 8: "Those who live according to the sinful nature ['flesh'] have their minds set on what that nature desires; but those who live in accordance with the Spirit have their minds set on what the Spirit desires. The mind of sinful man is death, but the mind controlled by the Spirit is life and peace; the sinful mind is hostile to God. It does not submit to God's law, nor can it do so. Those controlled by the sinful nature cannot please God. You, however, are not controlled by the sinful nature but by the Spirit, if the Spirit of God lives in you" (vv. 5–9).

Eduard Schweizer says of this characteristic theological use of the word by Paul, "Where *sarx* is understood in a full theological sense . . . it denotes the being of man which is determined, not by his physical substance, but by his relationship to God."[4]

The "Carnal" Christian?

Paul's use of the word *flesh* ("sinful nature") in Romans 7 and 8 is so clear that it would be unnecessary to elaborate this point were it not for an unfortunate misuse of the term in some areas of contemporary Christianity. This misuse is commonly known as "the doctrine of the carnal Christian"— "carnal" being only another word for "flesh." It leads to a serious misunderstanding of the next section of Romans, as well as other passages.

The idea of the carnal Christian is that human beings fall into three different classes: (1) those that are not saved; (2) Christians who are sinful, immature, or "carnal"; and (3) Christians who are "spiritual." In a study of Romans it is usually said that the "man" portrayed in Romans 7:14 and following is an example of the carnal Christian. He is saved, but he is not living that way. He is defeated. It is most often said that what he needs to do is get out of Romans 7 into Romans 8. He needs to live "in the Spirit."

Since we are going to deal with this at greater length in subsequent studies, what I have to say here is only preliminary. Still, even in a preliminary way, it is necessary to point out that the doctrine of the "carnal" Christian does not fit this context. It is important to see this, for we will never under-

---

4. For a thorough study of *sarx*, see the full article on the word by Eduard Schweizer in *Theological Dictionary of the New Testament*, vol. 7, ed. Gerhard Friedrich, trans. Geoffrey W. Bromiley (Grand Rapids: Wm. B. Eerdmans, 1971), pp. 98–151. The quotation is from p. 134.

stand Romans 7 and 8 correctly if we think of them as describing a defeated Christian who somehow becomes a victorious one. Paul is not talking about a carnal Christian *versus* a spiritual Christian at all, but rather about an unbeliever *versus* a Christian. The contrast is between what we were before our conversion and what we are now. It is the same contrast seen in being in Adam *versus* being in Christ, or being in slavery to the law *versus* being God's servants, which we have already seen in earlier sections of Romans.

That can be made quite clear to most people. Yet many will still ask quite understandably, "But what about 1 Corinthians 3?" In that chapter Paul writes to the Corinthians, "Brothers, I could not address you as spiritual but as worldly ("fleshly")—mere infants in Christ. . . . For since there is jealousy and quarreling among you, are you not worldly? Are you not acting like mere men?" (vv. 1, 3).

Those verses are often cited as the best support for the carnal-Christian doctrine in Scripture, but a close examination will show that that teaching does not follow from Paul's statements. They are mistakenly supposed to teach that men and women can become Christians and yet continue in a sinful or carnal state, passing on to a fuller commitment later. But that is precisely what 1 Corinthians 3 does *not* say. The Christians in Corinth were indeed acting badly, as Christians frequently do. In that area of their lives they were "worldly." That is, they were acting as if they were not Christians, as "mere men," unregenerate. But because they were not unregenerate but were actually Christians, they had to stop that bad behavior. Their sin was inconsistent with what they had become in Christ and was therefore intolerable.

This is precisely what Paul has been saying all along in these middle chapters of Romans. He has been teaching that the Christian is not what he was before he became a Christian and, for that very reason, he must (and will) live differently.[5]

Sin Aroused by the Law

The next thing Paul says, as he develops the contrast between what we were then and what by the grace of God we have become now, is that our relationship to the law has changed profoundly. That is, not only have we been changed; our relationships, beginning with the law, have changed, too.

Here again we have to look at a few terms carefully. The first is "passions," which occurs in the phrase "sinful passions" (*pathēmata tōn hamartiōn*). By itself the word *passions* is neutral and even somewhat passive. It is based on the Greek word from which we get our word *pathos*, and it cor-

5. For a helpful discussion of the doctrine of "the carnal Christian" see Ernest C. Reisinger, *What Should We Think of "the Carnal Christian"?* (Edinburgh, and Carlisle, Pa.: The Banner of Truth Trust, n.d.).

responds to what we usually mean when we speak of our natural appetites, impulses, or emotions. Impulses can be good or bad. That is, they can flow from good or bad desires, and they can be acted upon by good or bad influences. But here Paul links these normally neutral passions to sin, calling them "sinful passions," pointing out that when the law is allowed to work upon them it excites them not to good but to bad behavior.

What does this mean? Does it mean that the law of God, which is "good," as Paul is going to say in verse 12, itself turns morally neutral appetites or impulses into bad appetites or impulses? Not at all! The problem is that in the unregenerate man or woman these impulses, though not necessarily good or bad in themselves, are in fact bad, because they have been corrupted by our sinful natures. When the law tells us that we should not do something, our sinful natures rebel and do evil instead.

The law is good, but we are not good. Hence, before our conversions the law actually increased rather than reduced immorality.

Again, we will be considering this at greater length in future studies, for verses 5 and 6 are a seedbed of important ideas that Paul develops later. Still we need to see even here how profound Paul's statement is. What Paul is saying is that the cause of sinful acts lies in the sinful nature (or corrupted passions) of unregenerate people and not in the absence of good laws. In fact, there is a sense in which, because the problem is in *us*, good laws, even the good laws of God, merely aggravate or increase the sinful conduct. Because of our perversity, they actually make things worse.

D. Martyn Lloyd-Jones was very perceptive at this point, arguing (I think rightly) that there is a type of secular teaching of morality that does more harm than good, particularly among the young. This has bearing on our current efforts to teach sex education in the public schools. Morality can be taught by example and by a discussion of worthy values. We can talk helpfully about honesty, generosity, fair play, and such things. But trying to teach morality by introducing young people (or anyone else) to behavior they have not yet heard of or know little about—deviant sexual practices, for instance, or the use of drugs—does not prepare them to resist the sin but only instills in them a desire to commit the sin in question.

Here is what Lloyd-Jones says.

> To teach morality may be a positive danger, for it tends to inflame the passions; it encourages them. . . . A minister of religion once told me that the book that had done him the greatest amount of harm in his own personal life was a book entitled *The Mastery of Sex*. Avoid such books, for they will do more harm than good. The reason is that 'the motions of sins' are actually inflamed even by the Law of God. The very law that prohibits them encourages us to do them, because *we* are impure. So morality teaching can even be a positive danger. By teaching children about sex, and by warning them against the consequences of certain actions, what you are really doing is to

introduce them to the whole subject. Naturally they will greatly enjoy it, their curiosity will be aroused, and they will desire to read further.[6]

But I hear someone ask, "What shall we do, then? Are you telling us that we should never mention matters of morality to our children?" No, that is not it. There is a place for the right kind of moral teaching. But even with right moral teaching, you should know, if you are a Christian, that the important thing is not whether your children know what is right or wrong, though that is important, but whether they are Christians, too. For they are no different from ourselves. And what Paul is saying here is that before our conversion the law served only to arouse our sinful passions. It pushed us to sin. It was only after we had come to Christ that this changed and we found ourselves being drawn in the way of righteousness by God's Spirit.

Let us stop fooling ourselves about our children. The reason many of them are acting so badly is that they are not Christians. And let us also stop fooling ourselves about many of the grown-up churchgoers we know. The reason they do the sinful things they do is that they are not Christians either. Christians can sin, and they do. But they do not continue in it. What they do is what Paul says they do in verse 6: "But now, by dying to what once bound us, we have been released from the law so that we serve in the new way of the Spirit, and not in the old way of the written code."

Serving Him

That brings us to the final contrast in these verses. We have looked at the contrast between what we were and what we are now. We have looked at the contrast between our former and present relationships to the law. The final contrast is between what we did as unbelievers, the "fruit" we bore, and our present fruitfulness as Christians.

"What was the sum total of our work as unbelievers?" asks Paul. "We bore fruit for death" is his answer (v. 5). This is a different way of putting what he said in verse 4, though it amounts to the same thing. In verses 2–4, where he was using the marriage illustration, he was saying that we were fruitless while married to the law, because the law was impotent. He meant that we were unable to do good works. Now, in apparent contradiction, he says that we actually did bear fruit. However, his point is the same, for the fruit we bore then was fruit for death. Hence, we could do nothing to please God, and all we did do displeased him.

Even when we thought we were doing fine! Paul knew this by experience. He says in Philippians that before he met Christ he was so outstanding in his conduct that he could claim to have been "faultless" in respect to legal

6. Lloyd-Jones, *Romans: An Exposition of Chapters 7:1–8:4, The Law: Its Functions and Limits*, pp. 80, 81.

righteousness (Phil. 3:6). To use the terminology of Romans 7:6, he was indeed serving faultlessly "in the old way of the written code."

But it was not "in the Spirit." So not only was it not acceptable to God, it was actually evil. It was an exercise in self-righteousness, and it led even to the persecution of Christians. It was "fruit" of a sort. But it was fruit unto "death" quite literally.

What a difference when a person comes to Christ! In coming to Christ he or she is freed from a former unfruitful marriage to the law. The word Paul uses here (*katērgēthēmen*) is the word used in verse 2, where he spoke of a woman being freed from the law of marriage to her former husband by his death. Paul's point is the same. We died to the law in order to be brought into a new and fruitful relationship.[7]

But let me now apply this in a slightly different way than I have done before. Up to this point I have been stressing what Paul himself has been stressing: that if we have been saved by God through the work of Jesus Christ, we must (and will) live differently. I have said that if we are not living differently, if we are simply continuing in sin as before, we are not Christians, regardless of our outward profession. I have often said to fellow Christians that the fruit of conversion must be seen in our lives.

Now I want to say something more. If those about us who are Christians really are Christians, not only is it the case that they *must* bear fruit to God—serving "in the new way of the Spirit, and not in the old way of the written code"—they actually *are doing so*, regardless of whether or not they are doing it in precisely the way you and I are doing it. They may be very different from us and may be serving in very different ways. But if they are truly Christians, they are serving God, and we should acknowledge it.

I want to tell you an incident from the life of Donald Grey Barnhouse that illustrates this truth. He was at a luncheon of ministers, and one of them remarked on the frigidity of a certain denomination. He was bothered by how little its ministers seemed to accomplish. Barnhouse replied by probing the thoughts of the others a bit further. He told of a scholar in that denomination who went through theological seminary and was ordained. But he seldom preached. In fact, he never went to a prayer meeting and even absented himself from church for many weeks at a time. He was really a bookworm and spent his days in the library. Even worse, he was intemperate in certain of his personal habits. The man lived this way for more than twenty years.

7. This is one of the few passages in which the King James translators were entirely off base. They spoke of "that being dead in which we were held," meaning the law had died. But that was not the point of verse 4, and it is not the point here. Paul's argument in both places, as virtually all the commentators agree, is that *we* have died to the law by means of our union to Christ. His death was our death. Therefore, our old relationship to the law has ended and we have entered into a new and fruitful union to Jesus Christ. For a discussion of this point see Charles Hodge, *A Commentary on Romans* (Edinburgh and Carlisle, Pa.: The Banner of Truth Trust, 1972), p. 219.

"What is your opinion of such a minister?" Barnhouse asked.

The others agreed that a man like that was no credit to the ministry.

The conversation took another turn, and Barnhouse asked what study helps these ministers used in sermon preparation, especially what they considered to be the most helpful concordance. They were unanimous in preferring Strong's concordance. ("Strong's for the strong. Young's for the young. Cruden's for the crude," we used to say in seminary.) They seemed to prefer Strong's for its Hebrew and Greek helps and for its comparative word lists. It saved them hours of work each week and was, they agreed, their most valuable tool.

Barnhouse then said, "The man whom you said was no credit to the ministry was James Strong, the author of the concordance you all find so valuable."

The ministers quickly saw the point. God does not give his children identical jobs to do. The ways they are called to serve vary. But all are serving in some way, if they are truly Christians. Barnhouse wrote, "The most forlorn Christian in the most humble surroundings, living in penury on the lowest cultural scale, is serving a purpose in the divine plan. The convert from a savage tribe, the professor in his study, the flighty young girl—all are serving the Lord. We must not be satisfied with the way we are serving him, but we must be satisfied with the place where God has put us. He wants you exactly where you are today."[8]

Let's accept that—for others and for ourselves—and then make sure that we are actually serving him faithfully.

---

8. Donald Grey Barnhouse, *God's Freedom: Exposition of Bible Doctrines, Taking the Epistle to the Romans as a Point of Departure*, vol. 6, Romans 6:1—7:25 (Grand Rapids: Wm. B. Eerdmans, 1961), pp. 217, 218.

89

Sin's Sad Use of God's Good Law

Romans 7:7–12

What shall we say, then? Is the law sin? Certainly not! Indeed I would not have known what sin was except through the law. For I would not have known what coveting really was if the law had not said, "Do not covet." But sin, seizing the opportunity afforded by the commandment, produced in me every kind of covetous desire. For apart from law, sin is dead. Once I was alive apart from law; but when the commandment came, sin sprang to life and I died. I found that the very commandment that was intended to bring life actually brought death. For sin, seizing the opportunity afforded by the commandment, deceived me, and through the commandment put me to death. So then, the law is holy, and the commandment is holy, righteous and good.

A person would have to be extremely dense to have come as far as we have in our study of Romans and still not understand the limits of the law according to Paul's teaching. In the earliest chapters he has shown that law cannot justify a person. In the later chapters he has shown that neither can the law sanctify anyone. Therefore, if we are to be delivered from sin's penalty and power, it must be by the work of God in Jesus Christ and by the Holy Spirit.

But sometimes the very weight of an argument proves too much and appears to collapse because of it. That is what many people—perhaps you are one of them—might think here.

Someone might say: "Paul, you have shown that the law cannot justify or sanctify a person; it cannot declare him to be upright, and it cannot help him to become upright if he is not. If that is so, what is the value of the law? Doesn't that mean that the law actually has no worth and should just be thrown out entirely?" Or again: "You have said that sin is aroused by law so that those who hear the law actually do bad things they would not otherwise do. If that is the case, aren't you making the law of God sinful since it leads to evil?"

Since the law is from God, and God cannot do evil or produce anything that is evil, the gospel Paul teaches seems to collapse by this extension of it. However, these are faulty objections. The verses to which we come now show emphatically why the law is not sinful. In particular they speak of three good things the law does, even though it is powerless either to justify or sanctify a person.

The Law Reveals Sin As Sin

The first thing the law accomplishes, according to verse 7, is to reveal sin as sin. The verse says, "What shall we say, then? Is the law sin? Certainly not! Indeed I would not have known what sin was except through the law. For I would not have known what coveting really was if the law had not said, 'Do not covet.'"

There are two problems here, and it is important to understand both. The first problem is that if left to themselves, people never naturally think they are sinners. Take Genesis 6:5 as an example. It says that prior to the flood "the LORD saw how great man's wickedness on the earth had become, and that every inclination of the thoughts of his heart was only evil all the time." That is a description of sin as God sees it—*every inclination of the thoughts of our hearts only evil all the time.* But who really believes that? Who believes that his or her every inclination is to do evil? No one believes it apart from a supernatural illumination of his or her mind by the Holy Spirit.

Or take Romans 3:10–12, which we studied earlier: "'There is no one righteous, not even one; there is no one who understands, no one who seeks God. All have turned away, they have together become worthless; there is no one who does good, not even one.'" No one naturally believes that unless God reveals it to the person.

The second problem is this: Even if, by some means, we are able to admit that we have done bad things, we are never able to recognize those things as "sin" unless we can also be shown that they transgress the law of God. If we do things against the law of nature, or disregard standards of fair play or other moral criteria most people acknowledge, we may recognize those acts to be "wrong." We may violate the legal code of the country in which we live and recognize our acts to be "criminal." But we do not call either the morally wrong behavior or the criminal acts "sin" unless we see that these also violate God's law.

So the first good thing the law does is reveal that we are sinners. It does this by showing that the bad things we do are an offense to God. Leon Morris has it right when he says, "People without God's law do not see wrongdoing as it really is. . . . It takes the law to show wrongdoing to be sin."[1]

In the second half of verse 7, Paul gives an illustration that is apparently from his personal experience, since this is the first place in the chapter where he speaks in the first person. His example has to do with covetousness, which is condemned by the last of the Ten Commandments. Paul seems to be saying that this was the point at which the conviction that he was himself a sinner was activated.

We know what Paul thought of himself before God began to work with him, because he tells about it in the third chapter of Philippians. Did Paul think he was a sinner in those days? When he was going around hating Christians? And killing some? Not at all! On the contrary, he thought that he was a very moral man. He says that as far as "legalistic righteousness" is concerned he considered himself to be "faultless" (Phil. 3:6). He thought he was a model of virtue. It was only as the law began to work on him—starting with the words "Do not covet"—that he saw himself as a sinner.[2]

The Law Provokes Sin

The second good thing the law of God does is provoke sin, thereby drawing forth the realization of how bad sin really is. Here is the way Paul puts it: "But sin, seizing the opportunity afforded by the commandment, produced in me every kind of covetous desire . . ." (v. 8). This is what I call "sin's sad use of God's good law." We see it in several areas.

1. *Sin, seizing the opportunity afforded by the commandment, creates a surge of rebellion in our hearts.* The rebellion has been there all along, of course. That is what it means to be a sinner. It means to be a rebel against God. But when the law comes, this dormant rebellion is aroused from its slumber, as it were, and we discover what we are at heart.

Let me give two illustrations.

First, a biblical illustration. In the third chapter of Genesis we are told how Adam and Eve rebelled against God regarding the tree of the knowledge of good and evil. If God had not given them this law, there would have been nothing for them to have rebelled against and they would have contin-

---

1. Leon Morris, *The Epistle to the Romans* (Grand Rapids: William B. Eerdmans, and Leicester, England: Inter-Varsity Press, 1988), pp. 278, 279.

2. Murray says, "Apparently covetousness was the last vice of which he suspected himself; it was the first to be exposed" (John Murray, *The Epistle to the Romans* [Grand Rapids: Wm. B. Eerdmans, 1968], p. 249).

ued in innocence. However, as soon as God said, "You must not eat from the tree of the knowledge of good and evil, for when you eat of it you will surely die" (Gen. 2:17), this was the one thing Adam particularly wanted to do. Sin, seizing the opportunity afforded by the commandment, produced in him that covetous desire.

We know that Adam and Eve possessed an original innocence. So it is hard to explain—perhaps impossible to explain—how they could have rebelled against God's law. We cannot explain where sin came from. Nevertheless, the story of the fall is given to us in the form it is given to show how the law itself brings out our rebellion.

Here is an historical illustration. Saint Augustine in his *Confessions* tells of a time in his youth when he and a band of his friends went into a neighbor's field at night to steal pears. They shook the neighbor's pear tree, knocking down a large quantity of pears, then carried them off, eating a few but throwing most of them to some pigs. Why did Augustine steal the pears? With characteristic thoroughness, this great medieval theologian analyzes the question for many pages.

Was it the beauty of the pears? They were beautiful, it is true, since they were part of God's creation. But that was not why he stole them. He had others of even greater beauty at home.

Was he hungry and needed something to eat? That was not it.

Did he want to be approved by the others? That was part of the reason, he says. But it does not explain why the others, like himself, should have given approval for such a wrong act. Why should stealing be praiseworthy?

At last Augustine gets to the real reason, saying, "I only picked them so that I might steal. . . . I loved nothing in it except the thieving." It is a way of saying that the desire to steal was awakened by the prohibition.[3]

2. *Sin, seizing the opportunity afforded by the commandment, creates a desire to sin in ways that were not even thought of before.* In telling us not to do something, the law actually sets us to thinking about it, and because we are sinful people we soon find ourselves wanting to do that very thing.

Here is a personal illustration. One spring, when I was in the sixth grade, our school principal came into the classroom just before we were to be released to go home for lunch. He said he had heard that some of the students had been bringing firecrackers to school, and he wanted to say that this was definitely not allowed. Firecrackers were dangerous. They were against Pennsylvania state law. If any of his students even brought a firecracker into school, even if he did not set it off, he would be expelled from school immediately. He would never be able to come back.

Well! I did not own any firecrackers. I had not even been thinking about firecrackers. But, you know, when you get to thinking about firecrackers

3. Saint Augustine, *Confessions*, trans. R. S. Piné-Coffin (Harmondsworth, England: Penguin Books, 1961), pp. 47–53.

that really is an intriguing subject. And as I thought about them I remembered that one of my friends had some.

On the way home for lunch a friend and I went by this other friend's house, picked up a firecracker, and returned to school with it forty-five minutes later. We went into the cloakroom, invited another boy to come in with us, and said, "You hold the firecracker by the middle of the fuse. Pinch it very tight. Then we will light it. The others will think that it is going to explode. But when it burns down to your fingers it will go out, and everything will be all right."

What we had not counted on was that the lighted fuse would burn our friend's fingers. When it did, our friend dropped the firecracker. It exploded in an immense cloud of blue smoke and tiny bits of white paper, in the midst of which we emerged, a bit shaken, from the closet.

You cannot imagine how loud a firecracker sounds in an old school building with high ceilings, marble floors, and plaster walls! Nor can you imagine how quickly a principal can rush out of his office, down the hall, and into one of the classrooms. The principal was there even before my friends and I had staggered through the cloakroom's open door. He was as stunned as we were, though differently. I remember him saying over and over again, after we had been sent home and had come back to his office with our parents, "I had just made the announcement. I had just told them not to bring any firecrackers into school. I just can't believe it." He couldn't believe it then. But I am sure that our rebellion, as well as countless other acts of rebellion by thousands of children over the years, eventually turned him into a staunch, believing Calvinist—at least so far as the doctrine of total depravity of children is concerned.

That is what the law does. It provokes wickedness. Moreover, in doing so, it shows us not only that sin is sin, a violation of the law of God; it also shows how strong sin is. It must be very powerful if it can use even God's good law for such ends.

The Law Brings Us to the End of Ourselves

The third good thing the law does is bring us to the end of ourselves—to "death." This is what Paul is talking about in the latter half of this section, where he says: "Once I was alive apart from law; but when the commandment came, sin sprang to life and I died. I found that the very commandment that was intended to bring life actually brought death. For sin, seizing the opportunity afforded by the commandment, deceived me, and through the commandment put me to death" (vv. 9–11).

What does this mean? In what sense was Paul once "alive apart from the law"? Was he ever without knowledge of the law? And in what sense was he put to death?

The meaning of the passage seems to be quite clear. There was a time in Paul's life—we were talking about it earlier in regard to his claim to have been faultless as to legalistic righteousness—when Paul thought he was in good standing before God. God had told him what to do, and he had done it. If ever there was anyone who had pleased God, surely it was himself, Paul. As Leon Morris says, "He [was] alive in the sense that he had never been put to death as a result of a confrontation with the law of God."[4] But then the commandment came. That is, it came home to him. He had known it before. If he is still referring to covetousness at this point, as he may be, he had known not to covet from his youth. But now he began to understand the commandment, and with this his self-righteousness and self-confidence began to melt away. The words he uses are: "I died."

What happened to him is what I have been describing. When the law finally began to get through to Paul to do its proper work, he saw (1) that he was guilty of having broken it, and (2) that his nature was such that, instead of wanting to keep it, he actually wanted to break it. Instead of driving sin out, the law awakened sin. He saw how hopeless his sinful condition was.

But that was a good thing, you see! As long as Paul thought he was doing all right, he was on his way to perdition. It was only when he learned he was lost that he was ready to hear God's words about the Savior.

Is the Law Sin? Certainly Not!

Is the law sin, then? That is the question with which Paul started out. Here is his answer: "Certainly not!" (v. 7). Rather, as we have seen, "The law is holy, and the commandment is holy, righteous and good" (v. 12). The law does exactly what God sent it into the world to do, and that purpose, actually a threefold purpose, is good.

This leads to a few important conclusions.

First, *the law can never save anyone.* It never has saved anyone and it never will. It was not meant to. Therefore, if you have been thinking of yourself as a fairly decent person—who generally measures up to whatever moral standards seem reasonable—and believe that God should be glad to accept your self-assessment, bless you in life, and in the end receive you into heaven, it is not the case that you have been hearing and obeying the law. Rather, you have not really begun even to understand it. The law is condemning you, but you, in your ignorance, are supposing that everything is all right.

What has been happening to you is what Paul describes in verse 11. "Sin, seizing the opportunity afforded by the commandment, deceived" you. How? By making you think that everything is fine, when actually you are perishing.

How subtle sin is! In his commentary on these verses, D. Martyn Lloyd-Jones lists nine ways in which sin commonly deceives us.

4. Morris, *The Epistle to the Romans*, p. 281.

1. Sin gets us to misuse the law, convincing us that as long as we have not sinned outwardly and visibly, we are all right, forgetting that with God the thoughts and intentions of the heart are all important.

2. Sometimes sin changes its tactics and tells us that everything is hopeless and we might as well keep on sinning.

3. Sin tells us that it does not matter whether or not we are holy. It says, "Why don't you keep on sinning so that grace may abound?"

4. Sin deceives us by making us angry at the law, feeling that God is against us if he prohibits anything. If he were for us, we think, he would let us do what we want to do and be happy.

5. Sin gets us to believe that the law is unreasonable, impossible, and unjust.

6. Sin makes us think very highly of ourselves. It makes us ask why we should be bound by any law. Why shouldn't we become what Friedrich Nietzsche called a "superman" or a "superwoman" and be a law unto ourselves?

7. Sin tells us that the law is oppressive, keeping us from developing the wonderful gifts and talents we have within us, all of which would emerge if only we did not have to be held back by God's commandments.

8. Sin makes righteousness look drab and unattractive.

9. Sin causes us to discount the consequences of willful disobedience. It whispers what Satan said to Eve, "You will not surely die" (Gen. 3:4). It says that the most preposterous idea in the whole world is hell, forgetting that the Lord Jesus Christ spoke of hell more often than anyone else in the Bible.[5]

If you are expecting to be judged righteous by God on the basis of your own good works, which is a form of law-keeping, sin has tricked you by one or more of these common spiritual deceptions, and you have not even begun to know what the law has been given to us for—let alone know and understand the gospel. Let me say it again: The law was not meant to save anyone. It was given to reveal sin as sin, to provoke sin in sinners, and to make clear our completely hopeless condition apart from Jesus Christ.

The law points us to Christ, whom we need desperately, especially if we are blindly trusting in our ability to keep it for the sake of our salvation.

Second, *we need to teach the law to awaken people to their sinfulness and show them their need of a Savior.* This is what the Puritans did so brilliantly. They even spoke of it by the terminology Paul uses in Romans. They said it was the preacher's task to "slay" men by the law so that they might be "raised up" by the gospel. We need that kind of preaching today. People need to know the uselessness of their own good works and so-called righteousness. They need to know how utterly hopeless the situation is without a Savior.

---

5. D. M. Lloyd-Jones, *Romans: An Exposition of Chapters 7:1—8:4, The Law: Its Functions and Limits* (Grand Rapids: Zondervan, 1973), pp. 155–160.

They need to be convinced in their very bones that Jesus Christ is the only hope they have.

Instead, the majority of our churches provide largely self-help sermons and seminars designed to make people feel that they are doing very well, or at least are able to do very well, all by themselves. These churches do not use the law to bring them to the utter end of their self-confidence.

And it must be the *utter* end, which is why the Puritans spoke of "slaying" people with the law. To slay means to kill. It does not mean to wound or make sick. It means to destroy self-righteousness.

John H. Gerstner, Pittsburgh Theological Seminary's retired Professor of Church History, was preaching on Romans and expounding on the law. He was stripping away the veil on human wickedness. After the service, when he had gone to the back of the church, a woman approached him. She was holding up her hand with her index finger and thumb about a half-inch apart, and she said to Gerstner, "Dr. Gerstner, you make me feel this big."

Gerstner replied, "But, Madam, that's too big. That's much too big. Don't you know that that much self-righteousness will take you to hell?" He was right. The law was given to drive out *all* self-righteousness so that we might embrace Jesus Christ alone as our Savior.

90

Whatever Became of Sin?

Romans 7:13

Did that which is good, then, become death to me? By no means! But in order that sin might be recognized as sin, it produced death in me through what was good, so that through the commandment sin might become utterly sinful.

Whatever became of sin?"

As we have seen in our study of Romans 6:19–22, that is the question Dr. Karl Menninger, founder of the world-renowned Menninger Clinic in Topeka, Kansas, asked in the title of his best-selling book of 1973.[1] His answer was simple. In the lifetimes of many of us, Menninger argued, sin has been redefined: first, as crime—that is, as transgression of the law of man rather than transgression of the law of God—and second, as symptoms. Since "symptoms" are caused by things external to the individual, they are seen as effects for which the offender is not responsible. Thus it happened that sin against God has been redefined (and dismissed) as the unfortunate effects of bad circumstances. And no one is to blame.

1. Karl Menninger, *Whatever Became of Sin?* (New York: Bantam Books, 1978).

747

Yet sin *is* sin—and we *are* to blame. Sin, whether we acknowledge it or not, really is "any want of conformity unto or transgression of the law of God" (*The Westminster Shorter Catechism,* Answer 14).

This is what Paul has been talking about in Romans 7, of course. He has not begun at the point with which I have begun this chapter: with our lack of any true sense of being sinners. Rather, he has been approaching it from the other side, writing about the law and its functions. But the link between these two elements, sin and the law, is a matter of importance and is what Paul has been treating. His argument is that it is only by the law of God that we learn that sin really is sin and discover how evil it is.

Do you remember how Paul made these points in the paragraph containing verses 7–12? He argued that:

1. The law reveals sin to be sin.

2. Sin, seizing the opportunity afforded by the commandments of God, creates a surge of rebellion against those commands in our hearts and creates desires to sin in ways that we had not even thought of before.

3. In this way, the law, operated upon by sin, brings us to the end of ourselves.

And all this is good! Prior to receiving and understanding the law, we all think that we are doing pretty well, that we do not need a Savior or even God. It is only when the law has exposed our true nature to us, showing how bad we are, that we become open to the gospel.

This is now stated again in verse 13. In fact, what Paul says here is almost a direct echo of verse 7. "Did that which is good, then, become death to me? By no means! But in order that sin might be recognized as sin, it produced death in me through what was good, so that through the commandment sin might become utterly sinful."

Following up on that verse, I want to show in this study how the law actually operates. I want to do it by reviewing the Ten Commandments.

The First Commandment

The first commandment begins where we might expect it to begin, namely, in the area of our relationships to God. It says, "I am the LORD your God, who brought you out of the land of Egypt, out of the land of slavery. You shall have no other gods before me" (Exod. 20:2–3).

This command requires us to worship the true God and to worship him only. John R. W. Stott writes:

> It is not necessary to worship the sun, the moon and the stars to break this law. We break it whenever we give to something or someone other than God himself the first place in our thoughts or our affections. It may be some engrossing sport, absorbing hobby, or selfish ambition. Or it may be someone whom we idolize. We may worship a god of gold and silver in the form of safe investments and a healthy bank balance, or a God of wood and stone

in the form of property and possessions. . . . Sin is fundamentally the exaltation of self at the expense of God. What someone wrote of the Englishman is true of everyman: "He is a self-made man who worships his creator."[2]

To keep the first commandment perfectly, which is the only way rightly to keep this or any of the commandments, is, as Jesus taught, to "love the Lord your God with all your heart and with all your soul and with all your mind" (Matt. 22:37; cf. Deut. 6:5). It means giving him first place in everything, in all our loves, goals, and actions. It means using all we are and have in his service. No one has ever kept this command perfectly except Jesus.

The Second Commandment

The first commandment dealt with the object of our worship, forbidding the worship of any false deity. The second commandment deals with the nature of our worship, forbidding us to worship even the true God unworthily. It speaks of this at length, saying, "You shall not make for yourself an idol in the form of anything in heaven above or on the earth beneath or in the waters below. You shall not bow down to them or worship them; for I, the LORD your God, am a jealous God, punishing the children for the sin of the fathers to the third and fourth generation of those who hate me, but showing love to a thousand generations of those who love me and keep my commandments" (Exod. 20:4–6).

What does this mean? Is it a condemnation of idol worship only, a text forbidding us to worship by means of gold, silver, wood, or stone objects? Obviously it means more than that. It concerns the worship of God by any and all inadequate means.

One inadequate means, one "idol," is the mental images of God we carry about in our heads. J. B. Phillips wrote an entire book about this, calling it *Your God Is Too Small.* He spoke of our inadequate images of God by such chapter titles as: Resident Policeman, Parental Hangover, Grand Old Man, Meek-and-Mild, Absolute Perfection, Heavenly Bosom, God-in-a-Box, Managing Director, Perennial Grievance, Pale Galilean, and so forth.[3] We all have these inadequate ideas of God, which we prove by our irritation with God when he refuses to conform to our misunderstanding of him as "small," or when he declines to do precisely what we want him to do on some occasion.

A second way we worship unworthily is by going through the forms of worship without actually engaging our hearts or minds in our devotions. We go to church, but our minds are somewhere else. We pray, but it is only our heads that bow down, not our hearts.

2. John R. W. Stott, *Basic Christianity* (Downers Grove, Ill.: InterVarsity Press, 1971), p. 65.
3. J. B. Phillips, *Your God Is Too Small* (New York: Macmillan, 1967).

The Third Commandment

The third commandment says, "You shall not misuse the name of the LORD your God, for the LORD will not hold anyone guiltless who misuses his name" (Exod. 20:7). This law is widely flouted in our time, and not only by people who swear ferociously—or even mildly, by using the almost universal exclamation, "Oh, my God!" The commandment is broken when we confess Jesus to be "Lord" but do not follow him as Lord, or when we call God "Father" but do not trust him as the loving parent he is.

The great Puritan pastor and writer Thomas Watson said, "We take God's name in vain:

1. When we speak slightly and irreverently of his name. . . .
2. When we profess God's name, but do not live answerably to it. . . .
3. When we use God's name in idle discourse. . . .
4. When we worship him with our lips, but not with our hearts. . . .
5. When we pray to him, but do not believe in him. . . .
6. When in any way we profane and abuse his word. . . .
7. When we swear by God's name. . . .
8. When we prefix God's name to any wicked action. . . .
9. When we use our tongues any way to the dishonor of God's name. . . .
10. When we make rash and unlawful vows. . . .
11. When we speak evil of God. . . .
12. When we falsify our promise."[4]

Some people may take such ways of dishonoring God's name lightly, thinking them of no great account. But God says that *he* takes the third commandment very seriously. He says that he "will not hold anyone guiltless" who commits these offenses.

The Fourth Commandment

"Remember the Sabbath day by keeping it holy. Six days you shall labor and do all your work, but the seventh day is a Sabbath to the LORD your God. On it you shall not do any work, neither you, nor your son or daughter, nor your manservant or maidservant, nor your animals, nor the alien within your gates. For in six days the LORD made the heavens and the earth, the sea, and all that is in them, but he rested on the seventh day. Therefore the LORD blessed the Sabbath day and made it holy" (Exod. 20:8–11).

These verses contain the longest elaboration on any one of the Ten Commandments. Yet there are differences among Christians concerning their interpretation. Some insist that they require Christians to worship on Saturday, the Jewish Sabbath. Seventh-day Adventists are an example.

4. Thomas Watson, *The Ten Commandments* (London: The Banner of Truth Trust, 1970), pp. 85–91. (Original edition 1692.)

Others believe that Christians are to worship on Sunday, the Lord's Day, but want their observance to be according to Judaic tradition, that is, to observe the Sabbath by inactivity, as the ancient Jews did. Still others think of the Lord's Day as a Christian innovation, a new day given to the church by God for worship and joyful service.

I think the New Testament supports the latter view. But I ask whether we really observe either Saturday or Sunday in any special way. Do we use the whole of either day for worship or Christian service? Who among us truly keeps the Sabbath or the Lord's Day "holy"?

The Fifth Commandment

When we pass from the fourth to the fifth commandment, we also pass from the first table of the law, which concerns our relationships to God, to the second table of the law, which concerns our relationships to other people. It begins with family relationships: "Honor your father and your mother, so that you may live long in the land the LORD your God is giving you" (Exod. 20:12).

This chiefly has to do with human authority, for our parents are the first human authority God sets over us. Other authorities, all with different and variously restricted powers, include the state, the leaders of the church, and our employers. To fulfill this command we would have to do what Paul says further on in Romans: "Give everyone what you owe him: If you owe taxes, pay taxes; if revenue, then revenue; if respect, then respect; if honor, then honor" (Rom. 13:7). Yet we all rebel against authority, beginning in the home. At times it seems that the home is where we are particularly rude, unmannerly, disobedient, and ungrateful.

The Sixth Commandment

"You shall not murder" (Exod. 20:13). Jesus explained this command by showing that it concerns more than the taking of another person's life. It also concerns damaging his or her reputation in any way. "I tell you that anyone who is angry with his brother will be subject to judgment," Jesus said (Matt. 5:22).

This commandment searches the depth of our beings, for if we are honest with ourselves we will admit that we are often very angry and say things explicitly intended to hurt the target of our anger. But is there no such thing as righteous anger? Of course. Jesus displayed righteous anger when he drove the money changers from the temple. But our anger is seldom like that. Instead, our anger is generally aroused only by some real or imagined slight against ourselves. Do we commit murder? Yes, we do—by this definition. We murder by neglect, spite, gossip, slander, and many other acts flowing from our own enormous pride or jealousy.

Even preachers! Thomas Watson, himself a preacher, said, "Ministers are murderers [if they] . . . starve, poison or infect souls."[5]

The Seventh Commandment

The seventh commandment is the one most of us think about most often when we remember God's commandments, if we remember them at all. This is hardly a surprise, because most of us are thinking of sexual matters, even sexual sins, most of the time, and this is one command that speaks directly to this area of our lives. It is in light of our sexuality that we seem to feel most guilty.

"You shall not commit adultery" (Exod. 20:14).

Jesus commented on this commandment also and, as in his interpretation of the prohibition against murder, he showed its true intention: "You have heard that it was said, 'Do not commit adultery.' But I tell you that anyone who looks at a woman lustfully has already committed adultery with her in his heart" (Matt. 5:27–28). John Stott has written of this commandment:

> It includes flirting, experimenting, and solitary sexual experience. It also includes all sexual perversions, for although men and women are not responsible for a perverted instinct, they are for its indulgence. It includes selfish demands within wedlock, and many, if not all, divorces. It includes the deliberate reading of pornographic literature, and giving in to impure fantasies. . . . The commandment . . . embraces every abuse of a sacred and beautiful gift of God."[6]

The positive side of this command is chastity before marriage and faithfulness afterwards.

The Eighth Commandment

"You shall not steal" (Exod. 20:15). The ban against stealing is almost a universal standard of the human race. It is found in most cultures. But it is only biblical religion that explains why it is wrong to steal, in addition to the obvious fact that theft is socially disruptive and inconvenient. The real reason it is wrong to steal is that what the other person possesses has been given to him or her by God. "Every good and perfect gift is from above, coming down from the Father of the heavenly lights . . ." (James 1:17). Therefore, to take anything from one to whom it is given is to sin against God.

We do this in many ways. We steal from an employer when we do not give him the best work of which we are capable or when we waste time or leave work early. We steal from our customers if we charge too much for our

5. Ibid., p. 143.
6. Stott, *Basic Christianity*, pp. 67, 68.

products or services or if we knowingly sell what is inferior. We steal from others when we borrow from them but do not return what we have borrowed on time, if at all. We steal from ourselves when we squander our talents or time. We steal from God directly when we neglect to give him the worship, honor, thanksgiving, and obedience he deserves.

There is a positive side to this command, too. For Paul, when he was writing to the Ephesians, said to those who had been thieves, "He who has been stealing must steal no longer, but must work, doing something useful with his own hands, that he may have something to share with those in need" (Eph. 4:28). According to Paul, the eighth commandment remained unfulfilled until the offender began to help others who were in need.

The Ninth Commandment

The ninth commandment says, "You shall not give false testimony against your neighbor" (Exod. 20:16). This is a warning against perjury. But again, it is far more than that. Negatively, it condemns all slander, idle talk, gossip, unkind rumors, jokes at another person's expense, lies, and deliberate exaggerations or distortions of the truth. It concerns even listening to such unkind things uncritically. Positively, the commandment concerns our failures to rise to the defense of those we know to be verbally abused in any way.

The Tenth Commandment

The tenth commandment is in some ways the most revealing and devastating of all, for it deals explicitly with the inward and not merely the outward nature of the law. It concerns covetousness, which is an internal attitude that may or may not express itself in an outwardly acquisitive act. The text says, "You shall not covet your neighbor's house. You shall not covet your neighbor's wife, or his manservant or maidservant, his ox or donkey, or anything that belongs to your neighbor" (Exod. 20:17).

Covetousness is a root sin, for, as Watson says, when it is exercised fully it causes a breach of each of the other commandments.[7]

How relevant and modern this is, and how keenly it strikes at our excessively materialistic culture. We live in a grasping and thus very offensive society. One offensive element of materialism is our insensitivity to the needs of others, which it so often breeds, since it is often only at the expense of others that we are able to get ahead. Even more offensive is our unreasonable dissatisfaction with our abundance of wealth and opportunity. Those who have most seem often to be the most unhappy. Unfortunately, this restless desire for more is what the media seem determined to produce in us and

7. Watson, *The Ten Commandments*, pp. 177, 178.

fan to white hot flames. There are few who even recognize what is happening, let along resist it substantially.

There is probably no other command that so exposes this characteristic sin of our time and generation.

But where do we go from here? We have used the Ten Commandments to explore ten areas in which God requires certain standards of conduct from us, and we have found ourselves to be sinners by those standards. And not only have we been exposed as sinners, which is what Paul writes about in the first part of Romans 7:13 ("in order that sin might be recognized as sin"), we have also been shown to be exceedingly sinful, which is what he says in the second half ("so that through the commandment sin might become utterly sinful"). In other words, sin is always much worse than we imagine. In fact, the more we read and understand the law, the greater our sin will seem to be. And that will continue until, like Paul himself, we cry out, "Who will rescue me from this body of death?" and we are able to answer, "God—through Jesus Christ our Lord!" (Rom. 7:24, 25).

God cannot condone sin, however much we may wish it. He tells us that he will by no means clear the guilty. He teaches that "the wages of sin is death" (Rom. 6:23). His judgment will be executed. But at the very time he exposes the sin, he also points us to Jesus, who is sin's remedy.

Return now to Paul's questions about the law in the first half of Romans 7.

First question: "Is the law sin?"

Answer: "Certainly not! Indeed I would not have known what sin was except through the law" (v. 7).

Second question: "Did that which is good, then, become death to me?"

Answer: "By no means! But in order that sin might be recognized as sin, it produced death in me through what was good, so that through the commandment sin might become utterly sinful" (v. 13).

And the end of that is life! Why? Because only those who know they are dead in trespasses and sins seek a Savior. Only those who know they are spiritually sick seek the Great Physician.[8]

---

8. Parts of the preceding study of the Ten Commandments follow closely the study of these found in James Montgomery Boice, *Foundations of the Christian Faith: A Comprehensive and Readable Theology* (Downers Grove, Ill.: InterVarsity Press, 1986), pp. 226–245.

91

Who Is the "Man" of Romans 7?

Romans 7:14–20

We know that the law is spiritual; but I am unspiritual, sold as a slave to sin. I do not understand what I do. For what I want to do I do not do, but what I hate I do. And if I do what I do not want to do, I agree that the law is good. As it is, it is no longer I myself who do it, but it is sin living in me. I know that nothing good lives in me, that is, in my sinful nature. For I have the desire to do what is good, but I cannot carry it out. For what I do is not the good I want to do; no, the evil I do not want to do—this I keep on doing. Now if I do what I do not want to do, it is no longer I who do it, but it is sin living in me that does it.

There are few passages in the Bible over which competent Bible students have divided more radically than the last half of Romans 7, beginning with verse 14. This is a section of the letter in which Paul is speaking of himself, describing a fierce internal struggle with sin. And the question is: Of what stage in his life is he speaking? Is he speaking of the present, that is, of the time of his writing the letter—when he was a mature Christian, indeed an apostle? Or is he speaking of himself as he was in the past, before his conversion? Or is the true answer somewhere in between?

Who is the "man" of Romans 7? This question has divided Bible students from the earliest days of the church and continues to divide them today.

It is a serious question, too. Some problems of Bible interpretation may be of limited importance, the specifics of prophecy, for instance. But this is a section of Romans in which Paul is discussing the Christian life. He seems to be answering two related questions: How can I live a triumphant Christian life? How can I achieve victory over sin? Any true Christian wants the answer to those questions. So, unlike differing opinions concerning other, less practical parts of Scripture, we all instinctively take seriously the discussion of any diverse interpretations of this passage.

How should we proceed? In this study I want to present four main interpretations of these verses and evaluate each one.

The "Man" of Romans 7 Is Unsaved

The first view is that the "man" of Romans 7 is the apostle Paul as he was while unregenerate, that is, when he was not yet a Christian. This seems to have been the dominant view in the early church. In fact, the great Saint Augustine held it at first, though later, as a result of his maturing study of the Bible, he came to believe that what is said here is true of the regenerate person, too.[1] According to this view, Paul could not say the things he says here if he were truly a Christian.

What things?

Well, that he is "a slave to sin," for example (v. 14). This claim is particularly troublesome because Paul has previously said, "But thanks be to God that, though you used to be slaves to sin, you wholeheartedly obeyed the form of teaching to which you were entrusted. You have been set free from sin and have become slaves to righteousness" (Rom. 6:17–18). If Paul is speaking as a Christian, how can he say that Christians have been freed from sin's slavery in chapter 6 and then say that he is himself "a slave to sin" in chapter 7?

Paul also says, "Nothing good lives in me" (v. 18). True, he qualifies that at once by adding, "that is, in my sinful nature." But even so, can a believer really speak in these terms, knowing that God dwells within him and is working "to will and to act according to his good purpose" (Phil. 2:13)?

A bit further on Paul cries, "What a wretched man I am! Who will rescue me from this body of death?" (v. 24). Doesn't he know that he has been rescued by Christ? How can any true Christian make that statement?

In spite of the appeal of this interpretation, which is considerable, the view has several major flaws which in our day have caused most commentators to abandon it. Let me suggest a few.

1. For an excellent summary of the history of the interpretation of this passage from the days of the Fathers forward, see Charles Hodge, *A Commentary on Romans* (Edinburgh and Carlisle, Pa.: The Banner of Truth Trust, 1972), pp. 239, 240. (Original edition 1935.)

1. *What Paul says of himself in Romans 7:14–24 is not what Paul says of his pre-Christian state in other passages.* Paul is distressed over his inability to fulfill the law's just demands. He is wretched as a result of his failure. He is calling out for deliverance by someone outside himself. But what unbeliever ever thinks like that? What Paul thought of himself before his conversion is summarized in Philippians 3, where he claims to have been "faultless" as far as "legalistic righteousness" is concerned (v. 6). The unbeliever is not distressed by his failure to keep God's law. On the contrary, he is satisfied with his performance. He is self-righteous and self-confident. He does not even know he needs to be saved.

Here is the problem in a nutshell: In Romans 7:18, Paul says, "I have the desire to do what is good, but I cannot carry it out." But when he was an unbeliever he would have said, "I have the desire to do what is good, and I am doing it."

2. *Paul's delight in God's law, expressed in this passage, cannot be found in unbelievers.* What he says in Romans 7 is that "the law is good" and that "in my inner being I delight in God's law" (vv. 16, 22). Is that the attitude of the unbeliever? Not according to Paul's teaching elsewhere in Romans. Just before these verses, Paul has spoken of the effects of the law on sinners, saying that it exposes sin and provokes all kinds of evil desires, that is, rebellion against its demands. In the following section, in Romans 8, Paul argues that "the sinful mind is hostile to God. It does not submit to God's law, nor can it do so" (v. 7).

The "man" of Romans 7 is one who has moved beyond the hostility to God's law exercised by the unregenerate person.

3. *The present tense is used throughout the second half of Romans 7, and this is an apparently meaningful contrast with the past tense employed earlier.* In verses 7–13, the verbs are in the aorist tense: "Once I was alive apart from law; but when the commandment came, sin sprang to life and *I died*" (v. 9); "sin . . . *put me to death*" (v. 11); "sin . . . *produced death* in me through what was good" (v. 13). Those sentences (to which I have added italics) are written of a past experience. In verses 14–24, the present tense is used: "I *am* unspiritual" (v. 14); "I *do not* understand what I do" (v. 15); "I *agree* that the law is good" (v. 16), and so on. It is hard to deny that this is speaking of Paul's present, and therefore a truly Christian, experience.

As J. I. Packer says, "Paul's shift from the past tense to the present in verse 14 has no natural explanation save that he now moves on from talking about his experience with God's law in his pre-Christian days to talking about his experience as it was at the time of writing."[2]

2. J. I. Packer, *Keep in Step with the Spirit* (Old Tappan, N.J.: Fleming H. Revell, 1984), pp. 143, 144. Packer scatters discussions of Romans 7:14–24 throughout his evaluations of the various Christian views of holiness.

The "Man" of Romans 7 Is a "Carnal Christian"

The second view is a very popular one today. It is best known by the phrase "the carnal Christian." It holds that Paul is indeed speaking of himself as a Christian (for some of the reasons outlined above) but that he is speaking of himself (or of himself theoretically) as being in an immature or unsurrendered state. Defenders of this view observe that the "man" of Romans 7 is defeated and that this should not be true of the mature Christian. They observe how strongly the focus is on the self—the word "I" occurs twenty-six times in verses 14–24, and the words "me," "my" or "myself" twelve times more. The Holy Spirit, the secret to victory in the Christian life, is not mentioned in this chapter at all.

This view sees an enormous contrast between Romans 7, which is thought of as a chapter of defeat, and Romans 8, which is thought of as a chapter of victory through the Holy Spirit's power. Sometimes a Christian is told that the secret to victory is to get "self" off the throne of one's life and allow the Spirit to take control—to stop living in Romans 7 and get on to Romans 8.

Is this view valid? Is this what these verses are all about?

This is not my understanding, as I pointed out in a previous study. But let me begin by saying something positive. The truths in "the carnal Christian" theology are that Christians do indeed have a sinful nature and that they are not able to have victory in their lives apart from the Holy Spirit. This is the evident movement from chapter 7 to chapter 8. The victory that we are to have is not our doing. It is "through Jesus Christ our Lord" (v. 25) and by the Holy Spirit (Rom. 8).

Nevertheless, the weaknesses of this view (and I must add also the errors and dangers) far outweigh the truths. The chief weakness is the doctrine of "the carnal Christian" itself. This view postulates a two-stage Christian experience in which, in stage one, a person accepts Jesus as Savior only, without accepting him as Lord of his or her life, and then later, in stage two, goes on to receive him as Lord. This is just not biblical. Above all, it is not what Paul is saying or has been saying in Romans.

One rule of interpretation is that the meaning of any word or phrase must be determined by its context, and if this is applied to Paul's use of the word *carnal*, or *fleshly* (NIV translates "sinful nature"), in these chapters, the result is something quite different from "the carnal Christian" theology. If we look at Romans 8:5–8, we see that these verses contrast an individual controlled by the carnal, or sinful, nature with one controlled by the Spirit. But the contrast is not between worldly Christians and those who have "progressed" to the point of taking Jesus Christ as Lord. The contrast is between those who are Christians and those who are not Christians at all. Paul declares that "the mind of sinful man is death, but the mind controlled by the Spirit is life and peace; the sinful mind is hostile to God. It does not submit to God's law, nor can it do so" (vv. 6–7).

Does this mean, then, that when Paul uses the word *carnal* (or *fleshly*) of himself in Romans 7, he is speaking of himself as an unbeliever, the first of the views discussed? No, we have already seen reasons why that is not correct. What does it mean then? It means that the struggle Paul is describing is between himself as a new creature in Christ, the new man, and that old, sinful, un-Christian nature that he nevertheless retains in some measure. The struggle is part of what it means to be a Christian in an as-yet unperfected state. It does not mean that there is a first or early stage in the Christian life that may be described as "carnal."

We must remember that the flow of Romans 5 through 8 is *from* justification by faith *to* glorification and that chapters 6 and 7 are parentheses, inserted between chapters 5 and 8 in order to deal with Antinomianism (chap. 6) and the purpose and limits of the law (chap. 7). There is no two-stage doctrine of Christianity here at all.[3]

The "Man" of Romans 7 Is under Conviction

A third view has been advanced by D. Martyn Lloyd-Jones, following, it would seem, a suggestion made a century ago, though briefly, by Frederick Godet.[4] This approach takes everything that has been said thus far with full seriousness, drawing the apparently paradoxical conclusion that what Paul says here can be said of neither the unregenerate nor the regenerate man. The unsaved person cannot speak of the law as Paul does. He does not understand its good and spiritual character. He is in rebellion against it. On the other hand, the saved person cannot speak in such a defeated manner. He cannot cry out for deliverance, because he knows he has already been

3. Proponents of "the carnal Christian" theology will argue that, regardless of Paul's use of the word *carnal* in Romans, the essence of this view is nonetheless clearly spelled out in 1 Corinthians 3, where carnal Christians are defined as being "mere infants in Christ" (v. 1) and where it is said that one can be saved "but only as one escaping through the flames" (v. 15), that is, without any good works to show for that person's life. It must be acknowledged that, according to Paul's teaching, the Christians at Corinth were indeed acting in a carnal way—that is, as if they were not Christians—in the matter of their church's unspiritual divisions, which he is discussing. But this is quite different from saying that they were carnal in all areas or even that they could be. Indeed, in spite of this problem (and several others that he deals with later in the letter) they are also described as being "enriched in every way" and not lacking in "any spiritual gift" (1 Cor. 1:4, 7). As far as the destruction by flames is concerned, this is written of the fruit of Christian ministry specifically—that is, of converts and the building up of the church—and it is this that Paul says will be destroyed if the Christians of Corinth should continue to act in divisive and mutually competitive ways. For a discussion of this passage as well as the theology of "the carnal Christian" generally, see Ernest C. Reisinger, *What Should We Think of "the Carnal Christian"?* (Edinburgh, and Carlisle, Pa.: The Banner of Truth Trust, n.d.).

4. D. M. Lloyd-Jones, *Romans: An Exposition of Chapters 7:1—8:4, The Law: Its Functions and Limits* (Grand Rapids: Zondervan, 1973), pp. 176–224; cf. pp. 170–175 for a similar discussion of vv. 7–13; F. Godet, *Commentary on St. Paul's Epistle to the Romans*, trans. A. Cusin (Edinburgh: T. & T. Clark, 1892), vol. 2, p. 56.

delivered from the power of sin through the work of Christ. The "man" of Romans 7 is therefore one who does not yet know who can deliver him.

But where does that leave us? If Paul is not speaking of a regenerate or an unregenerate person, of whom is he speaking? Lloyd-Jones answers that he is speaking of one who has been awakened to his personal lawlessness and spiritual inability by the Holy Spirit but who has not yet been made a participator in the new life of Jesus Christ. He is one who, in the language of the American revivals of the eighteenth century, may be said to have been "awakened" to the truth of his condition but who is not yet "revived." The work has been started, but it has not yet come to fruition.

Here is how Godet put it: "The apostle is speaking here neither *of the natural man* in his state of voluntary ignorance and sin, nor *of the child of God*, born anew, set free by grace, and animated by the spirit of Christ; but of the man whose conscience, awakened by the law, has entered sincerely, with fear and trembling, but still *in his own strength*, into the desperate struggle against evil."[5]

What shall we say of this interpretation? It sounds reasonable, certainly. It is an attempt to take the data seriously, and it is advanced by sound scholars, particularly Martyn Lloyd-Jones, who examines each phrase carefully. Still, it has problems.

1. *It does not account for the change from the past tense of the verbs in verses 1–13 to the present tense, beginning with verse 14.* According to this view, what Paul says in verses 14–24 is of the past. It concerns the time of his own spiritual awakening, perhaps associated with his role in the martyrdom of Stephen when he began to "kick against the goads" (Acts 26:14). There would be no reason for the present tense at all. The only way Lloyd-Jones can deal with this is to say that the change is of no real importance.[6]

2. *It is not true that the "man" of Romans 7 does not yet know who can deliver him.* Paul is writing of a struggle we all feel at times, wanting to do what is right while being unable in himself to do it. But as soon as he cries out, "What a wretched man I am! Who will deliver me from this body of death?" he has the answer: "Thanks be to God—through Jesus Christ our Lord!" (vv. 24, 25). There is no reason to separate the problem from the answer temporally, as if Paul somehow passes from a state of conviction to a state of grace between the last two verses of the chapter.

The "Man" of Romans 7 Is a Mature Christian

The final view, which is that of most Reformed commentators from the time of the later Augustine forward, including Luther, Calvin, and the

5. Godet, *Commentary on St. Paul's Epistle to the Romans*, vol. 2, p. 56.
6. Lloyd-Jones, *Romans: An Exposition of Chapters 7:1—8:4, The Law: Its Functions and Limits*, pp. 183, 184.

Puritans, is that Paul is writing of himself as a mature Christian, describing the Christian's continuing conflict with sin, which we all experience, and teaching that there is no victory in such struggles apart from the Holy Spirit. To put it in other words, since Romans 7 is discussing the function and limits of the law, Paul is saying that just as the law of God is unable to *justify* a person (justification is made possible by the work of Christ), so also is the law unable to *sanctify* a person. Sanctification must be accomplished in us by the Holy Spirit.

Here is how Packer summarizes these verses:

> Alive in Christ, his heart delights in the law, and he wants to do what is good and right and thus keep it perfectly. . . . But he finds that he cannot achieve the total compliance at which he aims. Whenever he measures what he has done, he finds that he has fallen short (v. 23). From this he perceives that the anti-God urge called sin, though dethroned in his heart, still dwells in his own flawed nature. . . . Thus the Christian's moral experience (for Paul would not be telling his own experience to make theological points, did he not think it typical) is that his reach persistently exceeds his grasp and that his desire for perfection is frustrated by the discomposing and distracting energies of indwelling sin.
>
> Stating this sad fact about himself, renews Paul's distress at it, and in the cry of verses 24, 25 he voices his grief at not being able to glorify God more: "Wretched man that I am! Who will deliver me from this body of death?" Then at once he answers his own question: "Thanks be to God through Jesus Christ our Lord! . . ." The question was asked in the future tense, so the verb to be supplied in the answer should be in the future tense too: "Thank God! *He will deliver me* through Jesus Christ!"
>
> Paul here proclaims that his present involuntary imperfection, summed up in the latter part of verse 25, will one day be made a thing of the past through the redemption of the body referred to in chapter 8:23. . . . For that future redemption we must long and wait, maintaining always the two-world, homeward-traveling, hoping-for-glory perspective that pervades the whole New Testament.[7]

This is the point at which, in the next study, we are going to pick up the story of the continuing struggle of the Christian against indwelling sin. But even here we must make a few observations.

First, when Paul writes of "this body of death" in verse 24, which bemoans his wretched state, he is saying exactly what he said in Romans 6. (Notice the words I have italicized.) Paul spoke of our being crucified with Christ so that "*the body of sin* might be rendered powerless [done away with],

---

7. Packer, *Keep in Step with the Spirit*, pp. 128, 129. Packer has a discussion of "The 'Wretched Man' in Romans 7" in an appendix to this volume (pp. 263–270). See also the discussions in Leon Morris, *The Epistle to the Romans* (Grand Rapids: Wm. B. Eerdmans, and Leicester, England: Inter-Varsity Press, 1988), pp. 284–288; and John R. W. Stott, *Men Made New: An Exposition of Romans 5–9* (Grand Rapids: Baker Book House, 1984), pp. 70–79.

that we should no longer be slaves of sin" (v. 6); several verses later, he wrote, "Therefore do not let sin reign in *your mortal body* so that you obey its evil desires. Do not offer *the parts of your body* to sin, as instruments of wickedness, but rather offer yourselves to God . . ." (vv. 12–13). In Romans 6, Paul discussed the deliverance that is ours through our having been crucified and raised with Christ. But he also acknowledged the continuing presence of sin in us *through our bodies* and reminded us that we must struggle against it. It is the same in Romans 7, though here Paul is emphasizing the futility of the struggle if it is in our own strength.

Second, although stated in extreme terms in Romans 7, an honest acknowledgment of the hopelessly sinful nature of man apart from the Holy Spirit (which is what we find here), even after a person has become a Christian, is the first step to true holiness. In other words, to say, "I have passed out of Romans 7 into Romans 8," is not the mark of a mature Christian but of an immature one. The mature Christian knows that he is always in Romans 7 apart from the Holy Spirit. Moreover, he knows that dependence on the Holy Spirit is not something that is attained once for all but is the result of a daily struggle and a constantly renewed commitment.

What is sanctification? Is it an awareness of how good we are becoming? Or is it a growing sense of how sinful we really are, so we will constantly turn to and depend upon Jesus Christ? If we are mature in Christ, we know it is the latter.

92

The War Within

Romans 7:21-24

So I find this law at work: When I want to do good, evil is right there with me. For in my inner being I delight in God's law; but I see another law at work in the members of my body, waging war against the law of my mind and making me a prisoner of the law of sin at work within my members. What a wretched man I am! Who will rescue me from this body of death?

At the beginning of the last study I said that there are few passages in the Bible over which good Bible students have divided more radically than the last half of Romans 7, beginning with verse 14. Now, having finished that study, you can probably see why. In it I carefully worked through the four main interpretations of these verses, asking the important question "Who is the 'Man' of Romans 7?" We saw that the options are:

1. An unsaved person,
2. A "carnal Christian,"

3. A person who has come under conviction as a result of the Holy
   Spirit's work in his or her life, but who is not yet born again, and
4. A mature Christian.

In some ways, the last seems hardest to accept. But I tried to show reasons why the fourth of these possibilities is the right one and why it is necessary for us to know it, if we are to move ahead realistically in the Christian life. If we are Christians, we will never get anywhere by assuming that the seventh chapter of Romans is written about someone other than ourselves—someone who is not yet saved or not yet "mature" in the faith, as we are. Paul is writing about himself as a mature Christian and therefore about all who are true believers.

I ended our discussion in the last study by stating that sanctification is the process of coming increasingly to see how sinful we are so that we will depend constantly on Jesus Christ. And that is not easy! The Christian life is a warfare, a warfare within against our inherently sinful natures, as well as a warfare without against external forces. It is extremely important that we see this.

The Passage As a Whole

I think that Paul must have been concerned that we see this and that he recognized that it is difficult. I say this because in these verses Paul goes to considerable lengths to teach these truths to us.

Notice that in verses 14–24 Paul says almost exactly the same thing three distinct times. The first time is in verses 14–17. The second is in verses 18–20. The third is in verses 21–24. Each of these begins with a statement of the problem: "I am unspiritual, sold as a slave to sin" (v. 14); "nothing good lives in me, that is, in my sinful nature" (v. 18); and "when I want to do good, evil is right there with me" (v. 21). Each section then provides a description of the conflict: "what I want to do I do not do, but what I hate I do" (v. 15); "I have the desire to do what is good, but I cannot carry it out. For what I do is not the good I want to do; no, the evil I do not want to do—this I keep on doing" (vv. 18–19); and "in my inner being I delight in God's law; but I see another law at work in the members of my body, waging war against the law of my mind and making me a prisoner of the law of sin at work within my members" (vv. 22–23). Each section ends with a brief statement of why the problem exists: "it is sin living in me" (v. 17); "it is sin living in me" (v. 20); and "this body of death" (v. 24).

What distinguishes these three sections is that in the first Paul states the matter generally, in the second he states it in terms of his doing what he does *not* want to do, and in the third he says that he finds it impossible to do what he *does* want to do: "when I want to do good, evil is right there with me" (v. 21).

I repeat again that this describes the conflict of a mature Christian man, in fact, the conflict of an apostle of Jesus Christ in his later years. So the struggle Paul speaks of is a struggle we all face and will continue to face—if we are Christians. And the defeat he speaks of is the experience of all—even when we are well along in the Christian life—apart from the Holy Spirit.

"The American Way"

However, Paul is not writing these words to excuse our defeat, still less to encourage it. He is thinking of the victory that can and will be ours (see v. 25 and chap. 8). He wants us to achieve victory in the struggle against sin by the Holy Spirit. But the point here is that the victory we want comes only through this struggle and not by some secret formula for success or by some easy way of avoiding it.

I believe that at this point we Americans particularly need to hear what Paul is saying, for we hate conflict and are usually trying to avoid it by any means possible. Let me suggest three ways that American Christians try to avoid the struggle against sin, which (according to the teaching of Romans 7) will always be part of our lives.

1. *A formula.* The first way we try to avoid struggle in the Christian life is by hunting for some easy formula that will bring victory. This takes various forms: discovering a Christian book that will tell us what to do, following a three-step or four-step recipe for growth in the Christian life, ceasing to do some easy things (like going to movies), or starting to do more difficult things (like attending seminars). You know what I mean:

"Get out of Romans 7 and into Romans 8."
"Let go and let God."
"Get 'self' off the throne of your life and put Christ there."
"Just let Jesus take control."

The underlying motivation for these attempts is our lazy optimism—the expectation that life is meant to be easy, not hard. So, if we do find the Christian life hard, we assume that we are merely missing the right formula. Someone should be able to tell us what the formula is. If we do not find it—and we never will if ease is what we are seeking—we tend to get angry with our instructors or even with God.

2. *A new experience.* The second way we try to avoid struggle in the Christian life is by hunting for some new spiritual experience. This can be a charismatic-type experience—speaking in tongues, perhaps. It can be what used to be called "a second work of grace" in which we pass forever out of a defeated Christian state into a victorious one. Or it can be something as straightforward as an emotional experience in worship. In speaking of emo-

tion in worship I do not mean to suggest that this is bad. It is not. We have hearts as well as heads, and we are undoubtedly to worship with both. But emotion, even in worship, is bad if it is thought of as a substitute for or an escape from the fight against sin, which is an inescapable part of the life-long process of sanctification.

To come home from a church service saying, "Didn't we have a worshipful experience?" means nothing unless we have acquired the biblical knowledge with which we can fight against sin and a renewed commitment to do so.

3. *Avoidance.* The third way we try to escape struggle in the Christian life is typically "American": avoidance. That is, when we are defeated, rather than girding up our loins and turning to attack the problem again, we turn away from it and try to fill our minds with something else. Often this "something else" is television or other entertainment. Sometimes it is empty busy-ness—even in Christian activities. Just as with unbelievers, avoidance may be through alcohol or drugs for some.

Spiritual Realism

What I want to commend to you as we face the fact of the war within us is what J. I. Packer calls "spiritual realism." He talks about it toward the end of his study of the various Christian views of holiness, *Keep in Step with the Spirit.* As Packer defines it, "Realism has to do with our willingness or lack of will-ingness to face unpalatable truths about ourselves and to start making nec-essary changes.[1] In light of Romans 7:14–24, I want to suggest four state-ments with which this spiritual realism should start.

1. *When God called us to be Christian people he called us to lifetime struggles against sin.*

This should be evident from everything Paul says in this passage. But we seem to take extraordinary measures to avoid this truth. One way of avoid-ing it is by a kind of unrealistic romanticism in which we kid ourselves into thinking that everything is well with us spiritually or is at least well enough for us to get by with for now. This is particularly easy if we are affluent and do not need to worry about having enough to eat or paying the mortgage and if we can always battle occasional bouts of depression by going out for dinner or by taking a vacation. "No pain, no gain," we say, yet we labor rig-orously to avoid spiritual growth pains.

We also avoid this truth by shifting the blame, as Packer suggests in his discussion. It is what Adam and Eve did when God confronted them with their sin in the Garden of Eden.

Adam blamed Eve, saying, "The woman you put here with me—she gave me some fruit from the tree, and I ate it" (Gen. 3:12). But since he pointed

1. J. I. Packer, *Keep in Step with the Spirit* (Old Tappan, N.J.: Fleming H. Revell, 1984), p. 258. The discussion of "spiritual realism" is on pp. 258–261.

out that it was God who gave him the woman, Adam was really blaming God for his trouble.

Eve blamed the devil: "The serpent deceived me, and I ate" (v. 13). But since God had apparently allowed the serpent to come into the garden, this was only a slightly gentler way of also blaming God.

Packer says, "We are assiduous blamers of others for whatever goes wrong in our marriages, families, churches, careers, and so on. . . . Romantic complacency and resourcefulness in acting the injured innocent are among the most Spirit-quenching traits imaginable, since both become excuses for doing nothing in situations where realism requires that we do something and do it as a matter of urgency. Both states stifle conviction of sin in the unconverted and keep Christians in a thoroughly bad state of spiritual health."[2]

The starting place for achieving spiritual realism is to recognize that we are called to a constant spiritual warfare in this life and that this warfare is not easy, since it is against the sin that resides in us even as converted men and women. Realism calls for rigorous preparation, constant alertness, dogged determinism, and moment-by-moment trust in him who alone can give us victory. Here is the essence of the matter in the words of a great hymn by Johann B. Freystein (translated by Catherine Winkworth):

> Rise, my soul, to watch and pray.
> From thy sleep awaken;
> Be not by the evil day
> Unawares o'ertaken.
> For the foe, well we know,
> Oft the harvest reapeth
> While the Christian sleepeth.
>
> Watch against thyself, my soul,
> Less with grace thou trifle;
> Let not self thy thoughts control,
> Nor God's mercy stifle.
> Pride and sin lurk within
> All thy hopes to scatter;
> heed not when they flatter.

I do not know any hymn that describes the battle within us better or in more realistic language.

2. *Although we are called to a lifetime struggle against sin, we are nevertheless never going to achieve victory by ourselves.*

2. Ibid., pp. 258, 259.

This is another point that Americans in particular need to grasp. For while we are as a people very susceptible to either simple, quick-fix solutions or avoidance, we are also very confident of our ability to handle even the most difficult challenges. Like putting a man on the moon, we figure that, however tough the problem may be, with enough energy, skill, resourcefulness, and determination we can solve it. Live a victorious Christian life? Of course we can do it—if we really want to. So we say, "When the going gets tough, the tough gets going!" or, "You can if you believe you can."

In this we are perhaps more like the apostle Peter than anyone else in the Bible. Do you remember Peter's boast that, whatever might be true of the other disciples, he at least would never betray Jesus? "Lord, I am ready to go with you to prison and to death," said Peter (Luke 22:33). And he meant it! Peter loved Jesus, and he believed that the sheer intensity of his love would enable him to stand firm even in the midst of the greatest spiritual struggles.

But Jesus knew Peter, just as he knows us, and he replied, "I tell you, Peter, before the rooster crows today, you will deny three times that you know me" (v. 34).

In himself, Peter was unable to stand against Satan's temptation even for a moment. When the temptation came he fell. But fortunately this was not all Jesus said to Peter. Although Peter was boastful and self-confident and was wrong in both, Jesus had also told him, "Simon, Simon, Satan has asked to sift you as wheat. But I have prayed for you, Simon, that your faith may not fail. And when you have turned back, strengthen your brothers" (vv. 31–32).

If we could rephrase those words to express what Peter would probably say to us if he were writing this chapter, it would go like this: "When Jesus told me that he had prayed for me so that my faith would not fail, he meant that apart from him I could not stand against Satan even for a moment. I could not go it alone. However strong my devotion or determination, when the chips were down I would deny him. I did! And so will you—this is what I am to tell you—unless you are depending on Jesus every moment. Moreover, in the great battles of life it is certain that you will fall away and be lost unless he prays for you, which is what he has promised to do. 'Apart from me you can do nothing' is what he told us. I proved the truth of his words by my denial, and you will, too, unless you are depending on him constantly."

3. *Even when we triumph over sin by the power of the Holy Spirit, which should be often, we are still unprofitable servants.*

Why is this so? It is because our victories, even when we achieve them, are all nevertheless by the power and grace of God and are not of ourselves. If they were, we would be able to take some personal glory for our triumphs, and when we die we would bring our boasting into heaven. But our victories are not of ourselves. They are of God. And since they are not of our ourselves, we will not boast either on earth or in heaven but will instead give God all the glory.

Consider that great scene in Revelation in which the elders who represent the saints lay their crowns before the throne of God, saying, "You are worthy, our Lord and God, to receive glory and honor and power . . ." (Rev. 4:11). Why do you suppose they do that? And what does the scene mean? Clearly, the fact that the crowns are the elders' crowns mean that they represent the elders' own victories over sin and God's enemies. But, by taking them off and laying them before the throne of God, the elders indicate that their victories were achieved, not by themselves, but by the power of the Spirit of God that worked within them. In other words, in the final analysis the triumphs are God's alone.

4. *And yet, we are to go on fighting and struggling against sin, and we are to do so with the tools made available to us, chiefly prayer, Bible study, Christian fellowship, service to others, and the sacraments.*

We are never to quit in this great battle against sin. We are to fight it with every ounce of energy in our bodies and with our final breath. Only then, when we have finished the race, having kept the course, may we rest from warfare.

Isn't that what the Bible tells us everywhere?

Ephesians 6:10–12: "Finally, be strong in the Lord and in his mighty power. Put on the full armor of God so that you can take your stand against the devil's schemes. For our struggle is not against flesh and blood, but against the rulers, against the authorities, against the powers of this dark world and against the spiritual forces of evil in the heavenly realms."

Philippians 3:12–14: ". . . I press on to take hold of that for which Christ Jesus took hold of me. Brothers, I do not consider myself yet to have taken hold of it. But one thing I do: Forgetting what is behind and straining toward what is ahead, I press on toward the goal to win the prize for which God has called me heavenward in Christ Jesus."

Hebrews 12:1–4: "Therefore, since we are surrounded by such a great cloud of witnesses, let us throw off everything that hinders and the sin that so easily entangles, and let us run with perseverance the race marked out for us. Let us fix our eyes on Jesus, the author and perfecter of our faith, who for the joy set before him endured the cross, scorning its shame, and sat down at the right hand of the throne of God. Consider him who endured such opposition from sinful men, so that you will not grow weary and lose heart. In your struggle against sin, you have not yet resisted to the point of shedding your blood."

A Supernatural Gospel

I close this study by suggesting that a gospel in which we must do every-thing possible to attain a victory over sin—but in which, in spite of all we do or can ever do, the victory when it comes is by God alone and not by us or for our glory—a gospel like that must be from God; it could never have been invented by man. The very nature of our gospel is proof of its divine origin.

Left to ourselves, what do we do? We do one of two things. Either we cre-ate a gospel of works, so that our salvation depends upon our own righ-teousness and our sanctification likewise depends upon our own ability to defeat sin and choose righteousness. Or else we retreat into passivity and say, "Since the battle is God's and there is nothing I can do to achieve vic-tory, I might as well just sit back and let God work." To our way of thinking it seems that it must be either of those two choices. But the Bible, through Paul, says something quite different: "Therefore, my dear friends, as you have always obeyed—not only in my presence, but now much more in my absence—continue to work out your salvation with fear and trembling, *for it is God who works in you* to will and to act according to his good purpose" (Phil. 2:12–13, emphasis added).

The Christian life is not easy. No responsible person ever said it was. It is a battle all the way. But it is a battle that will be won. And when it is won, we who have triumphed will cast our crowns at the feet of the Lord Jesus Christ who worked in us to accomplish the victory, and we will praise him forever.

93

Victory! Through Jesus Christ Our Lord!

Romans 7:25

Thanks be to God—through Jesus Christ our Lord!
So then, I myself in my mind am a slave to God's law, but in the sinful nature a slave to the law of sin.

In the first chapter of 2 Corinthians the apostle is describing a time in his life with which you may be able to identify, particularly if you have been struggling against sin. Paul is not writing there of a struggle against sin—he is thinking of physical deprivation and danger—but he writes helpfully: "We do not want you to be uninformed, brothers, about the hardships we suffered in the province of Asia. We were under great pressure, far beyond our ability to endure, so that we despaired even of life" (v. 8).

You have probably felt like that when you have been struggling against some sin, almost in despair. In fact, I am sure you have, if you are really a Christian. The reason I say this is that, if our interpretation of Romans 7:14–25 is correct—if it is a description of the apostle Paul as a mature Christian and not as an unbeliever or a "carnal" Christian—then this

771

almost-despairing struggle against sin is the experience of us all, at least at times. All Christians find themselves wanting to do what is right (because of the life of Christ within) but of not being able to do what they would like to do (because of the continuing presence of indwelling sin). In fact, it is even worse than that. For, as we mature in the Christian life, growing closer to Jesus Christ and thus wanting to be more like him and please him more, the struggle actually grows stronger rather than weaker. Those who struggle most vigorously against sin are not immature Christians but mature ones. The hardest battles are waged by God's saints.

In the midst of our struggles we are sometimes brought to the very edge of despair, to use Paul's word in 2 Corinthians. But if you are close to that point and are thinking negatively, as most of us do at times, I want to say this: Although the struggle is a real one and difficult, the outcome is not bleak or uncertain but glorious—because of God.

That is what Paul comes to at the very end of Romans 7. After he has reached the absolute low point, asking, "Who will rescue me from this body of death?" he answers with what Charles Hodge calls "a strong and sudden emotion of gratitude"[1]: "Thanks be to God—through Jesus Christ our Lord!" (v. 25). That is, although the apostle was not able to find even the smallest ground for a hope of victory within himself, even at his weakest point the end is not grim because as a Christian he knows that God is for him. God has assured every believer victory through the work of Christ.

Interestingly enough, this is almost exactly what Paul says in 2 Corinthians where, as I said, he is speaking not of struggles against sin but of physical dangers and troubles. Immediately following his cry of despair ("in our hearts we felt the sentence of death"), he adds, "But this happened that we might not rely on ourselves but on God, who raises the dead. He has delivered us from such a deadly peril, and he will deliver us . . ." (vv. 9–10).

If you are struggling against sin—as I know you are, if you are a true Christian—that is what I want to leave with you as a result of this final study of Romans 7. *The reason for your struggle is to teach you to rely not on yourself but on God, who raises the dead.* And what I want you to be assured of is that *he has already delivered you from "deadly peril," and that he will deliver you again.*

Deliverance from Sin's Penalty

The deliverance from sin provided for us by God through Jesus Christ is in three stages, and the first is deliverance from sin's penalty, that is, from the judgment and wrath of God due us as the result of our being sinners. This is not the deliverance spoken of in Romans 7:25, but it is foundational,

---

1. Charles Hodge, *A Commentary on Romans* (Edinburgh, and Carlisle, Pa.: The Banner of Truth Trust, 1972), p. 238. (Original edition 1935.)

and Paul discussed it carefully in the opening chapters of the letter. It is upon this foundation that all further deliverance is built.

In a book of sermon illustrations H. A. Ironside tells of a young man who was the son of a friend of Czar Nicholas the First of Russia. He had been given the job of exchequer of a border fortress of the Russian Army, a responsible position in which he was to manage the czar's money and dispense wages to the troops. But the young man fell into gambling and began to cover his losses by borrowing little by little from the army treasury. One day he received notice that a government auditor was arriving to examine the books, so he sat down and added up what he had taken. It was a huge amount. He emptied out his own meager resources, subtracted that from what should have been in the government account and noted the great discrepancy. He then wrote under the amount due: "A great debt; who can pay?"

The young man knew it was impossible for him to make up the amount, and he did not know anyone who could be counted on to help him. So, rather than await arrest, trial, and disgrace, he drew his revolver and determined that he would kill himself upon the stroke of midnight. As he waited for the clock to strike, reflecting on how he had wasted his great opportunity, he became drowsy and drifted off to sleep.

It so happened that on that very night Czar Nicholas, dressed like a common soldier, entered the fortress to make an inspection of the battlements. According to regulations, every light should have been out. But when he passed the office of the exchequer, where the son of his friend was dozing, he noticed that the light was on and went in. There were the sleeping young man, the revolver, the open books, the total that was missing, and the cryptic note. It was all quite clear. The young officer had betrayed his trust. He had been stealing systematically for months.

At first the czar thought to awaken him and place him under arrest. But he felt sorry for the young man, and he remembered the father, his friend, and how brokenhearted he would be if his son were to be arrested. So, instead of proceeding harshly, he stooped over and wrote something below the young man's pathetic summation and went out.

The soldier slept for hours when suddenly, awakened by some noise, he sprang to his feet. It was long past midnight. He grabbed the revolver, pointed it to his head, and was about to pull the trigger when his eyes glanced down at the papers before him and he saw what had been written. Beneath his question, "A great debt; who can pay?" there was a single word: "Nicholas." Could it be? Had the czar been present? He sprang to some files where there were documents containing the czar's signature and made a careful comparison. The signature was authentic. "The czar has been here," he said to himself. "He has seen the papers; he knows what I have done; he knows my guilt, but he has undertaken to pay the debt himself." So instead of taking his life the young soldier waited for morning when, as he anticipated, a sack of gold coins arrived from Nicholas. The young man placed it in the safe, and when the inspector arrived for the audit the sack was found to contain exactly the amount needed.[2]

If you are a Christian, that is how Jesus Christ has delivered you from the penalty of your sin. You are guilty of transgressing the law of God and of trampling God's honor. You deserve to die. But Jesus has made payment for your transgressions. Only in your case the payment he made was not merely a sack of gold coins to balance out a finite monetary account but rather his very life, given in exchange for yours. Jesus died so that you might be delivered from sin's penalty.

Who can pay? Jesus! And he has!

Deliverance from Sin's Power

The second deliverance from sin provided for the believer by God through the work of Christ is from sin's power, that is, from constant defeat by sin in our struggles against it day by day. In my opinion, neither is this what Romans 7:25 is talking about primarily. The deliverance spoken of in our text is a future deliverance, not a present one. But present deliverance has bearing in this context, since Paul has been speaking of his present struggles against sin in chapter 7 and is going to talk about a present (as well as future) deliverance in chapter 8.

How does this present deliverance work out? To answer that, let me go back over some of the things we have already seen about the Christian life in Romans 5 through 7.

1. *We are sinners and will continue to be sinners throughout our Christian lives.* It follows from this that the Christian life will always be a struggle. That is not what we want to hear, of course. We want things to be easy. Nevertheless, if we study the Bible, we find that this is taught from beginning to end.

We find it by example, as when we think of an outstanding character like Job, who had God's own testimony that he was a righteous man. When Satan appeared before God, God called attention to Job, saying, "Have you considered my servant Job? There is no one on earth like him; he is blameless and upright, a man who fears God and shuns evil" (Job 1:8). Yet this is not what Job thought of himself. Job did not say, "Look at what a righteous man I am," even though he knew there could be no direct correspondence between his sins and the enormity of the tragedies he suffered. Instead, when he stood before God he said, "I am unworthy—how can I reply to you? I put my hand over my mouth. . . . My ears had heard of you but now my eyes have seen you. Therefore I despise myself and repent in dust and ashes" (Job 40:4; 42:5–6).

2. See H. A. Ironside, *Illustrations of Bible Truth* (Chicago: Moody Press, 1945), pp. 67–70.

David is another example, and not just in the period following his sin with Bathsheba. In the psalms he speaks often of his sins.

Isaiah, too, is an example. Isaiah was the greatest of the prophets. Yet when he had his great vision of God, recorded in Isaiah 6, he said, "Woe to me! I am ruined! For I am a man of unclean lips, and I live among a people of unclean lips, and my eyes have seen the King, the LORD Almighty" (Isa. 6:5).

It is always that way. It is the Bible's exceptional people who are most conscious of their transgressions.

Again, we learn that the Christian life is a constant struggle against sin from the Bible's explicit teaching in Romans and elsewhere. In Romans Paul will say, "Therefore, I urge you, brothers, in view of God's mercy, to offer your bodies as living sacrifices, holy and pleasing to God—which is your spiritual act of worship. Do not conform any longer to the pattern of this world . . ." (Rom. 12:1–2), and "The night is nearly over; the day is almost here. So let us put aside the deeds of darkness and put on the armor of light" (Rom. 13:12).

Ephesians 6:13 says, "Therefore put on the full armor of God, so that when the day of evil comes, you may be able to stand your ground, and after you have done everything, to stand."

In 1 Corinthians 9:24–27 we read: "Do you not know that in a race all the runners run, but only one gets the prize? Run in such a way as to get the prize. Everyone who competes in the games goes into strict training. They do it to get a crown that will not last; but we do it to get a crown that will last forever. Therefore I do not run like a man running aimlessly; I do not fight like a man beating the air. No, I beat my body and make it my slave so that after I have preached to others, I myself will not be disqualified for the prize."

These verses teach that the Christian life will be a struggle to the end and that the reason for this is that we carry the very root of the problem, which is sin, within our hearts.

Philip Doddridge, the famous eighteenth-century, nonconformist minister, said as he was dying, "The best prayer I ever offered up in my life deserves damnation." And Augustus Toplady, the author of the hymn "Rock of Ages" who reported those words of Doddridge, said, "Oh that ever such a wretch as I should be tempted to think highly of himself."[3] These are not the words of mentally unbalanced eccentrics but of mature believers infused with the same Holy Spirit who filled Paul.

2. *In spite of our being sinners, Jesus died to save sinners, and this is what he is doing.* The point I have just made—that we will have to struggle against sin throughout our lives—is something we learned largely from Romans 7. But

---

3. The quotations are from Robert Haldane, *An Exposition of the Epistle to the Romans* (MacDill AFB: MacDonald Publishing, 1958), pp. 307, 308.

here we go back a chapter, to Romans 6, to the teaching that when Jesus died we died in him and that when he rose from the dead we rose in him. In other words, as a result of Christ's work on our behalf we are not what we once were. We have died to the past. We have been given a new and happy future. Therefore there is no other direction for us to go in this life but forward. Do you remember how I put it when we were studying these themes in Romans 6? I said, "There is no going back. That possibility has been forever eliminated. There is no direction for us to go but forward."

Paul puts it like this, "In the same way, count yourselves dead to sin but alive to God in Christ Jesus. Therefore do not let sin reign in your mortal body so that you obey its evil desires. Do not offer the parts of your body to sin, as instruments of wickedness, but rather offer yourselves to God, as those who have been brought from death to life; and offer the parts of your body to him as instruments of righteousness. For sin shall not be your master, because you are not under law, but under grace" (Rom. 6:11–14).

It is *because* Jesus has saved us from sin's penalty and is saving us from sin's power that we struggle against it. Yet it is because *he* is saving us that we can be assured of final victory.

3. *We have the assurance of victory, also expressed as the inevitable triumph of God's grace.* The third element in our present deliverance from sin's power is what we were looking at in chapter 5, to go back still another chapter, and what we are coming to again in chapter 8. That leads to the last of the three stages of deliverance from sin provided for us by God through Jesus Christ.

Deliverance from Sin's Presence

When we were considering our deliverance from sin's *penalty* and our deliverance from sin's *power*, I said that Romans 7:25, our text here, is not really about either of those two deliverances, though, in the first case, deliverance from sin's penalty is foundational and, in the second case, there is a measure of overlapping. However, when we talk about deliverance from sin's *presence*, that is, about a future deliverance, we are right on.

We remember that the apostle has been describing his present struggle against sin, emphasizing that we can never hope to be entirely free from struggling against sin in this life. Moreover, he had come to the end of himself, so that he cried out, "What a wretched man I am! Who will rescue me from this body of death?" He then gives the answer, "Thanks be to God—through Jesus Christ our Lord!" The question—"Who will rescue me from this body of death?"—is in the future tense. Therefore, since the question is in the future tense, we must conclude that the answer should likewise be understood in the future tense, that is, not "Thanks be to God, who *has* rescued me through Jesus Christ," but rather, "Thanks be to God who *will* rescue me through Jesus Christ."

In other words, the deliverance Paul is looking for here is specifically a final deliverance from the very presence of sin, which has its hold on him now only through "this body of death," or "this dying body." Paul's final deliverance was to be through death and resurrection.

Let me add, before trying to wrap this up, that only this interpretation makes sense of the final sentence of the chapter. In that sentence, after having spoken of the victory that is ours in Christ, Paul returns to what he had been saying earlier, concluding, "So then, I myself in my mind am a slave to God's law, but in the sinful nature a slave to the law of sin."

If the deliverance of the first part of verse 25 were in the past (or even in the present), it would be a strange regression to conclude the chapter with a reiteration of the struggle Paul is describing. He should have gotten beyond that by the victory that is ours "though Jesus Christ our Lord." However, if the first part of that verse is referring to the future, as I have suggested, the summation makes sense. For Paul is saying that, although he is assured of a final victory over sin, he nevertheless knows that he must continue to fight a vigorous battle against sin daily until he dies.[4]

He has been saved from sin. He is being saved from sin. He will yet be saved from sin. But until the day of final deliverance it is his continuing responsibility to fight on.

The Winning Side

I conclude by pointing out that, although much of what Paul has written in Romans 7 sounds discouraging, it is not really discouraging at all. In fact, by contrast, there is enormous ground for genuine encouragement in what he says.

First, we are encouraged because the outcome of the battle against sin is certain. Our wrap-up of these themes has taken us back from chapter 7 through chapter 6 to chapter 5. But when we reach chapter 5, we return to verses that speak of the triumph of God's grace: "The law was added so that the trespass might increase. But where sin increased, grace increased all the more, so that, just as sin reigned in death, so also grace might reign through righteousness to bring eternal life through Jesus Christ our Lord" (Rom. 5:20–21).

"Through Jesus Christ our Lord." That is exactly the place to which we have come at the end of chapter 7, and the point is the same. Victory is ours. The triumph of grace is assured, regardless of how badly we may think we are doing now or how near despair we may be due to the intensity or duration of the struggle. It is the very knowledge of a final victory that will enable us to fight on.

4. For a good presentation of this position see John Murray, *The Epistle to the Romans* (Grand Rapids: Wm. B. Eerdmans, 1968), pp. 269, 270.

When the armies of Oliver Cromwell were winning battle after battle in the English Civil War, it was said of them that they could not lose because they knew, even before they started to fight, that God had given them the victory. I do not know how true that was of Cromwell's army. There were Christians on both sides of that conflict, and Cromwell's cause was not entirely free of base motives. But whatever the case with Cromwell's soldiers in those very human battles, the principle does hold true for us, the soldiers of Jesus Christ who are engaged in fierce spiritual warfare against sin.

Apart from Jesus, not one of us can prevail for a moment. But united to him, we not only can prevail. We will. The Bible promises that "he who began a good work in [us] will carry it on to completion until the day of Christ" (Phil. 1:6).

And there is this, too: Although your struggles may be prolonged and difficult, they are not essentially different from those of the many believers who have preceded you, including Paul and the other great personalities of Scripture. They triumphed, and so will you. Remember the text: "No temptation has seized you except what is common to man. And God is faithful; he will not let you be tempted beyond what you can bear. But when you are tempted, he will also provide a way out so that you can stand up under it" (1 Cor. 10:13).

PART NINE

Life in the Spirit

94

The Greatest Chapter in the Bible

Romans 8:1–39

Therefore, there is now no condemnation for those who are in Christ Jesus, because through Christ Jesus the law of the Spirit of life set me free from the law of sin and death. For what the law was powerless to do in that it was weakened by the sinful nature, God did by sending his own Son in the likeness of sinful man to be a sin offering. And so he condemned sin in sinful man, in order that the righteous requirements of the law might be fully met in us, who do not live according to the sinful nature but according to the Spirit.

With the words above, Paul opens what I consider the greatest chapter in Scripture. It is precarious and probably a foolish act to call any one chapter of the Bible "the greatest," if for no other reason than one is likely to get caught in a contradiction. This happened to me as soon as I had announced this subject. A friend pointed out that in my first volume on *The Minor Prophets* (1983), I have already called the third chapter of Hosea "the greatest chapter in the Bible," and obviously Hosea 3 and Roman 8 cannot both have that identical distinction.

Besides, a person is likely to change his mind over time. What appears as the greatest portion of the Word of God one year may appear less important later, and another book or chapter may take its place. I remember that

D. Martyn Lloyd-Jones said on one occasion that for a preacher the greatest book of the Bible should be the one he is expounding at that moment.

All that aside, there is a sense in which the eighth chapter of Romans truly is great, even superlatively great, and it would be wrong to begin our careful studies of this chapter without acknowledging that and then presenting a general outline. F. Godet, the Swiss commentator, called these thirty-nine verses great because they begin with "no condemnation" and end with "no separation,"[1] to which another writer, C. A. Fox, added that in between there is also "no defeat."[2]

Charles G. Trumbull, editor of the now deceased *Sunday School Times*, picked up on those earlier observations when he wrote:

> The eighth of Romans has become peculiarly precious to me, beginning with "no condemnation," ending with "no separation," and in between, "no defeat." This wondrous chapter sets forth the gospel and plan of salvation; the life of freedom and victory; the hopelessness of the natural man and the righteousness of the born again; the indwelling of Christ and the Holy Spirit; the resurrection of the body and blessed hope of Christ's return; the working together of all things for our good; every tense of the Christian life, past, present, and future; and the glorious, climactic song of triumph, no separation in time or eternity "from the love of God which is in Jesus Christ our Lord."[3]

An old German commentator named Spener said that if the Bible was a ring and the Book of Romans its precious stone, chapter 8 would be "the sparkling point of the jewel."[4] Many others have agreed.

How Many Sections?

It is not easy to outline Romans 8. The argument of the chapter is so carefully interwoven, with one thought following closely upon another, that dividing it into sections seems inevitably to be more or less "arbitrary," as Charles Hodge maintained.[5] This probably explains the surprising variety of outlines scholars give. Hodge himself divided the chapter into six sections, as Leon Morris also does. Godet found four sections. D. Martyn Lloyd-Jones has seven (or eight) sections. John R. W. Stott has two main parts, the first divided into four subsections and the second into two, plus an opening,

1. F. Godet, *Commentary on St. Paul's Epistle to the Romans*, trans. A. Cusin (Edinburgh: T. & T. Clark, 1892), vol. 2, pp. 56, 57.

2. Quoted by Leon Morris, *The Epistle to the Romans* (Grand Rapids: Wm. B. Eerdmans, and Leicester, England: Inter-Varsity Press, 1988), p. 299.

3. Quoted by Donald Grey Barnhouse, *Epistle to the Romans*, part 1 of the printed radio messages (Philadelphia: The Bible Study Hour, 1953), p. 1982.

4. Godet, *Commentary on St. Paul's Epistle to the Romans*, vol. 2, p. 57.

5. Charles Hodge, *A Commentary on Romans* (Edinburgh and Carlisle, Pa.: The Banner of Truth Trust, 1972), footnote, p. 263. Original edition 1935.

which he feels actually belongs with Romans 7, thus also making seven parts in all. The New International Version of the Bible has three sections and a total of nine paragraphs, which is a way of saying that the chapter could be treated in nine parts. Most commentators simply expound it as it comes.

Since we are going to be studying this chapter verse by verse, the way in which the verses are grouped is of little importance for us. Still, in order to give an overview of what the chapter is about, I want to suggest six divisions. These divisions follow Hodge and Lloyd-Jones most closely.

No Condemnation from the Law

We begin with verse 1. There is a sense in which this verse says everything the chapter really wishes to declare, for the sentence "therefore, there is now no condemnation for those who are in Christ Jesus" means that there is no condemnation now, nor will there ever be condemnation for those who are in Jesus. It is a statement of the believer's perfect and eternal security in Christ. But if that is so, then everything that follows in chapter 8 really follows. Above all, it follows that nothing "will be able to separate us from the love of God that is in Christ Jesus our Lord" (v. 39).

Verse 1 is the theme of the chapter, and the words "therefore, there is now no condemnation for those who are in Christ Jesus" are the triumphant cry growing out of the book's first half.

But why is there "no condemnation"? The first answer is that "through Christ Jesus the law of the Spirit of life set me free from the law of sin and death" (v. 2).

Very few of us have a proper sense of what it is to be under the law's condemnation, but we can get a glimpse of what is involved through watching others' trials. One day Jim Bakker is riding high as leader of a national television ministry and extensive business empire. But the funding appeals are dishonest, gifts are wrongfully used, and suddenly Bakker is on trial for fraud and is declared "Guilty." The condemned man now faces a maximum of 120 years in prison and $5 million in fines.

One day Ivan Boesky is a wealthy New York stockbroker. But suddenly he is convicted of insider trading and is condemned by the courts.

For months we follow the story of southern California's "Night Stalker" with its horrifying revelation of murders, rapes, and burglaries. Then Richard Ramirez is identified as the killer, convicted of thirteen counts of murder and thirty felonies by a jury of his peers. And he is sentenced to death for his atrocities.

"Guilty" was our status, too, as Paul has explained in the opening chapters of Romans. We were condemned sinners, subject to the outpoured wrath of God. But suddenly Jesus entered this world and died for us, bearing the wrath of God in our place, and there is now "no condemnation." The law tried to save us but could not. We had broken the law. The law could only condemn. But what the law could not do, God did through

Jesus. Instead of condemning us, God condemned sin so that "the righteous commandments of the law might be fully met in us, who do not live according to the sinful nature but according to the Spirit." This is the argument of verses 1–4.

Deliverance from Our Sinful Natures

But we have not only received deliverance from the law's condemnation as a result of God's saving favor to us through Jesus Christ. We have also been delivered from ourselves, that is, from our sinful natures. The first deliverance (vv. 1–4) is from sin's penalty. The second deliverance is from sin's power over us, which is what verses 5–14 describe.

In my judgment, these verses are the most important of the chapter if we consider them in terms of the weakness of the church of Jesus Christ today. They tell us that if we have been saved by Christ, then we have necessarily also been changed by him. In other words, not only have we who have believed on Jesus as Savior been justified, we have been regenerated as well. Therefore, if we are not living a new life in the power of the indwelling Holy Spirit, it is not simply that we are unfulfilled or defeated Christians. We are not Christians at all! As we will explore later, it is only "those who are led by the Spirit of God" who are the "sons of God" (v. 14). Many who are not living by the Spirit need to awaken to the fact that they are not truly Christians.

The other side of the picture is that, if we are so living, we can know that this is the Spirit's work and that it is another evidence that we are no longer under condemnation but have been saved forever.

Sons (and Daughters) of God

The Holy Spirit does not only change us, giving us a new nature and thus delivering us from our sinful former selves. The Holy Spirit also gives us a new standing before God, which is what the next section of the chapter teaches (vv. 15–17). What a standing this is! Before, we were slaves, wicked and condemned slaves at that. Now we have become God's daughters and sons, by which we cry, "*Abba*, Father," and confidently present our deepest questions, sharpest hurts, and most pressing needs to him.

Hope of Future Glory

Being a child of God means that we are also heirs of God together with Jesus Christ, God's unique Son. All that he has we have, and all that he experienced we are also to experience in some measure. This includes his sufferings, as Paul has said: "Now if we are children, then we are heirs—heirs of God and co-heirs with Christ, if indeed we share in his sufferings in order that we may also share in his glory" (v. 17).

But this suggests a great comparison to Paul. Share in his sufferings? Yes. But also in his glory, and "our present sufferings are not worth comparing with the glory that will be revealed in us" (v. 18). In these verses (vv. 18–25) Paul lifts the matter of our redemption to a cosmic level, asserting that the restoration of fallen men and women through the work of Christ is only one part of what God is doing in salvation. God is redeeming nature, too, which means that he is saving creation from the decay it experienced as the result of Adam's fall in Eden.

What a tremendous revelation this is! D. Martyn Lloyd-Jones says:

> The radical defect in so many of us is that we are so subjective and always thinking of our particular moods and states. The Apostle Paul reminds us that sin not only affects us and our fellow human beings, it has affected the whole creation—the animals, even inanimate nature, everything is affected. God's work, God's creation has been marred. Sin has come in, and evil has polluted it all. We are to look at salvation and ourselves as a part of the glorious scheme which is going to renovate the entire cosmos. And because God is going to do that to the whole cosmos he is going to do it to you![6]

This is yet another reason why there is "no condemnation" for those who are in Christ Jesus. By grace we have been caught up into this cosmic drama.

The Intercession of the Holy Spirit

The fifth reason that believers in Christ can be assured of their salvation and know that there can never be any "condemnation" is the intercession of the Holy Spirit: the third person of the Trinity interceding with the first person of the Trinity on our behalf (vv. 26–27). This does not mean that the Father needs to be persuaded to change his mind toward us, which some imagine either Jesus or the Holy Spirit doing. It means, as Paul points out, that the Holy Spirit interprets our prayers aright so that they are presented to the Father "in accordance with [his] will" (v. 27).

Have you ever tried to pray about something and been confused, not knowing exactly what you should pray for? I know I have. In fact, I find that as I grow older in the Christian life I am less and less certain of what I should pray for. When I was younger I had a more limited range of concerns and experience and saw only limited dimensions of a situation. Now I see more, and the situations in life for which I pray seem increasingly complex. In such situations it is good to know that, however I may pray, the Holy Spirit is constantly present to interpret my prayers correctly. I would not have it any other way. For whatever I may think I desire, in the final analysis it is not my will but the will of God that I want done.

6. D. M. Lloyd-Jones, *Romans: An Exposition of Chapters 7:1—8:4, The Law: Its Functions and Limits* (Grand Rapids: Zondervan, 1973), p. 266.

The Purpose and Character of God

The final section of Romans 8, verses 28–39, is the greatest of all. Martyn Lloyd-Jones calls it an argument involving the very character of God. So, if salvation "fails with respect to any believer, the character of God has gone."[7] Charles Hodge speaks of these verses as having two separate arguments: "the decree and purpose of God" (vv. 28–30) and "his infinite and unchanging love" (vv. 31–39).[8]

Verses 29 and 30 contain what commentators have called a golden chain of five links, each of which points to something God has done for believers. They stress the sovereignty of God in salvation. The links in this golden chain of God's sovereign acts are: foreknowledge, predestination, effectual calling, justification, and glorification. Paul calls these acts God's fixed "purpose" for his people.

John R. W. Stott has a wonderful way of handling this last section, and I share it here even though we will come back to it much further on. He calls verses 28–39 "the invincible purpose of God" and divides the section into two parts, the first presenting "five undeniable affirmations" (vv. 28–30) and the second "five unanswerable questions" (vv. 31–39).

The "undeniable affirmations" are the unbreakable chain of five links, which I have already mentioned. Says Stott, "This working together for good, God's purpose in the salvation of sinners, is traced from its beginnings in his own mind to its culmination in the eternal glory."[9] These verses comprise one of the grandest statements in the entire Word of God.

The unanswerable questions occur in verses 31–39:

1. "If God is for us, who can be against us?" (v. 31). Many are against us. Christians have many enemies. But the question is not "are they against us?" It is "can they be against us?" That is, can they prevail. The answer, if God is for us, is "Obviously not!"

2. "He who did not spare his own Son, but gave him up for us all—how will he not also, along with him, graciously give us all things?" (v. 32). Without the gift of Christ, we might wonder if God will give us all things. But since he has given us Jesus, what can he possibly be disposed to hold back? If he gave us the greatest of all gifts, he will certainly give all lesser ones.

3. "Who will bring any charge against those whom God has chosen?" (v. 33). Without the last word of that sentence, the earlier part would have some weight. Certainly there are many who could justly bring charges against us. Even our own consciences could do it. But not against those "whom God has chosen." Paul is speaking of people for whom Christ died,

7. Ibid.
8. Hodge, *A Commentary on Romans*, p. 283.
9. John R. W. Stott, *Men Made New: An Exposition of Romans 5–8* (Grand Rapids: Baker Book House, 1984), p. 101.

who have therefore been foreknown, predestined, called, justified, and glorified. No charges can stand against such people.

4. "Who is he that condemns?" (v. 34). No one, as long as Jesus has died and is even now in heaven making intercession for us.

5. "Who shall separate us from the love of Christ?" (v. 35). In response to this last question Paul brings out all possible separators he can think of: trouble, hardship, persecution, famine, nakedness, danger, or the sword. He acknowledges the troubles Christians face: "'For your sake we face death all day long; we are considered as sheep to be slaughtered,'" quoting from Psalm 44:22. He reviews the sources from which such trouble might be imagined to come: death and life, angels and demons, the present and the future, any powers whatever—height, depth, anything in the entire created order. But having reviewed it all and having placed it next to the eternal and invincible love of God, Paul concludes rightly that nothing will be able to separate us from that love in Christ Jesus our Lord (v. 39).

Disappointed with God?

Someone sent me a book by Philip Yancey, a free-lance author and editor-at-large for *Christianity Today*, titled *Disappointment with God*.[10] It grew out of counseling sessions the author had with young Christians, all of whom were disappointed with God and whose complaints boiled down to three accusations: (1) God is not fair; (2) God is hidden; and (3) God is silent—he does not answer prayers.

I am sure these accusations are genuine, and I appreciate Yancey's answers. He replies that "fairness" would send each and every one of us to hell; that God has unveiled himself as fully as possible in the person of the historical Jesus Christ; and that it is out of his periods of silence that God draws forth the precious perfume of human faith.

Yet what stuck with me most about the book is its title: *Disappointment with God*. For I found myself reflecting, particularly since I was beginning at the same time to work through this great eighth chapter of Romans, how any Christian could possibly be disappointed with God.

Disappointment with God? When he sent Jesus Christ to die for us so that we might escape his just wrath and condemnation?

Disappointment with God? When he sent his Holy Spirit to free us from our own sinful and debilitating natures and join us to Christ?

Disappointment with God? When he has made us his very own daughters and sons, with all the privileges that come from it?

Disappointment with God? When he has drawn us into a great cosmic drama of redemption, in which even the heavens and earth have a part?

10. Philip Yancey, *Disappointment with God: Three Questions No One Asks Aloud* (Grand Rapids: Zondervan, 1988).

Disappointment with God? When the Spirit intercedes for us, conforming our ignorant and incomplete prayers to the good, pleasing, and acceptable will of God?

Disappointment with God? When he has set in motion an invincible chain of saving actions, beginning with his affectionate choice of us in eternity past, proceeding through his predestination of us to be saved from sin and conformed to the image of his own blessed Son, his effectual calling of us to faith in Jesus as the Savior, and justification, and ending with glorification in which all the blessed purposes of God toward us are fulfilled?

Disappointment with God? When he has fixed such a lasting love upon us that nothing in all creation can separate us from it?

Disappointment?

Brothers and sisters, whatever are we thinking of? Or is it that we are not thinking? Or thinking only of ourselves? Perhaps our disappointment (if we have it) means only that we are unhappy because God has not done exactly what we wanted him to do when we wanted him to do it, regardless of the fact that he has a much better plan for us and is actually working it out day by day, and will until the end of time.

The only sure cure for our unseemly disappointment is getting our eyes off ourselves entirely and onto God, who has done these great things for us. The best way I know to do this is by a study of Romans 8, which at least in this respect really is "the greatest chapter in the Bible."

95

No Condemnation

Romans 8:1-4

Therefore, there is now no condemnation for those who are in Christ Jesus, because through Christ Jesus the law of the Spirit of life set me free from the law of sin and death. For what the law was powerless to do in that it was weakened by the sinful nature, God did by sending his own Son in the likeness of sinful man to be a sin offering. And so he condemned sin in sinful man, in order that the righteous requirements of the law might be fully met in us, who do not live according to the sinful nature but according to the Spirit.

Having surveyed the entire eighth chapter of Romans in our last study, we return now to the beginning of the chapter, concentrating on verses 1–4. The first verse tells us, "Therefore, there is now no condemnation for those who are in Christ Jesus." This sentence is the theme of the chapter, as I said in the last study. Everything else flows from it. The rest of the chapter is basically an exposition of this one idea.

But verse 1 is not only the theme of Romans 8. It is the theme of the entire Word of God, which is only another way of saying that it is the gospel. Indeed, it is the gospel's very heart.

789

This means that it is what Paul has been explaining all along. In Romans 1 he spoke of the gospel, saying that he was not ashamed of it "because it is the power of God for the salvation of everyone who believes" (v. 16). He spoke of the gospel again in Romans 3, adding that "now a righteousness from God, apart from the law, has been made known . . ." (v. 21). It is the same in Romans 5: "Therefore, since we have been justified through faith, we have peace with God through our Lord Jesus Christ" (v. 1), and "Since we have been justified by his blood, how much more shall we be saved from God's wrath through him!" (v. 9). He ended that chapter by saying, "But where sin increased, grace increased all the more, so that, just as sin reigned in death, so also grace might reign through righteousness to bring eternal life through Jesus Christ our Lord" (vv. 20–21).

These are only a few of the many statements of the gospel that have occurred thus far in Romans, and Romans 8:1 is but another. Always it is the gospel. Paul seems never to have grown tired talking about it.

Ah, but we do! Many of us find the gospel wearisome and grace boring.

Why is that, do you suppose? Why are we so different from Paul at this point? I think it is because of what Jesus alluded to in speaking of the woman who anointed his feet with her tears and then wiped them with her hair. She had a sinful past, and those who knew it objected, saying to themselves, like the Pharisee: "If this man were a prophet, he would know who is touching him and what kind of woman she is—that she is a sinner" (Luke 7:39). Jesus answered by telling of a man who had been forgiven a great debt and who therefore loved his benefactor greatly. Jesus' point was that "he who has been forgiven little loves little" (v. 47). Isn't that it? Isn't it true that the reason grace means little to most of us is that we do not consider ourselves to be great sinners, desperately in need of forgiveness?

Four Great Words

We cannot appreciate or even understand what Paul is saying unless we recognize that we are sinners and that we have been saved only by the grace of God. This is taught by the four great words in verse 1.

1. *Condemnation.* I spoke about condemnation in the last study, saying that we have a hard time appreciating what this means because few of us have ever been found guilty in a court of law. "Condemnation," as Leon Morris says, "is a forensic term which here includes both the sentence and the execution of the sentence."[1] But no human being has ever pronounced a sentence of "guilty" against most of us, and we think therefore that we are all basically fine people. We are not, of course. This is what Romans 1:18–3:20 has been teaching.

---

1. Leon Morris, *The Epistle to the Romans* (Grand Rapids: Wm. B. Eerdmans, and Leicester, England: Inter-Varsity Press, 1988), p. 300.

2. *Now.* "Now" is a time word, pointing to the change that has come about as the result of believers' entering into the justification that Jesus Christ made possible by his death. We stood condemned by God and were due to suffer the penalty of an eternal death for our sins, the "wages of sin" being "death" (Rom. 6:23). But that has been changed *now* because of God's great grace and favor to us.

3. *No.* This word is weak in the English translations. In our texts it is a simple negative, like most other negatives. In the Greek text "no" is strongly emphasized. First, it is not the simple negative *ou* but the compound and therefore stronger negative *oude.* Second, it occurs at the beginning of the sentence, which intensifies the negation. Commentators do not know how to render this well in English, but they write things like: "Not any therefore now of condemnation"[2] and "Not only is the Christian not in a state of condemnation now, he never can be; it is impossible."[3] It is a very strong statement.

4. *Therefore.* The fourth great word in this sentence is "therefore." To what does it refer? To the arguments immediately preceding this verse in chapter 7? To chapter 5 or chapter 3? Most agree that Paul's "therefore" is inclusive, pointing back to the entire argument of the epistle thus far. It is because of God's work in Jesus Christ and because of the application of it to us by the Holy Spirit that there is now "no condemnation."

God's Work, Not Ours

Here is a point at which we need to make sure we really understand what is being said. I have pointed out that there is no condemnation for us *because of what God has done.* But do we really believe that? Or do we still think that somehow, in some way, we are contributing to our salvation?

What Paul writes is that "there is now no condemnation for those who are in Christ Jesus." That is, there are two classes of human beings: those who are *in Christ Jesus* and who are therefore not under condemnation, and those who are not in Christ Jesus and who are therefore still under condemnation. What he is promising is for those in the first class only. But the question is: How do we get out of the one class and into the other. Is this something we do? Do we earn it? Do we attain it "by faith"? If you have understood what the apostle has been saying up to this point, you will know that it is none of the above. It is because of God's work in joining us to Christ. This is what the last half of Romans 5 and almost the whole of Romans 6 is about.

2. Donald Grey Barnhouse, *God's Heirs: Exposition of Bible Doctrines, Taking the Epistle to the Romans as a Point of Departure,* vol. 7, *Romans 8:1–39* (Grand Rapids: Wm. B. Eerdmans, 1963), p. 5.

3. D. M. Lloyd-Jones, *Romans: An Exposition of Chapters 7:1—8:4, The Law: Its Functions and Limits* (Grand Rapids: Zondervan, 1973), p. 271.

Here I must deal with a manuscript problem. Those who use the Authorized or King James text will notice the addition of the words "who walk not after the flesh, but after the Spirit" following the words "Christ Jesus" in verse 1. This is certainly an error, as even the famous Scofield Bible, which uses the King James text, acknowledges in a footnote.[4] It is worth pointing this out because, if the clause is retained, it suggests exactly the opposite of what the text actually says.

In its corrupt form the text reads, "There is therefore now no condemnation to them which are in Christ Jesus, who walk not after the flesh but after the Spirit" (KJV), which seems to be saying that if we continue to lead a godly life "in the Spirit" we will not be condemned, but that if we fail to lead a godly life we will be.

How did such a serious textual error come about? We do not know exactly, but it is not hard to imagine how this might have happened. For centuries before the invention of the printing press just prior to the Reformation, Bible manuscripts were copied by hand, and from time to time the copyists made errors, as we would have done ourselves. In the vast majority of cases the copyists were accurate. That is why we have such accurate texts today. Even where there are errors, we can correct them by comparing the errant copy with the multiplicity of other more perfect manuscripts. Still, mistakes were made, and this seems to have been the case here.

We can imagine a weary monk working his way through the Book of Romans, perhaps early in the morning when he was still sleepy or else late at night. He has finished chapter 7 and begins chapter 8, writing, "There is therefore now no condemnation to them which are in Christ Jesus. . . ." But at this point he either dozes off or perhaps, weary with the arduous work of copying, looks ahead to the end of the book to see how much more there is to do (he is only halfway through!). When he returns to his work his eye falls not on verse 2, where he should pick up, but on the latter half of verse 4, where he copies "who walk not after the flesh, but after the Spirit." This is a mistake, of course, a serious one, but it sounds right to him. It flows grammatically. So he continues by copying verse 2 and the verses after it.

Does this mean that we cannot trust the Bible? No! There are only a handful of such problems, and besides, they are well known to those who work with Bible texts. They have been corrected. Nevertheless, in this case the problem existed for quite a long time.

What I am saying is that these words do not belong. If they did, our escape from condemnation would last only as long as our next faltering step or sin; then we would be back under condemnation again. Thank God, salvation is not like that! Salvation is from God. It is by God. What the text says is that there is no condemnation for whose who have been joined to

4. The Scofield Bible says in its note to verse 1, "The last ten words were evidently copied from v. 4, where they properly express the result of 'no condemnation,' not its cause."

Jesus Christ by God the Father through the instrumentality of the Holy Spirit.

The Trinity at Work

Let me repeat that last statement: *There is no condemnation for those who have been joined to Jesus Christ by God the Father through the instrumentality of the Holy Spirit.* I repeat this because it is a Trinitarian statement—it speaks of God the Father, God the Son, and God the Holy Spirit—and because it is precisely in these terms that Paul goes on to explain what God has done for us and why "there is now no condemnation."

Can you see it in the text? After his opening statement in verse 1, Paul has two explanatory sentences, each beginning with the identical Greek word *gar*, translated either "because" or "for." The New International Version obscures this a bit, since it translates the Greek word as "because" at the beginning of verse 2 and as "for" at the beginning of verse 3, and because it divides the second of Paul's sentences (vv. 3–4) into two parts. But it is clear enough anyway. In verse 2 Paul says that there is no condemnation for those who are in Christ Jesus because "through Christ Jesus the law of the Spirit of life set me free from the law of sin and death." In verses 3 and 4 he says that there is no condemnation because "what the law was powerless to do in that it was weakened by the sinful nature, God did by sending his own Son in the likeness of sinful man to be a sin offering, [thus condemning] sin in sinful man, in order that the righteous requirements of the law might be fully met in us, who do not live according to the sinful nature but according to the Spirit."

When you put together those two parallel explanations of why there is now no condemnation, you see that each of the persons of the Godhead is involved.

1. *God the Father.* What has God the Father done for our salvation? The answer is in two parts. First, God sent Jesus in the likeness of sinful man to be a sin offering. Second, and by this means, God condemned sin in sinful man so that the righteous requirements of the law might be fully met in those who are joined to Christ.

Do you see now why I have called verse 1 not only the theme of Romans 8 but the very heart of the gospel? As Paul explains the basis of our deliverance, almost the entire gospel is presented in the next few verses. There is the doctrine of the incarnation, God's sending his Son Jesus to be like sinful man. The word *likeness* (v. 3) is important, of course, for it alerts us to the fact that although Jesus was a real man, which made him able to feel as we feel, endure temptation as we endure temptation, and eventually die, he nevertheless did not become like us in regard to our sinful nature. It is what the author of Hebrews means in noting that "we have one [high priest, that is, Jesus] who has been tempted in every way, just as we are—yet was without sin" (Heb. 4:15).

Paul's statement also contains the doctrine of the atonement. For his argument is that God sent his Son to be a sin offering. This picks up on all we learned about propitiation when we were studying Romans 3. God sent Jesus to die in our place and thus turn the divine wrath aside.

Finally, and by this means, "[God] condemned sin in sinful man, in order that the righteous requirements of the law might be fully met in us, who do not live according to the sinful nature but according to the Spirit." This refers to justification, God's work of condemning sin in Christ so that we might be able to stand before God in his perfect righteousness, and to the necessary work of sanctification that follows justification for all who have been saved. (We are going to look at the nature and necessity of sanctification carefully in the next study.)

2. *God the Son.* What has Jesus Christ done for our salvation? We have already touched on this by noting that he became like us in order to become a sin offering. In the context of what Paul worked out in Romans 3, this has two parts.

First, as a sin offering to God, Jesus made propitiation for our sins. When we were studying chapter 3, I pointed out that this is a term borrowed from the world of ancient religion. It refers to turning the wrath of God aside. Many in our time have judged this to be unworthy of the character of God and say such things as, "As if his wrath needs to be turned aside! God is not angry, he is love." But this can hardly stand in any honest study of Romans. What Paul has been saying from the beginning is that we are all under wrath because of our wickedness. The wrath of God is precisely our problem. It must be dealt with. How? We cannot turn it aside. All we do serves only to increase it, since we accumulate wrath against ourselves constantly by every thought we have and everything we do. Only God in the person of his Son can turn that wrath aside, and this he has done by Jesus' bearing it in our place. No one who fails to understand and believe this can be a Christian.

Second, Jesus did a work of redemption. Again, when we were studying chapter 3, I pointed out that redemption is a term borrowed from the ancient world of business, just as propitiation is borrowed from the ancient world of religion. It refers to buying something in the marketplace, and also to buying it *out* of the marketplace so it will not have to be sold there again. This means little if we think of it in regard to mere objects, but it means a great deal if we think of it in regard to people, especially slaves. To redeem a slave was to buy the slave out of the slave market so that he or she might be set free. This is what Jesus did for us. Paul touches on it in Romans 8 when he says that "through Christ Jesus the law of the Spirit of life set me free from the law of sin and death" (v. 2). He means that he was once a slave to sin and death. But Jesus freed him from that, as he has all who have been saved by him.

3. *God the Holy Spirit.* The third person of the Godhead is brought into the picture in verse 2 ("the law of the Spirit of life set me free from the law of sin and death") and in verse 4 ("who do not live according to the sinful nature, but according to the Spirit").

What has the Holy Spirit done for our salvation? He has joined us to Christ, so that we become beneficiaries of all Christ has done. When we were studying this doctrine in Romans 5, I pointed out two things. First, that it is terribly important and perhaps the most critical doctrine of salvation in Paul's writings. Paul used the phrases "in Christ," "in Christ Jesus," "in him," or their equivalents 164 times in his writings. We can hardly emphasize this enough.

Second, this union is hard to understand. We recognize that this was true for those living in Jesus' and Paul's day as well as for us, because instead of simply explaining the doctrine in abstract language, both Jesus and Paul used illustrations.

Jesus spoke of it as the relationship between a vine and its branches: "Remain in me, and I will remain in you. No branch can bear fruit of itself; it must remain in the vine. Neither can you bear fruit unless you remain in me. . . . Apart from me you can do nothing" (John 15:4–5). He also used the image of eating and drinking, which we adhere to literally every time we share in the Lord's Supper: "This is my body" and "This cup is the new covenant in my blood" (1 Cor. 11:24–25).

In his writings Paul illustrates the concept by three very powerful illustrations. The first is the union of the head and the body, in which he compares the members of the church to the various parts of Christ's body (cf. 1 Cor. 12:12–27; Eph. 1:22–23; Col. 1:18). The second is the union of the parts of a building, sometimes described as a temple that has the Lord Jesus Christ as its chief cornerstone (cf. 1 Cor. 3:9, 11–15; Eph. 2:20–22). The third and most powerful illustration is the union of a husband and wife in marriage. Paul ends his teaching about marriage by saying, "This is a profound mystery—but I am talking about Christ and the church" (Eph. 5:32).

By joining us to Christ, the Holy Spirit seals our salvation and makes possible the great declaration of this chapter: "Therefore, there is now no condemnation for those who are in Christ Jesus."

No, Nay, Never

I think of a popular Irish folksong called "The Wild Rover." Perhaps you know it. It tells of a young man's restless days and of his return home, ending with the chorus, "No, nay, never; no, nay, never, no more will I play the wild rover, no never, no more." It makes me ask, "Can there ever be a condemning judgment for those who are in Christ Jesus?" I answer, "No, nay, never—no more."

Do you remember Jesus' teaching about eternal security in John 10? He was speaking of how he and the Father hold us safely: "My sheep listen to my voice; I know them, and they follow me. I give them eternal life, and they shall never perish; no one can snatch them out of my hand. My Father, who has given them to me, is greater than all; no one can snatch them out of my Father's hand. I and the Father are one" (John 10:27–30).

When I was teaching John's Gospel I compared this to a carpenter who will sometimes join two boards by driving nails through them and then bending the protruding tip of the nails over sideways, embedding them in the wood, thus clinching the nail. I said that this is what Jesus does. His first nail is the doctrine of eternal life, a life that will never end. But lest we fail to appreciate that eternal life really *is* eternal life, he clinches it by the explanatory words "shall never perish." Then he drives the second nail, that we are secure in his hands. In case we fail to appreciate that, he clinches this nail, too, adding that the Father also has us in his hands, that no one can snatch us out of the Father's hands, and that he and the Father are one.

In the same way, Paul teaches that "there is now no condemnation"—(1) because of the Father's work; (2) because of the Son's work; and (3) because of the work of the Holy Spirit. Now it is "no, nay, never" for those who are in Jesus.

But do not presume on this security. This is a great doctrine for those who truly are in Christ, but it is only for those who are in him. Make sure you are. If you are not sure, give the matter no rest until the Holy Spirit himself plants upon your heart the assurance that you really are Christ's.

96

The Christian Doctrine of Holiness

Romans 8:3–4

. . . And so he condemned sin in sinful man, in order that the righteous require-
ments of the law might be fully met in us, who do not live according to the sinful
nature but according to the Spirit.

Our study of Romans 8 has brought
us to the third and fourth verses. But if we can set those aside for a moment,
I want to begin by a story drawn not from the eighth chapter of Romans but
from the eighth chapter of John.

Jesus had come from the Mount of Olives, where he had been praying, and
was met in the temple courts by a gathering of Pharisees and teachers of the
law who had devised a scheme to trap him. They had caught a poor woman in
adultery, and now they were bringing her before Jesus with a question:
"Teacher, this woman was caught in the act of adultery. In the Law Moses commanded us to stone such women. Now what do you say?" (John 8:4–5). It was a
disgusting situation. The law required that there be two or more eyewitnesses
to a crime, to the very act, and if this requirement had been met, as the leaders seem to have been claiming, the witnesses would also have had to see the

man who was involved. That they did not bring him before Jesus suggests that he may have been part of this plot and that it must have been a set-up, a trap. In other words, these leaders did not care either for the law or the woman but were only intent on trapping Jesus, whom they hated.

It was a clever trap, too. Jesus was known for being compassionate, so he would be expected to forgive the woman. But if he did that publicly, Jesus could be accused of violating or disregarding God's law. What kind of a prophet would do that? He would be discredited as a teacher sent from God. On the other hand, if he condemned the woman, the leaders would laugh him to scorn and mock his words. "Come to me, all you who are weary and burdened, and I will give you rest"? Oh, no! ". . . and I will kill you." They thought they had him in a box from which even God himself could not escape.

You know the story. Jesus fulfilled the law by demanding that all its requirements be met. Let those who witnessed the sin come forward and cast the first stones, as the law required. But let them be sure that they were not guilty themselves, which they would be, even of this crime, if they had been part of a plot to trap the woman. When the accusers failed to come forward, Jesus exercised the right to judge her not on the basis of the law, which she had indeed broken, but on the basis of his coming death for sinners—in exactly the way he saves us.

He asked the woman, "Where are they [the accusers]? Has no one condemned you?"

"No one, sir," she said.

He answered, "Then neither do I condemn you. Go now and leave your life of sin" (vv. 10–11). The King James Version says, "Sin no more."

No Condemnation

I tell that story because it is an exact illustration of what we find in the first four verses of Romans 8. The opening verse announces the great welcome news of freedom from condemnation for all who are in Christ Jesus. We have already studied this. It means that God has saved, and is saving, a great company of people by the work of Jesus Christ. We have the law. But, like the woman in John's Gospel, we are all unable to keep it. We are condemned by it. We cannot be set free from the law's condemnation by law, because the law is powerless. But what the law could not do, God did by sending his Son to be a sin offering. It is as if, in these verses, Jesus is saying to us, "Neither do I condemn you; go in peace."

But as we come to verses 3 and 4 we discover that it is not merely a question of our being delivered from the law's condemnation. Christ has delivered us from the law's power, too. He died to start the process of sanctification and not merely to provide propitiation from wrath, on the basis of which God has been able to justify believers from all sin. "And so he condemned sin in sinful man, in order that the righteous requirements of the law might be fully met in us, who do not live according to the sinful nature but according to the Spirit."

In other words, to go back to John 8, Jesus is saying, "You are free from all condemnation, but you must now leave your sin."

What this is teaching is that justification and sanctification always go together, so that you cannot have one without the other. Justification is not sanctification. We are not saved because of any good we may do. If that were the case, Jesus would have told the woman: "Leave your life of sin, and if you do that, neither will I condemn you." But Jesus did not say that. It was the other way around. No condemnation! But *then* a holy life! Nevertheless, just because justification is not sanctification and sanctification is not justification, we are not to think that sanctification is somehow unimportant. On the contrary, according to Romans 8:3–4, sanctification is the very end for which God saved us.

By sending his Son to be a sin offering, God "condemned sin in sinful man, *in order that* the righteous requirements of the law might be fully met in us, who do not live according to the sinful nature but according to the Spirit."

Let me back up and say this once again, though in different words.

1. *Two works.* In Romans 8:1–4 we have two great saving works of God. They are justification and sanctification. The first is deliverance from sin's penalty. The second is deliverance from sin's power. God accomplishes both for all Christians.

2. *Three agents.* In delivering us from sin's penalty and power, three divine agents are involved. God is the agent of our justification. It is he who pronounces us "not condemned." The Holy Spirit is the agent of our sanctification, since he accomplishes in us what the law was powerless to do. It is the remaining person of the Trinity, the Lord Jesus Christ, who makes both works possible by his death for sin. For Jesus not only bore God's just judgment upon sin for us in our place; he also broke its power over those who are joined to him by saving faith.[1]

---

1. The majority of Protestant commentators, as well as many in the early church, were so concerned to protect the doctrine of justification by faith apart from the merit of works that they rejected any thought of sanctification in this passage. Charles Hodge is an example. He writes, "If verse 3 is understood of the sacrificial death of Christ, and the condemnation of sin in him as the substitute of sinners, then this verse [v. 4] must be understood of justification, and not of sanctification" (Charles Hodge, *A Commentary on Romans* [Edinburgh and Carlisle, Pa.: The Banner of Truth Trust, 1972], p. 254 [Original edition 1935]). But this is a significant error in that it misses at least half of what Paul is saying and breaks the flow of the passage, since justification alone does not lead to "the righteous requirements of the law" being fully met in us. The problem Paul raises is not only that the law could not condemn sin by being a substitutionary sacrifice for it, which only Christ could do, but that it was unable to produce an actual righteousness in people. Christ accomplished this for his people, because his death not only dealt with sin's penalty, he bearing it in our place, but broke its power as well. See D. M. Lloyd-Jones, *Romans: An Exposition of Chapters 7:1—8:4, The Law: Its Functions and Limits* (Grand Rapids: Zondervan, 1973), pp. 301–307. Lloyd-Jones points out rightly that Paul speaks of the righteousness of the law being fulfilled "in [Greek, *en*] us" and not "with respect to [Greek, *peri*] us." The latter would be the right word if justification alone is in view.

John R. W. Stott says of Romans 8, "In verses 1 and 2 the scope of salvation is stated: no condemnation, no bondage. In verses 3 and 4 the way of salvation is unfolded: we are told how God affects it."[2]

3. *One goal.* All this is directed toward one goal, which is that "the righteous requirements of the law might be fully met in us, who do not live according to the sinful nature but according to the Spirit."

What Paul says here is the equivalent of what he says in his letter to the Ephesians, another great doctrinal book, where he teaches that God saved us apart from good works precisely so we might be able to do good works. The pertinent text says, "For it is by grace you have been saved, through faith—and this not from yourselves, it is the gift of God—*not by works*, so that no one can boast. For we are God's workmanship, created in Christ Jesus *to do good works*, which God has prepared in advance for us to do" (Eph. 2:8–10, emphasis added).

Four Important Truths

Because I have called this chapter "The Christian Doctrine of Holiness," what I need to do now is develop or unfold that doctrine. There are four important truths about "holiness" that we must examine.

1. *Holiness is justification's goal.* We could also say, since Jesus died to save us *from* and not merely *in* our sins, that the purpose of Jesus' incarnation and death was that all who are saved by him might live holy lives. God's sending his Son "in the likeness of sinful man" refers to the incarnation. "To be a sin offering" refers to Christ's death. Therefore, the incarnation and death of Jesus were so that "the righteous requirements of the law might be fully met in" Christians. Stott says, "God condemned sin in Christ, so that holiness might appear in us."[3]

We have the same idea in those important verses from Ephesians cited earlier, for there we are told that God has literally "ordained" or "appointed" us for good works. Ephesians is a great book about election, which is specifically taught in chapter 1. Then, in chapter 2, salvation is clearly said to be a result of God's choice and actions, rather than our own. So this is another case of God's appointing not only the ends but also the means to those ends. In this case, the end is good works. The means is our salvation by the work of Christ apart from human merit. In the language of Ephesians, God made us alive in Christ so that we might live for him. Or, as we can also say, he saved us by grace so that we might be gracious in how we treat other people.

2. *Holiness consists in fulfilling the law's just demands.* There are two errors to be avoided at this point. One is the error of the Pharisees. The Pharisees

---

2. John R. W. Stott, *Men Made New: An Exposition of Romans 5–8* (Grand Rapids: Baker Book House, 1984), p. 80.
3. Ibid., p. 81.

thought of themselves as being perfect fulfillers of the law. The law said tithe, so they tithed. They tithed not only their money but their goods, too, even down to the spices on their shelves. The law said keep the Sabbath, so they kept the Sabbath. They would not lift a finger to do even the smallest thing that might be construed as work. Yet the Pharisees were not righteous. They were self-righteous. Many were filled with pride, even to the point of hating those who were not like themselves. Their worst hatred was for Jesus, because his righteousness exposed their sin. Some of the most critical things Jesus ever said were about these people and their hypocrisy (cf. Matt. 23).

The other error is the exact opposite. It is a characteristic error of our times, the error of hedonistic Antinomianism. This view says, "What really matters is not the law but what I feel in my heart. So even if the law of God says that something is wrong, as long as I feel it is all right, it must be right. Or at least it is right for me."

Have you ever heard anybody say that? I am sure you have. It is the response made to moral demands by thousands of our contemporaries, many of whom want to be considered Christians but who really are not. They show they are not by their tragic disregard of God's requirements.

What, then, does fulfilling the righteous requirements of the law mean? The answer is in the word the New International Version translates as "live according to" but which actually means "walk" (*peripateō*). This word portrays the Christian life as a path along which we walk, following Jesus Christ who goes before us. The path has a direction, and it has boundaries. The direction is the character of God, which is expressed in the law but which we see fully in Jesus. The boundaries are the requirements God's law imposes. We must not cross over these requirements. If we do, we are not on the path. We are not following after Christ. On the other hand, if we do follow, our eyes are not fixed on the law primarily—that was the error of the Pharisees—but on Jesus, whom we love and desire to serve by our obedience.

Can Christians sin? Of course, they can—and do. We all do. But there is all the difference in the world between stumbling on the path, getting up and then going on, and not being on the path of discipleship at all. Those who are on the path may fall, but they are following after Jesus Christ and are never fully content unless they follow him.

3. *Holiness is the work of the Holy Spirit.* This is what we were studying at great length in Romans 7. Paul made two important points in that chapter. First, before his conversion he could not keep the law. He wanted to keep it, and at times he thought he had. But he actually could not. He was an impotent sinner. Second, even after his conversion he found that he was unable to keep the law of God *by himself.* He describes his struggle in this area toward the end of the chapter, showing that what he wanted to do he could not do, and that what he did not want to do he did. Paul discovered that it is only by the presence and power of the Holy Spirit that he or anybody else could or can be holy.

This suggests two obvious conclusions. First, if we cannot live a holy life apart from the Holy Spirit and yet must do so, then we must keep close to God in Bible study, where God speaks to us, and in prayer, in which we speak to God. We must seek the Spirit's blessing.

Second, we must work at this relationship. We must remember that in Romans 6 Paul developed the key to holiness by saying that we are to understand what God has done for us in Christ and then base our entire lives on it, conforming our conduct to what we know to be true. He said, ". . . count yourselves dead to sin but alive to God in Christ Jesus. Therefore do not let sin reign in your mortal body so that you obey its evil desires. Do not offer the parts of your body to sin, as instruments of wickedness, but rather offer yourselves to God, as those who have been brought from death to life; and offer the parts of your body to him as instruments of righteousness" (Rom. 6:11–13).

Paul does not mention the Holy Spirit in Romans 6, but, as we now learn in chapter 8, it is only by the power of the indwelling Spirit of God that we can do this.

4. *Holiness is mandatory.* Once I was asked to do a series of messages on Christian discipleship, and the first question I dealt with was this: "Is discipleship necessary?" I began by explaining the way the question needs to be interpreted. It should not mean, "Is discipleship necessary if we are to be obedient to Jesus?" That is obvious. Nor should it mean, "Is discipleship necessary in order to live a full and happy Christian life?" That should be obvious, too. What the question should mean (and the sense in which I treated it) is, "Is discipleship necessary for one to be a true Christian? Can you be a saved person without it?" The answer I gave, the answer that should be given by any true Bible expositor, is, "Yes, it is necessary! It is mandatory to follow after Christ to be a Christian."

We need to speak in exactly the same way about holiness. When we say that holiness is mandatory, we do not mean that it is merely good to be holy, and we certainly do not mean that we can be perfect or ever reach a point where we will no longer be in danger of sinning. We mean that we must be on the right path. We must actually be walking according to the Spirit of God, if we are Christians.

Unholy People and Churches

What does that say about us? What does it say about the state of Christianity in the United States today? If holiness is necessary, as we have seen it is, how do we account for the unholy state of so many alleged Christian people and their churches?

George Gallup, the founder and president of the American Institute of Public Opinion, asked this question several years ago and set out to find an answer. He had been struck by the fact that nearly half of all Americans can be found in a place of worship on a given Sunday and that high percentages have high levels of conservative religious belief. He found that:

Eighty-one percent of Americans claim to be "religious," which places them second only to Italians, whose rating is eighty-three percent.

Ninety-five percent believe in God.

Seventy-one percent believe in life after death.

Eighty-four percent believe in heaven.

Sixty-seven percent believe in hell.

Large majorities say they believe in the Ten Commandments.

Nearly every home has at least one Bible.

Half of all Americans can be found in church on an average Sunday morning. Only eight percent say they have no religious affiliation whatever.

Most say that religion plays an important role in their lives. One-fourth claim to lead a "very Christian life."

But although ninety-five percent say they believe in God and four out of five say they are religious, only one in five says that religion is the *most* influential factor in his or her life. Most want some kind of religious instruction for their children, but religious faith ranks far below many other traits parents would like to see developed in their offspring. Only one in eight says he or she would consider sacrificing everything for God or their religious beliefs. Gallup records "a glaring lack of knowledge of the Ten Commandments," even by those who say they believe in them. He observes "a high level of credulity, . . . a lack of spiritual discipline," and a strong "anti-intellectual strain" in the religious life of most Americans.

Gallup investigated this anomaly and found that those large numbers of people who claim to be religious—fifty to sixty million claim to be "born again"—are actually a terrible distortion. Those for whom religion actually makes a difference are about one in eight, or twelve-and-a-half percent. But, and this is the striking thing, when he studied the life of these people, Gallup learned that they were much happier, had more stable families (there were noticeably fewer divorces), were less prejudiced, and were involved regularly, mostly on a weekly basis, in some kind of service work for other people. And this was all by substantial percentage margins.[4]

What does this suggest? It suggests that many who consider themselves Christians, even in so-called evangelical churches, are not Christians. They may profess the right things. They may lead seemingly acceptable lives, if we don't scratch too far below the surface. But they are not on the path. They are not following hard after holiness. They are not born again.

Isn't it time we had a true revival of religion in our churches? If you have studied the revivals of the past, you know that they have had three characteristic stages. The first stage is an *awakening*. By that I mean an awakening on the part of alleged Christians to the fact that they are not really Christians.

4. George Gallup, Jr., "Is America's Faith for Real?" in Princeton Theological Seminary's *Alumni News* 22, no. 4 (Summer 1982): 15–17.

This is why the great eighteenth-century American revivals under the preaching of Jonathan Edwards, William and Gilbert Tennent, and George Whitefield were called the Great Awakening. What impressed those who lived through such times was how the Spirit of God worked first to awaken many professed but counterfeit followers of Jesus Christ to their true condition.

The second stage was the *revival* itself, which meant the coming to spiritual life of these former mere professors. In England the corresponding movement was referred to as the Wesleyan Revivals.

Finally, there was an *impact* on society in which many people outside the church pressed into it to find out what was happening and were converted also.

We need such a revival in our time. And what we need to see, as a first stage of this revival, is the awakening of many so-called evangelicals to the fact that they have been Christians in name only, which is proved by their lack of concern for Christian doctrine and their lack of holiness. They must awaken to their condition.

Assurance? It is the theme of Romans 8 and a great doctrine for those who are truly saved. But it is deadly presumption if we are not growing in holiness by following after and obeying Jesus Christ.

97

The Carnal Man and the True Christian

Romans 8:5–8

Those who live according to the sinful nature have their minds set on what that nature desires; but those who live in accordance with the Spirit have their minds set on what the Spirit desires. The mind of sinful man is death, but the mind controlled by the Spirit is life and peace; the sinful mind is hostile to God. It does not submit to God's law, nor can it do so. Those controlled by the sinful nature cannot please God.

In my first study of Romans 8, in which I surveyed the entire chapter, I said that in my opinion verses 5–14 are the most important of all if we consider them from the perspective of the weakness and need of the church of Jesus Christ at the present time. This is because they correct a mistaken but very popular understanding of what it means to be a Christian. This mistaken view, as we have already seen, divides people into three classes: (1) those who are not Christians, (2) those who are Christians, and (3) those who are Christians but who are living in an "unsaved" manner. The latter are often called "carnal Christians."

Not long ago I received a book written by two of my friends that (rather uncritically, I think) assumed this mistaken notion. It was a book for laymen and was intended to help them mature as Christians so they could function as leaders in the local church. It encouraged them to move beyond being mere "Christians" to being "disciples" of Jesus Christ. At one point it said, "All followers of [Christ] are his sheep, but not all sheep are his disciples."[1]

I have respect for my friends and applaud their intentions in this book. They are right in wanting laymen to assume their proper role in the church's life. But the problem lies in their procedure. They have adopted the three-category view, and this, I am convinced, inevitably leads the reader to think that—although it may be wise and perhaps even beneficial to become serious about the Christian life—becoming a "disciple" of Jesus Christ is, in the final analysis, merely optional. This conclusion is fatal, because it encourages us to suppose that we can be careless about our Christianity, doing little and achieving nothing, and yet go to heaven securely when we die.

I suppose it is this that has bothered me the most, the idea that one can live as the world lives and still go to heaven. If it is true, it is comfortable teaching. We are to have the best of both worlds, sin here and heaven, too. But if it is not true, those who teach it are encouraging people to believe that all is well with them when they are, in fact, not even saved. They are crying, "Peace!" when there is no peace. They are doing damage to their souls.

Two Classes of People

We come to this problem in the paragraph of Romans 8 that begins with verse 5, because in these verses, for the first time in the letter, the apostle gives a careful definition of the "carnal" person. The idea occurs five times in verses 5–8 ("sinful nature" in NIV). It has already occurred three times in verses 3–4.

"Carnal" is a rather straightforward translation of the Greek word *sarx*, which means "flesh." But *sarx* is one of those words that has several natural meanings. Basically, it refers to the fleshly parts of the body, which is why "carnal" (from the Latin word *caro*, meaning "meat") is used to translate it. But the meaning quickly goes beyond this in Bible passages to refer to certain aspects of what it means to be a human being. One thing it means is to be weak. This is a characteristic Old Testament usage, as in the words, "All flesh is grass" (KJV; NIV has "All men are like grass," to convey the real meaning). To be "fleshly" also means to be human rather than divine. This is because "God is spirit" (John 4:24), and we are mere flesh. A third thing "flesh" means is to be sinful. This is the most important meaning of *sarx* in the New Testament. It is why, in Romans 8, for instance, the word is translated by the New International Version as "sinful nature."[2] It means to be a

1. Walter A. Henrichsen and William N. Garrison, *Layman, Look Up! God Has a Place for You* (Grand Rapids: Zondervan, 1983), p. 23.

2. Because *sarx* has so many shades of meaning, NIV also renders it "unspiritual" (Rom. 7:14), "material" (Rom. 15:27; 1 Cor. 9:11), "worldly" (1 Cor. 3:1, 3; 2 Cor. 1:12; 10:4), "mere

merely sinful man, that is, man apart from the regenerating and transforming work of the Holy Spirit of God in salvation.[3]

This is what we have to keep in mind as we study Romans 8. For what Paul is talking about here is the difference between those who are Christians and those who are not. That is, he is speaking of two kinds of people only, not three.[4] Specifically, he is not speaking of how a "carnal Christian" is supposed to move beyond a rather low state of commitment in order to become a more serious disciple of the Lord.

The Carnal or Unsaved Person

What is it that most characterizes an unsaved person? These verses define the unbeliever in four important ways: (1) in regard to his thinking, (2) in regard to his state, (3) in regard to his religion, and (4) in regard to his present condition.

1. *His thinking.* The first verse of this paragraph concerns the unbeliever's thinking, telling us that "those who live according to the sinful nature have their minds set on what that nature desires" (v. 5). Here is a case in which the New International Version rendering of *sarx* by "sinful nature" has both a bad and a good side.

The bad side is this: When we hear the words *flesh* or *carnal,* most of us naturally think of what we term "fleshly sins," things like sexual promiscuity, drunkenness, a preoccupation with money perhaps, materialism, desire for praise from other human beings, pride, and other such vices. The term does include such things, and they are much of what the world sets its mind on. To replace "flesh" by "sinful nature" causes most of us to overlook these very things. We can forget that if our minds are set on these rather than on spiritual things, we are not Christians.

But the translation of *sarx* as "sinful nature" has a good side, too, because it frees us from thinking only of what we call fleshly sins. The word includes those sins, as I said, but it also includes many things that we do not associate with being fleshly. Take a very moral person, for example. He or she does

men" (1 Cor. 3:4), "ancestry" (Heb. 7:16), and "sinful [desires]" (1 Peter 2:11). See Lawrence O. Richards, *Expository Dictionary of Bible Words* (Grand Rapids: Zondervan, 1985), p. 283.

3. For a classic study of *sarx* and the related Greek terms, see the extensive article by Eduard Schweizer, Friedrich Baumgaertel, and Rudolf Meyer in *Theological Dictionary of the New Testament,* vol. 7, ed. Gerhard Friedrich, trans. Geoffrey W. Bromiley (Grand Rapids: Wm. B. Eerdmans, 1971), pp. 98–151.

4. This is perfectly obvious from the passage. Yet so entrenched has the doctrine of "the carnal Christian" become that one very able expositor, at least, while acknowledging that "there are only two kinds of people in the world, those who have been born once and those who have been twice," simply throws this aside after a few pages of exposition and declares inconsistently that "the primary application should be to Christians" (Donald Grey Barnhouse, *God's Heirs: Exposition of Bible Doctrines, Taking the Epistle to the Romans as a Point of Departure,* vol. 7, *Romans 8:1–39* [Grand Rapids: Wm. B. Eerdmans, 1963], pp. 23, 28).

not indulge in debauchery. Does this mean that such a person is therefore thinking spiritually rather than according to the sinful nature? Not at all. In an unsaved state, the cultured, well-spoken moral person is as devoid of the Spirit of God, and is therefore as lost, as any other.

Paul himself was once an example. Recall how he summarized his early life in the great testimony passage from Philippians. He said that before he met Jesus on the road to Damascus, he believed that he was right before God. He describes himself as being: "circumcised on the eighth day, of the people of Israel, of the tribe of Benjamin, a Hebrew of Hebrews; in regard to the law, a Pharisee; as for zeal, persecuting the church; as for legalistic righteousness, faultless" (Phil. 3:5–6). This is a portrait of a moral man. But it is no less a portrait of one whose mind was set on what his sinful self desired. What did Paul desire? He desired to prove himself to God, to prove that he was worthy of God's favor, to show that he could earn heaven. Nothing is so characteristic of the thinking of the unbeliever as this delusion.

2. *His state.* The next verse of this paragraph describes the state of the unbeliever. It is "death" (v. 6). Paul is not speaking of physical death, of course. He is speaking of spiritual death, and what he means is that the unsaved person is as unresponsive to the things of God as a corpse.

The Bible tells us that the power, wisdom, and glory of God are clearly revealed in nature: "The heavens declare the glory of God; the skies proclaim the work of his hands" (Ps. 19:1). The unsaved person does not see this. He may use the word *God* at times, but the word does not really mean anything to this person. He would far rather believe that the universe came into being by evolution or chance or in any other way rather than being created by a God who demands a proper respect and right moral conduct from those he has created.

The unbeliever's condition is even worse when it comes to the truths of the Bible. Either he cannot understand them at all or else they seem utterly foolish to him. Why? It is because it takes the Holy Spirit to provide such understanding. The Bible says, "The man without the Spirit does not accept the things that come from the Spirit of God, for they are foolishness to him, and he cannot understand them, because they are spiritually discerned" (1 Cor. 2:14).

D. Martyn Lloyd-Jones relates a classic case of this lack of spiritual understanding in an incident from the lives of William Wilberforce, the man who led the movement to abolish slavery throughout the British Empire, and William Pitt the Younger, who at one time was prime minister of England. Wilberforce was a Christian. Pitt was only a formal Christian, like so many others of that day. However, these two parliamentarians were friends, and Wilberforce was concerned for his friend's salvation. In those days there was a great preacher in London whose name was Richard Cecil. Wilberforce thrilled to his ministry and was constantly trying to get his friend Pitt to go with him to hear Cecil. Pitt kept putting Wilberforce off, but at last after many invitations Pitt agreed to go. Cecil was at his best, preaching in his most spirited manner. Wilberforce was ecstatic. He couldn't imagine anything more enjoyable or wonderful. He was delighted that Pitt was with him. But as they were leaving the service afterward, Pitt turned to his friend and said, "You know, Wilberforce, I have not the slightest idea what that man has been talking about."[5] Clearly, Pitt was as deaf to God as if he were a physically dead man.

3. *His religion.* At first glance it might seem strange to speak of the "religion" of those who operate according to the sinful nature, since we have just shown that they are unresponsive to God. But strange as it may seem, the unsaved do have a religion. The third verse of the paragraph speaks about this. It tells us that "the sinful mind is hostile to God. It does not submit to God's law, nor can it do so" (v. 7).

Not long ago I was reading an article in which the writer was speculating on the nature of things to come and in one place talked about religion. He used a phrase that struck me. He said that in the future we are likely to see a growth of "*a la carte* religion," meaning that people will choose the items they like from a potpourri of religions and then combine them to make their own comfortable little religious systems. I liked that description, because it struck me as something I had already observed. I had noticed that in our largely irrational age it is a common thing for people to hold many mutually inconsistent ideas, the only force holding them together being their own individual attractions to them. But, as I have thought about it, it seems to me that this is what all religions already are in one sense. They are collections of human thoughts held for no other reason than that they are comfortable. They are comfortable because what they actually do is to protect their adherents from the only truly valid claims of God.

This is why Paul says that people in their unsaved state are hostile to God and why they do not submit to his law. The two go together. They do not submit to God's law because they are hostile to him, and because they are hostile to God they inevitably try to construct a religion that will protect themselves from him.

4. *His present condition.* The last thing Paul says of the unsaved, or "fleshly," individual is that a person like this "cannot please God" (v. 8). How could he, if he is hostile to God and is doing everything humanly possible to resist and trample down his just law? Pleased with the wicked? Of course not. God is displeased with unbelievers constantly.

5. D. M. Lloyd-Jones, *Romans: An Exposition of Chapter 8:5–17, The Sons of God* (Grand Rapids: Zondervan, 1974), pp. 9, 10.

Characteristics of the Christian

The apostle is not writing only of unbelievers in these verses, however. He is also writing of Christians, contrasting them with unbelievers. He lists two of the Christian's contrasting characteristics specifically.

1. *The Christian's thinking.* In verse 5 the apostle contrasts the unbeliever and the Christian in terms of their thinking, saying that the unbeliever has his mind set on what the sinful nature desires but that the Christian has his mind "set on what the Spirit desires." This is a profound way of speaking, for it eliminates many misconceptions of what it means to be a Christian while it establishes the truly essential thing.

First, it eliminates the idea that the Christian is someone who is merely very "religious." To be religious and to be mindful of the things of the Spirit are two entirely different things. The Pharisees were religious, excessively so, but they killed Jesus. Before he was saved, Paul was religious, but he expressed his religion by trying to do away with Christians. Ironically, one function of religion is to try to eliminate God, as we have seen.

Paul's way of speaking also eliminates the idea that a Christian is anyone who merely holds to right theological beliefs. Much popular Christianity makes this destructive error, suggesting that as long as you simply confess that you are a sinner and believe that Jesus is your Savior and "receive him," whatever that means, you are right with God and will certainly go to heaven. Do not get me wrong here. I know that there are degrees of understanding on the part of Christians and that many true Christians are yet babes in Christ, perhaps because they have never been given adequate teaching. Many might be unable to describe their faith in any terms more adequate than those I have just given. I do not want to deny that they are Christians. But what I do want to say is that it is possible to confess those things and still not be a Christian, simply because being a Christian is more than giving mere verbal assent to certain doctrines. It is to be born again. And since being born again is the work of God's Spirit, it is right to insist that those who are truly born again will have their minds set on what God desires.

Finally, Paul's way of speaking eliminates the idea that a Christian is someone who has attained a certain standard of approved conduct.

What, then, does being a Christian mean? It means exactly what Paul says. The Christian is someone who has been born again by the work of the Holy Spirit and who now, as a result of that internal transformation, has his mind set on what the Spirit of God desires. If we are Christians, it does not mean that we have attained to this standard, at least not fully. But it does mean that we want to. Do you remember the illustration of the path? Being on the path does not mean that we have arrived at our destination. If it did, we would already be completely like Jesus. But it does mean that we are moving along this path, that we are following Jesus, who is going before us, that we are trying to be like him.

Having our minds set on what the Spirit desires takes us back to verse 4, in which the purpose of God in saving us is spelled out as our fully meeting the just requirements of the law. That is what the Spirit desires, and if we are Christians, our minds will be fixed on doing exactly that.

2. *The Christian's state.* The second specific characteristic of the Christian is his state, described as "life and peace" (v. 6). It is the opposite of "death," which describes the non-Christian. The Christian is a person who has been made alive by God's Spirit. Spiritual matters make sense to him now. Before, he was dead in his sins; now he is alive to a whole new world of reality. And he is at peace—peace with himself, as he never was before, in spite of many heroic efforts to convince himself that he was. Above all, he is at peace with God.

The word *peace*, as Martyn Lloyd-Jones points out, corresponds to the points of verse 7 step by step. "The natural man, the carnal mind, is 'enmity against God, is not subject to the law of God, neither indeed can be.' But of the Christian, you say at once: 'He can be subject to it, he is subject to it, he desires to be subject to it, and he goes out of his way to subject himself to it.' He 'hungers and thirsts after righteousness,' he desires to keep the commands which God has given."[6]

Signs of the New Life

I come to the end of this study, to the application, and it is very, very simple. Everything I have said is directed to one end only, and that is to have you look into your heart and take stock of whether or not you are a true Christian. I do not mean whether or not you are an exemplary Christian or a well-instructed Christian, certainly not a perfect Christian (no creature like that exists), but whether or not you are truly born again. Has the Holy Spirit of God made you alive in Jesus Christ so that your thinking, state, religion, and present condition have been changed?

More than two hundred years ago, when preaching in this country was vastly superior to what it generally is today, Jonathan Edwards wrote "A Treatise Concerning Religious Affections" in which he examined the "signs" of God's gracious work in a person and attempted to distinguish between signs that are true and certain and signs that are not. His subheads in the first part of the essay read:

Great effects on the body are no sign.
Fluency and fervor are no sign.
That they are excited by us is no sign.
That they come with texts of Scripture is no sign.
Religious affections of many kinds are no sign.

6. Ibid., p. 45.

Joys following in a certain order are no sign.
Much time and zeal in duty are no sign.
Much expression of praise is no sign.
Great confidence is no certain sign.
Affecting relations are no sign.[7]

Edwards was convinced, no doubt rightly, that none of these things, as powerful or moving as they may sometimes be, in itself proves that the person is being acted upon by God, rather than by the mere emotion of the moment, or that the individual is saved.

What is a sure sign, then? The answer boils down to whether the person has his or her mind set on the things of the Spirit of God and whether this is moving, as it must, in the direction of a true righteousness.

Are you born again? Do you have a new nature? Have you passed out of death into life, from being dominated by the sinful nature to being controlled by the Spirit of God? If you do not know the answer to that question, do not let the matter rest until you know that you really are in Christ. Nothing in all life comes close to that matter in importance. Pursue it with all your strength. And if by the grace of God—perhaps through the application of his Word to your heart through this study—you realize that you are not yet a new creature in Christ, call out for salvation. Trust that, as God has been gracious in opening your eyes to your true condition, he will also work in grace to bring you out of death into the utter newness of the Christian life.

---

7. Jonathan Edwards, "A Treatise Concerning Religious Affections" in *The Works of Jonathan Edwards*, vol. 1 (Edinburgh, and Carlisle, Pa.: The Banner of Truth Trust, 1976), pp. 234–343.

98

Who Is a Christian?

Romans 8:9-11

You, however, are controlled not by the sinful nature but by the Spirit, if the Spirit of God lives in you. And if anyone does not have the Spirit of Christ, he does not belong to Christ. But if Christ is in you, your body is dead because of sin, yet your spirit is alive because of righteousness. And if the Spirit of him who raised Jesus from the dead is living in you, he who raised Christ from the dead will also give life to your mortal bodies through his Spirit, who lives in you.

A few years ago, at one of the early Philadelphia Conferences on Reformed Theology, John Gerstner was speaking on the parable of the five wise and five foolish virgins from Matthew 25. He was arguing that, although each of these women seemed to be what we would today call believers, only five were actually taken to be with the bridegroom when he came, which means that only five were saved. He pointed out that: (1) all had been invited to the wedding banquet; (2) all belonged to what we would call the visible church; (3) all professed to have the bridegroom as their Lord; (4) all believed in the Lord's "second coming"; (5) all were waiting for Jesus; and (6) all even fell asleep while waiting. Nevertheless, five were not accepted. And when they cried to Jesus, "Lord,

813

Lord, open the door for us," he replied, "I do not know you" (see Matt. 25:11–12).

The point of Gerstner's message was that professing Christians should examine themselves to see if they really *are* Christians, knowing that a mere profession of faith is not enough. The study was so powerful that a number of people told me afterward that they did indeed begin to wonder whether they had truly been born again.

Self-Examination and Assurance

Perhaps you began to wonder about your own state at the end of the previous study. There I was trying to show that (according to Romans) there are not three categories of people in this life—those who are Christians, those who are not Christians, and those who are Christians but live as if they were not—but rather only two types—those who are dead in their sins and are therefore as unresponsive to God as dead people, and those who have been made spiritually alive by the Holy Spirit and are therefore following Jesus Christ in true discipleship. I acknowledged that Christians do sin, sometimes very badly. But a person who is on the path of discipleship gets up again and goes forward with Christ, while the unbeliever does not. In fact, the unbeliever is not on the path of true discipleship at all.

If teaching like this shakes you a bit, it is probably good for you to be shaken—particularly if you have been taking sin lightly. The Bible says that we are to examine ourselves to make sure of our calling (2 Peter 1:10). We should not be at ease in this matter. We should not rest until we are sure that we really do rest in Christ Jesus.

Yet we are studying Romans 8, and if you remember my introductory study, you will recall that the chapter's purpose is not to instill doubt in believers but rather the exact opposite. It is to give them assurance. Romans 8 teaches that if you are truly in Christ, nothing in all creation will be able to separate you from God's love (v. 39). I suppose that is why, having called us to examine ourselves by sharply contrasting those who live according to the sinful nature and those who live according to the Spirit (vv. 5–8), Paul continues by showing, in a most encouraging manner, who a Christian really is (vv. 9–11).

His outline is simple. He talks about the Christian's past, present, and future. The past is discussed in verse 9. The present is discussed in verse 10. The future is discussed in verse 11.

The Christian's Past

Verse 9 discusses the Christian's past. It is important, because it makes clearer than any other verse in this chapter the very point I have been making: that the description of those who are not controlled by the sinful nature but who live in accordance with the Holy Spirit applies to *all* Christians, not just to so-called spiritual ones. In other words, there is no ground for the doctrine of the "carnal Christian" here. Notice the apostle's ruthless logic: (1) if you do not have the Spirit of Christ, you do not belong to Christ; (2) if you belong to Christ, you have the Spirit of Christ; and (3) if you have the Spirit of Christ, you will not be controlled by the sinful nature but by the Spirit. In other words, if you belong to Jesus, you will live like it. If you do not live like it, you do not belong to him, regardless of your outward profession.

But this is meant to be encouraging, as I said, which is why Paul begins the first sentence as he does. He is writing to the believers in Rome and says to these believers, "You, however, *are controlled* not by the sinful nature but by the Spirit." That is, he is assuming that these professed Christians really are Christ's, and he is trying to explain the difference their new identification with Jesus has made and will make in the future.

What difference has it made? Well, when we look to the past, which is what the apostle does first, we see that as Christians we have been lifted out of our former sinful or fleshly state and into the realm of the Spirit. We are now "in the Spirit," and, as Paul also says here, the Spirit is "in" us.

This is an absolutely critical thing, for it means that being a Christian is not merely a matter of adopting a particular set of intellectual or theological beliefs, however true they may be. It involves a change of state, which is accomplished, not by us, but by God who saves us. D. Martyn Lloyd-Jones says, "It is not that a man just changes his beliefs and no more. No, he was in the realm of the flesh, and he is now in the realm of the Spirit. He was dominated by the flesh before, and governed by it. . . . He is now in a realm which is governed and controlled and dominated by the Spirit."[1] You and I cannot make this change ourselves. It is something God does.

Paul said the same thing in Romans 5, where he wrote that the Christian is no longer under the reign of sin unto death but instead has come under the reign of God's grace in Christ. The fact that it is "of grace" shows that God has done it.

This change also means that being a Christian is not a matter merely of living in a Christian manner either, important as that also is. If you are a Christian, you *will* live like one. That is what we have been seeing throughout our studies of Romans 5–8 and were discussing in the previous study especially. But living like a Christian, at least in an external, observable sense, does not in itself mean you are one. Many unbelievers live outwardly moral lives.

A Christian is someone who has been delivered from one realm, the realm of sin and death, and has been transferred to the realm of God's Spirit, which is life. This, of course, is something God has himself done, and it means that "salvation is of the Lord" and that it is all of grace. It is because of this—because salvation is of God and not of ourselves—that it is possible

1. D. M. Lloyd-Jones, *Romans: An Exposition of Chapter 8:5–17, The Sons of God* (Grand Rapids: Zondervan, 1974), p. 58.

to speak of the Christian's eternal security, as Paul does. The only reason we can be assured of our salvation is because salvation is a work of God, whose ways are always perfect, whose promises are never broken, and who does not change his mind.

The Christian's Present

Verse 10 describes the Christian's present state, saying that "if Christ is in you, your body is dead because of sin, yet your spirit is alive because of righteousness." In some versions of the Bible the word *spirit* in this verse is printed with a capital *S,* as if referring to the Holy Spirit, but this is certainly an error. The verse is referring to *our* spirit and should be printed with a lowercase *s,* as in the New International Version. It is a reference to our being born again.

The difficulty of this verse is with the clause "your body is dead because of sin." What does this mean? "Body" (Greek, *sōma*) clearly refers to our literal human bodies, not to some "mortal principle" within us. But in what sense is this body dead, since our mortal bodies are in this life clearly alive? Some have taken "your body is dead" to teach that the tendency of the body to draw us into sin has been completely destroyed or overcome. I discussed this several times in my treatment of Romans 6 and 7, where Paul does speak of having died to the past and of having been made alive to God. But the difficulty with this view is that in the earlier chapters it is the "self" who has died, that is, the old self. And when Paul speaks of the body, as he does in Romans 6:11–14, his point is not that the body is dead but, on the contrary, that it is the source of our continuing troubles and struggles. We have to overcome it.

In view of this, it seems best to take "your body is dead because of sin" to refer to the fact that our physical bodies have the seeds of literal death in them and will eventually cease to live: "For the wages of sin is death . . ." (Rom. 6:23).[2] Yet the contrast in verse 10 is the important thing. Although our physical bodies will die and are, in a certain sense, as good as dead now, our spirits have been made alive by the Holy Spirit whom the Father has sent to do precisely that.

What does it mean to have our spirits made alive by the Holy Spirit? Paul is talking about the present experience of the Christian, remember. So he means that by the new birth the Spirit has made us alive to things we were dead to before.

2. For discussions of these problems of interpretation see Charles Hodge, *A Commentary on Romans* (Edinburgh, and Carlisle, Pa.: The Banner of Truth Trust, 1972), p. 259; Robert Haldane, *An Exposition of the Epistle to the Romans* (MacDill AFB: MacDonald Publishing, 1958), pp. 342–346; John Murray, *The Epistle to the Romans* (Grand Rapids: Wm. B. Eerdmans, 1968), pp. 288–290; Leon Morris, *The Epistle to the Romans* (Grand Rapids: Wm. B. Eerdmans, and Leicester, England: Inter-Varsity Press, 1988), p. 309; and D. M. Lloyd-Jones, *Romans: An Exposition of Chapter 8:5–17, The Sons of God,* pp. 67–70.

1. *Alive to God.* The first thing we have become alive to is God himself. Before we were born again, we may have believed in God. Indeed, the Bible says that only the fool does not. But God was not real to us. We had no true sense of who he was or what he was like. When we prayed—if we did pray—God seemed far off and unresponsive. However, when we were born again this changed. Now, although there is still much we do not know about God and although his ways are still often strange and puzzling to us, we do not feel that God is unreal. On the contrary, he is more real to us even than life itself. We know that God loves us and is watching over us. We trust his wise management of our earthly affairs. God is particularly close in sickness and sorrow. We know that in the hour of our death we will pass from this world to the presence of the Lord.

2. *Alive to the Bible.* We have not only become alive to God as the result of the Holy Spirit's work; we have also become alive to the Word of God. It is in the Bible that God speaks to us clearly, regularly, and forcefully. Before we were born again, the Bible was a strange and closed book. Little in it seemed to make sense. We even found it to be boring. As Christians that has changed also. Today, when we read the Bible, we know that God himself is speaking to us in it. And not only does the Bible make sense; we know that it is true. Whatever the world may believe, whatever our nonbelieving teachers or friends may tell us to the contrary—we know that the words of the Bible pass the high standard of absolute truth and will endure forever, even when heaven and earth have passed away (Matt. 5:18).

We also find the Bible to be effective in our lives. We find that it changes us. We echo the words of Paul to young Timothy, when he said, "All Scripture is God-breathed and is useful for teaching, rebuking, correcting and training in righteousness, so that the man of God may be thoroughly equipped for every good work" (2 Tim. 3:16–17).

3. *Alive to the Spirit of God in other Christians.* Finally, we have also become alive to the Spirit of God in other Christians. For just as the Spirit of God bears witness with our spirit that we are children of God (Rom. 8:16), so does the Spirit within us bear witness with the Spirit in other believers that we are fellow members of the one spiritual family of God and that these others are our brothers and sisters in Christ.

I would suggest the following as excellent tests of whether a person is a Christian—whether *you* are a Christian.

First, is God real to you? I do not mean, "Do you understand everything about God and God's ways?" Of course, you do not, for you will never understand God completely. I simply mean: Is God real to you. When you pray do you know that you are really praying to him and that he is listening to you and will answer you? When you worship him in church, is it a real God you are worshiping?

Second, is the Bible a meaningful and attractive book to you? I do not mean, "Do you understand everything you read there?" Obviously you do not. But does it seem to be right when you read it? Are you attracted to it? Do you want to know more?

Finally, are you drawn to other Christians? Do you want to be with them? Do you enjoy their fellowship? Do you sense how much you and they have in common? If God is not real to you, if the Bible is not attractive, and if you are not drawn to other believers, why do you think you are a Christian? Probably you are not. On the other hand, if these things are true of you, you should be encouraged by them and press on in following after Jesus Christ.

The Christian's Future

Verse 11 describes the Christian's future, pointing forward to his or her physical resurrection. It is true, as verse 10 has said, that the "body is dead because of sin." But although we die we shall all nevertheless rise again. The text says that "if the Spirit of him who raised Jesus from the dead is living in you, he who raised Christ from the dead will also give life to your mortal bodies through his Spirit, who lives in you."

There are two common mistakes in the interpretation of this verse that we should not fall into. Lloyd-Jones discusses them.[3] The first misunderstanding is that the text is speaking not of a future physical resurrection but of some kind of moral resurrection now. True, there is a kind of "resurrection" in which we who have been dead in sin have been brought into newness of life and are now increasingly putting to death the deeds of the body and living to Christ and righteousness. But that is not what Paul is thinking of here. The comparison between the resurrection of Christ and our own resurrection makes his real meaning clear. The point is that God will raise us just as he raised Jesus.

The second mistake is to think of this in terms of "faith healing," which some have done, supposing it to be a promise of perfect health for those who believe God will heal them. This idea is simply foreign to the context.

The verse is speaking about a future resurrection, and it is regarding it as certain for all who are in Christ. Indeed, it could hardly be stated with greater certainty, for in developing the point the apostle brings in each member of the Trinity, as if to say that our final resurrection is as certain as God himself. Earlier we had a statement relating to the deity of Christ. When Paul spoke of the Holy Spirit he spoke of him as both "the Spirit of God" and "the Spirit of Christ" (v. 9). Things equal to the same thing are equal to each other. So these two verses together assert Christ's deity. Here, however, it is not just the divine Christ but also the divine Father and divine Spirit who are in view. All three combine to guarantee our final resurrection. At the res-

3. D. M. Lloyd-Jones, *Romans: An Exposition of Chapter 8:5–17, The Sons of God*, pp. 80–82.

urrection, being freed completely from sin's dread penalty, power, and presence, we shall be with God in heaven forever.

Such is the past, present, and future of the Christian.

Ironside and the Gypsy

Whenever I think of the past, present, and future of the Christian, as our text in Romans causes us to do, I remember an anecdote told by the great Bible teacher and former pastor of the Moody Memorial Church in Chicago, Harry A. Ironside. It is told in his study of Ephesians 2:1–10, which provides a similar description of what it means to be a Christian.

Ironside was riding on a train in southern California one Saturday when a gypsy got on and sat beside him. "How do you do, gentleman," she said. "You like to have your fortune told? Cross my palm with a silver quarter, and I will give you your past, present, and future."

"Are you very sure you can do that?" Ironside asked. "You see, I am Scottish, and I wouldn't want to spend a quarter and not get my full value for it."

The gypsy was very earnest. "Yes, gentleman," she said. "I can give you your past, present, and future. I will tell you all."

Ironside then said, "It is not really necessary for me to have my fortune told, because I have had it told already. It is written in a book. I have the book in my pocket."

The gypsy was astonished. "You have it in a book?" she said.

"Yes," said Ironside, "and it is absolutely infallible. Let me read it to you." He then reached in his pocket, pulled out his New Testament and began to read from chapter 2 of Ephesians: "'As for you, you were dead in your transgressions and sins, in which you used to live when you followed the ways of this world and of the ruler of the kingdom of the air, the spirit who is now at work in those who are disobedient. All of us also lived among them at one time, gratifying the cravings of our sinful nature and following its desires and thoughts. Like the rest, we were by nature objects of wrath.'

"That is my past," he said.

The woman had been startled when he pulled the New Testament from his pocket and now tried to get away. "That is plenty," she protested. "I do not want to hear more."

"But wait," Ironside said. "There is more. Here is my present, too: 'But because of his great love for us, God, who is rich in mercy, made us alive in Christ even when we were dead in transgressions—it is by grace you have been saved. And God raised us up with Christ and seated us with him in the heavenly realms in Christ Jesus. . . .'"

"No more," the gypsy protested.

"But," said Ironside, "you must hear my future, and you are not going to have to pay me a quarter for it. I am giving it to you for nothing. It says, '. . .

in order that in the coming ages he might show the incomparable riches of his grace, expressed in his kindness to us in Christ Jesus.'"

By now the gypsy was halfway down the aisle of the train, saying, "I took the wrong man!"[4]

We are dealing with a different text here, of course, and the specifics of the past, present, and future described in Romans 8:9–11 vary from what is said about them in Ephesians 2. But it is the same idea. Christians are people whose past has been altered. Before, they were dead in sin; now they are alive in Christ. Their present has been altered, too. They have been awakened to the reality of God, the beauty of the Scriptures, and the presence of the Spirit of God in other Christians. Theirs is a whole new world. Finally, they have a changed future before them. For in time death will be overcome, and they will be raised in a new resurrection body, like the resurrection body of Jesus, and will be with God and Jesus Christ forever.

Are you a Christian? By all means, ask that question of yourself. Be sure of the answer. But when you are sure, be sure of this truth, too: that nothing in heaven or earth will ever separate you from the love of God in Christ Jesus, and that your future will be even better than is your life with Jesus now.

---

4. H. A. Ironside, *In the Heavenlies: Practical Expository Addresses on the Epistle to the Ephesians* (Neptune, N.J.: Loizeaux Brothers, 1937), pp. 96–98.

99

Sanctification:
The Moral Imperative

Romans 8:12–13

Therefore, brothers, we have an obligation—but it is not to the sinful nature, to live according to it. For if you live according to the sinful nature, you will die; but if by the Spirit you put to death the misdeeds of the body, you will live.

I once received a letter from an old friend whom I had not seen for four or five years, and it contained an old problem. Two years earlier she had begun to date a man who was not a Christian. At the beginning of the relationship, when she had raised the question of religion, he had brushed it off, claiming to be an agnostic. My friend reasoned that the relationship would not last anyway, so she dropped the subject. But the relationship did last. And now it was two years later, and she was in love with a man who was not a Christian and had no interest in becoming one.

Of course, she had prayed. But God had not answered her prayer by bringing the man to faith. And now she had a twofold problem. One was how to find strength to break off the relationship, which she knew she should do. The second was with God. Why was God not intervening to bring her friend to faith? The relationship mattered to her. She had prayed for his salvation. There seemed to be no other men around who were Christians. What was wrong? In fact, in looking back over her life, she had begun to wonder if God had ever intervened in any special way to do anything just for her. And if he hadn't, why was she to assume she had a special relationship with him? Or, for that matter, why was she to believe that God was even there?

I think this letter expressed a very common dilemma, one you may have experienced yourself. Your specifics probably differ; the problem may be a job-related situation, a habit or sin needing to be overcome, some puzzling choice needing to be made. But the questions are the same. How can you do the right thing in your particularly difficult situation? And why doesn't God intervene in some way to work your problem out?

False Approaches to Sanctification

I want to suggest that the answers to those important questions are in the section of Romans 8 to which we come now, because in these verses Paul is talking about our obligation to do the right thing as Christian people. And he is implying—I am sure you will see this as we go on—that, as Christians, we not only have an obligation to live a holy life, doing the right things, but also the ability to live rightly. In fact, the obligation and ability are both grounded in the fact that we are Christians.

The place to begin this analysis is not with Paul's answer to how we are to live the Christian life, however, but by looking at a few of the inadequate approaches to sanctification that are often recommended in our day.

1. *A method.* In some circles what is recommended to believers who are fighting against sin, trying to live the Christian life, is a method. It may be a special approach to prayer or Bible study. It may be a special way of ordering one's daily life, or something else.

I do not want to be misunderstood at this point. Certain methods of organizing prayer, pursuing Bible study, and disciplining one's daily life are not bad. They may, in fact, actually be quite good. There is nothing wrong with keeping a list of items to pray for, or proceeding regularly through some personal program of Bible study, or having certain times of the day or week that we devote to specific Christian activities. I regularly recommend such items, and others. But what I want to say is that a method does not in itself guarantee sanctification or give us strength to do the right thing in some crisis.

As an illustration, we can think of Martin Luther's experience in the monastery of Erfurt before his conversion. Monasticism was a method. It was the very apogee of method; that was its genius. But although Luther fasted and prayed and kept vigils and confessed his sin, often for hours at a time, he was unable to find either peace or holiness in such practices. Luther's deliverance came in a different way entirely.

2. *A formula.* A second approach to godly living, which many recommend, is a formula. You have probably heard of some of them: "Let go and let God," "Give Jesus control of your life," "Let Christ have the throne," or "Take it by faith." The appeal of formulas is that they are easy to grasp and for a time may seem to provide the solutions we are seeking. But they are too easy, too simple, and in the end they just do not work. In itself no mere formula is adequate for the harsh realities of human life.

3. *An experience.* Perhaps most common today is the recommendation that believers seek some life-transforming experience, often described as a "second blessing" or "second baptism of the Holy Spirit." This experience is supposed to mark a major advance in the Christian life, after which the discouragements and defeats of earlier days are replaced by a new experience of holiness, joy, and victory. Proponents usually think this idea is supported by Paul's teaching in Romans 7 and 8. In Romans 7 Paul is describing what seems to be a stage of life characterized by defeat in spiritual matters, but in Romans 8 he is victorious. What is the difference? Obviously, so the argument goes, the difference is an experience of the Holy Spirit, who is not mentioned in Romans 7 but is mentioned repeatedly in Romans 8. We are told that if we have this special experience of the Spirit, the victories of Romans 8 will be ours.

Unfortunately, as we have seen, this is just not the teaching of Romans 8. Paul does talk about the Holy Spirit in the chapter, but his point is not that this is an experience a defeated Christian is somehow to attain in order to become spiritually victorious, but rather that the possession of the Holy Spirit is the very essence of what it means to be a Christian. This is not a *second* experience but an initial and determining one. Paul said it clearly in verse 9: ". . . if anyone does not have the Spirit of Christ, he does not belong to Christ." That is, he is not a Christian. The chapter argues that those who belong to Christ do have the Holy Spirit, and as a result, *they live like it.*

An Inescapable Obligation

What is the proper approach to sanctification, then? How are Christians to achieve victory over sin and grow in holiness? Paul gives the one and only adequate answer in these verses.

In some ways the most important word in verses 12 and 13 is the first, the word *therefore.* It points to what the apostle has just said. We have seen the same thing several times before. The first important occurrence of "therefore" was at the start of Romans 5, after Paul had explained the gospel in chapters 3 and 4. The word introduced the consequences of the salvation achieved for us by God through Jesus Christ, the most important being that our salvation is certain or assured. In fact, there is a sense in which everything we have been studying since (in Romans 5–8) has been a working out of that "therefore."

We saw this word again in Romans 5:12 and at the start of Romans 8. In each case it introduced a consequence following on what had previously been said. It is the same in verse 12.

Paul is arguing that Christians "have an obligation" to live according to the Holy Spirit, rather than according to the sinful nature. And the reason for this, which he has just stated, is that the Holy Spirit has joined them to Jesus Christ so that: (1) they have been delivered from the wrath of God against them for their sin and been brought into an entirely new realm, the sphere of God's rule in Christ; (2) they have been given a new nature, being made alive to spiritual things to which they were previously dead; and (3) they have been assured of an entirely new destiny in which not only will they live with God forever, but even their physical bodies will be resurrected. These are things God has done (or will do) for us. We have not done them for ourselves; indeed, we could not have. But, says Paul, because God has done them for us, "we have an obligation" to live like God has lived. We must—it is an imperative—live for him.

Let me say this another way. Everything that we have seen in Romans 8 up to this point has been a general description of the Christian: his status, present experience, character, and future expectation. Now, for the first time, Paul draws a specific conclusion, saying that the work of God for us and in us presents us with a serious obligation. It is to live for God and not according to our sinful natures.

In these two verses the specifics of this obligation are stated negatively, though positive expressions follow. We are *not* to live according to the sinful nature, and we are *not* to give reign to the misdeeds of the body. Yet the positive side is implied. Instead of living according to the sinful nature, we are obviously to live according to the Spirit. And instead of giving reign to the misdeeds of the body, we are to put the sins of the body to death and instead yield the members of our body to God for righteousness.

No New Teaching

Does this sound familiar? It should. If you remember our earlier studies, you will remember that this is exactly the teaching found when we were studying Romans 6:11–14.

In that chapter Paul was teaching about our union with Christ, following up on his introduction of that doctrine in the second half of Romans 5. He was teaching that, if we are Christians, we have been united to Christ in his death (so that his death becomes our death) and in his resurrection (so that his resurrection becomes our resurrection), and because of this union with Christ we are no longer what we were. We have a new status before God, and we are changed people. Therefore, he says, ". . . count yourselves dead to sin but alive to God in Christ Jesus . . . [and] do not let sin reign in your mortal body so that you obey its evil desires. Do not offer the parts of your body to sin, as instruments of wickedness, but rather offer yourselves to God, as those who have been brought from death to life; and offer the parts of your body to him as instruments of righteousness. For sin shall not be your master, because you are not under law, but under grace."

The key word in these verses is "count," or "reckon." It means to proceed on the basis of what is actually the case, in this case living precisely as a new creature in Christ because that is what one truly is as a Christian. When we studied these verses I pointed out that it is necessary that we do this. There is nothing else we can do. We cannot go back; our past is dead to us. The only direction we can go is forward.

This is exactly what Paul is teaching again in Romans 8. The only difference is that now his chief subject is not our union with Christ, which he was discussing in Romans 5 and 6, but rather the role of the Holy Spirit as the Father's agent in saving us. The Holy Spirit joins us to Christ. But this is the identical point! In other words, all Paul is doing in these chapters is approaching the subject of sanctification from two different directions. Yet, no matter what direction he comes from, the bottom line is the same. If we are Christ's, if the Holy Spirit has joined us to him, the past is dead for us and we must live now as what we truly are. To use Paul's words in verse 12, it is our "obligation."

Since Romans 8:12–13 are parallel to Romans 6:11–14, the earlier verses give an interpretation of the words "put to death the misdeeds of the body." They show that this means offering the parts of our body to God for righteousness rather than to sin.

"A Sin unto Death"?

I want to wrap up this study in a practical way. But before I do, there is one more matter that needs to be discussed. It concerns verse 13, which says, "If you live according to the sinful nature, you will die." What kind of a death is this? Is it physical or spiritual death? And, regardless of how we answer that first question, what would we actually have to do—how bad would we have to be—to experience it?

The most common way of answering these questions in evangelical circles is by thinking of this as "a sin unto [physical] death." The biblical phrase "sin unto death" comes from 1 John 5:16–17, in which John writes, "If anyone sees his brother commit a sin that does not lead to death, he should pray and God will give him life. I refer to those whose sin does not lead to death. There is a sin that leads to death ['a sin unto death,' KJV]. I am not saying that he should pray about that. All wrongdoing is sin, and there is sin that does not lead to death." These verses are difficult, but they seem to be speaking of some one sin or type of sin committed by Christians that is so bad that God will take the offending person to heaven early by death rather than allow him or her to stay in it.

If we look for illustrations of this in Scripture, we may have one in Paul's description of people who participated in the Lord's Supper in an unworthy

Life in the Spirit

manner. He wrote, "That is why many among you are weak and sick, and a number of you have fallen asleep" (1 Cor. 11:30). Paul seems to be saying that some of the Corinthian Christians died because of the way they dishonored the Lord's Supper. Another example might be found in the deaths of Ananias and Sapphira, who lied to the church about the selling price of some land (Acts 5:1–11).

This interpretation is attractive to teachers who find the doctrine of the carnal Christian in Romans 8. For it seems to say that if a Christian is "carnal" enough, he may die physically, though, of course, he will not lose his salvation.[1]

I want to repeat that 1 John 5:16–17 is a particularly hard passage to interpret. Various interpretations have been given.[2] To see it as dealing with physical death for sinning Christians seems to be one good possibility, though it is hard to reconcile this with the very next sentence in the passage, where John says, "We know that anyone born of God does not continue to sin . . ." (v. 18). If those born of God do not continue in sin, how can it be possible that any true Christian can sin so grievously that God would punish him or her by death? That, at the very least, is puzzling.

But even if 1 John 5 does concern punishment by physical death for some Christians, this is not an interpretation that fits the text we are studying. In Romans Paul is not talking about sinning Christians. He is distinguishing between Christians, who live by the Spirit, and unbelievers, who live according to the sinful nature. So his point seems to be rather that those who live according to the sinful nature, that is, unbelievers, will die spiritually—indeed, they are already spiritually dead—while those who live by the Spirit, that is, Christians, will live spiritually. Paul must be saying this, because it is what he has been saying all along.

Why, then, does he write as he does, saying to Christians, "For if you live according to the sinful nature, you will die"? The answer is that this is a general statement, like saying to a child, "If you put your finger in the fire, you'll get burned." It does not necessarily imply that a person hearing the words might ignore the warning or even be able to ignore it.

May I put it bluntly again? Paul is saying that if you live like a non-Christian, dominated by your sinful nature rather than living according to the Holy Spirit, you will perish like a non-Christian—because you are a non-Christian. "If you live according to the sinful nature, *you will die*." On the other hand, if you really are a Christian, you will not live according to the

1. For a thoughtful example of this "sin unto death" teaching applied to Romans 8, see Donald Grey Barnhouse, *God's Heirs: Exposition of Bible Doctrines, Taking the Epistle to the Romans as a Point of Departure*, vol. 7, *Romans 8:1–39* (Grand Rapids: Wm. B. Eerdmans, 1963), pp. 51–60.

2. For my own discussion of the major options, see James Montgomery Boice, *The Epistles of John* (Grand Rapids: Zondervan, 1979), pp. 172–176.

sinful nature. Instead, you will acknowledge what you actually are in Jesus Christ and live accordingly.

D. Martyn Lloyd-Jones concludes that here "the apostle teaches quite clearly that the way of sanctification is the way of realizing the truth about ourselves as Christians, and then putting it into practice."[3]

"You Can Do It!"

Now let me apply this teaching practically. At the beginning of this study I told of a letter I received from an old friend and that it had two questions: (1) How can I find the strength to do what is right; and (2) Why doesn't God intervene in my life in special ways to help out?

I want to return to that letter now, having looked at Paul's teaching about the way to sanctification, and share how I answered it. I called my friend, and after I had asked how she was doing—finding, incidentally, that she was doing remarkably well—I said something like this:

> I am sure you will find strength to do what is right in this situation, and the reason I am sure you will find strength is that I know you already have it. You can do it! I do not mean that you have the necessary strength or willpower in yourself, because none of us do. We can't do anything by ourselves or in our own strength. The reason I know you have the strength you need is that you have the Holy Spirit, which is true of every Christian. The reason you are troubled by the need to do right and are not willing simply to drift along in wrong living, as unbelievers do, is that you know you belong to Jesus Christ and therefore really want to please him. God's Spirit is within you. So if you were to say, "I don't have the strength to serve God," you would really be saying that the Holy Spirit is inadequate.
>
> And that is the answer to your other question, too. You want to know why God has not intervened in your life to do something special. I have heard many people ask that question—it is a natural one, particularly since we read about special interventions by God in people's lives in the Bible and in Christian biographies.
>
> But what do we mean when we ask that question?
>
> Do we mean that we want God to reorder events to suit our own personal wishes? If so, we have no right to ask that, nor should we want to. That would mean that we know better than God, that we can order the events of our lives better than he can. That would be terrible.
>
> Or do we mean—I think this is actually the case—that we want God to solve our problem by some external means, perhaps by removing the temptation, by changing our thinking so that we are no longer attracted by the wrong, or by providing an experience that will strip the temptation of its power? But if God were to do that, which he could, it would mean that what we are able to do as normal Christians unaided by some supernatural inter-

3. D. M. Lloyd-Jones, *Romans: An Exposition of Chapter 8:5–17, The Sons of God* (Grand Rapids: Zondervan, 1974), p. 110.

vention of God does not count. And this would mean that the Christian life ultimately has no meaning. What would be the point of being a Christian if, in crisis situations, God always has to intervene in some way.

To be a Christian means this. First, God has already done everything necessary to save you not only from sin's penalty but from its power, too. You have God's Holy Spirit within you, and as a result you can live for him. You do not need some secret method, esoteric formula, or mystical experience. God has already equipped you perfectly for every good work.

Second, you *will* live for him. And not only will you live for him, putting to death the misdeeds of the body and living in accordance with the Holy Spirit's desires, your doing that will also matter profoundly. What would it prove if God did the hard thing for you? Nothing at all! We already know that God is all-powerful. But when Christians do the right thing—even when it breaks their hearts or when they suffer for it—when they do it in utter dependence on God and out of love for him, then their obedience to God proves everything. It proves that they matter and that God matters. And that victory, their victory and yours, will endure to the praise of our great God throughout eternity.

My friend's two questions probably occur to every Christian at one time or another. My response was helpful to her—I hope it also furthers your own understanding of sanctification.

100

The Family of God

Romans 8:14

. . . because those who are led by the Spirit of God are sons of God.

One of the things I have said about Romans 8, as we have been working our way through it, is that basically Paul is not teaching anything new here but is instead reinforcing what he already stated. The general theme is assurance of salvation, but that doctrine was laid out in chapter 5. And, as I have explained, chapters 6 and 7 were a digression to answer several important questions growing out of chapter 5, after which the apostle picked up where he left off earlier.

But true as that is in general, we find something new when we come to Romans 8:14. This verse tells us that "those who are led by the Spirit of God are sons of God," and here the idea that we are "sons of God" appears in Romans for the first time.

This is not merely an incidental thought, although it would be possible for a new idea to appear at some point simply by accident, as it were. There is nothing accidental about this reference. Paul is talking about assurance of salvation and is arguing that one basis for this is our new relationship to God, which is a family relationship. Moreover, having introduced the theme

829

in our text, he then elaborates upon it in verses 15–17, speaking of such related concepts as "sons," "sonship," "children," and "heirs." Some of the words reappear later on in verses 19, 21, and 23. The idea is so important that a number of commentators, such as John R. W. Stott, treat verses 14–17 as a separate section, in spite of the fact that verse 14 is linked to the preceding verse by the word *because*, or *for*.[1]

Technically, verse 14 is introduced as proof of what has gone immediately before. Calvin saw this and said, "The substance . . . amounts to this, that all who are led by the Spirit of God are the sons of God; all the sons of God are heirs of eternal life; and therefore all who are led by the Spirit of God ought to feel assured of eternal life."[2] Therefore, Romans 8:14 is meant to be both a test of spiritual life and a comfort.

Verse 14 is one of those amazing verses, found often in the Bible, which is literally loaded with important teachings. I want to list five of them.

Two Fathers, Two Families

The first point is a negative one: *Not everyone is a member of God's family*. The reason this is important is that we have an idea in western thought, a product of older liberalism, which said that human beings are all sons or daughters of God and that therefore we are all members of one family. The popular way of putting this has been to speak of "the universal fatherhood of God" and "the universal brotherhood of man." I am sure you have heard those expressions.

There is a sense, of course, in which all human beings are brothers and sisters, having been created by the one God. This is the way the apostle Paul spoke in Athens when he quoted the Greek poets Cleanthes and Aratus to say to that particularly intellectual audience that "we are [all] his [that is, God's] offspring" (Acts 17:28). But that is not the way the words "sons of God" are used in Scripture, and it is certainly not the way the apostle is speaking here. When Paul writes of "those who are led by the Spirit of God," he is distinguishing between those who are led by the Spirit and those who are not led by the Spirit, which means that only a portion of humanity are God's *spiritual* children.

The clearest statement of this important truth is from the mouth of Jesus Christ. The relevant passage is John 8:31–47. Jesus had been teaching the people and had made a statement similar to what Paul has been saying in Romans: "If you hold to my teachings, you are really my disciples. Then you will know the truth, and the truth will set you free."

---

1. John R. W. Stott, *Men Made New: An Exposition of Romans 5–8* (Grand Rapids: Baker Book House, 1984), pp. 92–94.

2. John Calvin, *The Epistles of Paul the Apostle to the Romans and to the Thessalonians*, trans. Ross MacKenzie (Grand Rapids: Wm. B. Eerdmans, 1973), p. 167.

This offended his Jewish listeners, because they did not like to think of themselves as enslaved. "We have never been slaves of anyone," they said.

Their statement was absurd, of course. They had been enslaved by many nations during their long history, and even then were under the domination of the Roman Empire.

But Jesus ignored that point and answered instead that he had been speaking spiritually. "I tell you the truth, everyone who sins is a slave to sin. . . . I am telling you what I have seen in the Father's presence, and you do what you have heard from your father" (vv. 34, 38).

They answered that Abraham was their father.

Jesus denied it, saying that if they were Abraham's children, they would be like Abraham and would not be determined to kill him, which they were. He said again that, instead, they were acting like their true father.

They then replied that God himself was their only Father, at which point Jesus became most explicit: "If God were your Father, you would love me, for I came from God and now am here. . . . You belong to your father, the devil, and you want to carry out your father's desire. . . . The reason you do not hear is that you do not belong to God" (vv. 42, 44, 47).

It cannot be said any clearer than that. In these words Jesus made clear that there are two families and two fatherhoods, and that only those who love and serve God are God's children.

Born of God

This leads to the second important teaching of this verse. In fact, it is the main one: *All Christians are members of God's family*. This involves a change that is radical, supernatural, and far-reaching.

1. *It is radical.* To become a child of God means that the individual has experienced the most radical or profound change possible. This is because, before a person becomes a son or daughter of God, he or she is not a member of God's family but is a member of the devil's family (to use Jesus' terminology in John 8) or is merely "in Adam" (to use Paul's earlier teaching in Romans). We do not need to review Paul's earlier teaching in detail, because it was covered thoroughly in our studies of chapters 5 and 6. To be "in Adam" means to be in sin, a slave to wickedness, under divine judgment, and destined for eternal death. To be "in Christ" is the reverse. It means to be delivered from sin and its judgment, to be growing in holiness, and to possess eternal life. The change is as radical as passing from a state of slavery to freedom or from death to life.

2. *It is supernatural.* This change is not only radical. It is supernatural, too, which means that it is done for us from above by God. Here again we are helped by the very words of Jesus Christ, as recorded in John 3. He had been approached by Nicodemus, a ruler of the Jews, and had told

Nicodemus that he would never be able to understand spiritual matters unless he was "born again."

This puzzled the Jewish ruler, so he asked, "How can a man be born when he is old?"

Jesus replied, "I tell you the truth, no one can enter the kingdom of God unless he is born of water and the Spirit. Flesh gives birth to flesh, but the Spirit gives birth to spirit. You should not be surprised at my saying, 'You must be born again.' The wind blows wherever it pleases. You hear its sound, but you cannot tell where it comes from or where it is going. So it is with everyone born of the Spirit" (vv. 5–8). In these words Jesus made clear that becoming a child of God is a matter of spiritual birth and that this is something only the Spirit of God can do. The Greek word translated "again" implies that this birth is "from above," rather than from below, which means that this new spiritual life is divinely imparted.

3. *It is far-reaching.* This point will be developed more as we proceed through this section, but it is important to say here that the end of this spiritual rebirth is not only deliverance from sin's judgment—or, as many in our day seem to think, happiness now—but glorification. This is where chapter 5 began, and it is where chapter 8 will end. It is the point of this section of Romans: "Now if we are children, then we are heirs—heirs of God and co-heirs with Christ, if indeed we share in his sufferings in order that we may also share in his glory" (v. 17).

In his exceptional study of these verses, D. Martyn Lloyd-Jones stresses that the apostle's interest "is always in glorification," bemoaning the fact that the interest of today's church has settled on sanctification "because we are so miserably subjective."[3]

A Practical Result

Not every characteristic of our age is bad, however, though super subjectivity undoubtedly is a troublemaker. One potentially good characteristic is modern-day practicality. We are a down-to-earth people and want to see results. So I ask, what is the practical result of this important change that has happened to us? What does being a Christian mean in one's daily life?

Here is where Romans 8:14 provides us with a third important doctrine: *To be a Christian means to be led by God's Spirit.* Up to this point the doctrines I have been explaining might be thought to refer to a change of status only—before, we were "in Adam"; now we are "in Christ." Before, we were under condemnation; now we are delivered from condemnation. Before, we were spiritually dead; now we are spiritually alive. All that is true, of course, and Paul has taught it. But it is not the only truth he is teaching. Because our change of status has been accomplished by the Holy Spirit,

3. D. M. Lloyd-Jones, *Romans: An Exposition of Chapter 8:5–17, The Sons of God* (Grand Rapids: Zondervan, 1974), pp. 151, 152.

who lives within every genuine Christian, being a Christian also means that we will be led by that same Spirit. Or, as I have said in different words, it means that we will be growing in holiness increasingly.

This is the way verse 14 is tied to the preceding one. Verse 13 said that we will live spiritually, now and forever, "if by the Spirit [we] put to death the misdeeds of the body." Now verse 14 adds that we will indeed do that if the Spirit is within us, for this is the direction the Holy Spirit is leading.

A Test of Spiritual Paternity

From time to time we read in the papers of a "paternity suit," in which a mother sues for support of her child on the grounds that a certain man is the father though he denies it. In earlier ages this was a matter usually impossible to prove, which made a situation like this extremely difficult for the woman. But today a test can be made of both the alleged father's and the child's genetic makeup, and the relationship can be established (or disproved) with nearly 100 percent accuracy.

This introduces the fourth important teaching in this verse, which is, we might say, a test of paternity. It tells us *how we can know we are in God's family.* We are in God's family if the Spirit of God is leading us in our daily lives.

Do you remember what I said earlier about this being a new idea and a new section of Romans 8? Here I have to confess that it is not such a new idea after all, since we have really been noting this point all along. It is only another way of saying that those who are Christians will necessarily live accordingly. They are on the path of discipleship. Therefore, although they may fall while walking along that path, they also inevitably get up again and go forward. They grow in holiness.

A big question still remains: *How* does the Holy Spirit lead us?

People have a lot of ideas at this point, many of them unbiblical. Some answer in terms of outward circumstances, suggesting that God orders external events to direct us in the way we should go. Others look for special intimations or feelings or perhaps even special revelations. Some think of guidance almost magically, expecting God's Spirit to direct them to some verse supernaturally or to let them overhear some human remark that is actually from God. We have to be careful in this area since it is futile to deny that God does indeed sometimes lead in "mysterious" ways. Saint Augustine was converted by hearing a neighbor's child singing the words, "*Tole lege* (Take, read)." He received it as a word from God, picked up a Bible and, turning to a passage at random, fell upon verses that spoke to his specific need, and so was converted. We dare not say that this was not from God.

But is that sort of guidance what we are to expect normally? If so, the majority of us have not experienced it. If being "led by the Spirit" is what it means to be a Christian, and if that is what it means to be led, then most of us are not Christians! Of course, this is not what Paul is saying.

The place to start is by recognizing that the Holy Spirit works within us or, as we might say, "internally." Everything in the passage indicates this. Paul has been talking about our minds being set on what the Holy Spirit desires and about our having an obligation to live according to the Spirit rather than according to the sinful nature. In the next verses he will speak of an internal witness of the Spirit by which we instinctively call God "Father." God can order external events, of course, and he does. He orders everything. But that is not what is being discussed here. In this verse Paul is talking about what God's Spirit does internally within the Christian.

So we reduce the earlier question to this one: What does the Holy Spirit do internally in Christians to lead them? Let me suggest three things.

1. *He renews our minds.* The first area in which the Holy Spirit works is the intellect, and he does this by what Paul will later call "the renewing of your mind." This comes out very clearly in Romans 12. There, having laid down the great doctrines of the epistle, the apostle begins to apply them to the believer's conduct, saying, "Therefore, I urge you, brothers, in view of God's mercy, to offer your bodies as living sacrifices, holy and pleasing to God—this is your spiritual act of worship. Do not conform any longer to the pattern of this world, but be transformed by the renewing of your mind. Then you will be able to test and approve what God's will is—his good, pleasing and perfect will" (Rom. 12:1–2).

The person who discovers, tests, and approves what God's pleasing and perfect will is obviously is being led by God. But the key to this, according to Romans, is the mind's renewal.

How, then, are our minds to be renewed? There is only one way. It is by our reading and being taught by the Spirit from the Bible. That is what God has given the Bible to us for—to inform us, enlighten our minds, and re-direct our thinking. I hold the Bible and the Holy Spirit together in this, however, as the Reformers were particularly astute in doing. For alone, either is inadequate. A person who considers himself to be led by the Spirit apart from the Bible will soon fall into error and excess. He will begin to promote nonbiblical and therefore false teachings. But a person who reads the Bible apart from the illumination provided by the Holy Spirit, which is true in the case of all unbelievers, will find it to be a closed and meaningless book. The Christian is led by the operation of the Holy Spirit and the Bible together.

Here is a test for you. Has the Holy Spirit been leading you by enlightening your mind through Bible study? Have you discovered things about God, yourself, the gospel, and the ways of God that you did not know before? Do you realize that they are true? Are you beginning to live differently? Unless you are crazy, you will begin to live differently. Because a person who realizes that one way is true and another is false and yet takes the false path must be out of his or her mind, irrational. If your mind has been renewed, you will show it.

2. *He stirs the heart.* Figuratively, the heart is the seat of the emotions, and the Holy Spirit works upon it by stirring or quickening the heart to love God. In the verse that follows our text Paul speaks of an inner response to God by which we affectionately cry out, "*Abba,* Father." This verse does not actually mention the heart, but in a parallel text in Galatians Paul does, showing that he is thinking of the operation of the Holy Spirit upon our hearts explicitly. He writes, "Because you are sons, God sent the Spirit of his Son into our hearts, the Spirit who calls out, '*Abba,* Father'" (Gal. 4:6). In other words, the Spirit of God leads us by making us affectionate toward God and his ways. It is the Spirit who causes us, as Jesus said, to "hunger and thirst for righteousness" (Matt. 5:6).

This brings us to another test of whether or not you are a Christian. I mentioned it in an earlier study. Do you love God? I do not mean, "Do you love God perfectly?" If you think you do, you probably do not love him much at all. I mean only, "Do you try to please God? Do you want to spend time with him through studying the Bible and praying? Do you seek his favor? Are you concerned for his glory?"

3. *He directs our wills.* Just as the Spirit leads us by renewing our minds and stirring our hearts or affections, so also does he lead us by redirecting and strengthening our wills. Paul speaks of this in Philippians, where he writes: "Therefore, my dear friends . . . continue to work out your salvation with fear and trembling, for it is God who works in you to will and to act according to his good purpose" (Phil. 2:12–13).

God gives us a singleness of purpose—to do his will. It is the way God works. Has *your* will been redirected in that way? When you look deep inside, do you find that you really want to serve God and act according to his good purpose? God does not force you to be godly against your will. He changes your will by the new birth so that what you despised before you now love, and what you were indifferent to before you now find desirable.

John Murray had it right when he wrote, "The activity of the believer is the evidence of the Spirit's activity, and the activity of the Spirit is the cause of the believer's activity."[4] If you are trying to please God, it is because the Spirit is at work within you, leading you to want and actually do the right thing. It is a strong reason for believing you are in God's family.

Our Brothers and Sisters

There is one more important teaching in this short but potent verse, and it comes from the fact that the words we are dealing with are plural: "*those who are led* by the Spirit of God *are sons* of God." Therefore: *Those led by the Spirit of God are our true brothers and sisters.* We are part of the same divine family.

4. John Murray, *The Epistle to the Romans* (Grand Rapids: Wm. B. Eerdmans, 1968), p. 295.

The older, King James Version started this verse with "For as many as . . ." and I am almost sorry this has been changed, since it emphasized the inclusive nature of God's family better than "those" in the New International Version. Yet it is the same thing. And the problem is not so much our understanding the point as practicing it. There are many differences between believers within the church of Jesus Christ—differences of class, personality, background, economic status, temperament, abilities, drive, sensitivity, and thousands of other things. They have led to divisions in the church, for not all divisions (perhaps not even the majority) are doctrinal. Many divisions exist that should not exist, and sometimes these lead Christians in one camp to suspect and even fail to associate with those in another.

This should not be, for the text teaches that what makes other believers our brothers or sisters in Christ is not what denomination or movement they may belong to, but whether or not they are being led by God's Spirit. Anyone for whom that is true is our brother or sister in Christ, and we should recognize it and be willing to work with that person to fulfill God's purposes.

101

No Longer Slaves But Sons

Romans 8:15–16

For you did not receive a spirit that makes you a slave again to fear, but you received the Spirit of sonship. And by him we cry, "Abba, Father." The Spirit himself testifies with our spirit that we are God's children.

We are continuing to study the section of Romans 8 in which, for the first time in the letter, Paul introduces the thought of Christians being members of God's family. The section begins technically with verse 15 and continues through verse 17, though the phrase "sons of God" was introduced in verse 14 and the words "sons of God" and "children of God" are also used later. Paul's development of this idea makes these verses among the most important in the chapter.

It is important to see how they fit in. Remember that the apostle's overall theme in Romans 8 is assurance, the doctrine that Christians can know that they truly are Christians and that, because they are, nothing will ever separate them from the love of God. The experience of assurance demands that we actually be God's children. For this reason I have stressed the need to test our profession. It would be fatal to presume in this matter. However, the chapter has not been written to make us uncertain of our salvation, but to

837

give assurance of it, and that is where these verses come in. They give multiple and connecting reasons, one in each of the four verses, why the child of God can know that he or she really is a member of God's family.

Robert Haldane puts it like this:

> Here and in the following verses the apostle exhibits four proofs of our being the sons of God. The first is our being led by the Spirit of God; the second is the Spirit of adoption which we receive, crying, "Abba, Father," verse 15; the third is the witness of the Spirit with our spirits, verse 16; the fourth is our sufferings in the communion of Jesus Christ; to which is joined the fruit of our sonship, the Apostle saying that if children, we are heirs of God, and then joint heirs with Christ; if so be that we suffer with him, that we may be also glorified together.[1]

We looked at the first of these proofs in the previous study. We will look at the fourth in the next. In this study we will look at proofs two and three, adoption and the witness of the Spirit with our spirits, which belong together.

Adopted by God

We begin with verse 15: "For you did not receive a spirit that makes you a slave again to fear, but you received the Spirit of sonship. And by him we cry, 'Abba, Father.'" The chief idea in this verse, which is also a new idea, is "adoption," though this is obscured somewhat by the New International Version, which speaks of "sonship." But the Greek word is *huiothesia*, which means "to have an installation or placement as a son" and is the technical Greek word for "adoption" (the term used in KJV). Adoption is the procedure by which a person is taken from one family (or no family) and placed in another. In this context, it refers to removing a person from the family of Adam (or Satan) and placing him or her in the family of God.

Adoption is related to regeneration, or the new birth, but they are not the same thing. Regeneration has to do with our receiving a new life or new nature. Adoption has to do with our receiving a new status.

But first we need to back up and consider a problem. It comes from the way Paul uses the word *spirit* in this verse. You will notice that "spirit" occurs twice, once in the phrase "a spirit that makes you a slave again to fear" (KJV uses the words "spirit of bondage") and a second time in the phrase "Spirit of sonship [or adoption]." The question is: To what do these two words refer?

The word *spirit* can refer to either of two things in the Bible, either the Holy Spirit or a human spirit, or disposition. These two meanings, in various combinations, give us three possible interpretations of the verse.

---

1. Robert Haldane, *An Exposition of the Epistle to the Romans* (MacDill AFB: MacDonald Publishing, 1958), p. 353.

1. Both occurrences of "spirit" can be taken as referring to the human spirit. Those who think this way believe that Paul is talking about a person's disposition or feelings in both cases and would interpret the verse as saying that we used to be fearful but that now, following our conversion and because of it, we have a cheerful spirit of adoption by which we call God "Father." That is probably true enough. But there are good reasons for thinking that Paul is saying something considerably more important in this passage.

2. The second possibility is to take both occurrences of the word as referring to the Holy Spirit. Martyn Lloyd-Jones does this, referring the first to the time in our lives in which we are presumed to come under the conviction of sin but in which we have not yet come forth into the liberty of the gospel. This is an important point with Lloyd-Jones, since it is linked to his interpretation of Romans 7:7–25. He takes over two hundred pages to expound this and other points in his treatment of Romans 8:15–16.[2] Donald Grey Barnhouse also takes both occurrences as referring to the Holy Spirit, but he views the "spirit of bondage" as the time in which the people of God, the Jews, lived under the law of Moses, that is, before the coming of Christ.[3] John Murray refers both to the Holy Spirit but in a specialized sense, as meaning, "[You] did not receive the Holy Spirit as a Spirit of bondage but as a Spirit of adoption."[4]

3. The third view is a combination of the two, in which the first word is taken as referring to the human spirit and the second as referring to the Holy Spirit.[5] This is the view reflected in most translations, such as the New International Version, where the first "spirit" appears with a lowercase *s* and the second with a capital.

In my judgment, there is no question but that the second use of the word must refer to the Holy Spirit, if for no other reason than that it appears in precisely this way in the parallel verse in Galatians: "Because you are sons, God sent the Spirit of his Son into our hearts, the Spirit who calls out '*Abba*, Father'" (Gal. 4:6). However, it is not so easy to say what the first use of the word refers to. Clearly, it could refer to the Holy Spirit negatively, which is how Murray sees it ("You did not receive the Holy Spirit as a Spirit of bondage but as a Spirit of adoption"). But if we take the parallel passage in Galatians seriously and apply that context here, it seems that the bondage involved is bondage to the law and that the contrast is between

2. D. M. Lloyd-Jones, *Romans: An Exposition of Chapter 8:5–17, The Sons of God* (Grand Rapids: Zondervan, 1974), pp. 196–399.

3. Donald Grey Barnhouse, *God's Heirs: Exposition of Bible Doctrines, Taking the Epistle to the Romans as a Point of Departure*, vol. 7, *Romans 8:1–39* (Grand Rapids: Wm. B. Eerdmans, 1963), p. 89.

4. John Murray, *The Epistle to the Romans* (Grand Rapids: Wm. B. Eerdmans, 1968), p. 297.

5. There is a fourth logical possibility, of course: referring the first "spirit" to the Holy Spirit and the second to ours. But no one has proposed it seriously.

that bondage and the grace and freedom from trying to serve God by the law, which came through Jesus Christ (cf. Gal. 4:1–7).

Moreover, this interpretation fits Romans. For Paul has been talking about the Christian's former state—in which, being in Adam, we were enslaved to sin—and he has argued that we have been delivered from that former bondage by the Holy Spirit. Now he adds that this new state, which conveys freedom from bondage, also contains the privileges of sonship.

The word *adoption* is not common in the New Testament, being used only by Paul and that only five times (three times in Romans), and it does not occur in the Old Testament at all, since the Jews did not practice adoption. They had other procedures, polygamy and Levirate marriage, for dealing with the problems of widows and orphans and inheritance.

Paul took the idea of adoption from Greek and Roman law, probably for two reasons. First, he was writing to Greeks and Romans (in this case to members of the church at Rome), so adoption, being part of their culture, was something they would all very readily understand. Second, the word was useful to him because "it signified being granted the full rights and privileges of sonship in a family to which one does not belong by nature."[6] That is exactly what happens to believers in salvation.

Our Father in Heaven

I have spoken of adoption as giving the adopted one a new status. But "new status" may not be the best description of what happens. What is really involved is a set of new relationships—new relationships to other people, both believers and unbelievers, but above all a new relationship to God. When we speak of salvation as justification, we are thinking of God as Judge. That is a remote and somewhat grim relationship. When we think of regeneration, we are thinking of God as Creator. That, too, is remote. But when we think of adoption, we are thinking of God as our Father, which denotes a far closer relationship.

This is why the apostle says that the Spirit of adoption causes us to cry out, "*Abba*, Father."

It is important to recognize that our authority to call God "Father" goes back to Jesus Christ. It goes back to no less important a statement than the opening phrases of the Lord's Prayer, which begins, "Our Father in heaven . . ." (Matt. 6:9). Today we take the right to call God "our Father" for granted, but we need to understand how new and startlingly original this must have been for Christ's contemporaries. No Old Testament Jew ever addressed God directly as "my Father."

This has been documented in a thoroughly German way by Ernst Lohmeyer, in a book called "*Our Father*," and by Joachim Jeremias, in an

---

6. Leon Morris, *The Epistle to the Romans* (Grand Rapids: William B. Eerdmans, and Leicester, England: Inter-Varsity Press, 1988), p. 315.

essay entitled "Abba" and a booklet called *The Lord's Prayer*.[7] According to these scholars: (1) the title was new with Jesus; (2) Jesus always used this form of address in praying; and (3) Jesus authorized his disciples to use the same word after him.

No one would deny that in one sense the title of "father" for God is as old as religion. Homer wrote of "Father Zeus, who rules over the gods and mortal men," and Aristotle explained that Homer was right because "paternal rule over children is like that of a king over his subjects" and "Zeus is king of us all." In those days "father" meant "lord," or "master," which is what all kings (as well as fathers) were. The important point, however, is that the address was always impersonal. In Greek thought their God could be called a "father" in the same way that a king might be called a father of his country. So, too, do we call George Washington the father of our country. But the deity is never pictured as "*my* father" or "*our* father" in Greek writing.

The situation is similar in the Old Testament. Occasionally the word *father* will be used as a designation for God, but it is not frequent and it is never personal. In fact, it occurs only fourteen times in the whole of the Old Testament. God refers to Israel as "my firstborn son" (Exod. 4:22), and David says, "As a father has compassion on his children, so the LORD has compassion on those who fear him" (Ps. 103:13). Although Isaiah writes, "Yet, O LORD, you are our Father" (Isa. 64:8), in none of these passages does any individual Jew address God directly as "my Father." In fact, in most of these passages the point is that Israel has not lived up to the family relationship.

Thus, Jeremiah reports God as saying, "How gladly would I treat you like sons and give you a desirable land, the most beautiful inheritance of any nation. I thought you would call me 'Father' and not turn away from following me. But like a woman unfaithful to her husband, so you have been unfaithful to me, O house of Israel" (Jer. 3:19–20). Similarly, Hosea records God's words: "When Israel was a child, I loved him, and out of Egypt I called my son. But the more I called Israel, the further they went from me . . ." (Hos. 11:1–2).

Moreover, in the time of Jesus the distance between the people and God, suggested by the detached reverence by which God was customarily addressed, was widening rather than growing more narrow. The names of God were more and more withheld from public speech and prayers. And the great name for God, the Tetragrammaton (YHWH), usually translated "Jehovah" or "Yahweh," was so protected that we do not know even today precisely how it was pronounced.

7. Ernst Lohmeyer, "*Our Father*," trans. John Bowden (New York: Harper and Row, 1965); Joachim Jeremias, "Abba," in *The Central Message of the New Testament* (London: SCM Press, 1965), pp. 9-30, and *The Lord's Prayer*, trans. John Reumann (Philadelphia: Fortress Press, 1964).

The reason is that it was *not* pronounced, and no indication of how it should be pronounced was given. Whenever the word *Jehovah* appeared in the sacred text, the vowel pointing for the word *Adonai,* which means "Lord," was substituted for the vowel pointing of the divine name. This was to remind readers to say "Adonai" instead of "Jehovah," which is what they did. God was considered to be too transcendent to be directly addressed, and his name was considered too holy to be on human lips. So the distance between God and man continued to grow wider.

All this was completely overturned by Jesus Christ. He always called God "Father," and this fact must have impressed itself in an extraordinary way upon the disciples. Not only do all four of the Gospels record that Jesus used this address, but they report that he did so in all his prayers.[8] The only exception—the cry from the cross, "My God, my God, why have you forsaken me?" (Matt. 27:46; Mark 15:34)—enforces the importance of this point. That prayer was wrung from Christ's lips at the moment in which he was made sin for us and in which the relationship he had with his Father was in some measure temporarily broken. At all other times Jesus boldly assumed a relationship to God that was considered to be highly irreverent or even blasphemous by his contemporaries.

This is of great significance for our prayers. Jesus was the Son of God in a unique sense, and God was uniquely his Father. He came to God in prayer as God's unique Son. We are not like him. Nevertheless, Jesus revealed that this same relationship can be enjoyed by all who believe on him, all whose sins are removed by his suffering. They can come to God as God's children. God can be their own personal Father.

But even this is not all. When Jesus addressed God as Father he did not use the normal word for father. He used the Aramaic word *abba,* which is what Paul quotes in Romans 8:15 and the parallel text in Galatians 4:6. Obviously this word was so striking to the disciples that they remembered it in its Aramaic form and repeated it in Aramaic even when they were speaking Greek or writing their Gospels or letters in Greek. Mark used it in his account of Christ's prayer in Gethsemane (*"Abba,* Father, everything is possible for you," Mark 14:36). Paul used it in the texts we are studying.

What does *abba* mean specifically?

The early church fathers, Chrysostom, Theodor of Mopsuestia, and Theodore of Cyrrhus, who came from Antioch, where Aramaic was spoken, and who probably had Aramaic-speaking nurses, unanimously testified that *abba* was the address of small children to their fathers.[9] The Talmud confirms this when it says that when a child is weaned "it learns to say *abba* and *imma*" (that is, "daddy" and "mommy").[10]

8. See Matthew 11:25; 26:39, 42; Mark 14:36; Luke 23:34; John 11:41; 12:27; 17:1, 5, 11, 21, 24, 25.

9. Jeremias, *The Lord's Prayer,* p. 19.

10. *Berakoth* 40a; *Sanhedrin* 70b.

So this is what *abba* really means: daddy. To a Jewish mind a prayer addressing God as daddy would not only have been improper, it would have been irreverent to the highest degree. Yet this is what Jesus said in his prayers, and it quite naturally stuck in the minds of the disciples. It was something very unique when Jesus taught his disciples to call God "daddy."[11]

Now let me back up to something I said in the previous study when I was trying to explain how the Holy Spirit leads us. I spoke of his work upon our hearts, producing affection or love for God. A good illustration is the story of the prodigal son. When he came to his senses he remembered his father, his affection was quickened, and he determined to get up and go to him. That is the attitude the Holy Spirit creates in our hearts to assure us that we are no longer the devil's children but rather are God's sons and daughters. We now know that God is our loving Father, and because we know this we are drawn to him.

Witness of the Spirit

We come finally to the third verse in this four-verse section, a verse that gives another reason for knowing we are in God's family. It says, "The Spirit himself testifies with our spirit that we are God's children" (v. 16). There is no question what the two "spirits" refer to in this verse. The first is the Holy Spirit. The second is our human spirit. But it is not so clear about what this third proof of our being children of God consists.

One thing is clear. There is a contrast between verse 15, in which *we* give testimony to this new relationship, crying "*Abba*, Father," and verse 16, in which the Holy Spirit *himself* bears witness. Verse 16 concerns the Holy Spirit's witness, which is separate from our own. But what is this witness? How is it separate from what Paul has already said (and I have been discussing)?

I know that what I am going to say now will be misunderstood by some people and that a few may even condemn it as being wrong and dangerous, especially some in the Reformed tradition. But what I am convinced this teaches is that there is such a thing as a direct witness of the Holy Spirit to believers that they are sons or daughters of God, even apart from the other "proofs" I have mentioned. In other words, it is possible to have a genuine *experience* of the Holy Spirit in one's heart.

Experience of the Spirit? I know the objections. I know that no spiritual experience is ever necessarily valid in itself. Any such experience can be counterfeited, and the devil's counterfeits can be very good indeed. But the

11. I have borrowed a portion of this section, with variations, from James Montgomery Boice, *Foundations of the Christian Faith: A Comprehensive and Readable Theology* (Downers Grove, Ill.: InterVarsity Press, 1986), pp. 445–447.

fact that a spiritual experience can be counterfeited does not invalidate all of them.

I also know that those who seek experiences of the Holy Spirit frequently run to excess and fall into unbiblical ideas and practices. Every such experience must be tested by Scripture. But in spite of these objections, which are important, I still say that there can be a direct experience of the Spirit that is valid testimony to the fact that one is truly God's child.

Haven't you ever had such an experience? An overwhelming sense of God's presence? Or haven't you at some point, perhaps at many points in your life, been aware that God has come upon you in a special way and that there is no doubt whatever that what you are experiencing is from God? You may have been moved to tears. You may have deeply felt some other sign of God's presence, by which you were certainly moved to a greater and more wonderful love for him.

This has been a very common experience in revivals. Martyn Lloyd-Jones illustrates it by many dozens of pages of revival-time teaching and testimony. While I believe he is mistaken in referring to this as a "baptism of the Holy Spirit," I nevertheless believe that he is correct in calling it a genuine and desirable reality.[12]

If this idea is foreign to you or if it seems dangerous, perhaps you are not ready for it at this point. Let it go. You have plenty to occupy yourself with in what has already been taught in verses 14 and 15. But if you have had any of these intensely spiritual moments, perhaps in your quiet times or while sitting in a church service, thank God for them. Know that they do not replace any of the other things I have stressed. The Bible is primary. But rejoice that God also has a way of making himself so real to us that we are actually lifted up, even in hard times, and are assured by that spiritual whisper of divine love that we are and always will be God's children.

12. I recommend a careful reading of Lloyd-Jones's material, particularly his descriptions of this experience and his instructions on how to distinguish it from experiences that are false. See Lloyd-Jones, *Romans: An Exposition of Chapter 8:5–17, The Sons of God*, pp. 285–399.

102

The Inheritance of God's Saints

Romans 8:17

Now if we are children, then we are heirs—heirs of God and co-heirs with Christ, if indeed we share in his sufferings in order that we may also share in his glory.

Romans 8:17 introduces us to two important biblical ideas: suffering and glory. Or, as Ray Stedman says, "the hurts and hallelujahs."[1] The verse begins with the glory, talks about suffering, and ends with glory again. The first statement is that children of God are God's heirs and co-heirs with Jesus Christ.

What a marvelous thing this is, to be an heir of God himself! Sometimes children hope fondly for what they might inherit from their parents, but quite often these very human hopes are disappointing. One of the richest men who ever lived was Cecil Rhodes (1853–1902), an Englishman who emigrated to South Africa for health reasons and there amassed a vast fortune through diamond mining. He died when he was only forty-nine, and in his will he left most of his riches not to his immediate family, much to their resentment, but to endow the famous Rhodes scholarships.

1. Ray C. Stedman, *From Guilt to Glory*, vol. 1, *Hope for the Helpless* (Portland: Multnomah Press, 1978), p. 284.

845

"Well, there it is," said his brother Arthur when the disappointing news reached him. "It seems I shall have to win a scholarship."

The French writer of the Middle Ages, Francois Rabelais, who was also a Franciscan friar, made the following will: "I owe much. I possess nothing. I give the rest to the poor."

How different with God. God owes nothing, he possesses everything, and he gives it all to his children.

True and False Evangelism

There are certain things we need to know about our spiritual inheritance, however, and the first is that it is laid up for us in heaven, that is, in the future. This should be almost self-evident, but it is important to emphasize it in light of a certain kind of evangelism that has been developed in our age.

This evangelism says, "Jesus died to give you abundant life now, and this means that he has promised to provide all you either need or want. If you are in trouble, he will solve your troubles. If you are unhappy, he will make you happy. If you are discouraged, he will lift you up and give you a joyful and unquenchable heart song. Whatever your needs may be, Jesus is the provision for those needs. Tell him about them. Claim the answers to those needs by faith." In some of its more extreme expressions, this teaching has become what is called a "health and prosperity" gospel.

During their brief reign on religious television, Jim and Tammy Bakker preached this kind of evangelism. They taught that God would make believers rich and prosperous. Tammy said, "When I tell God what car I want, I even tell him the color."

Such a gospel forgets that Jesus came not to bring peace but a sword, and that his call to discipleship says, "If anyone would come after me, he must deny himself and take up his cross daily and follow me" (Luke 9:23). It is why, in our text, Paul follows his statement that if we are God's children, we are heirs of God with a sober reminder: "if indeed we share in his sufferings." True Christianity is honest at this point. It does not deny that there are very important promises for this life—promises that God will be with us in trouble, provide an inner peace in turmoil, minister comfort when we are distressed, and never leave us. But the basic idea is not that we shall escape trouble here but rather be given grace to go through it. And the blessings of our inheritance are almost entirely reserved for us in heaven.

D. Martyn Lloyd-Jones says, "True evangelism does not offer some panacea for all the ills in our life in this world; it does not promise to make us perfect in a moment or set the whole world right. It says rather, 'In the world ye shall have tribulation; but fear not, I have overcome the world.'"[2]

2. D. M. Lloyd-Jones, *Romans: An Exposition of Chapter 8:5–17, The Sons of God* (Grand Rapids: Zondervan, 1974), p. 405.

The Inheritance to Come

So we start from the truth that most of our rewards are in the future. But then we immediately what to ask: "Of what does our inheritance consist?" What will believers actually possess in heaven? There are a number of things that I call "lesser items," and then there is the greatest prize of all.

The Lesser Items

1. *A heavenly home.* The first thing that comes to mind here is the promise of a heavenly home that Jesus made to his disciples just before his arrest and crucifixion. He said, "Do not let your hearts be troubled. Trust in God; trust also in me. In my Father's house are many rooms; if it were not so, I would have told you. I am going there to prepare a place for you. And if I go and prepare a place for you, I will come back and take you to be with me that you also may be where I am" (John 14:1–3). This is a place prepared especially for all believers, and it is guaranteed by no less an authority than the Lord of glory himself, Jesus Christ.

2. *A heavenly banquet.* In several of his parables the Lord spoke of a heavenly banquet to which his own are invited. In one story he told of a great wedding supper to which many were invited who later refused to come, and of how the master sent to unexpected places to find guests (Matt. 22:1–14; cf. Luke 14:15–24). In another parable it is a banquet prepared for the prodigal son (Luke 15:11–32). In still another it is a wedding feast to which five wise women are admitted and five foolish women are shut out (Matt. 25:1–13). There are similar but passing references to other occasions of shared celebration.

These stories present our inheritance as joy and secure fellowship. We have a foretaste of these things in our observance of the Lord's Supper, which looks forward to the coming great marriage supper of the Lamb.

3. *Rule with Christ.* Another feature of our inheritance is that we will rule with Jesus in his kingdom. There is some difference among Bible scholars as to whether this refers to an earthly rule with Christ in some future age or to a heavenly rule only. But whatever its full meaning, there is no doubt that some important ruling authority is promised. Paul told Timothy, "If we endure, we will also reign with him" (2 Tim. 2:12). In one of his parables, Jesus spoke of servants who had shown their faithfulness during their master's absence being awarded cities over which to reign in the master's kingdom (Luke 19:11–27).

4. *Likeness to Christ.* One of the promised blessings, which means a great deal to me, is that we will be made like Jesus himself. John writes about it in his first letter, using language similar to Paul's in Romans 8. "Dear friends, now we are children of God, and what we will be has not been made known. But we know that when he appears, we shall be like him, for we

shall see him as he is" (1 John 3:1–2). It is hard to imagine a greater inheritance than to be made like the Lord Jesus Christ in all his attributes.

The Lord, Our Portion

In view of the magnitude of those last four items, why did I call them "lesser"? Because of the amazing and infinitely greater blessing that awaits us as "heirs of God."

Let me begin by reminding you of a grammatical distinction, namely that there are two kinds of genitives in most languages. One genitive is what grammarians call a subjective genitive, the other is what they call an objective genitive. Here are examples: "the love of money" and "the value of money." In each case the words "of money" are the genitive, having to do with possession. In the first phrase, "money" is the object, since it is the thing loved. The person involved has a love for money. In the second phrase, "of money" is still the genitive, but here it is the subject. The phrase does not refer to an individual who values money. It speaks of "money's value," value that money possesses.

Now take another phrase: "love of God." Is that a subjective genitive or an objective genitive? That answer is that, in this case, it can be either. If God is the subject, the phrase refers to God's love for us. If God is the object, it means that we have a love for God. Since the words can have either meaning, the interpretation has to be determined by the context.

With that distinction in mind, let's come back to our text to the phrase "heirs of God." Is this a subjective or an objective genitive? Again, it could be either. If it is a subjective genitive, then God is the subject and the meaning is that we belong to God as God's heirs. He has fixed his love upon us and made us his heirs by grace. If it is an objective genitive, then the meaning is that we have God as our inheritance. This is the boldest of the two possibilities, but it is what I am convinced Paul is saying here.

Here are my reasons.

First, this is taught in the Old Testament, which Paul certainly knew and from which he often borrowed. It is true that the Old Testament often speaks of the land of promise as the people's inheritance. This was a literal, earthly inheritance, though it was connected with God's greater promises to the patriarchs and their descendants. The important thing, however, is that it is transcended by passages that speak of God himself as their inheritance. Psalm 73:25–26, for instance, says:

> Whom have I in heaven but you?
>   And earth has nothing I desire besides you.
> My flesh and my heart may fail,
>   but God is the strength of my heart
>   and my portion forever.

Or Lamentations 3:24, "I say to myself, 'The LORD is my portion; therefore I will wait for him.'"

This greater reality was kept before the people in an interesting way in regard to the inheritance of the tribe of Levi, an inheritance given to them when the people invaded Canaan to possess it in the days of Joshua. You will recall that the land was divided tribe by tribe, along the lines specified by Moses even before the conquest. Each got its predetermined portion: Reuben, half tribe of Manasseh, Gad, Judah, Ephraim, the other half tribe of Manasseh, and all the others. Except Levi! Levi was the tribe of priests. They were scattered throughout the land in the forty-eight priestly towns, from which they were to serve the whole people in God's name. They had no inheritance because, as it was said of them, "the God of Israel, is their inheritance, as he promised them" (Josh. 13:33).

In the case of Israel, the land was certainly a good thing, promised from the time of Abraham. But the truly great inheritance was God himself. The purpose of scattering the Levites was to remind them of it.

Second, Romans 8:17 speaks of our being "co-heirs with Christ." That is, we inherit whatever we do inherit along with him. But as soon as we ask, "What does Jesus inherit?" all the items I mentioned earlier do not seem to fit. Jesus does not inherit heaven or a home in heaven; he has gone there to prepare a place for us. He does not actually inherit a kingdom over which he is to rule, though we can sometimes think of it like that; rather, he is already the ruler, the sovereign God. Similarly, neither the heavenly banquet nor his own character can rightly be said to be something willed to him or passed on to him by God.

What is Jesus' inheritance, then? The only thing that can properly be said to be his inheritance is the Father. This is what he had in mind in his great prayer just before his crucifixion. He prayed, "I have brought you glory on earth by completing the work you gave me to do. And now, Father, glorify me in your presence with the glory I had with you before the world began" (John 17:4–5).

Christ's inheritance is the glory of God, which means the vision of, participation in, and enjoyment of God himself. This is exactly the flow of the thought in Romans 8:17. For having spoken of our being heirs and having reminded us that we must enter into our possession by the gate of suffering, Paul ends up again with glory, reminding us that "we may also share in his [Christ's] glory," which is the glory of God.

Third, elsewhere in his writings, although not here, Paul speaks of the Holy Spirit who is given to us as the "earnest" (or "deposit") guaranteeing our inheritance (Eph. 1:14; cf. 2 Cor. 1:22, 5:5). An earnest is a pledge of something greater, but it is more than a mere document, bill of sale, or contract. It is a part of what is actually to come later. For example, when we buy a house we usually guarantee our intent to purchase it by making a prepayment of a small amount, a cash pledge of the greater amount to come. So, if the earnest of our inheritance is the Holy Spirit and the Holy Spirit is God—as he is, being the third person of the Trinity—then the full inheritance must be God himself.

Robert Haldane, who often writes brilliantly on the deepest subjects, says at this point, "God is the portion of his people, and in him, who is 'the possessor of heaven and earth,' they are heirs of all things. . . . God is all-sufficient, and this is an all-sufficient inheritance. God is eternal and unchangeable, and therefore it is an eternal inheritance—an inheritance incorruptible, undefiled and that fadeth not away. . . . It is God himself, then, who is the inheritance of his children. . . . He communicates himself to them by his grace, his light, his holiness, his life."[3]

If God is our inheritance, we can be assured of salvation, since nothing is going to move God. Nothing is ever going to dispossess us of our heavenly inheritance.

Looking Forward

All of this would be mere pie-in-the-sky if it did not have a practical effect on us, however. Yet that is precisely what it does have, if we truly believe this and are thinking this way.

Consider Abraham. The history of God's acts of redemption begins with Abraham when God called him out of his own country and sent him into a new land that he would show him, promising, "I will bless you . . . and all peoples on earth will be blessed through you" (Gen. 12:2–3). This calling contained the promise of a land, but it was far more than that. By promising a blessing to the nations through Abraham, God was also promising the Redeemer who was to come through his offspring. That promise was amplified throughout Abraham's long life, and it was this upon which Abraham's faith and hope fixed. This is why, when the author of Hebrews came to praise Abraham for his faith in the great chapter on the heroes of the faith (chap. 11), he says of Abraham, "By faith he made his home in the promised land like a stranger in a foreign country; he lived in tents, as did Isaac and Jacob, who were heirs with him of the same promise. For he was looking forward to the city with foundations, whose architect and builder is God" (Heb. 11:9–10).

"Heirs" of the promise? Yes, but the promise was not earthly. It was a promise of great spiritual blessing to be fulfilled ultimately in heaven.

It is the same with all the other heroes of the faith in this chapter. This is the point of Hebrews 11.

"By faith Abel offered God a better sacrifice than Cain did," and God accounted him to be "a righteous man" (v. 4). Abel received no earthly

3. Robert Haldane, *An Exposition of the Epistle to the Romans* (MacDill AFB: MacDonald Publishing, 1958), p. 365.

inheritance. He was murdered for his righteous stand. But he received a reward in heaven.

Enoch was a preacher. He preached of judgment before the great flood, warning the ungodly of his day to repent and flee from sin to God. He preached for three hundred years, but he had no reward here. He was utterly unsuccessful. No one was converted, and when the time for the flood came the only ones who were saved were Noah, his wife, and their immediate family. Enoch pleased no one on earth. But he has this testimony: "he was commended as one who pleased God" (v. 5b).

What did Noah inherit? Everything he had was swept away by the flood. Yet the writer says of him, "By his faith he condemned the world and became heir of the righteousness that comes by faith" (v. 7b).

Isaac and Jacob lived with Abraham in tents, having no real inheritance here. But they looked to the future and hoped for that (vv. 20–21), though they sometimes did it badly.

Joseph lost his home and his freedom for righteousness' sake. And even though God later advanced him and made him second in power only to Pharaoh of Egypt, Joseph's hopes were not there. He hoped in God's promise, in proof of which he gave instructions that his body was not to be buried in one of the Egyptian tombs but was to be carried from Egypt to Canaan when God eventually led the people out of slavery (v. 22; cf. Gen. 50:24–25).

Moses had no love for earth's treasures. He sought no earthly reward. Rather, he turned his back on the riches of Egypt, regarding "disgrace for the sake of Christ as of greater value than the treasures of Egypt, because he was looking ahead to his reward" (v. 26).

It was the same with all the Old Testament believers: Rahab, Gideon, Barak, Samson, Jephthah, David, Samuel, and the prophets. Such heroes of faith "were tortured and refused to be released, so that they might gain a better resurrection. Some faced jeers and flogging, while still others were chained and put in prison. They were stoned; they were sawed in two; they were put to death by the sword. . . . They wandered in deserts and mountains, and in caves and holes in the ground. These were all commended for their faith, *yet none of them received what had been promised*" (vv. 35–39, emphasis added).

Not then! But they have received it now. They have gone before us to take possession of the inheritance prepared in heaven for God's saints.

"Joy Hereafter"

Why should we expect it to be any different for us? It will not be. So why, when all Scripture teaches that our inheritance is in heaven and not on earth, should we spend so much effort trying to amass our fortunes here? Or why should we expect our lives to proceed along a gentle primrose path, when others gained heaven only by a sail through bloody seas?

I recently came across some wonderful words by Charles Haddon Spurgeon. They were written for preachers to encourage them to keep on in tough times, but the message is equally good for anyone. It goes like this:

Be not surprised when friends fail you: it is a failing world.

Never count upon immutability in man: inconstancy you may reckon upon without fear of disappointment. The disciples of Jesus forsook him; be not amazed if your adherents wander away to other teachers: as they were not your all when with you, all is not gone from you with their departure.

Serve God with all your might while the candle is burning, and then when it goes out for a season, you will have the less to regret.

Be content to be nothing, for that is what you are. When your own emptiness is painfully forced upon your consciousness, chide yourself that you ever dreamed of being full, except in the Lord.

Set small store by present rewards; be grateful for earnests by the way, but look for recompensing joy hereafter.

Continue with double earnestness to serve your Lord when no visible result is before you. Any simpleton can follow the narrow path in the light: faith's rare wisdom enables us to march on in the dark with infallible accuracy, since she places her hand in that of her Great Guide.

Between this and heaven there may be rougher weather yet, but it is all provided for by our covenant Head. In nothing let us be turned aside from the path which the divine call has urged us to pursue. Come fair or come foul, the pulpit is our watch-tower, and the ministry our warfare; be it ours, when we cannot see the face of our God, to trust under the shadow of his wings.[4]

---

4. Charles Haddon Spurgeon, "The Minister's Fainting Fits," in *Lectures to My Students* (Grand Rapids: Zondervan, 1972), pp. 164, 165.

103

Suffering:
The Path to Glory

Romans 8:17

Now if we are children, then we are heirs—heirs of God and co-heirs with Christ, if indeed we share in his sufferings in order that we may also share in his glory.

I do not think it was very good exegesis, but it was intriguing. A number of years ago a churchgoer asked a minister the meaning of the word *reproof* in 2 Timothy 3:16 ("All scripture is given by inspiration of God, and is profitable for doctrine, for *reproof*, for correction, for instruction in righteousness," KJV). The minister replied this way: "It means proof of doctrine, and then proof and proof again—*re*-proof." As I say, I do not think that is correct. I think the New International Version is right when it translates the Greek word *elegmos* as "rebuking." Still there is something to be said for "*re*-proofing."

In fact, it is what we have in Romans 8:14–17.

Several studies back, when we were in the midst of this section (at v. 15), I pointed out that verses 14–17 contain four proofs of our being sons and daughters of God, if the Holy Spirit has indeed brought us into God's family. First, we are led by God's Spirit. This refers to our conduct. If we are following after Christ in true and obedient discipleship, then we are Christ's and can be assured of salvation. Second, we have the internal witness of our spirits by which we cry "*Abba*, Father." We know that we have a new family relationship to God. Third, the Holy Spirit witnesses to us. I described this as an overwhelming sense of God's presence, something most Christians have experienced, though they may not understand it or know how to describe it. Fourth, we participate in Christ's sufferings.

These items are certainly proof and *re*-proof, being four good reasons why a child of God can know that he or she really does belong to God and that nothing in heaven or earth will ever snatch him or her away from God's love or break the family relationship.

The Problem of Suffering

But why should Paul introduce the idea of *suffering*, of all things—and at this point? None of us would do it. If we were trying to assure Christians that they really are Christians and their salvation is secure, suffering is probably the last thing we would mention. We think of it in the "problem" category. Hugh Evan Hopkins wrote a book called *The Mystery of Suffering*.[1] C. S. Lewis called his book *The Problem of Pain*.[2] Most of us are probably closest to Rabbi Harold S. Kushner's approach when he titled his problem-solving book *When Bad Things Happen to Good People*.[3]

We Christians acknowledge the problem of suffering and sometimes wrestle with it. But few of us would think of presenting it as a proof that the suffering person is a true child of God. It would seem to be the other way around.

So why does Paul drag the subject in here?

The first reason, surely, is that he was a realist. More than that, as an evangelist and a pastor, he knew that the people to whom he was writing were suffering. The early ministers of the gospel began to suffer for the gospel as soon as they began to obey Christ's Great Commission. Peter and John were jailed. Stephen was killed. Paul himself was imprisoned, beaten, shipwrecked, starved, threatened, and exposed to the elements. And what was true of these early preachers soon became true of their followers as well. They were ridiculed, hated, abused, and eventually martyred for their faith in great numbers. In addition, they endured the many disappointments, deaths, deprivations, and disasters common to all human life in a fallen and extremely sinful world.

1. Hugh Evan Hopkins, *The Mystery of Suffering* (Downers Grove, Ill.: InterVarsity Press, 1961).

2. C. S. Lewis, *The Problem of Pain* (New York: Macmillan, 1962).

3. Harold S. Kushner, *When Bad Things Happen to Good People* (New York: Avon Books, 1981).

Read the New Testament with suffering in mind and you will be startled to discover how extensively it is mentioned. Jesus said, "In this world you will have trouble" (John 16:33b). Most of the New Testament epistles have important discussions about suffering.

Suffering is as common to God's people today as in New Testament times. We need to understand that. It is true that most of us do not experience that special kind of suffering we call persecution, though our brothers and sisters in other parts of the world do. But we all know suffering. We suffer when we lose a husband or wife or other family member through death. We grieve when life itself or our friends or children disappoint us. We groan under pain, trauma, and sickness. We are hurt by prejudice, poverty, or sometimes a lack of rewarding work. The list is endless. Realism and pastoral concern undoubtedly caused the apostle to introduce this subject. Honesty did not allow him to talk about our inheritance without at the same time acknowledging that the path to glory involves a cross.

A second reason Paul probably introduced the subject is that he must have been aware of the many non-Christian approaches to suffering that were around. They were around then, and they are around today. His words, though quite brief, correct the following non-Christian approaches.

1. *Anger.* One response to suffering is anger. This is common with unbelievers, who blame or even curse God for their misfortunes. But it is also sadly true of some Christians. They blame God because he has not done something for them that they wanted—given them a loving spouse, for example—forgetting that Jesus has not promised us an easy life here, much less the fulfillment of our desires. He has called us to discipleship. The glory is hereafter.

2. *Avoidance.* A second approach is avoidance. If the path before them looks hard or even undesirable, some people turn from it and try to find something easier or more rewarding. Or, if the path cannot be avoided, they try to balance it with other things that are more attractive. The ancient name for this approach is hedonism. The Christian form of it is to ask God to remove the undesirable thing—sickness, for example, particularly a terminal illness. Christians who take this approach think the correct way is to ask God to remove the sickness so that afterward they might praise him for the healing. Of course, it sometimes is God's will to heal, so it is not wrong to ask for healing. But this is not the most profound or uniquely Christian approach to suffering.

A special form of this approach is used in some types of counseling. There the bottom line seems to be the individual's personal happiness or fulfillment. People are advised to do whatever makes them happy or "feels good," which ignores the truth that real growth comes by working through our hardships rather than by avoiding them.

3. *Apathy.* The third non-Christian approach is apathy, detachment from the problem. It is the attitude that says, "It just doesn't matter," and then tries to think about something else. One form of apathy is stoicism, the philosophy of the stiff upper lip. Stoicism may help you get by, but it is joyless and far removed from Christianity.

Paul was surrounded by these non-Christian philosophies, just as we are today, which is why I suggested that a second reason he introduced the subject of suffering at this point was to counter them. For our part, we need to know that these approaches are all less than truly Christian and come to understand suffering in a different light. We need to know that, for the Christian, suffering is the arena in which we are to prove the reality of our profession and achieve spiritual victories.

In the title of the fifth volume of my studies of John's Gospel, I called the Christian approach "Triumph Through Tragedy."[4] Of course, the key word is "through." We do not triumph by avoiding hardships.

Proof of Sonship

This brings us to the value of suffering according to a right theological framework or life-view. It has several important values, and the first is the chief reason Paul mentions it in Romans: He has been talking of Christians being sons and daughters of God; *now he speaks of suffering as proof of that relationship,* though the suffering may be in any of three different forms, each with a particular purpose.

1. *Persecution.* Some suffering is in the form of persecution, as I suggested earlier, and one value of persecution is that it proves to us that we really are children of God. Jesus taught this many times. In the Sermon on the Mount, near the beginning of his ministry, he said, "Blessed are you when people insult you, persecute you and falsely say all kinds of evil against you because of me. Rejoice and be glad, because great is your reward in heaven, for in the same way they persecuted the prophets who were before you" (Matt. 5:11–12). Again, in the Upper Room near the close of his ministry, he said, "If the world hates you, keep in mind that it hated me first. If you belonged to the world, it would love you as its own. As it is, you do not belong to the world, but I have chosen you out of the world. That is why the world hates you. Remember the words I spoke to you: 'No servant is greater than his master.' If they persecuted me, they will persecute you also . . ." (John 15:18–20).

There are two points here. First, Jesus suffered. Suffering was his lot, and it has always been the lot of God's godly people. It must be that way since

4. James Montgomery Boice, *The Gospel of John: An Expositional Commentary*, vol. 5, *John 18:1—21:25* (Grand Rapids: Zondervan, 1979). I discuss the various non-Christian approaches, though in different terms, and the uniquely Christian approach to suffering in chapter 1, pp. 13–21.

they were (and are) living in a sinful world. Second, suffering proves that we are on the side of Jesus and these godly people, for if we were not, the world would approve of us rather than being hostile.

Jonathan Chao, president of Christ's College, Taipei, and director of the Chinese Church Research Center in Hong Kong, has studied suffering in the context of the suffering of the church in China. He says, "One can almost say that suffering for Christ is a mark of discipleship."[5] D. Martyn Lloyd-Jones, who explores this line of thought extensively in his study of Romans 8:17, says, "If you are suffering as a Christian, and because you are a Christian, it is one of the surest proofs you can ever have of the fact that you are a child of God."[6] That is an important use of persecution. It proves that we are Christians and therefore disciples for Christ.

2. *Purification.* Not all suffering is in the form of persecution, however. Some of it is from God and is for no other reason than to produce growth and holiness. This is what the author of Hebrews was talking about when he wrote in reference to Jesus, "In bringing many sons to glory, it was fitting that God, for whom and through whom everything exists, should make the author of their salvation perfect through suffering" (Heb. 2:10).

That is a bold thing to say, of course, for it suggests that in some way Jesus was not perfect, which causes us to think immediately, though incorrectly, of some moral imperfection. We would be wrong to think that, since Jesus was utterly without sin. He was morally impeccable. Nevertheless, as Luke says, his life in the flesh included growth "in wisdom and stature, and in favor with God and man" (Luke 2:52). Perfection means wholeness, and Jesus grew into a wholeness of experience and trust in God through such things as poverty, temptation, misunderstanding, loneliness, abuse, and betrayal. God used these and many other experiences to "perfect" him. He also uses them to perfect us.

We are sinners, of course. So one image the Bible uses in speaking of this similar work in us is the refining of precious metal (Zech. 13:9; Mal. 3:3). It pictures God as a skilled refiner, heating the ore until the dross that has been mixed with it rises to the surface, where it may be scraped off. The refiner knows the metal is ready when he can see his face reflected in the glimmering molten surface. In the same way, God purifies us until he can see the face of Jesus Christ in his people.

One of our hymns puts it nicely:

> When through fiery trials thy pathway shall lie,
> My grace all-sufficient shall be thy supply;

5. Jonathan Chao, "Witness in Suffering," a paper prepared for the Second Asian Leadership Conference on Evangelism, Singapore, October 20–27, 1987, p. 7.

6. D. M. Lloyd-Jones, *Romans: An Exposition of Chapter 8:5–17, The Sons of God* (Grand Rapids: Zondervan, 1974), p. 433.

> The flame shall not hurt thee, I only design
> Thy dross to consume and thy gold to refine.

Another image of the Christian's suffering is of God disciplining us as an earthly father disciplines his children. The author of Hebrews writes of this, too, saying, "Endure hardship as discipline; God is treating you as sons. For what son is not disciplined by his father? If you are not disciplined (and everyone undergoes discipline), then you are illegitimate children and not true sons. . . . Our fathers disciplined us for a little while as they thought best; but God disciplines us for our good, that we may share in his holiness. No discipline seems pleasant at the time, but painful. Later on, however, it produces a harvest of righteousness and peace for those who have been trained by it" (Heb. 12:7–8, 10–11).

3. *Training.* A third kind of suffering also has value for Christians and can be likened to the suffering endured when a soldier is trained for combat by his commanding officer or, for that matter, the suffering endured in the battle itself. Paul wrote to Timothy, "Endure hardness with us like a good soldier of Christ Jesus" (2 Tim. 2:3). Elsewhere he changes the image and speaks of the rigorous preparation of an athlete: "I beat my body and make it my slave so that after I have preached to others, I myself will not be disqualified for the prize" (1 Cor. 9:27).

If you are called to endure any of these three kinds of suffering, you should be encouraged by them because they prove that you are a child of God and are being prepared to be used by him in the spiritual warfare that will lead to final victory.

The Power of the Christian's Witness

A second value of suffering is that *our witness to Christ is empowered by it.* I do not mean that we grow stronger in our ability to witness to Christ to the extent that we are called to endure persecution or some other form of suffering, though that is undoubtedly true. The blind man of John 9 grew stronger in his witness every time the religious authorities leaned on him to get him to modify his testimony. I mean, rather, that the witness of Christians carries particular weight when it is given under duress, when it is evident to everyone that it would be easier and apparently more rational to back off from one's witness or even, as Job was advised by his wife, to "curse God and die!" (Job 2:9).

Physical suffering gives particular clout to the witness of Christians. It means something special when a person can testify to God's grace when he or she is suffering from acute bodily pain or while dying. It is even more convincing when Christians bear witness to Jesus when they might suffer the loss of all things for it.

I previously mentioned Jonathan Chao and his insights into Christian suffering. He has studied the suffering church in China and reports many instances of this empowerment. One young Chinese pastor was imprisoned in 1960 and released in 1979. When he was released he discovered that during that nineteen-year period his parish had grown from 300 to 5,000 professing Christians. Today that same community has grown to 20,000.

In 1982 a Christian community in central China dispatched a missionary team in response to a Macedonian-type cry for help from another area. In a month of intense work they had established several new churches. But then most of the senior pastors were arrested. They were imprisoned for four years. However, their arrest forced the younger pastors to take over the leadership positions, and as a result not only were the home churches cared for, but the mission expanded and the growth in that area was phenomenal. People were persuaded to believe on Christ by the quality and duration of their leaders' suffering.

A fourteen-year-old girl understood this. She was one of nine young evangelists who were arrested by the local police and forced to remain kneeling in one place day and night. On the third day of this torture she fainted and was released. The others were made to suffer the same continuing torment for nine days and eight nights. Eventually they, too, were released, and when they were reunited the fourteen-year-old began to cry. "Why are you crying?" they asked.

She replied that she was crying because they had been called on to suffer for nine days while she had only been called on to suffer for three. Fourteen years old! But she understood the point of suffering for the sake of Jesus Christ and counted it not a burden but a privilege.[7]

Is it any wonder that the church in China is growing at a tremendous rate today while the church in America is barely holding its own in numbers and is declining markedly in devotion and character? Most of us want only the good life, not godliness. And our fourteen-year-olds think they are suffering if they have to turn off their personal TV and do their homework.

The Path to Glory

The final thing we need to say about the value of suffering is that *it is the ordained path to glory*. Paul says this explicitly in Romans 8:17: ". . . we share in his sufferings in order that we may also share in his glory." He also says this elsewhere. In 2 Corinthians 4:17–18 he writes joyfully, "For our light and momentary troubles are achieving for us an eternal glory that far outweighs them all. So we fix our eyes not on what is seen, but on what is unseen. For what is seen is temporary, but what is unseen is eternal."

There are two basic things to remember about suffering.

First, suffering is necessary. Jesus taught that it was necessary for *himself* when he said to the Emmaus disciples, "Did not the Christ have to suffer these things and then enter his glory?" (Luke 24:26). Then he proved that

7. These accounts appear in Jonathan Chao, "Witness in Suffering," pp. 19, 7, 8.

this was necessary by showing it to them in the Scriptures, beginning with Moses and all the prophets. Jesus taught that suffering is necessary for *us* when he said, "If they persecuted me, they will persecute you also" (John 15:20b) and "In the world ye shall have tribulation" (John 16:33a, KJV).

Second, although suffering is necessary (and has value), suffering is not the end of the story for Christians. Glory is! If suffering were the end, Christianity would be a form of masochism, suffering for suffering's sake. Since it is not the end, since suffering is the path to glory, Christianity is a religion of genuine hope and effective consolation.

The Christian who needs to worry about suffering is not the one who is suffering, particularly if it is for the sake of Jesus Christ. The person who should worry is the one who is *not* suffering, since suffering is a proof of our sonship, a means for the spread of the gospel, and the path to glory.

So let's hang in there! And let's encourage one another as we run the race and fight the long battles.

We need each other, but we have each other. That is what we are given to each other for. Thus, by the grace of God, we may actually come to the end of the warfare and be able to say as Paul did to his young protégé Timothy, "I have fought the good fight, I have finished the race, I have kept the faith. Now there is in store for me the crown of righteousness, which the Lord, the righteous Judge, will award to me on that day—and not only to me, but also to all who have longed for his appearing" (2 Tim. 4:7–8). May it be so for all God's people.

104

The Incomparable Glory

Romans 8:18

I consider that our present sufferings are not worth comparing with the glory that will be revealed in us.

There are times in every preacher's work when, if he takes the task of teaching the Bible seriously, he comes to themes that he knows are beyond him. In one sense everything in the Bible is beyond us. The Bible contains God's thoughts, and none of us is ever fully able to encompass the mind of the Infinite. Nevertheless, there are teachings that we do basically understand—because God has revealed them to us. Not so with every idea in the Bible. From time to time, we come to thoughts that we know we shall never fully understand, at least not until we get to heaven.

Glory is one of them. I call it "incomparable," not only because it resists comparison with anything we know in this life, particularly suffering, which is the contrast found in our text, but because glory is truly beyond our comprehension. At best we have only an intimation of it.

Glory is the word best used to describe God's magnificence and therefore also the dazzling magnificence of heaven and our share in it. But when

861

we look for descriptions of heaven in the Bible, in most cases the descriptions have a negative cast only. They tell us what heaven will *not* contain. The best description of heaven in the Bible is probably that of the New Jerusalem in Revelation 21. But think how the New Jerusalem is portrayed by the "loud voice from the throne"—"Now the dwelling of God is with men, and he will live with them. They will be his people, and God himself will be with them and will be their God. He will wipe every tear from their eyes. There will be no more death or mourning or crying or pain, for the old order of things has passed away" (Rev. 20:3–4). That God will dwell with us is positive. But the strength of the description is in the words: no tears, no pain, no death, no mourning! These are all negative ideas, no doubt because we cannot fully comprehend the positive things but can understand the removal of that which troubles our lives now.

And yet, the greatest word for what is in store for God's people is glory. Our text says, "I consider that our present sufferings are not worth comparing with the glory that will be revealed in us."

What Is Glory?

What is this "glory"? I find definitions of glory in the various commentaries, since incomprehensibility has never kept true scholars from defining anything. But the definitions seem inadequate to me. I want to suggest that in the case of the word *glory* we will make far better progress with the thinking of someone whose forte is literature, particularly poetry, rather than biblical scholarship. For that reason, I suggest an essay on glory by C. S. Lewis.

In the summer of 1941, Lewis was asked to give an evening sermon at the Oxford University Church of Saint Mary, and he responded by preparing the piece to which I refer. It was called "The Weight of Glory." Lewis, one of the greatest Christian apologists of the twentieth century, began by referring to a longing all human beings have for something that can hardly be expressed. He called it "a desire which no natural happiness will satisfy,"[1] and he found it in our wish to be approved by God. He argued that the biblical word for expressing this wish is glory.

At first, the idea of seeking divine approval seems to be unworthy, as it also did to Lewis when he began his study. But he said that he came to see that it is not unworthy at all but, on the contrary, expresses a natural and desirable order of things. A child wants approval from his parents and is right to want it. Creatures should want approval from their Creator. We are God's creatures, and we do. But the problem is that we behave in a way that destroys the possibility of that approval, unless God intervenes to save and transform us, which he does in Jesus Christ. One day we will appear before

---

1. C. S. Lewis, "The Weight of Glory" in *The Weight of Glory and Other Addresses* (New York: Macmillan/Collier Books, 1980), p. 8.

God for judgment. What will happen to us on that day? Lewis asked his listeners. He answered, "We can be left utterly and absolutely *outside*—repelled, exiled, estranged, finally and unspeakably ignored. On the other hand, we can be called in, welcomed, received, acknowledged. We walk every day on the razor edge between these two incredible possibilities."[2]

But there is more to glory even than this. Glory denotes not only "worth," "acceptance," or "approval." It also denotes "brightness," "splendor," and "luminosity," perhaps even "beauty." And we long for all that, too! In fact, we long not only to see what is beautiful. We want to participate in it, to be on the inside of this divine, heavenly beauty, rather than on the outside. In my judgment, it is here that Lewis, the poet, is at his best:

> We are to shine as the sun, we are to be given the Morning Star. I think I begin to see what it means. In one way, of course, God has given us the Morning Star already; you can go and enjoy the gift on many fine mornings, if you get up early enough. What more, you may ask, do we want? Ah, but we want so much more—something the books on aesthetics take little notice of. But the poets and mythologies know all about it. We do not want merely to *see* beauty, though, God knows, even that is bounty enough. We want something else which can hardly be put into words—to be united with the beauty we see, to pass into it, to receive it into ourselves, to bathe in it, to become part of it. . . .
>
> That is why the poets tell us such lovely falsehoods. They talk as if the west wind could really sweep into a human soul; but it can't. They tell us that "beauty born of murmuring sound" will pass into a human face; but it won't. Or not yet. For if we take the imagery of Scripture seriously, if we believe that God will one day give us the Morning Star and cause us to *put on* the splendor of the sun, then we may surmise that both the ancient myths and modern poetry, so false as history, may be very near the truth as prophecy.
>
> At present we are on the outside of the world, the wrong side of the door. We discern the freshness and purity of the morning, but they do not make us fresh and pure. We cannot mingle with the splendors we see. But the leaves of the New Testament are rustling with the rumor that it will not always be so. Some day, God willing, we shall get *in*. When human souls have become as perfect in voluntary obedience as the inanimate creation is in its lifeless obedience, then they will put on its glory, or rather that greater glory of which Nature is only the first sketch.[3]

Do we understand the meaning of glory now? No, I do not think we do, at least not fully. But we have a framework with which we can address the biblical teaching and uncover the specific contribution of our text.

2. Ibid., p. 15.
3. Ibid., pp. 16, 17.

Ichabod

The first thing the Bible adds to our understanding is that we long for glory because we once enjoyed it. I do not mean that individually we did. We did not exist prior to our births. I mean that we enjoyed glory once as a race—in Adam. Adam was made "in the image of God" (Gen. 1:26–27), which means, as D. Martyn Lloyd-Jones says, "that man at the beginning had a kind of glory."[4] He was like God, and he may even have been clothed with the splendor of God like a garment, as one commentator has suggested.

Yet what is man's condition today? Man is a disgrace compared to what he once was. He is a fallen being. Over him should be written the tragic Old Testament name "Ichabod," meaning "the glory has departed." It has departed from his body, from his soul, and from his spirit.

Man was once a beautiful physical specimen. The man Adam and the woman Eve were the glory of creation. They excelled the rest of the created order in every respect. But when they sinned, physical decay, sickness, suffering, and eventually physical death came upon them. God said, "Dust you are and to dust you will return" (Gen. 3:19b). They were not originally destined to die, but die they did. Man was also beautiful in soul, the most beautiful of all the creatures. He had a nobility that transcends our ability to fathom. But once Adam and Eve sinned, that beautiful soul was tarnished. Now they began to lie and cheat and shift the blame from their own failings to those of others. Most significant was the ruination of their spirits. The spirit was that part of Adam and Eve that had communion with God. They had walked and talked with God in the garden. But once they fell, they no longer sought God out. They hid from him, and the encounter that eventually came was a judgment.

We enjoyed glory once, which is why we long for it so much. But it is gone, gone with the wind. What a marvelous thing it is then, when we turn to the Bible, to find that the end of our salvation in Christ is not merely deliverance from sin and evil and their consequences, but glorification. God is restoring to us all that our first parents lost.

More Than Adam Lost

This is what Paul is beginning to deal with here in Romans, which brings us to our text. But as soon as we turn to that text and try to place it in its context, we notice that something greater even than the restoration of Adam and Eve's lost glory is involved. As we read on in Romans 8 we find that we are to have an enjoyment of God and a participation in God that surpasses Adam's.

Martyn Lloyd-Jones says,

4. D. M. Lloyd-Jones, *Romans, An Exposition of Chapter 8:17–39, The Final Perseverance of the Saints* (Grand Rapids: Zondervan, 1976), p. 4.

Adam was perfect man, but his perfection fell short of glorification. There was room for development, and it is clear that glorification was the ultimate that was intended for man. As man he was perfect; there was no blemish in him, there was no sin in him; there was no fault in him. He was in a state of innocence, but innocence falls short of glorification. But what is held before us and offered to us in Christ, and promised us in him, is nothing less than glorification. The thing to which man, if he had continued to keep God's commandments, would have arrived, and which would have been given to him as a reward for his obedience, is the thing that is now freely given us in and through our Lord and Savior Jesus Christ.[5]

Weighed in the Balance

All this brings me directly to the text. For in Romans 8:18 Paul is comparing the future glory to be enjoyed by God's people to their present sufferings, but saying that the glory far outstrips their suffering. That is obvious, isn't it? For if the glory we are to enjoy is to exceed even that minimal glory enjoyed by Adam, it is certain that it will exceed the trials we are enduring now.

Paul introduces an interesting though somewhat hidden image at this point in the verbal adjective translated "not worth comparing." It is the Greek word *axios*, from the verb *agō*, which means "to drive," "lead," or "cause to move." Figuratively used, it refers to something that is heavy enough to promote motion in a balance or, as we would say, to tip the scales. When we remember that the word *glory* itself denotes something that is weighty or has substance, it is clear what Paul is suggesting. He is saying that the future glory laid up for us is so weighty that our present sufferings are as feathers compared to it and that they cannot even begin to move the scales.

Paul provides a parallel to our text in 2 Corinthians 4:16–17, following a poignant mention of the many persecutions and sufferings he had endured for the sake of Christ. He says, "Therefore we do not lose heart. Though outwardly we are wasting away, yet inwardly we are being renewed day by day. For our light and momentary troubles are achieving for us an eternal glory that far *outweighs* them all" (emphasis added).

These two passages suggest several areas of comparison between our present sufferings and the glory that is to come.

1. *Their intensity.* The first area of comparison is between the intensity of the suffering and the intensity of the glory or, as we have been saying, between the "weight" of the two. Suffering is heavy. It hurts. It can hurt so intensely that we scream with terror or cry out with pain. But, says Paul, the intensity of our sufferings is not worth comparing with the glory. And he should know. Paul suffered as much as any man has suffered, judging from

5. Ibid., p. 7.

his descriptions in 1 Corinthians 4:9–13; 2 Corinthians 4:8–12; 6:4–10; and 11:16–33. But he also had a vision of heaven's glory, having been "caught up to the third heaven" (2 Cor. 12:2). In his opinion the intensity of the former is not to be compared to the grandeur of the latter.

2. *Their location.* The second area of comparison is between the location of our sufferings and the location of our glory. That is an awkward way of putting it, of course, but it is hard to think of something better. In Romans 8:18 Paul says that the glory of God is to be revealed "in us," using a word that literally means "internally" or "in our very being." This should be contrasted with the words "though outwardly we are wasting away," which he uses in the parallel text in 2 Corinthians.

The idea seems to be this: Suffering, though felt deeply, nevertheless only affects our outward persons, our bodies. It does not affect the real "us," those redeemed beings that, says Paul, are "being renewed day by day." It is that "real me," the inner me, that is going to participate in the glory. In other words, it is as C. S. Lewis said. We are not just going to observe the beauty; we are going to share in it: "God will one day give us the Morning Star and cause us to *put on* the splendor of the sun. . . . Some day, God willing, we shall get *in*." The endurance of outward suffering is not to be compared to our participation in this glory.

3. *Their duration.* The final point of contrast between suffering and glory concerns their duration. In Romans Paul distinguishes between "present sufferings," which means those belonging to this present age, and the glory "that will be revealed," meaning the unchanging and eternal glory of the age to come. In 2 Corinthians he calls the sufferings "momentary" and glory "eternal." You and I do not think much about eternity. But if we can make ourselves think this way, it is evident that there is no comparison between the glory of the eternal state and the sufferings of this passing earthly time, however painful our sufferings may be while we are going through them.

Breaking the Spell

I want to say finally that if we can appreciate what Paul is saying in this text and get it fixed in our minds, we will find it able to change the way we look at life and the way we live—more than anything else we can imagine. It will provide two things at least.

1. *Vision.* Focusing on the promise of glory will give us a vision of life in its eternal context, which means that we will begin to see life here as it really is. We have two problems at this point. First, we are limited by our concept of time. We think in terms of the "threescore years and ten" allotted to us, or at best the few years that have led up to our earthly existence or the few years after it. We do not have a long view. Second, we are limited

by our materialism. Our reference point is what we perceive through our senses, so we have the greatest possible difficulty thinking of "the spirit" and other intangibles. We need to be delivered from this bondage and awakened from our spiritual blindness.

In "The Weight of Glory" Lewis addressed the objection of those who might consider his talk about glory as only fantasy, the weaving of a spell. He replied by admitting that perhaps that is what he was trying to do. But he reminded his listeners that spells in fairy tales are of two kinds. Some induce enchantments. Others break them. "You and I have need of the strongest spell that can be found to wake us from the evil enchantment of worldliness which has been laid upon us for nearly a hundred years."[6] That is not the way I would say it. I would speak of truth as opposed to this world's falsehood. But it is probably the same thing. Both mean that we need to emerge from our darkness into God's light.

2. *Endurance.* "Breaking the spell" will give us strength to endure whatever hardships, temptations, persecutions, or physical suffering it pleases God to send us. Suppose there were no glory. Suppose this life really were all there is. If that were the case, I for one would not endure anything, at least nothing I could avoid. And I would probably break down under the tribulations I could not avoid. But knowing that there is an eternal weight of glory waiting, I will try to do what pleases God and hang on in spite of anything.

Here is the way hymnwriter Henry F. Lyte expressed it:

> Jesus, I my cross have taken,
> All to leave and follow thee;
> Destitute, despised, forsaken,
> Thou from hence my all shalt be.
> Perish every fond ambition,
> All I've sought or hoped or known;
> Yet how rich is my condition,
> God and heaven are still my own.
>
> Man may trouble and distress me,
> 'Twill but drive me to thy breast;
> Life with trials hard may press me,
> Heaven will bring me sweeter rest.
> O 'tis not in grief to harm me
> While my love is left to me;
> O 'twere not in joy to charm me,
> Were that joy unmixed with thee.
>
> Haste then on from grace to glory,
> Armed by faith and winged by prayer;

6. Lewis, "The Weight of Glory," p. 7.

Heaven's eternal day's before thee,
God's own hand shall guide thee there.
Soon shall close thine earthly mission;
Swift shall pass thy pilgrim days;
Hope soon change to glad fruition,
Faith to sight, and prayer to praise.

There is one more word in Romans 8:18 that we need to examine. It is the word *consider* (or "reckon" in KJV). We have seen it fifteen times in this epistle, noting that it has to do with reason. It is the process by which we figure something out. I stress it because, although I referred to the idea of "breaking a spell," I do not want you to suppose that there is anything magical about this. Magic *is* for fairy tales. But we are dealing with God's real world, and we are instructed to think this out clearly.

Paul writes, "I consider that . . ." meaning that he has thought it through and concluded that "the sufferings of this present time are not worthy to be compared with the glory which shall be revealed in us" (KJV). By using this word he invites us to think it through also.

If you are a Christian, I ask, "Isn't what the apostle says in this verse true? Isn't the glory to come worth anything you might be asked to face here, however painful or distressing?" D. Martin Lloyd-Jones challenged his congregation with these words: "The great reality is the glory that is coming. . . . Hold on to this idea, that we do not really belong to this present age, that 'our citizenship is in heaven.' This present world is passing, transient, temporary. 'The world to come' is the real, the permanent world. That is the one that has substance and which will endure forever."[7]

If you know that you are part of heaven's citizenry, you will endure—and say with the hymnwriter, "yet how rich is my condition."

---

7. D. M. Lloyd-Jones, *Romans, An Exposition of Chapter 8:17-39, The Final Perseverance of the Saints*, pp. 40, 41.

105

The Redemption of Creation

Romans 8:19–21

The creation waits in eager expectation for the sons of God to be revealed. For the creation was subjected to frustration, not by its own choice, but by the will of the one who subjected it, in hope that the creation itself will be liberated from its bondage to decay and brought into the glorious freedom of the children of God.

At the end of our previous study I wrote about the importance of the word *consider* in verse 18. It refers to a rational process by which a thinking person is able to figure something out. What Paul is thinking about is, as we would say, whether the Christian life is worth it. The Christian life is not easy. It involves rigorous self-denial, persecutions, even some sufferings. Unbelievers, worldly people, seem to have it better. Why should we, too, not live only for pleasure? What is to be gained by godliness?

As Paul considers this, it becomes perfectly evident to him why the Christian way is the only rational way—for two reasons we have already studied and for another that we are to investigate now. The first reason is the contrast between the short duration of our present sufferings and the timelessness of eternity. In verse 18 Paul uses the word *present* to refer to the shortness of this temporal age and does not actually mention eternity. But in the parallel text in 2 Corinthians 4:17 he contrasts our "momentary troubles" with "eternal glory," making the point explicit.

The second reason why the Christian life is "rational" lies in the contrast between the weight of our sufferings, which is light, and the weight of the glory yet to come. Paul does not deny that the earthly sufferings we experience are grievous. In 1 and 2 Corinthians he lists some of the tribulations he endured, and they were indeed heavy. But, he says, weighty as they are, "our present sufferings are not worth comparing with the glory that will be revealed in us."

Think it out, he says. Put both on a scale. If you do, you will find that our present sufferings are really inconsequential if compared with the glory to come: "Our light and momentary troubles are achieving for us an eternal glory that far outweighs them all" (2 Cor. 4:17).

The Hopeful Cosmos

The two arguments from verse 18 are alone adequate to prove Paul's point: that the Christian life is eminently worth it. But because Paul's was an extraordinary mind, he continues the argument into verse 19 and beyond. We miss this a bit in the New International Version since, in an effort to provide smooth English sentences, the translators have eliminated the conjunction "for," which actually begins the verse. You will see that word at the start of verse 20, but "for" actually begins verse 19 and verse 18 as well.

The verses literally say, *"For* I consider. . . . *For* the creation waits. . . . *For* the creation was subjected. . . ." In other words, verses 18–21 are all part of a long and carefully sustained argument.

The new element at this point is "the creation" or, as we would probably say today, "the cosmos." It is important to get this reference straight, for the word *creation* can obviously refer to every and all things God has made: man, the angels, demons, the physical universe, animals, whatever. But is that its meaning here? A little thought will show that in these verses creation must have a restricted meaning.

John Murray does the best job of anyone in analyzing this, for he shows in his commentary that verses 20–23 clearly delimit the term. *"Angels* are not included because they were not subjected to vanity and to the bondage of corruption. *Satan* and the *demons* are not included because they cannot be regarded as longing for the manifestation of the sons of God and they will not share in the liberty of the glory of the children of God. The *children of God* themselves are not included because they are distinguished from 'the creation' (vv. 19, 21, 23). . . . The *unbelieving* of mankind cannot be included because the earnest expectation does not characterize them." In other words, "all of *rational* creation is excluded by the terms of verses 20-23." The only thing that is left is the "non-rational creation, animate and inanimate."[1]

---

1. John Murray, *The Epistle to the Romans* (Grand Rapids: Wm. B. Eerdmans, 1968), pp. 301, 302.

And that is just it! Paul is talking about the physical world of matter, plants, and animals. His argument is that nature is in a presently imperfect state, but that it is longing for the day of liberation. Paul is personifying nature, of course, but he does not mean that inanimate nature has personal feelings that correspond to ours. He means only that nature is not yet all that God has predestined it to be. It is waiting for its true fulfillment. But if nature is waiting, we should be willing to wait in hope, too, knowing that a glorious outcome is certain. This is the third reason why Christianity is worth it.

The Blind (Unbelieving) Observer

This view of creation is radically different from the world's, of course, and this is worth pursuing. In general the world makes either one of two errors. Either it deifies the cosmos, virtually worshiping it as an ideal. Or else it regards the cosmos as gradually evolving toward perfection, accompanied by the human race, which is also so evolving.

I am sure many of us have in mind that powerful television image of Carl Sagan on the science series "Cosmos," standing before a large screen on which there is a display of a segment of the night sky in its brilliant starry splendor and saying in nearly mystical tones, "The cosmos is all that is or ever was or ever will be." That is what I mean by deifying the cosmos. In this series Sagan is a portrait of unbelieving man, standing on the very tips of his toes, peering off into the distant and mysterious heavens as far as his telescopes will allow, and declaring with blind arrogance, "The world is all that is."

But Paul gives us a different picture, although he, too, pictures something staring off into the distance. That is the meaning of the words "waits in eager expectation." J. B. Phillips captures this idea literally when he translates "is on tiptoe to see. . . ." But, according to Paul, it is not man who is on tiptoe looking. It is creation itself. In other words, if Carl Sagan could see as the Christian sees, he would say that the entire cosmos is actually looking beyond itself to God. And what creation is earnestly awaiting, as it looks beyond itself, is the "glorious freedom of the children of God" that it will share.

There are few images to equal this in all Scripture.

The world makes another error that is not entirely different from the first but is related to that idea. It sees in nature some kind of ongoing and automatic perfecting principle. This is almost like saying that the world is not God yet, but it is on the way. In cosmic terms this is the principle of evolution. In human terms it is the principle of inevitable perfection: "Every day in every way I am getting better and better." In other words, "I may not be God yet, but I will be, given time." Of course, a lot of time has gone by—millions of years according to L. S. B. Leakey and other evolutionists—yet man seems to be as much unlike God as he ever was. And man's world is woefully far from perfect.

A Christian World-View

The Christian's perspective, supplied by Scripture, is at this point far more balanced and mature than anything the blind and unbelieving world can devise. The Christian doctrine of the cosmos has three parts.

1. *This is God's world.* Everything in our passage presupposes this, not least the fact that the cosmos is called "creation." That term presupposes a Creator, which is exactly what the Christian maintains is the case. This world is not eternally existent. Scientific evidence for the Big Bang alone tells us that. Nor did the world come into existence by itself. Reason tells us that. For, in order for the creation to come into being "by itself," it would have to create itself, and that would mean it was in existence before it was created. In other words, it would have had to be and *not* be at the same time and in the same relationship, which is absurd. The only rational view of origins is that God made everything.

The consequence of this for Christians is that the cosmos—the creation—has value, not because humans ascribe value to it but because God created it and it is therefore valuable to him. Here we have a fundamental divergence between the Christian and the non-Christian outlooks.

Because Christians view the creation as God's handiwork, they respect and value the cosmos but do not worship it as an end in itself. Those who do not understand that God is Creator of the cosmos either worship the universe, which I have suggested Carl Sagan comes very close to doing, or else they abuse it, stripping it of anything that is of value to themselves. People cut down entire forests, allowing the earth to erode uselessly away. Or they poison their water, killing the fish and endangering their own health. Or they pollute the air, perhaps even damaging the protective ozone layer around the earth and thereby subjecting themselves and their descendants to the sun's destructive rays.

2. *This world is not what it was created to be.* The problems with the cosmos are not only those that the human race has inflicted on it, mostly destruction and pollution. The world has also been subjected to troubles as the result of God's judgment on man, rendered at the time of the fall. God told Adam, "Cursed is the ground because of you," and "It will produce thorns and thistles for you" (Gen. 3:17–18). Nature had not sinned; Adam had. But nature was subjected to a downgrading because of him and thus entered into his judgment. It is this trouble, the result of God's judgment on sin, that Paul is particularly concerned with in Romans. He uses three words to describe it.

First, *frustration.* This is the feeling we humans have when we know we should attain to some goal and are trying to reach it but are repeatedly thrown back or defeated. I want to go carefully at this point, since Paul does not explain exactly what he is thinking of. But let me suggest that (whether or not this is exactly what he has in mind) we have a picture of the creation's "frustration" in the way nature asserts itself in the annual renewal of springtime but is constantly defeated as spring passes into autumn and autumn into winter. It is as if nature wants always to be glorious but is impeded in its attempts to be so.

If that is a valid example, it leads me to think further to the way C. S. Lewis developed the idea in the first of his Narnia Chronicles, *The Lion, the Witch, and the Wardrobe*. You may recall that in the first section of that book, when Narnia was under the power of the wicked Witch of the North, the land was in a state of perpetual winter. Spring never came. But when Aslan died and rose again, a picture of Christ's resurrection, the ice began to melt, flowers began to bloom, the trees turned green, and an eternal spring was brought into existence. Using that image, we could say that the cosmos as we know it is in a state of winter now but is looking forward to that eternal spring of which the diurnal springs we know here are only hints of what is promised.

Our winters, the "winters of our discontent," link us to inanimate nature in its and our own frustrations.

Second, *bondage*. The bondage of nature is linked to its frustration and is the cause of it. But bondage speaks of the actual state of things, while frustration has to due with the resulting feelings. Bondage literally means slavery, wherein one entity is unwillingly subjected to the authority of another. This is what Paul means here. He is saying that although nature does not want to be as it is, it is powerless to do anything about it. The creation needs to be delivered by God.

This is what redemption is all about, of course, which is why I have called this chapter "The Redemption of Creation." The creation longs for redemption, and it will have it when the children of God are likewise fully redeemed.

Third, *decay*. Nothing Paul says about creation is as obvious to today's scientific observers as this: the cosmos is decaying or running down. This is called the second law of thermodynamics. It is another scientific axiom that neither mass nor energy are destroyed but are only converted from one to the other. Einstein's formula of relativity, $E=Mc^2$, is an expression of this. But although, by this formula, energy is not being destroyed, it is nevertheless becoming increasingly dissipated, which means that it is becoming increasingly less useful. For example, the sun's energy is not being lost even though its mass is being converted into energy. But that energy is being dissipated into space, where it is not accomplishing anything, and one day the sun will use up its energy and be gone. The whole universe is like that. It is all running down, dissipating, becoming increasingly useless.

However, Paul was probably thinking specifically of death, which comes to all living things, rather than the scientific principles I mentioned, since he would hardly have known of these "laws" except by general observation. It is not only the sun that is dying, of course. Living creatures die, too.

3. *The world will one day be renewed.* The third point in a Christian doctrine of creation is that, in spite of creation's current frustration, bondage, and decay, the day is coming when the world will be renewed. Spring will come, and the winter of creation's present discontent will be past history.

I am not sure how to understand this, though I know the options. Some people think of the redemption of creation in terms of the millennium, when Christ will rule on earth and a glorious "golden age" will be ushered in. Some think of this as a future eternal state, intangible and quite cut off from this present age of imperfection and suffering. Perhaps the closest we can come (and still be fairly sure we are on the right track) is by an analogy to the "redemption of our bodies," which is brought into the picture in verse 24. The redemption of our bodies means the resurrection of our bodies. So perhaps this is what creation will experience, a resurrection. In our resurrections we will have a continuity of our bodies (our earthly bodies will be raised), but our bodies will be different, heavenly, glorified. Creation will probably experience something like that, too.

Isn't this what the text must mean when it says, "Creation itself will be liberated from its bondage to decay and brought into the glorious freedom of the children of God" (v. 21)?

Paradise Regained

A few paragraphs back I traced the origin of the world's troubles to Genesis 3, where we are told that creation was subjected to the "frustration" described by Paul because of the sin of our first parents. I return to that chapter now, since in Genesis 3 we also find the promise of God's solution to the problem, which puts the redemption of creation in proper context.

What happened in the Garden of Eden is that Satan, the great enemy of God, tried to impede God's plans to create a world of men and women who would know and love him. Satan thought that if he could get the man and woman to rebel against God, he would defeat God's purpose. When he accomplished their fall, he thought he had done so. Indeed, he seemed to have done even better. For not only did he draw our first parents away from God, he brought the judgment of God upon creation itself. That beautiful world was tarnished, spoiled. It began to decay, and the creatures who had caused its fall and God's judgment soon added their own destructive efforts to its ruin.

Ah, but God intervened. It is true that God came in judgment on Satan and on the woman and the man and the world they had known. But even as he pronounced a judgment upon Satan, God also gave a promise of a future deliverer, saying, "And I will put enmity between you and the woman, and between your offspring and hers; he will crush your head, and you will strike his heel" (Gen. 3:15). This was a promise that Jesus would come one day to save all who would believe on him, but it was also more than that. It was a promise that in Christ God would frustrate Satan, undo his destructive works, and once again bring a redeemed human race into a redeemed creation. The promise was that Paradise will be perfected and regained.

As I said, I do not know what all this is going to mean, anymore than I know exactly what our resurrection bodies will be like. But I know how the prophet Isaiah speaks of it. In that day, he says:

> The wolf will live with the lamb,
>   the leopard will lie down with the goat,
> the calf and the lion and the yearling together;
>   and a little child will lead them.
> The cow will feed with the bear,
>   their young will lie down together,
>   and the lion will eat straw like the ox.
> The infant will play near the hole of the cobra,
>   and the young child put his hand into the viper's nest.
> They will neither harm nor destroy
>   on all my holy mountain,
> For the earth will be full of the knowledge of the LORD
>   as the waters cover the sea.
>
> Isaiah 11:6–9

Poetical? Of course, but what a powerful picture of the redeemed world that will be! The creation is waiting for that day, says Paul. And if it is, can we not wait in hopeful expectation, too? And be faithful children of God?

Looking to Jesus

What I am commending to you is a Christian perspective on this life and all we know in it, what the theologians call a world-and-life view. And I am suggesting, as Paul does, that adopting it will rearrange your values and change your approach to suffering and the disappointments of life. If you learn to reason as Paul does, you will experience the following:

1. *You will not be surprised when things go wrong in this life.* This world is not a good place. We live in a fallen environment. Your plans will misfire, you will often fail, others will destroy what you have spent long years and much toil to accomplish. This will be true even if you are a Christian and are trying to follow Jesus. But your successes are not what life is all about. What matters is your love for God and your faithfulness.

2. *You will not place your ultimate hope in anything human beings can do to improve this world's conditions.* This does not mean that you will fail to do what good you can do in this life as well as encourage others in their efforts to do good. As a Christian, you will. But you will not delude yourself into thinking that the salvation of the world's ills will be brought about by mere human efforts. You will feed the poor, but you will know that Jesus said, "The poor you will always have with you" (Matt. 26:11a). You will pray for your leaders, but you will know that they are but sinful men and women like yourself and that they will always disappoint you.

3. *You will keep your eyes on Jesus.* Where else can you look? All others are disappointing, and everything is crumbling about you. Only he is worthy of your trust. He has promised to return in his glory, and we know that when he does return and we see him in his glory, we will be like him (1 John 3:2). Moreover, when we are made like him in his glory, the creation that is also straining forward to that day will become glorious, too.

No wonder the early Christians prayed, "*Maranatha!*" Come, Lord Jesus!

106

The Redemption of Our Bodies

Romans 8:22-25

We know that the whole creation has been groaning as in the pains of childbirth right up to the present time. Not only so, but we ourselves, who have the firstfruits of the Spirit, groan inwardly as we wait eagerly for our adoption as sons, the redemption of our bodies. For in this hope we were saved. But hope that is seen is no hope at all. Who hopes for what he already has? But if we hope for what we do not yet have, we wait for it patiently.

In the passage of Romans 8 that begins with verse 22, and (in the following paragraph) ends with verse 27, we find a word that is repeated three times and yet is found nowhere else in this letter. In fact, it is found only six more times in the entire New Testament. It is the Greek word *stenazō* (variants, *sustenazō* and *stenagmos*), and it is translated "groan" (v. 23), "groans" (v. 26), and "groaning" (v. 22). The interesting thing is that it is applied to three different entities in these verses: to creation, to ourselves, and to the Holy Spirit.

Of creation Paul says, "We know that the whole creation has been groaning as in the pains of childbirth right up to the present time" (v. 22).

Of ourselves he says, "Not only so, but we ourselves, who have the firstfruits of the Spirit, groan inwardly as we wait eagerly for our adoption as sons, the redemption of our bodies" (v. 23).

Of the Holy Spirit he says, ". . . We do not know what we ought to pray for, but the Spirit himself intercedes for us with groans that words cannot express" (v. 26).

Two of these references are hard to understand. Since Paul is thinking of the inanimate creation and not men, angels, or demons in verse 22, it is hard to imagine how mere matter or even plants or animals can be conceived of as groaning. It is also difficult to envision the Holy Spirit's groans, though for different reasons. The one part of these verses that is not difficult to understand is *our* groaning, since groaning is a part of daily life with which almost anyone can easily identify.

Still, we need to see two things about this human groaning if we are to understand the verses to which we now come.

First, the groaning mentioned in verse 23 is that of believers in Jesus Christ and not that of all people generally. Paul makes this explicit when he writes that "we ourselves, who have the firstfruits of the Spirit, groan inwardly." I do not think this excludes the kind of groanings that Christians share with other people, expressions of grief caused by physical suffering or the loss of a loved one, for instance. But it means more. Christians grieve over the presence of sin in their lives, which unbelievers do not. In fact, believers grieve for sin increasingly as they grow in Christ. Christians also groan as the result of persecutions suffered for the sake of their life and witness, and this is also different from what non-Christians experience.

Second, the groaning of Christians is not mere grief over the things I mentioned. It is *expectant* grief, that is, grief that looks forward to a time when all that is causing pain will be removed and salvation will be consummated. Christian groaning is a joyful grief that gives birth to a sure hope and patient endurance.

The passage itself shows this, since hope and patience are the notes on which the verses end. But there is also a powerful image at the start of this paragraph that shows how the groans of Christians are to be interpreted. Paul uses the image of childbirth: ". . . the whole creation has been groaning as in the pains of childbirth" (v. 22), adding that "we ourselves . . . [also] groan" (v. 23). This is an important analogy, because it points beyond the cause of grief to its joyful consummation. The pains of childbirth are real pains, severe ones. But they are not endless; they last only for a time. Nor are they hopeless. On the contrary, they are filled with joyful expectation, since under normal circumstances they climax in the birth of a child.

Paul is saying that our griefs as Christians are like that. We groan, but we do so in expectation of a safe delivery.

Groans and Glory

This is a thoughtful continuation of the arguments Paul has been working out since the beginning of Romans 8. The theme of the chapter is the Christian's assurance that he or she has been saved by Christ and will be kept in this salvation by the love and power of God the Father.

The first part of the chapter distinguished between those who are truly saved and those who are not. Paul was aware of the dangers of presumption, of claiming an assurance that one has no right to unless one's conduct shows that the Spirit of Jesus Christ really is within. But having made that point—that those who are Christ's *will* live for Christ—Paul then got into his major argument, showing that true Christians can know they are saved and be confident in that assurance. We have seen that there are four proofs: (1) the fact that those who are Christians really do live for Christ; (2) the internal sense Christians have of being members of God's family; (3) the Holy Spirit's direct witness with our spirits; and (4) suffering. Paul said, "Now if we are children, then we are heirs—heirs of God and co-heirs with Christ, if indeed we share in his sufferings in order that we may also share in his glory" (v. 17).

But that is a problem, as we saw when we studied that verse. Sufferings? We would think that it would be the absence of sufferings, not their presence, that would prove we belong to Christ. If God loves us, shouldn't he keep us from suffering? Or isn't he able to? When things get hard it is natural that we begin to doubt God's favor rather than being assured of it.

That, of course, is why Paul has digressed to talk about suffering and why he is talking about our groanings now. It is why he has explained the involvement of creation in our present distress. What he is saying is that the sufferings we and "the whole creation" endure are the sufferings of childbirth and are therefore proof that the new age is coming. And it is why, although we do groan, we do not groan hopelessly. On the contrary, our groanings intensify our hope and enable us to wait patiently for the consummation.

The Resurrection of the Body

These verses also do something else that is important. They give substance to the Christian hope. That is, they begin to flesh out the main features of the consummation for which we are waiting. In verse 23 this is done by means of three word pictures or images: (1) "the firstfruits of the Spirit," (2) "our adoption as sons," and (3) "the redemption of our bodies." It is easiest to take them in reverse order.

What does Paul mean by the redemption of our bodies? This is an easy question to answer: he means the resurrection, the chief element in the hope of Christians.

This is an important idea to bring in at this point for at least two reasons. First, Paul has been talking about our sufferings, and it is chiefly in our bodies that we experience them. Physical suffering, whether from illness or abuse inflicted by persecutors, is experienced in the body. And there is even a sense in which psychological wounds are physical, though we do not usually think of them that way. We experience them in our minds, which are hard to distinguish from mere brain matter and neurological connections, but the effects are often directly physiological since they are seen in such things as sleeplessness, ulcers, hypertension, and other maladies.

Second, we are our bodies, as well as our spirits and souls. Therefore, salvation must include our bodies if it is to be complete.

Suppose someone should ask you, "Are you saved?" How would you answer? As a Christian it would be proper to answer in three ways. You could say, "Yes, I have been saved." In that case, you would be pointing back to the death of Jesus Christ on your behalf and to that past work of the Holy Spirit in turning you from a path of sin and joining you to Jesus. You could also say, "I am being saved." If you said that, you would be pointing to the continuing work of the Holy Spirit in your life, much as Paul did in the earlier part of this chapter. You would be thinking of the Spirit's work of sanctification. Finally, you could also say, "I am going to be saved." In that case, you would be thinking of the resurrection, when the work of God—begun by the death of Christ and continued by the work of the Holy Spirit in joining you to Jesus and sanctifying you—will be completed. Paul is thinking of that consummation here.

But there is one more question directly related to our text. Paul is writing about the Christian's resurrection, but that is not the word he uses to refer to it. He calls it "the *redemption* of our bodies." Redemption usually refers to the work of Christ in delivering us from sin's bondage by his death. Why does Paul use "redemption" instead of "resurrection" here?

Robert Haldane, one of the best of all commentators on Romans, suggests an interesting answer:

> When this term is . . . used, it commonly denotes two things—the one, that the deliverance spoken of is effected in a manner glorious and conspicuous, exhibiting the greatest effort of power; the other, that it is a complete deliverance, placing us beyond all danger. On this ground, then, it is evident that no work is better entitled to the appellation of redemption than that of the reestablishment of our bodies, which will be an illustrious effect of the infinite power of God. It is the work of the Lord of nature—of him who holds in his hands the keys of life and death. His light alone can dispel the darkness of the tomb. It is only his hand that can break its seal and its silence. On this account the apostle appeals, with an accumulation of terms, to the exceeding greatness of the power of God to us-ward who believe, according to the working of his mighty power, which he wrought in Christ when he raised him from the dead (Eph. 1:19, 20).[1]

1. Robert Haldane, *An Exposition of the Epistle to the Romans* (MacDill AFB: MacDonald Publishing, 1958), p. 377.

It is no wonder that we groan in these bodies. They are the seat of physical weakness, on the one hand, and of our sinful natures, on the other. But we groan in hope, knowing that these weak and sinful bodies are going to be transformed into bodies that are strong, sinless, and glorious, like the resurrection body of the Lord Jesus Christ.

Our Adoption as Sons

The second image that Paul offers of our sure hope of future glory is "adoption," speaking of "our adoption as sons." This is the same word that we have already seen in verse 15, where it was translated "sonship."

But that creates a problem. In verse 15 our adoption was treated as something that has already taken place. That is the way we considered it when we were at that point in the chapter. I spoke of our having been taken out of the family of Satan and having been brought into the family of God. It corresponds to the way a young couple today might adopt a child who has no parents or has parents who are unable to care for him or her. But in verse 23 adoption is treated as something still in the future, something for which "we wait eagerly." How can adoption be both past and future at the same time?

The answer, of course, is that the word is used in two senses. In one sense we have already received our adoption, since we have been brought into God's family. Nothing is ever going to change that family relationship. Yet in a second sense we still wait for our adoption, because we do not yet enjoy all its privileges.

I am convinced that when Paul speaks of "our adoption as sons" in verse 23, he is thinking of the special Roman custom of adoption and not of what we usually think of when someone uses that word. The Romans (as well as the Greeks) had adoption in our sense, that is, when a child is taken out of one family and is placed into another. But the Romans also had an important ceremony in which the son of a leading Roman family would be acknowledged publicly as the son and heir. It corresponded somewhat to the Jews' *bar mitzvah*, when a Jewish boy becomes a "son of the covenant," though among Romans it was less religious and more a matter of adulthood and the right of inheritance.

In the opening pages of Lloyd C. Douglas's religious novel *The Robe*, the young daughter of the Gallio family, Lucia, is reflecting on the day her brother Marcellus was adopted in such a ceremony. Marcellus was seventeen years old. Douglas writes, "What a wonderful day that was, with all their good friends assembled in the Forum to see Marcellus—clean-shaven for the first time in his life—step forward to receive his white toga. Cornelius Capito and Father had made speeches, and then they had put the white toga on Marcellus. Lucia had been so proud and happy that her heart had pounded and her throat had hurt, though she was only nine then, and couldn't know much about the ceremony except that Marcellus was expected to act like a man now—though sometimes he forgot to."[2]

Later Marcellus describes the occasion to a friend named Paulus: "When a Roman of our sort comes of age, Paulus, there is an impressive ceremony by which we are inducted into manhood. . . . Well do I remember—the thrill of it abides with me still—how all of our relatives and friends assembled, that day, in the stately Forum Julium. My father made an address, welcoming me into Roman citizenship. It was as if I had never lived until that hour. I was so deeply stirred, Paulus, that my eyes swam with tears. And then good old Cornelius Capito made a speech, a very serious one, about Rome's right to my loyalty, my courage, and my strength. I knew that tough old Capito had a right to talk of such matters, and I was proud that he was there! They beckoned to me, and I stepped forward. Capito and my father put the white toga on me—and life had begun!"[3]

As I say, I am convinced that this is what Paul has in mind in verse 23. You will recall that earlier he had spoken of our being "heirs of God and co-heirs of Christ, if indeed we share in his sufferings" (v. 17). We are sharing in the sufferings now, but the day is coming when we shall enter into the full rights of our inheritance in glory.

Firstfruits and the Full Harvest

The third picture of the consummation to which believers in Christ are moving is a harvest, suggested by the words "firstfruits of the Spirit." This does not refer to the fruit of the Spirit, as Paul does in Galatians ("But the fruit of the Spirit is love, joy, peace, patience, kindness, goodness, faithfulness, gentleness and self-control," Gal. 5:22–23). It refers to the Holy Spirit himself as the "firstfruits," which is a harvest image drawn from Jewish life.

The custom is described in Leviticus 23:9–14, which says in part, "When you enter the land I am going to give you and you reap its harvest, bring to the priest a sheaf of the first grain you harvest. He is to wave the sheaf before the LORD so it will be accepted on your behalf; the priest is to wave it on the day after the Sabbath" (vv. 10, 11). The portion of the harvest presented to the priest was called the firstfruits, and it was in the nature of an offering that consecrated the entire harvest. In this Old Testament ceremony the firstfruits were something the devout Jewish worshiper gave God. But in the New Testament Paul usually reverses this and speaks of the firstfruits as what God gives us as an earnest or down payment on the full blessings to come.

The full blessing is the harvest, a joyful time for which those who labor are willing to endure great hardship.

2. Lloyd C. Douglas, *The Robe* (Boston: Houghton Mifflin, 1945), p. 3.
3. Ibid., p. 66.

John Stott sums this up by saying, "So the Holy Spirit, who is the Spirit of sonship and makes us the children of God (v. 15), and then witnesses with our spirit that we are God's children (v. 16), is also himself the pledge of our complete adoption to be the sons of God, when our bodies are redeemed."[4] In this, as also in the development of the other two themes, we are reminded of some of the things Paul said earlier.

Hope and Patient Endurance

At the beginning of this study I discussed the word *groan*, pointing out that it is used of the creation, ourselves, and the Holy Spirit. I said that the usage we understand best is our own groaning, since we groan in our bodily weakness and fleshly sins. But groaning is not the only thing Paul says we do. He also says that "we hope" (v. 25) and "we wait" (vv. 23, 25), adding in the later case that we do it both "eagerly" and "patiently."

1. *We hope.* Hope is one of the very great words of the Christian vocabulary, occurring in such important phrases as our "blessed hope" (Titus 2:13) and "the hope of glory" (Col. 1:27). It is one of the three great virtues listed in 1 Corinthians 13:13 ("These three remain: faith, hope and love"). Paul has already written about hope in Romans 5: ". . . we know that suffering produces perseverance; perseverance, character; and character, hope. And hope does not disappoint us, because God has poured out his love into our hearts by the Holy Spirit, whom he has given us" (vv. 3–5).

The word *hope* has two senses: (1) an attitude of hopefulness, and (2) the content of that for which we hope. Both uses of the word occur in our text, the idea of content in verse 24 ("in this hope we were saved") and the attitude of hopefulness in verses 24 and 25 ("we hope").

What is striking about the Christian attitude of hopefulness is that it is a "sure and certain hope" and not mere wishful thinking. What makes it sure and certain is the content. The specific content is the return of Jesus Christ together with the things we have been mentioning in these verses: the resurrection of the body, the adoption of God's children, and the gathering of God's harvest. These things are all promised to us by God. Hence, the Christian hopes in confidence, a confidence grounded not in the strength of one's emotional outlook but on the sure Word of God, who cannot lie. If God says that these things are coming, it is reasonable and safe for us to hope confidently in them.

2. *We wait.* More specifically, we wait for them, which is the second verb Paul uses. Verse 23 says, "We wait eagerly." Verse 25 says, "We wait . . . patiently." It is important to take the two adverbs together, because biblical "patience" is not passivity. This is an active, though patient waiting. It

4. John R. W. Stott, *Men Made New: An Exposition of Romans 5–8* (Grand Rapids: Baker Book House, 1984), p. 97.

expresses itself in vigorous service for Christ even while we wait for his appearing.

The word *eagerly* makes us think of the creation waiting "in eager expectation for the sons of God to be revealed," which Paul introduced in verse 19, though the Greek words are not the same. In verse 19 Paul pictured creation standing on tiptoe, as it were, looking forward with outstretched neck in eager anticipation of the consummation. It is a grand picture, and it is what we are to be doing, too. It is one mark of a true Christian.

Here is how D. Martyn Lloyd-Jones puts it:

> Hope is the measure of true Christianity, which is through and through other-worldly. Pseudo-Christianity always looks chiefly at this world. Popular Christianity is entirely this-worldly and is not interested in the other world. But true Christianity has its eye mainly on the world which is to come. It is not primarily concerned even with deliverance from hell, and punishment, and all the things that trouble us and weary us. That really belongs to the past. True Christianity "sets its affection on things which are above, not on things which are on the earth." It is that which says, "We look not at the things which are seen, but at the things which are not seen: for the things which are seen are temporal, but the things which are not seen are eternal" (2 Cor. 4:17, 18).[5]

Paradoxically, of course, it is only these heavenly-minded people who are able to make any real or lasting difference in the world.

5. D. M. Lloyd-Jones, *Romans, An Exposition of Chapter 8:17–39, The Final Perseverance of the Saints* (Grand Rapids: Zondervan, 1976), p. 104.

107

The Holy Spirit's Help in Prayer

Romans 8:26–27

In the same way, the Spirit helps us in our weakness. We do not know what we ought to pray for, but the Spirit himself intercedes for us with groans that words cannot express. And he who searches our hearts knows the mind of the Spirit, because the Spirit intercedes for the saints in accordance with God's will.

I do not know of any subject that has caused more perplexity for more Christians than the subject of prayer, unless perhaps it is the matter of knowing God's will. And, of course, the two are related. They are related in this text as well as in other places, for the verses we are now studying speak of the Holy Spirit's help in prayer, concluding that "he who searches our hearts knows the mind of the Spirit, because the Spirit intercedes for the saints *in accordance with God's will*" (v. 27, emphasis added).

Christians who want to pray in accordance with God's will find themselves asking: What should I pray for? How should I pray? Can I pray with confidence, "claiming" things by faith? Or do I have to make my prayers tentative, adding always, "If it be your will"?

What happens if I pray wrongly? Can prayer do harm? Does prayer get God to change his mind? Can it change God's plans? If not, does it even matter if I pray?

As I say, I do not know any subject that has caused more perplexity and been more of a continuing problem for more believers than this one. But we have help in this area, the help of the Holy Spirit, which is great indeed. It is what Romans 8:26 and 27 are about.

"In the Same Way"

These verses begin with the phrase "in the same way." So we first need to ask what this refers to. It is a connecting phrase, of course, and most of the commentators link it to what immediately precedes. That is, they link it to the Christian's hope. The idea seems to be that we endure sufferings in this life but that we are able to handle them in two ways: first, by hope, that is, by a sure and patient looking forward to the final redemption of our bodies; and second, by the help of the Holy Spirit in prayer.

That is a valid connection, of course. But I think that D. Martyn Lloyd-Jones is right when he links the apostle's teaching about prayer in verses 26–27 to his teaching about prayer in verses 15–17. The earlier passage taught that the Holy Spirit enables us to pray, assuring us that we truly are God's children and encouraging us to cry out "*Abba*, Father." That teaching was followed by an extensive digression dealing with the sufferings endured in this life before we come into God's presence. But then, having dealt with sufferings, Paul returns once more to the Spirit's work in enabling us to pray, adding that the Spirit also "helps us in our weakness" (v. 26).

In other words, Paul returns to the subject of assurance, which is the chapter's main theme. The point of these two verses is that the Holy Spirit's help in prayer is another way we can know that we are God's children and that nothing will ever separate us from his love.[1]

Is Prayer a Problem?

A number of years ago the Bible Study Hour, on which I am the speaker, offered a small booklet containing several messages by another writer and myself and entitled "Is Prayer a Problem?" For most people it obviously is, as I suggested above. So the most important question is not the one in the title of that booklet but rather: *Why* is prayer a problem? Furthermore, what's to be *done* about it? At this point our text is extremely helpful.

Let's take the first question—Why is prayer a problem?—and deal with that. Paul answers that it is because of "our weakness."

When Paul speaks of our weakness, it is important to realize that he is not speaking of sin. Weakness is not sin. It is true that we are sinners and

1. D. M. Lloyd-Jones, *Romans, An Exposition of Chapter 8:17–39, The Final Perseverance of the Saints* (Grand Rapids: Zondervan, 1976), pp. 120–123.

often sin and that sin is a barrier to communication with God. David said of his prayer life, "If I had cherished sin in my heart, the LORD would not have listened" (Ps. 66:18). Isaiah told the Israelites, "But your iniquities have separated you from your God" (Isa. 59:2a). But that is not what is being spoken of here. The problem Paul is concerned with is weakness, and this is not sin but rather is grounded in our frailty as human beings.

What kinds of weakness are there? *Physical weakness* is one kind. The story of the disciples who were left by Jesus in the Garden of Gethsemane to pray provides one illustration. They kept falling asleep even though Jesus had instructed them to stay awake and pray with him.

But in Romans 8 the weakness Paul has in mind is *ignorance* or a *lack of understanding*. It is expressed in the fact that "we do not know what we ought to pray for." This is not a question of *how* to pray but of *what* to pray. Paul means that we do not know what we should ask of God. What is God's will for us or others? In our human limitations we simply do not know and therefore do not know how to pray rightly.

Notice that when Paul writes the word *weakness* he adds the word *our,* thereby putting himself in an identical position. In other words, the weakness that makes prayer difficult is not something that only new, baby, or immature Christians have. It is part of our common human condition. Even the greatest saints have had this difficulty.

Let me offer four illustrations.

First, there is the case of Job. I pick Job because he had the testimony of God that he was a righteous man: "Have you considered my servant Job? There is no one on earth like him; he is blameless and upright, a man who fears God and shuns evil" (Job 1:8). There was no outstanding sin in Job that might have been a barrier between him and God. Yet, because of the things that happened to him, Job was a confused man. He did not know why he was suffering as he was. His comforters thought they knew. They would not have had any difficulty praying, at least about Job. They had it all figured out—incorrectly. Job, who knew his heart, had no answers. He prayed, "Why have you made me your target? Have I become a burden to you? Why do you not pardon my offenses and forgive my sins? . . ." (Job. 7:20b–21).

Elijah is another example. This great prophet was a courageous man, having stood against the powerful prophets of Baal on Mount Carmel and by God's provision having won a great victory. Yet after the battle he was so emotionally and physically drained that he retreated to the desert fearing Jezebel, who had threatened to kill him. What did he pray? He asked to die, arguing, "I have had enough, LORD. Take my life; I am no better than my ancestors" (1 Kings 19:4). That much was true; he was no better. But it was still a confused and foolish prayer, since God had more for him to do.

Job teaches that a man can be righteous and still not know what to pray. Elijah teaches that a person can be courageous and have the same problem.

A third example is Mary Magdalene. Her chief characteristic was love. She loved Jesus greatly. Still, love was no defense against ignorance or a lack of understanding. She had not the faintest idea what God was doing in the death and resurrection of Jesus. So when she met Jesus in the garden after the resurrection, thinking him to be the gardener, she asked, "Sir, if you have carried him away, tell me where you have put him, and I will get him" (John 20:15). She was deeply devout, yet confused nonetheless.

And what about Jesus himself? This is a bold example; we have to be cautious how we use it. But we remember that in his flesh Jesus was subject to physical limitations, as we are. He grew hungry and tired as we do. He does not seem to have known everything (see Matt. 24:36). As for his praying, we know that in the garden he prayed for up to three hours that the cup of the wrath of God poured out against sin might be taken from him *if* it was God's will (Matt. 26:36–46). Jesus came to a position of quiet trust and confidence as a result of that prayer time. Still, we might say that he was praying for a while at least for something that turned out not to be God's will for him.

Is it any wonder that we have problems knowing what to pray for?

The "Burden Bearer"

But enough of the problem. We know it all too well. The point of the passage is that the Spirit "helps us" in the weaknesses I have been describing and, though we do not know what we should pray, he "intercedes for us with groans that words cannot express." We are weakness itself, but the Holy Spirit is all-powerful.

The first Greek word Paul uses for the Spirit's role in prayer is a long one, and the simple English translation "helps" does not even come close to doing it justice. The word is *sunantilambanetai*. Like many long Greek words it is put together from a few shorter ones, in this case three. The first is *sun*. It means "with," "along with," or "together with." The second word is *anti*. It means "for" or "in the place of." The main word, the verb, is *lambanō*. It means "to take," "take hold of," "remove," or "bear." All together the word refers to a person coming alongside another to take part of a heavy load and help him bear it.

This reminds us of the word Jesus used to describe the Spirit when he prophesied his coming to the disciples just before his crucifixion. He called him a *paraklētos*, which literally means "one called alongside of another" to help. It is sometimes translated "advocate" (which also means "to call alongside of"), or "comforter."

The idea of the Holy Spirit coming alongside a Christian to help is the same in both cases. But the special meaning in the word used here in Romans is to help by bearing the Christian's burden. It pictures our ignorance of what to pray for as a heavy load. We are struggling along under it, as it were. But the Holy Spirit comes alongside and helps us shoulder the load. He identifies with us in our weakness, as Jesus did by his incarnation, and he labors with us.

The second word Paul uses is intercession, saying that "the Spirit himself intercedes for us with groans that words cannot express." An intercessor is a person who pleads one's case. So the meaning is that the way the Holy Spirit comes alongside us to help and shoulder our burden is by pleading our case with God when we do not know how to do it. We do not know what to pray for, but the Holy Spirit does. So he prays for us, and God "who searches our hearts knows the mind of the Spirit" and answers his very correct and powerful prayers wisely.

Jesus did that for Peter in one of the best illustrations of intercession in the Bible. He told Peter that Satan wanted to sift him like wheat. Then he said, "But I have prayed for you, Simon, that your faith may not fail. And when you have turned back, strengthen your brothers" (Luke 22:32). Peter did not know what to pray. In fact, he probably wasn't praying at all. Later that evening he even fell asleep while praying. But Jesus prayed for him, and Jesus' prayers were answered, as a result of which Peter was strengthened and went on to many years of useful service.

But none of this is meant to suggest that we have nothing to do in prayer or have no responsibility to pray. We do have responsibility in prayer, which is made quite clear by the word *helps*. The apostle says that "the Spirit helps us in our weakness." He does not eliminate our need to pray regularly and fervently.

What about the word *groan*? This has been a problem among commentators since they cannot agree on who does the groaning. Is it the Spirit? The text seems to say that. Yet the majority feel that the Spirit, being God, does not groan, indeed cannot groan. Martyn Lloyd-Jones is emphatic on this point: "The Godhead does not groan; it is inconceivable for every reason."[2] However, if it is not the Holy Spirit who groans, it must be the Christian himself. Is this the correct interpretation?[3]

I think the context is a help here and that it is no accident that the word *groan* or *groanings* occurs three times in verses 22–27. The first occurrence refers to the inanimate creation, Paul writing that "the whole creation has been groaning as in the pains of childbirth right up to the present time" (v. 22). The second instance is ourselves. "Not only so, but we ourselves, who have the firstfruits of the Spirit, groan inwardly . . ." (v. 23). Since the word occurs a third time in reference to the Holy Spirit ("the Spirit himself intercedes for us with groans . . ."), there seems to be a meaningful progression

2. Ibid., p. 136.

3. Martyn Lloyd-Jones and Robert Haldane apply the "groaning" to ourselves. Leon Morris does also, though in a guarded fashion. John Murray and F. Godet apply the word to the Holy Spirit, although they suggest that his prayers only become groans as they are uttered through the lips of believers.

from inanimate nature to the redeemed to the third person of the Godhead. It is a bold progression, but it appears to be deliberate.

What does it mean? Obviously it does not mean that the Holy Spirit is unable to articulate his concerns. Yet, if the idea of bearing a heavy burden is still in view, it may be that this is what is governing the apostle's thought. A groan is appropriate to burden bearing.

Suppose you are helping someone carry a very heavy load. What is more expressive: a groan as you stagger along beneath it or a great deal of articulate chatter? Suppose your helper is saying, "My, this piano is heavy. They certainly do make pianos heavy, and awkward, too. Probably we should have spent the money and gone ahead and hired professional piano movers. I don't think I want to do this very often. Have you ever moved a piano before?" If you are struggling with the heavy load, too, that is probably the last thing you want to hear. If someone is chattering away like that, you would probably just want to tell this so-called helper to shut up and lift the piano. A real burden-bearer groans *with* you. I suggest that this is the image Paul is using.

The bearing of our prayer burdens does not have to be in words because, as the passage goes on to say, God "who searches our hearts knows the mind of the Spirit" and answers accordingly.

I think F. Godet has the right progression when he summarizes the three groaning agents in this way:

> What a statement of the unutterable disorder which reigns throughout all creation. . . . Nature throughout all her bounds has a confused feeling of it, and from her bosom there rises a continual lament claiming a renovation from heaven. The redeemed themselves are not exempt from this groaning, and wait for their own renewal which shall be the signal of universal restoration; and finally, the Spirit, who is intimate with the plans of God *for our glory* (1 Cor. 2:7) and who distinctly beholds the ideal of which we have but glimpses, pursues its realization with ardour.[4]

The last words refer to passion that goes beyond mere words.

A First Prayer Primer

Romans 8:26 and 27 imply or explicitly teach so many lessons about prayer that a number of them can be listed as a summary of what we have been learning. They constitute something of a prayer primer for Christians.

1. *We are supposed to pray.* Regardless of the problems we may have with prayer—and we are reminded that the saints have all had problems with prayer at times—we are nevertheless supposed to pray. In fact, the Word of

---

4. F. Godet, *Commentary on St. Paul's Epistle to the Romans*, trans. A. Cusin (Edinburgh: T. & T. Clark, 1892), vol. 2, pp. 103, 104.

God commands us to pray. Indeed, we are told to "pray continually" (1 Thess. 4:17). Anything God tells us to do is for our good, and we are poorer if we fail to do it. Prayer is one of the great spiritual disciplines.

2. *Do not expect prayer to be easy.* Why should it be? Nothing else in the Christian life is easy. Why should prayer be any different? When we were studying the last half of Romans 7, I pointed out that the Christian life is a struggle and that we should not expect simple or quick-fix solutions. Our contemporary American culture has conditioned us to want easy cure-alls. In the area of our sanctification we expect immediate victories either by a formula or spiritual experience. But God does not work that way. We are called to a struggle, and our perseverance in that struggle is itself a victory, even if the results are not visible or spectacular. And the Holy Spirit will help us bear our burden.

So also in prayer. You do not have to feel good about it, though you will in most cases. You do not even have to see results. What is important is that you keep on, and keep on keeping on. One bit of verse puts it like this:

> We are not here to play, to dream, to drift;
> We have hard work to do and loads to lift.
> Shun not the struggle; face it; 'tis God's gift.

3. *Realize what you are doing when you pray.* Although the discipline of prayer is itself a struggle and more often than not we do not know what we should be praying for, we nevertheless can know and need to know what we are doing. We are addressing ourselves to the great sovereign God of the universe and are presenting our adoration, confessions, thanksgivings and supplications to him. He is hearing these prayers and responding to them consistently, perfectly, and wisely out of his own inexhaustible abundance.

Does prayer get God to change his mind? Of course not! No reasonable person would want that—because if God's way is perfect, as it is, to get him to change it would be to get him to become imperfect. If that ever happened, the universe would fall into disorder! Any thinking person wants God always to run things according to his own perfect will, not ours.

But here is a parallel question: Does prayer change things? The answer to that is Yes—because God who ordains the ends also ordains the means, and he has made prayer a means to those ends. He has promised us that prayer is effective. Notice the difference between the two questions.

Does prayer get God to change his mind? No. It does not.

Does prayer change things? Yes, because God has ordained that it should be this way. Jesus has told us, "Ask and it will be given to you; seek and you will find; knock and the door will be opened to you. For everyone who asks receives; he who seeks finds; and to him who knocks, the door will be opened" (Matt. 7:7–8). James wrote, ". . . You do not have, because you do not ask God" (James 4:2), adding, "The prayer of a righteous man is powerful and effective" (James 5:16b). Remember, too, that when we are talking about change the chief thing that happens in prayer is that prayer changes *us*.

4. *Be encouraged by these verses.* It is true that "we do not know what we ought to pray for." But the Holy Spirit does, and the Holy Spirit has been given to us by God to assist precisely in this area, as well as in other ways. With his help we will make progress.

One commentator has compared learning to pray to a man learning to play the violin. At first he is not very good. But he gets the schedule of the classical music broadcasts in his area, buys the violin parts to the music that he knows will be played, and then tunes in the radio each afternoon and plays along as best he can. His mistakes do not change what is coming in over the radio in the slightest. The concertos continue to roll on in perfect harmony and tempo. But the struggling violinist changes. He gets better week by week and year by year, and the time eventually comes when he can play along with the orchestra broadcasts pretty well.

Prayer is like that. There are plenty of mistaken notes, and groans, too. But there is also progress and joy and encouragement, since God is continuing to conduct the perfect heavenly symphony, and the Holy Spirit is continuing to prepare us for the day when we will be able to take our place in the divine orchestra. In the meantime we can know that the Holy Spirit, the Paraclete, like a wise and faithful teacher, is by our side.

108

Knowing the Will of God

Romans 8:27

And he who searches our hearts knows the mind of the Spirit, because the Spirit intercedes for the saints in accordance with God's will.

At the beginning of the last study I said that I do not know of any subject that has caused more perplexity for more Christians than prayer, unless it is the matter of knowing God's will. I also said that the two are related. They are related in our text, as well as in other places, for the verse speaks of the Spirit's intercession for the saints "in accordance with God's will."

This verse introduces the matter of "God's will" at the level of the Spirit's part in prayer, not our part. "We do not know what we ought to pray for . . ." (v. 26). Nevertheless, it shows that there is such a thing as God's will, which inevitably raises the question of our relationship to it. In respect to prayer we ask questions like: What should I pray for? How should I pray? Can I pray with confidence? In respect to God's will we ask such closely related questions as: Does God have a perfect will for my life? Can I know what that will is? If I can, how do I find it? Can I ask God to show it to me? What is my responsibility for discovering it?

I can testify that in my own experience in pastoral counseling over a period of many years, I have been asked more questions about knowing or discovering the will of God than any others.

Alternative Views

A few years ago a very good book on this subject appeared in Christian bookstores. It was written by Garry Friesen, a professor at Multnomah School of the Bible in Portland, Oregon, together with J. Robin Maxson, pastor of the Klamath Evangelical Free Church, Klamath, Oregon. The title is *Decision Making & the Will of God.*[1] It is a good book because it examines the traditional evangelical views about knowing the will of God, critiques them, and proposes a helpful alternative. Let me summarize.

The traditional view distinguishes between three meanings of the phrase "will of God." The first is God's *sovereign will*, which the Westminster Shorter Catechism refers to as his eternal decrees "according to the counsel of his will, whereby, for his own glory, he hath foreordained whatsoever comes to pass" (Answer to Question 7). This sovereign will of God is hidden; it is not revealed to us, except as it unfolds in history. The second meaning of the term is God's *moral will*, which is known to us because it is revealed comprehensively in Scripture. It is what God wants or desires, as opposed to what he decrees. The third meaning is God's *individual will*, a term that refers to God's plan for an individual life and is what people are thinking of most often when they speak of searching for or finding God's will.

In their book Friesen and Maxson rightly accept the first two of these "wills": God's sovereign will and his moral will. But they dispute the third, that is, that God has an individual will for each life and that it is the duty of the individual believer to find it or "live in the center of it." The grounds for their critique are these arguments:

1. The existence of an ideal "individual will of God" for Christians cannot be established by reason, experience, biblical example, or biblical teaching.

2. The practice of looking for such an ideal will has created needless frustration in decision making for many.

3. The traditional view does not work out in most situations, if ever. It is hard to apply in the minor decisions of life or in deciding between genuinely equal options, for example.

4. The traditional view is hopelessly subjective. None of the usual ways of trying to find the supposed will of God are unambiguous: an inner witness, circumstances, counsel, personal desires, or special guidance.

In light of these obvious problems and their own examination of the biblical material, the authors propose an alternative view, which they call "the way of wisdom." A summary of their approach goes like this:

1. Garry Friesen with J. Robin Maxson, *Decision Making & the Will of God: An Alternative to the Traditional View* (Portland: Multnomah Press, 1980).

1. In those areas specifically addressed by the Bible, the revealed commands and principles of God (his moral will) are to be obeyed.

2. In those areas where the Bible gives no command or principle (non-moral decisions), the believer is free and responsible to choose his own course of action. Any decision made within the moral will of God is acceptable to God.

3. In non-moral decisions, the objective of the Christian is to make wise decisions on the basis of spiritual expediency.

4. In all decisions, the believer should humbly submit, in advance, to the outworking of God's sovereign will as it touches on each decision.[2]

My own evaluation of this book is that it is extremely helpful and is a significant breakthrough in cutting away many of the hangups on this subject that have nearly incapacitated some Christians. Its exposure of the weakness of subjective methods of determining guidance is astute. Its stress on the sufficiency of Scripture in all moral matters is essential. Its proposal of a "way of wisdom" in (most) decision-making matters is liberating. My only reservation is that it does not seem to deal adequately with special (and therefore also very important) situations.

I want to argue that Romans 8:27 makes an important contribution to this subject.

According to God's Will

The first and very obvious thing this verse does is to reinforce the idea of God's sovereign or hidden will—hidden, that is, from us. Sometimes scholars call this God's "secret" will, because it has not been revealed. It is, as the Westminster Shorter Catechism says, "whatsoever comes to pass."

The existence of this sovereign or hidden will is evident from Romans 8:27 and its context in two ways. First, the verse is talking about the role of the Holy Spirit in praying with us in situations in which we do not know what to pray for. It tells us that the Holy Spirit does know what to pray for and that the Spirit's prayers, quite obviously and naturally, are according to God's will. This teaches that there is a divine will and that it is hidden in these instances. The second way the existence of God's sovereign or hidden will is evident is in the fact that the phrase we are studying has a parallel in verse 28, which says, "And we know that in all things God works for the good of those who love him, who have been called according to his purpose." The last words, "according to his purpose," are the same thing as "in accordance with God's will" in the preceding verse. So what the Holy Spirit is praying for, among others, are the "things" in which God is working for the good of those who love him. These "things" are the events of life, which God controls for our good but which are unknown to us, at least until they happen.

2. Ibid., pp. 427, 428.

The context of these verses also deals with the moral will of God or, as we could say, the will of God for his people as disclosed in Scripture. This is what verse 29 speaks of. For no sooner does Paul speak of God's "purpose" (v. 28) than he goes on to declare in general terms what that purpose is: "For those God foreknew he also predestined to be conformed to the likeness of his Son, that he might be the firstborn among many brothers." At this point the sovereign will of God and the moral will of God clearly come together or overlap, for the text is making clear to us that God orders all events according to his sovereign plan in order that his people might become like Jesus Christ.

But let's go back to verses 26 and 27 at this point and ask: Is this what the things "we do not know what to pray for" are? Not exactly! Because if these things are merely our conformity to the character of Jesus Christ, then we already know this and should not be confused about it. We do not need the Holy Spirit's help in praying for the revealed will of God because it has already been revealed to us.

If we do need the Spirit's help, it is clearly in the area of things not revealed and for which we therefore do not know what or how to pray, and since the Holy Spirit prays for us in these areas "in accordance with God's will," there must be a will of God for us in these areas.

We may not know what it is.

We do not need to be under pressure to "discover" it, fearing that if we miss it, somehow we will be doomed to a life outside the center of God's will or to his "second best."

We are free to make decisions with what light and wisdom we possess.

Nevertheless, we can know that God does have a perfect will for us, that the Holy Spirit is praying for us in accordance with that will, and that this will of God for us will be done—because God has decreed it and because the Holy Spirit is praying for us in this area.

This should be an encouragement to everyone.

Special Guidance

And yet, it leaves an important question hanging. Does God ever reveal to us specific parts of this plan for our lives? Or to put it another way, Can we expect him to? Should we ever seek such direction? Actually, these three variations on the question have slightly different answers.

Does God ever reveal to us specific parts of his plan for our lives? Yes. Infrequently perhaps, but nevertheless sometimes.

Can we expect him to do? No, if by that we mean that we have a right to receive some special revelation.

Should we ever seek such direction? Of course, but we must be careful how we do it and not become frustrated or be made indecisive if God fails to answer these petitions.

Speaking personally, I have not experienced many specific directions for my life from God, but I have had several, the clearest being my call to the ministry. I was in grade school at the time and had been thinking about being a pastor and Bible teacher. I asked God for a specific sign, and he gave it to me clearly. I did not presume upon it. I recognized that it could have been what many would call coincidence or that I might have misunderstood what God was saying. I anticipated and received additional confirmation along this line as I grew older. Nevertheless I took the sign at face value and moved forward in the belief that God had called me to precisely the kind of work I am doing now. And obviously he had.

Moreover, there is the matter of growth. It is true that we never know entirely what we should pray for and that in some cases we do not have the slightest idea what to pray for. But that does not mean that this is always the case or that we will fail to become increasingly perceptive about the will of God in such matters as we mature. The text says that the Holy Spirit helps us in our weakness, praying for us when we do not know how to pray. Yet obviously we will grow stronger and wiser and will therefore increasingly know better how to pray and what to pray for as the Spirit works with us. This is why Paul could admonish the Ephesians, "Be very careful, then, how you live—not as unwise but as wise, making the most of every opportunity, because the days are evil. Therefore do not be foolish, but understand what the Lord's will is" (Eph. 5:15–17).

Remember the illustration of the violin player. It has been helpful to many. If prayer is like practicing the violin, it is also an exercise in coming to discover God's will. It is a way in which we progressively discover what it means to be like the Lord Jesus Christ and in that way increasingly become like him.

A "God's Will" Primer

At the end of the last study I offered what I called "a first prayer primer," listing some points to keep in mind about prayer. It strikes me that it would be helpful to offer a parallel primer on the subject of knowing God's will. This primer has six points.

1. *There is a perfect will of God for all people and all events, and therefore there is also a perfect will of God for each individual believer.* I do not think Garry Friesen and J. Robin Maxson deny this in their book, although they seem to, so intent are they in denying that there is a unique and special "individual will of God" for us to discover and live out. They say, "The idea of an individual will of God for every detail of a person's life is not found in Scripture." Therefore, "many believers are investing a great deal of time and energy searching for something that is nonexistent."[3]

3. Ibid., pp. 82, 83.

But if there is a sovereign though hidden will of God, as they admit, and if it is all-inclusive, as it obviously must be, then it must embrace an individual will for every detail of every person's life, believers as well as unbelievers, even if we do not or cannot perceive it. What Friesen and Maxson probably mean is that this "individual will of God for every detail of a person's life" is not something that is available to us to be discovered.

A person may object at this point that if such a will is not subject to discovery, then whether it exists or does not exist is meaningless. But that does not follow. On the contrary, it is of the greatest importance for us to know that God has a plan for our lives and is directing us in it, particularly when we do not know what it is. It means that we can trust him and go forward confidently, even when we seem to be walking in the dark, as we often are.

2. *The most important parts of the plan of God for our individual lives are revealed in general but morally comprehensive terms in the Bible.* Romans 8 contains some expressions of this plan, namely that we might be delivered from God's judgment upon us for our sin and from sin's power and instead be made increasingly like Jesus Christ. The decisive steps of God's plan include (1) foreknowledge, (2) predestination, (3) effectual calling, (4) justification, and (5) glorification (vv. 29–30), all of which we will examine in the next few studies.

But there are also many specifics.

The Ten Commandments contain some of these. It is God's will that we have no other gods before him, that we do not worship even him by the use of images, that we do not misuse his name, that we remember the Sabbath by keeping it holy, that we honor our parents, that we do not murder or commit adultery or steal or give false testimony or covet (see Exod. 20). The Lord Jesus amplified upon many of these commandments and added others, above all teaching that we are to "love each other" (John 15:12).

It is God's will that we be holy (1 Thess. 4:3).

It is God's will that we should pray (1 Thess. 5:17).

In the twelfth chapter of Romans Paul will say, "Do not conform any longer to the pattern of this world, but be transformed by the renewing of your mind. Then you will be able to test and approve what God's will is—his good, pleasing and perfect will" (v. 2).

3. *As concerns the parts of God's will for our individual lives that are not revealed in the Bible, it is impossible for us to know them by any amount of merely human seeking.* This does not mean that God cannot reveal these parts of his will to us or does not in some cases. (More of that later.) But it does mean that the only way we can know these hidden parts of God's will is if he reveals them to us and that, if they are not revealed to us in general moral categories in the Bible, their discovery is beyond our ability. We will not find the answer to our questions about the will of God in these areas by reading signs, following hunches, bargaining with God, or by any other similar folly.

4. Lest we be discouraged by this, however, we need to realize that *for the most part we do not need to know the will of God in hidden areas, because the Holy Spirit knows it and is praying for us in these areas in accordance with God's will.* This is what our text is chiefly saying, and it should be a great encouragement to us, as I suggested above.

Even if we knew what to pray for and prayed for it accurately or without distortion, and if our ability to walk in God's way depended on such personal prayers and understanding, we would still be uncertain. For one thing, we could not be sure we were praying according to God's will. How could we? We are usually off base on just about everything concerning prayer. For another thing, even if we prayed aright and knew we were doing so, we could still never be certain that we would actually walk in the way revealed to us. On the other hand, if the Holy Spirit is praying for us in these areas according to the sovereign and efficacious will of God, we can be confident and quite bold, knowing that this sovereign and efficacious will of God will be done.

Suppose Peter had been aware of the danger he was in at the time of the Lord's arrest. He might have prayed that God would keep him from falling by denying Jesus. That would have been a good prayer. But it was not what God had in mind for him, and when he actually did fall later Peter would have thought that God had not answered his prayer or had failed him. As it was, Jesus took the part of the Holy Spirit on this occasion and prayed for Peter that his faith would not fail, even though he would be allowed to deny Jesus. And Peter's faith did not fail. Moreover, Jesus prayed that Peter would be restored and that his restoration would enable him to strengthen his brethren when they later went through similarly dark days of failure. That, too, came to pass.

5. *Since we do not generally know God's will for our lives in areas not covered by the Bible's moral directives (and do not need to know it), we must learn to make the wisest decisions possible, knowing that God has given us freedom to do so.* In emphasizing this approach to life's decisions, Friesen and Maxson are entirely right and very helpful.

The authors recognize the proper place of many elements in making wise decisions, including some that they had previously discounted as ways to discover the supposed "individual will of God." They include items like open doors or opportunities, personal likes or dislikes, desires, impressions, and hunches. All these have a place as long as they are recognized for what they are, that is, not special revelations from God but important human factors that should rightly be taken into account. Planning is proper, though we must recognize that God can alter circumstances and thus force a redirection of our plans. Whatever happens, we need to be submissive to the will of God in advance and as it unfolds before us.

6. In spite of these careful remarks regarding the believer's normative guidance, *God is not in a box, and as a result he can (and from time to time does) reveal his will to individuals in special ways.* There are too many Christians who rightly attest to such leading to deny it.

I feel about this matter much as I do about the question of speaking in tongues. I do not believe there is anything in the Bible to teach that tongues-speaking is a gift to be particularly sought after or desired. I do not even believe that much of what passes for this gift today is from the Holy Spirit. I think it is largely psychological. Nevertheless, I cannot follow the hard logic of some, particularly of Reformed people (even though I am one), who argue that tongues cannot occur today because all supernatural occurrences have ceased. I follow Paul, who argues that we are not to "forbid" its practice (1 Cor. 14:39).

Let us think the same about special guidance. We cannot demand it. We recognize that much of what passes for special guidance is self-deception and must therefore be on guard against it. But we should also recognize that it can occur and be careful not to question it too rigorously in others—and if God guides us in this way, we must be quick to respond.

PART TEN

Unquenchable Love

109

All Things Working Together for Good

Romans 8:28

And we know that in all things God works for the good of those who love him, who have been called according to his purpose.

It is always a humbling experience to study the Word of God, and I have been humbled as I have moved from our last study about knowing the will of God to the tremendous text that is to occupy us now: Romans 8:28. "And we know that in all things God works for the good of those who love him, who have been called according to his purpose."

It seemed to me that the last study was rather difficult. At any rate, in writing it I had difficulty trying to distinguish between the various ways in which we use the term "God's will" and in trying to suggest what we can know and cannot expect to know about it. But then I came to our text, and the problems I had been laboring with in the last study suddenly seemed quite simple. Earlier Paul said, "*We do not know* what we ought to pray for." Now he writes, "*We know* that in all things God works for the good of those who love him." We do not know! We know! The first knowing concerns the details of what God is doing in our lives; we do not understand these things, we puzzle over them. The second knowing concerns the fact of God's great plan itself. Paul tells us that we do know this; we know that God has a plan.

He teaches this quite simply. If God has "called [us] according to his purpose," he must have both a purpose and a place for us in it. Moreover, we know that everything will obviously work together for our good in the achievement of that purpose. This is tremendous! Because of these truths this verse has been one of the most comforting statements in the entire Word of God for most Christians.

Faith and Circumstances

Yet this verse also poses an obvious problem. "In all things God works for the good of those who love him," the text says. But how can this be? How is this possible when the world is filled with hatred and evil, and when good people, as well as evil people, suffer daily?

Two days before I wrote this study, the ministerial staff of Tenth Presbyterian Church had its regular weekly meeting, and the ministers shared some of the problems they were dealing with. Three days earlier one of our members had been murdered. She was a lovely Korean girl, only twenty-one years old, and she had been very active in Tenth's ministries. Her name was Julee Yang. She sang in the choir, tutored disadvantaged children from one of the city's housing projects, and participated in a young people's group that is focused on the city. Julee worked in a jewelry store and was shot in the back when two young thugs came into the store to steal money. In a surprising turn of events, the murder was captured on a hidden video camera. According to some reports, it was the very first actual murder to have been captured on videotape. The funeral was the day of our staff meeting.

Other staff members shared counseling concerns. One was dealing with a person suffering from extreme personal setbacks, including a case of cancer. She had been thinking of suicide. Another was dealing with a young man who had been diagnosed as having AIDS.

The night before, I had conferred with another pastor who was planning a memorial service for a stillborn infant and wanted to talk about what comfort he could give the grieving parents. That same day, I was to visit another pastor who was under pressure in his church and was quite possibly going to be forced out of it, in spite of nearly two decades of faithful Bible teaching in that place. The combination of these seemingly tragic situations had depressed us all, and we spent a great deal of time praying about them. Later I went to the New Jersey shore, about an hour and a half away, to gain some breathing space and pray for the staff and these problems.

"We know that in all things God works together for the good of those who love him." But do we really know that?

When times are good—when we have steady jobs, when our families are doing well, when no loved one is sick, and there have been no recent deaths—in times like these, well, it is easy to say, "We know that in all things God works together for the good of those who love him."

But what about the other times?

What about times like those I was describing?

In such times we need to be sure we know what we are professing and are not merely mouthing pious nothings.

"All's Right with the World"

This great text has some built-in qualifications, and we need to begin with them. I call them "boundaries."

1. *For Christians only.* The first boundary is defined by a question: To whom does this promise apply? Obviously it does not apply to everyone, for Paul's statement says, "We know that in all things God works for the good of those who love him." That verse is talking about Christians. So, to read on to the closely linked verses that follow, it is saying that everything works for the good of those whom God has predestined to be conformed to the likeness of his Son, those he predestined and called and justified and glorified. This is not a promise that all things work together for the good of *all* people.

Do you remember Robert Browning's well-known couplet: "God's in his heaven—/All's right with the world"? The lines are a small capsule of nineteenth-century Victorian thinking, when the world was more or less at peace, and progress in all areas of human life and endeavor seemed unlimited and inevitable. Nobody thinks that way today, and rightly so. It is because all is not right with the world, and anybody who thinks so is either out of his or her mind or is just not seeing things clearly.

Several centuries before Browning, the German philosopher Gottfried Wilhelm Leibnitz developed a line of thought known popularly as "the best of all possible worlds" philosophy. But this, too, was an illusion and still is. For most people this is not the best of all possible worlds at all. In fact, for many millions of people this world and the things they endure in it are terrible.

According to our text, it is only of Christians, not of all people, that these comforting words can be said.

2. *To be like Jesus Christ.* The second boundary to our text comes from another question: What is meant by "good"? That is an important question to ask, because if "good" means "rich," as some would like it to mean, the text is not true, since most Christians have not been given a great supply of this world's goods. The same thing is true if "good" means "healthy." Not all believers have good health. Similarly, "good" cannot mean "successful" or "admired" or even "happy" in the world's sense, since God asks many Christians to endure failure or scorn or very distressing personal experiences or severe disappointments.

What does "good" mean, then, if it does not mean rich or healthy or successful or admired or happy? The answer is in the next verse: "For those God foreknew he also predestined to be conformed to the likeness of his Son."

That is what the "good" is: "to be conformed to the likeness of his Son," in other words, to be made like Jesus Christ. That is an obvious good. It is impossible to think of a higher good for human beings, to be like one's Maker. Pastor Ray Stedman rightly calls this "what life is all about."[1] But at the same time, seeing this allows us to see other not so obviously good things within the greater purpose. We can see how sickness, suffering, persecution, grief, or other ills can be used by God for this good end.

3. *A good use of bad things.* That leads to a third boundary for this text, and it comes from a third question: Are the things used in our lives by God for this good end necessarily good in themselves or only in their effect? The answer is the latter. In other words, this text does not teach that sickness, suffering, persecution, grief, or any other such thing is itself good. On the contrary, these things are evils. Hatred is not love. Death is not life. Grief is not joy. The world is filled with evil. But what the text teaches—and this is important—is that God uses these things (and others) to effect his own good ends for his people. God brings good out of the evil, and the good, as we saw, is our conformity to the character of Jesus Christ.

4. *Knowing rather than feeling.* The fourth and final boundary for the meaning of this text comes in answer to still another question: What is our relationship to what God is doing in these circumstances? The answer Paul gives is that "we know." He does not say that we "feel" all things to be good. Often we do not feel that God is doing good at all. We feel exactly the opposite. We feel that we are being ground down or destroyed. And it is not even that we "see" the good. Most of the time we do not perceive the good things God is doing or how he might be bringing good out of the evil. The text simply says, "we know" it.

Paul was no sentimentalist. He had been persecuted, beaten, stoned, and shipwrecked. He had been attacked and consistently slandered by the Gentiles as well as by his own countrymen. Paul did not go around saying how wonderful the world was or how pleasant his missionary endeavors had been. On the contrary, he reported that he had been "hard pressed on every side . . . perplexed . . . [and] struck down" (2 Cor. 4:8–9). But Paul came through the things that pressed down and perplexed him precisely because he knew that God was working out his own greater and good purposes through these events.

How did Paul know it? He knew it because God had told him this was what he was doing. And now Paul is telling us. He is saying that we, too, can

1. Ray C. Stedman, *From Guilt to Glory*, vol. 1, *Hope for the Helpless* (Portland: Multnomah Press, 1978), p. 298.

know it and be comforted in the knowledge that "in all things God works for the good of those who love him."

The Part Without Boundaries

We have spent the first half of this study looking at four qualifications for this text: (1) that it is for Christians only; (2) that the good is not our idea of the good but God's idea and that it is to be made like Jesus Christ; (3) that the things God uses for this supremely good end are not necessarily good in themselves; and (4) that we can "know" this even though we may not feel or see it. However, having established these boundaries, we can turn joyfully to the one part of the text that has absolutely no boundaries whatever.

It is the term "all things." This tells us that all things that have ever happened to us or can possibly happen to us are so ordered and controlled by God that the end result is inevitably and utterly our good. Even the worst things are used to make us like Jesus Christ.

What is more, when we begin to look at this closely, we see that they are used not only for our good but for the good of other people as well.

Here are three examples.

First, *Joseph.* Joseph's story shows how God controls circumstances. Apart from God's purpose, most of which was hidden from Joseph for a very long time, no one would suspect that God was doing anything good at all. Joseph was a young man favored of his father, with what we would call a bright future before him. His brothers hated him because of his righteousness and their own sin, and they conspired to do away with him. At first they threw Joseph into a dry cistern, planning to leave him there to die. But when some Midianite traders passed by, they seized the opportunity and sold him to them to be a slave. In their turn, the Midianites sold him to a military man in Egypt whose name was Potiphar.

What a horrible experience for a young man. Joseph was only seventeen years old, and he was now a slave in Egypt, where he could not even speak the language. But even this was not all. For a time he prospered as Potiphar's slave. But when Potiphar's wife tried to seduce him and he refused, Joseph was accused of trying to violate her and was thrown into prison where he spent the next two years as an abandoned and seemingly forgotten man.

All this, bad as it was, was only the path by which God was planning to raise him to the throne of Egypt to be second in power only to Pharaoh himself.

Pharaoh had a dream. No one could interpret it. Then Pharaoh's chief butler, who had been in prison with Joseph two years before, remembered how Joseph had interpreted one of his dreams. He told Pharaoh, and Joseph was removed from the prison and brought to court, where he easily supplied the explanation. Pharaoh was so impressed that he promoted the former slave on the spot, and Joseph was able to direct the Egyptian grain harvests and store large quantities of grain. Thus he saved many lives during the ensuing famine.

The favor of his father, his dreams, his brothers' hatred, the passing of the Midianite caravan, his being sold to Potiphar, the enthrallment of his master's wife, two years in prison, the Pharaoh's dream—all these diverse circumstances, some quite evil in themselves, were used by God for the great and ultimate good of Joseph and others.

His own testimony, uttered years later in a reassuring conversation with his eleven brothers, who had since been reunited to him, was this: "Don't be afraid. Am I in the place of God? You intended to harm me, but God intended it for good to accomplish what is now being done, the saving of many lives" (Gen. 50:19–20).

Second, *Job*. From the world's point of view the story of Job is one of the saddest in the Bible. Job was a mature and upright man, one who feared God and shunned evil. He had seven sons and three daughters, and his wealth consisted of seven thousand sheep, three thousand camels, five hundred yoke of oxen and five hundred donkeys. He had many servants. Then, suddenly, in one day all this was taken from him. Raiders carried off the donkeys and oxen. Lightning killed the sheep. Chaldean bandits stole the camels and killed the servants. Finally, a building collapsed and his children were all killed in an instant.

Satan, who was behind this, stood back and expected Job to curse God for his ill fortune. But instead Job "fell to the ground in worship and said: 'Naked I came from my mother's womb, and naked I will depart./The LORD gave and the LORD has taken away; may the name of the LORD be praised'" (Job 1:21).

The next stage of the story tells how Job was afflicted with ill health, being covered with boils from his head to his feet. Then his friends heaped even greater pain on him by their shallow counsel. Job did not understand this at all. Even at the end of the story, when God restored his wealth and gave him a new family, he seems not to have known what God was doing. God was developing Job's character and confounding the supposed wisdom of Satan, who had said that God's people serve him only because he makes them prosperous. Job did not see this or feel it. But everything was nevertheless working together for good in the life of this great patriarch.

Third, *Peter*. Peter sinned in his pride, telling Jesus that although the other disciples might deny him, Peter at least would not. Not Peter! Then, he, too, sinned in his weakness, doing precisely what he had told Jesus he would not do. Peter denied the Lord three times, the last time with oaths and cursings.

What was the outcome? Jesus turned even these very bad things to good. He interceded for Peter so that the apostle's faith would not fail, and he asked the Father to order things so that, when Peter was restored, he would be stronger for his fall and able to strengthen his brethren. This is what Peter did, for later he wrote to other Christians:

> Dear friends, do not be surprised at the painful trial you are suffering, as though something strange were happening to you. But rejoice that you participate in the sufferings of Christ, so that you may be overjoyed when his glory is revealed. If you are insulted because of the name of Christ, you are blessed, for the Spirit of glory and of God rests on you. If you suffer, it should not be as a murderer or thief or any other kind of criminal, or even as a meddler. However, if you suffer as a Christian, do not be ashamed, but praise God that you bear that name. For it is time for judgment to begin with the family of God; and if it begins with us, what will the outcome be for those who do not obey the gospel of God? And, "If it is hard for the righteous to be saved, what will become of the ungodly and the sinner?"
>
> So then, those who suffer according to God's will should commit themselves to their faithful Creator and continue to do good.
>
> 1 Peter 4:12–19

All Things

Years ago I had a watch that my father had given me when I graduated from high school. It was an unusual watch in that its back was transparent. You could look into it and see the mechanism working and the wheels turning. Some wheels went forward. Some went backward. Some turned quickly, others slowly. There was a large mainspring and a few small hairsprings. There were levers that were popping up and down.

The Christian life is like the parts of that watch. At times the events of our lives move forward quickly and we sense that we are making fast progress in being made like Jesus Christ. At other times events move slowly, and we seem to be going slowly ourselves or even slipping backward. Sometimes we seem to be going up and down with no forward motion at all. At such times we say that our emotions are on a roller coaster or that we just can't seem to get on track. Our lives have petty annoyances that spoil our good humor. Sometimes we are overwhelmed with harsh blows, and we say that we just can't go on. It may be true; perhaps we really can't go on, at least until we are able to pause and catch our spiritual breath again.

But God has designed this timepiece of ours—this plan for our lives. That is the point. It has been formed "according to his purpose," which is what our text is about, and it is because we *know* this, not because we feel it or see it, that we can eventually go on.

What can possibly come into our lives that can defeat God's plan?

There are many things that can defeat human planning. Our plans are often overturned by our sins and failures, others' opposition or jealousy, circumstances, or our own indifference. But not God's plans. He is the sovereign God. His will is forever being done. Therefore, you and I can go on in confidence, even when we are most perplexed or cast down.

What can happen to me that can defeat God's purpose?

Can some thorn in the flesh? Something to prick or pain me? Paul had his thorn in the flesh, but God's grace was sufficient for him and it was in his weakness that God was glorified.

Sickness? Job had boils, but God glorified himself in Job's sickness and even matured Job.

Death? How can death hurt me? "To be away from the body" is to be "at home with the Lord," says Paul (2 Cor. 5:8). Therefore, my physical death will only consummate the plan of God for me. And as far as those who remain behind are concerned, well, God will work his will for good for them also. No one is indispensable, so if I should die this afternoon, the next service of Tenth Presbyterian Church would still be held. The gospel would still be preached. Christians would still be strengthened and unbelievers won. This is because "in all things God works for the good of those who love him."

110

A Golden Chain of Five Links

Romans 8:29–30

For those God foreknew he also predestined to be conformed to the likeness of his Son, that he might be the firstborn among many brothers. And those he predestined, he also called; those he called, he also justified; those he justified, he also glorified.

When I was writing about Romans 8:28 in the previous study, I said that for most Christians that verse is one of the most comforting statements in the entire Word of God. The reason is obvious. It tells us that "in all things God works for the good of those who love him, who have been called according to his purpose." That is, God has a great and good purpose for all Christians and he is working in all the many detailed circumstances of their lives to achieve it.

Wonderful as that verse is, the verses that follow are even more wonderful, for they tell how God *accomplishes* this purpose and remind us that it is *God himself* who accomplishes it. The last reminder is the basis for what is commonly known as "eternal security" or "the perseverance of the saints."

Some time ago I came across an amusing but apparently true story. In 1966 the Hindu holy man and mystic Rao announced that he would walk on water. This attracted a great deal of attention, and on the day set for the feat a great crowd gathered around a large pool in Bombay, India, where it was to occur. The holy man prayerfully prepared himself for the miracle and then stepped forward to the pool's edge. A solemn hush fell over the assembled observers. Rao glanced upward to heaven, stepped forward onto the water, and then immediately plummeted into the pool's depths. Sputtering, dripping wet, and furious, he emerged from the pool and turned angrily on the embarrassed crowd. "One of you," he said, "is an unbeliever."

Fortunately, our salvation is not like that, because if it were, it would never happen. In spiritual matters we are all unbelievers. We are weak in faith. But we are taught in these great verses from Romans that salvation does not depend upon our faith, however necessary faith may be, but on the purposes of God.

And it is the same regarding love. The apostle has just said that in all things God works for the good of those who love him. But lest we somehow imagine that the strength of our love is the determining factor in salvation, he reminds us that our place in this good flow of events is not grounded in our love for God but on the fact that he has fixed his love upon us.

How has God loved us?

Let me count the ways.

These verses introduce us to five great doctrines: (1) foreknowledge, (2) predestination, (3) effectual calling, (4) justification, and (5) glorification. These five doctrines are so closely connected that they have rightly and accurately been described as "a golden chain of five links." Each link is forged in heaven. That is, each describes something God does and does not waver in doing. This is why John R. W. Stott calls them "five undeniable affirmations."[1] The first two are concerned with God's eternal counsel or past determinations. The last two are concerned with what God has done, is doing, or will do with us. The middle term ("calling") connects the first pair and the last.

These doctrines flow from eternity to eternity. As a result, there is no greater scope given to the wonderful activity of God in salvation in all the Bible.

Divine Foreknowledge

The most important of these five terms is the first, but surprisingly (or not surprisingly, since our ways are not God's ways nor his thoughts our thoughts), it is the most misunderstood. It is composed of two separate words: "fore," which means beforehand, and "knowledge." So it has been taken to mean that, since God knows all things, God knows beforehand who will believe on him and who will not, as a result of which he has predes-

1. John R. W. Stott, *Men Made New: An Exposition of Romans 5–8* (Grand Rapids: Baker Book House, 1984), p. 101.

tined to salvation those whom he foresees will believe on him. In other words, what he foreknows or foresees is their faith.

Foreknowledge is such an important idea that we are going to come back to it again in the next study and carefully examine the way it is actually used in the Bible. But even here we can see that such an explanation can never do justice to this passage.

For one thing, the verse does not say that God foreknew what certain of his creatures would do. It is not talking about human actions at all. On the contrary, it is speaking entirely of God and of what God does. Each of these five terms is like that: *God* foreknew, *God* predestined, *God* called, *God* justified, *God* glorified. Besides, the object of the divine foreknowledge is not the actions of certain people but the people themselves. In this sense it can only mean that God has fixed a special attention upon them or loved them savingly.

This is the way the word is frequently used in the Old Testament, Amos 3:2, for example. The King James Version translates God's words here literally, using the verb "know" (Hebrew, *yāda*): "You only have I known of all the families of the earth. . . ." But so obvious is the idea of election in this context that the New International Version sharpens the meaning by translating: "You only have I chosen. . . ."

And there is another problem. If all the word means is that God knows beforehand what people will do in response to him or to the preaching of the gospel and then determines their destiny on that basis, what, pray tell, could God possibly see or foreknow except a fixed opposition to him on the part of *all* people? If the hearts of men and women are as depraved as Paul has been teaching they are—if indeed "'There is no one righteous, not even one . . . no one who understands, no one who seeks God'" (Rom. 3:10–11)—what could God possibly foresee in any human heart but unbelief?

John Murray puts it in a complementary but slightly different way: "Even if it were granted that 'foreknew' means the foresight of faith, the biblical doctrine of sovereign election is not thereby eliminated or disproven. For it is certainly true that God foresees faith; he foresees all that comes to pass. The question would then simply be: whence proceeds this faith, which God foresees? And the only biblical answer is that the faith which God foresees is the faith he himself creates (cf. John 3:3–8; 6:44, 45, 65; Eph. 2:8; Phil. 1:29; 2 Peter 1:2). Hence his eternal foresight of faith is preconditioned by his decree to generate this faith in those whom he foresees as believing."[2]

Foreknowledge means that salvation has its origin in the mind or eternal counsels of God, not in man. It focuses our attention on the distinguishing love of God, according to which some persons are elected to be conformed to the character of Jesus Christ, which is what Paul has already been saying.

2. John Murray, *The Epistle to the Romans* (Grand Rapids: Wm. B. Eerdmans, 1968), p. 316.

Foreknowledge and Predestination

The chief objection to this understanding of foreknowledge is that, if it is correct, then foreknowledge and predestination (the term that follows) mean the same thing and Paul would therefore be redundant. But the terms are not synonymous. Predestination carries us a step further.

Like foreknowledge, predestination is also composed of two separate words: "pre," meaning beforehand, and "destiny" or "destination." It means to determine a person's destiny beforehand, and this is the sense in which it differs from foreknowledge. As we have seen, foreknowledge means to fix one's love upon or elect. It "does not inform us of the destination to which those thus chosen are appointed."[3] This is what predestination supplies. It tells us that, having fixed his distinguishing love upon us, God next appointed us "to be conformed to the likeness of his Son, that he might be the firstborn among many brothers." He does this, as the next terms show, by calling, justifying, and glorifying those thus chosen.

D. Martyn Lloyd-Jones points out that the Greek word that is translated "predestined" has within it the word for "horizon" (Greek, *proōrizō*). The horizon is a dividing line, marking off and separating what we can see from what we cannot see. Everything beyond the horizon is in one category; everything within the horizon is in another. Lloyd-Jones suggests therefore that what the word signifies is that God, having foreknown certain people, takes them out of the far-off category and puts them within the circle of his saving purposes. "In other words," he says, "he has marked out a particular destiny for them."[4]

That destiny is to be made like Jesus Christ.

Two Kinds of Calling

The next step in this golden chain of five links is what theologians call effectual calling. It is important to use the adjective *effectual* at this point, because there are two different kinds of calling referred to in the Bible, and it is easy to get confused about them.

One kind of calling is external, general, and universal. It is an open invitation to all persons to repent of sin, turn to the Lord Jesus Christ, and be saved. It is what Jesus was speaking of when he said, "Come to me, all you who are weary and burdened, and I will give you rest" (Matt. 11:28). Or again, when he said, "If anyone is thirsty, let him come to me and drink" (John 7:37). The problem with this type of call is that, left to themselves, no men or women ever respond positively. They hear the call, but they turn away, preferring their own ways to God. That is why Jesus also said, "No one can come to me unless the Father who sent me draws him . . ." (John 6:44).

---

3. Ibid., p. 318.
4. D. M. Lloyd-Jones, *Romans, An Exposition of Chapter 8:17–39, The Final Perseverance of the Saints* (Grand Rapids: Zondervan, 1976), p. 241.

The other kind of call is internal, specific, and effectual. That is, it not only issues the invitation, it also provides the ability or willingness to respond positively. It is God's drawing to himself or bringing to spiritual life the one who without that call would remain spiritually dead and far from him.

There is no greater illustration of this than Jesus' calling of Lazarus, the brother of Mary and Martha, who had died four days before. Lazarus in his grave is a picture of every human being in his or her natural state: dead in body and soul, bound with graveclothes, lying in a tomb, sealed with some great stone. Let's call to him, "Lazarus, Lazarus. Come forth, Lazarus. We want you back. We miss you. If you will just get up out of that tomb and return to us, you'll find that we are all anxious to have you back. No one here is going to put any obstructions in your way."

What? Won't Lazarus come? Doesn't he want to be with us?

The problem is that Lazarus does not have the ability to come back. The call is given, but he cannot come.

Ah, but let Jesus take his place before the tomb. Let Jesus call out, "Lazarus, come forth," and the case is quite different. The words are the same, but now the call is no mere invitation. It is an effectual calling. For the same God who originally called the creation out of nothing is now calling life out of death, and his call is heard. Lazarus, though he has been dead four days, hears Jesus and obeys his Master's voice.

That is how God calls those whom he has foreknown and predestined to salvation.

Calling and Justification

The next step in God's great chain of saving actions is justification. We spent a great deal of time discussing justification in volume 1 of this series, so we need not discuss it in detail here. Briefly, it is the judicial act by which God declares sinful men and women to be in a right standing before him, not on the basis of their own merit, for they have none, but on the basis of what Jesus Christ has done for them by dying in their place on the cross. Jesus bore their punishment, taking the penalty of their sins upon himself. Those sins having been punished, God then imputes the perfect righteousness of Jesus Christ to their account.

What does need to be discussed here is the relationship of the effectual call to justification. Or to put it in the form of a question: Why does Paul place calling where he does in this chain? Why does calling come *between* foreknowledge and predestination, on the one hand, and justification and glorification, on the other?

There are two reasons.

First, calling is the point at which the things determined beforehand in the mind and counsel of God pass over into time. We speak of "fore" knowledge and "pre" destination. But these two time references only have meaning for us. Strictly speaking, there is no time frame in God. Because the end is as the beginning and the beginning is as the end, "fore" and "pre" are meaningless in regard to him. God simply "knows" and "determines," and that eternally. But what he thus decrees in eternity becomes actual in time, and calling is the point where his eternal foreknowledge of some and his predestination of those to salvation finds what we would call concrete manifestation. We are creatures in time. So it is by God's specific calling of us to faith in time that we are saved.

Second, justification, which comes after calling in this list of divine actions, is always connected with faith or belief, and it is through God's call of the individual that faith is brought into being. God's call creates or quickens faith. Or, as we could perhaps more accurately say, it is the call of God that brings forth spiritual life, of which faith is the first true evidence or proof.

Romans 8:29–30 does not contain a full list of the steps in a person's experience of salvation, only five of the most important steps undertaken by God on behalf of Christians. If the text were to include all the steps, what theologians call the *ordo salutis*, it would have to list these: foreknowledge, predestination, calling, regeneration, faith, repentance, justification, adoption, sanctification, perseverance, and glorification.[5] The full list makes the point. After predestination, the very next thing is our calling, out of which comes faith which leads to justification.

The Bible never says that we are saved *because of* our faith. That would make faith something good in us that we somehow contribute to the process. But it does say that we are saved *by* or *through* faith, meaning that God must create it in us before we can be justified.

Glorified (Past Tense)

Glorification is also something we studied earlier, and we are going to come back to it again before we complete these studies of Romans 8. It means being made like Jesus Christ, which is what Paul said earlier. But here is one thing we must notice. When Paul mentions glorification, he refers to it in the past tense ("glorified") rather than in the future ("will glorify") or future passive tense ("will be glorified"), which is what we might have expected him to have done.

Why is this? The only possible but also obvious reason is that he is thinking of this final step in our salvation as being so certain that it is possible to refer to is as having already happened. And, of course, he does this deliberately to assure us that this is exactly what will happen. Do you remember how he put it in writing to the Christians at Philippi? He wrote, "I always pray with joy . . . being confident of this, that he who began a good work in

5. There is a classic exposition of the *ordo salutis* in John Murray, *Redemption Accomplished and Applied* (Grand Rapids: Wm. B. Eerdmans, 1970), pp. 79–181. (Original edition 1955.)

you will carry it on to completion until the day of Christ Jesus" (Phil. 1:4, 6). That is shorthand for what we are discovering in Romans. God began the "good work" by foreknowledge, predestination, calling, and justification. And because he never goes back on anything he has said or changes his mind, we can know that he will carry it on until the day we will be like Jesus Christ, being glorified.

All of God

I have a simple conclusion, and it is to remind you again that these are all things God has done. They are the important things, the things that matter. Without them, not one of us would be saved. Or if we were "saved," not one of us would continue in that salvation.

Do we have to believe? Of course, we do. Paul has already spoken of the nature and necessity of faith in chapters 3 and 4. But even our faith is of God or, as we should probably better say, the result of his working in us. In Ephesians Paul says, "For it is by grace you have been saved, through faith—and this not from yourselves, it is the gift of God—not by works, so that no one can boast" (Eph. 2:9). When we are first saved we think naturally that we have had a great deal to do with it, perhaps because of wrong or shallow teaching, but more likely only because we know more about our own thoughts and feelings than we do about God. But the longer one is a Christian, the further one moves from any feeling that we are responsible for our salvation or even any part of it, and the closer we come to the conviction that it is all of God.

It is a good thing it is of God, too! Because if it were accomplished by us, we could just as easily un-accomplish it—and no doubt would. If God is the author, salvation is something that is done wisely, well, and forever.

Robert Haldane, one of the great commentators on Romans, provides this summary.

> In looking back on this passage, we should observe that, in all that is stated, man acts no part, but is passive, and all is done by God. He is elected and predestinated and called and justified and glorified by God. The apostle was here concluding all that he had said before in enumerating topics of consolation to believers, and is now going on to show that God is "for us," or on the part of his people. Could anything, then, be more consolatory to those who love God, than to be in this manner assured that the great concern of their salvation is not left in their own keeping? God, even their covenant God, hath taken the whole upon himself. He hath undertaken for them. There is no room, then, for chance or change. He will perfect that which concerneth them.[6]

6. Robert Haldane, *An Exposition of the Epistle to the Romans* (MacDill AFB: MacDonald Publishing, 1958), pp. 407, 408.

Years ago Harry A. Ironside, that great Bible teacher, told a story about an older Christian who was asked to give his testimony. He told how God had sought him out and found him, how God had loved him, called him, saved him, delivered him, cleansed him, and healed him—a great witness to the grace, power, and glory of God. But after the meeting a rather legalistic brother took him aside and criticized his testimony, as certain of us like to do. He said, "I appreciated all you said about what God did for you. But you didn't mention anything about your part in it. Salvation is really part us and part God. You should have mentioned something about your part."

"Oh, yes," the older Christian said. "I apologize for that. I'm sorry. I really should have said something about my part. My part was running away, and his part was running after me until he caught me."[7]

We have all run away. But God has set his love on us, predestined us to become like Jesus Christ, called us to faith and repentance, justified us, yes, and has even glorified us, so certain of completion is his plan. May he alone be praised!

---

7. This story is told by Ray C. Stedman, *From Guilt to Glory*, vol. 1, *Hope for the Helpless* (Portland: Multnomah Press, 1978), p. 302.

111

Foreknowledge and Predestination

Romans 8:29

For those God foreknew he also predestined to be conformed to the likeness of his Son, that he might be the firstborn among many brothers.

There are quite a few misunderstandings about Reformed or Calvinistic Christians, and one is that we are always talking about predestination. That is probably not so, though there are Calvinists who like to beat this drum, just as those in other communions like to emphasize certain forms of church government, the gifts of the Holy Spirit, or modes of baptism.

This study is about foreknowledge and predestination. But if you are inclined to think that I am overemphasizing these truths by talking about them here, I need to point out that this is the first time in our long study of the Book of Romans that I have explicitly spoken about either. This is my hundred and twelfth study of Romans, but it is the first one specifically addressing these themes. The reason is obvious. This is the first place in Romans at which Paul introduces these two terms. God's foreknowledge of a chosen people and his predestination of them to be conformed to the image of Jesus Christ lies behind everything he has been teaching in the first seven and a half chapters. But Paul has not discussed these ideas until he has first presented our desperate condition due to sin and God's remedy for sin through faith in Jesus Christ.

Strikingly, this is also the procedure John Calvin followed in the *Institutes of the Christian Religion*. Calvin is known for teaching about predestination. But a discussion of the doctrine does not appear until near the end of Book Three, after more than nine hundred pages devoted to other themes and more than two-thirds of the way through the volume.

"According to His Purpose"

Where do we start in discussing this doctrine? We have already made a start in the last study, showing that foreknowledge and predestination are two of five great doctrines described as a golden chain by which God reaches down from heaven to elect and save a people for himself.

Yet Paul's own start is in verse 28, where he has written, "And we know that in all things God works for the good of those who love him, who have been called according to his purpose." Since the word *called* also occurs again as one of the five doctrines in this chain, we are alerted to the fact that the chain of divine actions merely explains how God achieves this purpose. In other words, it is not foreknowledge or predestination that is primary but the purpose of God itself. What is that purpose? Clearly, it is that from the mass of fallen and perishing humanity God might save a company of people who will be made like Jesus.

We could put it like this: God loves Jesus so much that he is determined to have many more people like him. Not that we become divine, of course. Nothing in the Bible teaches that. But rather that we might become like him in his many communicable attributes: things like love, joy, peace, holiness, wisdom, patience, grace, kindness, goodness, compassion, faithfulness, mercy, and other qualities.

In order to do that, God selects, predestines, calls, justifies, and glorifies this people. That is, verses 29 and 30 tell *how* God accomplishes the purpose of verse 28.

Foreknowledge

I said in the last study that foreknowledge is the most important of these terms and that it is the most misunderstood. I also said that I would be returning to it to discuss it further, which is what I want to do now.

The problem with this term is that if we break it down into its two constituent parts, the word itself suggests the wrong idea. The first part of the word is "fore," which means "before," and the second part is "knowledge." So the word seems to refer only to knowing something before it happens. Starting from this point, many people have gone on to supply what, in their judgment, God is supposed to know beforehand, concluding that what he foreknows or foresees is faith. According to such suppositions, it is on the basis of a faith which God foresees that he saves people.

That is not what the verse says, of course. It says that God foreknows people, not what they are going to do, and faith is not even mentioned. In the flow of these verses, what we are told is that God: (1) has a purpose to save certain people, and (2) does something to those people as a first step in a five-step process of saving them.

Actually, as soon as we begin to look at the word carefully, we discover that it is used in a very specific way in the Bible. And for good reasons! When we use the word *foreknowledge* in relation to ourselves, to refer to knowing beforehand, the word has meaning to us. We can anticipate what a person we know well might do, for instance. But that sense of the word is meaningless in relation to God. Because God is not in time, as we are, he does not know things *beforehand*. God simply knows. He knows all things. That is what omniscience means. But even if we think in time categories, which is all we can do as creatures locked in time, we have to say that the only reason God can even be said to foreknow things is because he predetermines them. As Robert Haldane says, "God foreknows what will be, by determining what shall be."[1]

No, the word *foreknowledge* has quite a different meaning in relation to God than it does in relation to us. It means that God "sets his special love upon" a person or "elects" a person to salvation.

This is a characteristic use of the word in the Old Testament. In Amos 3:2, which I mentioned in the last study, the King James Version has the words, "You only have I *known* [Hebrew, *yāda*] of all the families of the earth." That does not refer to God's knowledge in the usual sense of knowing all things, because in that sense God would have to be said to "know" all people and not just the people of Israel. In this verse the word has the meaning "set a special love upon" or "choose." In fact, as I have already pointed out, so obvious is the idea of election in this context that the New International Version sharpens the meaning by translating Amos 3:2 with the words, "You only have I *chosen*. . . ."

We see the same idea when we examine the use of "foreknowledge" (or "foreknew") in the New Testament, where the references occur seven times. Two of these occurrences are of man's foreknowledge, our common usage of the term. Five are of God's foreknowledge, and they are the determining passages.

1. *Acts 2:23*. This verse occurs in the middle of Peter's great sermon on the day of Pentecost, in which he was explaining the plan of salvation to the Jews of Jerusalem: "This man [Jesus] was handed over to you by God's set purpose and foreknowledge; and you, with the help of wicked men, put

---

1. Robert Haldane, *An Exposition of the Epistle to the Romans* (MacDill AFB: MacDonald Publishing, 1958), p. 396.

him to death by nailing him to the cross." In this speech Peter is not merely telling his listeners that God knew Jesus would be crucified. That is not the point at all. Rather, he is saying that God sent him to be crucified; that is, that God determined beforehand that this is what should take place. This is what foreknowledge means in Peter's context.

The same idea is present two chapters further on, although in this passage the word *foreknowledge* is omitted. There the believers are praying and say, "Indeed Herod and Pontius Pilate met together with the Gentiles [the "wicked men" of Acts 2:23] and the people of Israel in this city to conspire against your holy servant Jesus, whom you anointed. They did what your power and will had decided beforehand should happen" (Acts 4:27–28).

Both these passages say that human beings were merely carrying out what God had previously determined should happen in order to save sinners by Jesus' crucifixion.

2. *Romans 11:2.* In Romans 9–11 Paul is defending the doctrine of the eternal security of the elect against the argument that it cannot be true since many Jews have not believed in Jesus. There are six or seven answers to that objection in these chapters, and in chapter 11 there is one that includes the word *foreknew.* "I ask then: Did God reject his people? By no means! I am an Israelite myself, a descendant of Abraham, from the tribe of Benjamin. God did not reject his people, whom he foreknew" (vv. 1–2).

What does that mean? Does it mean that God does not reject those whom he sees in advance will not reject him? Of course not. That is not what Paul is talking about, and if it were, it would not help his case at all. What he means is that, even in the case of Israel, God has not elected each and every individual to salvation, instead choosing only a remnant, but that those whom he has elected to salvation are kept in that salvation. Paul introduces himself as an example. His argument is that those whom God has foreknown (that is, "chosen") will never fall away or be rejected—the same point he has been making in Romans 8.

3. *First Peter 1:2.* Peter was a great preacher of predestination, and two of the New Testament's explicit references to foreknowledge occur in his first letter. Writing to Christians scattered throughout the Roman provinces of what we call Turkey, he says at the very beginning of his epistle: "To God's elect, strangers in the world, scattered throughout Pontus, Galatia, Cappadocia, Asia and Bithynia, who have been chosen according to the foreknowledge of God the Father, through the sanctifying work of the Spirit, for obedience to Jesus Christ and sprinkling by his blood" (vv. 1–2). Verse 2 does not mean that God chose them because he foresaw that they would believe on or obey Jesus Christ, but rather the reverse. They believed and were being sanctified because God chose them to be saved.

4. *First Peter 1:20.* In verse 20 of the same chapter Peter is speaking of God's determination to send Jesus Christ to be the Savior. The text literally

says that God "foreknew him [that is, Jesus] before the creation of the world." But in this verse "foreknew" so clearly means "foreordained" (as in KJV) that the New International Version translators use the word *chosen:* "He was chosen before the creation of the world." In other words, God the Father appointed Jesus to be the Savior even before the creation of man or man's fall.

That same translation could have been used in each of the other passages I have mentioned:

Acts 2:23—"This man [Jesus] was handed over to you by God's set purpose and choice (or predetermination). . . ."

Romans 11:2—"God did not reject his people, whom he chose. . . ."

First Peter 1:2—"[To God's elect] who have been chosen according to the choice (or preordination) of God the Father. . . ."

5. *Romans 8:29.* The fifth New Testament reference to God's foreknowledge is in our text, and the meaning, as I have been arguing, is the same as in the other verses. Romans 8:29 means that God set his special or saving love upon a select group of people in order that his good purpose, namely, to create a people to be like his Son Jesus Christ, might be achieved.

Interestingly, some of the versions, knowing that this is the true meaning of the verb *foreknow,* have tried to suggest it by freer translations. The New English Bible says, "God knew his own before ever they were, and also ordained that they should be shaped to the likeness of his Son." Charles Williams rendered the verse, "For those on whom he set his heart beforehand he also did predestinate to be conformed to the image of his Son." Goodspeed wrote, "Those whom he had marked out from the first he predestined to be made like his Son." The Roman Catholic Jerusalem Bible is particularly sharp. It says, "They [that is, the ones called according to his purpose] are the ones he chose specially long ago." These all suggest the correct meaning nicely.[2]

Predestination

The second of our five golden terms is predestination, the one that bothers most people, though what bothers them is more accurately included in the word *foreknowledge.* That is, that God should set his love upon a special people and save them while overlooking others. Predestination means that God has determined the specific destiny of those he has previously decided should be saved and be made like Jesus.

---

2. The only version that misses the idea entirely is that of Kenneth N. Taylor, who did not translate from the Greek text and therefore unwittingly incorporates his own Arminian bias into *The Living Bible* paraphrase: "For from the very beginning God decided that those who came to him—and all along he knew who would—should become like his Son, so that his Son would be the First, with many brothers."

This is a good place to look at the objections people have to this doctrine, whether described by the word *foreknowledge* or *predestination*.

1. *If you believe in predestination, you make salvation arbitrary and God a tyrant.* Actually, there are two objections here. Let us take the second one first. Does predestination make God a tyrant, crushing justice by some willy-nilly saving of some and damning of others? We can understand how people who know little about the Bible's teaching might suppose this, particularly since they think of God as being unjust anyhow. But anyone who has studied the Bible (or even just the Book of Romans) knows how wrong this is. What will happen if we seek only an even-handed justice from God? The answer is that we will be lost. Justice is what Romans 1 is about. The justice of God condemns us and can only condemn us. If we seek justice from God, we will find it by being cast into outer darkness forever.

In order to be saved, we need mercy and not justice, which is what predestination is all about. It is God showing mercy to whom he will show mercy. As Paul says in Romans 9:18, ". . . God has mercy on whom he wants to have mercy, and he hardens whom he wants to harden."

As far as salvation being arbitrary is concerned, we must admit that from our perspective we cannot see why God chooses some and not others or even some and not all, and therefore his foreknowledge and predestination do seem arbitrary. But that is only because we are not God and cannot see as God sees. We cannot understand the full scope of his purposes in saving some and not others, but that does not mean that God is without such purposes. In fact, everything we know about God would lead us to conclude that he has them, though we do not know what they are. What we know about God shows that he is infinitely purposeful in his actions.

Ephesians 1:11 puts predestination in this framework, saying, "In him we were also chosen, having been predestined according to the plan of him who works out everything in conformity with the purpose of his will." That is the opposite of being arbitrary. Similarly, in Ephesians 3:10 and 11, Paul says, "His intent was that now, through the church, the manifold wisdom of God should be made known to the rulers and authorities in the heavenly realms, according to his eternal purpose which he accomplished in Christ Jesus our Lord."

2. *If you believe in predestination, you must deny human freedom.* This is a common objection, but it is based on a sad misunderstanding of the freedom we are supposed to have as fallen human beings. What does the Bible teach about our freedom in spiritual matters? It teaches that we are not free to choose God. "There is . . . no one who seeks God" (Rom. 3:10–11). "The sinful mind is hostile to God. It does not submit to God's law, nor can it do so" (Rom. 8:7). Predestination does not take away freedom. It restores it. It is because God foreknows me and predestines me to be conformed to the

image of his Son that I am delivered from sin's bondage and set free to serve him.

The matter can also be looked at practically, in answer to a related question: Does predestination destroy freedom in experience? Sinclair Ferguson answers, "We have a practical illustration in the life of that man who of all men was most clearly predestined by God, namely, Jesus. Jesus was the freest and most responsible man who ever lived. Has there ever been a life in which the sense of God's predestining purpose has been more clearly seen than in our Savior? Is he not spoken of as the elect, chosen and predestined one? Were not his ways determined for him in the pages of the Old Testament? Yet was there ever a freer man in all the universe?" Ferguson summarizes: "We may be told that the doctrine of predestination turns God into a tyrant and man into a slave. But we discover to the contrary that it shows God to be a God of great grace and the children of God to be the freest men and women."[3]

3. *If you believe in predestination, you will destroy the motivation for evangelism. For why should we labor to save those whom God has determined to save anyway?* The theological answer to this is that God determines the means to his ends as well as the ends themselves. So, if he has determined to bring the gospel to Mary Jones by a faithful witness to her by Sally Smith, then it is as important and necessary that Sally Smith be a witness to Mary Jones as it is that Mary Jones become a Christian.

But I would rather answer the objection in another way. Suppose God does not elect to salvation and thus, because he has determined to save some, does not commit himself to create new life within them that will break down their hard hearts and enable them to respond in faith to the message of the cross when it is made known. I ask: If God does not commit himself to doing that, what hope do you and I as evangelists have of doing it? If the hearts of men and women are as wicked and incapable of belief as the Bible teaches they are, how can you and I ever hope to present the gospel savingly to anyone?

To put it in even more frightening terms, if salvation depends upon *our* efforts to evangelize rather than the foreknowledge and predestination of God, what if I do something wrong? What if I give a wrong answer to a question or do something that turns others away from Christ? In that case, either by my error or because of my sin, I will be responsible for their eternal damnation. I do not see how that can encourage evangelism. On the contrary, it will make us afraid to do or say anything.

But look at it the other way. If God has elected some to salvation in order that Jesus might be glorified and that many might come to him in faith and be conformed to his image, then I can be both relaxed and bold in my wit-

---

3. Sinclair B. Ferguson, "Predestination in Christian History," *Tenth: An Evangelical Quarterly*, October 1983, p. 7.

ness. I can know that God will save those he has determined to save and will even use my witness, however feeble or imprecise it might be, if this is the means he has chosen.

Far from destroying evangelism, predestination actually makes evangelism possible. It makes it an expectant and joyful exercise.

Salvation Is of the Lord

As I close, I come back to something I said earlier. All five of these great terms—foreknowledge, predestination, calling, justification, and glorification—refer to things God does. Why is this? That is a meaningful question when we remember that there are also things that we are to do ourselves. Faith is something we do. God does not believe for us. Similarly, sanctification involves our efforts, though it is also of God. Why does Paul not mention these things in Romans 8:28–30?

The answer is obvious. The apostle is dealing with our eternal security, and he is emphasizing God's work so we might understand from the beginning that this wonderful plan of salvation cannot fail. It would if it depended on us. Everything we do fails sooner or later, and that would certainly be true of salvation. Our faith would fail. Our ability to persevere would be extinguished. Our hold on God would weaken, and we would let go and in the end fall into hell.

But salvation is not like that.

It is not our choice of God that matters, but rather God's choice of us. It is not our faith, but his call. It is not our ability to persevere, but the fact that he has determined beforehand to persevere with us to the very end and even beyond.

112

God's Effectual Call

Romans 8:30

And those he predestined, he also called. . . .

My wife Linda and I have many different personality traits, which is a natural thing for husbands and wives, and one of them is the way we respond to someone's call. If we are walking down the street and someone calls out so that we can hear the voice but cannot quite distinguish the words, my wife assumes that the person is calling her and turns around. I assume that the person is calling someone else and keep on going. The same thing is true if a driver of a car blows the horn. I ignore it; it must be for someone else. Linda thinks someone is trying to get her attention.

I do not know what that says about the two of us, perhaps only that Linda is more "people oriented" than I am and that I am more "task oriented" than she is. But it is an interesting observation in view of the word we need to look at in this study. The word is "called," and it occurs in the statement that "those he [that is, God] predestined, he also called . . ." (Rom. 8:30).

This word is the next link in the great golden chain of salvation by which God reaches down from eternity into time to save sinners. The point of this word, the third link, is that, unlike myself but like Linda, those whom God calls not only hear his call but actually respond to it by turning around and by believing on Jesus Christ or committing their lives to him.

Calling: External and Internal

But we need to back up at this point and review a distinction I made two studies ago, when I first introduced the golden chain. It is the difference between a call of men and women that is merely external, general, and (in itself) ineffective for salvation, and a call that is internal, specific, and regenerating.

The first call is an open invitation to all persons to repent of their sin and turn to Jesus. As I have mentioned, it was spoken by Jesus himself in many places. For example, he said in Matthew 11:28, "Come to me, all you who are weary and burdened, and I will give you rest." In Matthew 16:24 he explained, "If anyone would come after me, he must deny himself and take up his cross and follow me." He said in John 7:37, "If anyone is thirsty, let him come to me and drink."

This last invitation was spoken in Jerusalem on the last day of the Feast of Tabernacles, when people from many lands and nationalities were assembled. There were Jews from every part of Palestine as well as from many regions of the Roman Empire. There were also Gentiles, some who had become Jewish proselytes but also some who, no doubt, were merely interested bystanders. We get a feeling of what this audience must have been like by remembering the composition of the crowd that had assembled at Pentecost when Peter preached the first sermon of the Christian era, likewise extending a general call to all to believe on Jesus. We are told that on that occasion Jerusalem was filled with "Parthians, Medes and Elamites; residents of Mesopotamia, Judea and Cappadocia, Pontus and Asia, Phrygia and Pamphylia, Egypt and the parts of Libya near Cyrene; visitors from Rome (both Jews and converts to Judaism), Cretans and Arabs . . ." (Acts 2:9–11).

When Jesus (and later Peter) called such people to faith, the call was universal. It was (and is) for everyone. Anyone who wishes can come to Jesus Christ and be saved.

Today that same call flows from every true Christian pulpit and from all who bear witness to Jesus Christ as Lord and Savior in every land.

The difficulty with this external, universal, and (in itself) ineffectual call, however, is that if people are left to themselves, no one ever actually responds to it. People hear the gospel and may even understand it up to a point. But the God who issues the invitation is undesirable to them, and so they turn away. Jesus told a story about a man who had prepared a great banquet and invited many guests (Luke 14:15–24). When the feast was prepared he sent servants with the invitation: "Come, for everything is now ready." But the guests all began to make excuses.

"I have just bought a field, and I must go and see it," said one.

"I have just bought five yoke of oxen, and I'm on my way to try them out," said another.

A third replied, "I just got married, so I can't come."

That is the way it truly is, since Jesus was not making up this story out of thin air. That was the way the people of his day responded to his general call. They would not accept his invitation. They rejected it, preferring to go their own ways and about their own business.

One of the great newspaper organizations in this country is the Howard organization, and if you are acquainted with it, you may also be aware of the Howard Company logo. It is a lighthouse beneath which are the words: "Give the people the light, and they will find their way." The idea is that people make foolish mistakes and bad decisions because they do not know the right way. Show it to them and they will follow it, is what the motto means. But that is not the way the Bible describes our condition spiritually. When Jesus was in the world he was the world's light. The light was shining. But the men of his day did not respond to Jesus by walking in the right path. Instead they hated the light and tried to put it out. They crucified the lighthouse.

This is how people still respond to the universal invitation. It is why Jesus said, "This is the verdict: Light has come into the world, but men loved darkness instead of light because their deeds were evil" (John 3:19). It is why Paul wrote, "There is no one who understands, no one who seeks God" (Rom. 3:11). And it is why Jesus declared, "No one can come to me unless the Father who sent me draws him . . ." (John 6:44).

But this is where the second kind of call comes in, the kind that is actually spoken of in Romans 8:30. Unlike the first call, which was external, universal, and (in itself) ineffective, this second call is internal, specific, and entirely effective. In other words, it effectively saves those—and *all* those—to whom it is spoken.

The best discussion of the effectual call I know is in John Murray's small classic, *Redemption Accomplished and Applied*, where he begins by making the distinction I have just made, showing that there is such a thing as a general or universal call and that there are examples of it in the Bible. But then he points out rightly that "in the New Testament the terms for calling, when used with reference to salvation, are almost uniformly applied, not to the universal call of the gospel, but to the call that ushers men into a state of salvation and is therefore effectual. There is scarcely an instance where the terms are used to designate the indiscriminate overture of grace in the gospel of Jesus Christ."[1]

Here are some examples:

Romans 1:6–7—"And you also are among those who are called to belong to Jesus Christ. . . . called to be saints."

1. John Murray, *Redemption Accomplished and Applied* (Grand Rapids: Wm. B. Eerdmans, 1970), p. 88.

Romans 11:29—"For God's gifts and his call are irrevocable."

First Corinthians 1:9—"God, who has called you into fellowship with his Son Jesus Christ our Lord, is faithful."

Ephesians 4:1—"As a prisoner for the Lord, then, I urge you to live a life worthy of the calling you have received."

Second Timothy 1:8–9—"So do not be ashamed to testify about our Lord, or ashamed of me his prisoner. But join with me in suffering for the gospel, by the power of God, who has saved us and called us to a holy life. . . ."

Second Peter 1:10—"Therefore, my brothers, be all the more eager to make your calling and election sure. . . ."

In each of these texts and many others, including our text in Romans 8:30, the call of God is one that effectively saves those to whom it is addressed. Putting the above texts together, it is a call that unites us to Jesus Christ, bringing us into fellowship with him, and sets before us a holy life in which we will be sure to walk if we have truly been called. Putting the call into the context of Romans 8, it is the point at which the eternal foreknowledge and predestination of God pass over into time and start the process by which the individual is drawn from sin to faith in Jesus Christ, is justified through that faith, and is then kept in Christ until his or her final glorification.

Effectual calling is the central and key point in this great golden chain of five links.

The Power of God's Call

Now that we have distinguished between the external and internal calls, we need to ask why it is that the internal or specific call is so effective. Why does it bring those who hear it to salvation? The answer is not at all difficult to find. The reason the effective call *is* effective is that it is God's call. It issues from his mouth, and all that issues from the mouth of God accomplishes precisely that for which he sent it.

This is what Isaiah 55:10–11 teaches us, when it records God as saying:

> "As the rain and the snow come down from heaven,
> and do not return to it without watering the earth
> and making it bud and flourish,
>   so that it yields seed for the sower and bread for the eater,
> so is my word that goes out from my mouth:
>   It will not return to me empty,
> but will accomplish what I desire
>   and achieve the purpose for which I sent it."

God's words are always effective. They accomplish their purpose. But to be faithful to our text we need to point out that what we are dealing with in Romans 8:30, in terms of God's calling of sinners, is a call to salvation rather than another purpose. So we need to ask exactly how the effective call of God works in the achieving of this goal.

The chief thing the effective call of God in salvation does is to cause the *regeneration,* or *rebirth,* of the one thus summoned. In the study by John Murray that I referred to earlier, *Redemption Accomplished and Applied,* Murray says that it does not make much difference whether we put regeneration before effectual calling, or effectual calling before regeneration, since the critical determining act is God's in any case.[2] But when the relevant texts are carefully considered, the order nevertheless seems to be as I have indicated. That is, God calls the individual with a specific and effective call, and the call itself produces new spiritual life in the one who hears it, on the basis of which he or she is enabled to respond to the gospel.

In my judgment, the best illustration of how this works is that of the raising of Lazarus from the dead recounted in John 11, the illustration I introduced in the earlier, introductory study of these terms. We are encouraged to take it as an illustration, because it is in the midst of this story and in obvious reference to it that Jesus utters the well-known words, "I am the resurrection and the life. He who believes in me will live, even though he dies; and whoever lives and believes in me will never die . . ." (vv. 25–26).

What happens in this story? Jesus comes to the tomb of Lazarus and calls out to this dead man, "Lazarus, come out!" and Lazarus does. Clearly the call of Jesus created life in the formerly dead corpse, as a result of which Lazarus responded to Jesus by emerging from the tomb.

That is what happens when God calls us to salvation. His call creates spiritual life in the one called, and the proof that spiritual life is there is that we respond to him. How do we respond? We respond by turning from sin—the theological word is repentance—and by believing on Jesus Christ. In other words, the call of God produces life in the sinner, just as the word of God brought the heavens and earth into existence at the very beginning of creation. The first evidences of that new life are repentance from sin and faith in Jesus.

A moment ago I said that, according to John Murray, it makes little practical difference whether we put regeneration before calling, or calling before regeneration, and that is probably true, though the correct biblical picture seems to be calling first, then regeneration. However, this is not the case in regard to regeneration or calling, on the one hand, and faith and repentance on the other. In this case, the calling of God necessarily comes before the fruit of that calling. It is only after God calls and regenerates that one repents of sin and believes the gospel.

Which comes first, faith or life? The person who knows the Bible answers, "Life." Otherwise, salvation would depend on ourselves and our

2. Ibid., pp. 86, 93.

own ability, and none of the certainties that Paul is speaking about in Romans 8 would be possible.

Some Important Observations

There are a few important qualifications and observations on what I have been saying, and it would be a mistake to overlook them. Let me list three briefly.

1. *Two responses.* I said earlier that the trouble with the general call is that men and women do not naturally respond to it, meaning that they do not become Christians by this call alone. But I need to balance this by adding that, although they do not respond to the call of God unto salvation, they nevertheless can respond superficially by such outward things as coming forward at a religious meeting, making outward profession of faith, or even joining a church. And not only can they, many do. That is why Peter says in the text quoted earlier, "Therefore, my brothers, be all the more eager to make your calling and election sure . . ." (2 Peter 1:10). He means that we must be sure that we really have been called by God and are truly born again, and have not merely been called by the preacher.

Donald Grey Barnhouse, one of my predecessors as minister of Tenth Presbyterian Church in Philadelphia (1927–1960), wrote:

> If men heed no more than the outward call, they become members of the visible church. If the inward call is heard in our hearts, we become members of the invisible church. The first call unites us merely to a group of professing members; but the inward call unites us to Christ himself, and to all that have been born again.
>
> The outward call may bring with it a certain intellectual knowledge of the truth; the inward call brings us the faith of the heart, the hope which anchors us forever to Christ and the love which must ever draw us back to him who first loved us. The one can end in formalism, the other in true life. The outward call may curb the tendencies of the old nature and keep a soul in outward morality; the inward call will cure the plague that is in us and bring us on to triumph in Christ.[3]

2. *The importance of the general call.* My second qualification concerns the importance of the general call. Everything I have said thus far has stressed the necessity of the special, or internal, call of the individual to salvation by God. I have said that no one naturally responds to God on the basis of the general call alone. But now I need to add that although that is true, it is nevertheless also true that the general call is necessary, since it is through the general, or universal, call that God calls specifically.

3. Donald Grey Barnhouse, *God's Heirs: Exposition of Bible Doctrines, Taking the Epistle to the Romans as a Point of Departure*, vol. 7, *Romans 8:1–39* (Grand Rapids: Wm. B. Eerdmans, 1963), pp. 171, 172.

Let me say it this way: The effectual or specific call comes *through* the general call. That is, it is through the preaching of the Word by God's evangelists and ministers and through the telling of the Good News of the gospel by Christians everywhere that God calls sinners. He does not call everyone we Christians call. We sow the seed broadly; some of it falls on stony or shallow soil, just as some of it also falls on good soil. But when the seed falls on the soil God has previously prepared and when God, the giver of life, blesses the work of sowing—so that the seed takes root in the good soil and grows—the result is a spiritual harvest. People are saved, and they do pass into that great chain of God's saving acts, including foreknowledge, predestination, calling, justification, and glorification, that is outlined in the eighth chapter of Romans.

Let me put it still another way. If God calls effectively through the general call, it is as necessary that there be a general call if some are to be saved as it is that there be a specific and effectual call. Our call does not regenerate. God alone is the author of the new birth. All must be born "from above." Nevertheless, the way God does that is through the sowing of the seed of his Word, which is entrusted to us.

Nobody but God could invent this way of saving human beings. If it were left to us, we would say that either (1) God has to do it; we can do nothing, or (2) we have to do it; God can do nothing. As it is, the work of effectively calling people to Christ is of God, yet using human beings.

3. *Am I elect?* There is this last qualification. Sometimes people get bogged down by the subject of God's foreknowledge and predestination, and they end up saying, "Well, if God is going to elect me to salvation, he will just have to do it. There is nothing I can do." Or else they get hung up on knowing whether or not they are elect. They say, "How can I know I am elect? If I am not, there is no hope for me," and they despair. This question bothered John Bunyan, the author of *The Pilgrim's Progress*, for a long time and caused extraordinary despair in him.

But there is no reason for either such passivity or such despair. How do you know whether or not you are elect? The answer lies in another question: Have you responded to the gospel? In other words, have you answered God's call?

How do we know that the patriarch Abraham was an elect man? It is because, when God called to him to leave Ur of the Chaldeans and go to a land that he would afterward inherit, Abraham "obeyed and went, even though he did not know where he was going" (Heb. 11:8), and because he persevered in that obedience to the very end of his life.

How do we know that Moses was predestined to be saved? It is because, though raised in the lap of Egyptian luxury, when he had grown up he "refused to be known as the son of Pharaoh's daughter," choosing "to be mistreated along with the people of God rather than to enjoy the pleasures of sin for a short time" (Heb. 11:24–25). He sided with God's people.

How do we know that Paul was elected to salvation? It is because, though breathing out hatred against God's people and trying to kill some of them, when Jesus appeared to him on the road to Damascus, calling, "Saul, Saul, why do you persecute me?" the future apostle to the Gentiles was transformed. He saw his sin and turned from it. He saw the righteousness of Christ and believed on Jesus. He obeyed and served God from that time on. Moreover, when he wrote about salvation later, as he did in the letter to the Romans, he showed beyond any doubt that it was not he who chose God, but rather God who chose him and called him to be Christ's follower.

How do you know if you are among the elect?

There is only one way, and it is not by trying to peer into the eternal counsels of God, stripping the cover from the book of his divine foreknowledge and predestination. The only way you will ever know if you are among the elect is if you respond to the gospel. We are told in the Bible: "Believe in the Lord Jesus Christ, and you will be saved . . ." (Acts 16:31). Do it. Then you can know that God has set his electing love on you and that, having loved you, he will continue to love you and keep you to the end.

Will you believe? It would be a delight if God would use this study of the effectual call to call you effectually.

113

Justification and Glorification

Romans 8:30

. . . those he called, he also justified; those he justified, he also glorified.

Anyone who is involved in a business of any size knows the necessity of a long-range plan. There are one-year plans, five-year plans, and even ten-year plans. The longer these plans are the more often they need to be reviewed, revised, and updated. An executive who can create an accurate long-range plan, foreseeing most of the contingencies that will affect the company in future years, and then keep on top of it, is an extremely valuable asset to his or her organization.

We have been studying a long-range plan, in fact, the longest-range plan that has ever been devised or could be devised. It is a plan that has had its origins in eternity past and will find its consummation in eternity future. It is all-embracing. Everything that has ever happened or ever will happen in history is part of it. And it is utterly certain. So detailed is this plan and so wisely is it drafted that nothing will ever arise to upset it or even cause an alternative plan to be necessary. Of course, I am speaking of the plan of God outlined for us in Romans 8:28–30.

This plan begins with God's foreknowledge and predestination, expresses itself in time in the calling of individuals to faith in Jesus Christ as

Lord and Savior, includes justification, and ends in glorification, when these foreknown and predestined persons are made entirely like Jesus. We are to look at the last two steps of the plan in this study.

Justification by Faith

The first term we need to look at is justification, but we do not need to study it in detail here, since it was the chief focus of our study in volume one and has been mentioned many times since.

Justification is the opposite of condemnation. When a person is in a wrong relationship to the law and is condemned or pronounced guilty by the judge, condemnation does not make the person guilty. The person is only declared to be so. In the same way, in justification a person is declared by God to be in a right relationship to his law, but not made righteous. In a human court a person can be declared righteous or "innocent" on the basis of his or her own righteousness. But in God's court, since we humans have no righteousness of our own and are therefore not innocent, believers are declared righteous on the ground of Christ's atonement.

It helps to realize that the full New Testament doctrine is not merely justification alone, though this is the only word Paul uses in his abbreviated listing of it in Romans 8, but *justification by grace through faith in Jesus Christ.*

That definition has four parts.

1. *The source of our justification is the grace of God* (Rom. 3:24). Since "there is no one righteous, not even one" (Rom. 3:10), it is clear that no one can make or declare himself or herself "righteous" (v. 20). How, then, is salvation possible? It is possible only if God does the work for us—which is what "grace" means, since we do not deserve God's working. Paul frequently emphasizes this by adding the words *free* or *freely* to "grace," which is redundant but nevertheless strong writing.

2. *The ground of our justification is the work of Christ* (Rom 3:25). We saw this in volume one in our discussion of the word *propitiation*. It is because this work has been done that God has been able to justify us justly.

"Justification," writes John R. W. Stott, "is not a synonym for amnesty, which strictly is pardon without principle, a forgiveness which overlooks—even forgets (*amnēstia* is 'forgetfulness')—wrongdoing and declines to bring it to justice. No, justification is an act of justice, of gracious justice. . . . When God justifies sinners, he is not declaring bad people to be good, or saying that they are not sinners after all; he is pronouncing them legally righteous, free from any liability to the broken law, because he himself in his Son has born the penalty of their law-breaking. . . . In other words, we are 'justified by his blood.'"[1]

---

1. John R. W. Stott, *The Cross of Christ* (Downers Grove, Ill.: InterVarsity Press, 1986), p. 190.

3. *The means of our justification is faith* (Rom. 3:25–26). Faith is the channel by which justification becomes ours. This is not mentioned in the chain of God's saving actions listed in Romans 8:29–30, but it is the fruit of God's effectual calling and its result, which is regeneration. When we are born again we show it by repenting of sin and turning to Jesus Christ in faith, believing that he is our Savior.

Two things should be said about faith.

First, faith is not a good work. It is necessary, essential. But it is not a good work. In fact, it is not a work at all. Faith is God's gift, as Paul makes clear in Ephesians 2:8–9: "For it is by grace you have been saved, through faith—and this not from yourselves, it is the gift of God—not by works, so that no one can boast."

Second, although faith is the means of our justification, it is also the only means. Luther expressed this by the words *sola fide* ("by faith alone"), thus adding a word not present in the text of Scripture but by it nevertheless catching the essence of the idea. Clearly, if faith is not a good work but only receiving what God has done for us and freely offers to us, then it is by faith alone that we can be justified, all other acts or works being excluded by definition. The only means by which any person can ever be justified is by believing God and receiving what he offers.

4. *The effect of our justification is union with Christ.* This idea was developed fully in Romans 5 and in an earlier section of chapter 8. It is the ground of the benefits of our salvation unfolded in Romans 5:1–11 and of our victory over sin elaborated in Romans 5:12—8:17.

Stott explains it this way:

> To say that we are justified "through Christ" points to his historical death; to say that we are justified "in Christ" points to the personal relationship with him which by faith we now enjoy. This simple fact makes it impossible for us to think of justification as a purely external transaction; it cannot be isolated from our union with Christ and all the benefits which this brings. The first is membership of the Messianic community of Jesus. If we are in Christ and therefore justified, we are also the children of God and the true (spiritual) descendants of Abraham. . . . Secondly, this new community, to create which Christ gave himself on the cross, is to be "eager to do what is good," and its members are to devote themselves to good works. . . .
>
> To be sure, we can say with Paul that the law condemned us. But "there is now no condemnation for those who are in Christ Jesus."[2]

Hope of Glory

Glorification, the fifth and final term of Romans 8:29–30, is also a word we have studied earlier. In fact, we met the term as early as Romans 5:2

---

2. Ibid., pp. 191, 192. These four points are outlined by Stott. I discuss them in greater detail in volume one of these studies ("Just and the Justifier," Romans 3:25–26).

(which anticipates Rom. 8:28–30), where Paul spoke of Christians as rejoicing "in the hope of the glory of God."

What does Romans 5:2 mean?

It means that we know that one day we will be glorified and that we rejoice in this certainty. That is, we know that we will be like Jesus. He is God and is therefore like God in all respects; we will be like him. We will not become God, of course. But we will become like him in his communicable attributes: love, joy, peace, mercy, wisdom, faithfulness, grace, goodness, self-control and other such things (see Gal. 5:22–23). In that day sin will no longer trouble us, and we will enjoy the complete fullness and eternal favor of God's presence.

When does glorification take place?

There is a sense in which much of it takes place when we die, for then we will be freed from sin, which has taken up residence in our bodies, and will be like Christ. As John wrote, ". . . we shall be like him, for we shall see him as he is" (1 John 3:2). Yet I am sure John Murray is right when he insists in his treatment of this word that, in its fullest sense, glorification awaits the return of Jesus Christ and the resurrection of our bodies. In fact, the text in 1 John, which I have just quoted, says this. It does not say simply that "we shall be like him." It says, "*When he appears,* we shall be like him, for we shall see him as he is."

Here is how Murray puts it:

> 1. *Glorification is associated and bound up with the coming of Christ in glory.* . . . So indispensable is the coming of the Lord to the hope of glory that glorification for the believer has no meaning without the manifestation of Christ's glory. Glorification is glorification with Christ. Remove the latter and we have robbed the glorification of believers of the one thing that enables them to look forward to this event with confidence. . . .
>
> 2. *The glorification of believers is associated and bound up with the renewal of creation.* [This is the teaching of Romans 8:19–22, which we studied earlier. In those verses the glorification of our bodies, which means their resurrection, and the renewal of creation are placed together.]
>
> When we think of glorification, then, it is no narrow perspective that we entertain. It is a renewed cosmos, new heavens and new earth, that we must think of as the context of the believers' glory, a cosmos delivered from all the consequences of sin, in which there will be no more curse but in which righteousness will have complete possession and undisturbed habitation. "And there shall in no wise enter into it anything that defileth, neither whatsoever worketh abomination, or maketh a lie: but they which are written in the Lamb's book of life" (Rev. 21:27). "And there shall be no more curse: but the throne of God and of the Lamb shall be in it; and his servants shall serve him: and they shall see his face; and his name shall be on their foreheads" (Rev. 22:3, 4).[3]

3. John Murray, *Redemption Accomplished and Applied* (Grand Rapids: Wm. B. Eerdmans, 1970), pp. 177–179.

Past Tense, Future Blessing

The most striking feature of Paul's mention of glorification in Romans 8:30 is that it is in the past (aorist) tense, a fact noted when I first introduced this chain of words three studies back. Since glorification is clearly future from our perspective, this requires explanation.

Some commentators think that here Paul departs from strict accuracy or logic in order to stress the absolute certainty of this future event. That is, it is so assured that it can be spoken of *as if* it were past. D. Martyn Lloyd-Jones says this, writing, "The Apostle's argument is that, as we know most certainly that we have been called and justified, we can be equally certain of our glorification. Nothing can prevent it because it is a part of God's purpose for us."[4] Likewise Leon Morris: "So certain is it that it can be spoken of as already accomplished. It is in the plan of God, and that means that it is *as good as* here."[5]

Other scholars call this use of the past tense an aorist of *anticipation* or a *prophetic* aorist, which is almost the same thing. Since God has decreed it, it will happen and can be considered as having happened. Charles Hodge inclines to this explanation when he says, "God . . . sees the end from the beginning . . . so that in predestinating us, he at the same time, in effect, called, justified and glorified us, as all these were included in his purpose."[6]

F. Godet is also helpful, though to my way of thinking his explanation is probably not quite what Paul has in mind here. He reminds us that there is a sense in which we have been glorified. That is, our federal head Jesus Christ has been glorified, and we are glorified *in him*.[7] If this is the case, the verse would be matched by Ephesians 2:6, where Paul teaches that "God raised us up with Christ and seated us with him in the heavenly realms in Christ Jesus." This does not mean merely that taking our place in heaven is a future certainty but that we have actually already been seated in heaven in the person of Christ. The only reason I say that in my judgment this is not what Paul has in mind here is because in Romans there seems to be a flow from eternity past to eternity future, the middle portion of which dips into time. Paul seems to be describing something that began in the past, has affected us in the present, and will carry us into the future.

If we must make a choice among these three interpretations, I would side with either or both of the first two.

4. D. M. Lloyd-Jones, *Romans, An Exposition of Chapter 8:17–39, The Final Perseverance of the Saints* (Grand Rapids: Zondervan, 1976), pp. 257, 258.

5. Leon Morris, *The Epistle to the Romans* (Grand Rapids: Wm. B. Eerdmans, and Leicester, England: Inter-Varsity Press, 1988), pp. 333, 334.

6. Charles Hodge, *A Commentary on Romans* (Edinburgh, and Carlisle, Pa.: The Banner of Truth Trust, 1972), p. 286. (Original edition 1935.)

7. F. Godet, *Commentary on St. Paul's Epistle to the Romans*, trans. A. Cusin (Edinburgh: T. & T. Clark, 1892), vol. 2, p. 113.

Yet it may be—I think I prefer this—that the chain simply moves back into eternity at this point. We have seen that it begins in eternity and then dips down into time. The flow of the verses would be most satisfying if the chain simply moved back into God's timeless eternity once again, glorification being spoken of as past because it is indeed past (or eternally present) in the mind of God.

What about Sanctification?

As I close my detailed discussion of these specific terms, I want to ask a question that is also raised by Lloyd-Jones in his exposition—wisely, I think. It concerns the one obvious omission in this list: sanctification. Why is sanctification not included, particularly when it is supposed by many to be the central theme of Romans 5 through 8?

I have already addressed myself to the latter part of this question, namely, whether Paul *is* discussing sanctification in these chapters. I did that at the beginning of this volume, arguing that it is not Paul's purpose to discuss sanctification at all, though much of what he says necessarily touches on it. He is arguing the case for perseverance or eternal security, which is why he introduces the phrase "hope of glory" as early as Romans 5:2. That is the central and important theme, and it comes back at the end, in Romans 8, which is what we are studying now.

But that is not a full answer to the question.

Why not?

Well, Paul has not been discussing foreknowledge, predestination, or effectual calling in these chapters either, yet he mentions those terms here. If they are included, why not sanctification? Again, the apostle is unfolding the flow of salvation from the decrees of God in the past to our glorification in eternity future. Isn't sanctification an indispensable part of that flow? Isn't it as necessary and certain as the other items?

Why, then, is sanctification omitted?

Here are the reasons Martyn Lloyd-Jones offers.

1. *Sanctification is not part of the argument Paul has in mind at this point.* Paul is focusing on the acts of God for our salvation, and his point is that our salvation is certain because it is God who is thus acting. Our security depends upon what he has done, not on what we may or may not be able to do. To put it in other words, our security in Christ does not depend upon our sanctification. Eternal security is not the anticipated outcome of some process. Sanctification is a process while these other items are divine acts. From the point of view of Paul's argument in Romans 8, these are entirely different things.

2. *Sanctification is an inevitable consequence of justification.* Therefore, Paul does not need to mention it. As soon as a person is called by God and is justified, in that same moment sanctification begins. This is because of regen-

eration or the imparting of a new nature to the saved person. There is no justification without regeneration just as there is no regeneration without justification. So the one who is justified, who now also possesses a new nature, will inevitably show that new nature by beginning to live a new life. That is why we can say that a claim to justification apart from growth in holiness is presumption.

3. *Sanctification is inevitable also from the standpoint of our glorification.* Indeed, it is a preparation for it. To go back to the text I cited toward the beginning of this study, I note that when John, writing of glorification, says "We know that when he appears, we shall be like him, for we shall see him as he is," he immediately adds, "Everyone who has this hope in him purifies himself, just as he is pure" (1 John 3:2–3). In other words, it is the assurance of our glorification that spurs on our sanctification.

What the great Welsh preacher gets out of this (rightly, in my opinion) is that the proper way to teach sanctification is not by concentrating on "me," "my feelings," or certain steps to "personal holiness," but rather on what God has done for us. That is, the proper approach to sanctification is to fix our eyes on God and our minds on the great biblical doctrines.

How do most people teach sanctification today? Either it is by methods ("These are the steps; do this, and you will become holy"), or it is by experience ("What you need is a special filling of the Holy Spirit [or tongues or whatever]").

This is not the biblical pattern. As Lloyd-Jones says:

> The way to preach holiness is not to preach about "me" and "my feelings" and to propound various theories as to how I can be delivered; it is, rather, to preach justification and glorification. By so doing you will include sanctification. Such is the Apostle's method—"whom he justified, them he also glorified." It is because certain people do not know the truth about justification and glorification as they ought that they are defective in their teaching about sanctification. A man who has his eye on his future state of glorification will spend his time in preparing himself for it.[8]

Suppose you are invited to a party by the President of the United States. If you are normal, you would take some time to get ready, choosing a special dress or suit and making whatever other special preparations might be necessary. In the same way, the fact that we are going to be with Jesus Christ and be like him should influence our behavior and life choices.

When I was teaching on Romans 6:2 and 11, explaining how it is that we have "died to sin," I said that we have died to it in the sense that we have died to the past. And I developed a slogan: *You cannot go back; there is no place for you to go but forward.*

---

8. Lloyd-Jones, *Romans, An Exposition of Chapter 8:17–39, The Final Perseverance of the Saints*, p. 261.

That is absolutely true, of course. We cannot go back. The eternal purpose of God in saving us, unfolded in the five great acts of God described in Romans 8:29–30, makes that plain. But just as it is important to say that we cannot go back, so is it also important to say that we *are* going forward. God's foreknowledge of us is followed by his predestination of us to be conformed to the image of Jesus Christ. His predestination of us to be made like Jesus is followed by our being called to saving faith. Our calling is followed by our justification. Our justification is followed by our glorification. Therefore, it is as certain that one day we will be with Jesus, and be completely like Jesus, as it is that God exists and that his long-range plan is realistic, effective, and unchangeable.

This is God's great plan. So let's get on with our part in it and be thankful that his grace has drawn us in.

114

The Perseverance of the Saints

Romans 8:30

. . . those he justified, he also glorified.

W
e are all familiar with the saying about people who can't see the forest for the trees, and you must know people like that. You probably even know Bible teachers like that. I do not want this to be true of our study of Romans 8. So, at this point of our studies, having examined each of the five great terms of verses 28–30 in detail, I want to step back and look at the great doctrine of which they are all only individual parts.

It is not at all hard to recognize what that doctrine is, for we have been mentioning it in one way or another ever since we began the chapter. It is the perseverance of the saints, or eternal security. Or, as some say colloquially, "once saved, always saved." It is the truth that those who have been truly brought to faith in Jesus Christ—having been foreknown and predestined to faith by God from eternity past, having been called, regenerated, and justified in this life, and having been so set on the road to ultimate glorification that this culminating glorification can even be spoken of in the past tense—that these persons will never and can never be lost. Perseverance is implied in each of the terms we have studied, but this is the place to go back and look at the entire forest.

The Biblical Doctrine

Yet we do not want to distort the doctrine by oversimplification, as some do. We want to understand it as it is taught in Scripture—as Paul teaches it in Romans 8, for instance. Therefore, we need to begin our overview by excluding some common misunderstandings about perseverance.

First, perseverance does not mean that Christians are exempted from all spiritual danger, just because they are Christians. On the contrary, the opposite is true. They are in even greater danger, because now that they are Christians the world and the devil will be doggedly set against them and will try to destroy them—and would, if that were possible. We do not need to go very far in Romans to see this fact, for in the next section of this chapter Paul lists some of the hostile forces believers face. He will speak of trouble, hardship, persecution, famine, nakedness, danger, and sword, concluding, "For your sake we face death all day long; we are considered as sheep to be slaughtered" (v. 26, quoting Ps. 44:22).

It is because we really do face many spiritual dangers that the doctrine of perseverance is so important.

Second, the doctrine of perseverance does not mean that Christians are always kept from falling into sin, just because they are Christians. Sadly, Christians do sin. Noah fell into drunkenness. Abraham lied about his wife Sarah, saying she was his sister rather than his wife, thinking to protect his own life. David committed adultery with Bathsheba and then arranged for the murder of Uriah, her husband. Peter denied the Lord. Perseverance does not mean that Christians will not fall, only that they will not fall away.

Jesus predicted Peter's denial. But he added, "I have prayed for you, Simon, that your faith may not fail. And when you have turned back, strengthen your brothers" (Luke 22:31).

Third, perseverance does not mean that those who merely profess Christ without actually being born again are secure. This truth explains the many warnings that appear in Scripture to the effect that we should give diligent attention "to make [our] calling and election sure" (2 Peter 1:10). In this area Jesus' statements are among the most direct. He said, for example, "All men will hate you because of me, but he who stands firm to the end will be saved" (Matt. 10:22). We are able to stand firm only because God perseveres with us. But it is also true that we must stand firm. In fact, the final perseverance of believers is the only ultimate proof that they have been chosen by God and have truly been born again.

The Christian doctrine of perseverance does not lead to a false assurance or presumption, though some who claim to be saved do presume on God by their sinful lifestyles and willful disobedience.

Perseverance does not make us lazy.

Perseverance does not make us proud.

No, the real doctrine of perseverance is precisely what Paul declares it to be in Romans 8: that those whom God has foreknown and predestinated to be conformed to the likeness of his Son will indeed come to that great consummation. They will be harassed and frequently tempted. Often they will fall. Nevertheless, in the end they will be with Jesus and will be like him, because this is the destiny that God in his sovereign and inexplicable love has predetermined for them.

The Problem Passages

However, it is not possible to present this doctrine, even in the context of an exposition of Romans 8, without dealing with some of the biblical passages that seem to contradict it. These passages trouble some Christians and are often in their minds when they hear the security of the believer mentioned. Perhaps they trouble you.

Consider, for example, Hebrews 6:4–6, which says, "It is impossible for those who have once been enlightened, who have tasted the heavenly gift, who have shared in the Holy Spirit, who have tasted the goodness of the word of God and the powers of the coming age, if they fall away, to be brought back to repentance. . . ." Doesn't that imply that those who are saved can be lost?

Or what about 2 Peter 2:1–2? "But there were also false prophets among the people, just as there will be false teachers among you. They will secretly introduce destructive heresies, even denying the sovereign Lord who bought them—bringing swift destruction on themselves. Many will follow their shameful ways. . . ." Doesn't that say that people who have been redeemed by Christ can later deny him and thus fall away and perish?

Or what about Paul's words in 1 Corinthians 9:27? "I beat my body and make it my slave so that after I have preached to others, I myself will not be disqualified for the prize." Are believers subject to "disqualification"?

Or what about the four kinds of soil in Jesus' parable in Matthew 13? Some of the seed springs up quickly, but later it is scorched by the sun or else is choked by weeds. It perishes.

Or what about the five foolish virgins of Matthew 25? They are waiting for the bridegroom's coming, but because they went away to get oil and were not actually there when he came they were excluded from the wedding banquet.

I am sure you can add your own "problem" texts to these suggestions.

It is important to wrestle with these passages, of course, and not merely dismiss them with some glib statement of "once saved, always saved." Otherwise we will indeed be presuming, and we will miss the very important warnings the texts convey. However, a careful examination of these passages will show that although they can be said to put a proper hedge around perseverance, lest we presume upon it or take it lightly, they do not contradict the doctrine.

Three Categories

How do we approach these difficulties? Martyn Lloyd-Jones does it at great length in more than one hundred pages of careful argument in the second of two volumes on Romans 8. I do not want to take that much space to do the identical thing here. Those who want to examine the matter in greater detail can use the Welsh preacher's work.[1] However, Lloyd-Jones is helpful for us in that he puts the problem texts I have been introducing into a few manageable categories and treats them in that way. In a much briefer manner, I want to follow his procedure.

Category 1: *Passages that seem to suggest that we can "fall away" from grace.*

This category contains the most difficult and most frequently cited passages. Therefore, it is the one we need to explore at greatest length.

The first passage is the one in which the phrase "fallen away from grace" occurs, Galatians 5:4. An examination of the context shows that what Paul is addressing is the problem of false teaching that had been introduced into the Galatian churches by a party of legalistic Jews who were insisting that circumcision and other Jewish practices had to be followed if the believers in Galatia were truly to be saved. Here the contrast with grace is law, and the apostle is saying that if the believers should allow themselves to be seduced by this false teaching, they will have been led away from grace into legalism. This is not the same thing as saying that they will have lost their salvation, though the doctrine of the legalists was indeed a false doctrine by which nobody could be saved. Paul's argument is that the Galatian Christians should "stand firm" in the liberty Christ had given them and not become "burdened again by a yoke of slavery" (Gal. 5:1).

The parable of the four kinds of soil also falls into this category of problem texts. Does it teach that it is possible for a person to be genuinely born again and then fall away and be lost, either because of the world's scorching persecutions or its materialistic entanglements? The image we have of young plants suggests this, since the plants in the story obviously do have life. But if we examine Jesus' own explanation of the story, we will see that he makes a distinction between a person who only "hears" the word and a person who "hears the word and understands it" (Matt. 13:19, 23). The one who merely hears may receive the word he does not actually understand "with joy" and thus seem to be saved. But "he has no root" in him, which he proves by lasting "only a short time." Those who understand and thus have the root of genuine life in them show it by their endurance and fruit.

---

1. D. M. Lloyd-Jones, *Romans, An Exposition of Chapter 8:17–39, The Final Perseverance of the Saints* (Grand Rapids: Zondervan, 1976), pp. 263–366.

Jesus' point, since the parable concerns the preaching of the gospel in this age, is that not all preaching of the word will be blessed by God to the saving of those who hear it. Only some will be converted.

Another passage that falls in this category of problem texts is the story of the five wise and five foolish virgins. This is a disturbing parable because it teaches that there will be people within the visible church who have been invited to the marriage supper, profess Jesus as their Lord and Savior, and actually seem to be waiting for his promised return, but who are nevertheless lost at the end. It is meant to be disturbing. But if we compare it with the other parables in the same chapter—the parable of the talents and the parable of the sheep and the goats—it is clear that Jesus is saying only that in the church many who are not genuinely born again will pass for believers, until the end. It is only at the final judgment, when the Lord returns, that those who are truly saved and those who only profess to be saved will be differentiated.

The most difficult of the passages that seem to suggest that believers can fall away from grace is 2 Peter 2:1–2, which refers to people "denying the sovereign Lord who bought them." This sounds as if Peter is describing people who, having been redeemed by Jesus and having believed in him, later deny him and fall away.

We should be warned against this misunderstanding by the way the chapter continues. Then we see that Peter is actually speaking of people who have learned about Jesus Christ and have even escaped a considerable amount of the external pollution of the world by having the high standards of the Christian life taught to them, but who have repudiated this teaching in order to return to the world's corruption, which they actually love. Peter rather crudely compares them to "a dog" [that] returns to its vomit" and "a sow that is washed" but nevertheless goes back to "her wallowing in the mud" (v. 22). The reason they do this is because their inner nature is unchanged. They may have been cleaned up externally, but like the Pharisees, their insides are still full of corruption. These are the people who deny the Lord who bought them.

But how can Peter say that Jesus "bought" them? As I say, this is a difficult text and has proved so for many commentators. But the answer seems to be that Peter is also thinking of an external purchase or deliverance here. Since he begins by speaking of those who were false prophets among the people of Israel, what he seems to be saying is that just as they were beneficiaries of the deliverance of the nation from Egypt but were nevertheless not true followers of God, so there will be people like this within the churches. They will seem to have been purchased by Christ and will show outward signs of such deliverance, but they will still be false prophets and false professors.

None of these passages teach that salvation can be lost. They are either referring to something else, like falling from grace into legalism, or they are teaching that those who merely make an external profession of faith, however orthodox or holy they may seem, will fall away. As John writes in his first letter, "They went out from us, but they did not really belong to us. For if they had belonged to us, they would have remained with us; but their going showed that none of them belonged to us" (1 John 2:19).

Category 2: *Passages that seem to suggest that our salvation is uncertain.*

There are a large number of verses in this category, but they are much alike and therefore do not each require separate treatment. For example, there is Philippians 2:12: ". . . continue to work out your salvation with fear and trembling." And 2 Peter 1:10: "Therefore, my brothers, be all the more eager to make your calling and election sure. For if you do these things, you will never fall." And also Hebrews 6:4–6, "It is impossible for those who have once been enlightened, who have tasted the heavenly gift, who have shared in the Holy Spirit, who have tasted the goodness of the word of God and the powers of the coming age, if they fall away, to be brought back to repentance."

This last passage, which I have already mentioned, is particularly troubling to many. So let me begin with it. One observation is that even if the text does indirectly teach that a Christian can fall away and be lost, its specific teaching would be that such a person could thereafter never be saved a second time "because [they would be] crucifying the Son of God all over again" (v. 6). Few would want to accept that. So even those who do not believe in eternal security need to find another, better interpretation.

In this case, the answer is in the entire thrust of Hebrews, which was written to Jews who had been exposed to Christianity and had even seemed to accept it somewhat, to go on to full faith and not to draw back again into Judaism. Everything in the book points in this direction. So this "problem" passage is actually talking about people who might have had a taste of Christianity but who fall away without ever actually becoming true Christians. If this has happened, they cannot come back, because in a certain sense they have been inoculated against Christianity.

However, the real situation emerges in verse 9, where the author of the book writes, "Even though we speak like this, dear friends, we are confident of better things in your case—things that accompany salvation." In other words, the author considered his readers to be genuine believers, which meant that, in his opinion, they would not draw back but would go on to embrace the fullness of the doctrines of the faith, as he is urging them to do.

The other verses—Philippians 2:12 and 2 Peter 1:10—are not nearly so difficult. They merely remind us of what I said earlier: that the fact of God's perseverance with us does not suggest that somehow we do not have to persevere, too. We do. In fact, it is because God is persevering with us that we will persevere. Remember that Philippians 2:12, which tells us to "work out" our salvation, is immediately followed by verse 13, which says, "for it is God who works in you to will and to act according to his good purpose." That is, God gives us the desire and then enables us to achieve what he desires.

Category 3: *Warning passages.*

The final category of problem passages contains warnings, like Romans 11:20–21: ". . . Do not be arrogant, but be afraid. For if God did not spare the natural branches, he will not spare you either." Or Hebrews 2:1–3, which urges us to "pay more careful attention . . . to what we have heard" and ends with "How shall we escape if we ignore such a great salvation?" Or 1 Corinthians 9:27, where Paul issues a warning to himself: ". . . so that after I have preached to others, I myself will not be disqualified for the prize."

The reason for these passages is that we need warnings from God in order to persevere. Or, to put it in other language, they are one of the ways God has to ensure our perseverance. The proof of this is seen in the different ways unbelievers and believers react to them. Do the problem verses I have cited as "warnings" trouble unbelievers? Not at all. Either they regard them as mere foolishness and something hardly to be noticed, or they take them in a straightforward manner but assume that their lives are all right and that the verses therefore do not concern them. It is only believers who are troubled, because they are concerned about their relationships with God and do not want to presume that all is well with their souls when it may not be.

These passages provoke us to higher levels of commitment and greater godliness, which is what they are given for. And even this should encourage us. As Martyn Lloyd-Jones says, "To be concerned and troubled about the state of our soul when we read passages such as these is in and of itself evidence that we are sensitive to God's Word and to his Spirit, that we have spiritual life in us."[2]

God's Plan and God's Glory

As I said at the beginning of this study, I have taken a great deal of time to discuss these "problem passages" because I know that they loom large in the minds of Christian people whenever the doctrine of perseverance is discussed. And rightly so. We need to consider them carefully. But there is a danger in such close examination, for then we may give the impression that the related texts are all on the problem side and that there are very few passages that teach eternal security. That is not true, of course, even though in this study I will not balance my treatment of the problems with an equal number of passages on the positive side.

There are many such texts. I am sure you know some of them. There are two in the words of the Lord himself:

2. Ibid., p. 332.

"My sheep listen to my voice; I know them, and they follow me. I give them eternal life, and they shall never perish; no one can snatch them out of my hand" (John 10:27–28).

"And this is the will of him who sent me, that I shall lose none of all that he has given me, but raise them up at the last day" (John 6:39).

There are also the confident words of Paul that "he who began a good work in you will carry it on to completion until the day of Jesus Christ" (Phil. 1:6). And, of course, Romans 8:31–39, the end of the chapter:

> What, then, shall we say in response to this? If God is for us, who can be against us? He who did not spare his own Son, but gave him up for us all—how will he not also, along with him, graciously give us all things? Who will bring any charge against those whom God has chosen? It is God who justifies. Who is he that condemns? Christ Jesus, who died—more than that, who was raised to life—is at the right hand of God and is also interceding for us. Who shall separate us from the love of Christ? Shall trouble or hardship or persecution or famine or nakedness or danger or sword? As it is written:
>
> > "For your sake we face death all day long;
> >   we are considered as sheep to be slaughtered."
>
> No, in all these things we are more than conquerors through him who loved us. For I am convinced that neither death nor life, neither angels nor demons, neither the present nor the future, nor any powers, neither height nor depth, nor anything else in all creation, will be able to separate us from the love of God that is in Christ Jesus our Lord.

Why will we persevere? We will persevere because this is God's plan for us, and the end of it all will be God's glory.

115

Five Unanswerable Questions

Romans 8:31–36

What, then, shall we say in response to this? If God is for us, who can be against us? He who did not spare his own Son, but gave him up for us all—how will he not also, along with him, graciously give us all things? Who will bring any charge against those whom God has chosen? It is God who justifies. Who is he that condemns? Christ Jesus, who died—more than that, who was raised to life—is at the right hand of God and is also interceding for us. Who shall separate us from the love of Christ? Shall trouble or hardship or persecution or famine or nakedness or danger or sword? As it is written:

> *"For your sake we face death all day long;*
> *we are considered as sheep to be slaughtered."*

Anyone who has studied the Bible with care knows that there are times when we come to some soaring pinnacle of revelation and are left nearly breathless by the view. This is what happens when we come to the last great paragraph of Romans 8. Commentators have called these verses a "hymn of assurance," "a triumph song," "the highest plateau in the whole of divine revelation." But these accolades are surely

951

all too weak. This is a mountaintop paragraph. It is the Everest of the letter and thus the highest peak in the highest Himalayan range of Scripture.

I love the mountains, and some of my very best memories are linked to them. I remember a time some years ago, when my children were all young and our family was spending several weeks above Lake Geneva, near Montreux in Switzerland. There is a cable car there that takes people up a great massif called the Rocher de Nez, and on more than one occasion we went up the lift and spent many hours walking through the flower-filled meadows of the high Alpine slopes. Once on a perfect summer day we sat balanced on a ridge, looking off across the ranges and down into a valley where the cows were grazing, listening to the sonorous bells of the feeding herd and the chirping of the many birds—and reading *Heidi*, of course. One never forgets such experiences. I will never forget that day.

It is something like that to come to Romans 8:31–39. We have made our way up the steep ascent of doctrine in the first half of this great letter. We are able to look out over the beautiful but somewhat lower vistas of the book's second half. Yet now, for the time being, we are on the peak, and the experience is glorious.

John R. W. Stott has given me the title for this study, for in his short treatment of Romans 5–8, he speaks of "five undeniable affirmations" followed by "five unanswerable questions."[1] We have already looked at the undeniable affirmations. They are five words: foreknown, predestined, called, justified, and glorified. Now we are to look at the questions.

Strictly speaking, there are seven questions in these verses, two each in verses 31 and 35, and one each in verses 32, 33, and 34.[2] But the first question is not really part of the set. It is a formula Paul has for moving from exposition to the conclusion of an argument; we have already seen it several times in the letter.[3] It means, "In light of what I have been teaching, what conclusions follow?" And the last two questions (in verse 35) are actually part of the same inquiry. So there are five main questions in all. These five questions concern things that might be imagined to be able to defeat God's plan for us or harm us. But each is unanswerable, because there is nothing that can have this effect.

John Stott says, "The apostle hurls these questions out into space, as it were, defiantly, triumphantly, challenging any creature in heaven or earth or hell to answer them or to deny the truth that is contained in them. But there is no answer, for nobody and nothing can harm the redeemed people of God."[4]

1. John R. W. Stott, *Men Made New: An Exposition of Romans 5–8* (Grand Rapids: Baker Book House, 1984), pp. 101, 103.

2. In the New International Version text. Since ancient manuscripts had little or no punctuation, there have been various renderings of these verses in English with differing punctuations and varying numbers of questions.

3. In 6:1 and 7:7. Similar questions occur in 4:1 and 6:15.

4. Stott, *Men Made New*, p. 103.

These questions alone make this a mountaintop paragraph.

"Who Can Be Against Us?"

The first question is in verse 31: "If God is for us, who can be against us?" Taken by itself, the second half of this question is not at all unanswerable. Who can be against us? Why, many people and many things, of course! And not only *can* they be against us, they are. Theology has spoken of three great enemies of the Christian: the world, the flesh, and the devil. The world is against us because Christianity is an offense to it and is opposed to its God-rebelling ways. The world will get us to conform if it can; failing that, it will try to do us in. Our flesh is also an enemy because it contains the seeds of sin within it; we are unable to escape its baleful influence in this life. And, as if that were not enough, we have a powerful enemy in Satan, who is described by the apostle Peter as "a roaring lion looking for someone to devour" (1 Peter 5:8).

Yes, there are plenty of enemies out there who are against us, and there is even an enemy within. But what are these when they are put into a sentence containing the verse's first half, "If God is for us . . ."?

That is it, you see. I am sure you recognize that the word *if* in this sentence does not imply any doubt, for Paul has just banished doubt in the passage before this. He has shown how God has set his love upon us, predetermining that we are to be conformed to the likeness of his own beloved Son. Then, having made the predetermination, he has called, justified, and glorified us. In this verse "if" means "since"—"since God is for us"—and that makes the difference.

It is as if Paul is challenging us to place all the possible enemies we can think of on one-half of an old-fashioned balance scale, as if we were weighing peanuts. Then, when we have all the peanuts assembled on the scale, he throws an anvil onto the other side of the balance. That side comes crashing down, and the peanuts are scattered. "If God is for us, who can be against us?" Who can stand against God? The answer is "nobody." Nothing can defeat us if the Almighty God of the universe is on our side.

"How Will He Not Also . . . ?"

"Ah," someone says, "but that is assuming that God himself does not change. Nothing can stand against God, true enough. But what if God should grow weary of us, forget about us, and move on to something else?" Paul deals with this speculation in verse 32, asking, "He who did not spare his own Son, but gave him up for us all—how will he not also, along with him, graciously give us all things?"

Each of these five questions is unanswerable because each is grounded upon some undeniable truth, as we will see, and the undeniable truth in this verse is that God has given us his Son. If Paul had merely asked, "Will

God give us all things?" we might hesitate to answer, for how could we be confident he will? He has given us much, to be sure. But all things? Wouldn't we be right to think that even God might have limits to his grace and generosity? That might be reasonable were it not for the fact that God has already given us his Son. Jesus Christ, the divine Son of God, is the greatest thing God had to give. Yet he gave him—and not merely to be with us in some mystical way. He gave him over to death so that we might be rescued from the judgment due us for our sins.

Paul is challenging us to look at the cross and reason as follows: If God did that for us, sending his own Son, Jesus, to die in our place, is there anything he can possibly be imagined to withhold?

Some years ago a Bible teacher was speaking to a group of children, and he said that he would give a prize of ten dollars to anyone who could think of a promise that God might have made to us that he has not already made. The teacher might as well have offered a billion dollars, as he said, because our text tells us that God has already guaranteed us "all things" since he has not withheld his Son. The verse is a blank check for our true needs.

For example, we need strength to overcome temptation. By ourselves, we cannot resist temptations to sin. Will God give the strength we need to overcome it? Of course. Paul says elsewhere, "No temptation has seized you except what is common to man. And God is faithful; he will not let you be tempted above what you can bear . . ." (1 Cor. 10:13).

We also need a friend to be with us through life's dark places, so we will not despair and lose hope. Will God be a friend to us? Of course he will. Jesus said, "I no longer call you servants, because a servant does not know his master's business. Instead, I have called you friends . . ." (John 15:15); "And surely I am with you always, to the very end of the age" (Matt. 28:20).

Do we need direction for how we are to live and how we are to please God? God will provide that direction. God says, "I will instruct you and teach you in the way you should go" (Ps. 32:8a).

Do we need comfort when we have lost a loved one? God is the only sure source of comfort.

Will God be with us in death's dark hour? Of course. He will sustain us in death and bring us joyfully into his glorious presence at the last. The Bible says, "Precious in the sight of the LORD is the death of his saints" (Ps. 116:15). And lest we somehow think that some important need of ours has been overlooked, we remember Paul's words to the Philippians, spoken under the inspiration of the Holy Spirit: "And my God will meet all your needs according to his glorious riches in Christ Jesus" (Phil. 4:19).

Clearly, if God gave us Jesus, the greatest of all possible gifts, he can be counted on to give us all the lesser gifts. As John Stott says, "The cross proves [God's] generosity."[5]

5. Ibid., p. 104.

"Who Will Bring Any Charge?"

The third of these questions moves into the legal area, as if we were now in a court of law, asking whether someone might exist somewhere to accuse us and thus bring us into final spiritual condemnation. The question is in verse 33, "Who will bring any charge against those whom God has chosen?" Who could do that, Paul queries, since "it is God who justifies"?

Do you remember that great scene in the writings of the minor prophet Zechariah in which the high priest of that day, whose name was Joshua, is seen standing in the temple, no doubt preparing to present the people's sacrifice, and Satan is also there accusing him? Joshua is dressed in filthy clothes, symbolizing his sin. The devil is arguing that Joshua is unfit for his office, because he is a sinner. But God is also there, and he rebukes Satan through an angel, who says: "The LORD rebuke you, Satan! The LORD, who has chosen Jerusalem, rebuke you! Is not this man a burning stick snatched from the fire?" (Zech. 3:2). Then we are told how Joshua's filthy clothes are removed and how he is clothed with rich garments and a clean turban, symbols of his justification through the work of Jesus Christ. Who could accuse him now? The answer is clear: "No one, no one at all." Because God has justified him.

This is the picture conjured up by Paul's question. Apart from the work of God in Christ there would be many to condemn us—the devil, of course, and others, even our own hearts. But consider Paul's counter: "It is God who justifies," indeed, *has* justified us (see v. 30). Who could possibly secure our condemnation when we have already been acquitted by the highest court of all?

"Who Is He That Condemns?"

The fourth question is so closely related to the third that some have considered them to be asking the same thing. Yet there is a difference, as I will now explain.

Paul had earlier asked whether the good purposes of God toward us could change, concluding that they could not, since God has already given us Jesus, the greatest of all gifts (v. 32). Now Paul seems to go a step further, asking whether the attitude of Jesus could change. Verse 34 asks the question: "Who is he that condemns?" It answers, "Christ Jesus, who died—more than that, who was raised to life—is at the right hand of God and is also interceding for us."

The Bible teaches this truth in a striking image, using the word *paraclete* (or lawyer) for both the Holy Spirit and Jesus. A *paraclete* is "one called alongside another to help," which is also the exact meaning of the word *advocate*, the only difference being that one is derived from Greek and the other from Latin. Jesus used this word of the Holy Spirit when he told the disciples that he was going to send the Holy Spirit to them to be their

Counselor (John 16:5–15), and John used the term to speak of Jesus himself, saying that in him we have an "advocate" (KJV) who "speaks to the Father in our defense" (1 John 2:1). This is a picture of a divine law firm with two branches, a heavenly office and an earthly one. On earth the Holy Spirit pleads for us, interpreting our petitions correctly. In heaven the Lord Jesus Christ pleads the efficacy of his shed blood to show that we are saved persons and that nothing can rise up to cause our condemnation by God.

"Who Shall Separate Us from . . . Christ?"

The final, all-embracing, and climactic question is in verse 35: "Who shall separate us from the love of Christ?" and the development of the answer carries us to the chapter's end.

John Stott writes:

> With this fifth and last question, Paul himself does what we have been trying to do with his other four questions. He looks round for a possible answer. He brings forward all the adversaries he can think of, which might be thought to separate us from Christ's love. We may have to endure "tribulation," "distress" and "persecution"—that is, the pressures of an ungodly world. We may have to undergo "famine" and "nakedness"—that is, the lack of adequate food and clothing, which, since Jesus promised them to the heavenly Father's children, might seem to be evidence that God does not care. We may even have to experience "peril" and "sword"—that is, the danger of death and actual death, by the malice of men; martyrdom, the ultimate test of our faith. It is a real test, too, because (v. 36) the Scripture warns us in Psalm 44:22 that God's people are for his sake "being killed all the day long." That is, they are continuously being exposed to the risk of death, like sheep for the slaughter.
>
> These are adversities indeed. They are real sufferings, painful and perilous, and hard to bear. But can they separate us from the love of Christ? No! Verse 37: far from separating us from Christ's love, "in all these things"—in these very sufferings, in the experience and endurance of them—"we are more than conquerors."[6]

What Do *You* Say?

These five questions are so important that we are going to return to them and study them in detail in the next few studies, much as we returned to the "five undeniable affirmations" in verses 29 and 30, after having looked at them more generally. But before we do that I want to return to the question I separated out at the beginning, namely, the introductory question: "What, then, shall we say in response to this?" (v. 31a).

Paul asks this summary question in a plural form, "What shall *we* say?", including everybody to whom he is writing. But I want to ask it in the singu-

6. Ibid., pp. 105, 106.

lar. I want to ask it of you: "What do *you* say to these things? What is *your* response?"

This question is a divisive one, in the sense that it very clearly separates believers from unbelievers. Ask this question of a person who is not a Christian, and you will get one of two responses. One possibility is that the person will be utterly indifferent to the question and to the doctrines of God's grace that lie behind it. That is, he couldn't care less about the answer, because he thinks the whole thing is utter foolishness. Or else the person will respond with hostility: "Who are you to think that God has shown such special favor to you? To actually send Jesus to die for you and then promise to keep you through all the problems of this life and take you to heaven? What amazing arrogance!" If you talk about the Christian faith to unbelievers, I am sure you have met with both these responses.

But what is the case with Christians? Their response is quite different. They rejoice in what God has done for them.

I admit that there are Christians who are confused about these teachings and some who are timid. They are afraid to be too strong when talking about God's keeping power with his saints, believing that an emphasis on perseverance is dangerous. "Won't it cause people to grow careless about their faith?" they wonder. It does not, of course. But even though some are confused and some are timid, I maintain that there is nevertheless an enormous gulf between Christians' responses and the responses of those who are yet in their sins.

The heart of the believer warms to these truths, cautiously perhaps, but nevertheless responding with joy. For within all who truly know Christ there is the conviction that his is indeed a great love; that his love for us is the very foundation of our salvation; and that, because his is a divine love, all Christians can be assured that his love for us will never be shaken, weaken, vary, fluctuate, or change. On the contrary, believers know that the love of God in Christ is the greatest reality in the universe. It is the strongest, most steady, firm, unbending, solid, substantial, constant, uniform, dependable thing of all.

So I ask, "What do you say in response to these affirmations?" Do they strike a harmonious note within you? If so, it is proof that God has been at work in your life, bringing you out of darkness into his marvelous light. If these doctrines do not seem appealing to you—if they do not seem true or if you regard them with indifference—I warn you that you are not a Christian, that you do not know the Lord Jesus Christ in a saving way. I present him to you as your Savior. I challenge you to repent of your sin and turn to him.

It is this very gospel, the Good News of the fixed love of God in Jesus Christ, that is commended to you. As Paul wrote earlier in the letter, "But God demonstrates his own love for us in this: While we were still sinners, Christ died for us" (Rom. 5:8).

God used this great doctrine of the keeping power of the love of God in Christ to save Charles Haddon Spurgeon, one of the most powerful evangelists who ever lived. He became a Christian when he was only fifteen years of age. But he had already noticed that friends of his, who had begun life well, had made a wreck of their lives by falling into gross vices. Spurgeon feared that he might fall into them, too. In later years he explained his thinking: "Whatever good resolutions I might make, the probabilities were they would be good for nothing when temptation assailed me. I might be like those of whom it has been said, 'They see the devil's hook and yet cannot help nibbling at his bait.'" Spurgeon feared that he would disgrace himself and be lost.

It was then that he heard that Jesus will keep his saints from falling and will bring them safely to heaven. The doctrine had a particular charm for him, and he found himself saying, "If I go to Jesus and get from him a new heart and a right spirit, I shall be secured against these temptations into which others have fallen. I shall be preserved by him." It was this truth, with others, that brought C. H. Spurgeon to the Savior.[7]

"What do you say to these things?" This is a divisive question, as I said. But it is a decisive one too, and I urge you to decide. May God give you grace to respond to the message in faith and with joy.

7. The quotes are from Charles Haddon Spurgeon, "Perseverance Without Presumption" in *Metropolitan Tabernacle Pulpit*, vol. 18 (Pasadena, Tex.: Pilgrim Publications, 1971), pp. 347, 348.

116

Enduring Love

Romans 8:32

He who did not spare his own Son, but gave him up for us all—how will he not also, along with him, graciously give us all things?

John Calvin always expressed himself beautifully and frequently with great power. He has done both in his comments on Romans 8:31:

"'If God is for us, who is against us?'

"This is the chief and therefore the only support to sustain us in every temptation. If God is not propitious to us, no sure confidence can be conceived, even though everything should smile upon us. On the other hand, however, his favor alone is a sufficiently great consolation for every sorrow, and a sufficiently strong protection against all the storms of misfortune."

The great Reformer then cites a number of Bible texts in which believers dare to despise every earthly danger because of trusting God alone.

Psalm 23:4. "Even though I walk through the valley of the shadow of death, I will fear no evil, for you are with me."

Psalm 56:11. "In God I will trust; I will not be afraid. What can man do to me?"

Psalm 3:6. "I will not fear the tens of thousands drawn up against me on every side." Calvin then concludes, "There is no power under heaven or above it which can resist the arm of God."[1]

That is all very true, and it is what the apostle Paul wants us to conclude as the result of Romans 8:31, the first verse of the great defiant paragraph that concludes the eighth chapter. But a new question arises in our minds: Granted that nothing can be against us if God is for us, but *is* God really for us? How can we know that the great God of the universe is actually on our side?

Perhaps he is too busy to care about us.

Maybe we are too insignificant for him to give us even a second thought.

What if our sins have caused him to regret that he brought us into being in the first place?

Paul has no doubts along any of these lines, of course. But lest *we* do, he follows his first question with a second one, which is meant to blow these fearful musings to the winds: "He who did not spare his own Son, but gave him up for us all—how will he not also, along with him, graciously give us all things?" (v. 32). The verse means: We can know that God is for us and will be for us always because he has already given us his Son.

Facts Not Emotions

I want to examine Paul's statement in some detail because, like each of these great questions and statements, it is vitally important. But before I do, it is also important to notice what Paul does not say. If Paul were one of our contemporary Bible teachers or modern theologians, he might answer our doubts by saying, "You do not need to worry about the future, because God loves you. God is love."

That would be true, of course. In fact, that is the ultimate affirmation of this paragraph: Nothing in heaven or earth or "in all creation, will be able to separate us from the love of God that is in Christ Jesus our Lord" (v. 39). But Paul was a pastor, and he knew well that we can all easily doubt such statements, particularly when life becomes difficult. "All right," we may say, "I grant that God is love. But does he love *me*? How can I believe he loves me when I have lost my job, when my husband [or wife] has left me for someone else, when I have been diagnosed with an incurable disease? In fact, even when things go well, there are times when I just do not feel that God loves me or even that he cares about me at all."

Paul knew that mere assurances that God loves us are not effective. So, instead of dealing with our doubts on the emotional level—which is what "God loves you" does—he turns from emotional experience to sure facts. According to this verse, we can know that God is for us, not because we

1. The quotes are from John Calvin, *The Epistles of Paul the Apostle to the Romans and to the Thessalonians*, trans. Ross MacKenzie (Grand Rapids: Wm. B. Eerdmans, 1973), p. 183.

somehow sense that it is his nature to be loving, but because he has given us his Son to die for us. That is, we can know God's nature because of what he has already done in human history.

Actually, that is what Paul also does in verse 39, which I said was the ultimate affirmation of this paragraph. He says that nothing in heaven or earth or "in all creation, will be able to separate us from the love of God that is in Christ Jesus our Lord." But notice that even there, where he is speaking explicitly of God's love, it is nevertheless the love of God that is "in Christ Jesus our Lord." This is a way of saying that it is only in Christ and through the work of Christ that we can know and be assured of God's love.

Someone has noted rightly that there is hardly a verse in the Bible that speaks of God's love that does not also, either explicitly or by inference, speak of the cross of Christ or the atonement.

What Hath God Wrought?

The cross of Christ is so important to Paul that he will present various aspects of it in this and the next two verses. Yet Paul's purpose here is not to develop a theory of the atonement; he has done that already in Romans 3. His immediate purpose is to remind us of the factual elements of the atonement so that we will know that God is truly on our side.

What facts does he tell us in this verse?

1. *That this is God's action; God has done it.* This is the kind of point that is easy to pass over and not even think about. But it is actually extremely important, and a failure to see it leads to errors. I will present two of them.

The first error is made by people who think of the atonement as something accomplished by a loving Jesus to change the mind of God, who is imagined to be angry. To this way of thinking, God is ready to condemn us, but Jesus enters the picture to plead for us. "I love these people," he says. "Look, I am dying for them, in their place. Spare them for my sake." So God, who initially is reluctant or hostile, eventually agrees. "All right," he says. "I'll do it since you seem to care so much."

That is a travesty of what happened, of course. For whenever we read the Bible we find from beginning to end that the salvation of sinners by the death of Jesus is God's idea, that he, to use theological language, is the author or source of our salvation. Think of Isaiah 53:4:

> Surely he took up our infirmities
> and carried our sorrows,
> yet we considered him *stricken by God,*
> smitten *by him,* and afflicted.

The point of the verse, as emphasized by the added italics, is that God was responsible for Jesus's death. Isaiah makes the same point two verses further on, in verse 6.

> We all, like sheep, have gone astray,
>> each of us has turned to his own way;
> and *the Lord has laid on him*
>> the iniquity of us all.

Isaiah 53:6 is one of the clearest statements of substitutionary atonement in the Bible, but it is no less a statement of the fact that God the Father conceived and carried out this plan. God was not made to love us by Christ's death. He loved us from the beginning, and it is because he loved us that Jesus died. We can easily see how important this truth is to the argument for eternal security that Paul is making.

The second error people make in thinking of Christ's death is that they see it as a result of human actions only. "What a terrible day that was, when evil, jealous men killed the best man who ever lived," they might say.

It is true that evil men conspired to do away with Jesus. But the Bible never stops there when it speaks of the atonement. Do you remember how Peter put it when he addressed the Jews of Jerusalem on Pentecost, a few bare weeks after the crucifixion? He asserted their guilt. There was no escaping that. But he said this, "This man was handed over to you *by God's set purpose and foreknowledge;* and you, with the help of wicked men, put him to death by nailing him to the cross" (Acts 2:23, emphasis added). They were guilty, but the important thing is that Jesus' death had been planned and was accomplished by God.

So the atonement shows that God loved us from the beginning, indeed, has always loved us. It shows that he is truly on our side.

2. *That the atonement involved God's only Son.* The second point of fact Paul makes in verse 32 is that the atonement involved God's one and only Son. This teaches a number of things, one of them being Jesus' full deity. Indeed, this is basic to what comes next. For it is his being divine that gives the death of Jesus its full force and meaning. If Jesus were only another human being, his death would have no more value or significance than that of any other human being, a great example perhaps, but certainly not an atonement. It is because Jesus is the unique Son of God and therefore both holy and of infinite value that his death can be a true atonement for our sin.

John the Baptist introduced Jesus by saying, "Look, the Lamb of God, who takes away the sin of the world!" (John 1:29). This is important, too, because it adds something to the first statement. Showing that God is the author of our salvation points out that God has always been disposed to love us; indeed, he has loved us from eternity. But if that is all that can be said, a question would immediately arise: But how *much* does he love us? We, too, often love, though not well. Our love weakens. Could it be that God is like us in love, that he loves but not a whole lot—not enough to actually see us through all life's difficulties?

The answer, of course, is that God loves with an intensity and affection infinitely surpassing ours. And we know this because he has given us his own Son, his one and only Son. Jesus is the greatest gift God had to give. There is nothing in all the universe more precious to God than his Son and nothing greater than God's Son. So when God gave Jesus, he proved the greatness of his love by the most precious gift of all.

> The guilty pair, bowed down with care,
> God gave his Son to win.
> His erring child he reconciled
> and rescued from his sin.
> O love of God, how rich and pure,
> how measureless and strong.
> It shall forevermore endure,
> the saints' and angels' song.
>
> F. M. Lehman, 1917

3. *That God spared him not.* The third assertion in this verse carries us a step beyond even what we have seen so far, for it tells us that God "did not spare" Jesus. He could have spared him, but he did not.

Almost everyone who writes on this verse carefully recognizes that it contains a strong reference to the story of Abraham's near sacrifice of his son Isaac on Mount Moriah. This is because the Septuagint (Greek) translation of the Old Testament uses the Greek word for "spared" that is found in Romans 8:32 to translate one of God's words to Abraham following the patriarch's amazing obedience to God's command to sacrifice his son. The New International Version translates it as "withheld" in the Genesis text, but it is the same word. God said, ". . . because you have done this and have not withheld [spared] your son, your only son, I will surely bless you and make your descendants as numerous as the stars in the sky and as the sand on the seashore . . ." (Gen. 22:16–17).

The irony of the story, however, is that although Abraham was obedient to God up to the point of actually raising the knife to kill his son—that is, *he did not spare him*—God intervened to accomplish just that. God *did* spare Isaac, though Abraham was willing not to do so.

But the story also illustrates, and undoubtedly was also used by God to teach Abraham, that one day God literally would not spare his own Son but would allow him to die in order that Isaac and Abraham and all other believers down through the long ages of human history might be spared. Jesus is the only one who has ever deserved to be spared. Certainly none of *us* do. But by refusing to spare his Son, God spared us so that we might be saved and come to spend an eternity in glory with him. Somehow God taught that to Abraham on Mount Moriah, which is why Abraham named the place *Jehovah Jireh*, "The Lord Will Provide" (Gen. 22:14). God provided for us by giving up Jesus.

4. *That God delivered up Jesus for us.* This brings us to the fourth of the statements Paul has tucked into this single verse about the actions of God the Father in saving us through Jesus' death on Calvary. The previous statement was negative: "He did not spare his own Son." This statement is positive: "but gave him up for us all." It is a way of making the point more emphatic.

What does the statement mean when it says that God "gave him up" for us all? It means that God delivered him to death, of course. Jesus died, whereas Isaac did not have to die on Mount Moriah. But it is not just physical death that is meant here. This death was a spiritual death, involving a temporary separation from the Father when Jesus was made sin for us and actually bore the wrath of God against sin in our place. Do you remember the agony of the Lord Jesus Christ in the Garden of Gethsemane? Jesus prayed that "this cup" might be taken from him and in his grief sweat, as it were, great drops of blood (Luke 22:39–44). Later on the cross he prayed, "My God, my God, why have you forsaken me?" (Matt. 27:46). This was not a man shrinking from mere physical death. If it were, Socrates would be a better model for us than Jesus. Instead, it was the horror of the holy, eternal Son of God as he faced the experience of being made sin for us and of bearing the wrath of separation from the love of God in our place. He was delivered up so that we might be spared. He bore the wrath of God so that we might never have to bear it.

D. Martyn Lloyd-Jones writes:

> Such, then, is the measure of God's love, and it is the only adequate measure of a love which is "beyond measure." How pathetic and hopeless is the position of people who think that they safeguard the love of God by denying the substitutionary theory of the atonement, who say that our Lord did not cry out in an agony, and who imagine that the measure of the love of God is that God says, "Though you have killed my Son, I still love you, and am still ready to forgive you"! They believe that they safeguard and magnify the love of God by denying the truth concerning the wrath of God, and that God must and does punish sin. . . . What they actually do is detract from the love of God. The love of God is only truly seen when we realize that "He spared not his own Son" . . . .
>
> It is in such an action that you see the love of God. He loved such as we are, and to such an extent, that for us he punished his only Son, did not spare him anything, "delivered him up for us all," and poured upon him the final dregs of his wrath against sin and evil, and the guilt involved in it all.[2]

From the Greater to the Lesser

At this point it is easy to see how Paul's argument wraps up. For, having reminded us of the greater truth, indeed the greatest truth of all, the apos-

---

2. D. M. Lloyd-Jones, *Romans, An Exposition of Chapter 8:17–39, The Final Perseverance of the Saints* (Grand Rapids: Zondervan, 1976), pp. 396, 397.

tle insists that the lesser will certainly follow from it. It is like saying, "If a rich benefactor has given you a million dollars, he will certainly not withhold a quarter if you need it for a parking meter."

"He who did not spare his own Son, but gave him up for us all—how will he not also, along with him, graciously give us all things?" What are these "all things" Paul mentions? Well, *all things*, of course! Still, we have to understand this in the context of the terms Paul has been using. It does not mean all material things, as if Paul were promising that we would be rich. Or even good health necessarily. It is rather along the line of verse 28, which says that "in all things God works for the good of those who love him, who have been called according to his purpose." It means that God will overrule everything for our benefit, so that even evil will somehow be worked into God's great purpose, which is to make us like Jesus.

Whatever your circumstances, whatever trials, whatever pains, whatever persecutions, whatever hardships—God will use all of these things to make you like Jesus. Beyond that, he will provide all true necessities for your growth in holiness and perseverance in faith until the very end.

Love That Will Not Let Go

I want to end with a great hymn written by a Scottish minister of the last century whose name was George Matheson. He lived from 1842 to 1906. Matheson was blind, having lost his sight in his early youth, and his blindness gives great power and pathos to the words of the hymn, which clearly refer to it. But the occasion for the hymn was not the blindness but, in his own words, some "extreme mental distress," which had brought him great "pain." The story that grew up around this hymn, that his fiancée left Matheson when he lost his sight, seems to be unfounded. Nevertheless, something happened, something so painful that he never related it to anyone.

Matheson wrote this hymn on the evening of June 6, 1882, when he was alone in the manse in Inellen, Scotland, his family having all gone to Glasgow for his sister's wedding.

> O Love that wilt not let me go,
> I rest my weary soul in thee;
> I give thee back the life I owe,
> That in thine ocean depths its flow
>   May richer, fuller be.
>
> O Light that followest all my way,
> I yield my flickering torch to thee;
> My heart restores its borrowed ray,
> That in thy sunshine's blaze its day
>   May brighter, fairer be.

O Joy that seekest me through pain,
I cannot close my heart to thee;
I trace the rainbow through the rain,
And feel the promise is not vain
     That morn shall tearless be.

O Cross that liftest up my head,
I dare not ask to fly from thee;
I lay in dust life's glory dead,
And from the ground there blossoms read
     Life that shall endless be.

No one can read those lines without knowing that George Matheson knew the love of God in Christ Jesus and was assured that, whatever his circumstances might be, "he who did not spare his own Son, but gave him up for us all" would surely "along with him, graciously give us all things."[3]

Christian, reason it out. Do not be double-minded in your spiritual understanding. Know that God is working out all things for your good and that he will surely keep on doing so until the end.

---

3. The background of this hymn is from W. J. Limmer Sheppard, *Great Hymns and Their Stories* (Fort Washington, Pa.: Christian Literature Crusade, 1968), pp. 118, 119; and Daniel A. Polling, *A Treasury of Best-Loved Hymns* (New York: Pickwick Press, 1942), p. 38.

117

Our Perfect Salvation

Romans 8:33

Who will bring any charge against those whom God has chosen? It is God who justifies.

We have been dealing with the last full paragraph of Romans 8, and the focus of our discussion is the five unanswerable questions it contains. We have looked at two of these already: (1) "If God is for us, who can be against us?" and (2) "He who did not spare his own Son, but gave him up for us all—how will he not also, along with him, graciously give us all things?" In this study we come to the third unanswerable question.

The question asks: "Who will bring any charge against those whom God has chosen?" It is unanswerable because "it is God who justifies."

When I was writing about these five questions earlier, I pointed out that each is unanswerable because of some great spiritual truth. The truth behind the first great question is that God is for us. Therefore, "Who can be against us?" The truth in the second question is that God has already given us the best gift he could possibly have given. Therefore, "How will he not also, along with him, graciously give us all things?"

What is the truth in this third question? It is that God has justified us. No charge can be brought against those whom God has chosen if God, the supreme Judge of the entire universe, has acquitted them.

Let me state this another way. In the first question we are reminded that in God we have a Champion. In the second question we are reminded that in God we have a Benefactor. In the third question we are reminded that in God we have a Judge.

The Judge Appears

Ah, but that is just the problem. A judge? The very word triggers feelings of anxiety within us, and when we think of God as the Supreme Judge and of the fact that we must stand before him one day, our souls are rightly troubled and distressed. This thought filled the great Protestant Reformer Martin Luther with fearful contemplation, which he captured in one of his greatest hymns:

> Great God, what do I see and hear!
> The end of things created!
> The Judge of mankind doth appear
> On clouds of glory seated!
> The trumpet sounds, the graves restore
> The dead which they contained before:
>   Prepare my soul to meet him.

In our day a great deal of cultural energy has been spent trying to dispel these anxieties, lest we think about the final judgment and become troubled by the prospect. We numb ourselves by banal and unending entertainment, crowd our hours with frantic activity, bolster our sagging self-images by pop psychology and self-help programs. But in our quiet moments, if we have any, our subconscious thoughts surface to remind us that we are not what we should be, that we have willed to go astray like lost and foolish sheep, and that one day there will certainly be an accounting.

This disturbing realization is captured in a popular song by Billy Joel that says quite rightly, "I know that it'll catch up to me, somewhere along the line."

We are troubled on three counts.

First, our consciences accuse us. We put on a front for other people and sometimes fool them. We get them thinking that we are better or nicer or smarter or more godly than we actually are. But we do not do very well fooling ourselves. We know what our thoughts are in our secret moments—the lusts, angers, lies, and blasphemous ideas we harbor within. We may dull those thoughts, but we cannot escape them. This is what Paul was talking about in Romans 2:12–16, where he spoke of the final judgment day and of how even the thoughts of the heathen accuse them:

All who sin apart from the law will also perish apart from the law, and all who sin under the law will be judged by the law. For it is not those who hear the law who are righteous in God's sight, but it is those who obey the law who will be declared righteous. (Indeed, when Gentiles, who do not have the law, do by nature things required by the law, they are a law for themselves, even though they do not have the law, since they show that the requirements of the law are written on their hearts, their consciences also bearing witness, and their thoughts now accusing, now even defending them.) This will take place on the day when God will judge men's secrets through Jesus Christ, as my gospel declares.

As if it were not bad enough that our consciences accuse us, we also have Satan as our great "accuser." The Bible tells us this, in case we were not aware of it, for there he is called "the accuser of our brothers [that is, Christians], who accuses them before our God day and night" (Rev. 12:10). It is Christians whom Satan particularly accuses, for he already dominates unbelievers and does not want to awaken them to their sin.

If you are a Christian, Satan is accusing you to God. He is saying, "Did you see what John Smith did? That is no way for a Christian to act. That act is disgraceful, ungodly, secular. How can a person do that and still claim to be a Christian? How can you regard him as a Christian?"

Satan is saying, "Do you know what Mary Smith is thinking about right now? Her thoughts are unworthy of even a highly immoral woman, let alone a Christian. Aren't you ashamed of her conduct? I know I am."

Satan is saying, "I wouldn't have those people as my followers. How can you accept them? How can you have sent your Son to die for them?"

And Satan is making such accusations "day and night," according to the text in Revelation.

Yet it is not our own consciences or even Satan that really troubles us if we are at all spiritually perceptive. Rather, it is that we must stand before God, the Omniscient One, before whom all hearts are open, all desires known. That is the truly troubling prospect. That is what distressed Luther in the days before he came to understand the gospel and rejoice in what God had done for him in Jesus Christ. He used to tremble, asking himself, "How can I stand before God in the day of his judgment?" The wisdom of his age said that he could stand before God by good works. "But," said Luther, "what works can come from a heart like mine? How can I stand before the holiness of my Judge with works polluted in their very source?"[1]

Have you never thought this way? Have you never trembled at the thought that one day you must stand before God? In our day, of course, it is quite possible that such a thought has not crossed your mind. Much of our culture is designed to keep you from contemplating that awesome happening.

1. J. H. Merle D'Aubigne, *The Life and Times of Martin Luther* (Chicago: Moody Press, 1958), p. 32.

If you have never thought this way, if you have never trembled for your soul in light of your sins, then I say, "God help you." How can you believe in the gospel if you have never trembled under law? How can you be comforted by a text like Romans 8:33 if you have never seen your need to be saved from sin by Jesus Christ, to be justified by God on the basis of Christ's atonement and the gift of his righteousness?

It Is God Who Justifies

I am not unfolding the meaning of this great text in Romans to being you discomfort, of course. I do this only to awaken you to what the text says. The important thing is not merely that God, the author and accomplisher of our salvation, is our Judge. It is that this great, sovereign, and inescapable Judge has acquitted us through the work of Jesus Christ—if we have believed on Jesus Christ and trust him.

I want you to see two great things Romans 8:33 teaches us.

If you have been saved by God through the work of Jesus Christ, you are among those "whom God has chosen."

That is an interesting way of putting the statement, isn't it? Paul does not say, "Who will bring any charge against sinners?" For there are sinners whose sins are covered by the blood of Jesus Christ, and there are sinners whose sins are *not* covered by the blood of Christ. In the case of the latter, not only are the charges made—by their own consciences, by Satan, and by God himself—those charges stick! Those sinners are guilty, and there is no escape from the inevitable and resulting condemnation. It is only those "whom God has chosen" who will escape such sharp condemnation.

The word *chosen* takes us back to verses 28–30, which give the context in which the new status of "those whom God has chosen" is to be understood. Who are these persons? They are those "who have been called according to his [that is, God's] purpose" (v. 28). They are those whom "God foreknew" and "predestined to be conformed to the likeness of his Son, that he might be the firstborn among many brothers" (v. 29).

Using the five great words of that passage, they are those whom God "foreknew," "predestined," "called," "justified," and "glorified." What Paul is saying in our text is: How could anyone possibly bring any lasting or prevailing charge against such persons?

If you are among those whom God has chosen, it is also true that God has justified you of all sin.

It is God himself who has justified you! A few paragraphs back, I wrote that the greatest fear we have, if we think through our spiritual state carefully, is not that our consciences and/or Satan accuse us, but that the God who knows everything is our Judge. It terrifies us to consider that while we may harden our hearts or deaden our consciences and perhaps even fool Satan, we cannot avoid or fool God. It is God with whom we have to deal. Ah, but that very fact is our comfort. For if, instead of being condemned by

God we are actually acquitted or justified by him, then who is left to condemn us? If we have been saved by God, who can possibly overturn God's judgment?

Do you see how this works? If we have actually been justified by God, the fact that causes us most to tremble is actually that which gives us most assurance and comfort.

Let me spell this out in a few particulars:

1. *Our greatest offense is against God, however great our offenses against other persons may be.* So, if God has forgiven us, we are justified indeed. David sinned against Bathsheba, with whom he committed adultery, and against her husband Uriah, whom he arranged to have killed. But in his great psalm of repentance he rightly declared to God, "Against you, you only, have I sinned and done what is evil in your sight" (Ps. 51:4a). As a consequence, he knew that if God cleansed him from his sin, he would have complete restoration. That is why he says in that same psalm, "Cleanse me with hyssop, and I will be clean; wash me, and I will be whiter than snow" (v. 7). God did cleanse him, and he was washed from his iniquity. David was justified because of Christ's righteousness.

2. *God knows the law perfectly.* This second important aspect of our being justified by God is rooted in the fact that the law is God's law, after all, and God, who knows that law, has justified us. Therefore, we need not fear that some smart lawyer, like Satan (Rev. 12:10), will somehow find something we have done that has not been covered by the blood of Christ or some technicality that would make it impossible for God to justify us.

God is omniscient. He knows every stipulation of the law. He knows us in every particular. He knows our outward sins and our inward sins. He knows the sins of our heart as well as the sins of our minds. He knows the sins we would have done had we been given the chance to do them, and he knows the sins we sought out opportunities to commit. He knows our sins against others and our sins against ourselves. Nothing is outside the scope of God's knowledge. Nevertheless, knowing all this, God has justified us. And the reason he has justified us is that he also knows every detail of Christ's work and is fully aware of its value. He is aware—because he has so ordained—that "the blood of Jesus, his Son, purifies us from all sin" (1 John 1:7).

3. *God has satisfied all possible claims against us; he has done this himself, through Jesus Christ.* We have seen this before, but it is worth reminding ourselves that there is both a negative and a positive side to justification. The negative side has to do with the atonement: Christ's bearing the punishment of our sin in our place. It is what the New English Bible emphasizes in its translation of Romans 8:33: "It is God who pronounces acquittal." We are pardoned because of Christ's work—that is, not condemned. But justification is much more than this, which is why the New English Bible translation does not go far enough and why the New International Version is better.

"Acquittal" has only a negative connotation. It is true, but justification also involves the positive side of the transaction. If we are "justified," we are clothed with the very righteousness of Christ.

Elsewhere I have described justification as having these two parts: (1) our sin has been placed upon Jesus Christ and has been punished there, and (2) his righteousness has been placed on us. Or, as I have also said, it has been credited to our account.

Here is the way D. Martyn Lloyd-Jones puts it: "To justify means more than to pardon; it means more than to forgive. As we have seen repeatedly in our study of the first four chapters of this Epistle, it means that God makes a declaration, a judicial declaration, to the effect that he has not only forgiven us, but that he now regards us as just and righteous and holy, as if we had never sinned at all. . . . God not only imputes my sin to his Son, he takes his righteousness and imputes it to me."[2]

In the words of that great hymn, "Jesus, Thy Blood and Righteousness":

> Bold shall I stand in that great day;
> For who aught to my charge shall lay?
> Fully through thee absolved I am,
> From sin and fear, from guilt and shame.

"No one can lay any charge against me," writes Lloyd-Jones, "because I am arrayed in this righteousness."[3]

4. *The jurisdiction of God's court is universal.* Therefore, being acquitted by that court, we can never be condemned by any other. This aspect of our justification assures us and gives us comfort, even when our own thoughts and consciences accuse us.

We are aware of how lawyers will appeal to a higher court if they fail to get the verdict they are after in the lower court. In fact, they do it routinely. Even in a jury trial, a verdict can be appealed if there was an error in presenting evidence or if the judge erred in his instructions to the jury. Suppose, under rare circumstances, your case was appealed even to the Supreme Court of the United States and you were acquitted.

Even then there are situations in which you could conceivably still be in jeopardy. Suppose that jurisdiction in your case was challenged by another country. It might be possible for you to be acquitted here but then for you somehow to fall into the hands of people from that other country and be tried by them and found guilty.

On earth our status can be terribly uncertain. But not if we are judged and justified by God. The court of God is the Supreme Court of all Supreme Courts. His bench is the highest of all tribunals. There is no

2. D. M. Lloyd-Jones, *Romans, An Exposition of Chapter 8:17–39, The Final Perseverance of the Saints* (Grand Rapids: Zondervan, 1976), p. 408.

3. Ibid.

national government that can challenge God's judgment. Therefore, when Paul says, "Who will bring any charge against those whom God has chosen? It is God who justifies," he is asserting with great strength that those who are in Christ need fear no condemnation—not now, not ever. No one can overthrow the blessed judgment that has been rendered by God in our favor.

Prepared to Meet Him

All this is what Martin Luther discovered, of course, and it is why he became the prophet of the Reformation. In his early days, before he had studied the Bible and had learned that God has made the righteousness of Jesus Christ available for those who trust him, Luther feared for his soul. Earlier I referred to his great hymn on the judgment. It contains a verse about sinners who have not trusted Christ:

> . . . sinners, filled with guilty fears,
> Behold his wrath prevailing;
> For they shall rise and find their tears
> And sighs are unavailing:
> The day of grace is past and gone;
> Trembling they stand before the throne,
>   All unprepared to meet him.

That was once Martin Luther's fear. But then Luther discovered that God had made the necessary preparation through the death of Jesus Christ. He understood that justification can never be on the basis of our works, for it is our works that have gotten us into trouble in the first place. Rather, justification is provided on the basis of the work of Jesus Christ. Jesus died for sinners, and the righteousness in which believers are enabled to stand in the day of God's judgment is his righteousness that is imputed to them—and to us, if we are Christians.

That is the ground of our confidence. That is our security: the work of Jesus Christ and that alone. The last verse of Luther's hymn, picking up the theme of verse one, therefore cries,

> Great God, what do I see and hear!
> The end of things created!
> The judge of mankind doth appear,
> On clouds of glory seated!
> Beneath his cross I view the day
> When heaven and earth shall pass away
>   And thus prepare to meet him.

I have no desire to frighten you with thoughts of the final judgment. I want you to find comfort in Christ. But I need to say one more thing. If you are not in Christ—if your sins are not covered by his blood and you are not clothed in his righteousness—you *should* be frightened! There is no comfort for you. One day you will have to meet God, whom you have dishonored, and be judged by Christ, whom you have spurned. Who will save you in that day, if God himself is not your Savior? If you are not in Christ, in that day you will find God to be a stern, unyielding Judge.

But this is not yet that day. This is the day of God's grace. Jesus Christ is still proclaimed as Savior. Believe on him. Trust him. If you do, you will enter into a salvation that neither earth nor hell can shake and that God himself has made secure.

118

Our Wonderful Mediator

Romans 8:34

Who is he that condemns? Christ Jesus, who died—more than that, who was raised to life—is at the right hand of God and is also interceding for us.

Up to this point our study of the last part of Romans 8 has taught the doctrine of eternal security by presenting what God the Father has done on our behalf. This was particularly clear in verses 28–30, where it was a case of *God's* working, *God's* choosing, *God's* predestining, *God's* calling, *God's* justifying and *God's* glorifying. It was also the case in the following three verses in which Paul began to ask his unanswerable questions: (1) "If God is for us, who can be against us?" (2) "He who did not spare his own Son, but gave him up for us all—how will he not also, along with him, graciously give us all things?" and (3) "Who will bring any charge against those whom God has chosen?"

Even when the death of Jesus was mentioned, as it is in question two, it was mentioned from the viewpoint of God's giving up his Son.

With the fourth of these five questions, Paul's approach changes, as the work of Jesus Christ himself is suddenly brought forward. "Who is he that condemns?" Paul asks. Again there is no answer, because "Christ Jesus, who

975

died—more than that, who was raised to life—is at the right hand of God and is also interceding for us."[1]

In other words, having just said that God justified his people, Paul now speaks of the ground of that justification and offers four reasons why those who have been justified can be assured that they are forever free from condemnation. These reasons, all of which have to do with Jesus Christ's work, both past and present, are: (1) Christ's death, (2) Christ's resurrection, (3) Christ enthronement at the right hand of God, and (4) Christ's continuing intercession for us.

Christ's Death for Sin

As soon as we reflect on the teaching in this verse we are immediately impressed with how much doctrine Paul has compressed into it. He has done this with an economy of words, and nowhere is this more evident than in the first of his four statements. "Christ Jesus, who died" is all he says.

Why did he not elaborate on this a little bit?

The answer surely is that he has already done so in the earlier parts of the letter. In those earlier chapters we learn that Jesus died for sin, making an atonement for it. By means of his atonement he propitiated or turned aside the wrath of God, which sin deserved. Moreover, since Jesus had no sin of his own for which to atone, we learn that he did this on our behalf, or vicariously. Some years ago the great Swiss theologian Karl Barth was asked what was the most important word in the Bible, the questioner no doubt thinking that Barth would say "love" or some such godly quality. But instead Barth answered, "*Hyper.*" In Greek, *Hyper* is a preposition, meaning "on behalf of" or "in place of" another. Barth called this the most important word because it signifies that the death of Jesus was in our place and for us. He died so that we might not have to die spiritually.

I suppose the most common response to this, particularly from a Christian congregation, is that we already know all about it. Indeed, we have

1. The lack of punctuation in the original text has introduced uncertainty as to how the questions in verses 33–35 should be handled and, in particular, to what the question of verse 34 should be related. Is it to be taken with what immediately proceeds? If so, it would read: "It is God who justifies. Who is he that condemns?" That is, if God has justified, nobody can condemn. Or is it to be taken with what follows: "Who is he that condemns? Christ Jesus . . . is . . . interceding for us?" If it is the former, verse 34 should be divided, and the section dealing with the work of Jesus should be taken as introducing the further question: "Who shall separate us from the love of Christ?" The meanings are not very different in either case, but most commentators both ancient and modern take the questions as I am handling them, largely to preserve the parallel construction. In this handling, each question is matched to a corresponding answer, and the answer to this question ("Who is he that condemns?") is the work of Christ. For a fuller discussion of this problem see: D. M. Lloyd-Jones, *Romans, An Exposition of Chapter 8:17–39, The Final Perseverance of the Saints* (Grand Rapids: Zondervan, 1976), pp. 400–403; and John Murray, *The Epistle to the Romans* (Grand Rapids: Wm. B. Eerdmans, 1968), pp. 326–328.

known it for a long time. Why do we have to keep saying it again and again? Why repeatedly bring up the death of Jesus Christ?

Well, if you really do know this and really do live by faith in Christ and his atonement, there probably is no need to keep on repeating it, although those who know it best generally are those who love hearing it most often. Katherine Hankey's hymn says rightly, "I love to tell the story, for those who know it best/Seem hungering and thirsting to hear it like the rest."

But I suggest that we do need to hear it (and often), for the very reason Paul is repeating himself in Romans. Remember, he is writing about assurance. And the reason he is writing about assurance and at such length is that we tend to waver on this subject and doubt our salvation. This is particularly true when we fall into sin, whether outright sins of commission or those more subtle sins of the mind or spirit, perhaps even the sin of doubting God's word about salvation. In such a frame of mind we find ourselves wondering whether we really are saved or are still saved, assuming that we were saved once but have perhaps fallen away.

If you find yourself thinking like this, you need to hear that "old, old story" again. You need to hear what Jesus did for your sin, bearing the punishment of God upon it in your place.

"But suppose I sin?" you ask. Don't say "suppose." You have sinned and will continue to sin. That is not the right question. The question is rather, "Did Jesus die for my sin or did he not?" If he did, then the punishment for that sin has been undertaken by Jesus in your place, and there is no one (not even God) who can condemn you for it. Jesus took your condemnation.

"But suppose I question this?"

This questioning of yours—is it a sin or isn't it? If it is not a sin, if it is only a mere intellectual puzzling over the full meaning of what Jesus Christ has done and why, there is no problem. Christians are free to ask God questions and state what they do not understand. If it *is* a sin, that is, if it is outright disbelief of God's Word, even then why should this sin more than any other separate you from God's love and condemn you—if Jesus has, in fact, died for it?

I do not mean by this that your sin is covered by Christ's blood if you are among those who reject his atonement and scorn it. That is an unbelief that has never known faith. If you do this, you are not regenerate. I am speaking to those who are born again and love Jesus but who have doubts concerning their salvation. To them I say, as Paul does, "Christ died." He died for you.

When he hung on the cross, Jesus said of his atoning work, "It is finished" (John 19:30). And it was! It was finished forever. There is nothing that can ever be added to it or be taken away.

Christ's Resurrection

The second reason why we can be assured of our salvation on the basis of Jesus work for us is his resurrection, which Paul introduces with the words "more than that, who was raised to life."

That is a strange way of introducing the doctrine of the resurrection, because it is linked to Christ's death as if it adds something to it. And how can that be, if the atonement is a finished work, as I just said? Once again, this is something Paul explained earlier in Romans when he was dealing with the work of Jesus more extensively. Think back to what the apostle said at the end of chapter four, as he brought the first great section of the book to a close and prepared to move on into the second great section, which we are now studying: "He [Jesus] was delivered over to death for our sins and was raised to life for our justification" (Rom. 4:25).

What does that mean, "raised to life for our justification"? As the Bible describes them, both the resurrection and justification are works of God. So the verse is saying that God raised Jesus from the dead in some way that relates to his work of justification. Since justification is based on *Christ's* propitiation, the connection between resurrection and justification is not one of cause and effect. Rather, it must be one of demonstration. The point of the resurrection is to verify the justification, which is based upon the death. It is God's way of showing that Jesus' death was a true atonement and that all who believe on him are indeed justified from all sin.

Let me put it this way. When Jesus was alive on earth he said that he was going to die for sin, becoming a ransom for many. In time he did die and was placed in a tomb where he lay for three days.

Had he died for sin? He said that was what he was going to do, but the words alone do not prove his death was an atonement. Suppose Jesus was deluded? What if he only thought he was the Son of God and the Savior? Or again, suppose he was not sinless? He claimed to have been sinless. He seemed to be. But suppose he had sinned, even a little bit? In that case, he would have been a sinner himself, and his death could not have atoned even for his own sin, let alone for the sin of others. The matter would remain in doubt.

But then the morning of the resurrection comes. The body of Jesus is raised, and the stone is rolled back from the opening of the tomb so the women and later others can see and verify that he has indeed been raised. Now there is no doubt, for it is inconceivable that God the Father should thus verify the claims of Jesus if he was not his unique Son and was not therefore a true and effective Savior of his people.

As the great Bible teacher Reuben A. Torrey said in one of his writings, "I look at the cross of Christ, and I know that atonement has been made for my sins; I look at the open sepulcher and the risen and ascended Lord, and I know that the atonement has been accepted. There no longer remains a single sin on me, no matter how many or how great my sins may have been. My sins may have been as high as the mountains, but in the light of the resurrection the atonement that covers them is as high as heaven. My sins may have been as deep as the ocean, but in the light of the resurrection the atonement that swallows them up is as deep as eternity."[2]

"Who is he that condemns?"—who could possibly condemn us if Jesus has died for us and has been raised as proof of our justification?

Christ's Enthronement at God's Right Hand

We are climbing a grand staircase in studying these four phrases that speak of the saving work of Christ, both past and present. But we are likely to miss a step at this point if we are not very careful, because the third step deals with the ascension and enthronement of the Lord Jesus Christ, and this is not something heard a great deal about in most churches. (In the more liturgical churches there is a special day known as Ascension Day on which the doctrines associated with Jesus' return to heaven are often noted.)

There are two chief teachings involved. The first is Jesus' *glorification*. This was God's answer to the prayer Jesus uttered just before his arrest and crucifixion, recorded in John 17. He said, "I have brought you glory on earth by completing the work you gave me to do. And now, Father, glorify me in your presence with the glory I had with you before the world began" (John 17:4–5). Jesus laid this glory aside in order to become man to accomplish the work of redemption. But now, contemplating the end of his work, he asks for that glory to be restored.

And it has been! According to Acts, at the moment of his martyrdom Stephen saw the glorified Jesus "standing at the right hand of God" (Acts 7:56), and Paul was stopped and redirected by Jesus' voice while on the way to Damascus to persecute the early Christians (Acts 9:3–5). The apostle John later had similar visions of Jesus, according to the Book of Revelation.

The other teaching associated with Ascension Day is the one Paul seems chiefly to be concerned with here. It is Christ's "session," his being seated at God's right hand. Since the "right hand" was considered the place of honor, for Jesus to be seated there involves his exultation. That alone is significant in regard to our eternal security, for it means that the One who has achieved it for us by his death has been honored for precisely that achievement.

But there is more to the doctrine than even this. The most important thing about Jesus' being seated is that sitting implies a finished work. As long as a person is standing, there is still work to do. But once it is finished, the person rests from that work, as God rested from his "work of creating" (Gen. 2:2).

This point is developed carefully in the letter to the Hebrews, where a comparison is made between the work of Israel's earthly priests, according

2. R. A. Torrey, *The Bible and Its Christ* (London and Edinburgh: Fleming H. Revell, 1904–1906), p. 108.

to the pattern of temple worship that had been given by God, and the work of Jesus, who was the high priest to come. This theme dominates Hebrews, beginning as early as chapter 4 and continuing as far as chapter 10. The point is that Jesus' priestly work is superior to and replaces the preparatory work done by earthly priests.

Then comes this important statement in chapter 10: "Day after day every priest stands and performs his religious duties; again and again he offers the same sacrifices, which can never take away sins. But when this priest [Jesus Christ] had offered for all time one sacrifice for sins, *he sat down at the right hand of God.* Since that time he waits for his enemies to be made his footstool, because by one sacrifice he has made perfect forever those who are being made holy" (Heb. 10:11–14, emphasis added). The Jewish temple had no chairs in it, though there were other articles of furniture. This signified that the work of the priests was never done. Indeed, even the great sacrifice offered on the Day of Atonement had to be repeated year by year. But when Christ offered himself as a sacrifice, that sacrifice was the perfect fulfillment of the prior types and a true and utterly sufficient atonement for sin. It did not have to be repeated. Therefore, when Jesus had offered this sacrifice and it was accepted by God the Father, he showed that the work was completed by sitting down at God's right hand.

Where is Jesus now? He is seated at God's right hand. So whenever you doubt your salvation and are becoming disturbed by such thoughts, look to Jesus at the right hand of the Father, realize that he is there because his work of sacrifice is completed, that nothing can ever add to it or take away from it, and that you are therefore completely secure in him.

What would have to happen for you to lose your salvation, once you have been foreknown, predestined, called, justified, and glorified by God? For that to happen, God would have to throw the entire plan of salvation into reverse. Jesus would have to rise from his throne, go backward through the ascension (now a descension), enter the tomb again, be placed upon the cross, and then come down from it. For you to perish, the atonement would have had never to have happened. Only then could you be lost. But it *has* happened, according to the plan of God. And the fact that Jesus has been raised from the dead, brought to heaven, and been seated on the right hand of God the Father is proof that it has been accomplished. Your security is now as certain as the Lord's enthronement, which means that it is as unshakable as Jesus himself.

Christ's Present Intercession

The final reason why the believer in Christ can be assured of his salvation based on the work of Christ is Jesus' present intercession. Paul says that Jesus "is also interceding for us."

In light of the ideas of accusation, judgment, and acquittal that have appeared throughout this section, it is natural to see this intercession as

Jesus' pleading the benefits of his death on our behalf in the face of Satan or any other individual's accusations. Bible teachers have often spoken of the verse that way, and I have done so myself on occasion. But this is probably not quite the right idea. Why? Because Paul has introduced the verse with the question "Who is he that condemns?" and the answer to that is "no one," as long as Jesus has died, been raised, and is now seated at the right hand of God and making intercession for us. There is no need for that kind of intercession, because in view of Christ's finished work and God's judgment no one is able to accuse us.

D. Martyn Lloyd-Jones says, "There is no need . . . for our Lord to defend the believer. He has already done so, 'once and for ever.' But, in any case, it is God the Father himself who sent his Son to do the work. There can never be any query or question in God's mind with regard to any of his children."[3]

In view of that, what does intercession mean here? In this context it must refer to Jesus' prayers for his people, much like his great prayer of John 17, in which he prays for and receives all possible benefits of his death for them for the living of their Christian lives.

It means that there is no need you can possibly have to which the Lord Jesus Christ is indifferent.

It means that there is no problem to which he will turn a deaf ear or for which he will refuse to entreat his Father on your behalf.

Let me share a paragraph on this subject from the writing of Donald Grey Barnhouse, which has blessed me:

> You do not have a problem too great for the power of Christ. You do not have a problem too complicated for the wisdom of Christ. You do not have a problem too small for the love of Christ. You do not have a sin too deep for the atoning blood of Christ. One of the most wonderful phrases ever spoken about Jesus is that which is found on several occasions in the gospels. It is that "Jesus was moved with compassion." He loved men and women. He loves you. [Do] you have a problem? He can meet it, it does not matter what it is. The moment that the problem comes to you in your life, he knows all about it. . . . If there is a fear in your heart, it is immediately known to him. If there is a sorrow in your heart, it is immediately a sorrow to his heart. If there is a grief in your heart, it is immediately a grief to his heart. If there is a bereavement in your life or any other emotion that comes to any child of God, the same sorrow, grief or bereavement is immediately written on the heart of Christ. We find written in the Word of God, "In all their afflictions he was afflicted" (Is. 63:9).[4]

3. Lloyd-Jones, *Romans, An Exposition of Chapter 8:17–39, The Final Perseverance of the Saints*, p. 436.

4. Donald Grey Barnhouse, *Epistle to the Romans*, Part 53, *Romans 8:34–39* (Philadelphia: The Bible Study Hour, 1954), p. 11. The material in the booklets of radio sermons was condensed for the well-known Romans volumes, but the paragraph I have quoted was omitted in that revision.

Jesus intercedes for us in precisely those things. Moreover, he is heard in his intercession, and he ministers to you out of the inexhaustible treasure house of his glory. That is why Paul was able to write to the Philippians, "And my God will meet all your needs according to his glorious riches in Christ Jesus" (Phil 4:19).

Bobby McFerrin, the popular singer and entertainer, has a little song called "Don't worry; be happy." It made him famous. I like the song, even though I know it is misleading for anyone whose sin is not atoned for by the blood of Christ. A person in his or her sin *should* worry. There is no happiness for one who stands under God's dreadful condemnation. But "there is now no condemnation for those who are in Christ Jesus"! That first verse of Romans 8 tells us what the chapter is all about. There can be none because Jesus has died in our place, been raised for our justification, is seated at the right hand of God, and is even now carrying on a work of intercession for us.

Should people with such an intercessor worry? In their case, "don't worry" is a proper thing to say. And so is "be happy," though those words are undoubtedly too weak. We should rejoice with joy unspeakable.

119

No Separation from Christ's Love

Romans 8:35–36

Who shall separate us from the love of Christ? Shall trouble or hardship or persecution or famine or nakedness or danger or sword? As it is written:

> *"For your sake we face death all day long;*
> *we are considered as sheep to be slaughtered."*

Next to the bare facts of salvation, the greatest lesson a Christian can learn is that nothing can separate him or her from the love of Jesus Christ, which is the love of God. The world's values, entertainments, and sins are at odds with a believer's great calling and destiny. Yet all Christians can know that none of these things can triumph over them. Like a mountain climber ascending a dangerous precipice behind his guide, secured only by a rope, the Christian walks through life secured by the stout cord of God's love. Because the way is treacherous, any believer may often slip and fall. But a disciple of Jesus Christ is secure, because every Christian is bound to God by a gracious, unchanging, eternal, and indestructible love.

The Last Great Question

That is the point to which we come as we turn to the last of the five unanswerable questions Paul asks in the final paragraph of Romans 8. We have seen that the first three questions were unanswerable because of what God has done for us.

1. "Who can be against us?" No one can be against us, because God is for us, and God is the greatest force of all.

2. "He who did not spare his own Son, but gave him up for us all—how will he not also, along with him, graciously give us all things?" God will give the lesser gifts, because he has already given the greatest gift of all in Jesus.

3. "Who will bring any charge against those whom God has chosen?" No one will or can, because God has already justified his elect people.

The fourth question, which we looked at carefully in the previous study, is unanswerable because of what Jesus himself has done. "Who is he that condemns?" No one can condemn, because Jesus died, was raised from the dead, has ascended into heaven, is seated at the right hand of God the Father, and is even now interceding for us.

Having explored these four possible threats to our security—opposition, an imagined limit to God's gracious provisions for us, accusations, and condemnations—and having answered that in God we have a Champion, a Benefactor, a Judge, and an Intercessor, Paul now comes to the climax of his series of mounting rhetorical questions and asks the one that brings him to the very top of the mountain.

"Who shall separate us from the love of Christ?"

This question is also unanswerable, because there is no one nor anything that can be imagined to do it, even though Paul brings forth a long list of imagined separators. The only possible conclusion is the one we stated as we began these studies of Romans 8. As I said then, Romans 8 begins with "no condemnation" and ends with "no separation. There is "no separation," because nothing "will be able to separate us from the love of God that is in Christ Jesus our Lord" (v. 39).

When Hostile Forces Assail Us

Sometimes Christians are accused of being unrealistic. This is probably accurate in some instances. Yet it is not true of Paul. When Paul says that nothing "will be able to separate us from the love of God that is in Christ Jesus our Lord," he is not closing his eyes or shutting his ears to the hostile and destructive forces that surround the Christian at all times. On the contrary, he actually opens his arms to these forces and invites them to come forward, saying nevertheless and at the same time that they will never succeed in detaching us from Jesus Christ.

What are the forces arrayed against us? Paul lists seven in this verse, maybe choosing this number to suggest completeness. These are great forces, yet although they are great, all of them will fail.

1. *Trouble.* The first circumstance of life that might be thought able to separate a Christian from the love of Jesus Christ is "trouble" or, as the older King James Version of the Bible has it, "tribulation." I will focus on the KJV translation of this word, because "tribulation" does a better job of capturing the idea of hard circumstances pressing down upon us than does the less colorful "trouble" that the New International Version uses. The Greek word is *thlipsis*, which has to do with pressure.

The English word *tribulation* comes directly from the Latin noun *tribulum*, which meant a "threshing sledge." In the ancient world at the time of the grain harvest, the stalks of grain were brought to the threshing floor and a wooden threshing instrument, like a sled covered on the bottom with strips of metal, was dragged over the stalks to separate the heads of grain from the chaff. This instrument was called a *tribulum* because it pressed out the grain. This vivid picture produced the idea embodied in the word *tribulation*, because circumstances frequently press down on people so forcefully and unremittingly that it seems to them that they are being threshed like stalks of grain.

Perhaps you have experienced such harsh pressures. Life has been hard. You may have been abused as a child, have lost your job, have been deprived of a husband or wife or other family member, have undergone severe illness. Your strength may be nearly gone. But, says Paul, you may know that no tribulation, however severe, will separate you from Christ's love.

2. *Hardship.* The second circumstance of life that Paul thinks of as a possible separator is "hardship," which embodies a slightly different idea. The Greek word is *stenochōria*, and it is composed of two separate words, which mean "narrow" (*stenos*) and "space" or "territory" (*chōra*) respectively. So the idea is not so much that of being pressed down by circumstances, which is what "tribulation" means, but rather that of being confined within a narrow and oppressive space.

In our time I am convinced that many more people experience distress of this nature than outright pressures. Take the example of a man who is in a dead-end job. He entered his company with hopes for advancement, but he is now in his late forties and has been passed over for promotions several times. It is getting to where he cannot make a good lateral move, and he knows he will not move up much in the company, if at all. Meanwhile, he is married, with a wife and children to support and a mortgage to pay. He sometimes thinks of being free of these confining circumstances, but he knows that he cannot break free and still honor his commitments.

Or again, imagine a woman who is in her late thirties with two or three children who make tremendous demands on her, who has to survive on a rather meager budget, and who knows there is no future for her apart from the present circle of school, supermarket, baby-sitters, and the other marks of a most confined life.

How are you to triumph in such circumstances? The best way is to realize that Jesus Christ, the very Son of God, has fixed his love upon you and that nothing is ever going to separate you from his love. You may be in narrow straits now, but you are an heir of heaven, and one day your horizons will be as vast as the universe and as soaring as the stars. Nothing will deprive you of this destiny, because nothing, not even hardship, will be able to separate you from Christ's love.

3. *Persecution.* The Greek word for "persecution" (*diōkō*) contains the idea of being pursued by someone intent on our harm. It denotes harm that is relentless. What about such relentless persecutions? Very few of us suffer much outright persecution today, though Christians in other parts of the world endure it. But there are subtle persecutions, and there will undoubtedly be stronger and more outright persecutions if the present secularizing trends of western life continue.

Two things we can be sure of: (1) persecutions are a normal response to any forthright Christian witness or stand, and (2) we will experience them to the extent that we confront the world with Christ's claims. They may be as subtle as being shunned by those who regard themselves as quite sophisticated and Christians as being hopelessly "out of it" and dull. "Persecution" may mean being passed over for some honor or promotion. Ministers may experience this from a superior who pushes them into obscure posts because they are more interested in teaching the Word of God, with all its harsh edges, than in promoting the denominational programs. At times, particularly when Christians stand against some great national malaise, believers may even be sued in court to hush them up or render them ineffective.

Jesus said, "In this world you will have trouble. But take heart! I have overcome the world" (John 16:33b). Persecutions may separate us from a more lucrative worldly future or a more attractive image before the world, but persecutions will never separate us from Christ's love.

4. *Famine.* Most of the ancient world experienced famine at one time or another. Famine could result from lack of rain and the failure of crops; from natural disasters such as earthquakes, fires, floods, or locust plagues; or from war. Since those factors still exist today, hunger has not been eliminated for much of the world's population, despite technological advances in agricultural methods and the humanitarian efforts of those more fortunate. Hunger is a terrible thing. But even this cannot detach us from Christ, says Paul.

5. *Nakedness.* Today this word usually implies the state of undress normally associated with sexual activity or pornography. But in Paul's day it had to do more with poverty so severe that the person so afflicted was unable to buy the clothes he or she needed. It is a corresponding term to famine and, like it, may refer to economic hard times deriving from natural disasters or war.

6. *Danger.* Dangers, too, are of various types, though the focus here is on those to which Christians are exposed simply because they are Christians. Just as in New Testament times, in some countries Christians are arrested, tried, and imprisoned. In others they are attacked, beaten, and even killed.

I like what Robert Haldane wrote on this point:

> These [dangers], at some times, and in some countries, are exceedingly many and great; and at all times, and in all countries, are more or less numerous and trying. If God were not their protector, even in this land of freedom, the followers of the Lamb would be cut off or injured. It is the Lord's providence that averts such injuries, or overrules events for the protection of his people. This too is little considered even by themselves, and would be thought a most unfounded calumny or a fantastical idea by the world. But let the Christian habitually consider his safety and protection as secured by the Lord, rather than by the liberality of the times. That time never yet was when the Lord's people could be safe, if circumstances removed restraint from the wicked. Those who boast of their unbounded liberality would, if in situations calculated to develop their natural hatred of the truth, prove, after all, bitter persecutors.[1]

7. *Sword.* The last of these seven terms pushes the violence implied in the earlier ones to their furthest extremity, viewing circumstances in which Christians are executed or even murdered for their faith. This happened in the early church. Stephen was an early martyr. So was James. Others followed, and there was soon a trail of Christian blood to mark the progress of the gospel from land to land and through history.

So frequent and so vivid had this been, even by the time Paul wrote Romans, that the apostle felt compelled to establish martyrdom as a prophesied biblical datum, which he does by quoting Psalm 44:22: "For your sake we face death all day long; we are considered as sheep to be slaughtered." This has been literally true throughout history, which is Paul's point. Mission societies and organizations that deal with international violations of human rights say that even today as many as 600,000 Christians are killed every year for their faith. Even if, as is the case in our country, we are not literally being put to death for our religion, we are nevertheless regularly

---

1. Robert Haldane, *An Exposition of the Epistle to the Romans* (MacDill AFB: MacDonald Publishing, 1958), pp. 419, 420.

regarded in as low a fashion as the quotation from Psalms suggests—as sheep fit only for slaughter.

Christ's Love for Us

In view of these many dangers, toils, and cares that come into the lives of Christians, how can Paul say that there is nothing that can separate us from Christ's love? The answer, of course, is the nature of that love. It is high and long and broad and deep. It is eternal. The phrase "love of Christ" can mean either our love for Christ or Christ's love for us, but it is evident in this context that it is Christ's love for us and not our love for him that is the basis of our security and Paul's confidence.

Christ's love draws us out of ourselves and to him in the first place. It draws and wins disciples. Years ago, Tenth Presbyterian Church supported a missionary to Korea whose name was Harold Voekel. He was in Korea at the time of the Korean War. He was drafted into the army and assigned to the prisoner-of-war camps as a chaplain. Tens of thousands of North Koreans were imprisoned in these camps. Some were Communists. They were active in stirring up riots and rebellion. When Voekel entered the first camp he immediately won the men's interest because he could speak their language. He said he wanted to teach them a song. It was the Korean version of our familiar children's hymn, often taught in Sunday school.

> Jesus loves me! This I know,
> For the Bible tells me so.
> Little ones to him belong;
> They are weak, but he is strong.
>
> Yes, Jesus loves me,
> Yes, Jesus loves me,
> Yes, Jesus loves me,
> The Bible tells me so.

When Chaplain Voekel had finished teaching this in one camp, he went to a second camp and so on until he had covered all the POW camps in Korea. Then he went around again, this time teaching a few simple things about this person Jesus, who loved the Koreans. He did this for months. Thousands became believers. Discipline in the camps improved. The Communists had difficulty finding followers. When the truce finally came and the country was divided at the infamous 38th Parallel, thousands of these former prisoners of war refused to return to North Korea and Communism and instead chose to live in the south where they could continue to learn about and worship Jesus.[2]

2. This story is told in Donald Grey Barnhouse, *God's Heirs: Exposition of Bible Doctrines, Taking the Epistle to the Romans as a Point of Departure*, vol. 7, *Romans 8:1–39* (Grand Rapids: Wm. B. Eerdmans, 1963), pp. 189, 190.

There is no greater message than the message of the love of Jesus Christ for us. It has captured the imagination and won the hearts of widespread millions throughout history.

The love of Christ satisfies those it has drawn and won as disciples. And the proof is this: Once the soul has tasted Christ's love, it can never be satisfied with anything else. Not all the pleasures, not all the idols of this earth can satisfy the person who has known the love of Christ. One of our hymns puts it nicely when it says,

> Draw and win and fill completely,
> 'Til the cup o'erflows the brim;
> What have we to do with idols
> Who have companied with him?

The love of Christ not only draws and satisfies, it also keeps us safe forever. This is what Paul is chiefly saying in this paragraph. Here is a great passage on this theme by Donald Grey Barnhouse:

The love of Christ was eternal, for it was that love which moved him to leave heaven's throne and come down to this earth to redeem us. That love was deep, for it was that love which urged him on to the end of the road as he humbled himself to the death, even the death of the cross. That love was broad, for it was that love which opened the arms of God to all the world of sinners and made it possible for the very ones who nailed him to the cross to be forgiven and come back to the Father's heart. And that love is unchanging, for it is that love which comes to us today in the midst of our need, whatever it may be, and takes us out of darkness and into light, and from doubt to certainty, and from death to life.

In our text that love is presented to us in the phase of its permanence. God stoops to tell us that Christ is not fickle. What amazing condescension that such a verse should be in the Bible. The Lord leaves heaven and comes down to earth; he allows himself to be led to the judgment hall where he is buffeted and spat upon. He walks to Calvary and permits men to nail him to the cross. From that cross he cries out, "Father, forgive them, for they know not what they do." We see these things happen and he tells us that they have happened for us. . . . We look upon him with amazement, and wonder if he really means it. Then he smiles at us and tells us that he really does mean it and that he really does love us, and that nothing, nothing, nothing can separate us from that love.[3]

Paul's Sufferings and Christ's Love

I do not know how you are reacting to this, but I can guess how at least some are. There are some who will comment, "Well, that is all right for Paul

3. Ibid., pp. 190, 191.

to say, since he was an apostle and undoubtedly enjoyed special privileges. I am only a normal Christian. Can this really apply to me?"

If you are saying that, let me remind you of Paul's experiences. True, he was an apostle. But this meant that it was his lot to endure greater rather than lesser hardships than ourselves, in both quantity and degree. He writes about them in 2 Corinthians 11:23–29:

> . . . I have worked much harder, been in prisons more frequently, been flogged more severely, and been exposed to death again and again. Five times I received from the Jews the forty lashes minus one. Three times I was beaten with rods, once I was stoned, three times I was shipwrecked, I spent a night and a day in the open sea, I have been constantly on the move. I have been in danger from rivers, in danger from bandits, in danger from my own countrymen, in danger from Gentiles; in danger in the city, in danger in the country, in danger at sea; and in danger from false brothers. I have labored and toiled and have often gone without sleep; I have known hunger and thirst and have often gone without food; I have been cold and naked. Besides everything else, I face daily the pressure of my concern for all the churches. Who is weak, and I do not feel weak? Who is led into sin, and I do not inwardly burn?

Everything Paul speaks about in Romans 8 as a possible separator from the love of God in Jesus Christ is included in these verses as something Paul himself had experienced or was in danger of facing. Eventually, as we know, he was martyred. So Paul is not writing from some ivory tower or speaking "off the wall," as we say. He knew it all. Yet none of these things separated him from Christ's love, and today he is in the presence of Christ in heaven and will be forever.

So will it be for you, if you have truly tasted of Christ's love. This love is the greatest thing in the universe. Why settle for less?

120

More Than Conquerors

Romans 8:37

No, in all these things we are more than conquerors through him who loved us.

There are passages of the Bible that are so familiar that we often pass over truths that would be startling if we were coming to them for the first time. Romans 8:37 is an example. We have just been reminded in the previous verse, by a quotation from the Old Testament, that the people of God "face death all day long" and are "considered as sheep to be slaughtered" (Ps. 44:22). But now, in verse 37, we are told that nevertheless we are all "more than conquerors."

Sheep that conquer? We can think of lions that conquer, or wolves or polar bears or wild buffalo. Edgar Allan Poe even spoke of "the conquering worm," meaning that at last death comes to all. But sheep? The very idea of sheep as conquerors seems ludicrous.

This is figurative language, of course. But the image is not meaningless, nor is it as ludicrous as it seems. In contrast to the world and its power, Christians are indeed weak and despised. They are as helpless as a flock of sheep. But they are in fact conquerors, because they have been loved by the Lord Jesus Christ and have been made conquerors "through him."

Yet even that is not the most startling thing about this verse, for the victory of Christians is described as being *more than* an ordinary victory. In the Greek text a single compound verb, *hypernikōmen,* lies behind the five English words "we are more than conquerors." The middle part of the word is the simple verb *nikaō,* meaning "to overcome" or "to conquer." (The famous statue "Winged Victory" in the Louvre in Paris is called a Nike, which means "victory" and was the name given to the goddess of victory in Ancient Greece.) The first part of the verb, *hyper,* means "in place of," "over and above," or "more than." From it we get our word *super,* which means almost the same thing. When we put the two parts of the word together we find Paul saying that believers are all "super-conquerors," or "more than conquerors" in Jesus Christ.[1]

But how can that be? How can those who are despised and rejected—troubled, persecuted, exposed to famine and nakedness, danger and sword—how can such people be thought of as overcomers, super-overcomers at that?

It is a question worth pondering—and answering. Let me suggest a few reasons we may think like this.

Against Supernatural Forces

The first reason why the victory given to Christians by Jesus Christ is a superlative victory and why we are "more than conquerors" is that we are fighting against an enemy who is more than human.

This is the note on which Paul ends his letter to the Ephesians, reminding the Christians at Ephesus that "our struggle is not against flesh and blood, but against the rulers, against the authorities, against the powers of this dark world and against the spiritual forces of evil in the heavenly realms" (Eph. 6:12). In this passage Paul is thinking of the devil and his hosts, and he is saying that our battle, however human it may seem, is actually supernatural. It is a spiritual battle. If our enemies were mere human beings or mere natural forces, our victory, if we achieved it, would be a natural victory. But, as it is, our foes are supernatural, and therefore our victories are supernatural, too. We are more than conquerors.

The devil is the embodiment of these hostile spiritual forces, and he is a cunning foe. I have often said that we must not overrate Satan's strength, as if he were the evil equivalent of God. Satan is a creature. Therefore he is not omnipresent, omniscient, or omnipotent. Only God is that.

However, Satan is very dangerous.

---

1. "More than conquerors" is a particularly felicitous translation. It came into the King James Bible from the earlier Geneva Bible and has been retained in many later versions, including the New International Version. See Leon Morris, *The Epistle to the Romans* (Grand Rapids: Wm. B. Eerdmans, and Leicester, England: Inter-Varsity Press, 1988), p. 340.

And crafty! The devil devises more schemes in a minute than we can conceive in a lifetime, and all of them are directed toward our destruction. How can we stand against such an evil, crafty foe, let alone be a "superconqueror" of him and his forces? It is not in our own strength, of course. It is as the text says: "through him who loved us." Martin Luther stood against these spiritual forces, prevailed over them through Christ, and wrote about it in the hymn we know as "A Mighty Fortress":

> Did we in our own strength confide,
> Our striving would be losing;
> Were not the right Man on our side,
> The Man of God's own choosing.
> Dost ask who that may be?
> Christ Jesus, it is he;
> Lord Sabaoth his Name,
> From age to age the same,
> And he must win the battle.

None of us could stand against Satan's hostile forces even for a moment, but in Jesus Christ we can stand firm and fight on to victory.

Lifelong Battles

Second, Christians are "more than conquerors" because the warfare we are engaged in requires us to fight lifelong battles.

In his excellent study of this verse Donald Grey Barnhouse sharply contrasts our battles as Christians with the limited battles other soldiers fight: "In earthly battles soldiers are sometimes called upon to fight day and night. But there comes a moment when flesh and blood cannot take more and the struggle comes to an end through the utter exhaustion of the soldier. But in the spiritual warfare there is no armistice, no truce, no interval. The text is in the present tense . . . in the Greek: 'For thy sake we are being killed all the day long' (RSV). From the moment we are made partakers of the divine nature, we are the targets of the world, the flesh and the devil. There is never a moment's reprieve. It follows, then, that our conquest is more than a conquest, and thus we are more than conquerors."[2]

Eternal Results

The third reason why Christians are more than conquerors is that the spiritual victories achieved by God's people are eternal. This is a very important point and one we need to remind ourselves of constantly.

2. Donald Grey Barnhouse, *God's Heirs: Exposition of Bible Doctrines, Taking the Epistle to the Romans as a Point of Departure*, vol. 7, *Romans 8:1–39* (Grand Rapids: Wm. B. Eerdmans, 1963), pp. 202, 203. Barnhouse develops his own version of these five points on pp. 202–204.

We are creatures of time, and we live in a perishing world. Apart from spiritual battles and spiritual victories, everything we accomplish will pass away, no matter how great an earthly "victory" may seem in the world's eyes or our own. How can it be otherwise when even "heaven and earth will pass away" (Matt. 24:35)? Great monuments will crumble. Works of art will decay. Fortunes will be dissipated. Heroes will die. Even great triumphs of the human intellect or emotion will be forgotten. Not so with spiritual victories, for our spiritual victories impart meaning to the very history of the cosmos.

I am convinced that this is what our earthly struggles are about and that this is how we are to view them. When Satan rebelled against God sometime in eternity past, God was faced with a choice, humanly speaking. He could have annihilated Satan and those fallen angels, now demons, who rebelled with Satan against God. But that would not have proved that God's way of running the universe is right. It would only have proved that God is more powerful than Satan. So, instead of punishing Satan immediately, God allowed Satan's rebellion to run its course. In the meantime God created a universe and a new race of beings, mankind, in which the rebellion of Satan would be tested. Satan could have his way for a while. He could try to order things according to his will rather than God's. He would even be allowed to seduce the first man, Adam, and the first woman, Eve, into following him in his rebellion.

But God would reserve the right to call out a new people to himself, the very people Paul has been writing about in Romans 8. These individuals would be foreknown, predestined, called, justified, and glorified—all according to God's sovereign will. And when they were called they would be thrust into the spiritual struggle that Satan and his demons had brought upon the race. Satan would be allowed to attack, persecute, and even kill God's people. But for them, for those who have been brought to know the love of God in Christ Jesus, these sufferings would not be an intolerable hardship but would instead be a privilege that they would count themselves happy to endure for Jesus.

I am convinced that in his supreme wisdom God has ordered history in such a way that for every child of Satan who is suffering, a child of God is suffering in exactly the same circumstances. And for every child of Satan who enjoys the fullness of this world's pleasures, there is a child of God who is denied those pleasures.

The unbeliever curses his or her lot if deprived and made to suffer. The believer trusts and praises God and looks to him for ultimate deliverance. Unbelievers boast of their superiority if they are fortunate in securing this world's success or treasure. Believers acknowledge God as the source of whatever good fortune they enjoy, and if deprived of these things, as is frequently the case, they say, as Job did, "The LORD gave and the LORD has taken away; may the name of the LORD be praised" (Job 1:21b).

And the angels look on, as they also did in Job's case. "Is Satan's way best?" they ask. "Does the way of the evil one produce joy? Does it make him and God's other creatures happy? Or is the way of God best? Are believers the truly happy ones, in spite of their suffering?"

We, too, may pose such questions, and even wonder about the truth of Jesus' words in the Sermon on the Mount:

Blessed are the poor in spirit. . . .
Blessed are those who mourn. . . .
Blessed are the meek. . . .
Blessed are those who hunger and thirst for righteousness. . . .
Blessed are the merciful. . . .
Blessed are the pure in heart. . . .
Blessed are the peacemakers. . . .
Blessed are those who are persecuted because of righteousness. . . .

Matthew 5:2–10

Those words are indeed true! They are profoundly true. They are what God's people are proving every day of their lives as they suffer and in some cases are put to death, being literally counted "as sheep to be slaughtered."

"But the poor in spirit are despised," someone says.

True enough, but "theirs is the kingdom of heaven."

"But those who mourn, mourn alone," says another.

They often do, in human terms. But when they mourn an unseen presence stands beside them, Jesus himself, and they are truly "comforted." They know "the peace of God, which transcends all [human] understanding" (Phil 4:7).

"But the meek are crushed and beaten down."

In this world they are. Indeed, for God's sake "we face death all day long." But our kingdom is not here, any more than Jesus' kingdom was here, though in the end we will "inherit [even] the earth."

"But those who hunger and thirst after righteousness are strange, odd. Most people don't want to have anything to do with them."

True, but their longings will be satisfied by God himself, while those who seek earthly pleasures will fall short of joys here and in the end will be cast into the lake of fire, where thirst is never quenched.

"But the pure in heart have no welcome here, no secure place."

True enough, but they will see God. They have a home in heaven.

"Why do we need peacemakers?" asks another person. "We need strong armies to fight the world's conflicts." Peacemakers are despised. The strong and powerful are favored.

But those who make peace "will be called sons of God."

"Who would want to be persecuted, especially for righteousness' sake?"

No one, of course. But when Christians are persecuted, they count it a privilege, for it shows that they are standing with Jesus, belong to his kingdom, and have a reward laid up for them in "the kingdom of heaven."

Victories in such sufferings are eternal in the same way that the victory of our Lord upon the cross is eternal. Our sufferings endure for a moment, but they achieve an eternal victory. They point to the truth and grace of God forever. I am convinced that in the farthest reaches of heaven, in what we would call billions of years from now, there will be angels who will look on everyone who has been redeemed by Jesus Christ and thrust into spiritual warfare by him, and they will say, "Look, there is another of God's saints, one who triumphed over evil by the Lord's power!" Revelation 12:11–12 describes how they will exclaim of our great victories over Satan:

> "They overcame him
> by the blood of the Lamb
> and by the word of their testimony;
> they did not love their lives so much
> as to shrink from death.
> Therefore rejoice, you heavens
> and you who dwell in them!"

In achieving those eternal victories, we who love the Lord Jesus Christ will have indeed been more than conquerors.

Eternal Rewards

The fourth reason why we are more than conquerors in the struggles of life is that the rewards of our victory will surpass anything ever attained by earthly conquerors.

The kings of this world generally fight for three things: territory, wealth, and glory, often all three. And they reward their soldiers with a proportionate share of these attainments. The Romans settled their soldiers on land won from their enemies, though chiefly to consolidate their territorial holdings. Armies have usually been allowed to share in war's spoils. Napoleon said that men are led by "trinkets," meaning titles, medals, and other such glory symbols. The world's soldiers have their rewards, but they are earthly rewards. The people of God look for rewards in heaven. The apostle Paul wrote to the Corinthians, ". . . Run in such a way as to get the prize. Everyone who competes in the games goes into strict training. They do it to get a crown that will not last, but we do it to get a crown that will last forever" (1 Cor. 9:24–25).

In this life, like our Master, we may wear nothing but a crown of thorns. But in heaven we will wear crowns that are incorruptible and will possess an inheritance that will never slip away.

No Greater Cause

The final reason why we are more than conquerors is that the goal of our warfare is the glory of God, and that is an infinitely worthy and utterly superior thing.

A few lines back I wrote of our reward as being imperishable crowns, using the image the Bible itself gives us. With that in mind I call your attention to a scene in Revelation 4:1–11. The setting is the throne room of heaven, and there, before the throne of Almighty God, are twenty-four elders who represent the people of God saved from all nations and all ages. They, too, are seated on thrones and wear crowns, because the saints reign with Jesus. In the center, immediately surrounding the throne, are four living creatures who cry out day and night, "Holy, holy, holy is the Lord God Almighty, who was, and is, and is to come" (v. 8).

Whenever the four living creatures worship God with these words, the twenty-four elders rise from their thrones, fall before God, and worship him. Then—and this is the point for which I recall this picture—*they lay their crowns before the throne,* saying,

> "You are worthy, our Lord and God,
>   to receive glory and honor and power,
> for you created all things,
>   and by your will they were created
>   and have their being" [v. 11].

This picture is extremely beautiful, for it shows that the crowns of victory won by God's people are won by God's grace and therefore rightly belong to him. They are our crowns, but they are laid at the Lord's feet to show that they were won for his honor and by his strength. In this, as well as in all the other things I mentioned, we are more than conquerors.

But there is one more thing to say: The way to victory is not by "going up" to any self-achieved glory but rather by "stooping down" in suffering.

Remember the picture of Satan given in Isaiah 14? Satan said, "I will ascend to heaven; I will raise my throne above the stars of God; I will sit enthroned on the mount of assembly, on the utmost heights of the sacred mountain. I will ascend above the tops of the clouds; I will make myself like the Most High" (vv. 13–14). But God tells Satan, "You [will be] brought down to the grave, to the depths of the pit" (v. 15).

Where Satan aimed to sit is in some measure where the saints of the ages are raised, for they sit on the "mount of assembly," higher than anything except the throne of God, as we have just seen. But notice how they get there. Not by trying to dislodge the Almighty from his throne. Rather, they are exalted because they have followed in the steps of their Master, who

> . . . did not consider equality with God
>   something to be grasped,

but made himself nothing,
    taking the very nature of a servant,
    being made in human likeness.
And being found in appearance as a man,
    he humbled himself
    and became obedient to death—
        even death on a cross!
Therefore God exalted him to the highest place
    and gave him the name that is above every name,
that at the name of Jesus every knee should bow,
    in heaven and on earth and under the earth,
and every tongue confess that Jesus Christ is Lord,
    to the glory of God the Father.

Philippians 2:6–11

Jesus was the prototype—the true sheep fit only "to be slaughtered." He was "the Lamb that was slain from the creation of the world" (Rev. 13:8). But he was also a super-conqueror, and we are more than conquerors through him.

121

The Love of God in Christ Jesus

Romans 8:38–39

For I am convinced that neither death nor life, neither angels nor demons, neither the present nor the future, nor any powers, neither height nor depth, nor anything else in all creation, will be able to separate us from the love of God that is in Christ Jesus our Lord.

There are times in every Christian's life when what is called for is a clear and ringing testimony, and there are times when what is most needed is a careful and persuasive argument supporting Christian truth. Overall, both are essential, for a personal testimony is no adequate substitute for an argument, when that is needed. Conversely, an argument is no substitute for a testimony, when that is needed. In today's wishy-washy, subjective Christian climate we need arguments especially. But, and this is the point I am making, we need personal testimonies, too.

I say this because of the final verses of our chapter. Paul has been offering arguments for why we who believe in Christ can consider ourselves eternally secure. Indeed, he seems to have brought out every possible argument he can think of. These are the arguments behind each of the five undeniable doctrines and five unanswerable questions of verses 28–37. They are

999

basic to Christianity itself. But there is also a time for testimony and, being a good teacher and persuader, Paul does not forget it. That is why, in verses 38 and 39, he once again writes in the first person. It is the first time he has done so since verse 18. He has given his arguments. Now we are to hear his personal convictions.

What does he write? "For I am convinced that neither death nor life, neither angels nor demons, neither the present nor the future, not any powers, neither height nor depth, nor anything else in all creation, will be able to separate us from the love of God that is in Christ Jesus our Lord."

What a glorious testimony! There is no false optimism here, for what Paul says is based upon the sound arguments of the preceding verses. But this is no mere academic presentation either. For, as anyone can immediately sense, it flows from a great and dedicated heart and is so passionate, so stirring, that most people instinctively regard this as both the climax of the chapter and the highest point of the entire letter.[1]

In this testimony Paul faces all the possible "separators" of Christians from the love of God in Christ he can think of—he lists ten of them—and then dismisses each one.

The Gates of Death

For most people in our age, as also in the past, the most fearful of all adversaries is death—and rightly so. Apart from what we are told about death and the afterlife in Scripture, death is an unknown, save that it ends our existence here and is inescapable. That is frightening. Francis Bacon wrote rightly, "Men fear death as children fear the dark." They do. They tremble before it.

Moreover, death is the greatest of all separators. Obviously it separates us from life itself. But it also separates us from places and people we love. And it separates the soul and the spirit from the body, and separates both from God if the individual is not saved. Terrible! Yes, but for the believer in Christ this is not the final word. Death does separate us from things of the world, including other people. But it can never separate us from the love of God that is in Christ Jesus.

How do we know this? We know because Christ has conquered death. He has triumphed over it. Paul assured the Corinthians that, "'Death has been swallowed up in victory' [cf. Isa. 25:8]. 'Where, O death, is your victory? Where, O death, is your sting?' [cf. Hos. 13:14]. The sting of death is sin, and the power of sin is the law. But thanks be to God! He gives us the victory through our Lord Jesus Christ" (1 Cor. 15:54–57).

1. Ray C. Stedman calls this "the highest point of the letter," adding, "Paul cannot go beyond this, and neither can we" (*From Guilt to Glory*, vol. 1, *Hope for the Helpless* [Portland: Multnomah Press, 1978], p. 311).

Paul wrote to Timothy in the same fashion, saying that "our Savior, Christ Jesus, . . . has destroyed death and has brought life and immortality to life through the gospel" (2 Tim. 1:10).

As a matter of fact, death, far from separating believers from the love of God in Christ Jesus, actually ushers them into an even closer relationship with him. Alexander Maclaren, who calls death "the separator," puts it nicely: "The separator becomes the uniter; he rends us apart from the world that he may 'bring us to God.'"[2] We know God now, but only in part. In that day we shall know "fully," even as we also are known (cf. 1 Cor. 13:12). And there shall be no soul "asleep" and no purgatory for those who are in Christ Jesus. Paul said that "to be away from the body" is to be "at home with the Lord" (2 Cor. 5:8). His personal testimony was: ". . . I desire to depart and be with Christ, which is better by far" (Phil 1:23).

When William Borden of Yale lay dying in Egypt on his way to mission work in China, which he never reached, he left a farewell note that expressed a similar testimony. The note said, "No reserve, no retreat, and no regrets." Of course not! Death did not separate Borden from the love of God that is in Christ Jesus.

Nor Even Life . . .

The second possible separator that Paul mentions is "life," which at first glance seems to be a strange choice of word—until we remember that life sometimes seems even more cruel than death. It is why we sometimes call death a "release" or "mercy."

Life brings separations, just as death does. The political aftermaths of wars sometimes separate members of families from one another. This has happened in Eastern Europe, China, North and South Korea, and other divided countries in our lifetimes. Sometimes poverty forces people to move away from loved ones if they have to leave their homes to find jobs. And consider sickness or the encroaching limitations of old age. As we age, mobility becomes increasingly limited, eyesight and hearing fail, minds and memories dim. In these things we experience separation from the simple pleasures the world once offered us. But there is no separation from God's love.

Let me give you an example.

In the week I prepared this study I received a letter from a man who had attended Tenth Presbyterian Church about twenty-five years ago. His story was a sad one. He had slipped into homosexuality in his youth, and by his own confession his lifestyle had cost him his family—he had a wife and children—his profession, and his health. This man now had AIDS, and he was writing to say that during his terrible illness he had found the Lord and

2. Alexander Maclaren, *Expositions of Holy Scripture*, vol. 8, part 3, *The Acts, Romans* (Grand Rapids: Wm. B. Eerdmans, 1959), p. 212.

wanted to receive the weekly cassette version of "The Bible Study Hour," which he knew of and had found spiritually nourishing.

Here is what he wrote: "Unfortunately, I am losing my eyesight due to AIDS. I'm reading your material as fast as I can, before I find myself unable to do so. . . . Your tapes will enable me to continue my studies after the light fails. . . . I have become obsessed with God. I can't get enough of his Word. He literally has become my sole incentive to live. I have lost so much already and am losing everything else, but I cannot lose him. He is the only reason I hold on to life, miserable as it is. My living now is preparing me for eternity."

I found myself greatly touched by that letter, particularly at this point in our studies, since it is such a marvelous testimony to the truth that even life's misery cannot separate us from the love of God that is in Christ Jesus.

Neither Angels nor Demons

When Paul mentions "angels" and "demons" as his next pair of possible separators, he confuses most readers, since we cannot be absolutely certain of what he is referring to. The word *angels* usually means "*good* angels," but many have wondered how beneficent beings can be thought of as ever trying to separate believers from Christ. For that reason, some commentators have taken the word to refer to *fallen* angels or demons, and the second term to refer to the "principalities" or earthly "authorities" they are sometimes said to control.[3] The King James Bible and some other versions translate this second word as "principalities."

The problem with this is that Paul seems to be deliberately introducing contrasting pairs of terms in these verses: four pairs, with two single terms thrown in. If that is his pattern, the contrast in this pair must be between good and bad angels.

Can good angels ever try to separate us from Christ? No. But Paul may sometimes speak of them hypothetically as doing what we know they could never actually do, as in Galatians 1:8—"Even if we or an angel from heaven should preach a gospel other than the one we preached to you, let him be eternally condemned!" I favor this view and judge that here Paul is not thinking so much in rationally exclusive terms as he is simply sweeping over all creation to deny that anything or anyone anywhere could ever succeed in destroying our eternal security in Christ.[4] In the first pair of possible separators Paul has looked at our most immediate experiences: life and death. In the second he looks to the realm of spirit beings and declares that not

3. See D. M. Lloyd-Jones, *Romans, An Exposition of Chapter 8:17–39, The Final Perseverance of the Saints* (Grand Rapids: Zondervan, 1976), p. 452; and Leon Morris, *The Epistle to the Romans* (Grand Rapids: Wm. B. Eerdmans, and Leicester, England: Inter-Varsity Press, 1988), p. 341.

4. See John Murray, *The Epistle to the Romans* (Grand Rapids: Wm. B. Eerdmans, 1968), p. 333.

one of them, whatever that being may be like, can separate us from the love of God in Christ.

It is good for us to know this, because—although we do not fear the good angels (they are "ministering spirits sent to serve those who will inherit salvation," Heb. 1:14)—we are rightly on guard against the "spiritual forces of evil in the heavenly realms" (Eph. 6:12). These forces create havoc among all types of people. They produce separations, because evil divides. Indeed, the very name "devil" (Greek, *diabolos*) means "separator." But although the fallen angels can produce many kinds of divisions, there is nothing they can do that can ever separate us from Christ.

How do we know this? We know it because Jesus has defeated these evil forces at the cross. Paul told the Colossians, "When you were dead in your sins and in the uncircumcision of your sinful nature, God made you alive with Christ. He forgave us all our sins, having canceled the written code, with its regulations, that was against us and that stood opposed to us; he took it away, nailing it to the cross. And having disarmed the powers and authorities, he made a public spectacle of them, triumphing over them by the cross" (Col. 2:13–15).

The Tide of Time

Having addressed the experiences of life and death and expanded his circle of possible separators to include angelic forces, both good and evil, Paul now thinks in terms of time, arguing that neither present things nor future things can separate us from God's love in Christ. "Time is powerless against believers," says one commentator.[5]

The fact that Paul speaks of "present" and "future" and not "*past*" and "future" (which we might expect) shows that he is still thinking carefully, even though casting about in the broadest possible fashion. He does not say "past," because nothing in the past *has* separated us from Christ. We are in Christ now. Ah, but what of the present? What about those hard things that are pressing in on us at this very moment? They cannot separate us from Christ, says Paul. Jesus is equal to them. What about the future? What about things to come? They cannot separate us from Christ either, Paul adds.

In my judgment, there are two equally valid ways to think of this pair of words, and both may be correct.

On the one hand, we might think solely of earthbound circumstances, what we regard as the flotsam and jetsam of history and our daily lives. We are buffeted by circumstances now, and we will be buffeted by circumstances in future days until we die. But none of these circumstances will separate us from the love of God in Christ, because the God who has loved us in his Son controls history. He is the God of circumstances. So there is nothing that has come into our lives, is already in our lives, or will come into our

5. Morris, *The Epistle to the Romans*, p. 341.

lives that has not been filtered through the perfect and loving will of our heavenly Father and been directed by him to our good. That is why Paul was able to say just verses earlier, "And we know that in all things God works for the good of those who love him . . ." (Rom. 8:28).

Joseph said the same thing, in spite of the terrible experiences God allowed him to pass through. He told his brothers, "Don't be afraid. Am I in the place of God? You intended to harm me, but God intended it for good to accomplish what is now being done, the saving of many lives" (Gen. 50:19–20).

On the other hand, Paul's use of the words *present* and *future* may refer to what we would call "this life" and "the life to come." Nothing here and nothing hereafter can separate us from God's love. We have talked about "here." What about "hereafter"? We remember a verse saying that "man is destined to die once, and after that to face judgment" (Heb. 9:27). Ah, judgment! That is what lies in our hereafter and what we indeed must fear, if we are not in Christ. Yet how can we fear it if we *are* "in him"? In that case, we know there is nothing to fear, for Jesus has borne the judgment in our place. There are still judgments to come, true enough. But even these cannot separate us from the love of God that is in Christ Jesus.

Nor Any Powers

It is hard to know what Paul is thinking of when he speaks of "powers," particularly since he adds it as a freestanding term, without linking it to a matching word, as he has done with the other possible separators thus far. The word in Greek is *dynameis*, which can refer to miraculous signs or miracles, though here it would seem to mean heavenly or spiritual forces. The only problem is that we find it hard to think of spiritual powers that are not already included in the phrase "neither angels nor demons." I suspect that in this context "powers" probably looks back to those that have already been mentioned—powers of death and life, powers of angels and demons, powers of the present and of the future—and says in summary fashion that there are no powers anywhere that can divide us from Christ.

Can you think of any? Can any force anywhere separate you from the love of God in Christ Jesus, if neither death nor life, neither angels nor demons, neither the present nor the future can do so?

Neither Height Nor Depth

In the fourth (and last) of his matched pairs, Paul turns from human experience, spiritual powers, and time and considers space, saying that "neither height nor depth" will be able to separate us from the love of God in Christ Jesus.

What does this pair of terms mean? If the words merely describe space, the phrase means that nothing above us and nothing below us can separate us from Christ. Alexander Maclaren takes this view, expressing it well. He says, "The love of God is everywhere."[6] If this is the meaning, it would be an expression of the thought found in the well-known verses of Psalm 139:7–10:

> Where can I go from your Spirit?
>   Where can I flee from your presence?
> If I go up to the heavens, you are there;
>   if I make my bed in the depths, you are there.
> If I rise on the wings of the dawn,
>   if I settle on the far side of the sea,
> even there your hand will guide me,
>   your right hand will hold me fast.

On the other hand, it may be significant that the Greek words translated "height" (*hypsōma*) and "depth" (*bathos*) were used in the ancient world in astrology to describe a point directly overhead, above the horizon, and a point directly downward, below the horizon. These points were used in forecasting horoscopes. Some commentators find this to be their meaning.[7] If this is correct, the teaching is that even so-called astrological powers cannot separate us from the love of God in Christ Jesus.

Nor Anything Else

After the sweeping terms of the first part of these verses the closing single item "nor anything else in all creation" is almost an anticlimax. But that is all right. In fact, it is effective precisely for that reason, for it is as if Paul has run out of words in his verbal search for possible "separators" and ends up saying simply, "nor anything else, anything else at all."

What does "anything else in all creation" include? The answer is that it includes everything that exists except God, since God has created all these other things. Thus, if God is for us and if God controls everything else, since he has made it, then absolutely nothing anywhere will be able to separate us from his love for us in Christ Jesus.

That reminds me of the word we looked at briefly as we began this section, the word *convinced*. This is Paul's personal testimony, as I said, but it is a testimony based on the soundest evidence, evidence that had persuaded Paul and should persuade us also. What are the grounds of this persuasion? Paul's conviction is not based on the intensity of his feelings or a belief that the harsh circumstances of life are bound to improve or that any of these separating factors will somehow be dissolved or go away. Rather, it is based

6. Maclaren, *Expositions of Holy Scripture*, vol. 8, part 3, p. 217.

7. Morris, *The Epistle to the Romans*, pp. 341, 342; and Donald Grey Barnhouse, *God's Heirs: Exposition of Bible Doctrines, Taking the Epistle to the Romans as a Point of Departure*, vol. 7, *Romans 8:1–39* (Grand Rapids: Wm. B. Eerdmans, 1963), p. 230.

on the greatness of God's love for us in Christ, and that awesome love has been made known in that God sent his Son to die in our place.

There is nothing in all the universe greater or more steadfast than that love. *Therefore,* nothing in all the universe can separate us from it:

> Not death, not life
> Not angels, not demons
> Not the present, not even the future
> Not any power
> Not height, not depth
> Not anything else in all creation.

I do not know of anything greater than that. And I do not know of any better way of ending our studies of Romans 8 than to say again that this is Paul's testimony, born out of his own careful study of the Scriptures and his own personal experience of the love and grace of God.

So I ask of you: Is this *your* testimony? Have you been persuaded of these truths, as Paul was? Can you say, "I no longer have any doubts. I know that salvation is entirely of God and that he will keep me safe until the very end"? If you are not certain of these truths, it is because you are still looking at yourself. You are thinking of your own feeble powers and not of God and his omnipotence.

As far as I am concerned, I am persuaded and I am glad I am. There is nothing in all of heaven and earth to compare to this assurance.

Subject Index

Scripture Index